For Reference

Not to be taken from this room

7168

LIBRARY
ST. MICHAEL'S PREP SCHOOL
1042 STAR RT. - ORANGE, CA. 92667

French Novelists, 1900-1930

Dictionary of Literary Biography

Dictionary of Literary Biography • Volume Sixty-five

French Novelists, 1900-1930

7168

Edited by
Catharine Savage Brosman
Tulane University

A Bruccoli Clark Layman Book
Gale Research Company • Book Tower • Detroit, Michigan 48226

Advisory Board for
DICTIONARY OF LITERARY BIOGRAPHY

Louis S. Auchincloss
D. Philip Baker
John Baker
William Cagle
Patrick O'Connor
Peter S. Prescott

Matthew J. Bruccoli and Richard Layman, *Editorial Directors*
C. E. Frazer Clark, Jr., *Managing Editor*

Manufactured by Edwards Brothers, Inc.
Ann Arbor, Michigan
Printed in the United States of America

Copyright © 1988
GALE RESEARCH COMPANY

Library of Congress Cataloging-in-Publication Data

French Novelists, 1900-1930.

(Dictionary of literary biography; v. 65)
"A Bruccoli Clark Layman book."
Includes index.
1. French fiction—20th century—History and criticism.
2. French fiction—20th century—Bio-bibliography.
3. Novelists, French—20th century—Biography—Dictionaries. I. Brosman, Catharine Savage, 1934-   . II. Series:
Dictionary of literary biography; v. 65.
PQ671.T94   1988   843'.912'09   [B]   87-25822
ISBN 0-8103-1743-5

Nobel Prize citations, presentations, and acceptance
remarks reprinted by permission from
Nobel Lectures: Literature, 1901-1967,
edited by Horst Frenz (Amsterdam,
London & New York: Published for the
Nobel Foundation by Elsevier Publishing
Company, 1969).

For Paul and Kate

Contents

Plan of the Series

. . . Almost the most prodigious asset of a country, and perhaps its most precious possession, is its native literary product–when that product is fine and noble and enduring.

Mark Twain*

The advisory board, the editors, and the publisher of the *Dictionary of Literary Biography* are joined in endorsing Mark Twain's declaration. The literature of a nation provides an inexhaustible resource of permanent worth. We intend to make literature and its creators better understood and more accessible to students and the reading public, while satisfying the standards of teachers and scholars.

To meet these requirements, *literary biography* has been construed in terms of the author's achievement. The most important thing about a writer is his writing. Accordingly, the entries in *DLB* are career biographies, tracing the development of the author's canon and the evolution of his reputation.

The purpose of *DLB* is not only to provide reliable information in a convenient format but also to place the figures in the larger perspective of literary history and to offer appraisals of their accomplishments by qualified scholars.

The publication plan for *DLB* resulted from two years of preparation. The project was proposed to Bruccoli Clark by Frederick G. Ruffner, president of the Gale Research Company, in November 1975. After specimen entries were prepared and typeset, an advisory board was formed to refine the entry format and develop the series rationale. In meetings held during 1976, the publisher, series editors, and advisory board approved the scheme for a comprehensive biographical dictionary of persons who contributed to North American literature. Editorial work on the first volume began in January 1977, and it was published in 1978. In order to make *DLB* more than a reference tool and to compile volumes that individually have claim to status as literary history, it was decided to organize volumes by topic, period, or genre. Each of these freestanding volumes provides a biographical-bibliographical guide and overview for a particular area of literature. We are convinced that this organization–as opposed to a single alphabet method–constitutes a valuable innovation in the presentation of reference material. The volume plan necessarily requires many decisions for the placement and treatment of authors who might properly be included in two or three volumes. In some instances a major figure will be included in separate volumes, but with different entries emphasizing the aspect of his career appropriate to each volume. Ernest Hemingway, for example, is represented in *American Writers in Paris, 1920-1939* by an entry focusing on his expatriate apprenticeship; he is also in *American Novelists, 1910-1945* with an entry surveying his entire career. Each volume includes a cumulative index of subject authors and articles. Comprehensive indexes to the entire series are planned.

With volume ten in 1982 it was decided to enlarge the scope of *DLB*. By the end of 1986 twenty-one volumes treating British literature had been published, and volumes for Commonwealth and Modern European literature were in progress. The series has been further augmented by the *DLB Yearbooks* (since 1981) which update published entries and add new entries to keep the *DLB* current with contemporary activity. There have also been *DLB Documentary Series* volumes which provide biographical and critical source materials for figures whose work is judged to have particular interest for students. One of these companion volumes is entirely devoted to Tennessee Williams.

We define literature as the *intellectual commerce of a nation:* not merely as belles lettres but as that ample and complex process by which ideas are generated, shaped, and transmitted. *DLB* entries are not limited to "creative writers" but extend to other figures who in their time and in their way influenced the mind of a people. Thus the series encompasses historians, journalists, publishers, and screenwriters. By this means readers of *DLB* may be aided to perceive litera-

*From an unpublished section of Mark Twain's autobiography, copyright © by the Mark Twain Company.

ture not as cult scripture in the keeping of intellectual high priests but firmly positioned at the center of a nation's life.

DLB includes the major writers appropriate to each volume and those standing in the ranks immediately behind them. Scholarly and critical counsel has been sought in deciding which minor figures to include and how full their entries should be. Wherever possible, useful references are made to figures who do not warrant separate entries.

Each *DLB* volume has a volume editor responsible for planning the volume, selecting the figures for inclusion, and assigning the entries. Volume editors are also responsible for preparing, where appropriate, appendices surveying the major periodicals and literary and intellectual movements for their volumes, as well as lists of further readings. Work on the series as a whole is coordinated at the Bruccoli Clark Layman editorial center in Columbia, South Carolina, where the editorial staff is responsible for accuracy of the published volumes.

One feature that distinguishes *DLB* is the illustration policy–its concern with the iconography of literature. Just as an author is influenced by his surroundings, so is the reader's understanding of the author enhanced by a knowledge of his environment. Therefore *DLB* volumes include not only drawings, paintings, and photographs of authors, often depicting them at various stages in their careers, but also illustrations of their families and places where they lived. Title pages are regularly reproduced in facsimile along with dust jackets for modern authors. The dust jackets are a special feature of *DLB* because they often document better than anything else the way in which an author's work was perceived in its own time. Specimens of the writers' manuscripts are included when feasible.

Samuel Johnson rightly decreed that "The chief glory of every people arises from its authors." The purpose of the *Dictionary of Literary Biography* is to compile literary history in the surest way available to us–by accurate and comprehensive treatment of the lives and work of those who contributed to it.

The *DLB* Advisory Board

Foreword

DLB 65: French Novelists, 1900-1930 is the first of three *DLB* volumes devoted to French fiction writers of the present century. The second and third volumes will cover the periods 1930-1960 and since 1960. This chronological grouping of novelists whose careers often spanned more than one period was made on practical grounds more than on critical ones, and like other such classifications is somewhat arbitrary. The arrangement is not to be taken as an attempt to define literary schools and generations, although to some degree the authors grouped together share aesthetic and other concerns, and among their works there are similarities characteristic of their historical periods.

DLB 65 includes writers whose principal production appeared either before World War I or in the ten years or so following the war, and who are thus associated chiefly with the early decades of the century, even if they continued publishing well after 1930 and adopted new styles or topics. The second *DLB* French novelists volume will treat writers whose careers and literary concerns are associated mainly with the decade prior to World War II, the war years, the *après-guerre,* and the 1950s. The last volume will feature authors whose careers were established around 1960, or whose major works date from this period. These include the New Novelists, although in some cases their work began to appear well before 1960, because of their new departures from the dominant trends of previous decades and their continued and abundant production after 1960. In such a division there is necessarily some overlapping: authors such as François Mauriac, who produced much good fiction after 1930, would seem to belong in the second volume as much as the first; Georges Bernanos, who wrote almost as many novels in the 1920s as later, could have been assigned to the earliest group rather than to the middle one. In making the final decision, the editor took into consideration such factors as the amount and importance of the fiction each author produced in different periods and its characteristics.

The abundance of outstanding French fiction in the twentieth century is amply attested by the essays in these three volumes. Few critics in 1900 could have conceived of the variety and richness that the novel could display in France well before the end of the new century. A form that had been preeminently associated with the mimetic intentions of romanticism and realism—although certain of the symbolists also had adapted it to their ends—was to undergo, by midcentury or shortly thereafter, modifications so sweeping and numerous as to test its identity, eroding its generic distinctiveness and making it, in the term of more than one critic, an *anti-roman.* By interior ironies, redefinition of its contours, and restatement of its subject matter, the novel form has been called into question and taken on alternately the features of poetry, criticism, drama, autobiography, essay, history, and film. It has thus shown more of the remarkable resiliency that had already made it the preferred genre of postclassical France. Even as the poet Paul Valéry was writing that he would not compose a novel, because of the arbitrariness of the genre–that is, he could not deign to write a sentence such as "The marquise ordered her carriage and went out at five o'clock"–Marcel Proust, André Gide, and others were demonstrating how fictional structure could be like that of a great poem, or a great cathedral, or a piece of music, a puzzle, or a mathematical formula, with internal rigor and coherence as well as ornamental beauty. From the *roman*–the medieval term meaning a narrative, whether in prose or verse, in the vulgar or Romance tongue–through its late medieval, Renaissance, and numerous modern avatars, the romance or novel has proven itself to be both beloved of popular audiences and suitable for some of the loftiest and most ingenious expressions of sentiment and ideas of which the Western mind has proven itself capable. It is as if the very concept of story, with its linear structure corresponding to the temporal dimension of human experience, were singularly fitting for the rendering of this experience; even later fictions that are deliberately nonlinear and atemporal draw their identity from reference to the basic journey pattern which they seek to overturn.

Nor has any literary genre been more sensitive to the tremendous developments in the sciences as well as to the profound social and historical changes of the century. Even if analogies–such as those critics once sought to establish between Albert Einstein and Proust, to take but one example–have proven shaky, post-Newtonian physics and its vast technological consequences have affected, it would seem, the contents of fiction and its form alike, if only in certain writers' refusal to give their work a sense of closure, seeking instead the impression of expansion, as well as nonlinearity, distortions brought about by observers, and other parallels to physical phenomena. Mathematics itself is reflected in certain fictional undertakings, as the essay on Georges Perec in volume three will reveal. Philosophy, linguistics, and the social sciences have had an even greater impact; not only have individual writers been influenced by such figures as Friedrich Nietzsche, Sigmund Freud, Edmund Husserl, Henri Bergson, and, more recently, Ferdinand de Saussure, Claude Lévi Strauss, and Jacques Lacan: twentieth-century psychology, psychiatry, anthropology, and sociology have claimed the novel as one of their fields of investigation as well as a privileged form of expression. Such characteristics as fictional polyvalence and ambiguity, multiple plots and narrators, and competing levels of reality within the text mirror the multiplication of modes of knowledge in the twentieth century. Most of all, the modern French novel has shared with the sciences an epistemological function, calling into question previous modes of knowledge, proposing new ones, and questioning, by its ironic self-interrogation, the very possibility and value of knowledge. As for the great historical upheavals of the twentieth century–wars, economic crises, revolutions, colonial uprisings (some of which are referred to in the present volume)–there is no need to dwell here on their reflections in French fiction: as the individual essays reveal, the two world wars, class struggles, colonial unrest, and persecutions are the topics of numerous novels. The pace of the historical process, which, according to Jean-Paul Sartre, has begun to develop faster, has as its parallel the rapid evolution of fictional form as writers search for the new, or at least attempt to shape old forms to changing realities.

The desire to show the widest possible range of fictional types and experimentation, while giving full treatment to those authors who are now considered the greatest modern French novelists, is the principle underlying these volumes. Both historical importance and what now seems like lasting value have been weighed. While omitting late-nineteenth-century masters such as Maurice Barrès, Paul Bourget, Anatole France, and Pierre Loti, even though they pursued their work beyond 1900, these three volumes include essays on modern novelists whose work took root in the nineteenth century, particularly in *fin-de-siècle* aestheticism and on social and psychological novelists, some of whom renewed the formulas of realism and naturalism; the surrealist *prosateurs,* who disdained the novel and yet wrote narratives; the committed novelists of the 1930s and 1940s, who are among the most impressive of the century; the New Novelists, whose works first appeared in the 1950s and who are still writing now, though often in other genres; and the post-New Novelists, whose work ranges widely. Currents such as the poetic novel, the working-class novel, the feminist novel, the ideological novel, and the experimental novel occupy an important place in the selection. In this context the term *experimental* is not intended to denote any particular technique or content but merely a departure from previous norms; as Alain Robbe-Grillet rightly observed, Gustave Flaubert wrote the "new novel" of 1857, Marcel Proust that of 1913. In addition, these volumes treat numerous other figures, whose production does not fit entirely into the rough categories just mentioned. There is a wide range of aesthetic, ideological, and behavioral opposites: innovators and traditionalists, Communists and royalists, Catholics and atheists, feminists and misogynists, working-class writers and aristocrats, partisans of thought and partisans of action, activists and recluses, practitioners of the *roman-fleuve* and those of the terse narrative.

Readers will note, however, the predominant movement toward formal and ideological liberalism–that is, a loosening of forms and an ideological drift away from authoritarian nineteenth-century structures and standards toward a questioning of all inherited values. That these phenomena do not always appear together does not detract from their forcefulness in the modern French novel, which, it can be argued, has played more than once the role of an instrument of social change, while also reacting to change. On the one hand, for example, a great literary innovator such as Proust is in most respects a social conservative; on the other, a literary traditionalist such as

Roger Martin du Gard questions profoundly the society that preceded World War I.

Readers will observe also the significant place occupied by foreign literary influences, particularly American writers and such novelists as Fyodor Dostoyevski and Franz Kafka, and by other arts—painting, the cinema—whose aesthetic principles often underlie the fictional experimentation reflected here. It is more than a curiosity, furthermore, that many of the French novelists have traveled widely or have lived abroad; there are also in volumes two and three a number of foreigners who have made French their literary language, although they were born to others. This literary cosmopolitanism has been a major influence in the development of the modern French novel.

A further phenomenon to be noted is the importance of magazines, schools, literary friendships, and other connections among French novelists; despite, on the part of some, tendencies to iconoclasm and independence, occasionally to isolation, many, like their counterparts in previous centuries, played important roles in literary groups, notably those of the *Nouvelle Revue Française* and, later, of *Tel Quel*. Literary friendships have been strikingly important, as the essays on Gide and Martin du Gard, for instance, illustrate. Taken as a whole, the modern French novel illustrates in several ways what Julia Kristeva terms intertextuality—strictly speaking, the presence of one text in another, for instance, by allusion or quotation; more loosely construed, any reference of a text (thematic or formal) to previous ones. For these novelists have been voracious readers as well as writers, and they have written for those who know the canon, even when they have rejected it: Nathalie Sarraute's notion of character cannot be understood without reference to Honoré de Balzac. Reflected in these essays, moreover, is a web of personal relationships among authors, not just the friendships referred to above but also marriages and love affairs between writers that were central to their developments; the most striking illustration is furnished by two authors from volume two, Louis Aragon and Elsa Triolet, in the joint publi-

cation of their *Œuvres romanesques croisées* (1964-1974).

One further observation to be made on French literary life concerns the numerous and prestigious prizes for fiction, prizes which are mentioned time and again in the *DLB* essays. The announcements of the Goncourt, Médicis, Fémina, Renaudot, Interallié, and Académie Française awards are always major events of the literary year. A number of novelists treated in these three volumes won the Nobel Prize for Literature: Romain Rolland (1915), Roger Martin du Gard (1937), André Gide (1947), François Mauriac (1952), Albert Camus (1957), Jean-Paul Sartre (who rejected the 1964 prize), Claude Simon (1985). Elie Wiesel was awarded the Nobel Peace Prize in 1986. The Irish novelist Samuel Beckett, who wrote a large part of his work in French and was the Nobel laureate in 1969, is treated in volumes 13 and 15 of the *DLB*.

Three practical observations need to be added. First, the French novelist *DLB* volumes do not include essays on writers whose work belongs to a Francophone literature outside of France; the development of fiction in Black Africa, North Africa, and the Antilles is separate and significant enough to deserve treatment by itself, and Quebec novelists are treated in the *DLB* volumes on Canadian writers. Nor are novelists dealt with here who are considered Swiss and Belgian. Second, the claim is not being made that these three *DLB*s are exhaustive. There are other novelists in France in this century who, it might be argued, deserve a place in one of these three volumes. While some were omitted for practical reasons, others were excluded because, in one way or another, their work did not seem as representative or as significant as that of others. Such decisions inevitably reflect editorial preferences. Third, the lists of references following each essay do not include several major general bibliographies; along with suggestions for further reading, these are given at the end of each volume.

—Catharine Savage Brosman

Acknowledgments

This book was produced by Bruccoli Clark Layman, Inc. Karen L. Rood is senior editor for the *Dictionary of Literary Biography* series. Margaret A. Van Antwerp was the in-house editor.

Art supervisor is Gabrielle Elliott. Copyediting supervisor is Patricia Coate. Production coordinator is Kimberly Casey. Typesetting supervisor is Kathleen M. Flanagan. Laura Ingram and Michael D. Senecal are editorial associates. The production staff includes Rowena Betts, David R. Bowdler, Charles Brower, Cheryl Crombie, Mary S. Dye, Charles Egleston, Sarah A. Estes, Carol W. Farrington, Cynthia Hallman, Judith K. Ingle, Maria Ling, Warren McInnis, Kathy S. Merlette, Sheri Neal, Joycelyn R. Smith, and Elizabeth York. Jean W. Ross is permissions editor. Joseph Caldwell, photography editor, and Joseph Matthew Bruccoli did photographic copy work for the volume.

Walter W. Ross and Rhonda Marshall did the library research with the assistance of the staff at the Thomas Cooper Library of the University of South Carolina: Daniel Boice, Kathy Eckman, Gary Geer, Cathie Gottlieb, David L. Haggard, Jens Holley, Dennis Isbell, Jackie Kinder, Marcia Martin, Jean Rhyne, Beverley Steele, Ellen Tillett, Carole Tobin, and Virginia Weathers.

French Novelists,
1900-1930

Dictionary of Literary Biography

Alain-Fournier
(Henri Alban Fournier)
(3 October 1886-22 September 1914)

Helen T. Naughton
College of Notre Dame

BOOKS: *Le Grand Meaulnes* (Paris: Emile-Paul, 1913); translated by Françoise Delisle as *The Wanderer* (Boston & New York: Houghton Mifflin, 1928; London: Constable, 1929); enlarged edition, *Le Grand Meaulnes, suivi de Brouillons inédits*, annotated by Isabelle Rivière (Paris: Club des Libraires de France, 1953);

Miracles (Paris: Gallimard, 1924);

Le Grand Meaulnes, Miracles, Le Dossier du "Grand Meaulnes" (Paris: Garnier, 1986).

PERIODICAL PUBLICATIONS: "Le Corps de la femme," *Grande Revue* (25 December 1907);

"L'Amour cherche des lieux abandonnés," *L'Occident* (January 1910): 23-25;

"*Derniers Contes*, par Villiers de L'Isle Adam," *Nouvelle Revue Française*, no. 15 (March 1910): 414;

"*Sur la vie*, par Scantrel (André Suarès)," *Nouvelle Revue Française*, no. 16 (April 1910): 520;

"*Derniers Refuges*, par Jeanne Termier," *Nouvelle Revue Française*, no. 17 (May 1910): 679;

"Courrier littéraire," *Paris-Journal*, 9 May 1910-10 April 1912;

"Le Président Roosevelt à la Sorbonne," *Nouvelle Revue Française*, no. 18 (June 1910): 806;

"Le Miracle des trois dames de village," *Grande Revue* (10 August 1910): 564-568;

"La Partie de plaisir," *Schéhérazade* (15 September 1910);

"*Marie-Claire*, par Marguerite Audoux," *Nouvelle Revue Française* (November 1910): 606;

"Le Miracle de la fermière," *Grande Revue* (25 March 1911): 318-326;

"Portrait," *Nouvelle Revue Française* (September 1911);

"La Boîte aux lettres," by Alain-Fournier and others as Les Treize, *Intransigeant*, February 1912-July 1914;

"*Sur les champs de bataille. Souvenirs des anciens correspondants de guerre*," *Nouvelle Revue Française* (April 1912): 709;

"Madeleine," *Grande Revue* (June 1915): 532-539;

"Le Pari" (fragment of "Colombe blanche"), *Nouvelle Revue Française* (December 1922): 669-678;

"La Femme empoisonnée," *Poésie*, no. 18 (March-April 1944): 3-8.

Alain-Fournier's reputation rests principally on one widely acclaimed novel, *Le Grand Meaulnes* (1913; literally Big Meaulnes), and on his extensive correspondence with Jacques Rivière, critic and later editor of the prestigious *Nouvelle Revue Française*. Baptized Henri Alban Fournier, he adopted the demi-pseudonym Alain-

Alain-Fournier in Paris, 1913 (photograph by Dornac, by permission of Alain Rivière)

Fournier in December 1907 for his first publication, an essay entitled "Le Corps de la femme" (Woman's Body), in the *Grande Revue*.

Essential to an understanding of *Le Grand Meaulnes* is Alain-Fournier's nostalgia for his happy childhood and his intense attachment to the villages of his youth, especially Nançay, La Chapelle d'Angillon, and Epineuil-le-Fleuriel. Throughout his life he dreamed of happiness as a return to this period of wonder and innocence when the world was filled with mystery, marvel, and endless possibilities.

Alain-Fournier was born on 3 October 1886 in the home of his maternal grandparents at La Chapelle d'Angillon, thirty miles north of Bourges, in the center of France. His parents, Auguste and Albanie Barthe Fournier, were schoolteachers in various villages of the region around the Cher River until they were posted to Paris in 1908. Their only other child, Isabelle, was born in July 1889. She was to become her brother's lifelong confidante.

Fournier's father came from Nançay in Sologne, a wild and sparsely populated region of ferns and marshes, fir trees, and moors covered with heather. The boy's uncle Florent ran the village general store. At Nançay the young Fournier spent the last weeks of summer vacation hunting and wandering over the heath. He was entranced by the varied stores of goods spread over and under the counters of his uncle's store and was fascinated by the sudden arrival and departure of the numerous clients and guests. Nançay remained for him a wondrous place, strange and full of delightful surprises.

Throughout his life Fournier spent vacations in the quiet village of La Chapelle, home of his maternal grandmother, Maman Barthe, who entertained him with old songs and countless tales. Five miles to the south and hidden in the woods was the abandoned manor house of Loroy, with its reed-fringed lake, the spire and remains of a Cistercian abbey behind it. He was enchanted by its remoteness, its deserted air, its mysterious emptiness.

In October 1891, when Fournier was five years old, Monsieur Fournier was transferred to the village school of Epineuil-le-Fleuriel, in the extreme south of the Cher region. In this small secluded village, with the hamlet of Meaulnes to the north and the old chapel of Sainte-Agathe to the south, Fournier spent seven formative years of his childhood. The Fourniers lived on the left side of the vine-covered schoolhouse. The two schoolrooms lay between the tiny kitchen and the office of the mayor's secretary, a post Auguste Fournier also held.

The Fournier children, because of their parents' positions, were kept apart from the village youngsters, and they became inseparable companions. Fournier was fond of sports: swimming, fishing, hunting, cycling, hiking, and, later, rugby. As a child he delighted in the excitement of patriotic holidays and the processions of religious festivals, in the performances of wandering players on the village square, long walks and picnics on the banks of the river, and social visits with his mother. His special joy was to steal into the attic with Isabelle to read the eighty or so prize books awaiting distribution at the end of the school year.

Fournier was never able to overcome his nostalgia for these lost joys. He continued to search for what he called the *pays sans nom* (land without a name) where one keeps intact the sense of enchantment, the acceptance of miracle, and the purity of childhood.

Fournier's parents had ambitions for him beyond becoming a village teacher. In 1898, when he was twelve years old, he was sent to Paris where he became a day student at the lycée Voltaire, unhappy but scholastically successful. His deep-seated longing for adventure and a child's dream of the sea sent him next to the lycée in Brest in preparation for a career as a naval officer. In boarding school with its military discipline he felt like a prisoner. His dislike of mathematics and his rebellious spirit led him to renounce his naval ambitions after sixteen months, returning to the lycée of Bourges, where he passed his *baccalauréat* examination in 1903.

Since his parents' plans for him had always been entrance to the prestigious Ecole Normale Supérieure and a professor's career, he was enrolled next in the lycée Lakanal in Paris to prepare for the entrance examination, which only a small number of candidates passed each year. At Lakanal, he met his lifelong closest friend, Jacques Rivière, son of a well-to-do Bordeaux physician. Neglecting their school programs, the two young men became inseparable companions at plays, concerts, operas, and art exhibits, visiting bookstores and discussing literature at length.

On Ascension Thursday, 1 June 1905, the most important event in Fournier's life occurred, a meeting that Jacques Rivière was to describe as the event that gave birth to *Le Grand Meaulnes*. Coming from an art exhibit at the Grand Palais, descending the stone stairway to the Cours-la-Reine, Fournier saw in front of him an elderly lady accompanied by a beautiful blond girl. He followed them onto a *bâteau mouche* and later to a house on the Boulevard Saint-Germain. During the following ten days he returned to wait before the house whenever he was free from the lycée. On Pentecost Sunday the girl left the house; he followed her to mass at Saint-Germain-des-Prés, attempting to engage her in conversation. After several rebuffs she finally agreed to walk with him to the banks of the Seine. Her name was Yvonne de Quiévrecourt; she lived in Toulon, and her father was a naval officer.

Once back at Lakanal, he made feverish notes on every word, every gesture, every emotion of their time together. This meeting and Fournier's love for this *princesse lointaine*, told and retold, in notes, confidences to Isabelle, and letters to his friends Rivière and René Bichet (Le Petit B.), appear under the thinnest of disguises in *Le Grand Meaulnes*. Whenever possible he returned to the house on the Boulevard Saint-Germain and each anniversary of their meeting he spent in anguish and regret. During the next eight years she dominated his emotional life. In spite of all obstacles he continued to hope and actually to believe that she would one day become his wife.

In the summer of 1905 Fournier left for London to perfect his English with a view to earning a *licence* in that language. He held a post as secretary-translator in a wallpaper factory, but he continued to dream of Epineuil and Yvonne de Quiévrecourt. On his return to France he learned that Jacques Rivière, who had failed to pass the Ecole Normale examination, had obtained a scholarship to prepare his *licence* in Bordeaux. The separation of the two friends, prolonged by their periods of military service, gave rise to a voluminous correspondence, certainly one of the most fascinating and revealing in a period unusually rich in correspondences. The letters are a continuation of the long talks at recreation time on the bench of the *grande allée* in the park at Lakanal. Rivière tells Fournier about his visits to Gabriel Frizeau, a Bordelais art collector and friend of Paul Claudel, who introduced him to the painter André Lhote and to the future Saint-John Perse. He questions Fournier about the Paris salons and painters on exhibit there: Maurice Denis, Vuillard, Gauguin, Odilon Redon, Rouault, Degas, Laprade. They note their reactions to the music of Wagner, Debussy, Musorgski, Franck, Berlioz, Ravel. They discuss Claudel, Rimbaud, Francis Jammes, Jules Laforgue, André Gide, Paul Valéry, Charles Péguy, and their favorites among writers from other countries: Dickens, Shakespeare, Hardy, Stevenson, Emily Brontë, Ibsen, Dostoyevski, among others. They are eager subscribers to the little reviews of their day, hoping to place their own first literary efforts in these pages. They argue, explain, and criticize each other and, by so doing, enrich each other's work and sensibility. Fournier admitted that the only person who had been able to help him get close to the unknown and special world of his yearning was Rivière, with his limpid theories and his abstract writings.

Fournier's letters are an important part of his literary legacy. They not only serve to document his life and to record his aspirations and emotions but they also are often superior to rough drafts of his novel or short pieces of the same period. They give a picture of so appealing a man that many biographers have written hagiographic accounts of his life. His best letters were written to his parents and sister and to Rivière; others are to his friends Bichet, Lhote, and Péguy, while still others, and among them the most beautiful, are addressed to the women he loved.

At an early age Fournier seems to have realized that the only way to recover not only the detailed physical setting of his boyhood but also the emotions of the child he once was was to fix them in literary form. The first expression of this determination is in a nostalgic letter to his parents (March 1905) listing separate memories of Epineuil and expressing his desire to write "books and books" about his little corner of the earth. The genesis of *Le Grand Meaulnes* was long and difficult. Fournier's papers and rough drafts reveal a gradual evolution of style, plot, and characters drawn from his own experiences and letters, from events in other people's lives related to him by friends, and from secrets guessed or imagined in the faces to which he was irresistibly drawn.

Fournier's ambition to become a writer coincided with his first contact with Idealist philosophy at Lakanal and with the literary atmosphere of the second wave of symbolism which pervaded his adolescence, Debussy's opera *Pelléas et Mélisande* (1902) being the supreme manifestation of his artistic ideal. In a mechanistic, utilitarian age symbolism offered an escape from the pressures of a frigid world, from the rigidity and formalism of systems. It was a retreat from reality and an immersion in a subjective world of misty loves and dreams easier for Fournier to accept than the prison of lycée tasks and the unfulfilled promises of academic life.

But symbolism was a stumbling block to Fournier, both in subject matter and in style. He began his creative work with poems reminiscent of Vielé-Griffin, Henri de Régnier, and Francis Jammes, loose *vers libres* in which the dream remained vague, clouded, bafflingly out of contact with life, in contrast to his own peasant sense of humble reality, his love for the concrete aspects of a definite countryside.

In 1906 Fournier wrote his sister that he was working on the rough draft of a novel. He called it "Les Gens de la ferme" (The People of the Farm), a title he later changed to "Les Gens du domaine" (The People of the Domain). The pieces that remain from this period are impressions, short notations of childhood, or country scenes without plot or defined characters. He maintained in August of that year that his creed in art and literature was childhood; his goal, to succeed in expressing it without childishness but with its depths that reach into mystery.

Abandoning poetry in 1906 he turned next to the *poème en prose*, although his subject matter remained highly unrealistic. He still experienced difficulty freeing himself from the locale of the symbolists, which he felt uneasily was not the paradise that he was seeking, that *pays sans nom* so essential to his dreams that he used the phrase as the next working title for his novel. Writing of symbolism, Rivière recalls a paradise where the *lycéens* escaped from their troubles, a place of exile where the world no longer counted. But evasion, exile from the world was exactly what Fournier did *not* want, although in the beginning he envisioned a mysterious "other" world, a vague and magical dream land beyond and distant from the village of his youth. He came finally to realize that his nameless land was real and accessible to the believer who had retained the child's sense of the world's limitless marvel and was thereby worthy to discover it. In 1907 Fournier wrote André Lhote that he would not love this land with such passion if he were not sure that it existed somewhere in the universe.

When, in a state of nervous and physical exhaustion, Fournier first attempted to pass the Ecole Normale examination in July 1906, he made so poor a showing that he was not eligible for the orals. He returned to La Chapelle to recuperate and for a time was unable to read, study, or take part in long conversations. In the fall Maman Barthe, a widow since 1903, agreed to leave her tiny house in La Chapelle to take charge of her two grandchildren in Paris. Isabelle Fournier was enrolled in the lycée Fénelon and her brother was a prisoner once more, this time in the preparation classes of the lycée Louis-le-Grand. For Fournier this was the period of his first religious crisis, provoked among other things by the discovery of Claudel's collection of plays *L'Arbre* (1901). He was torn between the temptation to return to the faith of his childhood and a frantic desire to retain his freedom. His second failure at the Ecole Normale examination in July 1907, coupled with the news that Yvonne de Quiévrecourt was married, reduced him to a state of anguish and despair.

On 2 October 1907 Fournier began his two-year period of military service, a period marked by the engagement in December of Jacques

Fournier at Mirande, 1909, near the end of his first tour of military duty (by permission of Alain Rivière)

Rivière and Isabelle, who had met in April of the same year after Rivière's demobilization. Fournier detested the filth, the smell, the cramped quarters, the crudeness, the imbecility of army life and counted the days to his deliverance. Most of all he felt an immense pity and sympathy for the men. A soldier first in the cavalry and then in the infantry, he came in contact with a harsher reality and was introduced to a wider spectrum of men and human behavior than he had known before. The routine drudgery of the barracks and the physical exhaustion of maneuvers left him little time for literary activity. He began training as an officer-cadet at Laval in October 1908 and was commissioned a second lieutenant and sent in April 1909 to Mirande, in the southwest of France, where he remained for six months, until completion of his military service. He returned for additional periods of service in 1911 and 1913 and was mobilized at Mirande at the outbreak of the war in 1914.

The spring and summer of 1909, especially the months of May and June, were the bleakest and most depressing of Fournier's life. Loneliness and inactivity, added to disillusionment, a sense of failure, and anxiety about his future, contributed to another religious crisis much more serious and desperate than the first. It was the fourth anniversary of the meeting with Yvonne de Quiévrecourt. He was overcome with emotion at Lourdes and touched by conversations with the local priest and the chaplain of the hospice. He read Huysmans, the Old and New Testaments, Claudel, and Dostoyevski's *The Idiot* and prayed, as he put it, from the depths of his incredulity and his despair. Again he was strongly tempted to return to the Church but was held back by thoughts of the sacrifices that would be involved. He maintained that if he accepted faith he would become a monk or a missionary. The end of this crisis left him with the conviction that true happiness was not to be found in this world, that earthly happiness was too terrible to bear and was to be renounced in favor of a joy beyond. Six isolated fragments of the version of his novel entitled "Pays sans nom" exist, dating from 1909. All are melancholy and desolate, inferior to the letters of the same period. One of these fragments, "La Partie de plaisir" (The Outing), was refused by Gide for publication in the *Nouvelle Revue Française*.

In July 1909 Fournier's attempt to pass the *licence* examination in English resulted in another failure. Jacques Rivière and Isabelle Fournier were married in August at Saint-Germain-des-Prés, where Fournier had followed Yvonne de Quiévrecourt in 1905. Released from military service in September, he returned to Paris and, for the next six months, seems to have done very little, although his novel was taking shape in his mind. He was overwhelmed by a sense of the futility of life, a feeling of degradation due to carnal affairs at Mirande, thoughts of death, and the conviction that his life in a world where he felt himself a stranger would be a short one. Images of corruption, death, and decay had already appeared in his letters and imaginative pieces. He wrote that he was looking for a means to escape to the "lost domain" and that perhaps it was death after all. Yvonne de Quiévrecourt was lost forever. He was no longer first in the hearts of Jacques and Isabelle, the two people who had been his closest confidants. His academic projects had ended in failure; his work had been refused publication; he had no prospects or plans for a career.

Unfortunately very few of his letters date from this period, since he saw Jacques, Isabelle, and his parents daily, so it is difficult to follow the progress of his book, although some scattered, undated notes exist. In a letter dated April 1910, he wrote Rivière that he had chosen a new title, "Le Jour des noces" (The Wedding Day), for his work. He had a detailed outline, fairly close to the eventual novel, but only fragments were completed. His ultimate intention definitely was to write a novel of renunciation. The characters Meaulnes and Seurel now exist as well as a heroine, Anne-Marie, lost and found again, whom Meaulnes deserts on their wedding night, apparently to become a missionary.

An important change in Fournier's life was to affect drastically his plans for the novel. In February 1910 he met Jeanne Bruneau, a seamstress from Bourges who would become the Valentine of his novel. She had a timid and delicate face with something childish and tragic about her. He wrote his sister that Jeanne Bruneau was very beautiful and extraordinarily intelligent. She had all the best qualities except purity and because of her dubious past, he made her suffer cruelly. He was not interested in having a mistress; he was looking for love. Their liaison over the next two years was passionate and stormy, a series of ruptures and reconciliations. She once showed him a packet of letters from a former lover who had killed himself over her and whose explicit phrases offended him deeply. She threatened a life of prostitution if he abandoned her, but her relationship with Fournier enriched the novel by providing a realistic motive for Meaulnes's desertion of his bride. Although in rough drafts Valentine is Meaulnes's mistress, Fournier carefully eliminated all carnal scenes from the final version of the novel, thereby weakening both the character of Valentine and the reason for Meaulnes's overwhelming sense of remorse.

On 9 May 1910 Fournier began a two-year stint writing a column on literary events for the daily *Paris-Journal,* a post he disdained. He also contributed to the *courrier littéraire* in *Intransigeant* from February 1912 to the outbreak of the war. He served as French tutor to a young American poet named T. S. Eliot, who became his friend and whom he introduced to Rivière and to the milieu of the *NRF.* His godchild Jacqueline was born on 23 August 1911 after a difficult cesarean delivery that almost cost Isabelle Rivière her life. Fournier, who loved children, was enchanted by the baby.

Fournier worked simultaneously throughout 1910 on the realistic and the "dream" sections of his novel. From the beginning, the narrative was to be an imperceptible coming-and-going from dream to reality. The last hurdle Fournier had to cross was to be sure of what he meant by dream. The symbolist indifference to reality in no way appealed to him. The only things that interested him, he wrote, were things that had actually happened. In his book there would be no symbol, no theory, no hidden meaning.

At this juncture two writers helped him solve his artistic dilemma. Through his newspaper assignments he became a friend of Marguerite Audoux, a Sologne shepherdess whose novel *Marie-Claire* (1910) touched him deeply by its simple depiction of humble country life. Another close friend was Charles Péguy, with whom he had a great deal in common in spite of the difference in their ages. Péguy, who also felt the immanence of the marvelous in the world of reality, was of particular help. He strengthened Fournier's tendency to humanize the mysterious. Fournier discovered in the Scriptures the presence of the supernatural in human life, the mystery of the Incarnation being its supreme manifestation. There is no discontinuity between the "real" and the "other" world. The marvelous is not beyond or superimposed on reality but is an intrinsic part of it. To discover the secret wonder already existing in reality, to uncover in each detail of life its latent mystery became Fournier's goal.

During the eight years of the composition of *Le Grand Meaulnes,* Fournier continued to write short pieces, *poèmes en prose,* and stories of uneven quality, many of them published in reviews of the period. These works illustrate his struggle to find a subject and a style of his own and his slow progress to poetic realism. His last and best story, "Portrait," was published in the *Nouvelle Revue Française* in September 1911. His poems and short prose works were published after his death under the title *Miracles* (1924). Rivière's introduction to that volume, originally published in the *Nouvelle Revue Française* in 1922 and 1923, is essential reading for an appreciation of the false starts, wrong directions, and final discovery of his friend's path as a novelist.

A change in the directorship of *Paris-Journal* left Fournier jobless in April 1912. Péguy, who was a friend of Claude Casimir-Périer, remembered that the latter was looking for a secretary to help him write a book on Brest. Casimir-Périer

Composite photograph showing Fournier (at right) in 1913, his sister Isabelle Rivière and niece Jacqueline in 1912, and his brother-in-law Jacques Rivière in 1909 (by permission of Alain Rivière)

was the son of a former president of the Republic; his wife was the celebrated actress Simone (Pauline Benda). This was the wealthiest and most sophisticated milieu Fournier had ever known: Casimir-Périer's political world and the theater world of the last years of the *belle époque*. The post gave Fournier more time to devote to his novel, and the chapters began to accumulate. In October 1911 he wrote to Michel Lehl that his life was unhappy but his book was his consolation. He wanted it to sweep everyone off his feet; he hoped that all of France would read it and that all women would love it. By September 1912 he could inform Rivière that he was making an outline of the last chapter in the smallest detail and that he had ten chapters left to write. By November three chapters were still to be completed, one in the middle and two at the end. The novel was finished in early January 1913 but even then Fournier still spoke of inserting into it a long love letter written to Yvonne de Quiévrecourt the previous year, one which he had carried with him ever since.

In 1913 Marc Rivière, Jacques's younger brother, was at Rochefort preparing for entrance

to the Ecole de Médecine Navale and met the Quiévrecourt family. At the news, Fournier hurried to Rochefort to speak of Yvonne with her sister Jeanne. It was the eighth anniversary of the meeting at the Cours-la-Reine. He wrote Rivière that everything he had imagined of Yvonne was true. Several weeks later, he returned to Rochefort for an interview with Yvonne herself. She was, he reported, as he remembered and, although she was married and the mother of two children, she was the only person with whom he would have liked to spend his life. She remembered their first meeting in detail and promised him friendship but, after a brief exchange of letters, he realized that there was nothing further to expect from their relationship. In the love letter of 1912 which he gave her to read in his presence he had clearly indicated her role in his life. "Je n'avais qu'un moyen, vous ne m'aviez accordé qu'un moyen de vous rejoindre et de communiquer avec vous. C'était d'obtenir la gloire littéraire. . . . Un long roman que j'achève—et qui tourne tout autour de vous, de vous que j'ai si peu connue—paraîtra cet hiver" (I had only one way, you granted me only one way to reach you and to communicate with you. It was to attain literary fame. . . . A long novel that I am completing—and which revolves entirely around you, you whom I have known so little—will appear this winter).

Le Grand Meaulnes, dedicated to Fournier's sister Isabelle, appeared in serial form in the *Nouvelle Revue Française* from July to November 1913 and was published in book form by Emile-Paul in October of the same year. After eleven ballots it narrowly missed winning the Goncourt prize, an honor Simone was eager, through her influence, to secure for the young man with whom she had fallen in love. The attention of this famous older actress was flattering, and Fournier was soon involved in an intense and passionate relationship with a woman whom, as his letters to her reveal, his imagination transformed into an ideal young woman, a fiancée, a future wife. Their liaison brought him as much bitterness as joy, and her influence on his creativity was counterproductive. The work undertaken at this period of his life remains incomplete. There are fragments of a novel, "Colombe Blanchet," and a play, "La Maison dans la forêt" (The House in the Forest), in which his favorite themes are transformed or subverted, apparently under the influence of his relationship with Simone.

Called up immediately after the outbreak of war, Fournier joined his regiment at Mirande in August. On 22 September 1914 he was killed in battle in the Saint-Rémy wood near the village of Vaux-les-Palameix, just before his twenty-eighth birthday. His body was never found.

In its final form *Le Grand Meaulnes* is the story of Augustin Meaulnes, a tall, taciturn, adventurous boy of seventeen who becomes a boarder in the home of Monsieur and Madame Seurel, schoolteachers in the village of Sainte-Agathe. Their timid, hero-worshipping son François, the fifteen-year-old who narrates the story years later, falls immediately under his spell. On an escapade Meaulnes loses his way in the desolate Sologne forest and eventually arrives at a mysterious manor house hidden in the woods where a celebration is going on in honor of the engagement of the son of the house, the spoiled and chimerical Frantz de Galais.

At the party Meaulnes briefly encounters Frantz's sister, a beautiful girl named Yvonne, with whom he falls in love, encouraged by her promise to await his return. His search for her is complicated by the relationship that develops between Meaulnes and Frantz and by Frantz's rela-

tionship with his fiancée Valentine, who has rejected Frantz and refused to attend the engagement party. It is Valentine's deceit (she tells Meaulnes that Yvonne is married) that at first prevents Meaulnes from pursuing Yvonne; it is her disappearance, and Meaulnes's pledge to Frantz to find her again, that takes him from Yvonne almost immediately after their marriage and unwittingly involves him in an amorous relationship with Valentine. At the end of the novel, having brought together Frantz and Valentine, Meaulnes reappears to find that Yvonne has died giving birth to his daughter. The narrator, François, desolate, imagines Meaulnes setting out for further adventures with the little girl in his arms.

Rivière once wrote that no book is at the same time as enchanted and disenchanted as *Le Grand Meaulnes.* Admirers of the first part often fail to recognize that the novel is not a sentimental romance but essentially a tale of disillusionment, loss of faith, and failure. Fournier himself confirmed this view in a letter to Péguy in 1913 in which he stated that the little bit of voluptuousness in the book, the little bit of magic-lantern show, phantasmagoria, Russian ballet, and English adventure novel is compensated for by lasting regret and terrible suffering. The mysterious party scenes are only a part of the first section of the novel. They depict a paradise that in Meaulnes's case is irretrievably lost.

Meaulnes is a privileged soul. On the verge of manhood he has retained the child's idealism, his purity, his belief in the unforeseen and the miraculous, his unquestioning acceptance of the extraordinary. Three key utterances in Fournier's emotional vocabulary are essential to an understanding of the novel: *hauteur* (height), *trahir* (to betray), and *faire comme les autres* (to do as others do). He refers to Yvonne de Quiévrecourt as *haute* (lofty). He was sure that by dint of constant effort he would some day be so lofty—*si haut*—that they would be together again. Meaulnes says that when he discovered the Land Without a Name he had attained a height, a degree of perfection that he would never reach again. Only in death perhaps would he recapture the beauty of that time. But life on this plane is precarious. It involves, above all, belief and a continuous effort to remain *haut* and childlike. This does not mean clinging to childish ways. That is Frantz's mistake and François sees him as the pathetic, selfish, demanding child-man he has become at the end of the novel.

Meaulnes's principal error is losing his belief that, against all odds, he can find the Lost Domain and Yvonne again. He forgets her promise when he is told that she is married. He betrays the dream and slips without hope onto the easy path of ordinary adult life, thus causing the tragedy of the novel. Lonely and disillusioned like his creator, he says that a man who has made a leap into paradise cannot accept easy living as other people do. The compromise he must make to live *la dure vie basse* (the wretched lowly life) contrasts with the previous *hauteur*. This is why he turns so bitterly on Valentine and blames her for all that has gone wrong in their lives. She could not believe in Frantz's promises of happiness. She did not come to the celebration; she caused it to end in desolation.

François also betrays the dream he shared with his friend. He tells the story of Meaulnes's stay in the Lost Domain to the other boys, who see no mystery in the tale and even guess at the location of the place, and he becomes again a simple village boy whose vicarious leap into paradise has ended in failure. Yvonne alone has continued to believe, but she is condemned to death because she is the essential element in the magic world to which Meaulnes has lost all claim. There is, however, a final note of hope. François imagines Meaulnes setting out once more with his baby daughter. Another child—another point of departure. The cycle begins again.

It can also be said that few novels fuse so completely the real and the unreal as *Le Grand Meaulnes*. The reader closes the book with a memory of wonder and enchantment. But Fournier and those close to him have maintained that every element of the story is true to life. Fournier wrote that only reality can open the gates of dream. The school building with its attics, the life of the school and the village, even the names of the boys are authentic. Sainte-Agathe is Epineuil in the minutest detail. Uncle Florent's general store opens its doors in Vieux-Nançay. The Lost Domain is in part the château of Cornançay, near Epineuil, where a great celebration took place during Fournier's childhood. The strange celebration was inspired by a performance of Schumann's *Carnaval* danced by the Russian Ballet in 1910. The Seurels are recognizably the Fournier parents. Meaulnes's baby daughter is in part Fournier's niece Jacqueline.

The three male characters are differing aspects of Fournier's own personality, magnified and isolated so that none of them is he and he is

openly critical of each. Yvonne is certainly Yvonne de Quiévrecourt, whom Fournier had loved but never really known, and yet, in the last part of the novel, she also resembles Fournier's sister Isabelle, the young woman he knew best. Like Isabelle, Yvonne is closer than her parents to her brother Frantz, indulgent and accepting of his behavior, oblivious to his faults. Her good sense, maternal tenderness, courage, and generosity of heart make her the most memorable character of the novel.

Critics have pointed out that each of the three parts of the novel is dominated by one of the boys, Meaulnes, Frantz, or François. Meaulnes is definitely the hero of the first part. He stumbles into the Land Without a Name, falls in love with Yvonne, and sets the tone of mystery and enchantment that dominates the book. The second part relates the frustration of his efforts to rediscover the Lost Domain and is dominated by the quixotic Frantz, who steals Meaulnes's map, conceals his own identity, and disappears before giving further explanation. In the third part, François takes over and becomes Yvonne's loving friend. Most recent critics see François as the real hero of the book. Since he is the narrator, all the events are seen through his eyes and colored by his personality. He is responsible for the tone of wistfulness, regret, and nostalgia that permeates the story.

A great deal has been written about literary influences on Fournier: Nerval (*Sylvie*, 1854), Fromentin (*Dominique*, 1863), Gide (*La Porte étroite*, 1909), Rimbaud, Hardy, Dostoyevski, and the English adventure novelists, especially Stevenson. For a novel as intensely personal as *Le Grand Meaulnes* a more correct term would be spiritual affinities. Fournier's literary preferences naturally ran to books in which he found expressed tendencies and aspirations already existing in himself. Discovering a similarity to Dostoyevski in an episode of his novel, Fournier wrote that this was pure coincidence. No one will ever give it a thought, he said, because in his book he is putting the whole of himself—what he would like to have done and what he actually did. Fournier's letters authenticate the episodes and show how closely *Le Grand Meaulnes* reflects the temperament and experiences of the author.

The reaction to *Le Grand Meaulnes* in reviews of the period was varied, most critics failing to understand the novel. Valuable insight and information were provided by Rivière's *Nouvelle Revue Française* essay later published as the intro-

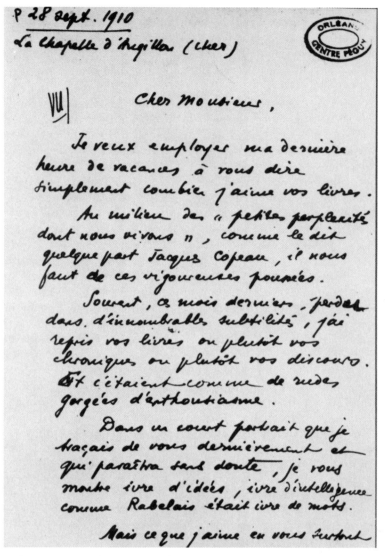

Page from Fournier's first letter to Charles Péguy (by permission of Alain Rivière)

duction to *Miracles*. Still more information came from the publication of the four-volume Rivière-Fournier correspondence (1926-1928) and of Fournier's letters to his family and to René Bichet in 1930. Because of Fournier's disappearance during the war and the appeal of these letters, he quickly became a romantic hero, and there was a spectacular increase of interest in him in France and abroad. A great number of books appeared from the 1930s through the 1950s—primarily biographical, many overly sentimental, varying considerably in quality. They tend to treat *Le Grand Meaulnes* as a reflection of its author's life rather than as a separate entity, often drawing conclusions from Fournier's letters rather than from the text. Many attempt to inter-

pret the novel from a preexisting point of view, particularly from a religious slant. The book has been variously described as a fairy tale, a dream fantasy, a rural novel, an adventure tale *à l'anglaise,* and a modern quest story. Simone's revelation in *Sous de nouveaux soleils* (1957) of her love affair with Fournier, Isabelle Rivière's authoritative refutation of her version of this affair in *Vie et passion d'Alain-Fournier* (1963), and Jean Loize's impressive accumulation of new details about Fournier's life in *Alain-Fournier, sa vie et "Le Grand Meaulnes"* (1968) have enriched understanding of Fournier's personality and temperament. Isabelle Rivière's book is also noteworthy for its inclusion of many previously unpublished letters. Perhaps the best book in English is Robert Gibson's *The*

Land without a Name: Alain-Fournier and His World (1975), a revision and amplification of his *The Quest of Alain-Fournier* (1954).

The 1960s ushered in a new phase of Fournier criticism, as critics began to study the novel itself. An early study indicative of this new trend is Robert Champigny's *Portrait of a Symbolist Hero: An Existential Study Based on the Work of Alain-Fournier* (1954). Other interesting and representative works include: Michel Guiomar's provocative psychocriticism based on concepts introduced by Gaston Bachelard, *Inconscient et imaginaire dans Le Grand Meaulnes* (1964), and Marie Maclean's study of the inner coherence and intricate structure of the novel, *Le Jeu suprême: Structure et thèmes dans "Le Grand Meaulnes"* (1973). A wealth of articles devoted to separate aspects of *Le Grand Meaulnes* have been published in scholarly journals, a great many in anglophone countries.

Le Grand Meaulnes has become a classic, published in many editions and formats. It has been translated into the major languages of the world. Françoise Delisle's English translation, the first, is entitled *The Wanderer* and appeared in 1928. Others have followed: *The Lost Domain*, translated by Frank Davison (1959) and *The Wanderer; or, The End of Youth*, translated by Lowell Blair (1971). *Le Grand Meaulnes* has been adapted for the stage and ballet. Jean-Gabriel Albicocco's 1967 film has been shown world wide. In the four years following its publication as a Livre de Poche (1963) more than 200,000 copies were sold annually.

Alain-Fournier himself has been variously honored. The lycée in Bourges was renamed for him. Plaques have been placed on Maman Barthe's house in La Chapelle where Fournier was born, on the schoolhouse in Epineuil, on Uncle Florent's store in Nançay, and on the house where Fournier lived in Mirande. A monument has been erected at Saint-Rémy and his name figures on the façade of the Pantheon in Paris. Streets bear his name and permanent exhibits can be seen in the Château de Béthune in La Chapelle and the Maison de la Culture in Bourges. Each year at Pentecost a bus takes devotees to the villages of Fournier's youth.

The Association des Amis de Jacques Rivière et Alain-Fournier, founded in 1975, publishes valuable studies and *inédits* in its quarterly bulletins. Alain-Fournier's papers, including notes, letters, and rough drafts, are at the archives of the association located in Viroflay. Alain Rivière, Fournier's nephew, and Hubert Blisson have created a poetic montage, *Les Etranges Paradis d'Alain-Fournier et du Grand Meaulnes*, which has been shown throughout France, in North Africa, behind the Iron Curtain, and in most of the countries of Western Europe.

Le Grand Meaulnes perhaps owes its popularity to the fact that every reader takes from it what he will. Some retain the memory of the marvelous *fête étrange* in the Land Without a Name. Others appreciate the concrete details of life in a French village. Some come away with a sense of desolation and loss as François carries downstairs the dead Yvonne, so long the object of Meaulnes's adolescent longings. Still others are impressed by the careful craftsmanship, the constant suspense as unforeseen events shape destiny. Some are drawn to the loving descriptions of the French countryside, and there are those who see in the novel new examples of the themes of sacred and profane love, innocence against experience, the fate of the idealist in a hostile world. All readers acknowledge the accomplished style and the haunting atmosphere. In the 19 April 1953 edition of *The Observer*, Harold Nicholson described Alain-Fournier's *Le Grand Meaulnes* as "the most impressive novel published in France during my lifetime," crediting it with giving him "a shock of delighted surprise, more sudden and concentrated than the prolonged pleasure that I have derived from the works of Fournier's great contemporaries." Praising "the genius with which Fournier handled his dream," Nicholson placed the novel "among those which every literate person should have read."

Letters:

Jacques Rivière et Alain-Fournier: Correspondance 1905-1914 (4 volumes, Paris: Gallimard, 1926-1928; revised and enlarged, 2 volumes, 1948);

Lettres d'Alain-Fournier à sa famille (1905-1914) (Paris: Plon, 1930; enlarged editions: Paris: Emile-Paul, 1940 and 1949; Paris: Fayard, 1986);

Lettres au Petit B. . . . (Paris: Emile-Paul, 1930)— comprises letters by Alain-Fournier to René Bichet; "La Fin de la jeunesse," by Claude Aveline; and "René Bichet," by Isabelle Rivière; enlarged edition (Paris: Fayard, 1986);

"Inédit: Les Lettres d'Alain-Fournier à Simone," *Le Figaro Littéraire*, 24-30 September 1964;

Charles Péguy et Alain-Fournier: Correspondance 1910-1914, edited by Yves Rey-Herme (Paris: Fayard, 1973);

"Correspondance 1910: L'Amitié entre André Lhote, Jacques Rivière, Alain-Fournier," edited by Alain Rivière, *Cahiers du Musée National d'Art Moderne,* no. 4 (April-June 1980): 214-256.

References:

Jean Bastaire, *Alain-Fournier ou l'anti-Rimbaud* (Paris: José Corti, 1978);

Bulletin des Amis de Jacques Rivière et Alain-Fournier (Viroflay, 1975-);

Robert Champigny, *Portrait of a Symbolist Hero: An Existential Study Based on the Work of Alain-Fournier* (Bloomington: Indiana University Press, 1954);

Jean-Marie Delettrez, *Alain-Fournier et le Grand Meaulnes* (Paris: Emile-Paul, 1954);

Fernand Desonay, *Le Grand Meaulnes d'Alain-Fournier* (Brussels: Editions des Artistes, 1941);

Robert Gibson, *The Land without a Name: Alain-Fournier and His World* (London: Elek, 1975);

Henri Gillet, *Alain-Fournier* (Paris: Emile-Paul, 1948);

Michel Guiomar, *Inconscient et imaginaire dans Le Grand Meaulnes* (Paris: José Corti, 1964);

Walter Jöhr, *Alain-Fournier, le paysage d'une âme* (Neuchâtel: Cahiers du Rhône, La Baconnière, 1945);

Daniel Leuwers, ed., *"Le Grand Meaulnes": Images et documents* (Paris: Garnier, 1986);

Jean Loize, *Alain-Fournier, sa vie et "Le Grand Meaulnes"* (Paris: Hachette, 1968);

Marie Maclean, *Le Jeu suprême: Structure et thèmes dans "Le Grand Meaulnes"* (Paris: José Corti, 1973);

Isabelle Rivière, *Images d'Alain-Fournier* (Paris: Emile-Paul, 1938);

Isabelle Rivière, *Vie et passion d'Alain-Fournier* (Monaco: Jaspard, Polus, 1963);

Jacques Rivière, Introduction to *Miracles* (Paris: Gallimard, 1924);

Simone (Simone [Benda] Porché), *Sous de nouveaux soleils* (Paris: Gallimard, 1957).

Papers:

Alain-Fournier's papers are in the archives of the Association des Amis de Jacques Rivière et Alain-Fournier, Viroflay, France.

Henri Barbusse
(17 May 1873-30 August 1935)

J. E. Flower
University of Exeter

SELECTED BOOKS: *Pleureuses* (Paris: Charpentier, 1895);

Les Suppliants (Paris: Charpentier, 1903);

L'Enfer (Paris: Librairie Mondiale, 1908); translated by Edward O'Brien as *The Inferno* (New York: Boni & Liveright, 1913); translated by John Rodker (London: Joiner & Steele, 1932);

Meissonier (Paris: Lafitte, 1911); translated by Frederick Taber Cooper as *Meissonier* (New York: Stokes, 1912);

Nous autres (Paris: Charpentier, 1914); translated by Fitzwater Wray as *We Others* (London & Toronto: Dent, 1918; New York: Dutton, 1918);

Le Feu: Journal d'une escouade (Paris: Flammarion, 1916); translated by Wray as *Under Fire: The Story of a Squad* (London & Toronto: Dent, 1917; New York: Dutton, 1917);

Clarté (Paris: Flammarion, 1919); translated by Wray as *Light* (London & Toronto: Dent, 1919; New York: Dutton, 1919);

L'Illusion (Paris: Flammarion, 1919);

La Lueur dans l'abîme (Paris: Editions Clarté, 1920);

Le Couteau entre les dents (Paris: Editions Clarté, 1921);

Paroles d'un combattant: Articles et discours (1917-1920) (Paris: Flammarion, 1921);

Quelques Coins du cœur (Geneva: Editions Coins du Sablier, 1921);

L'Etrangère (Paris: Flammarion, 1922);

Les Enchaînements (Paris: Flammarion, 1925); translated by Stephen Haden Guest as *Chains*, 2 volumes (London: Cape, 1925; New York: International Publishing, 1925);

Trois Films: Force–L'Au-delà–Le Crieur (Paris: Flammarion, 1926);

Les Bourreaux (Paris: Flammarion, 1926);

Jésus (Paris: Flammarion, 1927); translated by Solon Librescot (New York: Macaulay, 1927);

Les Judas de Jésus (Paris: Flammarion, 1927);

photograph by Manuel

Manifeste aux intellectuels (Paris: Les Ecrivains Réunis, 1927);

Faits divers (Paris: Flammarion, 1928); translated by Brian Rhys as *And I Saw It Myself* (New York: Dutton, 1928); translation republished as *Thus and Thus* (London & Toronto: Dent, 1929);

Voici ce qu'on fait de la Géorgie (Paris: Flammarion, 1929);

Ce qui fut sera (Paris: Flammarion, 1930);

Elévation (Paris: Flammarion, 1930);

Russie (Paris: Flammarion, 1930); translated by Warre B. Wells as *One Looks at Russia* (London & Toronto: Dent, 1931);

15

J'accuse (Paris: Bureau d 'Editions, 1932);

Zola (Paris: Gallimard, 1932); translated by Mary Balairdie Green and Frederick C. Green (London: Dent, 1932; New York: Dutton, 1933);

Staline: Un Monde nouveau vu à travers l'homme (Paris: Flammarion, 1935); translated by Vyvyan Holland as *Stalin: A New World as Seen through One Man* (London: Lane, 1935; New York: Macmillan, 1935);

Le Feu, journal d'une escouade, suivi du Carnet de Guerre, edited by Pierre Paraf (Paris: Flammarion, 1965).

The importance of Henri Barbusse is twofold: first as the author of *Le Feu* (1916; translated as *Under Fire,* 1917), the best known and most influential French antiwar novel written during World War I; second as a major left-wing writer and thinker during the first third of the twentieth century. More militant than Romain Rolland but less so than Louis Aragon or Paul Nizan, Barbusse had a career as a novelist, pamphleteer, and editor characterized by a deep concern for the underprivileged and exploited and for the educative role of art and writing in the class struggle. He believed that by virtue of his particular gifts, the writer had a perception of life which it was his duty to transmit to others. In 1919, in a letter to the Italian author Gabriele d'Annunzio, he wrote: "L'écrivain, le penseur, le guide, doit voir plus loin que les prétendus avantages immédiats, et plus loin que le temps présent" (The writer, thinker and guide has a duty to see beyond so-called immediate advantages of the present moment). In 1934 at the International Congress of Writers held in Paris he repeated in essence this remark: "Le devoir de l'écrivain est d'aider, dans la mesure de ses forces et dans la voie où il s'est engagé, les progrès et les perfectionnements de la collectivité à laquelle il est mêlé" (As far as his capabilities allow and given his sense of purpose the writer's duty must be to contribute to the improvement in the lot of the masses to whom he is committed).

Barbusse was born 17 May 1873 at Asnières in the *département* of the Seine into a family with a strong radical tradition. His mother, Annie (née Benson), was British; his father, Adrien, a French journalist and playwright. He was a brilliant student at Paris's Collège Rollin and had already begun writing his own verse and drama, for which he won prizes before graduating in 1895. He also contributed articles to the *Petit*

Parisien and the *Echo de Paris* and later, in 1903 was involved with the pacifist groups Revue de la Paix and Paix par le Droit. In 1895 his first volume of verse, *Pleureuses* (Hired Mourners), was published and in 1903 his second work, *Les Suppliants* (The Supplicants), a kind of verse novel, appeared. Both were influenced in form and tone by the symbolists and by a fin de siècle vogue for a rather effete aestheticism. However, *Les Suppliants* already gave some indication of his future preoccupations, and Barbusse would himself comment on it at a later date: "[son] originalité est d'être biblique, c'est-à-dire non de dépeindre mais de *prêcher* une vérité" (its originality is its biblical inspiration, that is to say it does not simply depict but it *preaches* a particular truth).

During these early years Barbusse earned his living through a series of civil service posts as well as from some writing and editorial work. In 1908 his novel *L'Enfer* (translated as *The Inferno,* 1913) was published. In it a young bank clerk rents a hotel room and, through a hole in the wall, spies on the various occupants of the adjoining room. This recording of human experience (not without a degree of prurient curiosity) has as its predominant theme the problem of communication. While there are comments of a political kind, they tend to be negative. Toward the end, for example, two doctors attend a person dying from cancer. The disease is likened by one of them to the spirit of nationalism and militarism which is killing France, but there are no suggestions for its cure or for an alternative course of action. In his 1932 book *Zola* (translated, 1932), Barbusse would criticize *L'Assommoir* for the same failure to suggest solutions. While certainly subversive—a quality which he acknowledged was shared by all truthful works—Zola's novel did not translate an awareness of the workers' plight into any recommendation for positive action. By the time Barbusse wrote *Zola,* his own *Le Feu* had already gone some way to meeting this objection and showed an important advance on his previous work.

Barbusse had completed his military service in 1893 and 1894. When war broke out twenty years later he joined up as an infantryman, later becoming a stretcher bearer before being invalided out in 1917. While like most, he considered Germany's overreaching imperialist ambitions to be principally responsible for the war, he (like Romain Rolland) could also see that France was not guiltless. Fundamentally opposed to war, he was nonetheless willing to fight in the hope that this would be the "war to end all wars." In a letter to *Humanité* (5 August 1914) he wrote that it would be "une guerre sociale qui fera faire un grand pas–peut-être le pas définitif à notre cause" (a social war which will cause a big, perhaps even definitive, step for our cause to be taken). Barbusse was mentioned several times in dispatches and in 1915 received the Croix de Guerre. Like most, he became rapidly disillusioned with war; early patriotism was replaced by cynicism and anger. The general inefficiency, the attitudes and the avoidance of duty by some in command, profiteering, and the idea of war much propagated by the jingoistic nationalist press as a colorful romantic adventure were frequent themes in his letters to his wife, published after his death in 1937. Like many novels of the war, *Le Feu* was based on a diary. (Its subtitle is *Journal d'une escouade,* The Story of a Squad.) Throughout his notebook or "Carnet de guerre," which he began in 1915, are passages which were eventually transferred to the novel. Already planned by the end of that year, the novel was completed by the middle of 1916; from August to November it was serialized in the left-wing review *L'Œuvre* with only one cut (chapter twelve) made by the censor. It was published in book form in December with this section restored and several new ones added; the novel was awarded the Prix Goncourt a year later and had sold nearly a quarter of a million copies by the end of 1918. Few, if any, novels of World War I have enjoyed such success or contributed so much to their author's subsequent career and reputation. *Le Feu* has been widely translated and is the high point of Barbusse's career as an imaginative writer.

On one level *Le Feu* describes and exposes the horrors and the futility of war. Descriptions are stark and frequently gruesome; men are threatened at every turn with being reduced to animals; quite ordinary objects (an egg or a box of matches) become disproportionately significant and prompt abnormal behavior among the soldiers. Barbusse's use of the essential diary form for the novel is particularly appropriate. The disjointed or, at best, tenuously linked episodes effectively underline the precarious, day-to-day nature of the soldiers' existence. This is not to say that the book is without structure. The title chapter comes three-quarters of the way through the novel as a natural climax; centrally placed is "Les Gros Mots" (Big Words) in which Barbusse discusses the problem of re-creating authentic French language; "L'Aube" (The Dawn) closes

Barbusse during World War I (courtesy of R. Laffont)

the novel with a vision of the future. Barbusse successfully emphasizes the elemental nature of front-line existence in this hell-like warscape: references to the fire of the title are matched by those to water (the ever-present rain) and mud. And against this background soldiers move either like animals or prehistoric creatures ("troglodytes sinistres") or like puppets, subject to forces beyond their control or understanding.

On a second level Barbusse makes his readers aware from the beginning of the novel's sociopolitical message. The men in the squad come from all parts of France and are representative of the working classes; Bertrand, the corporal, is used unequivocally as the author's spokesman; as narrator Barbusse intervenes at will to expand or interpret his soldiers' inadequately expressed ideas for them. And in the final chapter the register of language changes abruptly as the soldiers themselves articulate thoughts on equality, liberty, and fraternity, concepts whose significance they are beginning to grasp for the first time.

In later life Barbusse claimed it had been the Dreyfus Affair which had made him become socially aware: "le cas Dreyfus . . . me sortit de mon inertie individualiste" (the Dreyfus Affair . . . drew me out of my individualism and inertia). But it was the war which hardened his resolve, and he devoted the rest of his life to the pursuit and propagation of humanitarian and socialist ideals. His second war novel, *Clarté* (translated as *Light*, 1919), was not a success. As its title suggests, the novel is about enlightenment. Through his front-line action the hero, Simon Paulin, moves from passivity and individualism to an awareness of the exploitation and plight of the working-class masses and to action. His development is clearly intended to be educative. The description of his conversion as he lies wounded in a shell crater contains hints of the biblical conversion of Saint Paul; he is reborn: "Je me suis rendormi dans le chaos puis je me suis réveillé comme le premier homme" (I went to sleep amidst chaos and awoke like the first man). Parts of *Clarté* are effective: Paulin's delirium as he recovers from his injuries, the accounts of a provincial town's petty patriotism, moments of horror and destruction. But the object of the book is to preach. As a result, the symbolism is too often naive, the incidence of words indicating enlightenment (*clarté, lumière, soleil, aube, blancheur, éclair*) and Barbusse's authorial interference too obvious. Much of the language in the closing pages has an aphoristic tone more suited to the pamphlet or essay than to the novel, and by the close *Clarté* has developed into a statement of Barbusse's faith in the power of words and of books. After *Clarté* Barbusse turned to fiction less frequently. When he did so, as in his volumes of short stories, *Les Enchaînements* (1925; translated as *Chains*, 1925) and *Faits divers* (1928; translated as *And I Saw It Myself*, 1928), passages of sharply observed realistic description are overshadowed by a moralizing tone and by an emphasis on the plight of the enslaved individual and the absorbing powers of bourgeois society.

In March 1917 Barbusse founded the Association républicaine des anciens combattants (Republican Association of War Veterans) and, more important, the group Clarté, together with a periodical of the same name. Noted for its pacifist and internationalist character, *Clarté* attracted a wide spectrum of writers and was important in promoting in France the proletarian cultural movement which had its origins in the Soviet Union. Barbusse's own contributions to debates concerning both the role and the responsibility of the writer and intellectual and the value of art and literature appeared in a series of combative articles and essays, most of which were later published in book form: *Le Couteau entre les dents* (Knife between the Teeth, 1921); *La Lueur dans l'abîme* (The Light in the Abyss, 1920); and *Paroles d'un combattant: Articles et discours (1917-1920)* (A Fighter's Words: Articles and Speeches [1917-1920], 1921). His position remained consistent: "L'homme de lettres qui se tient systématiquement à l'écart des grandes idées sociales et politiques, atrophie sa mission d'écrivain et déshonore sa mission d'homme, puisque l'horreur universelle ne peut changer que par des mesures d'ordre politique" (The man of letters who systematically stands aside from the major social and political issues wastes and dishonors his vocation as a writer and as a man, since the horrors which exist throughout the world can be changed by political means only).

Barbusse joined the French Communist Party in 1923, a year after its foundation. During the 1920s he was active both as a political journalist and as a literary reviewer for the then-Communist paper *L'Humanité*; in addition to his volumes of short stories he also produced, in 1927, *Jésus* and *Les Judas de Jésus*, both poorly received by Marxist critics in a hardening political climate. In the former he portrays Jesus as a revolutionary defender of the exploited classes; in the latter he attempts to give historical and philosophical reasons for this portrait. His most significant act during this period was to create *Monde* in 1928. In many ways this weekly review, which continued until Barbusse's death, was a natural successor to *Clarté* in providing a forum for intellectual, artistic, and political debate. Its independence—proclaimed in its first issue—was genuine, but for all its value it was heavily criticized by the extreme left at the International Congress of Revolutionary Writers held at Kharkov in 1930. Barbusse's name was linked with that of the apolitical proletarian novelist Henri Poulaille, and *Monde* was seen as a reactionary publication. Probably because of his influential position in left-wing intellectual circles in France, Barbusse was spared some of the heavier criticism and was promised assistance in "re-educating" himself. As the political climate softened and as the period of the fellow travelers developed in the early 1930s, however, Barbusse continued to be active and influential. He was part of the group—including Paul Vaillant-Couturier, Jean Guéhenno, Romain Rolland, Paul Nizan, and Louis Aragon—which created the Association des Ecrivains et Artistes Révolutionnaires in 1932 and its review *Commune* a year later. At the same time he was much involved (again with Romain Rolland) in the European movement against the threat of fascism, and in 1933 he became president of the Comité Mondial contre la Guerre et le Fascisme. Already in 1932 in his essay *J'accuse* (1932), he attacked what he considered to be the pro-Hitler factions in France. In his 1932 study of Zola, despite his admiration, he underlined what he considered Zola's limitations and reiterated his views about socially committed writing. This was his last major contribution to the debate which would take a new direction with the attempt in France to promote socialist realism. During the last two years of his life his energy remained unabated. He traveled widely, attending conferences as far afield as New York. In 1935 his last work, *Staline* (translated as *Stalin*, 1935), was published, an undisguised eulogy of the man he saw as a natural heir to Lenin. In July he was invited to the Seventh International Congress in Moscow. Within days of arriving he developed pneumonia which proved fatal, and he died on 30 August.

In an interview with the journalist Frédéric Lefèvre in April 1925 Barbusse remarked: "Je ne suis pas un militant; je suis un homme de lettres" (I am not a militant; I am a writer). His career rather suggests otherwise, though he was certainly never militant in the way that Nizan and Aragon were. But he was fully and tirelessly committed to a campaign for peace and to a struggle on behalf of the mass of working-class people against the hegemony of the bourgeoisie. Almost without exception, his writings turned on this principle and on the insistence that art and literature should have a social purpose. At its best his essays and polemical writings have a drive and sense of purpose that were clearly effective; but only in *Le Feu* can his imaginative work be said to have reached an equivalent level.

Letters:

Lettres de Henri Barbusse à sa femme 1914-1917 (Paris: Flammarion, 1937).

References:

Danielle Bonnaud-Lamotte, "Les Ecrivains français du XXᵉ siècle en U.R.S.S.: La réception du *Feu* d'Henri Barbusse," *Œuvres et Critiques*, 2 (Spring 1977): 59-74;

Vladimir Brett, *Henri Barbusse. Sa marche vers la Clarté, son mouvement Clarté* (Prague: Editions de l'Académie Tchécoslovaque des Sciences, 1963);

David Caute, *Communism and the French Intellectuals, 1914-1960* (London: Deutsch, 1964);

Jacques Duclos and Jean Fréville, *Henri Barbusse* (Paris: Editions Sociales, 1946);

Frank Field, *Three French Writers and the Great War: Studies in the Rise of Communism and Fascism* (Cambridge: Cambridge University Press, 1975), pp. 21-78;

J. E. Flower, *Literature and the Left in France* (London: Macmillan, 1983), pp. 29-49;

J. H. King, *The First World War in Fiction*, edited by H. M. Klein (London: Macmillan, 1976), pp. 43-52;

Jacques Meyer, "*Le Feu* d'Henri Barbusse," *Europe* (January 1969): 16-67;

Nicole Racine, "The Clarté Movement in France 1919-21," *Journal of Contemporary History*, 2 (April 1967): 195-208;

Nicole Racine-Furland, *Les Ecrivains communistes en France 1920-1936* (Paris: Hachette, 1973);

Annette Vidal, *Henri Barbusse, soldat de la paix* (Paris: Editeurs Français Réunis, 1953).

André Breton
(19 February 1896-28 September 1966)

Anna Balakian
New York University

bibliography prepared by
Isabelle Lorenz
City University of New York

SELECTED BOOKS: *Mont de Piété* (Paris: Sans Pareil, 1919);

Les Champs magnétiques, by Breton and Philippe Soupault (Paris: Sans Pareil, 1920);

Clair de terre (Paris: Collection Littérature, 1923);

Manifeste du surréalisme; Poisson soluble (Paris: Editions du Sagittaire, 1924); republished with a preface and with *La Lettre aux voyantes* (Paris: Editions Kra, 1929);

Les Pas perdus (Paris: Gallimard, 1924; revised and corrected, Paris: Gallimard, 1969);

Légitime Défense (Paris: Editions Surréalistes, 1926);

Introduction au discours sur le peu de réalité (Paris: Gallimard, 1927);

Le Surréalisme et la peinture, avec soixante-dix-sept photogravures d'après Max Ernst, Giorgio de Chirico, Joan Miró, Georges Braque, Jean Arp, Francis Picabia, Pablo Picasso, Man Ray, André Masson, Yves Tanguy (Paris: Gallimard, 1928; enlarged, New York: Brentano's, 1945; revised, corrected, and enlarged, Paris: Gallimard, 1965); translated by Simon Watson Taylor as *Surrealism and Painting* (New York: Harper & Row, 1972; London: Macdonald, 1972);

Nadja (Paris: Gallimard, 1928); translated by Richard Howard (New York: Grove Press/ London: Evergreen Books, 1960); revised edition (Paris: Gallimard, 1963);

Ralentir travaux, by Breton, René Char, and Paul Eluard (Paris: Editions Surréalistes, 1930);

L'Immaculée Conception, by Breton and Eluard (Paris: Editions Surréalistes, 1930);

Second Manifeste du surréalisme (Paris: Editions Kra, 1930);

L'Union libre, anonymous (N.p., 1931);

Misère de la poésie: L' "Affaire Aragon" devant l'opinion publique (Paris: Editions Surréalistes, 1932);

photograph by Lipnitzki

Le Revolver à cheveux blancs (Paris: Editions des Cahiers Libres, 1932);

Les Vases communicants (Paris: Editions des Cahiers Libres, 1932);

Qu'est-ce que le surréalisme? (Brussels: René Henriquez, 1934); translated by David Gascoyne as *What Is Surrealism?* (London: Faber & Faber, 1936);

L'Air de l'eau (Paris: Editions Cahiers d'Art, 1934);

Point du jour (Paris: Gallimard, 1934; revised and corrected, 1970);

Du temps que les surréalistes avaient raison (Paris: Editions Surréalistes, 1935);

Position politique du surréalisme (Paris: Editions du Sagittaire, 1935);

Notes sur la poésie, by Breton and Eluard (Paris: G. L. M., 1936);

Le Château étoilé (Paris: Editions du Minotaure, 1937);

L'Amour fou (Paris: Gallimard, 1937); translated by Mary Ann Caws as *Mad Love* (Lincoln: University of Nebraska Press, 1987);

Fata Morgana (Buenos Aires: Editions des Lettres Françaises, 1942); translated by Clark Mills (Chicago: Black Swan Press, 1969);

Arcane 17 (limited edition, New York: Brentano's, 1944; trade edition, 1945);

La Situation du surréalisme entre les deux guerres (Paris: Fontaine, 1945);

Young Cherry Trees Secured Against Hares/Jeunes Cerisiers garantis contre les lièvres, bilingual edition, English translations by Edouard Roditi (New York: View/London: Zwemmer, 1946);

Les Manifestes du surréalisme, suivis de Prolégomènes à un troisième manifeste du surréalisme ou non (Paris: Editions du Sagittaire, 1946);

Yves Tanguy, bilingual edition, English translations by Bravig Imbs (New York: Pierre Matisse, 1946);

Arcane 17 enté d'ajours (Paris: Editions du Sagittaire, 1947);

Ode à Charles Fourier (Paris: Fontaine, 1947); translated by Kenneth White as *Ode to Charles Fourier* (London: Cape Goliard, 1969; London: Cape Goliard/New York: Grossman, 1970);

Martinique, charmeuse de serpents (Paris: Editions du Sagittaire, 1948);

La Lampe dans l'horloge (Paris: Robert Marin, 1948);

Poèmes (Paris: Gallimard, 1948);

Flagrant Délit; Rimbaud devant la conjuration de l'imposture et du truquage (Paris: Editions Thésée, 1949);

La Clé des champs (Paris: Editions du Sagittaire, 1953);

Les Manifestes du surréalisme, suivis de Prolégomènes à un troisième manifeste du surréalisme ou non,

Du surréalisme en ses œuvres vives, et d'Ephémérides surréalistes (Paris: Editions du Sagittaire, 1955);

L'Art magique, by Breton with the assistance of Gérard Legrand (Paris: Club Français du Livre, 1957);

Joan Miró. Constellations, gouaches by Miró and prose poems by Breton (New York: Pierre Matisse, 1959);

Manifestes du surréalisme (Paris: Pauvert, 1962); translated by Richard Seaver and Helen R. Lane as *Manifestoes of Surrealism* (Ann Arbor: University of Michigan Press, 1969);

Clair de terre. Précédé de Mont de Piété. Suivi de Le Revolver à cheveux blancs et de l'Air de l'eau. (Paris: Gallimard, 1966);

Les Champs magnétiques. Suivi de S'il vous plaît et de Vous m'oublierez, by Breton and Soupault (Paris: Gallimard, 1967);

Signe ascendant. Suivi de Fata Morgana, les Etats généraux, Des Epingles tremblantes, Xenophiles, Ode à Charles Fourier, Constellations, Le La (Paris: Gallimard, 1968);

Selected Poems: André Breton, bilingual edition, English translations by White (London: Cape, 1969);

L'Un dans l'autre (Paris: Losfeld, 1970);

Perspective cavalière, edited by Marguerite Bonnet (Paris: Gallimard, 1970);

Poems of André Breton: A Bilingual Anthology, edited and translated by Jean-Pierre Cauvin and Caws (Austin: University of Texas Press, 1982).

OTHER: Max Ernst, *La Femme, 100 têtes,* preface by Breton (Paris: Editions Carrefour, 1929);

Le Surréalisme au service de la révolution, nos. 1-6, edited by Breton (Paris, 1930-1933; republished, New York: Arno Press, 1968);

Achim Arnim, *Contes bizarres,* introduction by Breton (Paris: Editions des Cahiers Libres, 1933);

Dictionnaire abrégé du surréalisme, edited by Breton and Paul Eluard (Paris: Galerie Beaux Arts, 1938);

Trajectoire du rêve, compiled by Breton (Paris: G. L. M., 1938);

Anthologie de l'humour noir, edited by Breton (Paris: Editions du Sagittaire, 1940; revised and enlarged, 1950);

Almanach surréaliste du demi-siècle, edited by Breton and Benjamin Péret (Paris: Editions du Sagittaire, 1950);

Charles Robert Maturin, *Melmoth ou l'homme er-rant,* preface by Breton (Paris: Pauvert, 1954).

André Breton, a twentieth-century French poet and essayist, also a novelist and founder and theoretician of the surrealist movement, was born in Tinchebray, Normandy, on 19 February 1896, died in Paris on 28 September 1966, and was buried in the cemetery of Batignoles. His family originated in Brittany and Lorraine. His first years were spent in Lorient on the Brittany coast, which was to leave in his poetry indelible impressions of shell-studded seashore and luminosity of sky. He was educated in Paris at the lycée Chaptal from 1906 to 1913 and entered medical school at the University of Paris on the eve of World War I. He continued his medical studies intermittently during the war years although he had been mobilized. He served in the ambulance corps and neurological wards for the war-injured in Nantes, in Saint-Dizier (in the region of the Marne), and later in Val-de-Grâce, where he did an internship. It was while a medical student that he became acquainted with the works of Sigmund Freud and of Freud's French predecessors, Dr. Pierre Janet and Dr. Jean-Martin Charcot. During the years of service at the front and in hospitals, Breton shuttled to and from Paris and mingled with the literati, getting to know established figures such as Paul Valéry and Marcel Proust, avant-garde poets such as Pierre Reverdy and Guillaume Apollinaire, who frequented the cubist circles, and aspiring poets yet unknown who gathered at the bookstore of Adrienne Monnier.

It was in Apollinaire's *Les Mamelles de Tirésias (The Breasts of Tirésias),* a play first performed in 1917, that Breton heard the word *surrealist*; he later used it, in memory of Apollinaire, as the name of the movement he created in 1924. In 1917 he met Louis Aragon, a fellow student at Val-de-Grâce, and Philippe Soupault in the entourage of Apollinaire. With Soupault he wrote in 1919 the first presurrealist automatic text, *Les Champs magnétiques* (Magnetic Fields, 1920), an application of lessons in psychic automatism learned in the medical textbooks of Janet. At the end of the war he was writing poetry for avant-garde magazines such as *Sic* and *Nord-Sud,* directed by Reverdy, and with Aragon and another young poet just returned from war, Paul Eluard, he founded the magazine *Littérature* (the word taken in its derogatory sense) to which con-

tributed those who, with Breton, were to initiate the surrealist movement.

In addition to the psychiatry he discovered in medical school, the most important influences on Breton's poetic formation were Rimbaud and Lautréamont, two revolutionary poets of the nineteenth century who had not come to serious literary attention until the second decade of the twentieth century. Rimbaud had wanted to create a new language for poetry, and Lautréamont had tried, with horrendous imagery, to destroy the notion of an anthropocentric universe. The latter, as the basis of his metaphoric imagery, compared incomparables in such phrases as "beautiful like the encounter of an umbrella and of a sewing machine on a dissecting table." The literary principle underlying this image became the nucleus of what Reverdy in poetry and Max Ernst in painting termed "the fortuitous juxtaposition of disparate realities," which was to become standard and basic practice in surrealist poetry.

By 1919 Breton, with his friends Aragon and Eluard, learned of the Dada activities in Zurich, and with the support of painter Francis Picabia they persuaded Tristan Tzara to come to Paris and continue the iconoclastic activities of Dadaism in collaboration with French recruits. Drawn at first by the nihilism and antiart attitudes of Tzara, Breton soon turned to a more positive form of subversion in which antipathies for the social order might not exclude the restructuring of art forms and renewal of faith in youth, love, poetry, and liberty, which were to become the signposts of the surrealists' philosophy, first promulgated in Breton's *Manifeste du surréalisme* in 1924. Of the two definitions of surrealism which mark all the writings of Breton, the first stresses the need to utilize the unconscious mechanism of the mind to overcome the moral and aesthetic constraints that reason has imposed upon free-thought processes and analogical practices; the second projects the power of a mental state which may introduce the dream into the world of action to resolve human problems in general. Illustrations of these definitions were to become the principal objective of Breton's writings both in poetry and in prose.

In their battle against rationalism in favor of the potentials of the imagination, the surrealist group under the leadership of Breton assumed a laboratory format, centered in café meetings and at the home of Breton, 42 rue Fontaine in Montmartre, which he established after his marriage on 25 September 1921 to

Simone Kahn, the first of his three wives, ended in 1931. The breakup of this marriage caused him considerable anguish, even though it took place at his instigation, while he was involved in a passionate affair with "Madam X." He kept his Montmartre domicile until the end of his life. Under his direction the group studied transcriptions of dreams and practiced hypnosis, psychic automatism in writing and painting, and aleatory (random) walking in the streets of Paris; they even attempted a simulation of the verbal communication of the deranged—all this to free the creative imagination from the shackles of rational training. The group included, besides Aragon and Eluard, poets such as Robert Desnos, René Crevel, Benjamin Péret, Philippe Soupault (very briefly), Antonin Artaud, as well as artists from all over the world: Salvador Dali, Max Ernst, Marc Chagall, Victor Brauner, René Magritte, Yves Tanguy, Man Ray, Mata, Toyen, and others.

The coterie was always in a state of flux as joiners turned into dissenters; surrealist activities peaked in the period between 1924 and World War II. Many of the writings and paintings first emerged in the numerous successive journals which were founded and floundered under surrealist direction. In the 1930s Breton, along with many of his colleagues, wished to participate in political action and joined the French Communist Party. Many stayed within its framework. Breton was quickly disillusioned. The 1935 pamphlet *Du temps que les surréalistes avaient raison* (When the Surrealists Were Right), which explains Breton's position, can be read in English translation in *Manifestoes of Surrealism* (1969). The concept of revolution had two meanings for him: on the one hand it was the revolution of the human spirit; on the other it signified a sporadic adherence to the Marxist objective of transforming society.

Although the political applications of Breton's philosophical theories went awry, his literary activities multiplied. Simultaneously, he wrote some of his major poetic texts and produced a trilogy in prose, *Nadja* (1928; translated, 1960), *Les Vases communicants* (Communicating Vessels, 1932), and *L'Amour fou* (1937; translated as *Mad Love*, 1987), followed during World War II by *Arcane 17* (written and published in a limited edition in 1944). Collectively these works constitute Breton's self-study of his affective life and the related process of creativity in writing. These prose works are Breton's contribution to the contemporary novel, as critics view it *in retrospect*, not according to the structure of the novel as it was at the

time of Breton's writing, but as the genre developed and was transformed in subsequent years. *Les Vases communicants* reflects his love affair or "free union" with "Madam X." *L'Amour fou* was written under the inspiration of his love for Jacqueline Lamba, whom he met in 1935 and married that same year. Although including autobiographical elements, they are closer to fiction in some ways—a poetic fiction, to be sure—because their aim is not conveying information but creating, or re-creating, states of mind (in various characters) through literary means, in order to relegate fact to its proper subordinate place and give to psychic reality its full and universal importance.

It should be noted that his first, 1924 manifesto begins with a severe attack on the profusion of novels available and popular at the time. He criticizes them for nurturing positivist and naturalist techniques, for the "vacuity" of their descriptive style, and his dissatisfaction extends to novelists' psychological analysis of characters, which Breton finds reductive even in such prestigious models as Stendhal and Dostoyevski. He states flatly that he has no intention to add to the pile of such "ridiculous" novels and burden the reading public with what he calls the empty moments of his life. Since a major element of Breton's poetics was also to eliminate barriers of genres, it may be an anomaly to classify him as a novelist; yet ironically, most of those who have read Breton, or even become familiar with his general reputation as a writer, associate him chiefly with his work *Nadja*, which can be considered either as his critique of the standard novel of his time or as a forerunner of the New Novel. Indubitably Breton's impact has been recognized by free-form novelists such as Alain Robbe-Grillet, Michel Butor, and Claude Simon. *Nadja* has gained justification as a novel because, instead of destroying the novel as Breton had hoped, he contributed strongly to the shaping of the antinovel as a form.

Nadja, Les Vases communicants, L'Amour fou, and *Arcane 17* are held together by their rejection of narrative discourse and their displacement of sequence of events by the sequence of analogies of perceived images that reflect the subjectivity of the voice in the text. Except for a brief simulation of dialogue in *Nadja*, these works are interior monologues in which the stream of consciousness of the *I* designates and interprets the objects and sites toward which he gravitates and the persons he encounters. The first three of

Tristan Tzara, Breton's first wife, Simone Kahn Breton, and Breton, Paris, 1922

these works can be viewed as a trilogy which takes place in Paris, with, in each of the volumes, a brief interlude of escape from the city; the autobiographical events are conveyed in documentary fashion; and, to preserve Breton's truth-claim, the descriptions one might expect are replaced by photographic illustrations. As theoretically stated in the first manifesto, all events that are exogenous to people's lives–that is, those which do not relate to the fate of their souls and the meaning of their existences–are eliminated.

Nadja opens with the question–"Who am I?"–and in the opening pages Breton gives an overview of his humdrum routines and of the persons he regularly visits. The young woman "who calls herself Nadja," and whose name contains the first two syllables of the Russian word "to hope," enters his life through chance encounter, one of those cherished outcomes of aleatory walking in which the group indulged as an act of faith in the benign powers of chance. Breton thereafter, between the clearly stated dates of 4 and 13 October 1926, becomes Nadja's companion and intrudes into the penumbral experiences of a young woman who has let down the barriers between the rational and the irrational and who "cares little but marvelously for life." It is an adventure for Breton to share the perceptions in high gear that make Nadja see a blue wind in the

trees and a hand in flame in the Seine river. However, though disenchanted with his own conjugal life, he does not fall in love with Nadja–perhaps an indication of the limits of his propensity for the irrational. After Nadja's disappearance from almost daily meetings, and a period of silence, he learns that she has been committed to an institution; this news catalyzes his protest against society's inability to cope with any infringement of its static definition of propriety and its concept of rational behavior. Breton casts his social protest into a philosophical metaphor of the prison-house in which so-called civilized humanity lives under the yoke of mores that curtail its intrinsic liberty. The lesson in freedom that Nadja contributes to Breton's understanding of life has a corollary: she opens his particular life to a new capacity for love.

The subsequent texts continue the analogical sequence of objects catalyzing actions, actions leading to images, pictorial and verbal, that generate or support philosophical meditations, all contributing to a cumulative answer to the search for identity, articulated in the opening question of *Nadja*. Each of these texts highlights one of the facets of the unconscious which aims to destroy the linguistic dichotomy Western civilization has developed between *real* and *unreal*, *rational* and *irrational*, *physical* and *spiritual*, *causal* and *marvelous*, whereas in Breton's surrealist vision they are perceived in continuity and unity.

In *Les Vases communicants* Breton places the dream in the world of the material phenomena of man's wakeful state with its accumulation of desires and frustrations. He asserts that its active relationship with the dream is at the heart of the surrealist vision. Summing up his quasi-scientific inquiries, he envisages "*a conducting wire* between the not too dissociable worlds of wakefulness and sleep, of exterior reality and interior, of reason and insanity, of the serenity of knowledge and of dream, of life for life and for revolution, etc." He opens with a theoretical study of dreams beginning in the eighteenth century and including Freud's methodologies, proceeds to autoanalyses of his dreams and their relation to his daily life and unsuccessful pursuit of lady X with whom he has become infatuated, and concludes that the dream is not only a residue of past experiences in the realm of desire and its obstacles, but also has the power of prophetic wish-fulfillment. This belief explains why the tone of despondency on which the book opens is overcome by faith in the power of poets to transform unacceptable realities.

L'Amour fou is the happy justification of that faith as he seeks out the miracle of objective chance, the moments of coincidence between our voluntary movements, impelled consciously or unconsciously by human desire or necessity, and their concordance with objective chance. At the end of the peripatetic journey through his labyrinth in these three volumes is not the Minotaur but "the scandalously beautiful" Jacqueline. The love which was undirected in *Nadja* and impeded in *Les Vases communicants* reaches in *L'Amour fou* its realization in the figure of Jacqueline Lamba, the woman who was to become Breton's second wife in August 1934 and the mother of his only child. It is interesting to note that the forces of the unconscious manifested in mental derangement (*Nadja*), dreams (*Les Vases communicants*), and law of probabilities (*L'Amour fou*) are all benign for Breton: Nadja leads him to a broader appreciation of freedom, dreams are sublimating rather than nightmarish in their effects, and chance supports his pursuit of happiness. Neither in medical or mathematical sciences nor in the literary or painterly practices of other surrealists have these forces operated so propitiously in favor of man.

Arcane 17, the last of the prose works, which negates both the basic narrative and descriptive styles of the novel and the format of autobiography, takes place not in Paris but in North America, where Breton spent the war years 1941-1945 in self-exile. (He went to New York in 1941, after a short stay in Martinique, where he was briefly interned as a political suspect.) *Arcane 17* opens like *Les Vases communicants*, on a note of solitude and despondency, the biographical context being this time the separation from his wife Jacqueline, which took place in the early 1940s and deprived him of seeing daily his beloved daughter, Aube, born in 1936, and separation from his country during the war. Aleatory chance remedies the former situation by the unexpected encounter of a new love, Elisa Bindhoff, with whom he undertakes a journey to Acadia (the Gaspé Peninsula) and was to marry the following year after divorcing Jacqueline in Reno. There in 1944 he writes his fourth analogical prose, which, according to contemporary loosening of genre definitions, can qualify as novelistic. He combines in the network of emblems the great forces of eroticism and political destiny, the commitment of the human will to personal love and to universal fraternity. The triumph of light over darkness is embodied in the Percé Rock, which at the tip of the peninsula acts as a curtain that produces light and darkness intermittently, and, in the medieval legend with whom Melusine's new love Elisa is identified, brings physical and moral strength. The mythical half-human half-divine mermaid/wife ever protected the House of Lusignan though she was stripped permanently of her human form through the (human) weakness of character of her spouse. In the same manner Elisa is the great protector of the exiled poet, and by extension Breton reaches out to the universal power of woman, long neglected but essential, he thinks, for the hope of future social reconstruction and human salvation.

Arcane 17 ends on a note of fervent optimism as Breton affirms the possibilities of harmony through the application of the alchemical principle of conciliation of opposites in nature to human relationships. Perhaps nowhere more than in this prose of 1944 is Breton primarily a poet. His orchestration of images to arouse ecstasy out of the strictures of anguish is his hymn to life and to its indestructibility in the midst of man's gigantic efforts for universal anthropocide.

Other prose writings of Breton include his collection of articles on modern art entitled *Le Surréalisme et la peinture* (1928); the English translation, *Surrealism and Painting* (1972), includes all

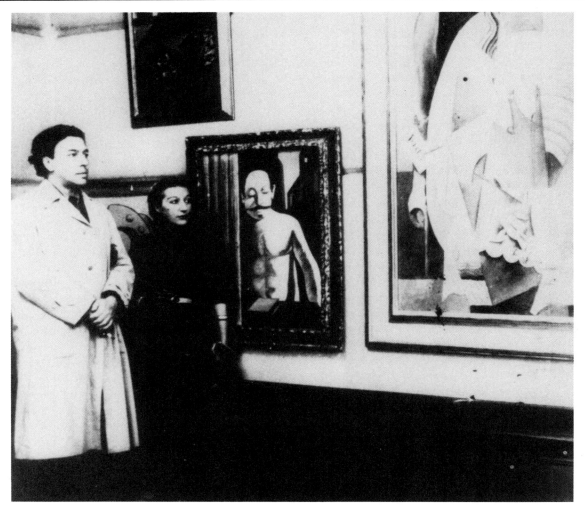

Breton with his second wife, Jacqueline Lamba Breton, at the 1936 surrealist exposition held in London (photograph by D. R.)

the essays of the enlarged edition of 1965. In the opinion of Breton the essential common factor among poets and painters associated with surrealism is the freedom of the eye which he describes in the first sentence of the first article: "L'œil existe à l'état sauvage" (the eye exists in a savage state). In French *sauvage* means primeval, virginal, as well as possessing the connotation of violence it has acquired in English. The freedom of the eye, whether in the construction of metaphors or of painterly visions, was for Breton the stripping of code-connotations in favor of individual powers of association. The *Second Manifeste du surréalisme,* published in 1930, responded to his detractors and suggested that surrealism should move in the direction of occultism and toward a monistic view of the universe where "la vie et la mort, le réel et l'imaginaire, le passé et le futur, le communicable et l'incommunicable, le haut et

le bas cessent d'être perçus contradictoirement" (life and death, the real and the imaginary, the past and the future, the communicable and the incommunicable, the high and the low, cease to be perceived as contradictory), in the manner of the hermetists' conciliation of opposites. Breton differed from the romanticists by transforming the dualistic metaphor into a circular mode tying together the animal, vegetable, and mineral kingdoms in a holistic unity. And love became a union very similar to the oneness of the physical world.

This monistic philosophy underlies Breton's poetry, which is his major achievement, although little of it has yet appeared in English translation. Beginning with his first collection, *Clair de terre* (Earthshine, 1923), gathering the poetry of the 1920s, and proceeding to *Le Revolver à cheveux blancs* (The Revolver with White Hair, 1932), which in terms of hermetic imagery signifies the union of protest and magic, his poetry reveals the sensuality and imagination of a visionary, and love is always the motivating element: love of woman, the embrace of the cosmos, and the perception of metamorphosis in every human and natural phenomenon. His most famous poem, *L'Union libre* (Free Union), published anonymously in 1931, belongs to this period. It consists of a long series of metaphors identifying the power of a woman loved within the dynamics of the four alchemical elements of water, fire, earth, and air. Breton continues the ritualistic handling of eroticism in his next series of poems, *L'Air de l'eau* (The Air of Water, 1934), dedicated to Jacqueline Lamba. While in Marseilles during his passage from occupied France to the United States he wrote the first of his long poems, *Fata Morgana* (1942), in which the themes of exile, love, and voyage are transmitted not in circumstantial narrative but through enigmatic alchemical symbols and nonreferenced metaphors of displacement and faith in the power to overcome. "Les Etats généraux," written in New York in 1943 and included in *Poèmes* (1948), is a trilevel poem about rebellion and liberty, using elliptical language and applying historical figures to contemporary situations. In New York Breton was employed as a speaker for the Voice of America. The third of his long poems, *Ode à Charles Fourier* (1947; translated and explicated by Kenneth White, 1969), was inspired by a cross-country trip he took during which he perceived the "savage eye" of America. In this poem he takes the nineteenth-century Utopian socialist Fourier as the emblematic figure of harmony.

Breton returned to Paris at the end of World War II, and he spent the last decades of his life in Paris or at his summer home in Saint-Cirq-la Popie. He had confrontations with the existentialist writers popular in the postwar period and he adhered to the short-lived World Citizens movement of Garry Davis since it was compatible with the notion of "A Planet without a Visa," which he had promoted in the early surrealist tracts to highlight the international character of surrealism and the surrealist antipathy for national barriers and ethnocentricities.

His last major poetic work was *Constellations* (1959), a series of prose poems paralleling twenty-two gouaches by Miró. In these brief pieces Breton writes of the poet in terms of artisan, prestidigitator, weaver, and painter. He highlights links in the total creation—plants such as ivy,

Breton's summer home at Saint-Cirq-la Popie (photograph by Dr. Michel Lanoote)

birds that carry pollen, woman who carries the seed—all working together for the unity of earth and sky.

He wrote his memoirs in the form of a dialogue in which friends and reporters engage with him; the work, entitled *Entretiens 1913-1952* (1952, Conversations 1913-1952), gives comprehensive coverage of his intellectual life and explains his motives, his enthusiasms, and his contacts and recurring breaks with friends and fellow artists.

During the war Breton had compiled *Anthologie de l'humour noir* (1940), an anthology of black humor beginning with selections from Swift and ending with works by Dali. This anthology and other works, long out of print, have reappeared in Pauvert or Gallimard paperback editions of Breton's works. Visitors from all over the world have continued to find their way to his studio even after his death.

In a literary world full of misogynists, Breton blazed a trail of loving which set a style among his followers, bringing woman and eroticism back in a resurgence of love poetry in France. Breton's poetic work, not widely available in English, has had little effect on writers in the United States. It has, however, been of seminal importance to Latin American writers. He has also had an impact on black writers such as West Indian poet Aimé Césaire and African poet and statesman Léopold Senghor, who have been guided to explore the forces of native geography and folklore and the inherent compulsion for liberation as fundamental elements of a universal surrealism.

Interviews:

Jean Duché, *André Breton nous parle,* special issue of *Le Figaro Littéraire,* no. 25 (5 October 1946);

André Parinaud and others, *Entretiens 1913-1952* (Paris: Gallimard, 1952; revised and corrected, 1973).

Bibliography:

Michael Sheringham, *André Breton: A Bibliography* (London: Grant & Cutler, 1972).

References:

Ferdinand Alquié, *Philosophie du surréalisme* (Paris: Flammarion, 1955); translated by Bernard Waldrop as *The Philosophy of Surrealism* (Ann Arbor: University of Michigan Press, 1965);

Anna Balakian, *André Breton, Magus of Surrealism* (New York: Oxford University Press, 1971);

Marguerite Bonnet, *André Breton: Naissance de l'aventure surréaliste* (Paris: José Corti, 1975);

Clifford Browder, *André Breton, Arbiter of Surrealism* (Geneva: Droz, 1967);

Mary Ann Caws, *André Breton* (New York: Twayne, 1971);

J. H. Matthews, *André Breton* (New York & London: Columbia University Press, 1967).

Papers:

The Fondation Doucet in Paris has Breton's papers, which will not be made available until the year 2016, the fiftieth anniversary of his death.

Jean Cocteau

(5 July 1889-11 October 1963)

James P. Mc Nab
Guilford College

SELECTED BOOKS: *La Lampe d'Aladin* (Paris: Société des Editions, 1909);

Le Prince frivole (Paris: Mercure de France, 1910);

La Danse de Sophocle (Paris: Mercure de France,
1912);

Le Coq et l'arlequin: Notes autour de la musique
(Paris: La Sirène, 1918); translated by Rollo
H. Myers as *Cock and Harlequin: Notes Concern-
ing Music* (London: Egoist Press, 1921);

Le Potomak (Paris: Société Littéraire de France,
1919; revised edition, Paris: Stock, 1924);

*Carte Blanche: Articles parus dans "Paris-Midi" du 31
mars au 11 août 1919* (Paris: La Sirène,
1920);

Poésie, 1917-1920 (Paris: La Sirène, 1920);

Le Secret professionnel (Paris: Stock, 1922); translated by Margaret Crosland as *Professional Secrets* in her *Cocteau's World: An Anthology of
Writings by Jean Cocteau* (London: Owen,
1972; New York: Dodd, Mead, 1973);

Vocabulaire (Paris: La Sirène, 1922);

Le Grand Ecart (Paris: Stock, 1923); translated by
Lewis Galantière as *The Grand Ecart* (New
York & London: Putnam's, 1925); translated
by Dorothy Williams as *The Miscreant* (London: Owen, 1958);

Dessins (Paris: Stock, 1923);

Plain-Chant (Paris: Stock, 1923);

Thomas l'imposteur (Paris: Gallimard, 1923); translated by Galantière as *Thomas the Imposter,*
(New York & London: Appleton, 1925); translated by Williams as *The Imposter* (London:
Owen, 1957; New York: Noonday Press,
1957);

Les Mariés de la Tour Eiffel (Paris: Gallimard,
1924); translated by Michael Benedikt as
The Wedding on the Eiffel Tower in *Modern
French Plays,* edited by Benedikt and George
Wellwarth (London: Faber & Faber, 1965);

Poésie, 1916-1923 (Paris: Gallimard, 1925);

Le Rappel à l'ordre (Paris: Stock, 1926); translated
by Myers as *A Call to Order* (London: Faber
& Gwyer, 1926);

photograph by Sima

Opéra, œuvres poétiques, 1925-1927 (Paris: Stock,
1927);

Orphée (play) (Paris: Stock, 1927); translated by
Carl Wildman as *Orpheus: A Tragedy in One
Act and an Interval* (Oxford: Oxford Univer-
sity Press, 1933); translated by John Sava-
cool in *The Infernal Machine and Other Plays*
(Norfolk, Conn.: New Directions, 1964);

Le Livre blanc, anonymous (Paris: Les Quatre Chemins, 1928); translated as *The White Paper*
(Paris: Olympia Press, 1957); enlarged as *Le
Livre blanc suivi de quatorze textes érotiques inédits; illustré de dix-huit dessins* (Paris: Persona,
1981);

Oedipe-roi, Roméo et Juliette (Paris: Plon, 1928);

Antigone; Les Mariés de la Tour Eiffel (Paris: Gallimard, 1928);

Les Enfants terribles (Paris: Grasset, 1929); translated by Samuel Putnam as *Enfants Terribles* (New York: Brewer & Warren, 1930); translated by Rosamund Lehmann as *Children of the Game* (London: Harvill Press, 1955);

Opium, journal d'une désintoxication (Paris: Stock, 1930); translated by Ernest Boyd as *Opium: The Diary of An Addict* (London & New York: Longmans, Green, 1932; London: Allen & Unwin, 1933);

La Voix humaine (Paris: Stock, 1930); translated by Wildman as *The Human Voice* (London: Vision Press, 1951);

Essai de critique indirecte: Le Mystère laïc. Des beaux arts considérés comme un assassinat (Paris: Grasset, 1932);

La Machine infernale (Paris: Grasset, 1934); translated by Wildman as *The Infernal Machine* (London: Oxford University Press, 1936); translated by Albert Bermal in *The Infernal Machine and Other Plays* (Norfolk, Conn.: New Directions, 1964);

Portraits–souvenir, 1900-1914 (Paris: Grasset, 1935); translated by Crosland as *Paris Album 1900-1914* (London: Allen, 1956);

Soixante Dessins pour "Les Enfants terribles" (Paris: Grasset, 1935);

Le Fantôme de Marseille (Paris: Gallimard, 1936);

Mon Premier Voyage (tour du monde en 80 jours) (Paris: Gallimard, 1936); translated by Stuart Gilbert as *Round the World Again in Eighty Days* (London: Routledge, 1937);

Les Chevaliers de la table ronde (Paris: Gallimard, 1937); translated by W. H. Auden as *The Knights of the Round Table* in *The Infernal Machine and Other Plays* (Norfolk, Conn.: New Directions, 1964);

Les Parents terribles (Paris: Gallimard, 1938); translated by Charles Frank as *Intimate Relations* in *Four Plays* (London: MacGibbon & Kee, 1962);

La Fin du Potomak (Paris: Gallimard, 1940);

Les Monstres sacrés (Paris: Gallimard, 1940);

La Machine à écrire (Paris: Gallimard, 1941); translated by Ronald Duncan as *The Typewriter* (London: Dobson, 1947);

Allégories (Paris: Gallimard, 1941);

Renaud et Armide (Paris: Gallimard, 1943);

Léone (Paris: Gallimard, 1945);

Poèmes (Lausanne: H. Kaeser, 1945);

La Belle et la bête, journal d'un film (Paris: Janin, 1946); translated by Duncan as *Diary of a Film (La Belle et la bête)* (New York: Roy, 1950; London: Dobson, 1950; revised edition, New York: Dover, 1972);

L'Aigle à deux têtes (Paris: Gallimard, 1946); translated and adapted by Duncan as *The Eagle Has Two Heads* (London: Vision Press, 1948; New York: Funk & Wagnalls, 1948);

La Difficulté d'être (Paris: Morihien, 1947); translated by Elizabeth Sprigge as *The Difficulty of Being* (New York: Coward McCann, 1967);

Le Foyer des artistes (Paris: Plon, 1947);

Poésies, 1946-1947 (Paris: Pauvert, 1947);

Poèmes (Paris: Gallimard, 1948);

Le Sang d'un poète (Monaco: Editions du Rocher, 1948), translated by Lily Pons as *The Blood of a Poet* (New York: Bodley Press, 1949);

Lettre aux Américains (Paris: Grasset, 1949);

Maalesh: Journal d'une tournée de théâtre (Paris: Gallimard, 1949); translated by Mary C. Hoeck as *Maalesh: A Theatrical Tour in the Middle East* (London: Owen, 1956);

Jean Marais (Paris: Calmann-Lévy, 1951);

Orphée (film) (Paris: La Pavade, 1951);

Bacchus (Paris: Gallimard, 1952); translated by Hoeck as *Bacchus* in *The Infernal Machine and Other Plays* (Norfolk, Conn.: New Directions, 1964);

Reines de France (Paris: Grasset, 1952);

Journal d'un inconnu (Paris: Grasset, 1953); translated by Alec Brown as *The Hand of a Stranger* (London: Elek Books, 1956; New York: Horizon, 1956);

Clair-obscur (Monaco: Editions du Rocher, 1954);

Discours de réception de M. Jean Cocteau à l'Académie Française et réponse de M. André Maurois (Paris: Gallimard, 1955);

The Journals of Jean Cocteau, edited and translated by Wallace Fowlie (New York: Criterion Books, 1956; London: Museum Press, 1957);

Poèmes, 1916-1955 (Paris: Gallimard, 1956);

La Corrida du premier mai (Paris: Grasset, 1957);

Poésie critique, 2 volumes (Paris: Gallimard, 1959,1960);

Le Testament d'Orphée (Liège: Dynamo, 1960);

Le Cordon ombilical: Souvenirs (Paris: Plon, 1962);

Le Requiem (Paris: Gallimard, 1962);

La Comtesse de Noailles. Oui et non (Paris: Librairie Académique Perrin, 1963);

Le Cap de Bonne-Espérance, suivi de Le Discours du grand sommeil (Paris: Gallimard, 1967);

Entre Picasso et Radiguet, edited by André Fermigier (Paris: Hermann, 1967);

My Contemporaries, translated by Crosland (Philadelphia: Chilton, 1968);

Faire-part, edited by Claude Michel Cluny (Paris: Chambelland, 1968);

Two Screenplays: The Blood of the Poet; The Testament of Orpheus, translated by Carol Martin-Sperry (New York: Orion, 1968; London: Calder & Boyars, 1970);

La Belle et la bête, bilingual edition of the shooting script, edited by Robert M. Hammond (New York: New York University Press, 1970);

Professional Secrets: An Autobiography of Jean Cocteau Drawn From His Lifetime Writings, edited by Robert Phelps, translated by Richard Howard (New York: Farrar, Straus & Giroux, 1970);

Three Screenplays: L'Eternel Retour, Orphée, La Belle et la bête, translated by Martin-Sperry (New York: Grossman, 1972);

Cocteau's World: An Anthology of Writings by Jean Cocteau, edited and translated by Crosland (London: Owen, 1972; New York: Dodd, Mead, 1973);

Le Passé défini I, 1951-1952, journal, edited by Pierre Chanel (Paris: Gallimard, 1983); translated by Howard as *Past Tense, Volume I, Diaries* (New York: Harcourt Brace Jovanovich, 1986);

Poèmes (Appogiatures, Clair-Obscur, Paraprosodies) (Monaco: Editions du Rocher, 1984);

Le Passé défini II, 1953, journal, edited by Chanel (Paris: Gallimard, 1985).

Collections: *Œuvres complètes,* 11 volumes (Lausanne: Marguerat, 1947-1951);

Théâtre, 2 volumes (Paris: Gallimard, 1948);

Nouveau Théâtre de poche (Monaco: Editions du Rocher, 1960);

Théâtre inédit et textes épars (Paris: Gallimard, 1981);

Vocabulaire, Plain-Chant et autres poèmes (Paris: Gallimard, 1983).

PLAY PRODUCTIONS: *Le Dieu bleu,* ballet by Cocteau and Frédéric de Madrazo, Paris, Théâtre du Châtelet, June 1912;

Parade, ballet by Cocteau; collaboration of Cocteau, Diaghilev, Massine, Picasso, Satie; Paris, Théâtre du Châtelet, 18 May 1917;

Le Bœuf sur le toit, musical spectacle; scenario by Cocteau, music by Milhaud; Paris, Comédie des Champs-Elysées, 21 February 1920;

Les Mariés de la Tour Eiffel, Paris, Théâtre des Champs-Elysées, 18 June 1921;

Antigone, Paris, Théâtre de l'Atelier, 20 December 1922;

Roméo et Juliette, Paris, Théâtre de la Cigale, 2 June 1924;

Orphée, Paris, Théâtre des Arts, 15 June 1926;

La Voix humaine, Paris, Comédie-Française, 17 February 1930;

La Machine infernale, Paris, Théâtre Louis Jouvet, 10 April 1934;

Les Chevaliers de la table ronde, Paris, Théâtre de l'Œuvre, 14 October 1937;

Les Parents terribles, Paris, Théâtre des Ambassadeurs, 14 November 1938;

Les Monstres sacrés, Paris, Théâtre Michel, February 17 1940;

La Machine à écrire, Paris, Théâtre Hébertot, 29 April 1941;

Renaud et Armide, Paris, Comédie-Française, 13 April 1943;

L'Aigle à deux têtes, Paris, Théâtre Hébertot, November 1946;

Un Tramway nommé Désir, adapted by Cocteau from Paule de Beaumont's translation of *A Streetcar Named Desire* by Tennessee Williams, Paris, Théâtre Edouard VII, 17 October 1949;

Bacchus, Paris, Théâtre Marigny, 20 December 1951;

L'Impromptu du Palais-Royal, Tokyo, 1 May 1962.

MOTION PICTURES: *Le Sang d'un poète,* scenario and direction by Cocteau, 1932;

L'Eternel Retour, scenario and dialogue by Cocteau, 1943;

La Belle et la bête, scenario and direction by Cocteau, 1946;

L'Aigle à deux têtes, scenario and direction by Cocteau, 1947;

Ruy Blas, scenario and dialogue by Cocteau, 1948;

Les Parents terribles, scenario and direction by Cocteau, 1948;

Orphée, scenario and direction by Cocteau, 1950;

Les Enfants terribles, adaptation and dialogue by Cocteau, 1950;

Le Testament d'Orphée, scenario and direction by Cocteau, 1960.

Jean Cocteau was first introduced to the Parisian public in 1908, when he was eighteen. The colorful and popular actor Edouard de Max, with colleagues from the Comédie-Française, gave a public reading of his friend's poems at a theater on the Champs-Elysées. For the remaining fifty-five years of Cocteau's career, until the last hours of his life, he was rarely far from the public eye. His accessibility, his versatility, and his constant willingness to change artistic direction made him newsworthy, but often led to a view of him as brilliant but shallow. Proust was the first to formulate the reproach, in 1908, begging his friend to approach his artistic mission with more gravity. Eleven years later, Gide attacked the younger writer publicly. He claimed that Cocteau was no more than an entertainer, a nimble squirrel in the tree of the arts, and advised him to stick to this role. This assertion of a basic lack of depth continued to haunt Cocteau and to a large extent is still attached to his name. While this negative assessment has a kernel of truth, it is much too extreme and one-sided.

Cocteau's willingness and ability to turn his hand to the most disparate creative ventures do not fit the stereotypical image of the priestlike–or Proust-like–writer single-mindedly sacrificing his life on the altar of an all-consuming art. But the best of his efforts, in each of the genres that he took up, enriched that genre. For example, his presentation of the "realist ballet" *Parade* (Side-show, 1917), with the joint participation of Erik Satie, Picasso, Massine, and Diaghilev and the Ballet Russe, is now widely recognized as the first truly modern ballet. The best of his theater continues to enjoy wide respect and success. *La Voix humaine* (published in 1930 and translated as *The Human Voice*, 1951) is one example of a play of his that has been translated into many languages and staged with regularity. Since the first perfomance at the Comédie-Française in 1930, this one-act monologue has been a vehicle for virtuoso performances by such well-known actresses as Berthe Bovy, Ingrid Bergman, and Anna Magnani. The importance of Cocteau's films, including *La Belle et la bête* (Beauty and the Beast, 1946) and *Orphée* (Orpheus, 1950), is freely granted by the public and movie critics alike, as well as by such filmmakers as Alain Robbe-Grillet and François Truffaut, who have found in Cocteau's cinema a radically new approach. And while Cocteau wrote few novels, in this genre too he was an innovator. His crowning accomplishment, *Les Enfants terribles* (1929; translated as *Enfants Terribles*, 1930) is without precedent in its representation of the alienation of adolescence and was unusually prophetic in anticipating the disaffection of generations of teenagers. Hailed as a masterpiece by Albert Thibaudet when it first appeared, *Les Enfants terribles* continues to exercise an almost uncanny fascination, raising the dark side of youth to a twentieth-century sacral myth.

Les Enfants terribles is Cocteau's most complete, comprehensive treatment of childhood. But this theme is present throughout much of his production. Ultimately, the childhood that fascinated Cocteau the most was his own. He was born Jean Maurice Eugène Clément Cocteau into a distinguished, well-to-do family. His maternal grandfather had a brokerage firm for which Georges Cocteau, Jean Cocteau's father, worked. His father's side of the family pales when compared to the Lecomtes, his mother's people. Cocteau's mother, Eugénie Lecomte, was beautiful, elegant, and, thanks in part to her diplomat brother Raymond, well connected to the Parisian world of government officials and ministers. Raymond Lecomte cut a dashing figure in his various diplomatic assignments, though he was accompanied by a trace of scandal regarding his apparent homosexuality.

In his recollections of childhood, Cocteau presented a picture of graceful Parisian life quite untouched by real worries or any significant unhappiness. In a volume of recollections entitled *Portraits–souvenir, 1900-1914* (1935; translated as *Paris Album 1900-1914*, 1956), one particularly telling sketch describes his parents' departure for the theater. The setting is a room in the family house. The principal accessory is a large mirror that reflects the mother and the child, Jean. The boy looks adoringly at his mother, who has the grace, dignity, and beauty of a Spanish Madonna. This is a scene of beauty, harmony, and mystery, in which the child is marvellously at ease. The theater, for which the mother soon departs, is a distant, magic kingdom. Present here are many of the elements around which Cocteau would compose much of his fictional universe, including a closed space endowed with a life of its own, a boy, a fascinating, powerful woman, a mirror, and the magic appeal of the theater.

Whereas Cocteau's mother is described in loving detail in this scene, his father is given the briefest of mentions: "Ma mère et mon père allaient à la Comédie-Française ou à l'Opéra" (My mother and my father used to go to the Comédie-Française or to the Opéra). The father is largely missing from Cocteau's memoirs and from the fictional world he composed. Instead, the reader typically finds a weak youth and a female presence so strong–very positive, very negative, or both—that one is justified in talking about a female archetype as a major structural element of his work. This is surely related to the death of his father when the boy was nine. Georges Cocteau committed suicide by shooting himself in his bedroom at home. There is some indication that his homosexuality, latent or exposed, may have played a part in his decision to take his own life.

Throughout his career, Cocteau appears to have sought to associate himself with well-known artists and celebrities, often having his name linked to theirs through collaborative ventures. These personalities include Diaghilev, Stravinsky, Satie, and Picasso. He was tireless in his quest for publicity and the pursuit of official honors and distinctions, for example his election to the Académie Française in 1955. He felt a compulsive need to see his own worth and even identity revealed, confirmed, and validated externally. His doubts were never resolved, a sense of personal equilibrium never achieved. The death of his lover, the young writer Raymond Radiguet, in 1923, left Cocteau disconsolate, adrift. In the 1920s, opium addiction, a brief return to the Church, and the discovery of new lovers, hailed as prodigies, reflected the need to find some kind of security, a sense of belonging, a mooring. Until the end of his life, a radical feeling of insecurity and estrangement set in motion a countervailing effort to achieve recognition and well-being. His work continued to chronicle the domination of life by death and suffering. This neurotic vision, grounded in Cocteau's childhood, came to be sublimated, as he chose to rename his neurosis poetry, identifying it as a sacred mission and himself as the poet quintessential, Orpheus incarnate.

Cocteau's novels represent a small but very important part of his large output. In an effort to give a unified core to his diverse creations, he labeled each of the many genres in which he worked "poésie." Under the title "poésie de roman" (poetry of the novel) he listed *Le Potomak* (The Potomak, 1919), *Le Grand Ecart* (literally The Big Split, 1923; translated, 1925) and *Thomas l'imposteur* (1923; translated as *Thomas the Imposter*, 1925), *Les Enfants terribles*, and *La Fin du Potomak* (The End of the Potomak, 1940). In fact, neither *Le Potomak* nor its sequel *La Fin du Potomak*, with their erratic, discontinuous segments, have much in common with the novel. On the other hand, *Le Livre blanc*, first published anonymously in 1928 and translated as *The White Paper* in 1957, has a straightforward narrative,

with recognizable if unconventional plot, themes, and characterization. Cocteau was less than forthright in admitting that he wrote *Le Livre blanc*, though it is unquestionably his.

The 1920s were by far Cocteau's most productive decade, especially with regard to his novels. Certainly *Le Potomak* precedes this decade. It was composed just before World War I and published a year after the war's end. With its mélange of text and drawing (some sixty pages of drawings form the heart of the book) and even verse, and its probable source in automatic writing, *Le Potomak* is a remarkable anticipation of surrealism. It recounts visits to see the Potomak, a formless marine monster kept in an aquarium, and chronicles the lives of two families, the Mortimers, who are dull and placid, and the cruel, barbaric Eugènes. It was not until Cocteau fell under the influence of Raymond Radiguet, from 1920 on, that he espoused that return to "classicism" of which the composition of more traditional or recognizable novels formed a significant part.

By 1920, although Cocteau was considered a leader of the avant-garde, it had become very difficult for him to exercise that role. The avant-garde was Dada, whose collaborators, most notably André Breton, hated Cocteau. That year, Radiguet broke with Breton and aligned himself with Cocteau. In part in response to Radiguet's natural preference for order over disorder, in part because a position at the side of the other avant-garde writers had been ruled out by Breton, but also because of a desire to try something "new," Cocteau returned to the old, the traditional.

In the summer of 1921 in the company of Radiguet, Cocteau wrote *Le Secret professionnel* (1922; translated as *Professional Secrets*, 1972), probably the most important critical essay he ever composed. In it he set forth a program for himself as artist, vowing to divorce himself from the avant-garde and the public alike in order to find a personal center; and he placed great emphasis upon clarity, classicism, and simplicity. The following summer, still in the company of Radiguet and under his influence in this most extraordinarily creative period, he wrote the two novels *Le Grand Ecart* and *Thomas l'imposteur*, as well as a volume of traditional verse, *Plain-Chant* (Plainsong, 1923), and an adaptation of Sophocles' *Antigone* for the theater, produced in 1922.

Le Grand Ecart, like Cocteau's other novels, presents a young man trapped between the

Cocteau in 1921 (photo: Segalab)

world of childhood, which he finds hard to leave, and the adult world of well-defined personal identity and responsibility. In none of the works is the transition from one world to the other successfully completed. Two (*Thomas l'imposteur* and *Les Enfants terribles*) end in the hero's death. *Le Grand Ecart* concludes with a failed attempt at suicide and a sense of utter hopelessness for the protagonist.

Jacques Forestier, the protagonist of *Le Grand Ecart,* is about nineteen when the novel begins. He has just had an unhappy affair with Germaine, a part-time actress and cocotte. The bulk of the novel is a flashback. When he was eleven, Jacques was first made to realize that it was his fate to be deeply moved by beauty but never to attain it. He was in a hotel in Mürren, Switzerland, when a vision of total beauty in the form of a young Armenian couple captivated him. The young man and woman moved on without even speaking to Jacques. But from then on, the pattern was set: he would always be wounded by beauty which would remain beyond his grasp. Other episodes confirmed this fate. Then, at the

age of eighteen, a boarder in Paris, Jacques becomes involved with Germaine. The account of their affair forms the major part of the narrative. The imbroglios in which they are involved are often amusing, but the conclusion is somber. After losing Germaine to Peter Stopwell, an English schoolboy and fellow boarder at the pension, Jacques tries to kill himself, is unsuccessful, and faces an uncertain future, filled with feelings of inadequacy, with only his mother to succor him. The epilogue closes a cycle opened by the initial portrait of Jacques.

Cocteau's technique of making the greater part of his novel a flashback may have been inspired by cinematic techniques, given Cocteau's abiding fascination with the cinema. But the chronology of the events is far from clear and in no way corresponds to chapter divisions. The uncertainty of the time scheme in *Le Grand Ecart* fits inside a larger pattern of uncertainty. The narrative point of view, for example, is disturbingly inconsistent. At first Jacques is presented by the third-person omniscient narrator from the outside, as something of a curiosity. But, by the end of the novel, Jacques's vision of reality comes to be corroborated by the narrator and presented as valid. Therefore, Peter Stopwell, Jacques's rival in love, is transformed from an indolent, foppish schoolboy into the representative of a race of super beings, an envoy of destiny. There is a jarring lack of consistency here and elsewhere in the novel, as irrational or mythical elements are introduced without adequate justification into a fictional world that is otherwise governed by the same laws as the natural world of everyday reality.

In *Le Grand Ecart* there is a regrettable unevenness and dispersal of interest. A number of characters, mere painted surfaces, appear and disappear without adding to the reader's understanding of Forestier's dilemma. Were Jacques Forestier depicted in a fully delineated, detailed setting, the extraneous characters and episodes would be of little consequence. But, since the locale is presented as little more than a jumble of names, a chase from Switzerland to the Italian lakes, to Venice, to Paris, the overall picture is blurred, rather like a film run at high speed.

In spite of its defects, *Le Grand Ecart* is one of Cocteau's more important works. Jacques Forestier anticipates most of Cocteau's later heroes, who come ill-equipped to meet the challenges of society and the adult life. Whereas, in subsequent works, this basic situation is sublimated and reinterpreted mythically, the inability to cross the threshold leading out of childhood is undisguised in *Le Grand Ecart*. It presents the basic, raw material out of which Cocteau's imaginative universe is built.

Both *Le Grand Ecart* and *Thomas l'imposteur* were published in early October 1923, *Thomas l'imposteur* just a week after the story of Jacques Forestier. Cocteau claimed that *Thomas l'imposteur* was inspired by another work, Stendhal's *La Chartreuse de Parme* (*The Charterhouse of Parma*, 1839) just as Radiguet had sought inspiration for his novel *Le Diable au corps* (*The Devil in the Flesh*) in an outside source, Mme de La Fayette's *La Princesse de Clèves* (1678). *Le Diable au corps* was published in March 1923.

Whereas the initial response to *Le Grand Ecart* was quite favorable, those critics who did respond to the appearance of *Thomas l'imposteur* expressed misgivings that it should treat World War I without the seriousness it deserved. Much the same reproach had been leveled at Radiguet concerning *Le Diable au corps*. In later years it was *Thomas l'imposteur* and not *Le Grand Ecart* that would enjoy success, especially with a young reading public, and was frequently reprinted in paperback form.

Thomas l'imposteur has none of the structural flaws that detract from *Le Grand Ecart*. Its considerable popularity with young readers, which continues to the present day, surely derives from Cocteau's ability to present the living-out of a childhood fantasy. There is no hesitation on the author's part. From beginning to end, the narrative is located firmly outside the realm of banal, everyday life. It is the tale of a very unusual hero in very exceptional circumstances–rendered possible by the war–in a world where magic and mystery have a place. War suspends natural law, instead of reinforcing it.

The youthful protagonist, Guillaume Thomas, is mistakenly identified as Guillaume Thomas de Fontenoy, nephew of the famous military commander. He innocently acquires a uniform, assumes the new identity of a soldier with a famous family name, and plays the role to the very end. Notwithstanding the dreadful suffering he witnesses, Guillaume goes through the years 1914 to 1917 (the time frame of *Thomas l'imposteur*) as a participant not in history but in a great game.

The leader of the game is Clémence, Princesse de Bormes. She organizes an ambulance service that goes from her house in Paris to tend the wounded at the front in Flanders and Champagne, the areas in which Cocteau himself saw service as a medical orderly in the early years of World War I. Clémence has many of the features of a character of folklore or myth. Her origins are mysterious; she was raised as an orphan in Russia and has Polish blood. She radiates an unearthly quality and has the sibylline gift of prophecy. Above all, although she has mysterious, preternatural attributes, her psychological makeup is simple; she is all of one piece, entirely pure and noble in heart, thought, and deed.

It is thanks to the princess that Guillaume is able to lead a life of adventure. When he places himself under her tutelage, he is reborn to a new life, and his new name and his new uniform are the outward signs of a change of identity. His rebirth is not the adolescent's awakening to adult sex, life, and responsibility, but rather a reentry into the world of childhood. *Thomas l'imposteur* is the account of a dream-wish fulfilled. For example, his love implies no striving for possession or for marriage. Instead, it is extraordinarily diffuse. It is directed in turn–or simultaneously–toward the princess, her daughter Henriette, who, like her mother, is in love with Guillaume, and the marines with whom the boy spends time at the battle-front! Similarly, Guillaume, like the princess, shows courage in the face of German gunfire. But their boldness is not the resolute determination of the hero. It is rather the lack of awareness or the sense of invulnerability of children at play.

Wherever he goes, Guillaume appears to be enveloped in a blanket of security and confidence. From one childlike situation of dependence he passes easily to another, leaving the princess, who is no longer able to organize the convoys, for the Belgian front, where he is adopted by the marines. Although he is of an age with them, they treat him as a mascot, an infant brother, or a pet. At no time does Guillaume show any sign of inner doubt or anxiety or turmoil. The Germans as such do not exist for him. He is not enlisted in support of a national cause against an adversary. Instead, the enemy soldiers are merely a kind of catalyst, allowing his game to go on.

Inevitably, this protracted game cannot go on forever. It implies an emptiness as well as a plenitude, a death to one world–that of harsh reality–at the same time that it is an initiation into another. It comes as no surprise when death, the ultimate form of reality, catches up

Cocteau, Jean Hugo, Raymond Radiguet, and Pierre de Lacretelle in Lavandou, 1922 (photo: Segalab)

with Guillaume Thomas. He is felled at night by a German sniper's bullet. Here, as in *Le Grand Ecart*, the transition into adult life is never made, and the hero remains a child until his death.

There is an important, basic difference between the story of Jacques Forestier and that of Guillaume Thomas, quite apart from the artistic superiority of the second work over the first. Whereas Jacques Forestier made futile, despairing attempts to leave childhood behind him, Guillaume, far from suffering in his role as child-hero, accepts it totally, fully. He does not even consider crossing the threshold into the world of adults, but rather exults in being a *puer aeternus*, a boy forever.

The change from one work to the other perhaps coincides with a change in Cocteau's own vision. Cocteau's sense of persecution and psychological isolation was strong by 1923. His definitive choice of homosexuality and his quarrel with the surrealists brought to the surface what was a very fundamental sense of being cut off from and excluded by society. Now lamenting this exclusion (this is the stage at which Forestier remains), now seeing it as a source of strength, Cocteau

came to fix his gaze upon the time when the sentence of exclusion was passed. Much of his work returned to paradise lost, to childhood, innocent and fascinating, just before the fall: that critical moment in adolescence when childhood could no longer be preserved and the road into a conventional life with heterosexual relations and shared responsibilities was blocked. In an inevitable, corollary movement, a female figure, based on the mother, the guardian of childhood, assumes great importance. She is a source of fascination, pure protector when viewed positively, hated jailer, blocking progress and stunting growth, when seen in a negative light.

Confronting the princess in *Thomas l'imposteur* and related to her antithetically is the curious Mme Valiche, an amateur actress who accompanies the convoy of ambulances to the front where she works as nurse and entertainer of the troops. She is about the same age as the princess and sees herself as a performer just as the princess treats life as a stage. She too has a gift of prophecy and second sight, but this allows her to ferret out news of casualties and to gloat over them. She is described as "ce vampire," and derives special pleasure from being the first person in Paris to know that Guillaume has died. She is filled with glee as she runs to break the news to the princess and her daughter. She invents details about his death in order to increase their suffering. Her natural element is death and suffering and the stench of gangrene. The princess, in contrast, is always associated with life and pure love. She wastes away when she finds out about Guillaume's death, and her daughter cannot bear to live without him, so she commits suicide. At every level, be it moral, physical, social, religious, or spiritual, Mme Valiche is painted black, as the negative counterpart of the princess.

It is not surprising that critics should have been shocked by Cocteau's apparent lack of gravity in treating the suffering and solemnity of World War I. But from *Thomas l'imposteur* on, it becomes clear that Cocteau's work is grounded not in a confrontation with history, but just the opposite. Cocteau has nothing in common, for example, with Malraux or Sartre, for whom the reach of historical event—often in the form of catastrophe—was ineluctable and omnipresent. Cocteau grounds his work in a denial or a rejection of history, preferring the world of childhood, myth, and romance. Indeed, Cocteau's natural inclination would be permanently in the direction of what Henry James called, in the preface to *The American* (1877), experience "liberated . . . experience disengaged, disembroiled, disencumbered, exempt from the conditions that we normally know to attach to it": in other words, toward romance rather than toward mimetic fiction. Again and again he would borrow his settings and his character silhouettes from the world of everyday reality or the recognizable world of natural law. But the rules of that world, the substance of his characters, themes, and plot, derived from an archetypal or mythical pattern rather than a realistic one.

Just two months after the publication of Cocteau's novels, the death of Raymond Radiguet from typhoid, in December 1923, precipitated a crisis in his mentor's life. Cocteau's name had been—and would again be—linked with the death or ruin of other young men, his intimates. But Radiguet's case was unique. Dead at twenty, Radiguet was an authentic genius who left a significant corpus of works of quality, including the novels *Le Diable au corps* (1923; translated as *The Devil in the Flesh*, 1932) and *Le Bal du comte d'Orgel* (1924; translated as *The Count's Ball*, 1929). Though there was without question a self-

destructive impulse in Radiguet, Cocteau did nothing to check this. He initiated Radiguet into a fast-paced life that came to include heavy drinking bouts and the use of opium. When he did become sick, the younger man had been weakened by years of dissipation.

After the death of Radiguet, Cocteau did create works of great significance. His greatest novel, *Les Enfants terribles,* would come several years later. His major work for the theater still lay ahead of him; it would include *Orphée,* his first independent, original, full-length play, which was performed in 1926, and *La Voix humaine,* as well as *La Machine infernale* (1934), his retelling of the story of Oedipus. It was not until 1930 that he would make his first movie, *Le Sang d'un poète (The Blood of a Poet),* not shown publicly until 1932. Two of his finest films, *La Belle et la bête* and *Orphée,* were not conceived, written, and directed until the late 1940s and early 1950s. The fact remains that, in losing Radiguet, Cocteau appears to have lost some of his consistency. The quality of his work after 1923 fluctuated considerably. It seems clear that Radiguet was as much of an influence on Cocteau as Cocteau was on him.

In writing *Le Livre blanc,* a homosexual "confession," Cocteau tried to duplicate the circumstances that had surrounded the composition of his earlier novels. He wrote it late in 1927 in the company of Jean Desbordes, an aspiring writer in whom he thought he saw a reincarnation of Radiguet: "Il y a un miracle du ciel, Raymond est revenu sous une autre forme" (There is a heavenly miracle, Raymond has returned in another guise). Cocteau's enthusiasm for Desbordes's volume of effusive verse *J'adore* (1928) was not at all shared by others. Desbordes was not Radiguet. And while *Le Livre blanc* is of considerable documentary interest, it has none of the artistic coherence or intensity of Cocteau's better work. The influence of Desbordes was not the salutary aesthetic influence that Radiguet's presence had been.

Le Livre blanc first appeared in a limited edition of twenty-one copies in 1928, with no signature. Two years later it was republished in an edition of four hundred fifty copies with seventeen drawings by "M. B. Arrington" (the drawings are clearly Cocteau's). Cocteau coyly refused to admit the novella was his. This was true also of a 1949 edition, limited to five hundred copies. The English translation of 1957, published by Olympia Press, is also unsigned, although it bears

Cocteau in the drawing-room of the Villa Santo-Sospir, St. Jean Cap Ferrat, his principal home from 1950 until his death in 1963. The fresco on the wall is by Cocteau (Les Reporters Associés).

the legend that the preface and illustrations are by Jean Cocteau of the Académie Française: Cocteau had been elected to the French Academy in 1955. It was not until after the author's death that his name appeared on the book. His early reluctance to claim the work may have stemmed from a fear of hurting his mother (the reason he gave to his friends), but later he was probably indulging a lifelong fondness for mystification, especially after his mother died in 1943.

Le Livre blanc takes the form of a first-person account of the narrator's life centered upon his homosexuality. Outside literary influences are rather obvious. The first-person narration, the self-justification, and the curious admixture of religion in a narrative where it seems scarcely to belong are features reminiscent of Rousseau's *Confessions* (1781, 1788), which Cocteau was reading about the time he composed *Le Livre blanc*. Its salaciousness and rapid passage from one episode to another without much development of character or setting recall many novellas of the eighteenth century. There is even a distinct echo of Chateaubriand's *René* (1805) in

Le Livre blanc's persistent melancholy and religiosity, as well as in the narrator's family circumstance: his birth causes the death of his mother, leaving him with a brooding, sad father. Finally, it seems likely that *Le Livre blanc* was a response to Gide's *Corydon* (1924), a defense of homosexuality: the rivalry between the two writers and Cocteau's preoccupation with the older man's work were intense throughout the 1920s, all the more so since Gide had satirized Cocteau in the form of the character Passavant in his 1926 novel *Les Faux Monnayeurs* (*The Counterfeiters*).

The novella begins with early childhood memories of the initial awakening to homosexuality. The first is of a farm boy naked on a horse. This centaurlike image, witnessed by the narrator when he was a child, is so powerful that he faints. Subsequent events, involving gypsies, the schoolboy hero Dargelos of the lycée Condorcet, two-way mirrors, and the sailor PAS DE CHANCE (NO LUCK) in Toulon, are given their first appearance in *Le Livre blanc* and go on to become staple elements of Cocteau's poetic mythology. They confirm his fascination with ocular imagery and his voyeurism. This material, like many other parts of *Le Livre blanc*, is autobiographical, though the narrator alters the chronology of events.

The conclusion of *Le Livre blanc* is quite arbitrary, although similar to that of many eighteenth-century tales. The narrator decides to leave France, where he is tolerated but not respected, in order to seek love and liberty. A series of imbroglios, including the suicide of a boy out of jealousy–his sister was going to marry the narrator, whom *he* loved–had culminated in the narrator's decision to enter a monastery. But his first encounter there is with a monk who resembles Dargelos, PAS DE CHANCE, and other fateful paramours. It is then that the narrator decides there is no happiness for him in France and that he has to leave the country.

Although the aesthetic interest of *Le Livre blanc* is quite slim, it is as rich a compendium of Cocteau's obsessions as any single work he ever wrote. Some of the elements that Cocteau used rather crudely are reworked and presented with consummate artistic skill in the 1929 novel *Les Enfants terribles,* a work of genius. Cocteau wrote *Les Enfants terribles* while undergoing a cure for opium addiction in a clinic in Saint-Cloud, in the suburbs of Paris. He had received his first treatment in 1925. The death of Radiguet had left him disconsolate and in casting around for a palliative, he had briefly returned to the Church and –with greater application–taken up heavy use of opium. His second cure, paid for by Gabrielle "Coco" Chanel, began in December 1928 and lasted for over three months. The notebook he kept, *Opium, journal d'une désintoxication* (1930; translated as *Opium: The Diary of an Addict,* 1932), is a fascinating account of the stages of withdrawal. The worst of the cure was behind him when he wrote *Les Enfants terribles.*

Les Enfants terribles is a restatement of Cocteau's abiding, neurotic interest in the theme of adolescence. Insofar as Paul, the protagonist, is a weak, uncertain schoolboy who is unable to leave childhood behind and grasp adult life and responsibility, he resembles Jacques Forestier of *Le Grand Ecart.* But in *Les Enfants terribles* Cocteau transcends the raw material of neurosis to create a twentieth-century sacral myth that attains a high level of artistic consistency and intensity.

As a boy of fourteen, Paul is hurt in the schoolyard by a snowball hurled by his hero, the bully Dargelos. He is then obliged to leave the lycée Condorcet and stay at home, where his sister Elisabeth, two years his elder, guards him jealously. Throughout the story, the memory of Dargelos never leaves Paul. He and his sister are joined for a time by Gérard, a youth who loves first Paul, then Elisabeth, and later by Agathe, who falls in love with Paul. In a brief interlude, Elisabeth marries Michaël, a young American who is killed in an accident before the marriage is consummated. On becoming aware of the love shared by Paul and Agathe, Elisabeth intervenes. She marries off Gérard and Agathe and, in despair, Paul kills himself with poison sent by Dargelos. Elisabeth's destiny is wholly linked to that of her brother. She too commits suicide, dying at the very instant that he does. The two rise together to heaven in the "spirit" of the bedroom in which they had spent so much of their time together.

In the 1920s Cocteau came to insist upon a dialectic opposing life, love, and society on the one hand, and art and immortality on the other and to stress his preference for art. Paul's life, death, and rebirth–the apotheosis of the final scene–need to be seen against this background. The children's lives are pure, sacred experience, a quasi-religious mission, a form of the absolute, a poem or work of art in contradistinction to the world of shared reality, which is fallen, relative, debased. The image of Dargelos is assimilated into the children's room in the form of memory and a photograph: he is made the divinity or godhead or spirit of the room. Elisabeth's tenacious hold on Paul, her refusal to let him be like or associate with others make of her a kind of priestess in the service of Dargelos, childhood, their room, and the rites with which they surround themselves that they call "le jeu" (the game). Left alone, Paul is weak and supine with a natural disposition toward lethargy. In saving Paul from himself and from the banality of mediocre existence, of which the principal representative is Agathe, Elisabeth is a kind of muse. She controls the fate of all those around her. Her extraordinary power is seen in her relations with Michaël. His reasoning, problem-solving intelligence is the complete denial of Paul and Elisabeth's closed, instinctive, mysterious childhood world. Consummation of Elisabeth's marriage to him would thrust her fully into contact with this adult world. Instead, he is killed on the road between Nice and Cannes: his long scarf is caught in the wheels of his car, strangling and decapitating him. The episode is of course patterned upon Isadora

Duncan's similar death in Nice. Elisabeth remains the sacred virginal priestess of an exclusive cult.

Elisabeth is one of the most complex, fascinating characters created by Cocteau. She is protective, attentive, nurturing: with the death of the children's mother early in the story (the father has died before the narrative begins), she assumes fully the role of mother which was partly hers before their mother died. She also has for Paul "une passion violente"; she is like a harpy with its hapless prey, a nocturnal spider, and, in her bloody death-dealing, she even resembles Lady Macbeth. She is both giver and taker of life, cradle of birth and uterine trap, Sophia and Gorgon.

The children's bedroom, over which Elisabeth presides, is like a temple, endowed with an intensity of its own that derives from its shared identity with Elisabeth herself as controlling presence. The theme of childhood as prison and paradise, central to *Les Enfants terribles,* is given an appropriate setting: the confined space of the orphans' bedroom, largely at night, which is a place of magic and mystery.

Les Enfants terribles reveals a darker side of childhood that had never been adequately chronicled before Cocteau. He was the first to show those instinctual, inchoate strivings, that sense of ritual, those destructive and self-destructive urges that would become common currency in literature and especially cinema after World War II. Cocteau is here at his most effective, shaping a myth out of his material, presenting an absolute reality that obeys its own laws and its own ineluctable dynamic, making no attempt to follow natural law, the laws of the world, realism. In elevating the difficult years of adolescence into an archetypal reality, a cohesive whole going from beginning to death to apotheosis, he presented an exemplar that would enjoy extraordinary success. *Les Enfants terribles* became the handbook of generations of young people both in France and elsewhere.

Les Enfants terribles is in effect Cocteau's last novel. He did list *La Fin du Potomak,* written in 1939 and published in 1940, with his novels. In its recollection of characters from *Le Potomak*—the Eugènes for example are now said to have spread their misery over much of the world—this work is a sequel. But its shapelessness deprives it of any of the features of the novel. And it does not have any of the freshness of the first work.

In the 1920s, when all of his novels were written, Cocteau uncovered and presented what would become the core of his artistic vision. His gravitation toward a mythopoeic vision, his fascination with a strong female presence and with the theme of adolescence, as well as the poetic intensification of the very space inhabited by his characters, are features that can be traced back to his novels. In his subsequent work in all genres, from the film *Le Sang d'un poète* to the plays *La Voix humaine* and *La Machine infernale,* or *Les Parents terribles,* as to his poetry and graphic work, the core elements from his novels continued to dominate Cocteau's artistic vision.

Letters:
Lettres à Milorad 1955-1963, edited by Milorad (Paris: Saint-Germain-des-Prés, 1975);
Correspondance avec Jean-Marie Magnan (Paris: Belfond, 1981);
Lettres à Jacques Maritain (Paris: Stock, 1984).

Interviews:
André Fraigneau, *Entretiens autour du cinématographe* (Paris: A. Bonne, 1951); translated by Vera Traill as *Cocteau on the Film: An Interview Recorded by A. Fraigneau* (New York: Roy, 1954);
William Fifield, "Jean Cocteau, An Interview," *Paris Review,* 32 (Summer-Fall 1964): 13-37;
Fraigneau, *Jean Cocteau: Entretiens avec André Fraigneau* (Paris: Union Générale d'Editions, 1965);
André Bernard and Claude Gauteur, *Entretiens sur le cinématographe* (Paris: Belfond, 1973).

Biographies:
André Fraigneau, *Cocteau par lui-même* (Paris: Editions du Seuil, 1957);
Frederick Brown, *An Impersonation of Angels: A Biography of Jean Cocteau* (New York: Viking, 1968);
Jean-Jacques Kihm and Elizabeth Sprigge, *Jean Cocteau: The Man and the Mirror* (New York: Coward-McCann, 1968);
Pierre Chanel, *Album Cocteau* (Paris: Tchou, 1970);
Francis Steegmuller, *Cocteau: A Biography* (Boston: Little, Brown, 1970).

References:
Cahiers Jean Cocteau, nos. 1-10 (Paris: Gallimard, 1969-1985);
Pierre Chanel, ed., "Raymond Radiguet, Jean Cocteau," *Cahiers Jean Cocteau,* no. 4 (Paris: Gallimard, 1973);

Chanel, ed., "Le Romancier," *Cahiers Jean Cocteau,* no. 8 (Paris: Gallimard, 1980);

Lydia Crowson, *The Esthetic of Jean Cocteau* (Hanover, N.H.: University Press of New England, 1978);

Arthur B. Evans, *Jean Cocteau and His Films of Orphic Identity* (Cranberry, N.J.: Art Alliance, 1975);

William Fifield, *Jean Cocteau* (New York: Columbia University Press, 1974);

Wallace Fowlie, *Jean Cocteau: The History of a Poet's Age* (Bloomington: Indiana University Press, 1966);

René Gilson, *Jean Cocteau* (Paris: Seghers, Collection Cinéma d'aujourd'hui, 1964); translated by Ciba Vaughan as *Jean Cocteau* (New York: Crown, 1969);

Jean-Marie Magnan, *Cocteau* (Paris: Desclée de Brouwer, 1968);

James P. Mc Nab, "Mythical Space in *Les Enfants terribles,*" *French Review,* 47 (Spring 1974): 162-170;

Mc Nab, *Raymond Radiguet* (Boston: Twayne, 1984);

Milorad, "Romans-jumeaux ou de l'imitation," *Cahiers Jean Cocteau,* no. 8 (Paris: Gallimard, 1979): 87-107;

Gérard Mourgue, *Jean Cocteau* (Paris: Editions Universitaires, 1965);

Neal Oxenhandler, *Scandal and Parade: The Theatre of Jean Cocteau* (New Brunswick, N. J.: Rutgers University Press, 1957);

Arthur King Peters, *Jean Cocteau and André Gide: An Abrasive Friendship* (New Brunswick, N. J.: Rutgers University Press, 1973).

Papers:
Manuscripts by Cocteau are at the Archives Jean Cocteau, Milly-la-Forêt (Essonne), France.

Colette
(Sidonie Gabrielle Colette)
(28 January 1873-3 August 1954)

Margaret Davies
University of Reading

SELECTED BOOKS: *Claudine à l'école,* as Willy (Paris: Ollendorff, 1900); translated by Janet Flanner as *Claudine at School* (London: Gollancz, 1930); translated by H. Mirande (New York: A. & C. Boni, 1930);

Claudine à Paris, as Willy (Paris: Ollendorff, 1901); translated as *Claudine in Paris* (London: Gollancz, 1931); translated by James Whitall as *Young Lady of Paris* (New York: A. & C. Boni, 1931);

Claudine en ménage, as Willy (Paris: Mercure de France, 1902); republished as *Claudine amoureuse* (Paris: Ollendorff, 1902); translated by Frederick A. Blossom as *The Indulgent Husband* (New York: Farrar & Rinehart, 1935);

Claudine s'en va: Journal d'Annie, as Willy (Paris: Ollendorff, 1903); translated by Blossom as *The Innocent Wife* (New York: Farrar & Rinehart, 1935);

Minne, as Willy (Paris: Ollendorff, 1904); revised with *Les Egarements de Minne* (1905) as *L'Ingénue libertine* (1909);

Dialogues de bêtes, as Colette Willy (Paris: Mercure de France, 1904); enlarged five times, fifth enlargement published as *Douze Dialogues de bêtes* (Paris: Mercure de France, 1930);

Les Egarements de Minne, as Willy (Paris: Ollendorff, 1905); revised with *Minne* (1904) as *L'Ingénue libertine,* as Colette Willy (1909);

La Retraite sentimentale, as Colette Willy (Paris: Mercure de France, 1907); translated by Margaret Crosland as *Retreat from Love* (London: Owen, 1974; Bloomington: Indiana University Press, 1974);

Les Vrilles de la vigne, as Colette Willy (Paris: Editions de la Vie Parisienne, 1908);

L'Ingénue libertine, as Colette Willy (Paris: Ollendorff, 1909); translated by R. C. B. [Rosemary Carr Benét] as *The Gentle Liber-*

tine (New York: Farrar & Rinehart, 1931; London: Gollancz, 1931);

La Vagabonde, as Colette Willy (Paris: Ollendorff, 1910); translated by Charlotte Remfry-Kidd as *Renée la Vagabonde* (Garden City: Doubleday, 1931); translated by Enid McLeod as *The Vagabond* (London: Secker & Warburg, 1954);

L'Envers du music-hall, as Colette (Colette Willy) (Paris: Flammarion, 1913); translated by Anne-Marie Callimachi as *Music-hall Sidelights,* published with Helen Beauclerk's translation of *Mes Apprentissages* (London: Secker & Warburg, 1957); Callimachi's translation republished with Raymond Postgate's translation of *Mitsou* (New York: Farrar, Straus & Cudahy, 1958);

L'Entrave, as Colette (Colette Willy) (Paris: Librairie des Lettres, 1913); translated by Viola Gerard Garvin as *Recaptured* (London: Gollancz, 1931; Garden City: Doubleday, Doran, 1932);

Prrou, Poucette et quelques autres, as Colette Willy (Paris: Librairie des Lettres, 1913);

La Paix chez les bêtes (Paris: Georges Crès, 1916);

Les Heures longues, 1914-1917 (Paris: Fayard, 1917);

Les Enfants dans les ruines (Paris: Editions de la Maison du Livre, 1917);

Dans la foule (Paris: Georges Crès, 1918);

Mitsou; ou, Comment l'esprit vient aux filles, published with *En camarades, pièce en deux actes* (Paris: Fayard, 1919); translated by Jane Terry as *Mitsou; or, How Girls Grow Wise* (New York: A. & C. Boni, 1930);

La Chambre éclairée (Paris: Edouard Joseph, 1920);

Chéri (Paris: Fayard, 1920); translated by Flanner (New York: A. & C. Boni, 1930; London: Gollancz, 1931);

La Maison de Claudine (Paris: Ferenczi, 1922; revised edition, Paris: Ferenczi, 1930); translated by McLeod and Una Vicenzo Troubridge as *My Mother's House,* published with McLeod's translation of *Sido* (London: Secker & Warburg, 1953; New York: Farrar, Straus & Young, 1953);

Le Voyage égoïste (Paris: Editions d'Art Edouard Pelletan, 1922);

Chéri, comédie en quatre actes, by Colette and Léopold Marchand (Paris: Librairie Théâtrale, 1922);

Le Blé en herbe (Paris: Flammarion, 1923); translated by Ida Zeitlin as *The Ripening* (New York: Farrar & Rinehart, 1932); translated by Roger Senhouse as *Ripening Seed* (London: Secker & Warburg, 1955; New York: Farrar, Straus & Cudahy, 1956);

Rêverie du nouvel an (Paris: Stock, 1923);

La Femme cachée (Paris: Flammarion, 1924); translated by Crosland as *The Other Woman* (London: Owen, 1971);

Aventures quotidiennes (Paris: Flammarion, 1924);

Quatre Saisons (Paris: Philippe Ortiz, 1925);

L'Enfant et les sortilèges (Paris: Durand, 1925);

La Fin de Chéri (Paris: Flammarion, 1926); translated anonymously as *The Last of Chéri* (New York: Putnam's, 1932); translated by Senhouse (London: Secker & Warburg, 1951);

La Naissance du jour (Paris: Flammarion, 1928); translated by Benét as *A Lesson in Love* (New York: Farrar & Rinehart, 1932); republished as *Morning Glory* (London: Gollancz, 1932);

Renée Vivien (Abbeville: Edouard Champion, 1928);

La Seconde (Paris: Ferenczi, 1929); translated by Garvin as *The Other One* (New York: Cosmopolitan Book Corporation, 1931); Garvin's translation also published as *Fanny and Jane* (London: Gollancz, 1931);

Sido ou les points cardinaux (Paris: Editions Kra, 1929; revised edition, Paris: Ferenczi, 1930); translated by McLeod, published with McLeod and Troubridge's translation of *La Maison de Claudine* (London: Secker & Warburg, 1953; New York: Farrar, Straus & Young, 1953);

Prisons et paradis (Paris: Ferenczi, 1932; revised edition, Paris: Ferenczi, 1935);

Ces Plaisirs (Paris: Ferenczi, 1932); translated by Edith Dally as *The Pure and the Impure* (New York: Farrar & Rinehart, 1933); translated as *These Pleasures* (London: White Owl, 1934); republished as *Le Pur et l'impur* (Paris: Armes de France, 1941);

La Chatte (Paris: Grasset, 1933); translated by Morris Bentinck as *Saha the Cat* (New York: Farrar & Rinehart/London: T. W. Laurie, 1936);

Duo (Paris: Ferenczi, 1934); translated by Blossom (New York: Farrar & Rinehart, 1935);

La Jumelle noire, 4 volumes (Paris: Ferenczi, 1934-1938);

Discours de réception à l'Académie Royale de Langue et de Littérature Françaises de Belgique (Paris: Grasset, 1936);

Mes Apprentissages: Ce que Claudine n'a pas dit (Paris: Ferenczi, 1936); translated by Helen Beauclerk as *My Apprenticeships,* published with Callimachi's translation of *L'Envers du music-hall* (London: Secker & Warburg, 1957);

Bella-Vista (Paris: Ferenczi, 1937);

Le Toutounier (Paris: Ferenczi, 1939);

Chambre d'hôtel (Paris: Fayard, 1940); translated by Patrick Leigh Fermor as *Chance Acquaintances,* published with his translation of *Julie de Carneilhan* (London: Secker & Warburg, 1952), and with his translations of *Gigi* and

Julie de Carneilhan (New York: Farrar, Straus & Young, 1952);

Mes Cahiers (Paris: Armes de France, 1941);

Journal à rebours (Paris: Fayard, 1941); translated by Le Vay with *De ma fenêtre* (1942) as *Looking Backwards* (London: Owen, 1975; Bloomington: Indiana University Press, 1975);

Julie de Carneilhan (Paris: Fayard, 1941); translated by Fermor with *Chambre d'hôtel* (London: Secker & Warburg, 1952) and with *Gigi* and *Chambre d'hôtel* (New York: Farrar, Straus & Young, 1952);

De ma fenêtre (Paris: Armes de France, 1942); enlarged as *Paris de ma fenêtre* (Geneva: Milieu du Monde, 1944); translated by Le Vay with *Journal à rebours* (1941) as *Looking Backwards* (London: Owen, 1975; Bloomington: Indiana University Press, 1975);

De la patte à l'aile (Paris: Corrêa, 1943);

Flore et Pomone (Paris: Galerie Charpentier, 1943);

Nudité (Paris: Mappemonde, 1943);

Le Képi (Paris: Fayard, 1943);

Broderie ancienne (Monaco: Editions du Rocher, 1944);

Gigi et autres nouvelles (Lausanne: La Guilde du Livre, 1944); *Gigi* translated with *Julie de Carneilhan* and *Chambre d'hôtel* (New York: Farrar, Straus & Young, 1952) and with *La Chatte* (London: Secker & Warburg, 1953);

Trois . . . six . . . neuf (Paris: Corrêa, 1944);

Belles Saisons (Paris: Galerie Charpentier, 1945);

L'Etoile Vesper (Geneva: Milieu du Monde, 1946); translated by Le Vay as *The Evening Star* (London: Owen, 1973; Indianapolis: Bobbs-Merrill, 1974);

Pour un herbier (Lausanne: Mermod, 1948); translated by Senhouse as *For a Flower Album* (New York: McKay, 1959);

Trait pour trait (Paris: Fleuron, 1949);

Journal intermittent (Paris: Fleuron, 1949);

Le Fanal bleu (Paris: Ferenczi, 1949); translated by Senhouse as *The Blue Lantern* (London: Secker & Warburg, 1963; New York: Farrar, Straus, 1963);

La Fleur de l'âge (Paris: Fleuron, 1949);

En pays connu (Paris: Manuel Bruker, 1949);

Chats de Colette (Paris: A. Michel, 1950);

Creatures Great and Small: Creature Conversations; Other Creatures; Creature Comfort, translated by McLeod (New York: Farrar, Straus & Cudahy, 1957);

Paysages et portraits (Paris: Flammarion, 1958);

Notes marocaines (Lausanne: Mermod, 1958);

The Stories of Colette, translated by Antonia White (London: Secker & Warburg, 1958); republished as *The Tender Shoot and Other Stories* (New York: Farrar, Straus & Cudahy, 1959);

Découvertes (Lausanne: Mermod, 1961);

Earthly Paradise: An Autobiography Drawn From Her Lifelong Writings, edited by Robert Phelps, translated by Helen Beauclerk and others (London: Secker & Warburg, 1966; New York: Farrar, Straus & Giroux, 1966);

Places, translated by Le Vay (London: Owen, 1970; Indianapolis: Bobbs-Merrill, 1971);

Journey for Myself: Selfish Memories, translated by Le Vay (London: Owen, 1971);

The Thousand and One Mornings, translated by Margaret Crosland and David Le Vay (London: Owen, 1973; New York: Bobbs-Merrill, 1973).

Collections: *Oeuvres complètes,* 15 volumes (Paris: Flammarion, 1949-1950);

Oeuvres complètes de Colette, 16 volumes (Paris: Club de l'Honnête Homme, 1973);

Colette: Oeuvres, 2 volumes to date, edited by Claude Pichois (Paris: Gallimard, 1984, 1986).

No other writer appears to have told so much about herself as Colette, to have plundered so markedly her own life in each of its stages in order to create her different fictional aliases: Claudine, Renée Néré, Léa, Julie de Carneilhan. The first person, her favorite narrative stance especially in the early part of her career, deceives; the lyrical outbursts seduce and seem to deliver her to her readers in all her intimacy. And the facts of her life, at that time scandalous and even now intriguing, have tended to attract not only biographers' but also critics' attention. Like Rimbaud, she has become something of a legend and indeed was already partly so while she was alive: Colette the author and model of the Claudines and at the same time the last lyric writer; Colette the mime and dancer who appeared on stage scantily clad; Colette who was stranger to no sensual pleasure, including lesbian affairs and the seduction of her stepson as well as the scoffing of truffles; Colette, eventually, the wise old lady, a sort of Mother Earth who "knew all about" men and wine and animals; and finally Colette the great writer, whom even Proust called "maître."

What remains incontrovertible behind all the scandal and the anecdotes and her eventual adulation by some as a cult figure is the ample evidence of Colette the writer. Her real story, not only for later readers but also for herself, is of the process of writing, of its dynamic, transforming powers and its interaction with life. As with Montaigne, the lived feeds the writing, but the art of writing creates the model, and life is altered, pushed onward in a new synthesis. Indeed it is this creative power of writing over her own life which seems to be the most remarkable quality of Colette. Sometimes like the true "maîtresse de maison" that she was she looks backward, turns out the cupboards, airs them at the open windows of the world, digs out the weeds in her garden, and nurtures the best blooms. Occasionally her writing is in advance of experience, and she fleshes out in fiction the path she is later to tread in real life. Colette, one should be warned, is the woman who, when she was awakened during a train journey to see a beautiful moonlit landscape, uttered a single swear word and promptly went to sleep again, only to produce the following day an incomparable description of this dramatic marvel.

She was born on 28 January 1873 in Saint-Sauveur-en-Puisaye in the *département* of Yonne, as Sidonie Gabrielle Colette, daughter of Jules and Sidonie Colette. Her mother, the daughter of journalists and writers, had been married before and had two children by her first marriage, although recent research has suggested that the second son might already have been fathered by Jules Colette, a retired army officer who had lost a leg at Marignan and was, at the time of his daughter's birth, employed as a tax inspector. Sidonie Colette was a remarkable woman who later figured importantly in Colette's autobiographical works and, as Sido, was the model which Colette idealized in the later part of her life. Her father was more remote and so preoccupied with his obsessive love for Sido that the child felt he had little time for her. Nevertheless, Colette had a happy childhood. She ran wild in garden and fields but knew that she would always come back to the maternal fold. The Colettes, however, were plagued by increasing financial difficulties, and when "Gabi," as she was called, reached the age of seventeen her future seemed threatened. In France at the end of the nineteenth century the only prospect for a respectable middle-class girl was marriage, and where would be found a husband willing to take a young woman without a dowry? Fortune seemed to smile on the family in the shape of the thirty-five-year-old Henry Gauthier-Villars, son of a well-known publisher and with whom Jules Colette

had been friendly. Henry Gauthier-Villars was better known as Willy, music critic, journalist, and manager, as it were, of a veritable writing factory. Well-known writers would accept to "ghost" for him because they needed the money, and he had a flair for management and publicity. Willy, although notorious for his womanizing, had been living for three years in a stable relationship with a woman named Germaine Servat who had recently died and left him with a small son. The Colette family were friendly enough with him for Sidonie Colette to have at certain periods helped to look after the child, and Gabi had often met Willy on family trips to Paris. With his rather dubious background Willy could no more hope for a dazzling social marriage than could the dowryless Gabi. More important the eighteen-year-old girl fell passionately in love with the middle-aged Parisian man of the world. Letters of Sidonie Colette at the time reveal that Willy seemed the answer to their prayers. Letters of Willy show a different picture. Still very much affected by the loss of his mistress he could hardly respond emotionally, although he was not immune to the charms of the lively, independent young girl and her intense curiosity about all life had to offer.

In 1893 Sidonie Gabrielle Colette became Madame Willy, and her life for the next thirteen years in Paris was a story of swift and continued disillusion, for Willy soon reverted to his old ways. In the airless, confined space of a Paris flat, she became very unhappy despite the friendship of several of Willy's ghostwriters, and for a long period she was seriously ill with an unexplained malady. It was soon after her recovery that Willy suggested to her that she should write down some of the stories about her childhood that she had told him and add some salacious details—which she obediently did. At first he put them aside, but he later decided that he had made a mistake and rushed them into print under his own name. Thus was the first of the Claudine series, *Claudine à l'école* (1900; translated as *Claudine at School*, 1930), born; thus too did Sidonie Gabrielle Willy become Colette the writer.

The main feature of *Claudine à l'école* is the figure of Claudine, wild, clever, sensual, outspoken, both tender and cruel to her schoolmates, an anarchic version of Colette herself. The story consists of a loosely strung series of anecdotes which center on Claudine's discovery of the lesbian love affair between the headmistress and one of the younger teachers, to whom Claudine had also been attracted. There is one male character–the doctor, a delegate of the canton, who comes from time to time to visit the school and submit the girls to his lascivious attentions. A caricatural weak male, he is also the lover of the headmistress, and, with a parody of an orgy, the book ends at a school dance where the two are discovered in bed by the headmistress's mother. *Claudine à l'école* has many faults, but the dialogue is racy and accomplished and the use of local dialect gives a sense of authenticity. In the figure of Claudine, Colette managed, perhaps unconsciously, to create a type. *La garçonne* (the tomboy) already existed in literature, but *Claudine à l'école* invested her with a particular, dynamic charm, and the book was an immediate success. Willy was congratulated, but the more perspicacious began to be aware of Colette.

As the Claudine series progressed, the title character became public property. There were Claudine collars, Claudine scent, Claudine haircuts (modeled on Colette's). In 1902 Willy directed a play based on the second book, *Claudine à Paris* (1901; translated as *Claudine in Paris*, 1931). In the starring role was the Parisian music-hall actress Polaire, whom Willy called one of his "twins." He was often seen on opening nights with Polaire on one arm and her "twin," Colette, on the other.

Although the Claudine books are the least accomplished of Colette's works of fiction, they do bear some of her hallmarks. In *Claudine à Paris* there is even less of a plot than there is in *Claudine à l'école*. The kind of exaggeration, caricature, and obvious titillation evident in *Claudine à l'école* is, however, exploited even more in the figure of Marcel, the young homosexual, and in Luce, one of Claudine's old schoolmates, who at a certain moment is seen crawling obediently about on all fours for her septuagenarian uncle. The story line, such as it is, has to do with Claudine's infatuation and eventual marriage to the handsome Renaud.

Renaud, Colette was later to admit, was modeled on one aspect of Willy but is totally unsuccessful as a fictional creation, hollow, unreal, and, as Colette once put it, like a decoration on a Christmas tree. His is very much the supernumerary role, and in the third novel, *Claudine en ménage* (1902; translated as *The Indulgent Husband*, 1935), it is Claudine's involvement with another woman, Rézi, which occupies the center of the scene and which is most powerfully and subtly portrayed. Claudine's senses have been awakened by Renaud, and with her usual avidity (what Colette

later called her own cannibalism for "la chair fraîche" [fresh flesh]) she finds that she is drawn to the ultrafeminine, curvaceous Rézi; at the same time she hopes that Renaud will become jealous. Instead, however, he encourages her, and the sultry affair between the two women is carried on behind the closed curtains of the Parisian "cinq à sept" (rendezvous spot). There is never one explicit detail, but Colette manages to convey by images and rhythm the abandonment to voluptuousness, and equally, when in a moment of shock Claudine realizes that Renaud is actually sharing Rézi with her, the other side of the coin, the escape into the outside world, the flight into nature, the freedom of the wild, tomboy spirit from the feminine flesh. *Claudine en ménage* is the first assured expression of Colette's lyrical prose, which here movingly delineates those two forces which were to dominate both Colette's life and her writing: the centripetal urge toward the claustrophobic, self-obsessed world of love, sex, jealousy and that centrifugal yearning toward liberty and the marvels of the world.

At the end of *Claudine en ménage* Claudine leaves her country retreat and returns to Renaud. But the next novel, *Claudine s'en va: Journal d'Annie*, published in 1903, a year after *Claudine à Paris* had been staged as a play, and translated as *The Innocent Wife* in 1935, clearly marks the beginning of the end of Claudine. A new heroine appears as the first-person narrative is transferred to Annie, one of Claudine's friends. At a time when Colette was beginning to brace herself to envisage a separation from Willy, it is interesting that she created a character who, although diametrically opposed to Claudine in her passivity and dependence on love and security, is also, because of the unexplained departure of her husband, obliged to envisage a life of solitude. In *Claudine s'en va*, which Colette regarded along with *Claudine à Paris* as the low point of the series, this development does not take full shape, and instead Colette fills in the pages with padding which includes the Willy-like character of Maugis and anecdotes set in Bayreuth at the time of the Wagner festival. The book is obviously a result of forced labor but the ending is significant. Annie's final decision is indeed a variation on the centrifugal theme; she accepts her solitary destiny by turning outward and embracing variety in the form of travel. But this apparent freedom is merely a travesty, for she is fleeing only in order to find the hoped-for miracle–the figure of a man who will block the next turning. Freedom is

Colette at twenty, spring 1893

still a mirage on the horizon.

Both Annie and Claudine were to appear in a later work, but in the meantime Colette's own journey on the road to freedom was being accomplished slowly in other ways in her writing. In 1904 she produced *Dialogues de bêtes* (Animal Dialogues), a collection of stories featuring two animal characters, the cat Kiki-la-Doucette and the dog Toby-Chien, and carrying the dedication "To amuse Willy." Colette's relationship with the animal world, although a potent part of her legend, still remains mysterious and unexplained. She seemed not merely to have loved animals but to have felt a particular affinity with them, and toward the end of her life said that one of her great regrets was that she had left no lasting monument in the animal world. In *Dialogues de bêtes* these two characters act as a mask for Colette: they speak and behave as if they were cat-and-dog-

like human beings but in the voice of Colette herself, airing some of her favorite observations about male and female characteristics and about the marvels of the natural world. Although the idea was not original (there was a certain vogue for animal studies at the time; Kipling's *Jungle Book*, Jules Renard's *Histoires naturelles*, Apollinaire's *Le Bestiaire* also identify human and animal characteristics), *Dialogues de bêtes* established Colette as a writer independent of Willy. In his preface to an enlarged edition of the dialogues, Francis Jammes declared that here was a true poet, who (despite her dubious legend) would manage to overthrow all those affected muses who had previously been occupying the slopes of Parnassus.

In the rather rudimentary figure of Annie and in the animal characters, Colette can be seen attempting to project herself outward. With the very young heroine of the 1904 story *Minne* she moves away from the hitherto obsessive relationship with Willy and looks backward in time. Interestingly, the slight and touching story of Minne turns out to be similar, as one later discovers in *La Maison de Claudine* (1922; translated as *My Mother's House*, 1953), to one of Colette's own childhood fantasies, but in the story it is acted out in more melodramatic circumstances. Minne, the spoiled, cossetted child of a bourgeois family living in a district near the "fortifications" of Paris, weaves her adolescent desires around the figure of a gangster whom she reads about in the paper. The fantasy threatens to become real disaster when she really believes this hero of her dreams has come to take her away and seeks him out in the streets. Her innocence protects her in various strange encounters, and she is eventually returned to the fold. *Minne* is, in fact, an interesting early example of that mysterious mingling of imagination and reality which informs what Colette later called the "lie" of fiction. A sequel, *Les Egarements de Minne* (Minne's Wildness) was published in 1905, and in 1909 Colette revised and combined the two works under the title *L'Ingénue libertine* (translated as *The Gentle Libertine*, 1931). The sequel takes Minne, now a married woman, on a search for sexual fulfillment which she, finally and unexpectedly, finds with her despised husband. Speaking of *L'Ingénue libertine* Proust declared his admiration for Colette's insight and sureness of touch.

From 1904 to 1907 Colette actively prepared her departure. As the royalties of all her works except *Dialogues de bêtes* belonged to Willy

Colette with her first husband, Henry Gauthier-Villars, who had several of her early books published under his own pseudonym, Willy

(both *Minne* and *Les Egarements de Minne* were published under his name), she was completely dependent financially and so set about training herself for a new career as dancer and mime. Physical expression, rhythm, musicality, and, above all, the limelight–these were the attractions and would remain so for a long time. The sessions with the mime Georges Wague were arduous, but Colette was prepared to discipline herself, and in 1906 she left her husband and launched herself successfully as a mime at the Théâtre des Mathurins and at L'Olympia.

There is no trace of this new life in the next Claudine novel, *La Retraite sentimentale* (translated as *Retreat from Love*, 1974), which Colette began writing in 1904 and published under the name of Colette Willy in 1907. But the old life is clearly being sloughed off. The actual fact that Willy was really abandoning her emotionally (he had embarked on what looked like a serious liaison) is transformed into the illness and then the death of Claudine's husband. The two women, Claudine and Annie, are together in an old coun-

try house which is clearly modeled on Les Monts Boucons in the Jura, which had belonged to the Willy couple. The women enact in their conversations the two opposing solutions to this death of love which Annie has already experienced and with which Claudine is learning to come to terms. For Claudine, this unique, idealized love can be followed only by a retreat into solitude and nature and the company of animals. The narrative here is not presented through the first person, but as recounted by Claudine to the narrator Annie, in that characteristic rhythmic, richly decorated prose in which Colette sublimates her own sensuality. Annie, unlike Claudine, is too restless and dispersed for retreat and meditation. She chooses, as she did before, to go off again into the world.

Clearly these two possibilities were ever present for Colette, neither perhaps better than the other, each with its solace and its dangers. She herself seemed immediately and perforce to be following the Annie path, not only in her peripatetic, active life as a mime, with its chance acquaintances and constant change, but also in the fulfillment of her sexual curiosity and desires. Much has been written about her various lesbian liaisons of this time, most notably with Natalie Barney (to whom Remy de Gourmont addressed his 1914 *Lettres à l'Amazone*) and with the Marquise de Belbeuf, known as Missy (scion of a prestigious family, who protected Colette almost maternally, if one can use this word about such an apparently masculine figure), for the next six years. Colette later, in *Ces Plaisirs* (1932; translated as *The Pure and the Impure*, 1933), wrote percipiently and from her own experience about the way in which women who are hurt by men defend themselves by turning toward other women for affection and sympathy. She was never any more explicit in writing about the physical side of these pleasures than she had been in *Claudine en ménage*. In life, however, she did not hesitate to blazon them abroad by appearing with Missy in 1907 at the Moulin Rouge in a pantomime called *Rêve d'Egypte*, written by Missy, in which the two women embraced passionately. There had been controversy enough when Colette had danced practically naked, but this public act of bravado created an uproar nearly as sensational as the "battle" which had attended the opening performances of Victor Hugo's *Hernani* in 1830. The curtain had to be rung down, and Colette Willy the mime became the talk of the town.

Three months later Colette Willy the author produced a short story which firmly proved her powers as a lyrical writer and also embodied her determination to continue. "Les Vrilles de la vigne" (The Tendrils of the Vine), which was published in 1908 as the title piece of a story collection, is perhaps one of the most musical and eloquent of her set pieces. Hardly a story, it is a reworking of the legend of the bird who in order not to be caught in the tendrils of a swift-growing vine sings ceaselessly throughout the night. Like the bird, the narrator refuses to be smothered by the threat of new attachments: "j'ai craint les vrilles de la vigne, et j'ai jeté tout haut une plainte qui m'a révélé ma voix!... Je voudrais dire, dire, dire, tout ce que je sais, tout ce que je pense, tout ce que je devine, tout ce qui m'enchante et me blesse et m'étonne" (I feared the tendrils of the vine and I cried out aloud in a lamentation that revealed to me my own voice!... I want to say, say, say everything I know, everything I think, everything I guess, everything which delights and hurts and astonishes me).

To live and live to the fullest, to say and say everything: once she was liberated from Willy who had, for all his faults, set her on her path, this now becomes the burning theme. *La Vagabonde*, which first appeared in serial form in *La Vie Parisienne* (1910), was published in book form the same year, and was translated as *Renée la Vagabonde* in 1931, could well be this "lamentation" which revealed to her her own voice. It is not merely the best of her works so far but one of the best of all her novels. Another double is the focal point, and the references back to the real Colette are obvious. Renée Néré is a writer and has been married to the well-known artist Taillandy, who treated her as badly as Willy did Colette. She, also like Colette, is earning her living as a mime and her partner is called Georges. This explicit use of the apparent double soon reveals itself to be a metaphor for the fundamental theme of the book. The name Renée Néré turning back on itself, the surname a near anagram of the first name; the initial important image of the mirror where Renée faces herself and sees a heavily made-up "counselor" who actually talks to her and questions her decision to lead an independent life; the dichotomy between the glitter and the bright rowdiness of the music-hall stage and the loneliness, fatigue, and introspection of the writer and blue stocking; past love, present lack—this series of reflections and oppositions sets the situation.

Into this world of make-up and makeshift comes Max, slightly ridiculous with his aristocratic name of Maxime Dufferein-Chantel and his stilted bearing, his money and his doglike devotion: the "grand serin" (big canary) as Renée calls him because he merely sings and does not work for a living. Similarly, Colette, conscious of her own superiority of character and intellect but faced with the physical attractiveness and the love of an "inferior male," had christened the rich young man Auguste Hériot, who was vying for her affections with Missy, "the little canary." Max is, like most of Colette's adult males, not convincingly drawn. He is a good example in her work of what has been called "the man object." More movingly portrayed is Renée's struggle between the temptation of the sheer physical pleasure and the general warmth and protectiveness that Max offers and her own sense of hard-won independence. To give in to this "large dense male," to diminish herself into a mere wife and mother, to become, in short, a "woman object," is revealed finally, despite the lure of the senses and the strong and instinctive leaning toward man, a dangerous snare.

In *La Vagabonde* the tension mounts dramatically as Colette shows her skill in mastering the techniques of suspense. In a final kaleidoscopic section which, in fragmented images, mirrors the theme of escape and the force of the centrifugal movement, Renée, the "vagabond," throws herself into the world. It is as if the "large dense male" had threatened to block the marvels that surround her, and once again possession of the world of nature is seen as the ideal, the ultimate independence. Now, however, something new and all-important is added. Colette had hinted at this in *Les Vrilles de la vigne* (1908), but now the crucial self-fulfillment of the "vagabond" lies not merely in experiencing the marvels of the world but in finding words in which to express them. To her surprise she finds that she has forgotten Max:

> Pendant combien de temps venais-je pour la première fois, d'oublier Max? Oui, de l'oublier, comme si je n'avais jamais connu son regard ni la caresse de sa bouche, de l'oublier, comme s'il n'y avait pas besoin plus impérieux dans ma vie, que de chercher des mots, des mots pour dire combien le soleil est jaune, et bleue la mer, et brillant le sel en frange de jais blanc.... Oui de l'oublier, comme s'il n'y avait d'urgent au monde que mon désir de posséder par les yeux les merveilles de la terre! C'est à cette même heure qu'un esprit insidieux m'a soufflé: "Et s'il n'y avait d'urgent, en effet, que cela? Si tout, hormis cela, n'était que cendres?" (For how long had I for the first time, forgotten Max? Yes, forgotten him as if I had never known his look, nor the caress of his touch, forgotten him as if there were no more imperious concern in my life than the search for words, words to say how yellow is the sun and blue the sea and brilliant the salt in its fringe of white jet.... Yes, forgotten him as if there were nothing urgent in the world except my desire to possess through my eyes the wonders of the world! It is at this moment that an insidious spirit whispered in my ear: "And if nothing else did matter? If everything, apart from that, were merely ashes?")

Expressed eloquently and yet tentatively ("an insidious spirit"), this passage formulates and epitomizes Colette's credo, one which underpins her creative drive for the rest of her long

life. Words, and also rhythm. The only reality is the translation of one's ideas into rhythm, Renée declares at the beginning of *La Vagabonde,* and at the end her desire for Max has been transformed: "Ce n'est plus une pensée, c'est un refrain, un bruit, un petit croassement rythmé" (no longer a thought but a refrain, a noise, a rhythmical little croak). Colette later declared that she would have liked to compose music. In a sense she did. All her works have a marked rhythmical quality not merely within the sentence or the paragraph but also in their overall composition.

La Vagabonde was perhaps the first work to evidence this overall harmony of construction, and it was the first to receive wide acclaim as a major literary achievement. It is a classic example of the *roman d'analyse,* both restrained in tone and tightly knit in structure. It also has a lively and convincing setting, and, especially, it is a moving and profound study of a very individual woman who, in Colette's hands, becomes a new type. Renée, the "new woman," is very much a product of the epoch, but at the same time she has characteristics which remain significant today. Hers is, it would seem, a continuing feminine dilemma; but it is, as well, that of any human being who, in isolation, faces up to the realization that he or she is responsible for his or her own destiny. The final part of the novel in particular exudes a poignant existential sadness. The critic and journalist André Billy declared at the time that Colette merited the terms of praise that had once been applied to Chateaubriand: "She has invented a new way of being sad." The novel was presented in 1910 for the Prix Goncourt—at the same time as Apollinaire's *L'Hérésiarque et Cie*—and although it received only three votes, Remy de Gourmont, while criticizing the unsuitable milieu, found in *La Vagabonde* an example of "un détachement vraiment nietzschéen, un arrachement au bonheur par amour de la liberté, où se lit la philosophie la plus haute, la plus féminine et la plus vraie" (a Nietzschean detachment, a denial of happiness through love of liberty, the highest, most feminine, truest kind of philosophy).

Dialectically, having refused love in writing, Colette in her life was heading right back to it. Both Missy and Auguste Hériot were being superseded by a very different kind of lover. In December 1910 Colette, who had recently had a short story, "Le Poison," published in the daily paper *Le Matin,* made the acquaintance of one of the subdirectors, Henry de Jouvenel. Jouvenel was of aristocratic descent and, like Willy, something of a

Colette (seated) with the Marquise de Belbeuf ("Missy") in 1907 (photograph by Roger Viollet). During the summer of that year, Colette and Missy shared Missy's villa in Picardie while Willy and his current mistress lived next door.

womanizer. He was also very ambitious, later finding a career in politics and the foreign service. This combination was a potent one for Colette, and after a melodramatic period when she had to cope with the jealousy of both Missy and Hériot and also threats to her life from the recently cast-off mistress of Jouvenel, she went to live with him in September 1911. They were married in December of the following year when Colette was two months pregnant. The marriage took place three months after the death of her mother, an event which had no repercussions in her writing at the time but which was to reveal its significance a good ten years later. Colette in 1912 seemed content and settled. She had been continuing her career as a mime and was still writing, particularly the short stories for which she acquired such a reputation, and even taking on some reporting.

The crystallization in novel form of this real-life fulfillment is disappointing and would seem to bear witness to the claim that happiness (albeit, as it proved, temporary) does not produce great works of art. And yet the title of Colette's next novel, *L'Entrave* (1913; translated as *Recaptured*, 1931), may harbor the suggestion of future trouble. After the free soul Renée of *La Vagabonde*, Colette depicts a Renée in chains, "hobbled" to her physical and emotional needs. Renée has become independent, not by her own doing but because of an unexpected legacy, and is full of nostalgia and regret for her old career in the music hall. The whole movement of the work is the exact opposite of that of *La Vagabonde*. After the frenzied outward turning, there is a retreat inward into idleness, introspection, a sort of void. Again against Renée's will a masculine figure intrudes into her solitude, and he is again inferior to her in talent and intelligence but much more dominant physically than Max. To him and to sheer sensual pleasure she succumbs in some of the most explicit and forceful scenes that Colette, who generally deployed an art of suggestion, ever wrote.

L'Entrave as a whole, however, is lifeless; the characters and their dialogue have a hollow ring. It is, above all, the ending which is disappointing in more ways than one. At the level of the plot

Colette in costume for the 1907 pantomime Rêve d'Egypte, *written by Missy (Collection of Mme Dreyfus-Valette)*

Renée submits, becomes the slave to this version of the "big dense male." Also Colette's writing seems perfunctory. The masochistic tone is exaggerated so that the last scene with the overly explicit symbolism of the little homebound wife waiting for the hunter (here the fisher!) to return is a mere parody. Colette herself judged this ending inadequate— "ce couloir insuffisant par où j'ai voulu que passint mes héros amenuisés" (this inadequate corridor through which I wanted my diminished heroes to pass). But there was a good excuse. Perhaps Colette's attention, as she wrote *L'Entrave,* was divided between the book and the baby. Colette-Renée de Jouvenel, whom Colette nicknamed Bel-Gazou, was born on 3 July 1913.

Much more successful was the collection of short stories *L'Envers du music-hall,* published the same year as *L'Entrave* and woven around Colette's experiences in the theater. Slight, but full of penetrating observations and lively dialogue, Colette's short stories tended to focus on the very ordinary people she had met but who to her were not at all ordinary. Even the humblest of these characters, and particularly the women, in their conditions of near-starvation and illness, were capable of touching devotion, generosity, and self-sacrifice. Love, sensuality, sacrifice, jealousy—these were themes which Colette saw enacted everywhere.

It was not long before Colette's euphoria about her baby daughter was superseded by the same sort of jealousy that she had known with Willy, for Jouvenel, while remaining attached to her, could never resist a new conquest. In fact it has been claimed that had it not been for the enforced separation caused by the war (Jouvenel as a reserve officer was mobilized immediately in August 1914), the marriage might not have lasted as long as it did—until 1923.

Life, however, had become very different for Colette. She was now La Baronne de Jouvenel and before the war dutifully played the role of hostess for Jouvenel, who had been elected as *député* for Corrèze, where the family owned a château. Occasionally they would both be invited to dine at the Elysée Palace. But more important to her was her own career. Colette the mime had bowed out before Colette the journalist; and for the war years she was caught up in a constant round of activity. She traveled as a reporter to Venice and later accompanied Jouvenel to Rome when in 1917 he became French delegate to the commission for the petite entente. Her journalistic pieces are collected in the volume *Les Heures longues, 1914-1917* (The Long Hours, 1917). They show how, even in what might seem casual writing, Colette was a scrupulous craftsman, always in search of the right words in which to couch her poetic perceptions. Proust, in a letter to her, declared himself delighted by her portrayal of Venice "hiding itself under the sand like a flat-fish when seagulls swoop." It was at this time also that, not surprisingly after her own career in the theater, she became interested in the cinema and contributed to the review *Le Film.*

By the end of the war the Jouvenel couple seemed to embody success. Jouvenel was well launched in his career as politician and was sent in 1918 to Geneva as a member of the French delegation to the disarmament commission. In 1919 Colette became dramatic critic of *Le Matin* and editor of their story section. She, having published no work of fiction during the war, made an impressive return, first with *Mitsou; ou, Comment l'esprit vient aux filles,* a long story, in 1919, and then with what is perhaps her best-known novel, *Chéri,* in 1920.

The theme of *Mitsou* (translated as *Mitsou; or, How Girls Grow Wise,* 1930) is in fact typically Colette. The young heroine is a music-hall artist who falls in love with an officer on leave, whom she symbolically calls "the blue lieutenant." He is not able to think that their one night together has been anything more than a *passade.* She, however, for all her frivolity and vulgarity, is capable of that transcendence through love which Colette found in her humble companions of the music hall, the most banal heroism of accepting the difference in their stations and wishing that for him her memory will prove to be worthy of his love. Proust was full of admiration for this work. He wrote to Colette that he had been moved to tears and that one particular restaurant scene had made his own attempts at similar scenes look pathetic. Proust spoke advisedly of scenes, for the story has a curious form. It is partly conceived as dialogue with stage directions and is partly told through Mitsou's letters. The theater had obviously had a potent influence on Colette, for *Chéri,* although it was not published until 1920 (translated, 1930), had been conceived by Colette in 1912 and had shape in her mind as a play.

By the time *Chéri* appeared Colette was in her late forties. Hitherto her writing had spun itself out of memory or out of her present preoccupations. Only in the short stories had she projected herself into totally other characters.

Chéri marks a strange phenomenon, for the nub of its story is the love between a woman of forty-nine and a young man barely out of adolescence, a kind of love which had not yet been enacted in the life of Colette but which was to become a reality the following year when Colette took over the *éducation sentimentale* of her stepson Bertrand de Jouvenel. Against the usual background of disapprobation and scandal their affair became public knowledge. Despite his own liaisons and his serious relationship with the Princesse Marthe Bibesco, Jouvenel was to find the situation intolerable and left home in 1923, leaving Colette and Bertrand together. It was in 1924 that Bertrand's marriage was announced, but Colette, unlike her heroine in *Chéri,* was not prepared to let him go. As Bertrand wrote much later, he left because it was inevitable and because of the general "climat de scandale" that was surrounding them.

Thus *Chéri* is in some sense a premonition of things to come, a case of life modeling itself on art, and not, as is commonly supposed, the other way round. The imagination has its own ways of fulfilling itself. If one wishes to look at the novel in the context of Colette's past experience, Chéri, the slim, androgynous adolescent, could well be another facet of Colette and Léa a mother figure standing in for Sidonie Colette who had died eight years before and remained so far unsung. As long ago as 1911 Colette had in fact been trying out in several stories which appeared in *Le Matin* the figure of a rich, lost adolescent called Clouk, but he was adenoidal and ugly, and she soon replaced him with the beautiful Chéri in other parallel stories.

At first, then, it seemed Colette's intention to make Chéri the main figure, and indeed he inaugurates in her work a series of lost young men who are searching for the mother in various guises, unable to bear reality without her. Maurice Goudeket, Colette's third husband, once told a strange story about Colette's own explanation of Chéri: that he was like a creature from the animal kingdom striving to be born into the human, and certainly he appears in this novel and in its 1926 sequel, *La Fin de Chéri* (translated as *The Last of Chéri,* 1932), as an ill-starred, damned soul, a representative of the spirit world. In any event in this spoiled, handsome boy, Colette had created yet another type, not acknowledged, so she said, by men but recognized by countless women who claimed that they had met him.

In the final version of the novel it is Léa who monopolizes the center of the scene: Léa the sybaritic Ceres, the full-fleshed, pink-cheeked, blue-eyed courtesan, amoral and marginal according to a bourgeois code but good-natured, easy-going, a thoroughly good sort. "Donne-le-moi, ton collier de perles!" (Give me your pearl necklace!): Chéri's first words reveal him as vain, greedy, and rather feminine, whereas Léa's strength is symbolized by her magnificent wrought iron bedstead. The strong woman and the weak male, this inversion of the traditional topos, exploited to the fullest here, is in fact a constant throughout the rest of Colette's fiction.

One of Colette's techniques which is carried out with great skill in the two Chéri books is that of contrast, the inversion of sex, contrast of color or of musical note (for it was in terms of music that Colette later said that she envisaged Chéri). Against the pink sheets and curtains and sunlight the black figure of Chéri is like a graceful devil transforming the whole décor into a satanic furnace. Léa is presented throughout at the symbolic level; her room is womblike, pink like a watermelon, slaking thirst, giving life; Colette handles this symbolism discreetly, in occasional images which thread through the down-to-earth story about the inevitability of Chéri's departure and the way in which both will tackle it. The plot, dependent on Chéri's arranged marriage to the young girl Edmée, unfolds against the chatter and gossip of Léa's pals, those other courtesans, including Chéri's mother, who have made a material success of their lives. Colette, with her sharp eye and her keen ear, by now excelled in dialogue of this sort. It is funny, bitchy, revealing.

Léa's first preoccupation is with her age, not only because it is the major obstacle to her love but also because it marks the end of her career. She is being forced into retirement, and she simply does not know what to do. In the same way that Colette has no pity for her (indeed is perhaps using her in order to show no pity toward herself), she looks in her mirror and judges what she sees. Once again the mirror, as in the Claudine series and in *La Vagabonde*, with its implications of the double and the gap between appearance and reality, plays an important role in the action. The mirror represents Léa's pride but also her strength. After Chéri's departure she resists the temptation of giving up and buys new clothes to "disguise that monster, the old woman." (What restrained and resigned irony is here being turned against the world of men!) In fact she is simply waiting for him to come back.

Faithful to its conception as a play, *Chéri* is divided, as it were, into three acts. The middle part of the novel is given over to Chéri, for Léa, in order to save face, goes away, supposedly with a new lover. Chéri cannot cope without her. Above all he finds his young wife's love and eventual jealousy of the past intolerable, and, like a somnambulist, simply leaves home, to hide in a hotel room and haunt Léa's empty house. The final "act" returns to Léa, living in the hope of Chéri's return. When he does come back to her it is without warning or explanation. At first they are both wary, and the mirror announces the coming confrontation; Léa watches Chéri watching her, and appropriately the reader's attention is focused on this play of appearances, for it is Léa's physical appearance that is the insurmountable obstacle to love, and this, in her heart of hearts, she already knows. It is also significant that Chéri is presented as a child coming home and nestling in his mother's arms and that Léa treats him as such. Such reactions serve ironically to point forward to the inevitable outcome, but there are many twists and turns on the way, and Léa and Chéri's lovemaking in the blindness of night overwhelms Léa's fears and obscures her normal lucidity, although even in the course of their encounter she has a moment of premonition. As so often in Colette's writing, abandonment to physical pleasure is seen as a defeat, a torture even, "an abyss from which love emerges, pale, taciturn and full of nostalgia for death." However, with her usual robustness, Léa soon returns to an overweaning confidence. With the cold light of day and Chéri's awakening this confidence is soon shown to be the antique sin of hubris. Again Chéri watches Léa, notes the physical signs of old age as she sleeps, her thinning hair, her double chin, her flabby neck. But with dramatic irony, Léa, unconscious of his observance, makes herself fit to face him again and misguidedly continues to treat him like a child, even (with what effects of bathos!) advising him to take rhubarb tablets for his constipation. The blow when it comes is, nevertheless, a shock, to the reader, to Léa, and even to Chéri himself; it is significant that in this skillfully crafted piece of writing, it is in the use of language that the blow is delivered. The signifier simply takes over: "Toi, tu as été pour moi . . . " (You have been for me . . .), says Chéri, and the past tense reveals all. It is again entirely characteristic of Colette in her own reactions and in her writing that Léa registers this rejection in musical tones as a refrain, "une grande lamentation intérieure" (an interior lamentation). To counteract the blow she shouts at Chéri, attacking his young wife in vulgar fishwife terms. It is only when Chéri reminds her that this is not worthy of the "chic type" she has always been for him, that she is in fact destroying her own image, that she finds the strength to live up to this ideal.

The transcendence is of the spirit, the tragedy is of the flesh and is seen in the flesh, in the wrinkled hands that Léa sees lying in her own lap. And flesh and spirit are still combined in appearance, in "son visage noble et défait" (her noble ravaged face). It is flesh and its appearance which continue to suffer. Léa cannot bear to separate her flesh from his: "ma force me quitte dès que ta chair s'éloigne de moi!" (my strength leaves me when your flesh goes away from me!). Even when she has sent him away to "chercher [sa] jeunesse" (search out his youth) she still hopes that he will come back, then catches sight of herself in the mirror. There she sees not the self she recognizes, only a crazy, gesturing old woman. The mirror has its final say in the tragedy of this woman whose whole life has been based on the pleasures of the flesh. It can also be seen as a metaphor in the wider context of the dialectical relationship between life and writing. The reflection of life in the mirror of writing acts, like Renée Neré's looking-glass double, both as revelation and counselor. But, as Colette later noted in the epigraph of *La Naissance du jour* (1928; translated as *A Lesson in Love*, 1932), "Imaginez-vous, à me lire, que je fais mon portrait? Patience: c'est seulement mon modèle" (Do you imagine when you read me that I am painting my portrait? Patience: It is only my model). In life she took the opposite course from Léa. When Bertrand de Jouvenel left to go to his young fiancée, Colette threw down from her window a piece of paper with the scribbled words "Je t'aime." He promptly returned.

Chéri, which was published in July 1920, had a success deserved above all for the beauty and the economy of the form. As André Gide said, " . . . Pas une faiblesse, pas une redondance, pas un lieu commun" (There is not one weakness, not one redundancy, not one commonplace). *Chéri* is another *roman d'analyse* in the classical French tradition. The subject matter, however, awakened many doubts particularly among male critics: the milieu was doubtful, Léa was, after all, a courtesan, and Chéri could be seen as her gigolo. Women were less squeamish: they rec-

ognized not only Chéri but much of themselves in Léa, and wherever Colette went they expressed praise and admiration. Indeed Léa, this latter-day earthy Bérénice, is a magnificent creation. She is a woman presented both as others see her, magnetic and splendid, and from the inside as only another woman could portray her. It is, one can argue, not an exaggerated claim to say that in comparison with Léa even those admired fictional women Emma Bovary and Anna Karenina seem lacking in substance.

Although the actual composition of *Chéri* owed nothing to the influence of Bertrand de Jouvenel, he did play a role in the two works which followed: *La Maison de Claudine* (1922; translated as *My Mother's House,* 1953) and *Le Blé en herbe* (1923; translated as *The Ripening,* 1932). It was he who, utterly fascinated by the stories which Colette told him of her childhood, suggested that she should gather them together in a volume. It has already been suggested that in the character of Chéri Colette might have been projecting the imaginative possibility of a return to the source. Certainly *La Maison de Claudine* marks the first explicit stage of her journey back to the lost paradise of her childhood. In this book loosely strung, pithy anecdotes are intertwined with nostalgic and lyrical evocations of the womblike house and garden, the trees and birds, and, at night, the glowing security of the lamp. Like Proust, Colette invests memory with magic, and the past becomes a timeless fairy world. Dominating it all, indeed herself the "nourishing domain," is the figure of Sido, Colette's mother, idealized into another version of the Mother Earth, stoical and dignified, a cornucopia of generosity and female wisdom, in tune with the secrets of nature and with the animals she gathers around her.

Bertrand de Jouvenel's contribution to the novel *Le Blé en herbe* was a story he had told Colette about an adolescent infatuation, which in fact had never come to anything, between himself and a young English girl, daughter of friends of his mother's. This idea at first, like that for *Chéri,* took shape in Colette's mind as the basis of a short play in which in complete darkness two lovers would be heard talking. When the curtain went up they would be revealed as adolescents. Colette had already tried her hand at the treatment of young or adolescent love, in Claudine, in Minne, in Mitsou, and in Edmée, Chéri's young wife. In *Chéri* the two young people had been used as a foil to the Chéri-Léa rela-

Colette with her second husband, Baron Henry de Jouvenel, whom she married on 19 December 1912

tionship. In *Le Blé en herbe* it is the older woman, Madame Dalleray (Bertrand de Jouvenel's apartment was in the rue d'Alleray), the mysterious temptress, strangely masculine despite her sultry, seductive airs, who acts as foil to the two young lovers, initiating the boy Phil and thus setting up the chain of jealousy which finally leads the girl, Vinca, to show that she too is a grown woman.

It is a simple, even banal, story, more shocking at the time than it is now. Perhaps its most remarkable quality is the exquisite setting in the Brittany summer and the way in which the sights and colors, the texture of sand and shrub, the pristine feel of the air are evoked for all the senses. It is the quintessence of summer and holiday, Colette's parallel to Proust's Balbec. As with *Chéri*, a symbolic thread weaves its way through this limpid story. The girl herself, with her flower name (Vinca, the periwinkle) and her blue

eyes, seems to incarnate the freshness of earth and sea, not Ceres but Persephone.

It is she, the female, who has all the qualities which are traditionally thought to be masculine–strength, practicality, a no-nonsense attitude–and the boy who is weak, romantic, and ill at ease in life. At one moment he almost gives in to a sort of generalized death wish, letting himself gently slide down the cliff's side, being pulled back by Vinca. The inversion of masculine and feminine characteristics sets off a chain of paradoxes, and each chapter seems to end with a new one. The mysterious Madame Dalleray, the sexual, sultry seductress, is in fact rather masculine and authoritarian. It is Phil who is worried at the thought of Vinca losing her virginity, and the girl who makes little of it. And yet the narrator, who is named Colette, takes pains at the end to underline the possible consequences which, despite Vinca's insouciance, could make her a victim. If *Le Blé en herbe*, for all the delights of its setting and sympathetic insights into young love, seems less perfect than *Chéri*, it is, perhaps, precisely because of this rather moralizing interference of Colette the narrator. There was always in Colette, along with the desire to tell all, the sense that she knew more than most. "Colette knew about food and wine and clothes and gardens and men and cats"–how often in her work one finds this and similar cries of admiration! "What wine would Colette have chosen with truffles?" Sometimes it irks. The temptation to comment is great in *Le Blé en herbe* because her characters are so young. Like the omniscient Balzac, she knew only too well the pitfalls on their way.

Critical acclaim for *Le Blé en herbe* was divided between those who were shocked and those who praised the purity of the style and the sureness of the storytelling. The last of Bertrand de Jouvenel's traces in Colette's work comes in the sequel to *Chéri*, which she began in December 1924 soon after he had left her and which was published in 1926 under the title *La Fin de Chéri*. Obviously, on one level Colette can now be seen to be doing what she did with Willy/Renaud in *La Retraite sentimentale*–killing him off–and in the process she is possibly airing her resentment against her husband, Bertrand's father. This view, however, underrates the logic and dynamic of the whole conception of *Chéri*. *Chéri* had always been conceived as a lost soul, incapable not merely of growing up but also of inserting himself into a full, human reality. Chéri, the married man, without his "Nounoune," as he used to call Léa, and all that she gave him of health, vitality, and pleasure, is a mere shadow. As in the earlier novel, the story takes shape against a background of contrasts and oppositions. Instead of Léa's rosy-pink boudoir, there is the smart modern house of Chéri and Edmée with its dominating colors of black and white and silver and the funereal, sickly touches of purple and yellow. The courtesans of the *belle époque* have now in this postwar period turned to good works in the hope of obtaining honors. Women have become independent and indeed even seem to have taken over from men. The efficient, clever Edmée has become a doctor, and there is simply no role for Chéri. Against this hard background is played out Chéri's existential anguish–his sense of the void and his own inability to fill it.

Once again Colette is intuitively in accord with the prevailing mental climate. The atmosphere of pointlessness and alienation that per-

vades *La Fin de Chéri* is similar to that which engulfs Proust's narrator in *Le Temps retrouvé* before he comes to his own personal salvation. But there is to be no salvation for Chéri. In search of one, still hoping for incarnation, still believing in the possibilities of transformation, he returns yet again to Léa. The ensuing scene is the heart of the book and magnificently conducted in just as dramatic a manner as the last scene of *Chéri*. The presence of Léa has always been enlivening for the reader as well as Chéri, and readers as well as he expect a miracle. Even at sixty Léa perhaps has been able to transcend the passage of time. The rosy light in which her room is still bathed builds up illusions, and with Chéri, readers experience the shock as Léa turns round. There is no superfluous commentary, only the sequence of Chéri's reactions, from the incredulity: " 'Qu'est-ce que c'est que cette bonne femme-là?' . . . Elle n'était pas monstrueuse, mais vaste. . . . La jupe unie, la longue veste impersonnelle entr'ouverte sur du linge à jabot annonçaient l'abdication, la rétraction normales de la féminité . . . " (Who is this old girl, vast, masculine, like a jolly old gendarme?), to an inner prayer for Léa to shake off this disguise and to reappear intact, and finally, as she shatters all his illusions: "Tu devrais faire analyser tes urines; tout ça, l'estomac. . . . Et le reste c'est de la littérature" (Have your urine analyzed; look after your stomach. . . . All the rest is only literature), total abdication.

Léa's inner reactions are not revealed. It is clear from her appearance that she has shaken off what Colette always regarded as the burden of femininity and is settling into the peaceful virility of old age. It is as if for Colette masculinity were the norm and femininity a temporary additional burden. At least for Léa this abdication has been her salvation. She is now robust and content: nevertheless one sees signs of her emotion, and as always with Léa they manifest themselves physically. Pathetically she attempts to pull in her stomach, and the whole mass of flesh trembles; she plays with the beautiful pearl necklace which has stayed intact whereas her neck has thickened and reddened. But the miracle does not happen.

Perhaps, in contrast to the final scene of *Chéri*, there is a hint of caricature. Léa is too big, too masculine, the sound of the cushion being squashed under the enormous behind too much of a parody, but structurally this exaggeration is necessary. These are Chéri's reactions, and the shock has to be traumatic, for after it he simply drifts toward death. His end is symbolic. He retreats into a dark hotel room and endlessly re-lives his memories of Léa. When he finally shoots himself his fate seems inevitable.

In *La Fin de Chéri* Chéri has become a rather different character from the spoiled boy of the first book. Colette has invested him with something of the romantic, hopeless idealism which is one facet of the topos of the return to the source. There are other variations on this neg-ative aspect to her fiction, but in her nonfictional works the way back proves on the contrary to be fruitful, a powerful stimulus for both life and writing.

Predictably now, Colette behaved in exactly the opposite way from her fictional character. In-stead of renouncing him, she had tried to keep Bertrand de Jouvenel, and when in 1925 he even-tually left her, she embarked (almost on the re-bound) on a new and passionate affair with a man not so young as Bertrand but still younger than she, Maurice Goudeket, who did in fact be-come her third husband and faithful companion for the rest of her life. No wonder that the mon-strous Léa seems a caricature. After all the toss-ing on turbulent seas and initial concern on the part of her friends that she was once again submit-ting herself to a master and becoming a slave to love, Colette's emotional life had found a peace-ful haven. Naturally enough then, for "l'amour heureux n'a pas d'histoires," Maurice Goudeket does not appear in totally fictional work, al-though as himself, "mon meilleur ami," he is a con-stant presence in Colette's later meditations on life.

The phrase "totally fictional work" is used here advisedly, because the work in which he does figure thinly disguised, *La Naissance du jour,* is a hybrid. Throughout there is a strong autobio-graphical thread holding together the different moments in time and depending on the first-person narrative of what appears to be the real present-day Colette in her Saint-Tropez house, La Treille Muscate, with her plants and trees and dogs and her painter friends. The focal point of this Colette's memories is the real Sido, clearly the model which she is setting up for herself, and from more recent times she speaks of a sec-ond husband, charming but unfaithful, and the sort of "cannibalism" which has led her to a much younger lover. It may not be immediately clear to the reader but in fact autobiography is being constantly modified, not merely in the way in which memory tampers with the past, confus-ing and selecting and embellishing, but also con-

Colette with her daughter Colette-Renée de Jouvenel, nick-named Bel-Gazou, at Castel-Novel, 1917

sciously in the direction of wish fulfillment: only the enchanting sequence of the Saint-Tropez hours, the changes in light, the sights, the smells, the natural feel of garden and sea are left intact.

In particular the real-life mother, who some-times irritated Colette, is taken one step further than she was in *La Maison de Claudine* to become a completely idealized, poetic figure, the fount of all wisdom and generosity, and Colette addresses her in the impassioned tones of a litany. Now that the Cape of Middle Age has been turned, the new art to be mastered is the "chic suprême du savoir-décliner" (the supreme chic of knowing how to decline). From now on it is renunciation, abdication of egoism and greed and possessive love, a joyous turning outward to the marvels of the world, a return to the pristine, symbolized by Sido's getting up ever earlier to catch the first light of dawn, a positive cultivation of the will to be reborn and to create each day. This heroic re-nunciation and the sublimation of human emo-tion into a dazzled wonderment at the mystery of life itself are delineated at the beginning of *La Naissance du jour* in a quotation from a letter of

Sido's thanking her son-in-law for his invitation to come to see her daughter but declining because she is old and does not want to miss her last chance of seeing the flowering of her rare pink cactus. The letter is a memorable document which provides both the theme and its dénouement. But again this is a literary device and the reality was just the opposite. A letter of Sido's did indeed furnish the point of departure for *La Naissance de jour,* but in fact she accepted the invitation, expressing the regret that she would not see the flowering of her cactus. Just as Colette is aiming to create her own future life she is taking the liberty of re-creating the past. The divisions between fact and fiction are fluid and interconnect in the most complex fashions.

In *La Naissance du jour* the brave claims that "man my friend" has ceased to be a problem are tested, for the temptation of giving in to the love of a younger man is still strong. It is here that autobiography begins to diverge clearly from fiction, because although one can see some traits of Goudeket in the figure of Vial, the decision that Colette the narrator makes is, once again, the opposite of the one which Colette the woman had already made in real life. She welcomes the birth of day with that movement toward transcendence which seems to represent her most basic, imaginative urge. Opening out onto "le monde sphérique tout bondé de saveurs" (the spherical world stuffed full with savors), itself a symbol of the perfect circular form at which Colette is aiming in her art, she sends her lover away and declares her power to transform the fleeing figure into that symbol of her mother's renunciation, the pink cactus. The ending of *La Naissance du jour,* like that of *La Vagabonde* but joyous, is a declaration of faith in the transforming, creative powers of the writer. The real lover has still not had time to change shape. "Mais que je l'assiste seulement et le voici halliers, embruns, météores, livre sans bornes ouvert, grappes, navire, oasis . . . " (But let me come to his aid and he will be changed into thickets, spray, meteors, open boundless text, bunches of flowers and fruit, ship, oasis . . .). Lived experience becomes symbol, the world becomes the open boundless text, the text becomes a model for the life that is to come. Birth, rebirth, creativity: the so aptly titled *La Naissance du jour* is not only the most poetic of Colette's works but also in itself a most moving statement about the role of art itself.

It is hardly surprising that in her work *Sido,* published the following year in 1929 (translated,

1953), Colette should return again to her "model," fleshing out now her memories in the more explicit fashion of *La Maison de Claudine.* Sido, dignified, wise, and generous, appears even more touching and admirable in her old age. But also Colette returns to the great love between her mother and her father, and to the enigmatic and rather ineffectual figure of her father who in retirement seemed to live in Sido's shadow. One can do no more here than air the suggestion that Colette may well have been affected by her memories of him in some of her male portrayals.

As a counterpoint to these lyrical creations of the past, *La Seconde* (1929; translated as *The Other One,* 1931), written almost in parallel to *Sido,* returns to the fictional form. If it swings forward in time to a Jouvenel-inspired relationship, it also lurches heavily backward into the claustrophobic world of emotional dependence, the atmosphere, as Colette put it, of "the harem," with the unfolding of the relationship between two women, wife and mistress, who seek refuge together from the dominating yet essentially weak Farou, a celebrated dramatist. It was transparently obvious that Colette had drawn on the real-life relationship between herself and Germaine Patat, one of Jouvenel's mistresses in the early days of their marriage. There is also the recognizable figure of Farou's son, who is infatuated with Jane, the secretary and mistress. The scandal that so often attended Colette's work soon broke and like *Le Blé en herbe,* which also had been first published as a serial, *La Seconde* had to be withdrawn.

It is certainly, like *L'Entrave,* one of Colette's least successful novels, despite its insights into the women's desire to defend themselves against the male. As in *L'Entrave,* the movement is centripetal and the characters seem shadowy. Colette seems to have found her best inspiration when her characters move toward transcendency.

Love, its pleasure and woes, had not been done with yet. In *Ces Plaisirs* of 1932, Colette proffers her views on the stranger shores of love and, in particular, homosexuality. Her own opinion, which she shared with her close friend the actress Marguerite Moréno, was that everybody has both masculine and feminine characteristics and that both she and Moréno possessed a large share of the masculine. In this view she is within the traditionally conventional framework, for she classes rationality, strength of will, power of intellect as masculine, and emotional dependence, servility, and humility as feminine. This outline reflects the way in which Colette plays with the sexual traits of her characters, sets them in conflict, even inverts them. Particularly noticeable are the tensions acted out by the fictional women who are overtly modeled on herself.

Male homosexuality is not the central focus of *Ces Plaisirs,* because from the woman's point of view (which she naturally enough takes), men create a world for themselves and can quite easily shut out women. This autonomy is, she considers, rare for women who, even in lesbian relationships, seem always to be acting over and against men. The most moving part of the book is the account of the two ladies of Llangollen who manage to live out their idyll in isolation from the world; they are figures completely suffused by Colette's lyricism. Similarly idealized is the figure of Charlotte in the opium "fumerie," who honors her young lover by giving public voice to the pleasure she feigns. *Ces Plaisirs* (republished in 1941 as *Le Pur et l'impur*) took its original title from a self-quotation: "ces plaisirs qu'on nomme à la légère physiques" (those pleasures which are lightly called physical). Charlotte is an example of the way in which physical love can lead to a certain kind of heroism. For Colette herself the mysteries of the flesh lead back to the delights of the imagination and their distillation in the word; "De ce mot *pur* qui montait du vide, j'écoutais, j'écoute encore le tremblement bref, l'*u* plaintif, l'*r* de glace limpide. Les lèvres qu'il entrouvait prolongeaient sa résonance unique. Il n'éveillait rien en moi, sinon le besoin d'entendre encore le mot *pur* et de savourer le délice imaginaire que nous nommons pureté" (In this word *pur* which rose from the void, I listened, I am still listening to the brief quiver of the plaintive *u,* the limpid ice of the *r.* The lips it forces open prolonged its unique resonance. It awakened nothing in me except to hear the word *pur* again, and to savor the imaginary delight that we call purity).

The public was more concerned with impurity. The scandal that seemed to be her natural habitat broke out again. She was also criticized for going on stage again to act the part of Léa in the play of *Chéri* that she had made with Léopold Marchand. (It had been originally produced in 1921; Colette had played the role of Léa in several subsequent productions, including a 1925 revival in Paris.) Colette had been brilliant as a mime, but she was much less successful as an actress. People came to see her although, as André Rouveyre told her, they came mainly out of curiosity about this by now famous lady of nearly sixty.

Writing alone, for all her proclamations, had never satisfied her totally. Involvement with the world and its marvels included relationships with other people from all walks of life and even the physical movement which had impelled her into her career as a mime. Colette's next venture seemed unexpected but in fact was completely in character. In 1932 she opened an Institut de Beauté with the backing of the Sultan of Marrakech and the Princesse de Polignac and presided there herself, mulling over her own recipes for quince cream and cucumber lotions, brewing and stirring the resulting potions, blending her own perfumes and actually carrying out beauty treatments. This occupation satisfied her desire to liberate women by making them look and feel better thanks to her particular secrets from her knowledge of the natural world. In a sense this liberation had also become one of her motivations for writing. Unfortunately she was not as successful a businesswoman as she was a writer. Like Balzac the only way in which she could make money was by her pen, and despite her constant activity as a journalist, drama critic, essayist, short-story writer, scriptwriter, she was often in financial difficulties. The Institut de Beauté had to close, but the publication of her books continued in full spate.

The year 1933 saw the appearance of another novel, *La Chatte,* which revealed once again her skill in exploring normally unsung regions of the psyche. Fundamentally this work is yet another variation on the theme of the return to the source, expressed in the drama of the young man Alain, a more sensitive and poetic version of Chéri, but who, like Chéri, has to be cast out of a womblike existence. In Alain's case, this existence is symbolized by the maternal house and garden with its presiding genius, "la chatte," the female cat in whom all his tenderness and dreams of idealized love have crystallized. His mental climate is poeticized in images of dream and moonlight and in the mysterious shadows of lush garden and elusive cat. For Alain, as for Chéri, the rite of passage into adulthood is enacted in marriage, and the new young wife is his exact opposite. Practical and robust, she and her physical demands leave him with a sense of disgust, and this is expressed in Colette's characteristic notation of intimate detail. The sight of some stray black hairs in the washbasin makes him feel sick. Their new flat too is diametrically opposed to the maternal house. It is high up in a new block exposed to the glaring sunlight which reverberates against the hard, shiny, geometrical surfaces and far removed from the beneficent shade and moistness of the earth. Alain is as alienated and as miserable as the cat who, so he has insisted, should live with them.

It is with the development of this strange triangular relationship, Alain/Camille/the cat, in that symbolically triangular apartment that Colette is concerned, and indeed the buildup of jealousy and tension in the scene in which Camille thrusts her rival from the balcony into space is accomplished with all the skill and economy that one now expects from Colette. The action in this scene is tremendously exciting, present to all one's senses, so that one participates in the fall and in Camille's horror at what she has done: "Elle eut le temps d'entendre le crissement des griffes sur le torchis, de voir le corps bleu de Saha tordu en S, agrippé à l'air avec une force ascendante de truite, puis elle recula et s'accota au mur" (She had the time to hear the scratching of claws on the plaster of the wall, to see the blue body of Saha twisted into an S, clutching the air with the leaping power of the trout, then she retreated and leaned against the wall). But the cat's fall is miraculously broken, and Alain appears with her unhurt in his arms. The tension is released only to mount again the higher, for Saha now tries to tell Alain what has happened: "tout le félin visage s'efforçait vers un langage universel, vers un mot oublié des hommes" (her feline face forcing itself toward a universal language, toward a word forgotten by men). And Alain eventually understands by the physical manifestation of Saha's fear in front of Camille that his wife is an assassin. Human contacts are too dangerous. Alain retreats into his fantasy world–"I have neglected my dreams too much"–and back he goes into the night with the cat, through the monochrome colors of dream, to the house, the flower smells, and the maternal lamp. He falls asleep: garden, trees, and cat fuse into his dreams, and time stands still.

Like so many of Colette's books, *La Chatte* seems to be written out of a yearning toward the impossible. Sometimes, as in *La Naissance du jour*, the yearning is a model for the future. Here it is seen as a temptation to retreat from the real world into dream, imagination, the past, and Colette ends on a warning which might well be addressed to herself more than to the reader. For despite the seductiveness of the writing with its rhythmical prose and its lush imagery (even as far back as *Les Vrilles de la vigne*, she had been re-

minding herself of the druglike qualities of both music and poetry), Colette makes it clear that it is Alain, not Camille, who is the monster, having definitively chosen the ideal in lieu of the real, animals rather than humans, the Lost Paradise of the past instead of the vital source of the present. The writer may sublimate, but her fictional character becomes less than human. At the end Camille looks back and sees Alain, half supine, playing with the first green, prickly chestnuts of August "d'une paume adroite et creusée en patte" (with an agile palm that was hollowed out like a paw).

In a way which was hardly reassuring to a masculine audience, Colette's males are ill fated. The series of weak men incapable of coming to terms with life and contrasted to stronger, more earthly females comes to an end with the figure of Michel in the slighter work, *Duo*, published a year after *La Chatte*, in 1934, and translated into English in 1935. Michel too is an idealist, and although this ideal seems to have been realized in his marriage, the discovery of a letter which reveals in the crudest of terms a past infidelity of the wife's undermines his ideal world and destroys his desire to live. In fact this affair had been of no significance for his wife Alice, but he, like Chéri, simply retreats into death, walking like a somnambulist into the waters of a nearby river. Once again this portrayal of a lost soul is conceived of in terms of music. For Colette, Chéri had been like a symphony. In the 1934 book, as the title indicates, it is by a "duo" between the man's and the woman's voices that the story is presented. This musicality, always such a potent feature of Colette's writing, is at its most evident in Michel's abandonment to death, as his body is covered by the little waves beating an almost imperceptible rhythm in that fading echo of a beat which so often rounds off a work by Colette.

Colette had now finished in fiction with the male idealist unable to cope with life. In April of 1935 she and Goudeket were married, ostensibly to solve the problems of traveling as a couple to New York which they thought might have stricter standards about such matters than Paris. The fictional "way back" was being accompanied in real life by emotional fulfillment and contentment, and it is fair to say that from this point of view, she and her husband "lived happily ever after."

Her next task in what now seemed an alternating pattern of fiction and autobiography was, however, *Mes Apprentissages: Ce que Claudine n'a pas dit* (1936; translated as *My Apprenticeships*, 1957), a return to her first marriage to set

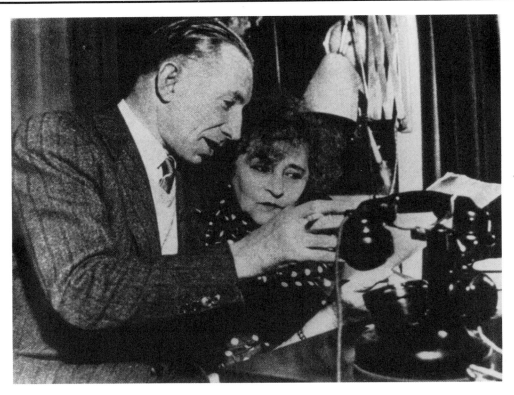

Colette with her third husband, Maurice Goudeket (photograph Lipnitzki-Viollet)

straight the score for herself and for the world about her life with Willy. Willy had died in 1929, and it was only now, as she wrote in *Mes Apprentissages*, that she was capable of attempting anything like an objective analysis. He had been her first love and also her literary mentor. Not only was he responsible for making her write in the first place but also, as is more rarely acknowledged, he had been a useful critic, pruning her tendency to the "purple patch" and encouraging her to make smooth transitions. But as her husband he had been the cause of much pain and disillusionment, and she declares that she can only summon up a sort of "cold pity, a laugh without much charity," although she admits that in their relationship she also does not show up very well. Now that she is happily married and, despite all the scandals, an honored public figure (in 1936 she was made a Commandeur de la Légion d'Honneur, after having been appointed chevalier in 1920 and officer in 1928, and in the same year she was also elected to the chair of Anna de Noailles in the Académie Royale de Langue et de Littérature Françaises), she has the self-confidence to acknowledge the shortcomings of the past. From the vantage point of age she admits her youthful readiness to be initiated into all

aspects of sensual pleasure. In a comment worthy of Laclos she writes: "En peu d'heures, un homme sans scruples fait, d'une fille ignorante, un prodige de libertinage, qui ne compte avec aucun dégoût. Le dégoût n'a jamais été un obstacle. Il vient plus tard comme l'honnêteté. J'écrivis autrefois: 'la dignité, c'est un défaut d'homme.' J'aurais mieux fait d'écrire que 'le dégoût n'est pas une délicatesse féminine' " (In a few hours, an unscrupulous man can make of an ignorant girl a prodigy of libertinage who knows of no disgust. Disgust has never been an obstacle. It comes later, like integrity. I wrote once: "Dignity is a man's weakness." I should have done better to write that "disgust is not a feminine delicacy"). Certainly also squeamishness is not a weakness in her writing.

Willy was a complex character and in *Mes Apprentissages* Colette gives searching glimpses into his activity as impresario for his literary factory. Did his frenzied urging on of others mask an insuperable writer's block? Why was he so mean in money matters? It had always rankled Colette that she had not been able to use her own name on the Claudine series and had never had the right to her royalties. But here her resentment is not expressed overtly: she regards Willy as a curiosity and a phenomenon. After all, he had not only taught her how to love and to write but also, and more important, he had showed her how to live without being happy and how eventually to recover her self-esteem. The designation "My Apprenticeships" is, like all of Colette's titles, well chosen. Not until she was past the age of fifty, on "l'autre versant" (the downward slope), did she feel that she might be able to turn the cry of pain into a festive note.

This transforming power is not immediately visible in her next work of fiction, the slight sequel to *Duo* entitled *Le Toutounier* (The Doggie Bed, 1939), which takes up the story of Alice after her husband's suicide. Devastated because she had loved him despite her momentary infidelity, Alice seeks solace in characteristic Colette fashion in a return to the source, in this case her girlhood home, her sisters, and the symbolic divan which they had called the "dogs' bed" and in which they had all slept together. But this retreat to the womb of the family, to a closed, female, infantile world, proves to be just as impossible as Chéri's love for Léa and Alain's for the cat. The two sisters are about to leave and follow their respective lovers. Alice will remain alone and will have to face the claims of reality. The temptation of retreat has to be enacted by Alice (and written once again by Colette), but there is no real doubt about the outcome. In Colette's world, the female of the species is always the tough one.

Equally tough but much more attractive is the figure of Julie de Carneilhan, the eponymous heroine of Colette's last novel, which appeared in 1941 just after Goudeket, who was Jewish, had been rounded up in one of the dawn raids of the occupying German forces and sent to an internment camp. As always, Colette did not write her fiction about her present concerns, and the anxiety of the first two years of the war and her profound distress at the temporary disappearance of her faithful "meilleur ami" did not find expression until this particular trial was over and she produced her actual "souvenirs" of wartime Paris in *L'Etoile Vesper* of 1946 (translated as *The Evening Star*, 1973). In that work she admitted that, ever afterward, if there was an unexpected ring at the door she would react with a nervous tic, a trembling of the mouth. Her overt reaction at the time was practical: to hide as much as she could of her sorrow, to do her best to have Goudeket released, which she managed after a few months, to support him when he then lived a hounded exis-

tence, and above all to keep on writing. She had been so effective in modeling herself on Sido that she was widely regarded as a source of practical wisdom not merely for "le savoir-décliner" but for an essential "savoir-vivre" in the face of the occupier, and she was much in demand as a journalist and broadcaster.

With the customary delay in time, *Julie de Carneilhan* looks back to her second husband, Henry de Jouvenel, who had died in 1935. It also contains another male figure who is so clearly modeled on real life that his name is barely changed. Colette's brother Léo, who had died in March 1940, becomes Julie's brother Léon. Julie's background is, however, very different from Colette's, but her circumstances have much that is recognizable. She is an aristocratic forty-year-old whose ex-husband is an influential political figure who has remarried a millionairess. Julie is living in straitened circumstances with the characteristic Colette fortitude, keeping up her spirits, and maintaining, as Léa did, the appearance that she offers to the world. Her pride is her strength, pride in her class (she is always asking herself how a Carneilhan should behave), pride in her robust physical strength and her healthy body, a feminine pride in her looks and in the sureness of her taste (one of her favorite remarks as, like all Colette's heroines, she surveys herself critically in the mirror, is "Well, that's got style"), and pride in at last being able to keep dignity and emotional independence in the solitary life she leads with its more casual relationships. Again like many of Colette's heroines, she has many of the characteristics which in her world would normally be considered masculine, above all physical courage and endurance.

In *Julie de Carneilhan* once again the masculine and feminine tendencies are at war, and it is the feminine emotional weaknesses which lead to Julie's tragedy and to an eventual return to the source, which, for all Colette's poetry, is clearly a defeat. When Julie's ex-husband, Herbert d'Espivant, desperately ill, begs her to come to see him, she gives in, and against her better judgment lets herself be inveigled into an unworthy plot involving money. The story line is more complicated than has been the case in past Colette novels. It is as if it molded itself formally on the deviousness of Espivant's character, as layer upon layer of deceit is accumulated, and Julie proceeds on her path from gullibility based on pity and even hope toward ever greater disillusionment.

Colette is at her best in describing the encounter between Julie and Espivant's new wife, a flamboyant, gorgeous Jewish woman, revealing, through Julie's perceptions only, the suspense and subtle shifts of feeling. First the two women eye each other as rivals, Julie, the aristocratic French woman, snobbishly criticizing Marianne's lack of taste and her invasive scent, but secretly, as another female, acknowledging the marvelous hair and flesh fit for the harem. At one point, however, Julie—and this is a characteristic reaction of Colette's women—wonders whether the two of them might join forces against the man. She is torn between the desire to vindicate her own honor and pride by revealing Espivant's despicable nature and the female desire to give in to love by protecting the weak male. It is (of course) this self-sacrificing tendency which prevails. "Human contacts are too dangerous": this realization of Alain's in *La Chatte* is not repeated, but, as inevitably as Alain, Julie is drawn to the way back. Her brother Léon, who lives in a world of his own with his horses and dogs, is planning to take them back to the childhood home, the Château de Carneilhan. Like Alain, without appearing to make a conscious decision, she gets up in the middle of the night—the predawn hour so loved by Sido—and begins to polish her riding boots. As she contemplates the journey, she too begins to lose all sense of time and reality, the hours and seasons mingle, and the way back, through dream and memory, seems to be an enactment of the death wish that follows upon the loss of love. The nostalgic images of the natural world are blocked once again by memories of a lover, and Julie is invaded by a searing sense of loss. The return to the source offers her no joy. As his beloved horse nuzzles her brother's hand, she thinks "Lui du moins il emmène, en partant, ce qu'il aime le plus au monde" (He at least, when he leaves, can take with him the thing that he loves most in all the world).

Solitude, deprivation, the retreat into memory: these were indeed elements in Colette's life during the Occupation. The years also were taking their toll, and she was becoming more and more crippled by arthritis. Nevertheless, she kept on working as a journalist and broadcaster to give heart to the French public and particularly to French women whose main task, she felt, should be to uphold both the spiritual and material values in order to show their dignity in the face of the occupants. Prolonged work on a novel was now proving to be too demanding, but writ-

ing was a necessary part of her life, and for a while several volumes of short stories appeared at regular intervals: *Chambre d'hôtel* in 1940 (translated as *Chance Acquaintances*, 1952), *Le Képi* (The Kepi) in 1943, and *Trois . . . six . . . neuf* (Three . . . Six . . . Nine) in 1944 show her in characteristic form. Keen observation, lightness of touch, humor, and above all sympathy with the underprivileged of this world with all their quirks and limitations, and their heroism—these are Colette's hallmark.

The most famous of these stories is "Gigi" which appeared as the title piece in the 1944 volume *Gigi et autres nouvelles* (Gigi and Other Stories). This joyous return to youth—to the figure of the adolescent girl and to the world of the fashionable cocottes (the highest class of kept women) whom Colette had known—is a limpid and brilliant fairy story shot through with indulgent humor. The spontaneous young Gigi is being trained by two generations of women to follow in their footsteps, and this education, ironically, is as rigorous as any course at a finishing school. How to choose the right wine, how to eat ortolans, how to look after one's personal hygiene—all "les habitudes honorables des femmes sans honneur" (the honorable habits of women without honor)—provide the basis for a structure of oppositions and inversions. At every level the reader encounters the unexpected: dignity in dishonor, strict morality within immorality made concrete finally in the surprise of the little heroine, the reward of virtue instead of what is commonly known as vice. For Gigi, prepared to accept both her destiny and a protector, finds instead the love of a veritable Prince Charming. A dream of youth, high spirits, and hope comes true. Even in her fiction, Colette's last words on love are, in essence, "They lived happily ever after."

It would seem that Colette had at last succeeded in living up to her model. If an account of her life in her last years could be used as a manual of the art of "savoir décliner," her own last writings are exquisite examples of an art form which she made peculiarly her own—so much so that one hesitates to give them any single label: essays, diaries, memoirs? Immobilized in her bed, looking out at the gardens of the Palais Royal, noting the passing of the hours, the changes of sky and season, and the games of children, receiving the friends who flocked to see her and the letters from an admiring public, Colette, the obsessive writer, wrote down her daily thoughts, her meditations, memories, and daydreams. These works were in fact to be her swan song. The deservedly best known are *L'Etoile Vesper* of 1946 and *Le Fanal bleu* of 1949 (translated as *The Blue Lantern*, 1963); when the latter was published she felt, at the age of seventy-six, that she had definitely entered the night of old age.

L'Etoile Vesper makes it clear that even in old age Colette used writing in order to live better. Because of her infirmity she needed to resign herself to her lot, and for this her past and her present needed to be in harmony. Accordingly, she developed a "virtuosity of the memory." This phrase not only helps to characterize so much of her writing but it also underlines its therapeutic value. In *L'Etoile Vesper* Colette ascribes to her enforced immobility the fact that she has given up fiction. It is also revealing that, because she no longer can go out and meet and observe people, she feels that the *romanesque* (the "fictional") is absent from her life. Like Balzac, whom she so much admired, she could boast of a highly developed sense of observation. Unlike Balzac, however, since she no longer had the opportunity to put herself into the skin of other people, the temptation of "lying" as she described it, of being something other than herself, was removed. In *L'Etoile Vesper* she presents fiction as an "imposture." The invention of dialogue between imagined people and the imposition of an arbitrary conclusion have always been tasks, which she now willingly casts off for the sheer pleasure of being "truthful" from time to time. There is, as always with Colette, the hint of provocation, the self-indulgent delight in parading a paradox; this tendency is even more extreme and pronounced in the work of her old age when all is permitted. Nevertheless, many novelists might share her views. They also throw light on the nature of her fiction and the intricate ways in which its "lies" are enmeshed with "the truth." Perhaps the real truth of Colette is to be found in that meshing.

In *L'Etoile Vesper* one sees that writing has become fused with her lifelong habit of "wonderment." She marvels at the world, what she can still see of it from her window and what she can still cull from books and pictures and the dried flowers and objects that are around her, even the fire, her last pet, and its delicate white ash. Everything is an object of delight. She is after all, she says, again provocatively, a normal old person. The old are cheerful by nature; if they are sad they are abnormal or ill or wicked. But the heart of her wonderment is still the word. Still she continues her search, like a gourmet, for a better word, a word better than better. With Colette everything is of a piece–her sensuality, her appetite, her unflagging curiosity, her sureness of taste–all these find their consummation in writing. *L'Etoile Vesper* ends with another provocation: she must, she asserts, learn to give up the old habit of writing; tapestry and the rhythmic plying of the needle will now accompany and perhaps replace the tracery of the pen. But three years later *Le Fanal bleu* appeared, a book as lively and full of wonderment over past and present as any. If the world now seems dimmer and more muffled, Colette sees no reason to be anxious: it is just that she, with her now blunted senses, is drifting away from it. Writing remains. Indeed she comes to think that, having used it throughout as a model for her life, it has come full circle. Model and life are one. Writing leads only to writing. And she realizes that contrary to her tentative resolution at the end of *L'Etoile Vesper,* writing is not like other tasks. One can never say: "Now that's finished": in the very sands of time are written the words "to be continued." The world itself as she foresaw at the end of *La Naissance du jour* has become text.

Honors and acclaim rained on Colette in the last decade of her life. In 1945 she was the first woman to be elected to the Académie Goncourt. Four years later she became its president. In 1953 she received the Médaille d'Or de la Ville de Paris and also was promoted to Grand Officier de la Légion d'Honneur. Her name was still known in the worlds of the theater (*Chéri* was still being played, and *La Seconde* and *Gigi* were adapted for the stage) and of film (*Gigi*, the 1958 movie with Leslie Caron in the title role, was particularly successful).

Even Colette's death was remarkable. Maurice Goudeket's account of it showed how she managed to create even to the last. He wrote: "Elle m'avait, pendant trente ans d'un bonheur sans faille, fait vivre dans un monde féerique, . . ." (For thirty years, she enabled me to live in a fairy world). Her death was a long, slow ecstasy, punctuated by cries of " 'Regarde,' me dit-elle, 'Maurice! Regarde!' " (Look, oh look!) even when she could see nothing of the marvels that had so delighted her in the external world. It is his opinion that she had entered her Lost Paradise. It is that creative spirit both in living and in writing which the crowds who flocked to the national funeral with which the state (if not the church) honored her on 7 August 1954 so justly acknowledged. It is that spirit also which ensures her continuing renown.

Letters:

Une Amitié inattendue: Correspondance de Colette & Francis Jammes, edited by Robert Mallet (Paris: Emile-Paul, 1945);

Lettres à Hélène Picard, edited by Claude Pichois (Paris: Flammarion, 1958);

Lettres à Marguerite Moréno, edited by Pichois (Paris: Flammarion, 1959);

Lettres de la Vagabonde, edited by Pichois and Roberte Forbin (Paris: Flammarion, 1961);

Lettres au Petit Corsaire, edited by Pichois and Forbin (Paris: Flammarion, 1963);

Lettres à ses pairs, edited by Pichois and Forbin (Paris: Flammarion, 1973).

Biographies:

Claude Chauvière, *Colette* (Paris: Firmin Didot, 1931);

Margaret Crosland, *Madame Colette, A Provincial in Paris* (London: Owen, 1953);

Francis Carlo, *Colette mon amie* (Paris: Rive Gauche, 1955);

Yvonne Mitchell, *Colette: A Taste for Life* (New York: Harcourt Brace Jovanovich, 1955);

Maurice Goudeket, *Près de Colette* (Paris: Flammarion, 1956); translated by Enid McLeod as *Near Colette* (New York: Farrar, Straus & Cudahy, 1957);

Goudeket, *La Douceur de vieillir* (Paris: Flammarion, 1965);

Paul Hollander, *Colette, ses apprentissages* (Paris: Klincksieck, 1978);

Hollander, *Colette et Willy: Claudine en ménage* (Paris: Klincksieck, 1978);

Michèle Sarde, *Colette libre et entravée* (Paris: Stock, 1978); translated by Richard Miller as *Colette, Free and Fettered* (New York: Morrow, 1980);

Joanna Richardson, *Colette* (London: Methuen, 1983).

References:

Marcelle Biolley-Godino, *L'Homme-objet chez Colette* (Paris: Klincksieck, 1972);

Bulletin de la Société des Amis de Colette en Puisaye, 1-12 (Puisaye, 1966-1972);

Cahiers Colette (Paris: Flammarion, 1977-   );

Le Capitole, special issue on Colette (December 1924);

Catalogue de l'exposition Colette (Paris: Bibliothèque Nationale, 1973);

Margaret Davies, *Colette* (London: Oliver & Boyd, 1961);

Fernand Desonay, "Quelques Thèmes d'inspiration chez Colette," *Bulletin de l'Académie Royale de Belgique* (October 1954);

Erica Mendelson Eisinger and Mari Ward McCarthy, *Colette: The Woman, The Writer* (University Park & London: University of Pennsylvania Press, 1981);

Europe, special issue on Colette (November-December 1981);

Figaro Littéraire, 8, special issue on Colette (24 January 1953);

Amélie Fillon, *Colette* (Paris: Editions de la Caravelle, 1933);

Louis Forestier, *Chemins vers la maison de Claudine et Sido* (Paris: Société d'Enseignement Supérieur, 1968);

Elaine Harris, *L'Approfondissement de la sensualité dans l'œuvre romanesque de Colette* (Paris: Nizet, 1973);

Nicole Houssa, "Balzac et Colette," *Revue d'Histoire Littéraire de la France,* 60 (January-March 1960);

Houssa, *Le Souci de l'expression chez Colette* (Brussels: Palais des Académies, 1958);

Anne A. Ketchum, *Colette, ou La Naissance du jour. Etude d'un malentendu* (Paris: Minard, 1968);

Maria Le Hardoin, *Colette* (Paris: Editions Universitaires, 1956);

Lettres Françaises, special issue on Colette, no. 529 (12-19 August 1954);

Elaine Marks, *Colette* (New Brunswick: Rutgers University Press, 1960);

Thierry Maulnier, *Introduction à Colette* (Paris: La Palme, 1954);

Ilene Olken, "Imagery of *Chéri* and *La Fin de Chéri,*" *Studies in Philology,* 60 (January 1963);

Claude Pichois and Vincette Pichois, eds., with the assistance of Alain Brunet, *Album Colette* (Paris: Gallimard, 1984);

Madeleine Raaphorst-Rousseau, *Colette, sa vie, son art* (Paris: Nizet, 1964);

Yannick Resh, *Corps féminin, corps textuel* (Paris: Klincksieck, 1973);

Pierre Trahard, *L'Art de Colette* (Paris: Jean Renard, 1941);

Gonzague Truc, *Madame Colette* (Paris: Corrêa, 1941).

Papers:

The Bibliothèque Nationale holds a large collection of Colette's manuscripts.

Eugène Dabit

(21 September 1898-23 August 1936)

David O'Connell
University of Illinois at Chicago

BOOKS: *L'Hôtel du Nord* (Paris: Denoël, 1929);
translated by Homer P. Earle as *Hotel du
Nord* (New York: Knopf, 1931);

Petit-Louis (Paris: Gallimard, 1930);

Villa Oasis; ou Les Faux Bourgeois (Paris: Gallimard, 1932);

Faubourgs de Paris (Paris: Gallimard, 1933);

Un Mort tout neuf (Paris: Gallimard, 1934);

L'Ile (Paris: Gallimard, 1934);

La Zone verte (Paris: Gallimard, 1935);

Train de vies (Paris: Gallimard, 1936);

Les Maîtres de la peinture espagnole (Paris: Gallimard, 1937);

Le Mal de vivre (Paris: Gallimard, 1939);

Journal intime (1928-1936) (Paris: Gallimard,
1939);

*L'Hôtel du Nord, suivi de Au Pont-Tournant, version
théâtrale inédite* (Paris: Union Bibliophile de
France, 1946).

Eugène Dabit's corpus of novels and shorter
fiction represents one of the more important
achievements among the many left-wing French
writers of the 1930s. Although he left school at
an early age and was largely self-taught, he over-
came a number of social and educational handi-
caps in order to become a painter and an art
critic as well as a fiction writer.

Born of a mother who was illegitimate and
a father who worked as a teamster, Dabit produced five novels, a volume each of novellas,
short stories, and childhood reminiscences, and a
great many book reviews and short pieces of art
criticism in the seven-year span beginning at the
end of 1929. Not long after his death, his publisher, the prestigious house of Gallimard,
brought out three more volumes of his work: a
book of art criticism, an uncompleted novel, and,
finally, his private diary.

Not only did Dabit earn the respect of the ex-
acting readers at Gallimard, he also maintained a
high degree of visibility on the Parisian literary
scene and garnered for himself a good deal of respect in that milieu with the many short pieces of

his work that appeared during the period
1930-1936 in such major literary reviews as *La
Nouvelle Revue Française, Les Nouvelles Littéraires,*
and *Europe.* Furthermore, Dabit seems to have
been known and admired by many of the major literary figures of the era, including André Malraux, Louis-Ferdinand Céline, Louis Guilloux,
and Jean Guéhenno. Both André Gide and
Roger Martin du Gard were literary advisers and
confidants as well as friends. Dabit's untimely
death in 1936 during a trip to the Soviet Union
with a delegation of left-wing French writers
caused him and his work to lose much of the recognition that they deserve. Only in recent years
have scholars begun to restore to Dabit the place
that is his in the history of the novel of the
interwar years.

Dabit's life can be divided into four distinct
periods: childhood and adolescence until his enlistment in the artillery in 1916; the four subsequent years of military service until his release
(after almost two years with the occupation forces
in Germany) in 1920; the period during which,
until the late 1920s, he attempted to establish himself as a painter; and the literary period, overlapping the previous one for several years, from
probably as early as 1926, and ending with his
death in 1936. Since his fictional *œuvre* leans so
heavily on the immediate social environment, including neighborhood, friends, and family, it is
important to know something of Dabit's life in
order to appreciate the full significance of his novels and shorter fiction.

Dabit was a highly sensitive only child who,
if he had been born into a more privileged environment, would perhaps have developed the
means of self-expression at an earlier age. As it
was, however, Dabit was thirty-one when his first
novel was published at the end of 1929. His
mother seems to have been a kind, gentle, and sensitive woman, and it was she who exercised the
greatest influence over her son's early years. This
childhood was spent in the dreary working-class
quarters of the northern end of Paris (rue de

Dabit (in back, at left) with Pierre Herbart and André Gide in the Soviet Union, 1936 (courtesy of Catherine Gide). During this tour of the USSR with a delegation of French writers Dabit died unexpectedly, at the age of thirty-seven.

Ménilmontant and then rue Calmels), and this part of Dabit's life is described in both *Faubourgs de Paris* (Neighborhoods of Paris, 1933) and *Petit-Louis* (1930). When, in 1923, his parents borrowed a large sum of money from one of Mme Dabit's brothers in order to make a down payment on a hotel (they already had experience as concierges), Dabit moved with them to the Hôtel du Nord and then later gave the establishment's name to his first and best-known novel.

Dabit's father, Emile, and his immediate family seem to have exercised little or no measurable influence on Dabit and his work. The maternal side, however, more than made up for this deficiency. Mme Dabit, née Louise Hildanfelger, was the daughter of an Alsatian woman who had never bothered to regularize her union with her common-law husband. This man, Dabit's maternal grandfather, was the subject of a kind of mythology that Louise Dabit communicated to her son in his youth–and it consisted essentially in im-

buing the boy with strong anticlerical convictions and in proposing to him as a model of conduct this very grandfather, Louis Guyot, who had been an anarchist and, as a *communard*, had been deported from France after the suppression of the popular uprising of 1871.

Two of Louise Dabit's brothers also served as models for her son. In their case the influence is much easier to document because each was taken as the point of departure for one of Dabit's novels. Her older brother, Auguste, an officer during World War I and later a successful traveling salesman specializing in leather goods, died suddenly in 1933, and his death became the inspiration for and subject of the novel *Un Mort tout neuf* (1934). Her younger brother Emile, who had made his fortune as the owner of a bordello established behind the lines in Champagne during the closing years of the war, and then later owned and operated a more luxurious establishment of the same kind near the Place Clichy in

Paris, became the subject of *Villa Oasis; ou Les Faux Bourgeois* (1932). In addition to these striking examples, Dabit also routinely transposed various working-class friends and acquaintances—as well as the tenants of the Hôtel du Nord—for his fiction.

Dabit quit school in 1910 to become an apprentice tradesman. He began as a locksmith and worked at a variety of jobs until his enlistment in the army in 1916. The final years of this first period of his life as well as the beginning years of the second period are described quite vividly in the novel *Petit-Louis*. The third period of Dabit's life is marked essentially by his attempt and subsequent failure to become a painter. After his release from the service, he enrolled in art schools, meeting his future wife, Beatrice Appia, whom he married in 1924, at one of them. But despite his efforts to express himself and to find an audience as a painter, he continued to feel a void within himself. Whether this problem resulted from dissatisfaction with his work, from the continued and discouraging lack of recognition, from the realization that painting would never enable him to come into intimate contact with the common man (for whom and to whom he was feeling an ever stronger urge to speak), or, finally, from the simple need to purge himself of deeply experienced feelings and memories that he could not express through painting, one cannot know with certainty. In all likelihood, each of these reasons contributed to his decision, in 1926, to spend less time painting and to devote himself to trying to capture in words his wartime experiences. About a year later, he had in hand a manuscript of almost 300 pages which he sent to André Gide. Gide read it with interest and summoned Dabit for an interview. For the rest of Dabit's short life they would be friends. Gide felt, however, that Dabit's inspiration was more like that of the novelist Roger Martin du Gard. He thus provided Dabit with an introduction to him, and this professional relationship turned out to be an extremely close one. It was Martin du Gard who advised Dabit about his work for the last nine or ten years of Dabit's life and Martin du Gard who, at the very beginning, urged him to put aside his first attempt at a novel (the manuscript of what would later become *Petit-Louis*) and write instead about his neighborhood.

Following this advice, Dabit wrote *L'Hôtel du Nord*, which deals with the daily life of the proletarian lodgers in the hotel that Dabit's parents bought after the war. The book, which was awarded the Prix Populiste in 1929, has continued to enjoy a solid and respectable readership over the past fifty years. It has been frequently republished in paperback editions, and in 1938 it was made into a film by Marcel Carné that has become a classic in its own right.

There are about a dozen characters in the novel, which, eschewing unity of action, is built upon the notion of unity of place. Among them is Renée Levesque, a girl from the countryside who is abandoned by her lover, a factory worker, after she becomes pregnant. Later, when her neglect of her offspring is a major factor in the child's death and when her subsequent promiscuous conduct shocks even the highly tolerant owners of the hotel, she is thrown into the street. Others are Ladevese, abandoned by his wife, who comes to the hotel to die of tuberculosis; the Pellevoisin sisters, two suffocating spinsters consumed by erotic frustration, who pledge fidelity to each other but then furtively seek lovers on the side; Adrien, the homosexual, who dresses as a woman every Saturday night before setting out on his adventures; and old man Deborger, formerly a resident of the hotel, but now slowly dying at the poorhouse in Nanterre, who comes back once a week to have a drink on his day out. What these and other characters in the book have in common is a painful sense of solitude and of spiritual impoverishment. The dream of almost every female in the book is marital security, for which she is willing to pay with her body. As for the men, their most pressing need seems to be for perpetual movement and noise: chasing women, lengthy card games, and boisterous, vapid conversation about the day's headlines. Any spiritual needs that they have can be satisfied by the local palmreader who, for a fee, will assure them that the future holds both wealth and happiness. In creating this little universe, Dabit well realized that both his characters and those real people upon whom they were based had had the benefit of little or no formal education and were forced to work long hours for little pay. But still, he seems to suggest that condition is no justification for the sacrifice of one's dignity. In fact, the narrative voice that speaks through the deliberately restrained and unadorned style that characterizes this work (as well as all the later volumes) asserts that if these people harbor little or no inner life and are almost all promiscuous, greedy, small minded and bored with life, it is no one's fault but their own. Their dream of happiness and wealth in the future will never prove more than an illusion, he intimates, for they are so accustomed to living on a more or less sensual level that they can have no future different from the existence they are presently living. It is significant that the one child born in the course of the novel should die of neglect—and, all things considered, it is probably better off.

Petit-Louis, a first-person *récit*, is in several ways Dabit's best novel. Touching and confessional in nature, its deep emotion, perhaps inevitable in a first novel that tells of a boy's experience of war, is held in check and disciplined by a clear, diaphanous style. In subject matter it is also the antithesis of that masterpiece of all the novels written about World War I, Raymond Radiguet's *Le Diable au corps* (*Devil in the Flesh*, 1923) for whereas the latter chronicles the coming of age of a bourgeois adolescent too young to be drafted, *Petit-Louis* deals with a Parisian proletarian of eighteen who enlists in the artillery to avoid being drafted into the infantry. What makes this novel especially significant, and like *L'Hôtel du Nord,* is the characters' constant concern for money, their obsession with achieving financial success under the assumption that money automatically begets happiness. Early in the novel, just after young Louis has quit school so he can work in order to earn money that will be turned over to his parents, his father, who had been called to active duty at the beginning of the war, comes home on leave. While in Paris, he buys cigarette lighters, candy, and other such items in order to sell them at a fancy profit to his comrades in the trenches. Later, when Louis himself is moved to the front, he works full time in a brothel in a rear area during his rest periods and then invites his own mother to work in the same establishment as a cleaning woman. Since she entertains the dream of setting up her own business after the war, she and her son put up with an overbearing boss. In other words, the war for these people represents an opportunity. Although it is dangerous and one must avoid being taken in by capitalist propaganda that seems to want to prolong the war, for Louis and his family the war is also a means of moving ahead in society while the vigilance of those who control the rigid structures of French society has been temporarily suspended.

Villa Oasis; ou Les Faux Bourgeois, which Gide considered to be Dabit's best novel, tells of two people, Julien and Irma Monge, from the same kind of sordid background depicted in *L'Hôtel du Nord,* but in this case the couple, based on Dabit's

uncle Emile and his wife, has become wealthy. As the novel begins, Irma, age thirty-nine, gets word that her daughter, whom she had simply abandoned as an infant twenty years earlier, has discovered Irma's whereabouts and is on her way to Paris. The girl, Hélène, moves in with Julien and Irma but, owing principally to neglect on their part, dies of tuberculosis. With the odor of death permeating their lives in Paris, Julien and Irma decide to sell their brothel, invest their money, and retire to Fontainebleau, where they plan to live as idle *rentiers*. But once they are in the country, the dream turns into a nightmare. Irma, who has spent her life caring only about herself and has even been, during the past fifteen years, the secret lover of her husband's best friend, discovers that with no work to do and no money to strive for, she is beginning to think. Inevitably, her thoughts turn to her daughter, for whose death she is largely responsible; to her husband, who already spends as much time as possible in the sleazy neighborhoods of Paris that he loves best; and to her lover, who, she now realizes, has been after her money all these years. In a fit of despair she decides one night to leave her country home and return to Paris. But in leaving Villa Oasis in the dark she stumbles and falls into a swimming pool where she drowns. Ironically, it is this pool, a symbol for Dabit of idle luxury, that destroys her. Left alone, Julien realizes that he has betrayed his origins. Hated as an outsider by the local peasants, dismissed as a grotesque and amusing *parvenu* by the wealthy bourgeois in nearby country homes, and now condemned in his own turn to begin thinking about the meaning of life, he concludes that he must sell the villa and go back to Paris where he belongs. Unfortunately, before he is able to complete the transaction and buy a share of a new business in Paris, he dies of a heart attack.

In Dabit's view, Julien, like Irma, has been deceived by a god—money—that fails. In his fourth novel, *Un Mort tout neuf* (A Fresh Corpse), as well as in *La Zone verte* (The Countryside, 1935), the last novel published during his lifetime, this same theme is reworked. In *Un Mort tout neuf,* based on the experience of the death of his uncle Auguste, he once again brings together working-class family and friends. The plot is simple: a minute description of death, four days of mourning, and burial. The selfishness of each character is underlined as they fight over the belongings of the deceased and learn things about him that they had never known. Dabit courageously depicts the vulgar, self-serving banality of the small and limited worlds in which they live.

In *La Zone verte,* Dabit attempts to chronicle the adventures of an unemployed Parisian sign painter in the country. Finding work in a small restaurant-hotel, his hero sleeps with the owner's wife and reflects upon the differences between the life of low-class people in the city and in the country. On balance, the third-person narrator seems to feel that workers are better off in the city because they have more distractions and better public services. The deep, essential meaninglessness of their lives, however, is equal to the emptiness of the lives of their country counterparts.

Among Dabit's other publications, *L'Ile* (The Island, 1934) and *Train de vies* (Slices of Life, 1936) contain pieces of short fiction, and *Faubourgs de Paris* is an autobiographical volume disguised as a novel that re-creates life in and around Paris in the early years of the twentieth century. After Dabit's death, Gallimard published his thoughts on Spanish art, the result of many summers spent in Spain as a painter before deciding to give himself completely to literature. *Les Maîtres de la peinture espagnole* (Masters of Spanish Painting) appeared in 1937 and was followed two years later by the unfinished novel *Le Mal de vivre* (The Pain of Living), a highly autobiographical work in which the hero is torn between love of his wife and of her best friend. The transposition of this real-life triangle is not very successful and the end result is a self-portrait of Dabit as a self-centered person who cruelly and destructively uses each of these women. This impression of Dabit as a selfish and insecure man is reinforced by reading his diary, *Journal intime (1928-1936),* published at the same time as *Le*

Mal de vivre. Here too, one sees Dabit as the private man concerned with little more in life than casual affairs with women as the world is about to go to war. Ironically, during his 1936 trip to Russia, where he allegedly contracted scarlet fever and died in mysterious surroundings, Dabit was consumed by doubts about his own ability and obsessed by the thought of dying. To put off thoughts of death and to convince himself that he was living as intensely as possible, he gave himself in his last years to a series of sentimental attachments to women who were really of no consequence to him. Finally, in 1946, Dabit's widow published *Au Pont-Tournant,* a stage adaptation of *L'Hôtel du Nord.* Written by Dabit in 1932, it has never been produced.

Dabit's accomplishment as a novelist is considerable, especially in view of the fact that he was an authentic representative of the Parisian working class, a group that French intellectuals, preponderantly of bourgeois origin, are usually quite willing to speak for without having any inside knowledge of their life. In the history of the French novel of the interwar years, Dabit's name is emerging more and more as one to be reckoned with. In a period during which the French novel as a whole displays an overwhelming interest in social and political questions, his novels take the reader inside the social class that was often at the heart of such questions. *L'Hôtel du Nord, Petit-Louis, Villa Oasis,* and *Journal intime* remain important literary reflections of that era.

Reference:

David O'Connell, "Eugène Dabit: A French Working-Class Novelist," *Research Studies,* 41 (December 1973): 217-233.

Roland Dorgelès
(Roland Lécavelé)
(15 June 1886-18 March 1973)

David O'Connell
University of Illinois at Chicago

SELECTED BOOKS: *Les Croix de bois* (Paris: Albin Michel, 1919); translated as *Wooden Crosses* (New York & London: Putnam's, 1921);

Le Cabaret de la belle femme (Paris: Edition Française Illustrée, 1919; enlarged edition, Paris: Albin Michel, 1922; enlarged again, 1928); translated by Brian Lunn and Alan Duncan as *The Cabaret Up the Line* (London: Lane, 1930);

La Boule de gui (Paris: Editions de la Banderole, 1922);

Saint Magloire (Paris: Albin Michel, 1922); translated by Pauline de Chary (London: Collins, 1923; New York: Doran, 1923);

Le Réveil des morts (Paris: Albin Michel, 1923);

Le Cadastre littéraire ou une heure avec M. Barrès (Paris: Emile-Paul, 1925);

Montmartre, mon pays (Paris: M. Lesage, 1925);

Sur la route mandarine (Paris: Albin Michel, 1925); translated by Gertrude Emerson as *On the Mandarin Road* (New York & London: Century, 1926);

Partir (Paris: Albin Michel, 1926); translated by Pauline E. Rush as *Departure* (London: Gollancz, 1928; New York: Simon & Schuster, 1928);

Le Promeneur nocturne (Paris: A la Cité des Livres, 1926);

La Caravane sans chameaux (Paris: Albin Michel, 1928);

Ecrit sur l'herbe (Paris: Cahiers Libres, 1928);

Souvenirs sur les Croix de bois (Paris: A la Cité des Livres, 1929);

Chez les beautés aux dents limées (Paris: Laboratoires Martinet, 1930);

Entre le ciel et l'eau (Paris: Georges Crès, 1930);

Le Château des brouillards (Paris: Albin Michel, 1932);

Si c'était vrai? (Paris: Albin Michel, 1934);

Quand j'étais montmartrois (Paris: Albin Michel, 1936);

Vive la liberté! (Paris: Albin Michel, 1937);

Frontières (Paris: Albin Michel, 1938);

Retour au front (Paris: Albin Michel, 1940);

Sous le casque blanc (Paris: Editions de France, 1941);

Route des tropiques (Paris: Albin Michel, 1944);

Carte d'identité, récit de l'Occupation (Paris: Albin Michel, 1945);

Bouquet de Bohème (Paris: Albin Michel, 1947);

Bleu Horizon (Paris: Albin Michel, 1949);

Portraits sans retouche (Paris: Albin Michel, 1952);

Tout est à vendre (Paris: Albin Michel, 1956);

La Drôle de guerre, 1939-1940 (Paris: Albin Michel, 1957);

Au beau temps de la Butte (Paris: Albin Michel, 1963);

A bas l'argent (Paris: Albin Michel, 1965);

Lettre ouverte à un milliardaire (Paris: Albin Michel, 1967);

Le Marquis de la Dèche (Paris: Albin Michel, 1971);

Images (Paris: Albin Michel, 1975);

Vacances forcées (Paris: Albin Michel, 1985).

Roland Dorgelès is usually associated with his first novel, *Les Croix de bois* (*Wooden Crosses*), written during World War I and published shortly thereafter, in 1919. Its portrait of desperate but essentially patriotic and courageous men facing an almost hopeless situation in the trenches made it an immediate and overwhelming success. For the past sixty years the book has been republished from time to time, and it remains to this day, of the more than thirty books that Dorgelès wrote, his major achievement.

Dorgelès, who signed all of his published works with that pseudonym, was born Roland Lécavelé in Amiens, the ancient provincial capital of Picardy, on 15 June 1886. As a youth he received a traditional petit bourgeois Catholic upbringing but set out in a new direction when, in late adolescence, he moved to Paris, hoping to become a painter, and enrolled in the Ecole des

Roland Dorgelès on the jury for the 1946 Prix Goncourt. Left to right: André Billy, Francis Carco, Colette, Léo Larguier, Dorgelès, and Lucien Descaves (Keystone).

Beaux-Arts. Most of his time was spent in Montmartre, the gathering place for artists and painters. At the famous *belle époque* café called Le Lapin Agile, he associated with Pierre Mac Orlan, Francis Carco, Kees van Dongen, and Pablo Picasso. Montmartre at the time was at the height of its fame, and Dorgelès was responsible for one of the best-known acts of tomfoolery of the era. He was the principal instigator of a gag pulled off under the name Borondi, whose painting, entitled *Le Soleil se couche sur l'Adriatique* (Sunset on the Adriatic), was entered in the 1910 competition of the Salon des Indépendants and hailed by the majority of critics as a masterpiece. Only later was it revealed that Dorgelès and some of his friends had orchestrated the hoax by tying a paint brush to a donkey's tail.

These early years of his life would later serve him well as a professional writer, inspiring touching and lighthearted evocations in a number of books, including *Montmartre, mon pays* (Montmartre, My Homeland) in 1925, *Le Château des brouillards* (Castle of Fogs) in 1932, *Quand j'étais montmartrois* (When I Lived in Montmartre) in 1936, *Bouquet de Bohème* (Bouquet of the Bohe-

mian Lifestyle) in 1947, and, finally, *Portraits sans retouche* (Portraits Without Alteration) in 1952.

By 1908 Dorgelès seems to have felt that his personal gifts could be put to better use and that he could achieve a fuller form of self-expression through writing. He dropped out of the Ecole des Beaux-Arts and left behind its formal restrictions in order to begin working as a reporter for such popular newspapers and magazines of the day as *Paris-Journal* (1909-1912) and *Comoedia* (1908-1914). His early journalistic efforts are characterized by humor and a biting sense of irony in favor of the average man and his need for freedom. Ironically he would soon have the opportunity to serve the same cause, human freedom, in the Great War that was only a few months away.

Dorgelès volunteered for duty as soon as war was declared. As he stated later in speaking of the feelings that impelled him and other young Frenchmen to enlist in the service of their country: "Nous nous pensions tous être les champions de la conscience humaine" (We all thought ourselves to be champions of human conscience). He also found in the struggle on behalf of freedom and democracy new meaning for his life, since by this time he had lost the religious faith of his youth.

To his credit Dorgelès remained faithful to his personal cult of heroism and service to the nation throughout the course of the war, serving in the infantry until 1916 when combat wounds forced him into aviation duty. These years, even more than the earlier Montmartre period, were the central experience of his life as well as of his subsequent career as a writer.

When *Les Croix de bois* appeared in 1919, it narrowly missed receiving the Prix Goncourt by a vote of six to four in favor of Marcel Proust's *A l'ombre des jeunes filles en fleurs*. As a kind of consolation prize, his novel was awarded the important but less prestigious Prix Fémina. The novel became a monumental popular success, was widely translated into other languages, and was often republished throughout the 1920s. The first English translation, *Wooden Crosses*, appeared in 1921.

The responsive chord struck by *Les Croix de bois* can be explained by the narrator's sincere, patriotic, and nonideological style. Although the succession of *tableaux* that constitutes the novel is based on invention and is a creation of the novelist's imagination, it is nonetheless informed by his experiences. Since Dorgelès's goal in the novel is to tell of *the* war, and not *his* war, he took the people and events of his own experience and transformed them in order to evoke in his reader, especially readers who had themselves been through the war, the feeling that he was recounting also their experiences. Another reason for transposing his experiences was to preserve the dignity of the many friends whom he had seen suffer and die.

In Dorgelès's re-creation of the daily life of the man in the trenches, the average soldier emerges much as he must have been in reality, neither a hero nor a coward, neither a superman nor an automaton, but rather a man resigned to his fate and capable of great endurance in the face of a grueling war. Various ranks and social classes, with their differing but ultimately reinforcing points of view, are introduced. They all share, however, the ideal of service to the nation under siege.

At the heart of *Les Croix de bois* is the voice of the author (transposed into the first-person narrator Jacques Larcher), who tells very little about himself and even less about his own exploits and experiences. It is only upon occasion that he even speaks of himself, preferring to narrate the adventures of those few soldiers he knew best: Bouffioux, Fouillard, Bréval, Broucke, and Sulphart. The last, a factory worker who survives more than three years in the trenches only to return to Paris to learn that those who have sacrificed so much for their country have already been forgotten, and Gilbert Demachy, a character who has much in common with the narrator and who dies at the close of the novel, receive the most extended development.

When Sulphart is finally released from the army after being treated for wounds, he openly states that he does not want to return to the front and risk being killed. When he learns the good news that he has been awarded a pension and can return to civilian life, he seems lost and unable to adapt to the new realities. Unable to find a job at the Rouen factory where he used to work, he wanders off to Paris and turns increasingly to drink. At the end of the novel his fate is uncertain. Considering himself as a victor in the war for the simple reason that he personally has survived, he is still seriously disoriented from the stress of years of combat. Demachy, who is just the opposite of the tough-guy, street-corner philosopher Sulphart, is portrayed with great tenderness, and his death, described over four pages, is among the most touching in modern French literature. Wounded in the abdomen and left behind on the battlefield, he attempts to maintain consciousness in the hope that a stretcher bearer will pass nearby. Trying to retain his strength to call out for help when the time comes, he dies slowly, bleeding to death before help comes. A former law student in Paris, Demachy shared with the narrator love of good books, of the theater, and of Paris and its beautiful women. With his death a part of the narrator also dies, and by this time the reader has a clear understanding that Demachy is someone who could have made an important contribution to society after the war. The waste and futility of war are all the more striking as one watches him die slowly, drawing his last breath as two tears fall upon his cheeks.

In comparison with other war novels written later in the interwar period, or with the many novels to come out of subsequent conflicts, *Les Croix de bois* seems tame and well mannered. It contains no swear words and no vulgarity, although Dorgelès has his predominantly working-class characters speak in slang, changing the spelling of many nonslang words to indicate pronunciation, while maintaining a certain stylistic decorum. This is the kind of novel that did not shock the public of its day. At the same time, however, its content can still move readers. Although a contemporary reader might be tempted to extract a pacifist message from the novel, it is not a pacifist work. It details the absurdity of war and the sacrifice that some are forced to make, but it also contains a muted but potent patriotic undertone. While seeming to admit that the war is insane and that the sacrifices demanded are immense, it also assures the reader that there was no other choice. Until the Germans are expelled from France, a true patriot knows where his duty lies. Its only lament is that the sacrifices will soon be forgotten.

Later books by Dorgelès came back to the theme of the Great War. For instance, his *Le Cabaret de la belle femme* (1919; translated as *The Cabaret Up the Line*, 1930) is a collection of stories in which the common soldier once again emerges as the hero. Also included in this book are three chapters that military censors had deleted from the original edition of *Les Croix de bois*. Dorgelès's novel *Le Réveil des morts* (The Reawakening of the Dead, 1923) takes up the problem of memory as related to the sufferings of those who had served and died in the trenches. The novel's action is set in the Aisne region, northwest of Paris, where almost everything has been destroyed. A local village is being rebuilt, in fact resurrected. In a moving style, the narrator asks what the dead think of the speculators, builders, and developers who are now reaping fortunes on the basis of their sacrifices. One night they all reappear in a dream that takes place in the mind of the village's chief architect, the man appointed by the state to restore the village and bring it back to life. As the dream unfolds, the speculators and crooked businessmen tremble, and those who have been swindled take heart, while the state, through its bureaucratic representatives, attempts to right the wrongs that are taking place. But as the dream ends, the return to reality is abrupt. In the new postwar world, the dead have been forgotten, and human selfishness is on the rise again.

After the war Dorgelès continued to earn his living as a writer. A series of travel books appeared during the interwar years. In *Sur la route mandarine* (1925; translated as *On the Mandarin Road*, 1926), for example, he chronicles a voyage to French Indochina. While not going so far as to question France's self-appointed civilizing role there, he does point an accusing finger at exploiters and manipulators who take advantage of the

natives. The following year a novel, entitled *Partir* (translated as *Departure*, 1928), appeared. Taking as its subject matter life aboard a steamship headed for the Far East, the book lacks the inspiration and sincerity that had made *Les Croix de bois* so successful. Contrasting the wonders of nature with the selfishness and sordidness of his characters, Dorgelès was forcing his hand and showed himself to be writing without conviction.

His next travel book, *La Caravane sans chameaux* (Caravan Without Camels), came out in 1928 and tells of his experiences in the Middle East, from Alexandria to Jerusalem. A few years later he had the opportunity, like many French writers of the 1930s, to visit the Soviet Union. He also visited Nazi Germany and Fascist Italy and reported on his impressions of the three dictatorships in *Vive la liberté!* (1937). In this work he exhorts his compatriots not to take their freedom for granted nor to dissipate their strength in internal squabbles between the left and the right. In 1938 Dorgelès repeated his message of the need for national reconciliation and unity against the threat of the rising dictatorships in *Frontières* (Borders), which took as its point of departure the absorption of Austria into the Third Reich. During the Occupation he wrote more travel books, this time about Africa: *Sous le casque blanc* (Under the White Helmet) and *Route des tropiques* (Road to the Tropics) appeared in 1941 and 1944 respectively.

As war approached in 1939, Dorgelès was dispatched as a reporter to cover activities at the front. After war was declared in 1939, he was widely acknowledged as having coined the expression "la drôle de guerre," or "the phony war," to describe the situation in which the Allies found themselves: at war with Germany but afraid to attack her; he later used the expression as the title of one of his books.

Dorgelès was a literary personality in Paris for over half a century. As a member of the influential Goncourt jury for much of that time and as its president for many years, he was able to play an important role in making literary reputations. His novels are largely forgotten. Written half-heartedly, without the conviction that characterizes *Les Croix de bois*, such works as *Saint Magloire* (1922; translated, 1923), *Si c'était vrai?* (If It Were True, 1934), *Tout est à vendre* (Everything for Sale, 1956), and *A bas l'argent* (Down With Money, 1965) stand out as isolated works of fiction among the many travel and souvenir books that tell of the colorful characters who populated Montmartre in its heyday before World War I.

As a fiction writer, Dorgelès is weak, from *Les Croix de bois* until the end of his career, in evoking the psychological inner workings of his characters. Indeed, *Les Croix de bois* succeeded precisely because his characters were not so much real people as types that a vast public needed and wanted to read about in the aftermath of the war. In addition Dorgelès was never a great stylist. If anything, his style is conversational and journalistic, and this is what has made his books about Montmartre, for instance, so endearing. They are easy to read, full of sincerity and discretion, but no great works of literature. Dorgelès's life as a man

of French letters was a long and, on the whole, distinguished one, but he was not a writer of the first rank. His patriotism and love of country were always very strong. It was this quality that enabled him to write *Les Croix de bois* and that subsequently endeared him to the next two generations of French readers.

References:

Michel Brunet, *Roland Dorgelès: De Montmartre à l'Académie Goncourt* (Paris: Bibliothèque Nationale, 1978);

Armand Lanoux, *Colloque Roland Dorgelès* (Paris: Hôtel de Massa, 1978).

Georges Duhamel

(30 June 1884-13 April 1966)

Elizabeth Richardson Viti
Gettysburg College

SELECTED BOOKS: *Des Légendes, des batailles* (Paris: Editions de "L'Abbaye," 1907);

L'Homme en tête, poème (Paris: Editions "Vers et Prose," 1909);

Notes sur la technique poètique by Duhamel and Charles Vildrac (Paris, 1910);

Selon ma loi, poèmes (Paris: Figuière, 1910);

La Lumière, pièce en quatre actes (Paris: Figuière, 1911);

Compagnons, poèmes (Paris: Nouvelle Revue Française, 1912);

Dans l'ombre des statues, pièce en trois actes (Paris: Nouvelle Revue Française, 1912); translated by Sasha Best as *In the Shadow of Statues* (Boston: Badger, 1914);

Propos critiques (Paris: Figuière, 1912);

Le Combat, pièce en cinq actes (Paris: Mercure de France, 1913);

Paul Claudel; Le Philosophe–le poète–l'écrivain (Paris: Mercure de France, 1913);

Les Poètes et la poésie, 1912-1913 (Paris: Mercure de France, 1914; revised and enlarged, 1922);

Vie des martyrs, 1914-1916 (Paris: Mercure de France, 1917); translated by Florence Simmonds as *The New Book of Martyrs* (London: Heinemann, 1918; New York: Doran, 1918);

Civilisation, 1914-1917 as Denis Thévenin (Paris:

Mercure de France, 1918); translated by T. P. Conwil-Evans (London: Swathmore Press, 1919); translated by E. S. Brooks (New York: Century, 1919);

Entretiens dans le tumulte: Chronique contemporaine 1918-1919 (Paris: Mercure de France, 1919);

La Possession du monde (Paris: Mercure de France, 1919); translated by ·Eleanor Stimson Brooks as *The Heart's Domain* (New York: Century, 1919);

Confession de minuit, volume 1 of *Vie et aventures de Salavin* (Paris: Mercure de France, 1920); translated as *Confession at Midnight* in *Salavin* (1936);

L'Œuvre des athlètes, comédie en quatre actes . . . Suivi de Lapointe et Ropiteau, comédie en un acte (Paris: Gallimard, 1920);

Elégies (Paris: Bloch, 1920);

Les Hommes abandonnés (Paris: Mercure de France, 1921);

Trois journées de la tribu (Paris: Gallimard, 1921);

Lettres d'Aupasie (Paris: Editions du Sablier, 1922);

Les Plaisirs et les jeux: Mémoires du Cuib et du Tioup (Paris: Mercure de France, 1922); translated by R. Wills Thomas as *Days of Delight* (London: Dakers, 1939);

Deux hommes, volume 2 of *Vie et aventures de Salavin* (Paris: Mercure de France, 1924);

Le Prince Jaffar (Paris: Mercure de France, 1924);

La Journée aux aveux, comédie en trois actes, suivie de Quand vous voudrez, comédie en un acte (Paris: Mercure de France, 1924);

Délibérations (Paris: Cahiers de Paris, 1925);

Essai sur le roman (Paris: Lesage, 1925);

La Pierre d'Horeb (Paris: Mercure de France, 1926);

Essai sur une renaissance dramatique (Paris: Editions Lapina, 1926);

Lettres au Patagon (Paris: Mercure de France, 1926);

Journal de Salavin, volume 3 of *Vie et aventures de Salavin* (Paris: Mercure de France, 1927); translated as *Salavin's Journal* in *Salavin* (1936);

Maurice de Vlaminck (Paris: Les Ecrivains Réunis, 1927);

Le Voyage de Moscou (Paris: Mercure de France, 1927);

Images de la Grèce (Paris: Editions du Sablier, 1928);

La Nuit d'orage (Paris: Mercure de France, 1928);

Les Sept Dernières Plaies (Paris: Mercure de France, 1928);

Chant du nord (Paris: Editions du Sablier, 1929);

Le Club des Lyonnais, volume 4 of *Vie et aventures de Salavin* (Paris: Mercure de France, 1929); translated as *The Lyonnais Club* in *Salavin* (1936);

Scènes de la vie future (Paris: Mercure de France, 1930); translated by Charles Miner Thompson as *America: The Menace, Scenes from the Life of the Future* (Boston & New York: Houghton Mifflin, 1931; London: Allen & Unwin, 1931);

L'Alsace entrevue; ou, L'aveugle et le paralytique (Strasbourg: Librairie de la Méssange, 1931);

Géographie cordiale de l'Europe (Paris: Mercure de France, 1931); republished in part as *Mon Europe* (Paris: Flammarion, 1931);

Les Jumeaux de Vallangoujard (Paris: Paul Hartmann, 1931);

Mon Royaume (Paris: Paul Hartmann, 1932);

Tel qu'en lui-même, volume 5 of *Vie et aventures de Salavin* (Paris: Mercure de France, 1932); translated as *End of Illusion* in *Salavin* (1936);

Querelles de famille (Paris: Mercure de France, 1932);

L'Humaniste et l'automate (Paris: Paul Hartmann, 1933);

Le Notaire du Havre, volume 1 of *Chronique des Pasquier* (Paris: Mercure de France, 1933); translated by Béatrice de Holthoir as *News from Havre* (London: Dent, 1934); translated by Samuel Putnam as *Papa Pasquier* (New York & London: Harper, 1934);

Discours aux nuages (Paris: Editions du Siècle, 1934);

Le Jardin des bêtes sauvages, volume 2 of *Chronique des Pasquier* (Paris: Mercure de France, 1934); translated as *The Garden of the Wild Beasts* in *The Fortunes of the Pasquiers* (1935);

Remarques sur les mémoires imaginaires (Paris: Mercure de France, 1934);

Vue de la terre promise, volume 3 of *Chronique des Pasquier* (Paris: Mercure de France, 1934); translated as *Canaan Glimpsed* in *The Fortunes of the Pasquiers* (1935); translated by Holthoir as *In Sight of the Promised Land* (London: Dent, 1936);

La Nuit de la Saint-Jean, volume 4 of *Chronique des Pasquier* (Paris: Mercure de France, 1935); translated as *St. John's Eve* in *The Pasquier Chronicles* (1937);

The Fortunes of the Pasquiers, translated by Putnam (New York & London: Harper, 1935)—comprises *Le Jardin des bêtes sauvages* and *Vue de la terre promise;*

Discours de réception de M. Georges Duhamel à l'Académie Française; Réponse de Henri Bordeaux (Paris: Mercure de France, 1936);

Fables de mon jardin (Paris: Mercure de France, 1936);

Salavin, translated by Gladys Billings (New York: Putnam's, 1936; London: Dent, 1937)—comprises *Confession de minuit*, *Journal de Salavin*, *Le Club des Lyonnais*, and *Tel qu'en lui-même;*

Défense des lettres. Biologie de mon métier (Paris: Mercure de France, 1937); translated by E. F. Bosman as *In Defense of Letters* (London: Dent, 1938; New York: Greystone Press, 1939);

Le Désert de Bièvres, volume 5 of *Chronique des Pasquier* (Paris: Mercure de France, 1937); translated as *The House in the Desert* in *The Pasquier Chronicles* (1937);

Deux Patrons, suivi de Vie et mort d'un héros de roman (Paris: Paul Hartmann, 1937);

Les Maîtres, volume 6 of *Chronique des Pasquier* (Paris: Mercure de France, 1937);

The Pasquier Chronicles, translated by Holthoir (London: Dent, 1937; New York: Holt, 1938)—comprises *Le Notaire du Havre, Le Jardin des bêtes sauvages, Vue de la terre promise, La Nuit de la Saint-Jean,* and *Le Désert de Bièvres;*

Cécile parmi nous, volume 7 of *Chronique des Pasquier* (Paris: Mercure de France, 1938); translated by Holthoir as *Cécile Among the Pasquiers* (London: Dent, 1940), Holthoir's translation republished as *Cécile Pasquier* (New York: Holt, 1940);

Le Dernier voyage de Candide, suivi d'un choix de nouvelles (Paris: Fernand Sorlot, 1938);

Le Combat contre les ombres, volume 8 of *Chronique des Pasquier* (Paris: Mercure de France, 1939);

Mémorial de la guerre blanche (Paris: Mercure de France, 1939); translated by N. Hoppé as *The White War of 1938* (London: Dent, 1939);

Positions françaises (Paris: Mercure de France, 1940); translated by Basil Collier as *Why France Fights* (London: Dent, 1940); Collier's translation republished as *The French Position* (London: Dent, 1940);

Lieu d'asile (Paris: Mercure de France, 1940);

Les Confessions sans pénitence, suivi de trois autres entretiens: Rousseau, Montesquieu, Descartes, Pascal (Paris: Plon, 1941);

Suzanne et les jeunes hommes, volume 9 of *Chronique des Pasquier* (Paris: Mercure de France, 1941); translated as *Suzanne* in *Suzanne and Joseph Pasquier* (1946);

La Passion de Joseph Pasquier, volume 10 of *Chronique des Pasquier* (Paris, 1941); translated as *Joseph Pasquier* in *Suzanne and Joseph Pasquier* (1946);

Chronique des saisons amères, 1940-1943 (Paris: Paul Hartmann, 1944);

Civilisation française (Paris: Hachette, 1944);

Inventaire de l'abîme, 1884-1901 (Paris: Paul Hartmann, 1944); translated in *Light on My Days: An Autobiography* (1948);

Biographie de mes fantômes, 1901-1906 (Paris: Paul Hartmann, 1944); translated in *Light on My Days: An Autobiography* (1948);

La Musique consolatrice (Monaco: Editions du Rocher, 1944; revised and enlarged, 1950);

Paroles de médecin (Monaco: Editions du Rocher, 1946);

Souvenirs de la vie de paradis (Paris: Mercure de France, 1946);

Suzanne and Joseph Pasquier, translated by Holthoir (London: Dent, 1946); republished as *Suzanne; Joseph: Two Novels from the Pasquier Chronicles* (New York: Holt, 1949)–comprises *Suzanne et les jeunes hommes* and *La Passion de Joseph Pasquier;*

Consultation aux pays d'Islam (Paris: Mercure de France, 1947);

Homère au XXᵉ siècle: Croquis et lettres de voyage de Berthold Mahn (Paris: Union Latine d'Editions, 1947);

Semailles au vent (Monaco: Editions du Rocher, 1947; Montreal & New York: Cercle du Livre de France, 1947);

Le Temps de la recherche (Paris: Paul Hartmann, 1947);

Tribulations de l'espérance (Paris: Mercure de France, 1947);

Light on My Days: An Autobiography, translated by Collier (London: Dent, 1948)–comprises *Inventaire de l'abîme, 1884-1901* and *Biographie de mes fantômes, 1901-1906;*

La Pesée des âmes, 1914-1919 (Paris: Mercure de France, 1949);

Le Voyage de Patrice Périot (Paris: Mercure de France, 1950); translated by Bosman as *Patrice Periot* (London: Dent, 1952);

Cri des profondeurs (Paris: Mercure de France, 1951); translated by Bosman as *Cry out of the Depths* (London: Dent, 1953; Boston: Little, Brown, 1954);

Manuel du protestataire (Paris: Mercure de France, 1952);

Le Japon entre la tradition et l'avenir (Paris: Mercure de France, 1953);

Les Espoirs et les épreuves, 1919-1928 (Paris: Mercure de France, 1953);

Les Voyageurs de l'Espérance (Paris: Gédalge, 1953);

Refuges de lecture (Paris: Mercure de France, 1954);

La Turquie nouvelle, puissance d'Occident (Paris: Mercure de France, 1954);

L'Archange de l'aventure (Paris: Mercure de France, 1956);

Les Compagnons de l'Apocalypse (Paris: Mercure de France, 1956);

Israël, clef de l'Orient (Paris: Mercure de France, 1957);

Les Livres du bonheur (Paris: Mercure de France, 1957);

Problèmes de l'heure (Paris: Mercure de France, 1957);

Le Complexe de Théophile (Paris: Mercure de France, 1958);

Travail, ô mon seul repos! (Paris: Wesmael-Charlier, 1959);

Nouvelles du sombre empire (Paris: Mercure de France, 1960);

Traité du départ, suivi de Fables de ma vie (Paris: Mercure de France, 1961);

Problèmes de civilisation, précédé de Traité du départ, Fables de ma vie, La Médecine au vingtième siècle (Paris: Mercure de France, 1962);

Le Livre de l'amertume: Extraits du journal de Blanche et Georges Duhamel (Paris: Mercure de France, 1983).

PLAY PRODUCTIONS: *La Lumière,* Paris, Théâtre de l' Odéon, 8 April 1911;

Dans l'ombre des statues, Paris, Théâtre de l' Odéon, 26 October 1912;

Le Combat, Paris, Théâtre des Arts, 14 March 1913;

L'Œuvre des athlètes, Paris, Théâtre du Vieux-Colombier, 10 April 1920;

Lapointe et Ropiteau, Geneva, Théâtre Pitoëff, 28 April 1920;

Quand vous voudrez, Geneva, Théâtre Pitoëff, 5 February 1921;

La Journée des aveux, Paris, Studio des Champs-Elysées, 24 October 1923.

Georges Duhamel characterized the major portion of his extraordinarily varied and prolific production as "littérature de témoignage": his mission was to bear witness to a world in crisis, to understand and explain it to his contemporaries and, in so doing, to impose order where there was seemingly nothing but chaos. The writer's ultimate goal was to provide his readers with some calm, some hope during a difficult time–the first half of the twentieth century. These efforts to transform the irrational into the rational began first in the author's immediate experience, and because Duhamel never hesitated to enhance his writing with the autobiographical, there is an indisputable interrelatedness between his life and his work.

Born in Paris on 30 June 1884 to parents of peasant stock, Georges Duhamel was one of eight children, although four died quite young. His mother, Emma Pionnier Duhamel, was exemplary but his father, Pierre-Emile Duhamel, was a quixotic man. He changed jobs (past forty, he decided to begin medical studies), lodgings, and mistresses with regularity, forcing his family to put up with the emotional and financial consequences. Duhamel, a myopic and frail child diagnosed as having a weak spinal column, not only had to suffer the cups of blood from slaughterhouse animals that the doctor requested he drink but also had to withstand the taunts of his schoolmates who ridiculed his thick glasses and slight stature. Catholicism, which Duhamel abandoned when he was thirteen, did not console him; however, the boy found other sources, such as music, to mitigate his pain. He played the flute, and whenever he had a few sous he went to the opera and to concerts. Nature soothed him as well, but it was undoubtedly his love of learning which most effectively lent a sense of security to these years. An inveterate reader gifted with an intuitive and penetrating mind, Duhamel was an exceptional student. He decided early on both a scientific and a literary career.

At eighteen Duhamel moved into his own room in the Latin Quarter, quickly appreciating his solitude and independence. The following year, in 1903, he began his medical studies at the University of Paris, ironically two years after his father had completed his, and enrolled simultaneously in classes at the Institute of Biology. Following his father's advice, Duhamel not only acquitted himself admirably of the assigned work but almost daily he observed various operations in the city hospitals in order to learn as much as possible. Most evenings were devoted to study, but there were also those which were given over to the reading and discussion of books. An interest in literature was claiming more and more of the young man's time, and he knew and loved the classics yet also was interested in current works. Among those with whom he shared this interest were Charles Vildrac, his future collaborator as well as future brother-in-law, and about a half dozen other young men who planned on conquering the literary world. However, in 1904 Duhamel had to suspend this frenetic pace when, run down, he became ill with rheumatic fever.

Two years later Duhamel's friendly association with literary men crystalized into the communal living experiment known as the Abbaye. Duhamel and Vildrac, later a distinguished playwright, persuaded René Arcos, a poet and novelist-to-be, Albert Gleizes, an aspiring artist, and Henri Martin-Barzun, a future critic and essayist, to live together in a house that they had rented in Créteil, a Parisian suburb. The men were going to support themselves by learning a trade, printing, and were going to spend their free time in creative pursuits. The Abbaye did, in fact, print several books, for its members and for such noteworthy writers as Anatole France. Duhamel's first literary publication, *Des Légendes, des batailles* (Legends, Battles), a volume of poetry, appeared in 1907. Unfortunately, life was difficult at Créteil. Money was scarce and arguments abundant; thus, the Abbaye de Créteil group disbanded in 1908.

This same year Duhamel, who had commuted to medical school and to the Institute of Biology during his stay in Créteil, received his *licence ès sciences* and, the following year, his medical degree. He also married Blanche Sistoli, an aspiring actress (stage name Blanche Albane) whom he had met at an Abbaye get-together. During the early years of their marriage, an exceedingly happy one which brought them three sons, Duhamel worked in an industrial laboratory doing research on animals and, in the evenings, wrote poetry. Although perhaps an improvement over *Des Légendes, des batailles* which suffers from poor technique, undeveloped thought, and little originality, Duhamel's four subsequent volumes of verse, *L'Homme en tête* (Man at the Head, 1909), *Selon ma loi* (According to My Law, 1910), *Compagnons* (Companions, 1912) and *Elégies* (1920), are not particularly noteworthy. Duhamel himself decided that he was actually more gifted for prose and turned to, among other literary activities, the theater. But although his first play, *La Lumière* (The Light, 1911), was mounted by the celebrated slice-of-life director André Antoine and was relatively well reviewed by the noted critic Paul Souday, his plays are not remarkable either. For the most part they are *pièces à thèse* such as *Dans l'ombre des statues* (In the Shadow of Statues, 1912) and *Le Combat* (1913) or mediocre imitations such as *L'Œuvre des athlètes* (The Work of Athletes, 1920), an updated *Tartuffe*, and *Quand vous voudrez* (When You Wish, 1924), a Marivaux-like comedy.

Duhamel's true gifts first emerged in his chronicles of World War I. Duhamel, the doctor, served fifty-one months in a mobile surgical unit not far from the front, performed two thousand operations and cared for four thousand wounded. To relieve the shock and revulsion he felt during the day, Duhamel frequently wrote at night or in spare moments and produced four prose works. *Vie des martyrs, 1914-1916* (1917; translated as *The New Book of Martyrs*, 1918) and its companion piece, *Civilisation, 1914-1917* (1918; translated, 1919), protest against war and

Members of the Abbaye de Créteil, the communal living experiment Duhamel helped organize in 1906: (front row) Charles Vildrac, René Arcos, Albert Gleizes, Henri-Martin Barzun, Alexandre Mercereau; (back row) Duhamel, Berthold Mahn, Jacques D'Otémar

its atrocities through a series of sketches in which the writer not only realistically describes his daily army experiences but also successfully captures in words the souls of the men he describes. *Vie des martyrs* created but a slight stir whereas *Civilisation,* published initially under the pseudonym Denis Thévenin because Duhamel wanted the work seen strictly as a social document, not only won public acclaim but the prestigious Prix Goncourt and a special award from the Académie Française as well. (Duhamel was not pleased with his success, feeling that rather than inspiring contempt for war, he had inured people to its horrors.) In the second two volumes, *Entretiens dans le tumulte: Chronique contemporaine 1918-1919* (Conversations During the Tumult: Contemporary Chronicle, 1919) and *La Possession du monde* (1919; translated that year as *The Heart's Domain*) he tries to formulate a philosophy of life. After having witnessed so much death, Duhamel viewed happiness as life's ultimate goal, a spiritual happiness available to all who have open minds and are sensitive to life's many facets.

Duhamel followed these war chronicles with what would eventually become one of the solid bases of the writer's reputation as a novelist, his *Vie et aventures de Salavin* (1920-1932). In this cycle of five novels and one short story the protagonist, Louis Salavin, not coincidentally is also seeking the meaning of life. Duhamel felt that if a novel were to be meaningful the hero had to be an outgrowth of the writer himself, and there is no doubt that Salavin is, in many respects, an embodiment of the author. Furthermore, the Salavin series differs from other well-known cycles, Emile Zola's *Rougon-Macquart* novels, for example, in that it insists upon the psychology of the character, analyzing his every thought while virtually ignoring environment and plot.

In the first volume of the cycle, *Confession de minuit* (1920; translated as *Confession at Midnight* in *Salavin*, 1936), Salavin, the narrator, recounts his immediate past to a stranger whom he meets in a bar late one night. Salavin says that he was fired from his position at the firm of Socque et Sureau for having given in to the impulse to touch the earlobe of M. Sureau, his boss. He spends the remainder of the novel first looking for another position and then disheartened, meandering through the streets of Paris. The monotony is only sometimes interrupted by visits to his sole friend Lanoue or by evenings spent with his mother, with whom he lives, and who sits and sews with their neighbor Marguerite to support herself and her son. Salavin prefers, instead, introspection and, wallowing in self-involvement, cannot accept himself as he is. *Confession de minuit* documents his slow, steady mental and emotional decline. Critics questioned Duhamel about Salavin's capacity for self-castigation, and the author heatedly denied that Salavin was mentally unbalanced. On the contrary, Duhamel saw Salavin as alienated modern man, mediocre perhaps, but a man, nonetheless, with whom everyone could find something in common.

In the succeeding works Salavin's personality does not change. Rather, each book serves to reinforce character traits which determine Salavin's inexorable nature. In the short story "Nouvelle Rencontre de Salavin" (Another Encounter with Salavin), from the collection *Les Hommes abandonnés* (The Abandoned Men, 1921), Salavin admits to a theft, a suicide attempt, and the seduction of Lanoue's wife. However, the reader discovers that Salavin has been dreaming when a bartender awakens him. The effect is one of suspense, but certainly Duhamel's belief that the dream is revelatory also influenced his choice: Salavin, as he did with the unusual gesture of touching M. Sureau's ear, wishes to disobey society.

The second novel of the series, *Deux hommes* (Two Men, 1924), is the study of Salavin's friendship with Edouard Loisel, whom he has met by chance in a café. Now married to the seamstress Marguerite, Salavin invites Loisel and his wife over for the evening because the two men have very quickly decided that they wish to share one another's lives completely. As their friendship deepens Loisel becomes more and more Salavin's benefactor: he finds Salavin a job where he works and assumes the responsibility of caring for his friend's sick child. Salavin finds himself dependent, passive, and resentful, and as their friendship careens toward its end, he accuses Loisel of making him his slave. In truth, the relationship is doomed from the start because Salavin, not having the integrated personality necessary to its success, is incapable of friendship. Salavin, on the other hand, feels that a complete

break will allow him to grow as an individual, not realizing that his self-absorption makes this impossible.

Journal de Salavin (1927; translated as *Salavin's Journal* in *Salavin*, 1936) follows the quest for a new and different self. In this, his diary, Salavin resolves to become a lay saint and to keep a record of his progress. He intends to do good deeds whenever and wherever he can but discovers, ironically, that people are as ungrateful as he had been with Loisel. When, for example, his fellow worker Jibé Tastard steals money from petty cash, Salavin replaces the money in order to give the young man a second chance. Instead, Tastard steals again, and when he is finally fired from Cilpo, a milk company, not only has Tastard stolen money but he has also stolen large quantities of milk and is responsible for the pregnancy of a company secretary. After a variety of failed attempts at heroism, most notably during a crowd's panic in a theater, Salavin decides to appeal to religion. He writes to a Reverend Croquet, a Protestant minister who proves to be more a businessman-psychologist. His encounter with the Catholic confessional is routine and unsatisfactory except for his confession to Abbé Pradelles whom he deems a saint. His own unsaintliness all the more clear, Salavin, as a final gesture, gives his only overcoat to the down-and-out Jibé in the dead of winter. Salavin catches pneumonia, enters a charity hospital, and is close to death. Because Salavin seems more human than before, *Journal de Salavin* is probably the best volume of the series. His search for goodness and his belief that it is within reach are touching, as is his discovery that in a world where people are only relatively honest and decent, those who deal in absolutes are unacceptable.

In contrast, *Le Club des Lyonnais* (1929; translated as *The Lyonnais Club* in *Salavin*, 1936) is the least interesting volume because the psychological study of Salavin, so prominent heretofore, is virtually nonexistent. Salavin becomes involved with a Communist group which meets in the shoemaker's shop of an old idealist and revolutionary named Legrain who wants to change the world for his dying daughter. Salavin is attracted to these half-a-dozen Communists because, unlike himself, they have strong convictions. But Max Aufrère, one of the hangers-on who introduced Salavin into the group, tries to pull him in the opposite direction, for Aufrère claims to be nothing but a spectator in life. However, when the Communists need to have a check cashed by someone

Blanche Sistoli at the time when she was a member of Jacques Copeau's experimental Théâtre du Vieux-Colombier.
She and Duhamel were married in 1908.

not suspected of party affiliation, Aufrère volunteers out of vanity. Meanwhile, the police close in on the Communist cell and everyone, including Salavin, is arrested, although he is soon set free. The book is overly involved with politics and, as a thesis novel, was Duhamel's attempt to expose the Communists. Salavin has not evolved and continues to neglect his family which, after his mother's death in this volume, is reduced to Marguerite. Marguerite has greater importance because of the humanity and compassion she shows her husband; she suffers her fate in silence and deserves the sainthood her husband sought. When, in the end, Salavin leaves to realize a personal revolution, Marguerite stoically sits in her armchair to await her husband's return.

In the final novel, *Tel qu'en lui-même* (1932; translated as *End of Illusion* in *Salavin*, 1936), Salavin assumes a new name, Simon Chavegrand, and is traveling to a new life in Tunis. On the train to Marseilles, he meets Louis d'Argoult and his wife and child who are also going to North Africa. While in Marseilles Salavin saves the child's life after she has wandered into the path of an oncoming train. Once in Tunis, Salavin tries to continue his heroic performance: he attempts to reform his Arab servant boy; he cares for pa-

tients in a hospital; and he exposes himself to typhus in order to test a new vaccine. But his acts are fruitless because, only ostensibly altruistic, they are motivated by selfishness. When at the end of the novel Salavin tries to persuade his Arab servant, wanted by the police, to give up, the boy shoots Salavin in the leg, which becomes infected and is amputated. Marguerite, summoned from France, brings Salavin back to their Paris apartment to die. Yet death is the expected conclusion to Salavin's story. Salavin was doomed to failure because, although he was able to know himself, he was unwilling to accept himself. Thus he duplicated in Tunis the life he had lived in France. Salavin's tragedy was that he could never be other than Salavin.

After the appearance of the last book many critics, far from charitable, attacked the work for its negativism, its lack of religiousness, and the hero's selfish manner. John Charpentier, writing in *Mercure de France,* expressed such distaste for Salavin that he confessed to being glad that he was dead, saying that it had taken all of Duhamel's considerable talent to interest him in Salavin's life story. But the public apparently thought otherwise, because interest in Salavin continued to grow even after the cycle's close. Finally, in response to repeated questions about the origin and development of Salavin's adventures, Duhamel explained in an addendum to *Deux Patrons* (Two Bosses, 1937) entitled "Vie et mort d'un héros de roman" (Life and Death of a Novel's Hero), how he had composed the series. Time has softened early criticisms, and most contemporary critics agree that the Salavin cycle is one of Duhamel's admirable achievements. Certainly as long as people's relation to the universe and to each other is unresolved, Salavin will live.

Duhamel wrote additional novels while the Salavin series was appearing: *Le Prince Jaffar* (1924), a novel that includes elements of both essay and travelogue, *La Pierre d'Horeb* (Horeb's Stone, 1926), a heavily autobiographical work describing the author's school days and life in the laboratory among his coworkers; and *La Nuit d'orage* (The Stormy Night, 1928), a dramatization of psychosomatic illness. However, the writer's extraordinary energy and interest in the world around him compelled Duhamel to examine a wide range of subjects, from art, as in *Maurice de Vlaminck* (1927), a tribute to his friend the Fauvist painter; to other countries as he did in his volume of travel essays *Géographie cordiale de l'Europe* (1931); to parenting as he did in the humorous *Les Plaisirs et les jeux: Mémoires du Cuib et du Tioup* (1922; translated as *Days of Delight*, 1939). But of particular interest is, in contrast to these upbeat pieces, his commentary on the dehumanization of society. Certainly *Scènes de la vie future* (1930; translated as *America: The Menace, Scenes from the Life of the Future*, 1931), an anti-American diatribe written after a trip to the United States and for which the writer won the Grand Prix de l'Académie Française, is a vigorous campaign against twentieth-century machines and their misuse. Duhamel speaks out against French mechanization as well in *Les Jumeaux de Vallangoujard* (The Twins of Vallangoujard, 1931), whereas *Querelles de famille* (Family Quarrels, 1932) castigates modern civilization as a whole for creating individuals who cannot catch up emotionally and morally to technocratic and industrial advances. Finally, in *L'Humaniste et l'automate* (The Humanist and the Automaton, 1933) Duhamel, the doctor, analyzes the pathology of a machine-guided civilization.

Duhamel was approaching fifty and so it is no surprise that in 1933 the first volume of what is considered his masterpiece, *Chronique des Pasquier* (The Pasquier Chronicles) also appeared: his opinion was that a good novel is the product of a mature mind, and indeed, seemingly all of

Duhamel's interests and personal experiences come together in this highly autobiographical ten-volume series. Written primarily during the 1930s at a time when the novel was flourishing in France, the cycle is seductive for its masterfully simple view of a bourgeois family in which Duhamel depicts the psychological and intellectual evolution of its members.

In *Le Notaire du Havre* (1933; translated as *News from Havre* and as *Papa Pasquier,* 1934) Laurent Pasquier, narrating his family story about forty years later, introduces the readers to this lower-middle-class family struggling for survival and eager to get ahead. The father, Raymond Pasquier, is beyond forty yet about to begin medical studies. Irascible, impractical, and flamboyant, Papa Pasquier, one of the prime movers of the cycle, provides some of its most comic moments. In obvious contrast, his wife, Lucie Delahaie, is a gentle, kind, and self-effacing mother who lovingly tends to her children. Mama Pasquier is both a martyr and a magician, seen throughout the novel either sewing, cleaning, or cooking and always making very little go a long way. The Pasquier children are only sketchily drawn in this first volume: Laurent is intelligent but a dreamer; Ferdinand is hardworking but dull witted; Joseph is a crude realist, and Cécile has a gift for the piano. Suzanne, the fifth child, does not appear until a later novel. One day Madame Pasquier receives a letter from the notary in Le Havre informing her of an inheritance. In the main the novel consists of waiting for this inheritance, the legal complications involved, and the anxieties aroused. Duhamel artfully uses suspense, but he uses irony as well, for when the inheritance finally arrives, most of it must be used to pay debts accrued by Papa Pasquier after dealing with his neighbors the Courtois and Wasselins. Clearly, this irony is most evident in the presence of the notary who hovers over the entire family as some omnipotent regulator of destinies. For the French, there is no more obvious symbol of the bourgeoisie and its preoccupation with money than the notary.

Le Jardin des bêtes sauvages appeared a year after *Le Notaire du Havre,* in 1934 (and was translated as *The Fortunes of the Pasquiers,* 1935). The title comes from the Pasquier children's name for the Jardin des Plantes, formerly the location of the main Paris zoo, where they walked and played, as did Duhamel and his children. Laurent is about fourteen now and breaking away from the family which he no longer per-

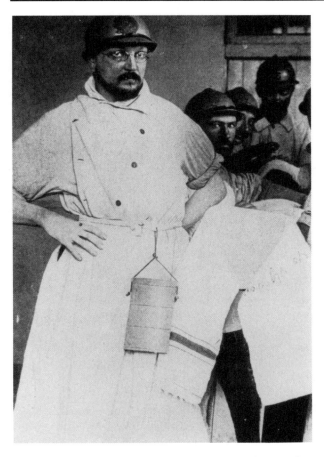

Duhamel at Verdun, 1916. During World War I he served as a doctor with a mobile surgical unit.

ceives as a warm, nurturing unit. In fact the key reason for Laurent's disillusionment with the family is the focal point of the novel: Laurent discovers his father's sordid liaison with a cheap-looking mistress, Solange Meesemacker. Moreover, he is amazed by other family members' reaction. Joseph accepts it matter-of-factly and his saintly mother suggests that in life one must accept the good with the bad. In this novel Justin Weill, Laurent's school chum, emerges as one of the cycle's important characters and reveals Duhamel's profound understanding of the Jew, his beliefs, his feelings, and his sense of despondency in the face of extermination and persecution. When Justin falls in love with Cécile, the reader feels his awkwardness not only because he is an adolescent but also because he is the member of a minority and instinctively fears rejection. Cécile herself takes on greater importance in this volume. She is a burgeoning genius, recognized as such by her piano instructor Valdemar Henningsen, a virtuoso manqué who vacillates be-

tween awe at her monumental talent and frustration at his own lack of it. Cécile provides the Pasquier household with a respite from worry through what Duhamel called "la nourriture céleste" (heavenly nourishment)–music.

When *Vue de la terre promise* (1934; translated as *Canaan Glimpsed* in *The Fortunes of the Pasquiers*, 1935) opens, Cécile is a concert pianist engaged to Henningsen; Suzanne is eight; Ferdinand is an accountant, and Joseph is a successful businessman. The family is still living together but in Créteil where Papa Pasquier, now a doctor, practices medicine. Laurent, almost twenty and a scientist working in a Paris laboratory, is becoming increasingly disenchanted with his family. In fact there is a great deal of unpleasantness to test Laurent in this third volume. He discovers his sister's fiancé stealing morphine from Dr. Pasquier's medicine chest and, later, when Henningsen is deprived of the drug, he shoots his mother and kills himself. Furthermore, Laurent receives a letter from his lab colleague, Hélène Strohl, for whom he has great affection, announcing her imminent marriage to his brother Joseph. Worse, he discovers his father is responsible for the pregnancy of a poor relative, Paula Lescure, whom Mme Pasquier had taken into their home. Thus, the novel's title refers to Laurent who vacillates between his family's set of values and attraction to a new world, a promised land that would permit him to decide these values for himself. Laurent tests his faith in the ideal world of scientific discovery which contradicts the real world of money that had always obsessed the Pasquiers. He throws his inheritance, a thousand-franc note, into the Seine in front of the most money-minded family member, Joseph. However, he confesses to Justin Weill that he had had the note changed and had thrown away only five hundred francs. Although clearly a sensitive idealist, Laurent is not sufficiently evolved to disavow the material completely. Rather, he realizes that neither the insulated existence of the laboratory, nor the ethereal world of music for that matter, can provide escape from life. Laurent is ready to get on with his and moves into a Paris apartment.

Published the year that Duhamel was elected to the Académie Française, *La Nuit de la Saint-Jean* (1935; translated as *St. John's Eve* in *The Pasquier Chronicles*, 1937) is supposedly derived from a posthumous account of events written by Justin Weill and given by his mother to Laurent. Now twenty-five, Laurent is still working in a laboratory and also in a hospital, and his materialist brother Joseph is a very wealthy businessman. In order to show off a newly acquired large property which he calls La Pâquellerie, Joseph invites his family and a few others there to celebrate Saint-John's Eve, an occasion traditionally associated with unusual happenings. Indeed, the party turns unpleasant: Laurent's much-admired superior at the laboratory, Renaud Censier, expresses his infatuation with Laure, a young woman to whom Laurent himself is attracted; Delcambre, an artist, indulges in questionable jokes and flirts with the thirteen-year-old Suzanne; and Laurent walks in on his father who is flirting with the nurse who cares for Joseph's two sons. There is little more than a restatement of what is already known–Joseph's cupidity, Papa Pasquier's infidelity, and Mme Pasquier's silent suffering–which makes this volume one of the least interesting of the series. Only Justin Weill's personality is further developed, for having traveled to Palestine, he has a new vision of his place in society. Laurent's evolution is limited to his change in attitude toward Joseph. He begins to understand Joseph's veritable need for money and belief that it is a creative agent. Laurent even realizes that the Josephs of the world are necessary for society's survival and, therefore, have a positive function in life.

The fifth volume, *Le Désert de Bièvres* (1937; translated as *The House in the Desert* in *The Pasquier Chronicles,* 1937), is the most blatantly autobiographical. Laurent, along with a group of idealistic youths like those of the Abbaye at Créteil, participates in a communal living experience outside of Paris, inspired and arranged by Justin. The group's goal is to live the life of free men and philosophers while supporting themselves through a trade, printing. The members are Bernard Jusserand and his wife; Testevel, a moody bachelor; Jean-Paul Sénac, an alcoholic poet; a painter, Brénugat, and his wife and child; and Armand Larseneur, a pianist. Picquenart is the typographer who teaches them the printing trade and Mme Clovis is their housekeeper, soon fired for stealing wine. Unfortunately, because of their idealism the group forgets to cope with the exigencies of daily life as well as the foibles and flaws in each other; thus, meager funds and disparate personalities eventually break up this ostensibly idyllic experiment. Justin feels that if people of supposed intelligence and good will are incapable of getting along then harmony in the everyday world must be impossible. Yet, though he

cannot make the group members love and respect him enough to follow his leadership nor make them love and respect one another as he does them, Justin cannot turn away from these aspirations. Duhamel illustrates superbly both the disparity between real and ideal worlds and, through Justin, his own desire always to strive for the latter.

Les Maîtres (The Masters, 1937) consists of letters from Laurent, once again working in a Paris laboratory, to Justin, employed in a Roubaix factory. The novel describes Laurent's contact with two superiors whom he very much admires: Nicolas Rohner, the cerebral scientist, and Olivier Chalgrin, the humanitarian. His association with these brilliant men eventually reveals their rivalry which Laurent, amazed at such pettiness, follows. The one-upmanship becomes so intense that every member of the scientific community feels obliged to take sides. In a final and moving scene, Chalgrin walks up to Rohner at an Academy of Science meeting to extend his apologies, but Rohner refuses them and the sensitive Chalgrin suffers a stroke. Their competition serves to establish the dichotomy between two types of individuals. Rohner represents the cold, rational, and objective scientist who thinks only of his work and not the people involved. The autopsy of Catherine Houdoire, a lab assistant who had contracted the disease that she was studying, illustrates this vividly. Rohner dissects her body to prove his theories on the cause of death and, worse, distorts his findings to support his hypothesis. However, Chalgrin, the objective yet understanding scientist involved in humanity's problems, is overly compassionate and hypersensitive and, thus, represents another extreme. Laurent tries valiantly to adopt a middle-of-the-road attitude, reasoning that no one should be so weakly structured as to be swayed by extremes. He is working on a formula for his future which now precludes hero worship in what, with each volume, becomes increasingly an account of Laurent's progress toward wisdom.

Cécile parmi nous (1938; translated as *Cécile Among the Pasquiers,* 1940) concentrates on Cécile's unfortunate marriage to the self-centered dilettante Richard Fauvet. Unhappy with her husband, Cécile concentrates all her love on her son Alexandre and on her music. Richard, aware and ashamed that he cannot inspire love in his wife, devotes his time to literary endeavors. However, as the head of a literary group, he faces this same problem: he is a sterile being who never prompts affection in anyone. Furthermore, the more deeply Fauvet feels his deficiencies, the greater is his desire to hurt his wife. He is at his cruelest when he flirts with Suzanne in full view of his wife who is performing on the concert stage. The last bond disappears when Alexandre dies. There is no reason for the couple to remain together, for as Cécile admits, the desire to have a child is the reason she married. The mother's love for her child is the most touching aspect of the novel. Alexandre is the center of Cécile's world and brings her the most intense of all joys, making his death all the more unbearable. Laurent is seen as Cécile's support (as is her newly found religious fervor), and their closeness to and understanding of one another, evident from the time they were children, reaches a crescendo in this volume. Laurent is by now Duhamel's ideal human being, endowed with all the traits necessary to a doctor and humanitarian.

Laurent is thirty-three when *Le Combat contre les ombres* (The Struggle Against Shadows, 1939) opens. It is 1914, just before the outbreak of World War I, and he is director of the service which prepares vaccines and serums at the National Institute of Biology. The institute's director, Larminat, places an inept assistant, Hippolyte Birault, in Laurent's laboratory. When Laurent dismisses Birault because of incompetence, Larminat reinstates him. Apparently, the director gave the position to Birault as a favor to a minister who had done much for the institute. Laurent, infuriated by his boss's lack of integrity, follows the suggestion of a fellow scientist, Vuillaume, and writes a newspaper article about the political manipulations which go on in the laboratories. This unleashes a torrent of articles and places Laurent in the center of a controversy. As time passes, he realizes that his friends are either too weak to side with him or remain uninvolved. Laurent resigns his position, and ironically, it is offered to Vuillaume. Only Jacqueline Bellec, with whom Laurent falls in love and whom he eventually marries, alleviates the pressure. Duhamel's message is clear in what comes very close to being a thesis novel: science and politics do not mix. There is no room in the laboratory for a political appointee because the researcher, whose task it is to help humanity as a whole, should be above such concerns and move, instead, toward a scientific goal.

The ninth volume, *Suzanne et les jeunes hommes* (1941; translated as *Suzanne*, 1946), is the least interesting, perhaps because its central character is as boring as she is beautiful. The novel deals almost exclusively with the twenty-nine-year-old Suzanne's theatrical career, to which she has devoted herself entirely. In fact, she boasts to Eric Vidame, director of the Théâtre des Carmes and for whom she works, that she knows fifty different roles. Nonetheless, instead of giving her the female lead in *King Lear* which she wants and merits, Vidame gives it to an unqualified actress who is the mistress of the company's producer. Furious, Suzanne leaves the troupe and accepts the invitation of a friend, Philippe Baudouin, to stay with his family in the country. But when a member of the troupe arrives and suggests that Suzanne leave with them on a South American tour, she does, forty-eight hours later and much to the distress of Philippe and his love-struck brothers. There is virtually nothing of interest in this novel. Only Duhamel's ironic view of the theater world has any bite. Furthermore, there is little suspense because the tension which might have been created by a woman struggling to reconcile love and career simply is not there. Suzanne, too preoccupied with her appearance, is not up to it. Nor is Duhamel, who seems content to fall back on the familiar themes of nature and the family. However, both the harmonious Baudouin clan and their idyllic bucolic backdrop are too good to be true and only serve to stretch credulity. France was occupied by the Nazis when Duhamel wrote this volume, and it appears that he wanted to provide for himself and his readers a diversion from their painful reality rather than a well-constructed novel.

The last of the Pasquier cycle, *La Passion de Joseph Pasquier* (1941; translated as *Joseph Pasquier*, 1946), analyzes Joseph's world and downfall. Inestimably rich now, Joseph decides that the height of recognition would be to become a member of the Académie Française. The novel follows his fruitless efforts as well as some business undertakings mishandled because of his new obsession. Furthermore, his egocentrism blinds him to the unhappiness of his entire entourage. His assistant Blaise Delmute resigns because he finds Joseph no longer a cutthroat businessman. Joseph's mistress is unfaithful, and his unfaithful wife leaves him. His three children are maladjusted, although Lucien, the older of the two sons, survives by being a carbon copy of his father. His younger son, Jean-Pierre, whom he had always disparaged because of his desire to be a painter, jumps out the window of their home and is

Duhamel with his grandchildren at his country home in Valmondois

gravely injured. The volume ends as Laurent, coming to the boy's aid, cannot tell Joseph if his son will survive or not. A sense of doom and futility reigns, in large part because of Joseph's attitude that money is the sine qua non of life.

But not only does disorder dominate Joseph and his family, it marks the original Pasquier clan as well. Papa Pasquier is dead; Suzanne is still in South America; Cécile is on tour in the United States and Ferdinand, always in the shadows, is lost in his hypochondria, even more so than before. Laurent, with whom Mme Pasquier now lives, is the only one to have found true happiness in life. And ironically, although critical opinion of Duhamel's *Chronique des Pasquier* was uniformly favorable, the dissent that did emerge was provoked by the last five volumes which focused on an individual family member, leaving the others either partially or totally eclipsed. Nonetheless, even today readers finish the series understanding the Pasquiers and feeling that the family's struggles are theirs, and for many, the warmth of the Pasquier clan and the human sentiments which permeate their chronicles have made Duhamel a French Dickens.

During the 1930s, while the majority of the Pasquier books were being published, Duhamel was also producing political commentary, in large part inspired by the rise of the Third Reich. These publications document Duhamel's movement from the desire for a rapprochement with Germany after World War I to total repudiation of the country after World War II. *Défense des lettres* (1937; translated as *In Defense of Letters*, 1938) is a group of essays and meditations in which the writer speaks out against Hitler's methods and plans, while the title work of *Le Dernier voyage de Candide, suivi d'un choix de nouvelles* (Candide's Last Voyage and Other Stories, 1938) is a short story which voices the writer's fear of a holocaust. Written after Germany's invasion of Czechoslovakia, *Mémorial de la guerre blanche* (1939; translated that year as *The White War of 1938*) portrays the Munich Pact as an armistice rather than a peace treaty since it had only served to delay Germany's march. *Positions françaises* (1940; translated that year as *Why France Fights*) uses a plant analogy to explain why France would have to fend off conquest and destruction anyway she could. *Lieu d'asile* (Place for

Shelter, 1940) is a journal which Duhamel kept while working once again as a doctor for war casualties, a text which serves as a sequel to *Vie des martyrs* and *Civilisation*. Finally, in 1944 Duhamel spoke out against the German occupation in the aptly titled *Chronique des saisons amères, 1940-1943* (Chronicle of the Bitter Seasons).

While several types of novels flourished in France after World War II–psychological and antipsychological, those with plots and the plotless, those with heroes and with antiheroes–Duhamel's novels were all written in a traditional manner. His postwar texts center almost exclusively upon religious matters: God, the soul, evil, and human destiny. The first of these, *Le Voyage de Patrice Périot* (1950; translated as *Patrice Periot*, 1952), is the story of a man who looks for an answer in God when his son commits suicide. Also preoccupied with God is *Cri des profondeurs* (1951; translated as *Cry out of the Depths*, 1953), the study of a coward, Félix Tallemand, who wishes to give the impression of being on the side of God and justice. *Les Voyageurs de l'Espérance* (The Voyagers of Hope, 1953) is an update of the story of Noah in which the Fromond family finds safety in their ship, Hope, after an atomic blast has almost covered the earth with water. *L'Archange de l'aventure* (The Archangel of Adventure, 1956) focuses on Cyprien Ricord who, suffering from the loss of his wife, finds faith through his son. Published in the same year, *Les Compagnons de l'Apocalypse* (Companions of the Apocalypse) satirizes self-styled missionaries through its principal character, Dan Traveler. Finally, *Le Complexe de Théophile* (Théophile's Complex, 1958) is another attempt to define God.

However, as he did while he was writing *Chronique des Pasquier,* during this period Duhamel continued to produce a variety of essays. In *Manuel du protestataire* (Manual of the Protestor, 1952), he insists that the state is becoming too powerful, a theme he repeats in *Problèmes de l'heure* (Problems of the Hour, 1957). Duhamel

the humanist speaks out when in *Refuges de lecture* (Reading, a Refuge, 1954) he suggests reading as an escape from a humdrum existence. And in *Problèmes de civilisation* (1962), the writer expresses his most fundamental belief when he says that man must partake of life as profoundly as possible. Significantly, this attitude is also found in *Nouvelles du sombre empire* (News of the Somber Empire, 1960), Duhamel's last novel. The hero, Lestrangier, commits suicide and is sent to Gehenna, a hell which is a replica of his earth life. At the novel's end, Lestrangier realizes that the incident was a bad dream. He is not dead at all and, indeed, is very grateful to be alive. Duhamel's philosophy is clear: while it is true that there is much to correct in the world, there is no greater experience than life itself. Duhamel's own life was a testimony to this belief.

Georges Duhamel died on 13 April 1966 in his country home in the Valmondois. His books, though still read, are no longer the best-sellers that they once were; yet the message of harmony which pervades all his works remains pertinent today.

Bibliographies:
Marcel Saurin, *Les Ecrits de Georges Duhamel* (Paris: Mercure de France, 1951);
Jacques J. Zéphir, *Bibliographie duhamélienne: Essai de bibliographie des études en langue française sur l'œuvre de Georges Duhamel* (Paris: Nizet, 1972).

References:
William Falls, *Le Message humain de Georges Duhamel* (Paris: Boivin, 1948);
L. Clark Keating, *Critic of Civilization* (Lexington: University of Kentucky Press, 1965);
Bettina L. Knapp, *Georges Duhamel* (New York: Twayne, 1972);
César Santelli, *Georges Duhamel, l'homme, l'œuvre* (Paris: Bordas, 1947);
Pierre-Henri Simon, *Georges Duhamel* (Paris: Les Editions du Temps Present, 1946).

Maurice Genevoix

(29 November 1890-8 September 1980)

Alain D. Ranwez

Metropolitan State College

BOOKS: *Sous Verdun, août-octobre 1914* (Paris: Hachette, 1916); translated by H. Grahame Richards as *Neath Verdun, August-October, 1914* (London: Hutchinson, 1916; New York: Stokes, 1917); revised in *Ceux de 14* (1950);

Nuits de guerre (Hauts de Meuse) (Paris: Flammarion, 1917); revised in *Ceux de 14* (1950);

Au seuil des guitounes (Paris: Flammarion, 1918);

Jeanne Robelin (Paris: Flammarion, 1920);

La Boue (Paris: Flammarion, 1921); revised in *Ceux de 14* (1950);

Rémi des Rauches (Paris: Flammarion, 1922);

Les Eparges (Paris: Flammarion, 1923); revised in *Ceux de 14* (1950);

Euthymos, vainqueur olympique (Paris: Flammarion, 1924);

La Joie (Paris: Flammarion, 1924);

Raboliot (Paris: Grasset, 1925);

La Boîte à pêche (Paris: Grasset, 1926);

Les Mains vides (Paris: Grasset, 1928);

Cyrille (Paris: Flammarion, 1929);

L'Assassin (Paris: Flammarion, 1930);

Rroû (Paris: Flammarion, 1931); translated by Alice Grant Rosman (London & New York: Putnam's, 1932; New York: Minton Balch, 1932);

Gai-l'Amour (Paris: Flammarion, 1932);

Forêt voisine (Paris: Flammarion, 1933);

Jours de la Marne (Paris: Flammarion, 1933);

Marcheloup (Paris: Flammarion, 1934);

Tête baissée (Paris: Flammarion, 1935);

Le Jardin dans l'île (Paris: Flammarion, 1936);

Bernard (Paris: Flammarion, 1938);

Les Compagnons de l'Aubepin: Livre de lecture courante, by Genevoix and Pierre Carré (Paris: Hachette, 1938);

La Dernière Harde (Paris: Flammarion, 1938); translated by Warre Bradley Wells as *The Last Hunt* (London: Allen & Unwin, 1940; New York: Random House, 1940);

L'Hirondelle qui fit le printemps (Paris: Flammarion, 1941);

Maurice Genevoix

Laframboise et Belle humeur (Paris: Editions de l'Arbre, 1941);

Eve Charlebois (Paris: Flammarion, 1944);

Canada (Paris: Flammarion, 1945);

Sanglar (Paris: Flammarion, 1946); revised as *La Motte rouge* (Paris: Seuil, 1979);

L'Ecureuil du Bois-bourru (Paris: Flammarion, 1947);

Discours de réception de Maurice Genevoix à l'Académie Française et réponse de André Chaumeix de l'Académie Française, 18 novembre 1947 (Paris: Flammarion, 1948);

Afrique blanche, Afrique noire (Paris: Flammarion, 1949);

Ceux de 14 (Paris: Flammarion, 1950)—comprises *Sous Verdun, Nuits de guerre, La Boue,* and *Les Eparges;*

L'Aventure est en nous (Paris: Flammarion, 1952);

Fatou Cissé (Paris: Flammarion, 1954);

Vlaminck (Paris: Flammarion, 1954);

Le Dernier Quart d'heure . . . (Paris: Table Ronde, 1955);

Le Roman de Renard (Paris: Presses de la Cité, 1958); translated by Margaret Crosland as *The Story of Reynard* (London: Hamilton, 1959);

Mon Ami l'écureuil (Paris: Bias, 1959);

Poissons (Paris: Chêne, 1959);

Routes de l'aventure (Paris: Presses de la Cité, 1959);

Au cadran de mon clocher (Paris: Presses de la Cité, 1960);

Le Petit Chat (Paris: Arts et Métiers Graphiques, 1960);

Vaincre à Olympie (Paris: Livre Contemporain, 1960);

Jeux de glaces (Paris: Wesmael-Charlier, 1961);

La Loire, Agnès et les garçons (Paris: Presses de la Cité, 1962);

Les Deux Lutins (Paris & Tournai: Casterman, 1962);

Derrière les collines (Paris: Presses de la Cité, 1963);

Beau-François (Paris: Presses de la Cité, 1965);

Christian Caillard (Neuchâtel: Ides et Calendes, 1965);

La Forêt perdue (Paris: Plon, 1967);

Jardins sans murs (Paris: Plon, 1968);

Bestiaire enchanté (Paris: Plon, 1969);

Tendre Bestiaire (Paris: Plon, 1969);

Maurice Genevoix. Trois Textes de l'auteur, suivis d'articles critiques (Paris: Diderot, 1970);

Bestiaire sans oubli (Paris: Plon, 1971);

Le Bestiaire d'Edouard Marcel Sandoz, by Genevoix and Sylvio Acatos (Lausanne: Bibliothèque des Arts, 1972);

La Mort de près (Paris: Plon, 1972);

La Grèce de Caramanlis; ou, La Démocratie difficile? (Paris: Plon, 1972); translated by Constantin Tsatsos as *The Greece of Karamanlis* (London: Doric, 1973);

Terre natale (Geneva: Edito-Service, 1973);

La Perpétuité (Paris: R. Julliard, 1974);

Un Jour (Paris: Seuil, 1976);

Solognots de Sologne (Paris: Chêne, 1977);

Lorelei (Paris: Seuil, 1978);

Je verrai, si tu veux, les pays de la neige (Paris: Flammarion, 1980);

Trente Mille Jours (Paris: Seuil, 1980).

Collections: *Œuvres complètes de Maurice Genevoix*, 20 volumes (Paris: Diderot, 1970-1972);

Œuvres complètes, 22 volumes (Geneva: Edito-service, 1973-1978).

OTHER: *Orléannais*, introduction by Genevoix, photographs by Jacques Boulas, notes by Georges Monmarché (Paris: Hachette, 1956).

Early in his literary career Maurice Genevoix emerged as an important witness of his time because of his personal experience at the battle of the Marne, recounted in his tetralogy *Ceux de 14* (The Men of 1914), whose title refers to the soldiers of World War I. This work remains one of the most poignant accounts of the war. Genevoix's acute sense of observation was later transferred to the world of nature, and he became a well-known author of regional novels. His success was assured when he received the Prix Goncourt in 1925 for *Raboliot*, a regional novel which, in his typical manner, exalts the visible beauties of nature and its hidden secrets. Continuing in the literary style of the nineteenth-century writer Guy de Maupassant, Genevoix's realism accentuates those individuals who are frustrated in their desire to remain apart from the laws of the socialized world. An internationally recognized lecturer, he was elected to the Académie Française on 24 October 1946 and was formally inducted the following year. From 1958 until 1973 he served as its Secretary in Perpetuity, a position which he used to become one of France's most ardent defenders of the native language.

Maurice-Charles-Louis-Genevoix was born on an island in the River Loire at Decize (Nièvre). He was the son of Gabriel Genevoix, a notary's clerk, and his wife, Camille Balichon Genevoix. He spent his childhood in the town of Châteauneuf-sur-Loire, which would become an important literary background for his fictional work. Some of his childhood experiences are reflected in his masterly and mellow volume of memoirs, *Trente Mille Jours* (Thirty Thousand Days, 1980). He first attended the local school, then transferred to the lycée of Orléans in 1901; he later studied at the Lycée Lakanal in Sceaux in order to prepare for the Ecole Normale Supérieure in Paris, where he was accepted in 1912. A superior student, Genevoix was first in his class (1914) and seemed destined to become one of France's most renowned academicians–the scholarly treatise he wrote on Guy de Maupassant for the *Diplôme d'Etudes Supérieures* attests to his promise–but World War I ended his university life. Mobilized in 1914, he was quickly promoted to lieutenant and fought heroically on the front. Genevoix was seriously wounded on 25 April 1915 at the battle of the Marne and returned to Paris, where later he did charity work for French orphans. The battle left a deep impression on the young soldier, and he devoted his many months of convalescence to recounting his war experiences. His first book, entitled *Sous Verdun, août-octobre 1914* (1916; translated that year as *Neath Verdun*), was the initial volume of the tetralogy *Ceux de 14,* which also includes *Nuits de guerre (Hauts de Meuse)* (Nights of War [Heights of Meuse], 1917), *La Boue* (The Mud, 1921), and *Les Éparges* (Eparges, 1923). *Sous Verdun* provides a straightforward account of the horror of the war experience and was well received by the press. Genevoix's talent in achieving an acute realism made him a celebrated witness and also quickly labeled him an "écrivain de guerre" whose words represented a protest against all war and a pacifist cry against those forces which would shatter man's harmony with nature.

For reasons of health (he had had Spanish influenza) Genevoix returned to his beloved Loire region in 1919; the area remained his home for thirty years. At first he lived in what he called "la maison paternelle" in Châteauneuf, with his father. He was married twice, the first time to Yvonne Montrosier, the second to Suzanne Neyrolles. He returned to Paris in 1950 and assumed in 1958 his responsibilities as secretary of the Académie Française. The Loire years proved to be prodigious for the writer. Genevoix seemed to rediscover his subconscious self and his harmony with nature–most notably with the Loire river itself. In 1922 he received a Florence Blumenthal Foundation grant to help him develop as a professional writer. The judging panel consisted of a number of well-known individuals, among the most renowned of whom were André Gide, Marcel Proust, and Paul Valéry. With these funds Genevoix was able to devote his time to the novel he had been preparing. *Rémi des Rauches* (1922) perhaps best reflects the harmonious relationship Genevoix experienced with his native countryside. It is a regional novel falling into the well-defined category of fictional works dealing with an existing geographical location which is not only the setting for the action but a moving force behind events as well. Typically, reality is minutely observed and the description is as important as the narration. The characters are integrated into the landscape and form a part of it,

giving the area an animate expression. Genevoix set his first regional novel in the area he knew best, although instead of Châteauneuf he used the pre-Revolutionary name of Portvieux. This region had not been generally featured in French literature, and consequently, his novel proved to be informative about the area's topography and the various occupations of its inhabitants. *Rémi des Rauches,* one of Genevoix's most celebrated novels, was considered a strong candidate for the Prix Goncourt but it failed to win the award because of internal politics. In a naturalistic manner similar to that of Emile Zola, Genevoix stresses the ambivalent relationship man has with nature, which both fascinates and destroys. This theme continues to be evident in other books, including his prize-winning novel *Raboliot.*

In this novel Genevoix makes use of a rural setting where his hero, Raboliot, suffers the nostalgia of a paradise lost. Rich in regional vocabulary and dialect, this novel traces the life of a poacher pursued by the law who finds refuge and solace in the woods. The themes of man separated from nature and menaced by the progress of the mechanized world reappear in many of Genevoix's works, most notably in *Rroû* (1931; translated, 1932), *La Dernière Harde* (1938; translated as *The Last Hunt,* 1940), and *La Forêt perdue* (The Lost Forest, 1967). The first, the story of a cat's adventures, is rich in local lore and colloquialisms. In it Genevoix proves himself to be, along with Colette, one of the outstanding writers of animal stories in early-twentieth-century France.

In 1928 Genevoix's father died and Genevoix left Châteauneuf and the house he had shared with his father, moving to Vernelles in the nearby Loiret, where he bought a home in 1929. It was also at that time that he began his series of travels abroad: Canada, Scandinavia, Mexico, and Africa. Africa was preferred by the author for its primitive beauty; he dedicated a long essay to it in 1949 entitled *Afrique blanche, Afrique noire* (White Africa, Black Africa), but Canada was likewise important. Besides novels in which the heroes are primitive and instinctive beings refusing to bend to man's social law, Genevoix wrote a number of works devoted to the description of nature and its wonders–*La Boîte à pêche* (The Fishing Tackle Box, 1926), *Forêt voisine* (Nearby Forest, 1933), for example–and short narratives depicting animals, such as *L'Hirondelle qui fit le printemps* (The Swallow Who Made Spring, 1941) and *L'Écureuil du Bois-bourru* (The Squirrel of Gruff Woods, 1947). He also wrote a curious sports novel, *Euthymos, vainqueur olympique* (Euthymos, Olympic Conquerer, 1924), and a somber tragedy, *Cyrille* (1929), whose characters belong to the peasantry. His trilogy, comprising *Marcheloup* (1934), *Tête baissée* (Bowed Head, 1935), and *Bernard* (1938), provides an astute portrayal of French rural life between the two world wars. In *Beau-François* (Handsome Francis, 1965), he recounts and develops in a flavorful style which imitates oral recitation provincial legends that are centuries old.

Throughout his literary work, whether it be fiction or nonfiction, Genevoix remains faithful to his desire to be an objective observer. Even his relatively few essays on literature avoid a theoretical approach, preferring that the literary work define itself. His principal aim was to capture the impressions nature makes upon man, for Genevoix believed that understanding nature led directly to a truer understanding of oneself. This attempt was no easy task, for it required Genevoix to interpret many characters, as in his *Bestiaire enchanté* (Enchanted Bestiary, 1969) and *Tendre Bestiaire* (Tender Bestiary, 1969), whose awareness was on a nonverbal level.

In 1970 Genevoix, who was the president of the program committee of French state radio, inaugurated a television series dedicated to presenting French authors. That same year he was awarded the Grand Prix National de Lettres. Although he was often criticized for not considering a philosophy or a specific moral commitment in his literary work, his collective opus is still appreciated by a public sensitive to the idea that man must remain faithfully integrated with nature. It is also the work of a superb stylist. With sensitivity to speech and literary nuance, his language combines colloquial terms with learned words and imperfect subjunctives and similarly blends charming wit and familiar observations with astute judgments and, ultimately, with the views of a *moraliste,* or critic of behavior. He is likewise important for his portrayals of two regions—the Orléanais and Sologne—some of whose provincial legends and customs are reflected in his work; in this respect he represents the continuation in twentieth-century France of an important literary tradition.

André Gide

(22 November 1869-19 February 1951)

Elaine D. Cancalon
Florida State University

SELECTED BOOKS: *Les Cahiers d'André Walter*, anonymous (Paris: Didier-Perrin, 1891); translated by Wade Baskin as *The Notebooks of André Walter* (New York: Philosophical Library, 1968; London: Owen, 1968);

Le Traité du Narcisse (Paris: Librairie de l'Art Indépendant, 1891); translated as *Narcissus* in *The Return of the Prodigal . . .* (1953);

Les Poésies d'André Walter, anonymous (Paris: Librairie de l'Art Indépendant, 1892);

La Tentative amoureuse (Paris: Librairie de l'Art Indépendant, 1893); translated as *The Lovers' Attempt* in *The Return of the Prodigal . . .* (1953);

Le Voyage d'Urien (Paris: Librairie de l'Art Indépendant, 1893); translated by Baskin as *Urien's Voyage* (New York: Philosophical Library, 1964; London: Owen, 1964);

Paludes (Paris: Librairie de l'Art Indépendant, 1895); translated in *Marshlands and Prometheus Misbound* (1953);

Les Nourritures terrestres (Paris: Mercure de France, 1897); translated in *The Fruits of the Earth* (1949);

Le Prométhée mal enchaîné (Paris: Mercure de France, 1899); translated by Lilian Rothermere as *Prometheus Illbound* (London: Chatto & Windus, 1919); translated again in *Marshlands and Prometheus Misbound* (1953);

Philoctète (Paris: Mercure de France, 1899)—comprises *Philoctète, Le Traité du Narcisse, La Tentative amoureuse,* and *El Hadj;* translated in *The Return of the Prodigal . . .* (1953);

Feuilles de route, 1895-1896 (Brussells: Printed by Vandersypen, 1899);

Lettres à Angèle, 1898-1899 (Paris: Mercure de France, 1900);

Le Roi Candaule (Paris: Revue Blanche, 1901);

L'Immoraliste (Paris: Mercure de France, 1902); translated by Dorothy Bussy as *The Immoralist* (New York: Knopf, 1930; London: Cassell, 1930);

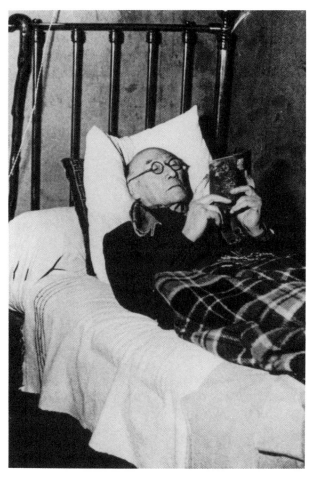

André Gide (Dominique Darbois)

Saül (Paris: Mercure de France, 1903); enlarged edition (1904)—adds a preface by the author and his "De l'évolution du théâtre"; translated in *The Return of the Prodigal . . .* (1953);

Prétextes: Réflexions sur quelques points de littérature et de morale (Paris: Mercure de France, 1903; enlarged, 1913); translated by Angelo P. Bertocci and others as *Pretexts: Reflections on Literature and Morality,* edited by Justin

O'Brien (London: Secker & Warburg, 1959; New York: Meridian, 1959);

Amyntas (Paris: Mercure de France, 1906); translated by Villiers David (London: Bodley Head, 1958);

Le Retour de l'enfant prodigue (Paris: Edité par "Vers et Prose," 1907); translated in *The Return of the Prodigal . . .* (1953);

La Porte étroite (Paris: Mercure de France, 1909); translated by Bussy as *Strait is the Gate* (New York: Knopf, 1924; London: Jarrolds, 1924);

Oscar Wilde: In Memoriam (souvenirs); Le "De Profundis" (Paris: Mercure de France, 1910); translated by Bernard Frechtman as *Oscar Wilde: In Memoriam (Reminiscences). "De Profundis"* (New York: Philosophical Library, 1949); translated as *Oscar Wilde* (London: Kimber, 1951);

Nouveaux Prétextes: Réflexions sur quelques points de Littérature et de Morale (Paris: Mercure de France, 1911);

C.R.D.N., anonymous (Bruges: Imprimerie Sainte-Catherine, 1911); enlarged as *Corydon* (1920); trade edition, signed by Gide (Paris: Gallimard, 1924; enlarged, 1929); translated anonymously (New York: Farrar, Straus, 1950; London: Secker & Warburg, 1952);

Isabelle (Paris: Nouvelle Revue Française/Marcel Rivière, 1911); translated in *Two Symphonies* (1931);

Bethsabé (Paris: Bibliothèque de l'Occident, 1912); translated as *Bathsheba* in *The Return of the Prodigal . . .* (1953);

Souvenirs de la cour d'assises (Paris: Nouvelle Revue Française, 1914);

Les Caves du Vatican, 2 volumes (Paris: Nouvelle Revue Française, 1914); translated by Bussy as *The Vatican Swindle* (New York: Knopf, 1925); Bussy's translation republished as *Lafcadio's Adventures* (New York: Knopf, 1927) and as *The Vatican Cellars* (London: Cassell, 1952);

La Symphonie pastorale (Paris: Gallimard, 1919); translated as *The Pastoral Symphony* in *Two Symphonies* (1931);

Si le grain ne meurt, 2 volumes (Bruges: Imprimerie Sainte-Catherine, 1920, 1921); translated by Bussy as *If It Die . . .* , 1 volume (New York: Random House, 1935; London: Secker & Warburg, 1950);

Morceaux choisis (Paris: Gallimard, 1921);

André Gide [Pages choisies] (Paris: Georges Crès, 1921);

Numquid et tu . . . ?, anonymous (Bruges: Imprimerie Sainte-Catherine, 1922); trade edition signed by Gide (Paris: Editions de la Pléiade/J. Schiffrin, 1926); translated in *The Journals of André Gide* (1947-1951);

Dostoïevsky (Paris: Plon-Nourrit, 1923); translated by Arnold Bennett as *Dostoyevsky* (London & Toronto: Dent, 1925; New York: Knopf, 1926);

Incidences (Paris: Gallimard, 1924);

Les Faux-Monnayeurs (Paris: Gallimard, 1925); translated by Bussy as *The Counterfeiters* (New York: Knopf, 1927; London & New York: Knopf, 1928); republished as *The Coiners* (London: Cassell, 1950);

Le Journal des Faux-Monnayeurs (Paris: Editions Eos, 1926); translated by Justin O'Brien as *Logbook of The Coiners* (London: Cassell, 1952);

Voyage au Congo (Paris: Gallimard, 1927); translated in *Travels in the Congo* (1929);

Le Retour du Tchad: Carnets de route (Paris: Gallimard, 1928); translated as *Return from Lake Chad* in *Travels in the Congo* (1929);

L'Ecole des femmes (Paris: Gallimard, 1929); translated by Bussy as *The School for Wives* (New York: Knopf, 1929);

Travels in the Congo, translated by Bussy (New York: Knopf, 1929)–comprises *Voyage au Congo* and *Le Retour du Tchad;*

Essai sur Montaigne (Paris: J. Schiffrin/Editions de la Pléiade, 1929); translated by Stephen H. Guest and Trevor E. Blewitt as *Montaigne: An Essay in Two Parts* (London: Blackamore Press/New York: Liveright, 1929);

Robert (Paris: Gallimard, 1930); translated in *The School for Wives . . .* (1950);

Œdipe (Paris: Editions de la Pléiade, 1931); translated in *Two Legends* (1950);

Two Symphonies, translated by Bussy (New York: Knopf, 1931; London: Cassell, 1931)–comprises *Isabelle* and *La Symphonie pastorale;*

Pages de journal (1929-1932) (Paris: Gallimard, 1934);

Les Nouvelles Nourritures (Paris: Gallimard, 1935); translated in *The Fruits of the Earth* (1949);

Nouvelles Pages de journal (1932-1935) (Paris: Gallimard, 1935);

Geneviève (Paris: Gallimard, 1936); translated in *The School for Wives . . .* (1950);

Retour de l'U.R.S.S. (Paris: Gallimard, 1936); translated by Bussy as *Return from the U.S.S.R.* (New York: Knopf, 1937; London: Secker & Warburg, 1937); Bussy's translation republished as *Back from the U.S.S.R.* (London: Secker & Warburg, 1937);

Retouches à mon Retour de l'U.R.S.S. (Paris: Gallimard, 1937); translated by Bussy as *Afterthoughts: A Sequel to "Back from the U.S.S.R."* (London: Secker & Warburg, 1938); Bussy's translation republished as *Afterthoughts on the U.S.S.R.* (New York: Dial, 1938);

Journal. 1889-1939 (Paris: Gallimard, 1939); translated in *The Journals of André Gide* (1947-1951);

Théâtre (Paris: Gallimard, 1942); translated by Jackson Mathews as *My Theater* (New York: Knopf, 1952);

Interviews imaginaires (Yverdon & Lausanne: Editions du Haut Pays, 1943);

Interviews imaginaires. La Délivrance de Tunis (New York: J. Schiffrin, 1943); translated by Malcolm Cowley as *Imaginary Interviews* (New York: Knopf, 1944);

Pages de journal (1939-1942) (New York: J. Schiffrin, 1944; Alger: Charlot, 1944; enlarged edition, Paris: Gallimard, 1946); translated in *The Journals of André Gide* (1947-1951);

Thésée (New York: J. Schiffrin, 1946; Paris: Gallimard, 1946); translated by John Russell as *Theseus* (London: Horizon, 1948; New York: New Directions, 1949);

Le Retour (Neuchâtel & Paris: Ides et Calendes, 1946);

Et nunc manet in te (Neuchâtel: Richard Heyd, 1947); translated by Keene Wallis as *The Secret Drama of My Life* (Paris & New York: Boar's Head Books, 1951); enlarged edition of original French version, *Et Nunc manet in te, suivi de Journal intime* (Neuchâtel: Ides et Calendes, 1951); translated by Justin O'Brien as *Madeleine* (New York: Knopf, 1952); translated by O'Brien as *Et nunc Manet in te and Intimate Journal* (London: Secker & Warburg, 1952);

Paul Valéry (Paris: Domar, 1947);

Poétique (Neuchâtel & Paris: Ides et Calendes, 1947);

Le Procès; Pièce tirée du roman de Kafka, by Gide and J. L. Barrault (Paris: Gallimard, 1947); translated by Jacqueline and Frank Sundstrom as *The Trial, from the Novel of Franz Kafka* (London: Secker & Warburg, 1950);

The Journals of André Gide, 4 volumes, translated by O'Brien (New York: Knopf, 1947-1951; London: Secker & Warburg, 1947-1955);

Préfaces (Neuchâtel & Paris: Ides et Calendes, 1948);

Rencontres (Neuchâtel & Paris: Ides et Calendes, 1948);

Les Caves du Vatican. Farce en trois actes (Neuchâtel & Paris: Ides et Calendes, 1948);

Eloges (Neuchâtel & Paris: Ides & Calendes, 1948);

Notes sur Chopin (Paris: Arche, 1948); translated by Frechtman as *Notes on Chopin* (New York: Philosophical Library, 1949);

Feuillets d'automne (Paris: Mercure de France, 1949); translated by Elsie Pell as *Autumn Leaves* (New York: Philosophical Library, 1950);

The Fruits of the Earth, translated by Bussy (New York: Knopf, 1949; London: Secker & Warburg, 1949)—comprises *Les Nourritures terrestres* and *Les Nouvelles Nourritures;*

Journal, 1942-1949 (Paris: Gallimard, 1950); translated in *The Journals of André Gide* (1947-1951);

The School for Wives. Robert. Geneviève; or, The Unfinished Confidence, translated by Bussy (New York: Knopf, 1950; London: Cassell, 1953);

Two Legends: Theseus and Oedipus, translated by Russell (New York: Knopf, 1950); Russell's translation republished as *Oedipus and Theseus* (London: Secker & Warburg, 1950);

Ainsi soit-il ou les jeux sont faits (Paris: Gallimard, 1952); translated by O'Brien as *So Be It; or, The Chips are Down* (New York: Knopf, 1959; London: Chatto & Windus, 1960);

The Return of the Prodigal, Preceded by Five Other Treatises, with Saul, A Drama in Five Acts, translated by Bussy (London: Secker & Warburg, 1953)—comprises *Le Traité du Narcisse, La Tentative amoureuse, El Hadj, Philoctète, Bethsabé, Le Retour de l'enfant prodigue,* and *Saül;*

Marshlands and Prometheus Misbound: Two Satires, translated by George D. Painter (New York: New Directions, 1953; London: Secker & Warburg, 1953)—comprises *Paludes* and *Le Prométhée mal enchaîné;*

Ne jugez pas (Paris: Gallimard, 1969);

Le Récit de Michel, edited by Claude Martin (Neuchâtel: Ides et Calendes, 1972).

Collections: *Œuvres complètes d'André Gide,* edited by L. Martin Chauffier, 15 volumes (Paris: Gallimard, 1932-1939);

Le Théâtre complet, 8 volumes (Neuchâtel & Paris: Ides et Calendes, 1947-1949);

Romans, récits et soties, œuvres lyriques, edited by Yvonne Davet and Jean-Jacques Thierry (Paris: Gallimard, 1958).

PLAY PRODUCTIONS: *Le Roi Candaule,* Paris, Nouveau Théâtre, 9 May 1901;

Philoctète, Paris, private performance, 3 April 1919; reading, Paris, Comédie des Champs-Elysées, 16 October 1937;

Saül, Paris, Théâtre du Vieux-Colombier, 16 June 1922;

Le Retour de l'enfant prodigue, Monte-Carlo, Théâtre de Monte-Carlo, 4 December 1928; Paris, Théâtre de l'Avenue, 23 February 1933;

Œdipe, Antwerp, Cercle Artistique, 10 December 1931; Paris, Théâtre de l'Avenue, 18 February 1932;

Les Caves du Vatican, adapted by Gide from his novel, Montreux, Société des Belles-Lettres, 9 December 1933; revised, Paris, Comédie-Française, 13 December 1950;

Perséphone, libretto by Gide, Paris, Opéra, 30 April 1934;

Le Treizième Arbre, Marseilles, Rideau Gris, 8 May 1935; Paris, Théâtre Charles de Rochefort, 13 January 1939;

Robert ou l'intérêt général, Tunis, Théâtre Municipal, 30 April 1946.

OTHER: *Anthologie de la poésie française* (Paris: Gallimard, 1949; New York: Pantheon, 1949).

TRANSLATIONS: Joseph Conrad, *Typhon* (Paris: Nouvelle Revue Française, 1918);

Walt Whitman, *Œuvres choisies,* translated by Gide and others (Paris: Nouvelle Revue Française, 1918);

William Shakespeare, *Antoine et Cléopâtre* (Paris: Lucien Vogel, 1921);

William Blake, *Le Mariage du Ciel et de l'Enfer* (Paris: Claude Aveline, 1923);

Shakespeare, *Hamlet,* bilingual edition (New York: Schiffrin, 1944; Paris: Gallimard, 1946).

André Gide is one of the most important novelists of the first half of the twentieth century. His place in the development of the genre is equal to that of other innovators such as Marcel Proust, James Joyce, and Virginia Woolf. His novels have been translated into more than twenty languages, including Serbo-Croatian, Hebrew, and Bulgarian. The English-speaking world is especially well served since Gide's mastery of written English was excellent, and the numerous translations of his novels by his good friend Dorothy Bussy were done under his direct supervision.

Gide's importance and his influence on the twentieth century extend to several domains: the thematics of his novels champion emancipation in all forms of human behavior; he renewed the form of the novel through aesthetic innovation; his essays and documentary narratives make of him a discerning witness of his times; and multiple prefaces and articles attest to his influence as a literary critic. Gide's international standing was recognized four years before his death, in 1947, when he was awarded the Nobel Prize for literature.

André Paul Guillaume Gide was born on 22 November 1869 in Paris. Gide's family belonged to the rich, upper middle class and to the Protestant faith. Although his mother's family had been Catholic until the eighteenth century, the marriages of his maternal great-grandfather Rondeaux and of his grandfather to Protestant women had well established the Calvinist tradition before Gide's birth. Gide's paternal family came from Uzès, a small town in southern France, while the Rondeaux were of Norman stock. Gide would later use the diversity of his origins to support one of the major themes of his work, that of the necessity and value of contradiction within the individual psyche.

Paul Gide was a respected professor of law at the University of Paris. His son's recollections of him up to his early death in 1880, as expressed in the memoirs *Si le grain ne meurt* (1920, 1921; translated as *If It Die . . . ,* 1935), evoke the image of a gentle, caring person who took time to walk and talk with his *petit ami* but who left more serious decisions concerning the boy's upbringing to his wife. Madame Paul Gide (Juliette Rondeaux) was a perfect example of puritan severity. Every aspect of her son's life, from the clothes he wore to the books he read, was regulated by his mother, who continued to give him advice until her death in 1895, when her son was twenty-five.

This severity, coupled with a precocious sensuality, provoked a struggle within the child which would mark his attitudes and behavior for life. In the Calvinist ethic taught to him by his mother, any outward manifestation of sexuality was equated with sin. Two events narrated in *Si le grain ne meurt* were especially significant. At the age of nine Gide was expelled from school for masturbation and subsequently threatened with castration by a doctor; later on, in 1882 (at age thirteen), the young Gide discovered his aunt in the presence of her lover and consoled his very distressed cousin Madeleine, whom he vowed to protect for the rest of her life. From that time on, sexual love for women was impossible. Gide became emotionally and intellectually attached to Madeleine, and the writer Gide told and retold their story in almost all his works; but the various incarnations of his cousin present an idealized image of woman as sacrificial saint.

After finishing his *baccalauréat* in 1889, Gide decided not to go on to the university, but rather to devote himself immediately to his chosen career as a writer. He had already meditated on a book which he believed would express all he had to say. In 1890 he withdrew to a mountain retreat in Switzerland where he composed *Les Cahiers d'André Walter* (1891; translated as *The Notebooks of André Walter*, 1968). This work, which precedes Gide's contact with the symbolist school, was obviously nourished by the romantic theme of the young, suffering, and misunderstood artist as portrayed in such books as Goethe's *The Sorrows of Young Werther*, which Gide knew through other writers, including Senancour and Novalis. The narrative, written in diary style, contains passages from Gide's personal journal begun years before. It consists of two notebooks, "Le Cahier blanc" ("The White Notebook") and "Le Cahier noir" ("The Black Notebook"), which tell the story of Walter's love for his cousin Emmanuèle, his renunciation of that love in favor of a desired purity, and his final insanity and death. Despite its uncontrolled adolescent lyricism, which Gide himself criticized in a preface written in 1930, these "Notebooks" are of utmost importance for the understanding of the mature works to come. Although they could not possibly represent the sum of his desires and his art, they do establish certain essential aesthetic precedents.

Les Cahiers d'André Walter represents Gide's first experiment in the form of self-conscious fiction which will pervade his entire narrative production. The real author, André Gide (without revealing his identity, the book being published anonymously), writes a story using entries from his own diary about a fictitious character, André Walter (note the obvious reflection created by the use of the same first name and the reference to German romanticism: Werther/Walter), who in turn is writing a book entitled *Allain*. In order to increase the number of layers of composition and to further obscure the fine line between reality and fiction, the manuscript is left posthumously (since Walter dies) to Pierre C. (Pierre Chrysis, pseudonym of the *real* person, Gide's friend Pierre Louÿs, pseudospelling of Louis!) who writes a short explanatory note in which he speaks of Walter as of a real person. In addition to the illusion of depth created by this play of mirror images, the constant reflexivity draws the reader's attention to the actual composition of the work, thereby forcing awareness of the aesthetic devices being used and inviting participation in the creation of the text.

Les Cahiers d'André Walter may not have been the ultimate work its young author hoped it would be, but it pointed the way to the major developments to come. Printed at his own expense, the book sold only a few copies to a small elite, and this "public" failure too signaled a problem not soon to be resolved.

Rather than satisfy the young Gide, the extremism expressed in *Les Cahiers d'André Walter* provoked the need to experiment with an opposing point of view. Already in the first years of his career, Gide's dialogical nature would cause him to write works whose "theorems" represent contradictory poles. Whereas *Les Cahiers d'André Walter* demonstrates the impossibility of happiness through renunciation, *La Tentative amoureuse* (1893; translated as *The Lovers' Attempt* in *The Return of the Prodigal* . . . , 1953), written two years later in 1893, expresses the failure of requited physical love. Luc and Rachel satisfy their desire but are soon bored with their happiness. They fail to realize that anticipation brings greater joy than satisfaction. However, if the characters fail in their experiments because they attempt to carry them out *materially*, Gide, the author, succeeds in exorcising his own demons by giving them an *ideal* expression. This short narrative begins a series of works through which Gide will accomplish a kind of catharsis of his psychic contradictions by expressing them, one by one, in exaggerated literary figures.

The discrepancy between material and ideal manifestations, which Gide expressed in comments on *La Tentative amoureuse,* is certainly a problem raised by his contact with the symbolist movement. Gide had been attending the Tuesday evening meetings at Mallarmé's house ("les mardis de la rue de Rome") since the beginning of 1891. The influence of the school is overpowering in his works written from 1891 to 1893. During this period Gide abandoned the lyrical, romantic style of *Les Cahiers d'André Walter* in order to adopt the subtle conceits and sometimes stereotyped vocabulary of the symbolist poets. And, for a time, he refused all descriptive expression of material and psychological reality in favor of the search for an absolute ideal. His memoirs attest to this conversion: "je tenais pour 'contingence' . . . tout ce qui n'était pas 'absolu.' . . . Pour chacun de mes compagnons il en allait à peu près de même; et l'erreur n'était pas de chercher à dégager quelque beauté et quelque vérité d'ordre général de l'inextricable fouillis que présentait alors le 'réalisme'; mais bien, par parti-pris, de tourner le dos à la réalité" (I considered everything that was not *absolute*–that is to say, the whole prismatic diversity of life–*contingent.* . . . It was very much the same with every one of my companions. But our error did not lie in trying to extract some beauty and some truth of a general order out of the inextricable medley presented at that time by *realism*, but rather in deliberately turning our backs upon reality).

Two works written during this period especially represent the influence of the symbolist school. *Le Traité du Narcisse* (1891; translated as *Narcissus* in *The Return of the Prodigal*, 1953) is a manifesto of symbolist doctrine, and *Le Voyage d'Urien* (1893; translated as *Urien's Voyage*, 1964) is a demonstration of one of its major techniques. *Le Traité du Narcisse* represents Gide's first attempt at reinterpreting the myths of classical antiquity. The meditation occurs in three stages, each centered around a major figure (Narcisse, Adam, and the Poet). In the first stage Narcisse's love of his own image is a symbolist attempt to accomplish fusion between form and idea. By becoming one with his reflection Narcisse would realize the fusion of the material body with the spiritual soul. But Narcisse does not see only himself. In the river of time he observes the multiplicity of things, so many forms which, through multiplication, attempt to attain one absolute, ideal form.

This meditation causes Narcisse, in the second stage, to dream about the perfection of the first paradise. In the Garden of Eden, idea and form, being and appearance were one until Adam dared to question this pure state by breaking a branch of the tree of knowledge. This act caused a schism: perfection was broken into multiple forms, each of which is only an imperfect variation on the original idea. The third stage focuses on the story of the human race as a constant struggle to rejoin form and idea and thereby to return to the lost paradise. Foremost in this struggle is the poet, whose language re-creates a partial paradise and whose work (as Symbol) must "manifest" (suggest, represent) the ultimate truth which lies beyond appearance. The poet is a seer who, like the scientist, searches for the archetype of things and the laws of their succession; but whereas science uses logical reasoning, the poet can "see" through things, penetrate them and arrive at their Essence, which he then endows with his own eternal (artistic) form.

In *Le Voyage d'Urien* Gide gives a perfect demonstration of the symbolist technique according to which the form a work takes is meant not simply to correspond to its content, but also to fuse with that content to such an extent that the two become inseparable. Here, as in any mythic quest, the voyage *is* the search for self and the description of its various stages *is* the soul as it passes from one "landscape" to another. The spiritual odyssey is divided into three symbolic steps: the Pathetic Ocean, warm, delicious, and tempting, represents sensual awakening and desire; the voyage on the Sargasso Sea indicates the stagnation of self-introspection leading to Baudelairean ennui; and the third stage on the Glacial Sea suggests the frozen sterility of metaphysical systems. None of these attempts seems to work, for *Le Voyage d'Urien* (du Rien = of nothing) already contains a hint of the self-criticism and irony with which, a few years later, Gide will attack the impotence and stagnation of literary attitudes at the end of the century.

It was in fact time in Gide's life for a real voyage. In order to escape the stifling atmosphere of the literary salons (of which he had become a faithful participant) as well as the puritanical rigor of his mother's control, Gide left, in the fall of 1893, for a trip to North Africa, which would last until the following spring, leading from Tunis to Biskra by way of Zaghouan, Kairouan, and Sousse. During this trip, Gide discovered the value of the senses. Up to this time his most fervent experiments had been either spiritual or intellectual. The power of sensual awareness had been denied, owing mainly to the constraints imposed by his Calvinist upbringing. Now, coming into contact with a rich, luxuriant nature and a more primitive native population which lived without the comforts of European civilization, Gide was able to discover that knowledge can be gained also through the sensual penetration of an environment. It was also during this first adventure that Gide was to become consciously aware of and express his homosexuality through an en-

*Gide in Biskra, Algeria, during his first visit to Africa, 1893
(Bibliothèque Nationale)*

counter with a young Arab boy. A chance meeting with Oscar Wilde during a second trip to North Africa at the beginning of 1895 further helped him affirm what he would come to consider as his "special nature," homosexuality limited to encounters with adolescent boys (that is, pederasty).

Two works published in 1895 and 1897 attest to the importance of the North African experience: they are *Paludes* (translated as *Marshlands*, 1953), a comical satire of the stifling atmosphere from which Gide had fled, and *Les Nourritures terrestres* (translated as *The Fruits of the Earth*, 1949), a lyrical celebration of the liberation he had experienced.

Paludes is a short piece whose many-leveled irony first signaled a side of Gide's talent later to be developed in the form known as the *sotie*. Not only does *Paludes* (first labeled "treatise" and twenty years later "sotie") satirize the atmosphere of the literary salons but it also calls into question, through parody, Gide's favorite structural

device, the *composition en abyme* (interior reproduction of the text). The young author had taken himself seriously when he invented a suffering romantic hero, André Walter, whose notebooks told of a novel, never to be written, entitled *Allain*. In *Paludes* the protagonist is also writing a story entitled "Paludes," which he describes to the reader in his journal. The main character of his "Paludes," Tityre, also keeps a journal, of which selections are likewise revealed. This multiplication of layers of writing, intertwined with layers of supposed "reality," draws attention to the ambiguity of the process of creation and casts doubt upon its capacity for representation. Even though the author within the story constantly proposes the writing process as proof of the validity of his life, the truth of this claim is questioned by the continual play of mirror reflections which always turns the writing process back on itself and makes it as circular and stagnant as the social behavior which the author shuns.

In Virgil's *Bucolics* Tityrus is happy with his marshy homeland and lacking any desire for adventure. Gide's Tityre lives in the middle of a swamp, "recumbent" and contented to observe the plants and animals which surround him. The protagonist claims that he invents Tityre as an allegorical figure of social and intellectual stagnation. One of his friends acts as a model by exemplifying the routine of a reasonable marriage, thankless work, and conventional fidelity. Most of his other friends spend their time gravitating from one salon to another, engaging in subtle and meaningless gibberish, splitting hairs over pseudointellectual, psychological, and metaphysical problems, repeating the same time-worn ideas in the same clichés. But despite this (not so) implicit criticism of his society, the protagonist is just as incapable of action and experience as his contemporaries. Acts are more virtual than real, listed as possible events in his written agenda. When he fails to live up to this schedule, he simply chalks up the failure on the side of "deficits."

In addition to literary and social criticism, Gide also ridicules his own personal weaknesses in *Paludes*. His inability to tear himself away from the milieu of the Parisian salons (before his African trip) is satirized by the "voyage" the protagonist takes with his companion Angèle. This trip, which is dramatically and repeatedly announced to his friends ("Je pars"–"I am leaving"), gets only as far as a near suburb of Paris. Angèle and the protagonist must come back the same day (Saturday) so as not to miss Sunday church services (certainly a comic allusion to the religious demands of Gide's childhood). Angèle herself is a satirical version of Gide's image of Madeleine Rondeaux as an interceding angel; even though Gide continued to idealize his cousin he was able to rise above his own obsession through the objectivity provided by writing. *Paludes* even goes so far as to poke fun at the platonic relationship between the protagonist and Angèle, a situation which foreshadows the sexual failure of Gide's marriage to Madeleine, which would take place only a few months after the publication of the piece.

Two years later (in 1897) with the publication of *Les Nourritures terrestres*, Gide offered still another example of the evolution of his writing process through statement and counterstatement. Whereas Tityre was borrowed from Virgil and encrusted in the paludian marshland, in *Les Nourritures terrestres* Ménalque is the spokesman for adventure and detachment (Virgil's Menalcus went off to see the city of Rome). *Paludes* was meant to ridicule the artificial intellectuality from which Gide had fled, while *Les Nourritures terrestres* is a spontaneous celebration of the sensual liberation experienced during his African trip.

Les Nourritures terrestres is written in a lyrical style, full of enthusiastic exclamations and enumerations. It has no plot per se but consists rather of descriptions and advice given by the narrator (who has received the same from his mentor Ménalque) to a young disciple known as Nathanaël(=gift of God). It is certainly a major work since it explicitly states and defends Gide's doctrine of individual liberation and establishes that doctrine's basic terminology which will pervade almost all his succeeding works. These key concepts can be best summarized through the use of the terms *dénuement, disponibilité,* and *déracinement.*

Dénuement (denuding) is at the heart of the narrator's explanation to Nathanaël that his first duty is to peel off all the outer layers imposed upon his being by cultural convictions, constraints, and rules, and also by the artificiality of book learning. He must become "nude," pure and innocent as a newborn child, so that his being (like the tabula rasa) is prepared to absorb and benefit from each new experience. In a preface to *Les Nourritures terrestres* written in 1927 Gide emphasized this return to original purity and its relationship to a quasi-religious experience, so as to answer his detractors, who saw in

the book a simple apology for the free reign of instinct.

Disponibilité (availability, openness) follows *dénuement*. Once having peeled away the layers imposed by culture, the individual is free to receive the greatest pleasure possible from each new experience. Each present moment has value in and of itself and must be totally detached from all past and future occurrences. But more important still than the value of the moment itself is the psychic and sensual power with which it is approached. This almost drunken readiness to indulge completely in each brand-new offering of nature is called "fervor."

Dénuement and *disponibilité* assume *déracinement* (uprooting). The young acolyte must learn to break off his roots, to reject both family and friends in order to strike out on his own. One is of course reminded here of Gide's often quoted reply to Maurice Barrès and of the latter's defense of *enracinement* (taking root): "Né à Paris d'un père uzétien et d'une mère normande, où voulez-vous, Monsieur Barrès, que je m'enracine?" (Born in Paris, of a father from Uzès and a mother from Normandy, where, Mr. Barrès, do you expect me to take root?).

Ménalque himself pronounces the celebrated and often criticized aphorism "Familles je vous hais!" (Families I despise you!). For in order to be completely free and *disponible* one must also reject all family ties and material possessions, which can only weaken fervor through subtle offerings of false security. This type of willing detachment goes even further, for the very act of giving advice to a disciple is contrary to the doctrine of complete individual liberty which that advice proposes. One cannot be free if one is bound by obedience to any doctrine, no matter how liberal. This is why the ultimate expression of love from the narrator to Nathanaël is also an ultimate form of detachment: "Nathanaël, jette mon livre; ne t'y satisfais point. Ne crois pas que ta vérité puisse être trouvée par 'quelque autre.... Jette mon livre; dis-toi bien que ce n'est là qu'une des mille postures possibles en face de la vie. Cherche la tienne" (Nathanaël, throw away my book; do not let it satisfy you. Do not think that your truth can be found by some other.... Throw away my book; tell yourself that it represents only one of the thousand possible approaches to life. Seek your own).

The doctrine of total detachment raises the question of responsibility and this discrepancy was also expressed in Gide's private life. After his

Madeleine Rondeaux at Cuverville. Gide's obsession with his cousin culminated in their marriage in October 1895.

first two North African trips, his mother was frightened by the radical turn of his thought. Her objection to Gide's proposed marriage to his cousin was reversed by her desire to see him come under a moderating influence which would eventually replace her own. Madame Gide died in fact in May 1895, and the wedding took place the following October. Gide was not unaware of the sexual problems that his marriage was likely to cause. When he consulted a doctor for advice he was told that marriage would bring out his "real" heterosexual feelings and that he should have no fears. This idyllic situation did not, of course, materialize. If Gide could not have physical relations with Madeleine it was paradoxically because of the intensity of his love for her: in his mind, spiritual and physical love were distinctly separate. His attachment to his wife remained strong and constant, for Gide always believed that she brought out the finest expression of his being: yet, he also realized that complete freedom of expression could only be gained away

from her domination and often in secret. This conflict explains his multiple visits to and departures from Cuverville, their home in Normandy, throughout the years.

Gide's contact with North Africa turned his thoughts away from the artificiality of symbolism and toward a more realistic approach to the novel. His major production from *L'Immoraliste* (1902; translated by Dorothy Bussy in 1930 and by Richard Howard in 1970) consists of novels which depict real characters, well entrenched in a specific social and historical time period. This approach constitutes a definite break with the symbolist school, whose characters were legendary, symbolic figures lacking in individuality and meant to serve the Idea. The novels do, however, consistently demonstrate the influence of Gide's early symbolist training by their emphasis on the intimate relationship between form and content. Any aesthetic interpretation of the works must necessarily point to the integral role of structure in the evolution of thought.

Gide's major novelistic production began in 1902 with *L'Immoraliste* and continued until 1926 with the publication in book form of his most important novel, *Les Faux-Monnayeurs* (1925; translated as *The Counterfeiters*, 1927). It also includes the *récits*, *La Porte étroite* (1909; translated as *Strait is the Gate*, 1924), *Isabelle* (1911; translated in *Two Symphonies*, 1931); *La Symphonie pastorale* (1919; translated as *The Pastoral Symphony* in *Two Symphonies*, 1931), and a *sotie*, *Les Caves du Vatican* (1914; translated as *The Vatican Swindle*, 1925, and later republished as *Lafcadio's Adventures* and as *The Vatican Cellars*). Three more short novels which form a trilogy were published in 1929, 1930, and 1936: *L'Ecole des Femmes* (translated in 1929 as *The School for Wives*), *Robert*, and *Geneviève* (translated with *L'Ecole des femmes*, 1950), but they are of inferior quality. *Thésée* (1946; translated as *Theseus*, 1948) is a short narrative work believed by some critics to summarize Gide's life. Most of the works were first published in successive issues of the *Nouvelle Revue Française*.

L'Immoraliste, *La Porte étroite*, *Isabelle*, and *La Symphonie pastorale* represent variations on the psychological novella, a form which Gide was to make specifically his own. These stories are all told in the first person by a narrator-protagonist who attempts to explain and/or justify certain events in his past, although the complexity of structure increases as other points of view are added. Gide labeled three out of four of these works *récits* (narratives), refusing to call them novels, in a "Projet de Préface" written for *Isabelle* (1911) in 1910: "Le roman, tel que je le reconnais ou l'imagine, comporte une diversité de points de vue, soumise à la diversité des personnages qu'il met en scène; c'est par essence une œuvre déconcertée" (The novel, as I recognize it or conceive of it, includes a diversity of points of view, dependent on the diversity of characters it portrays; it is by its very essence a complicated work of art). If taken as an ensemble, however, these four *récits* already contain all the elements which will be recombined, enriched, and/or satirized in the two major novels. The psychological "case histories" illustrated by the *récits* represent the extreme limits to which each of Gide the man's major preoccupations (obsessions) could be carried. Each protagonist and his or her struggle represent a variation on the quest to attain or produce the absolute. *L'Immoraliste* and *La Porte étroite* set in opposition total freedom and perfect obedience, whereas in *Isabelle* and *La Symphonie pastorale* the narrator-protagonist attempts, through the use of language, to re-create a world of total innocence. By thus giving literary existence to his own multiple contradictions Gide was able to use his writing as a kind of personal catharsis. The complexity of his own nature prevented him from ever espousing only one direction of thought.

The ambiguity of such a multifaceted approach is increased by the use of the first-person narrative perspective. Each one of the *récits* is told by a narrator who is removed in time (to a greater or lesser extent) from the events he is recounting. This distancing creates doubts and questions in the reader's mind as to the reliability of the information transmitted, and eventually as to the credibility of narration itself as a representative act. Such a complex of questions engages the reader in the formation of the text and creates a type of "disquieting fiction" in which the author refuses to conclude or to lead the reader toward the "right" answer. Gide's belief in the merit of this type of writing is evidenced by his preface to *L'Immoraliste* is which he states: "Mais je n'ai voulu faire en ce livre non plus acte d'accusation qu'apologie, et me suis gardé de juger" (But I intended to make this book as little an indictment as an apology and took care to pass no judgment).

The story of *L'Immoraliste* was obviously taken to a large extent from Gide's North African experience, but most of the elements were largely transformed. The protagonist, Michel,

asks three of his friends to come to his retreat at Sidi b. M., to tell them his story and ask for their help. He reviews for them his sheltered, studious youth with a severe Huguenot mother who died young and a scholarly father whose deep devotion to his research was transmitted to his son. A death-bed promise to his father brings about Michel's marriage to Marceline, a family friend. During their wedding trip to North Africa, Michel falls gravely ill with tuberculosis and almost dies. But he so systematically cares for his body that he begins to get well, and with this renewed interest in living comes the realization of all of man's possibilities as well as a brand-new joy from the sensuous contact with nature. When he is cured, Michel tries to reestablish a "normal" life in Paris and Normandy: he takes on a teaching job and is about to become a father. But when Marceline loses her baby and as a result becomes seriously ill herself, Michel cannot stop himself from forcing her to relive all the stages of their first trip until she dies. Once freed, Michel is at loose ends and asks his friends to give him a reason for living.

L'Immoraliste is, very much like *Les Nourritures terrestres*, an illustration of the concepts of *dénuement* and *disponibilité*. When he is forced to deal only with his body, Michel undergoes a transformation which strips him of all of society's layers of fiction, conventions, and constraints. He describes this discovery of his original being as that of a palimpsest, an ancient manuscript hidden beneath a more recent one. Once having reached this stage of absolute readiness (tabula rasa) he can derive total pleasure and profit from each new experience since it is in no way limited by the past. Little by little Michel detaches himself from all his possessions and finally even from his wife, but this psychological evolution occurs gradually and to a large extent unconsciously.

Certain key episodes clarify Michel's thought both for the narrator and the reader. At one point he observes an Arab boy steal a pair of scissors but makes no move to stop him. Later on, Ménalque, who acts here as in *Les Nourritures terrestres* as the spokesman of *disponibilité*, explains to Michel that what he is lacking is not so much a sense of morality as a sense of property. Because he feels detached from all things, possession of material objects means little to him. The episode in which Michel describes the delight he took in poaching on his own land reinforces this idea and also points to the theme of disintegration on which the story will end. By poaching on his own land Michel destroys the unity and system which made it productive. He finally demonstrates that by refusing possession he is actually refusing responsibility, for when he is told by the manager's young son that ownership presupposes certain duties, he decides instantly to put the farm up for sale. This total breakdown in unity affects the very texture of Michel's being, and after Marceline's death his Nietzschean will abandons him and he must turn to others for direction.

L'Immoraliste, like all of Gide's important works, demonstrates the close relationship between form and content that is a positive carryover from the symbolist period. Since there is very little dialogue interspersed with the narrative, perception and interpretation are mainly restricted to Michel's own. Marceline hardly ever speaks and seems to be eliminated as a character by Michel the narrator, just as her physical being is destroyed by Michel, the immoralist. Although the style retains some of the *précieux* elements of symbolism, it is already indicative of the clarity and balance of the classical form for which Gide soon became famous. But like his other early works, *L'Immoraliste* attracted the attention of only an elite readership. Foreseeing this problem, Gide gave orders to print only 300 copies of the first edition. His disappointment caused him to wait five years before writing *Le Retour de l'enfant prodigue* (1907; translated as *The Return of the Prodigal*, 1953).

This short prose poem is based on the biblical parable but completely transforms its lesson. It was written as a partial response to Paul Claudel and Francis Jammes, whose attempts to convert Gide to Catholicism had been going on for some time. Whereas the passage from the Gospel of Luke would teach the importance of individual salvation and the return to the fold of those who were deemed "lost," Gide's version celebrates the need for individual liberation. To the three biblical characters (father, elder brother, and prodigal son) Gide adds the mother and, especially important, a younger son. The prodigal comes back home but his return is provoked by hunger and despair and not by genuine repentance. In dialogues with the members of his family he shows both physical and emotional weakness and continued rebellion against rules imposed from without. At the end of the tale he encourages his younger brother to set out on his own, hoping that he will have the strength to succeed where the prodigal failed.

The thematic structure of the work is based on an extended symbolic system which creates two parallel levels: the family is a metaphor for organized religion; the house is the Church (more specifically the Catholic Church); the father and mother together can be seen as composing God (discipline plus love); the unbending rigor of the elder brother represents the rigidity of doctrine as expressed by the clergy. The story is structured in dialogues presenting successive confrontations between the prodigal and each of the other actors. Gide's lesson seems to be that strict adherence to doctrine is necessary only for the weak. The younger brother will succeed because he leaves completely detached from all material possessions. He takes no money with him and cannot therefore be "softened" by comfort at the beginning of his venture as was his brother.

Unlike his other works, which underwent a long gestation period, Gide wrote *Le Retour de l'enfant prodigue* in a space of two weeks. Its composition interrupted that of *La Porte étroite*, which proved to be a much more difficult endeavor.

La Porte étroite is considered by most critics to be a mirror image of *L'Immoraliste*. Whereas Michel conceives of being as a constant becoming, detached from all a priori notions, ideologies or constraints, Alissa accepts the limitations imposed by religion, family, and society and reasons according to preconceived moral precepts. In Michel one can see the danger of total rebellion against a puritanical (that is, Calvinist) background and in Alissa the danger of its total acceptance.

Like *Les Cahiers d'André Walter*, *La Porte étroite* is a love story of two cousins who will never marry. It is told in the first person by Jérôme and clarified by the addition of Alissa's diary. Jérôme describes their childhood vacations in Normandy and how their love grew, nurtured by common interests and bonds. In one key episode Jérôme finds Alissa crying while her mother and the other children laugh and joke with the mother's lover. Jérôme swears to protect his cousin for the rest of his life and to search, with her, for the rewards which lie on the other side of the "strait gate." When Alissa's sister Juliette reveals her love for Jérôme, Alissa is all too ready to make the sacrifice. But Juliette marries another, and Alissa still refuses to announce her engagement. Finally she changes her clothes and hairstyle and no longer will read the books she and Jérôme loved or play the piano. After one final meeting Jérôme gives up, and Alissa falls ill and dies. It is only upon reading her diary that Jérôme (and the reader) understands her struggle.

As is usually the case, the structure of the narrative relates intimately to the problems it poses. The story is told by a narrator, Jérôme, who comes closer to fulfilling the role of "I" as "witness" than that of protagonist. Jérôme's character is weak; he is constantly afraid to act and unlike Michel, who makes things happen, allows events to provoke and rule his behavior. On the story level this weakness results in Alissa's victory in renunciation. Without a strong hand to direct her, Alissa reverses the roles and makes the final decision affecting their lives. On the level of narration, Jérôme's weakness and confusion produce a desired ambiguity during the first part of the book. No one, neither Jérôme (who has not the courage and energy to discover the truth) nor the reader, can really understand the reasons for Alissa's withdrawal.

These reasons are clarified by Alissa's diary. Alissa believes that earthly love will keep Jérôme from the complete realization of divine love. She aspires to a kind of sainthood through self-sacrifice and renunciation. By giving up Jérôme she hopes to save both him and herself. Her diary is a perfect example of the struggle of a psyche to achieve total sincerity and self-knowledge, and of the difficulty of recognizing sincerity despite the barriers created by the necessity of language. This was a concern which remained foremost in Gide's writings throughout his life. The expression of total sincerity was one of the major objectives of his *Journal* which covers the years 1889-1949, published—at first anonymously—in several volumes over the course of the years 1931 to 1950.

La Porte étroite demonstrates an increased complexity of form: there are really two protagonists and two points of view; there are many secondary characters who are described in relative detail and whose dialogues are both informative and performative. With this second realistic *récit* Gide was on his way toward the form he would someday call *roman*.

Isabelle is told with a certain ironic detachment absent from the preceding *récits*. The narrator, Gérard, explains his adventure at La Quartfourche, where he goes to consult papers on the seventeenth-century prelate Jacques Bénigne Bossuet, under the direction of a certain Monsieur Floche. A strange old couple, the Saint-Auréols, also live in the château. Gérard gradu-

ally is taken up by what he can discover of the romantic life of their daughter Isabelle. Her crippled son, the resident priest, a mysterious nocturnal visit to which Gérard is a witness, and an old letter from Isabelle to her lover which Gérard finds, all provide clues to a sordid drama. Finally Gérard leaves the château, unsatisfied, only to return later to find the Floches and Baron Saint-Auréol dead, the château in ruins, and Isabelle in charge. His romantic dream is shattered by the superficiality of the real Isabelle he finally meets.

There is a definite distinction in *Isabelle* between the narrator and the character that is not present in the other *récits*. The young man who enters La Quartfourche is, like Flaubert's Emma Bovary, imbued with the adventurous spirit of the romantic novel and the magic and innocence of the fairy tale. He sees Isabelle as a Cinderella character, poorly treated by her family and forced to flee. But at the same time, Gérard the narrator looks back upon this time of his youth and with tongue in cheek satirizes his own naïveté. This satire is achieved through the use of subverted forms of discourse, taken from narrative subgenres. In this way Gérard mocks not only his own youthful fantasies but also the very forms of writing in which such fantasies are usually celebrated. The following narrative techniques make of *Isabelle* the most "critical" (or ironic) of Gide's *récits*: the use of exaggerated details in the description of characters, which successfully turns them into caricatures; the reversal of the value of objects from fairy tales (the horse fails to pull the carriage up the hill; the door handle falls off; the coachman is annoyed and distasteful, and so forth); the mediocre nature of Gérard's adventures, which makes them a parody of a nineteenth-century adventure novel.

Gérard's recounting of the events according to the order in which he experienced them reveals his interest in the relationship between narration and reality and points to the connection between all narrative and the detective story. By forcing the reader to participate in the creation of the story, Gérard proves that, unlike Michel, Jérôme, and Alissa, he is consciously aware of creating a work of art. *Isabelle* is a transitional work whose theme is further detached than that of the preceding *récits* from Gide's personal preoccupations and whose style announces the satirical imagination and detailed creation of caricature thoroughly developed in *Les Caves du Vatican*.

Although it was not published until 1919, *La Symphonie pastorale* was conceived by Gide much earlier. It is known that a conversation about the theme had taken place between Gide and his friend Paul Laurens as early as 1893. It was composed after *Les Caves du Vatican*, but its structure, style, and psychological preoccupations tie it intimately to the other *récits* and its theme especially suggests its relationship to *Isabelle*.

On the surface *La Symphonie pastorale* is a very simple story. A Protestant pastor living in a small Swiss village finds a young blind girl and brings her home, despite his wife's objections, to educate. The girl, brought up by a deaf grandmother who never spoke to her, barely acts human. The pastor teaches her to speak, think, read, and feel and soon falls in love with her. He hides all evil from her so that she believes that the world is pure. When his son Jacques declares his intention to marry Gertrude (as she has been named by the family), the pastor refuses and separates the couple. An operation restores Gertrude's sight, and with it she gains a realization of suffering and sadness, especially that of the pastor's wife. She commits suicide, and the pastor learns that both she and Jacques had converted to Catholicism.

Several events and inner conflicts in Gide's life influenced the writing of this *récit*. Gide's love for the young Marc Allégret, to whom he was mentor, was an impetus for the Pygmalion theme linking the pastor to his creation, Gertrude. The necessity of love between student and teacher is a platonic theme that much influenced this episode in Gide's life. But the most important conflict was the religious turmoil which Gide experienced in 1916 and which is documented in the lyrical work *Numquid et tu . . . ?* (published anonymously in 1922; translated in *The Journals of André Gide, 1947-1951*). As is often the case, *La Symphonie pastorale* (which Gide included among what he called his "critical" works) was meant to demonstrate the danger of taking to extremes an idea which is elsewhere celebrated. In *Numquid et tu . . . ?* Gide presents Christ as the prime example of what man can become, when, unfettered by the constraints of the law, his acts are directed only by love. All orthodoxy, whether it be Pauline or Calvinist, is rejected in favor of a free interpretation of the Gospel which teaches that love can lead humankind to happiness *on earth*.

In *La Symphonie pastorale* the pastor attempts to put this freedom into practice by teaching Gertrude that all is true and good in a world of

Gide and Marc Allégret during their travels in England, 1918

love and beauty. He hides from her both the possibility of sin and the scriptural passages from Saint Paul that establish laws and regulations demanding obedience. He believes and teaches Gertrude to believe that aesthetic beauty is equivalent to ethical good. When he finally realizes that his love for Gertrude is more than charity, he convinces himself that it must be condoned by God, simply because it *is* love: "S'il est une limitation dans l'amour, elle n'est pas de Vous, mon Dieu, mais des hommes. Pour coupable que mon amour paraisse aux yeux des hommes, oh! dites-moi qu'aux vôtres il est saint" (If there is any limitation to love, it is set by man and not by Thee, my God. However guilty my love may appear in the eyes of man, oh tell me that in Thine it is sacred). One might note that the pastor's error is similar to Michel's since he pushes individual freedom to its limit. In the same way, the pastor's son's failing resembles that of Alissa, for both see only the severity and interdictions of Christian doctrine and conclude in favor of its limitations.

As Germaine Brée has pointed out in *André Gide, l'insaisissable Protée* (1953), it is the conflict between the pastor and Jacques which kills Gertrude, who *is* pure love and innocence.

Both the style and the structure of *La Symphonie pastorale* reinforce the pastor's inner struggle. Gide's original title for the work, "L'Aveugle" (The Blind Person—masculine or feminine, the French is ambiguous), would have pointed explicitly to the opposition between physical and mental blindness. It is of course the pastor who really blinds himself to the facts through the superimposition of a beautiful theory on brute reality. His construction of that theory is reinforced by his use of expressions and metaphors which he takes directly from the scriptures. This ready-made language acts as a screen that prevents him from "seeing" beyond certain clichés, and helps him justify his actions. By constantly using biblical language to describe an earthly love, he eventually convinces himself of the divine character of that love. The clever reader "sees" through this screen long before the pastor himself does.

As in the case of the other *récits*, the first-person narration engages the major character in a reliving of his predicament, deforms its objective reality, and represents this limited view to the reader. But in *La Symphonie pastorale* several dialogues that reveal the ideas and feelings of the pastor's family help the reader see more clearly. The pastor's own slow realization is also achieved through an element of structure. The absolute distance between narrator and character which was maintained in the other *récits* (all narration occurring after the events) is modified by the diary structure of *La Symphonie pastorale*. The book is divided into two parts. The first part traces events which begin with the discovery of Gertrude (two-and-one-half years before) and reach a period very close to the present of narration. It is upon rereading this first notebook that the pastor realizes the nature of his love. In the second notebook there is a moment when events actually catch up and coincide with the present of narration. This moment is followed by a rapid acceleration of the concluding actions, which seem to be out of control. It can easily be seen how this temporal structure follows and corresponds to the pastor's state of mind: attempt at justification and gradual awareness; the moment of truth; a cascade of confused thoughts and erratic actions which conclude the story.

Despite the increased complexity of the linear *récit*, Gide had by this time exhausted the possibilities of the form. He had already written *Les Caves du Vatican* and was about to embark on his major novel, *Les Faux-Monnayeurs*. The form and obsessive preoccupations of the *récits* seemed to him at this point to be things of the past.

Les Caves du Vatican was the result of a long gestation. Originally conceived in 1893, it was first published in *Nouvelle Revue Française* in 1914. The intervening twenty years saw the publication of several *récits* whose preoccupations and characters are satirized in *Les Caves du Vatican*, demonstrating the consistent unity of Gide's work. Along with *Paludes* and *Le Prométhée mal enchaîné* (1899; translated as *Prometheus Illbound*, 1919, and again as *Prometheus Misbound*, 1953), *Les Caves du Vatican* is labelled "sotie" by its author. A *sotie* was originally a satirical farce (fifteenth century) played by actors dressed as buffoons who represented various imaginary characters. It originated in the "fête des fous" (fools' play) which parodied religious ceremonies. When eventually banned by the Church, the parody turned its irony on social customs. *Sotie* comes from *sot*, meaning "stupid fool." In *Les Caves du Vatican* the characters are marionettelike figures, devoid of psychological depth, whose existence is determined solely by the network of relationships linking one to another and to the social institutions which "pull their strings."

In 1893 (the year in which the *sotie* is set) rumor had it that Pope Leon XII had been kidnapped, imprisoned in the Vatican, and a false pope put in his place. The rumor was spread by a group of swindlers whose purpose was to extort money from fervent Catholics. Gide used this rumor (described in newspaper articles) as a pretext for the main story line of *Les Caves du Vatican*, which revolves around an extortion plot to collect money for the deliverance of the pope.

The title of the novel has several possible meanings. This ambiguity immediately points to one of the major themes, that of the multiple meanings of signs and the deceptive character of appearance. "Cave" in its feminine form means "cellar," the obvious meaning of the title referring to the pope's supposed imprisonment. But it is also a Latin verb meaning "beware" (of facile interpretations, of confidence men, of false appearances, and so forth) and in its masculine form is a French slang term for "dupe" or "fool." "Vatican" is of course the seat of the papacy, but it also means "capital" or "high place" and can therefore be taken as the symbol of absolute truth. The characters in the novel are all "caves," duped by the institutions to which they blindly adhere in their search for a stable meaning which does not exist.

The plot of *Les Caves du Vatican* is extremely complex. It is, however, tied together by family relationships and also by the supposed imprisonment of the pope. The main story line revolves around three brothers-in-law (all "caves") whose names provide the titles for the first three books. Anthime Armand-Dubois begins as a Freemason, undergoes a miraculous cure and conversion, but returns to atheism when he learns of the "false" pope. Julius de Baraglioul writes psychological novels and hopes to be elected to the Académie. He questions his traditional principles upon meeting his illegitimate half-brother Lafcadio but regains confidence in logic and convention by convincing himself that the Church's indifference is the fault of the "false" pope. Amédée Fleurissoire is completely taken in by the plot to raise money to "free the pope" and goes off as a "crusader" to Rome where, owing to his naiveté, he encounters all kinds of problems. Book four is entitled "Le Mille-Pattes" (Centipede). It outlines the activities of the swindler Protos and his attempts to raise money from contributions by fervent Catholics who believe his story that the pope has been kidnapped. Book five, "Lafcadio," tells the story of Julius's half-brother, who has developed into a free spirit, detached from all social convention. Finding himself, by chance, in the same train compartment as Amédée, he pushes him out the window in order to prove that gratuitous actions are possible. But Lafcadio is not completely free, since his action has unforeseen consequences, and his emotions (desire to become part of a family, attraction to Julius's daughter, for example) create attachments despite himself.

Like most of Gide's works, *Les Caves du Vatican* is a criticism of the search for absolutes and the adherence to rigid systems which limit individual freedom. But because of the satirical style and complex structure of the book, the simple rejection of absolutes goes much further and actually raises doubt as to the very existence of any essential values. The perpetual motion of the topsy-turvy world of the novel tends to belie the attempt by each character to achieve a fixed attitude toward life. None of them is capable of accepting human contradictions, and although a few vacillate between systems, none can remain for very long detached from *all* systems.

Anthime exchanges atheistic determinism for Catholic providence and therefore hardly changes at all. Julius's rejection of the psychological motivation of his novels in favor of gratuitous action cannot stand up to the test of reality: when Lafcadio tells him that such an act has actually occurred he rejects it. Amédée (like Don Quixote or Emma Bovary) lives an illusion created by a tradition of adventure novels and tales of religious crusades. His total separation from reality makes his death a logical consequence. He dies as he lived, a character in a melodrama. Even Lafcadio is an avatar of the Gidian bastard-child, free of all family attachments and totally *disponible*. Lafcadio is scarcely less of a puppet than the other characters, for he attempts to achieve his freedom in a most rigid and systematic manner: by way of example, his use of self-inflicted wounds to punish himself for deviations from his self-made code of behavior is reminiscent of religious fanaticism. Lafcadio can be seen as the ultimate parody of Michel, as Fleurissoire, the crusader, is of Alissa. Lafcadio's gratuitous act, of which much has been made by critics, is yet another example of his resemblance to the other characters, for by attempting to act without motive, Lafcadio tries to become equal to God, going beyond human functionalism and thereby equating himself with the absolute.

Protos is the character who demonstrates the fallibility of all systems by moving freely from one to another. By disguising himself in the systems' outer garb (the clothing of a priest, for example) he proves to what extent each system is superficial and depends on its outward appearance. He takes advantage of the dupes ("caves") by pretending to be a part of the structure which controls them. But even Protos is defeated when he attempts to ensnare Lafcadio in the paradoxical system of those who act supposedly without regard for order, the *hors-la-loi* (outlaws).

With *Les Caves du Vatican* Gide rejects the psychological linearity of the *récits* and develops the satirical and more complex style and structure that were foreshadowed in *Isabelle*. The actors of *Les Caves du Vatican* are caricatures (as were the Floches and Saint-Auréols) whose features and behavior are stereotyped by the use of exaggerated description and playful onomastics: "Protos" comes from Proteus, the sea god who changes form at will; the three sisters are given names of flowers and "budding" is also suggested by the name given to the naive "Fleurissoire"; a prostitute is called Carola "Venitequa" ("come here" in Italian) and Julius's father, who is the symbol of bourgeois tradition (but yet engendered the illegitimate Lafcadio during a trip to Romania), is baptized "Juste." Even though the narrator presents his characters as marionettes, he at times seems to endow them with real life when he pretends that he cannot completely explain their actions: "Lafcadio, mon ami, vous donnez dans un fait divers et ma plume vous abandonne!" (Lafcadio, my friend, here you require the pen of a newspaper reporter–mine abandons you!). And yet the narrator is ubiquitous, following his characters from city to city and revealing their secrets. Such structural contradictions act as an aesthetic symbol for the impossibility of imposing order on the world. The characters desire this order, but the novel continually refuses and belies it. It will be left to *Les Faux-Monnayeurs* to develop this problem and to propose several possible solutions.

During the period from 1902 to 1925, when he wrote his major novels, Gide's emotional life and intellectual activities greatly intensified. In 1909 Gide and several other literary figures (including Henry Ghéon, Jacques Copeau, Jean Schlumberger) founded *La Nouvelle Revue Française* (NRF), a scholarly journal whose only criteria were aesthetic quality and intellectual honesty and which refused to support any single ideology. In 1911 in conjunction with the *NRF*, a publishing branch, under the direction of Gaston Gallimard, was established. Gallimard, which began by serving the contributors to the review on a very limited basis, would eventually become one of the major publishers in France.

During World War I Gide devoted much of his time to helping the Belgian refugees at the Foyer Franco-Belge. The war and his religious crisis of 1916 caused a dark period to which his *Journal* attests, but Gide would never remain despondent for long. Indeed, this was the last period of religious anxiety and emotional soul-searching that he was to undergo. Although he retained from his Protestant upbringing reverence for the figure of Christ and devotion to elements of the evangelical message, after the 1916 crisis he abandoned all other vestiges of religious belief. In subsequent decades, and to the end of his life, he would maintain what Paul Claudel called his Goethean serenity. Moreover, his growing love for the young Marc Allégret soon brought him back to his more natural state of joy. Up until this time Gide had disassociated physical and emotional love. His encounters with young boys had always remained purely sensual and his only emotional attachment was to his wife Madeleine. With Allégret Gide discovered the fulfillment of a complete love. If Madeleine had known about his sensual adventures she had been able to ignore them, but she considered the affair with Allégret certain betrayal. During the trip to England which Gide took with his young companion in 1918, she burned all of Gide's letters. This act caused one of the lowest points in Gide's emotional life, for he believed that the letters had contained the very best of himself.

The period after the war saw Gide finally attain a celebrity which extended beyond the intellectual elite. His constant search for absolute sincerity interested members of the growing surrealist movement, to whom Allégret had introduced him. His fame was especially heightened by a series of attacks against himself and other contributors to the *NRF:* one by a minor novelist, Henri Béraud, who berated the supposed "snobism" of the review, and another, more important, by Henri Massis, a writer associated with the Catholic journal *La Revue Universelle*. Gide himself reveled in the criticism for it helped him clarify and formulate his own ideas.

During the 1920s several works attested to Gide's attempt to attain complete sincerity and express his convictions despite the possibility of public outcry. His study of Dostoyevski, published in 1923, emphasized the novelist's psychological insight, demonstrated by the creation of characters who are prey to multiple contradictions. Gide of course saw a relationship between Dostoyevski's characters and his own, all of whom belie the classical unity of self which Massis believed threatened.

With the commercial publication of *Corydon* in 1924 (it first appeared anonymously as *C.R.D.N.* in 1911), Gide took the risk of losing the respected position he had finally achieved in the world of letters, that of the "contemporain capital" (capital contemporary) as he was called by André Rouveyre that same year. But the outcry was less than he and his colleagues had feared, for the French public was probably ready for such a text. *Corydon*, written in the form of a Socratic dialogue and translated into English in 1950, is a systematic defense of homosexuality, which Gide attempts to demonstrate is not "against nature" but has merely been suppressed by Western society. The treatise, which he once called his most important book, also defends the idea that the emotional, intellectual, and social development of adolescent boys be directed by the love of an older companion.

In his memoirs, *Si le grain ne meurt,* Gide attempts to achieve the same ultimate sincerity as is evidenced by the diary he kept throughout his life and whose object was to "tell all." The memoirs outline and explain his early formation and the severity of his Calvinist upbringing and attempt to shed light on his relationship with Madeleine. These latter revelations were to become even clearer by the publication of *Et nunc manet in te* (1947; translated as *The Secret Drama of My Life,* 1951, and as *Madeleine,* 1952) after her death, a text in which Gide's self-accusations reach their peak.

Les Faux-Monnayeurs is one of the major novels of the experimental period of the 1920s. It was first published in 1925 in several *NRF* installments; that was also the year of *Mrs. Dalloway* by Virginia Woolf. Only three years earlier Joyce had produced *Ulysses,* and during the years 1913-1927 Marcel Proust's masterpiece, *A la recherche du temps perdu* (*Remembrance of Things Past*), appeared. All of these novelists broke with tradition. They rejected the "well-made" nineteenth-century novel with its carefully developed plot and its "flesh-and-blood" characters. Their ideas and final products may have greatly differed, but they were all eager to redefine the novel as a genre and, following the lead of an innovator like Flaubert, were especially concerned with form.

Gide's attitude toward this need for change is clear from comments made both in his *Journal* and in *Le Journal des Faux-Monnayeurs* (1926; translated as *Logbook of The Coiners,* 1952), which was a running diary that followed the composition of the novel in most of its stages. One of the comments speaks of the need to make of *Les Faux-Monnayeurs* a crossroads, a rendezvous of problems, the ultimate work into which all experience is poured. Others attempt to define the "pure" novel from which must be eliminated all extraneous material. These seemingly contradictory concepts should no longer surprise the reader who has learned to recognize the richness of Gide's work and its refusal of all monolithic structures. *Les Faux-Monnayeurs,* like *Les Caves du Vatican,* raises problems concerning the definition of the genre, and in so doing already announces the *nouveau roman,* or new novel, of the 1950s and 1960s. In his rejection of the carefully evolving chronological intrigue and through the creation

Gide in his study (Laure Albin-Guillot)

of characters whose individual weights can be measured only insofar as they fit into a system of relationships, Gide creates the link between the precursors of the nineteenth century (Flaubert, Stendhal) and the New Novelists to come (Butor, Robbe-Grillet, Sarraute, Simon, and others).

One of the major innovations in the novel is its use of narrative perspective. The "story" is told both by an omniscient narrator (who, however, disclaims his omniscience and thereby raises the question of the credibility of the Balzacian form) and by Edouard, a novelist himself, who keeps a diary and is also attempting to write a novel entitled *Les Faux-Monnayeurs* about a novelist writing *Les Faux-Monnayeurs* . . . This technique, *la composition en abyme,* creates a series of reflections and counterreflections; by their very existence and relationships, they raise the question of the substance of reality and its representation. Once again the form of the work directly manifests its content, for as Edouard says: "A vrai dire, ce sera là le sujet: la lutte entre les faits proposés par la réalité, et la réalité idéale" (To tell the truth, that in itself will be the subject: the struggle between the facts proposed by reality and ideal reality). The creation of layers of representation is even more complex here, for other characters also add their perspectives through the use of letters and dialogue (the reader often feeling like a voyeur) and Gide's comments in the *Journal* and *Le Journal des Faux-Monnayeurs* add still another dimension.

This novel represents the culminating point of Gide's career. Most of the preoccupations dealt with in the *récits* are reconsidered and intertwined in *Les Faux-Monnayeurs* (as they were satirized in *Les Caves du Vatican*). In fact, Gide had considered the possibility of writing another series of *récits*, but following the advice of his friend Roger Martin du Gard, he achieved the complex synthesis of a major novel. Whereas each *récit* has a central character on whom all others depend, in *Les Faux-Monnayeurs* there are no secondary characters. Each actor plays out his own version of the major themes; each becomes in turn a "hero," disappears, and sometimes reappears. Each character seems therefore to remain independent even of his creator (who is not the omniscient narrator, who seems only to be an observer) and certainly of Edouard, who shows, in some ways, the same blindness as the heroes of the *récits*, by his belief in his ability to control reality.

As with most of Gide's works, the concept of *Les Faux-Monnayeurs* went through a long process of maturation. The original impetus for the novel was a story in the *Journal de Rouen* about a band of counterfeiters and another in the same paper dealing with the suicide of several adolescents in Clermont-Ferrand. As usual these news items were only a beginning and would be completely transformed. The actual composition of the work was begun in 1919, just after Gide's trip to England with Marc Allégret and Madeleine's desperate reaction. Again, although the relationship with Allégret is definitely a factor in the novel, it is only one small part. As Gide himself stated, there may be much of him in Edouard, but Edouard is not Gide.

The characters and incidents in the novel combine, separate, and recombine in numerous ways to create a vast, complex, and ever-changing network of relationships. The intricacy is such that only a brief idea of the "story" can be given here. The task is made even more difficult by the fact that Gide chose not to allow a central plot to develop continuously, but rather broke up each story line, so that the reader is forced to put the pieces together much like a jigsaw puzzle ("Ne

jamais profiter de l'élan acquis"–Never take advantage of the acquired momentum,–said the author). The incidents in the novel primarily concern three families: Profitendieu, Molinier, and Azaïs-Vedel. Both Albéric Profitendieu and Oscar Molinier are judges. In the Profitendieu family there are four children: Charles, Bernard, Cécile, and Caloub. At the beginning of the novel, Bernard discovers letters proving that he is illegitimate and leaves home. He spends his first night with his friend Olivier Molinier, who has two brothers, Vincent and Georges. Olivier tells Bernard that Vincent seems to have abandoned a woman (Laura), who was left weeping in the stairwell; he also tells Bernard about the impending visit of his Uncle Edouard (a novelist), his mother's half-brother, whom he admires. Laura is one of the children of the Azaïs-Vedel family, who run a boarding school. The grandfather, Azaïs, as well as the father/pastor Vedel, are oblivious to the goings-on of a band of young counterfeiters. Rachel sacrifices her health trying to keep the school going while her brother Armand cynically refuses to make any attempt to improve his life.

After having managed to come into possession of Edouard's valise, Bernard reads his diary and a letter from Laura, finds Laura, and persuades Edouard to allow him to accompany them to Saas-Fée, where Edouard must go to find an old friend's grandson (Boris), and where Laura can hide her pregnancy from her family. In the meantime, Vincent becomes connected with a cynical English woman (Lilian) and her novelist friend (Passavant, enemy of Edouard), with whom Olivier goes off in spite. At the end of the novel Edouard brings Boris back to the boarding school, where he kills himself in order to prove his courage to the band of young hoodlums. Bernard decides to return to his family, and Olivier and Edouard are finally united. The novel, which is open-ended, finishes with the words "Je suis bien curieux de connaître Caloub" (I'm very curious to get to know Caloub).

Despite the complexity of the intertwining plots, several structural and thematic elements act as organizing factors. The most immediately discernible is the title. Although the original impetus for the novel came from a newspaper story involving a ring of actual counterfeiters, the theme of false appearances goes far beyond the distribution of coins and monetary notes. To a certain extent, every character in the novel (including Edouard) is engaged in some sort of counterfeiting, whether it be moral, intellectual, social, or aesthetic. All are eager to present an appearance which will camouflage their inauthenticity. One of the prime examples of this phenomenon is the Azaïs-Vedel boarding school, with which most of the characters have some contact. The apparent atmosphere of the school is that of a rigid Calvinist training ground where youth are taught the value of hard work; fidelity to family, church, and country; and purity of morals. The old grandfather Azaïs refuses to see beyond the appearance of probity created by the boys who form la Société des Hommes Forts (Society of Strong Men), a club actually dealing in extortion and the passing of counterfeit currency, while pretending to defend the innocent.

Individual examples of "counterfeiting" abound in the novel. Rather than act spontaneously, according to their own needs and feelings, many of the characters attempt to imitate the stereotyped behavior celebrated by the myths and fictions of society. Bernard refuses to believe in his father's love (since myth suggests that men whose wives have affairs which produce children will despise and reject those children) and thinks that he must leave home. Laura's husband, Douviers, talks of fighting a duel with Vincent in order to live up to a heroic image. The Comte de Passavant seduces young boys but uses the cover of a literary magazine of which they become "editors."

The most interesting example of counterfeiting is presented by the novel itself and by Edouard's attempt to create a novel within the novel. Although he claims to want to pour all of his experience into the work, he rejects certain elements of "reality," either because he does not understand them, or because they do not conform to certain preconceived notions. But art is, after all, the creation of the appearance of reality (as is a false coin) and as such may be accused of a certain "inauthenticity." By making the writing of a novel the central issue, Gide raises the entire problem of the definition of art. Edouard's function, however, also suggests a necessary relationship between morality and aesthetics, for not only does his narration (diary) act as a unifying factor but also he is endowed with a certain moral responsibility with regard to several of the characters. At times he fulfills this role sincerely (his advice to Bernard to return to his father), but at others his desire to experiment with human behavior despite the consequences (his decision to bring Boris back to the boarding school) raises moral

and aesthetic questions at the same time. Did Edouard bring Boris back to please his grandfather, La Pérouse? Or was he creating an experimental situation to provide matter for his novel? Why did he not realize that the stifling atmosphere of the school would be dangerous for Boris's fragile nature? And finally, why does he refuse to use the suicide scene in *his* novel?

Another thematic element which unifies the novel is that of "coming of age." The preponderance of adolescents and episodes which emphasize their emotional, intellectual, social, and moral development make of the novel a bildungsroman in the style of *L'Education sentimentale*. Like Flaubert, Gide offers very few definitive answers. The theme is touched on in the cases of Olivier, who learns how to express his true feelings, and his younger brother Georges, who learns the danger of going along with the crowd. But it is most thoroughly developed through the story of Bernard who learns, thanks to Edouard's advice, how to reject stereotyped behavior and "trouver [la] règle en soi-même; . . . avoir pour but le développement de soi. . . . suivre sa pente, pourvu que ce soit en montant" (find one's rule in oneself; . . . have self-development as one's final goal. . . . follow one's inclination provided that it goes uphill).

Certain structural elements also facilitate the comprehension of the text despite its complexity. The novel is divided into three parts: "Paris," "Saas-Fée," and "Paris." Both parts entitled "Paris" contain eighteen chapters, consisting of passages from Edouard's diary and "omniscient" narration. "Saas-Fée" (which contains seven chapters) is itself framed by two letters, the first from Bernard to Olivier, and another near the end, from Olivier to Bernard, followed by a most interesting and curious chapter in which the narrator withdraws like a "voyageur, parvenu au haut de la colline" (traveler having reached the top of the hill) to judge and analyze the individuals he has created. Gide is playing here with theories that deal with the acquired "autonomy" of literary beings and is raising problems akin to those in many modern works (for example, *Sei personnaggi in cerca d'autore—Six Characters in Search of an Author,* by Pirandello). This externally narrated chapter, far from provoking a belief in the "reality" of the characters, emphasizes their creation by the artist and is thus another element which places the novel in the realm of self-conscious fiction. The reader is constantly reminded that he or she is a participant in writing and not simply an observer. This theme is also reinforced by the literary dialogues that consume a good part of the "Saas-Fée" section and in which Edouard explains his theories about the novel.

The tripartite structure of the novel, which at first may seem overly symmetrical and reductive, is expanded through the use of techniques which create a new conception of narrated time. The first part, told by the omniscient narrator, begins at 4:00 P.M. and ends the next day at 7:00 P.M. It therefore covers a little more than a day. This narration, however, contains all the passages from Edouard's diary which were written "last year." The "day" therefore seems to be infinite since it "contains" the past year. The novel in this way opens up into the past in the same way as it continues into a projected future, and usual temporal distinctions within a strict chronological time span are blurred. From Gide's comments, quoted by Roger Martin du Gard in his *Notes sur André Gide* (1951), it is clear that his desire was not to present, as did the traditional novel, a *horizontal* narration following the main characters through chronological time but rather a *vertical* narration in which a fragment of time is expanded to include the activities of many actors.

This temporal expansion naturally creates an impression of spatial ubiquity and suggests (as does Proust's novel) a reappraisal of the absolute laws of nature. Human endeavors which refuse the domination of chronological time and limited space gain their only value from their relative position within an ever-changing network of relationships. It is clear from this relativism that neither a single point of view (like those in the *récits*) nor an omniscient narrator pretending to be a god could have sufficed in *Les Faux-Monnayeurs*. In fact, the multiple perspectives and reflections of perspective in the novel caused it to be labeled, in an innovative 1949 article by Wylie Sypher, "Gide's Cubist Novel." In a cubist painting concrete reality is broken down into various parts, each seen from a different angle. This deconstruction must be reconstructed by the spectator, who plays an active role. The picture is therefore not static but its various elements are in constant motion as different spectators reconstruct them in different ways. Each element has meaning only insofar as it enters into a system of relationships. In much the same way, the episodes in *Les Faux-Monnayeurs* are told and retold in various fragments from various angles; the reader must put these versions together and realize an individual interpretation. The choice becomes more difficult and complex as the reflections multiply, reflect one another, and distance themselves from all objectivity.

Les Faux-Monnayeurs is a novel which proves the impossibility of ever attaining that sought-for objectivity. It states once again, as did the *récits*, the error of the search for any type of absolute, for truth is not a preconceived essence given before experience but rather the dynamic functioning of experience. A true novel must incorporate as many reflections as possible, but, when taken as a whole, it does not provide a definitive answer but is simply in itself yet another reflection, which will be re-reflected in the vast chain of intertextuality. *Les Faux-Monnayeurs* foreshadows thus not only existentialist thinking but also recent deconstructionist theory.

Les Faux-Monnayeurs represents Gide's ultimate achievement in the creation of narrative fiction. Attempts to return after 1925 to a more limited form like the *récit* were not very successful. The trilogy written from 1929 to 1936 is certainly aesthetically inferior. It does, however, reveal some of Gide's more socially directed concerns, and in fact the late 1920s and the 1930s were a period in which Gide attempted to represent his social and political attitudes in works both of fiction and nonfiction.

In 1923 Elisabeth van Rysselberghe gave birth to a girl, Catherine, of whom Gide was the father. Elisabeth was the daughter of Maria van Rysselberghe, otherwise known as "La Petite Dame," who occupied an apartment immediately adjacent to Gide's in the Rue Vaneau for twenty-four years. In the 1970s Gallimard published *Les Cahiers de la Petite Dame*, a running diary kept by Maria van Rysselberghe without Gide's knowledge, which contains a wealth of information about his life and relationships during the years 1918 to 1951. Gide's affair with Elisabeth was linked to his growing concern for women's rights. Elisabeth wanted a child out of wedlock and Gide was the perfect father. Gide's paternity was kept secret from Madeleine.

The trilogy of *récits* entitled *L'Ecole des femmes*, *Robert*, and *Geneviève* deals partly with the need for a new definition of women's roles in family and society. In the first book Eveline tells the story of her marriage to Robert, who covers up his hypocrisy and opportunism under the guise of religion and social conformity. The second book is Robert's attempt to defend himself and the third is the story of their daughter Geneviève, who has learned from her mother's ex-

Gide with his infant daughter, Catherine, and, from left to right, Catherine's mother, Elisabeth van Rysselberghe, grandmother Maria van Rysselberghe, and Gide's friend Roger Martin du Gard (Collection of Mme Christiane Martin du Gard)

perience a woman's need to lead a more independent life. In one of the dialogues Geneviève expresses her desire to have a child without the ties of marriage. One of Gide's objects in writing a trilogy was, again, to provide several reflections of a given situation, but the work lacks the spontaneity and compassion of the earlier *récits* without demonstrating the complexity of the novels. This lack may very well be the result of an attempt to write didactic fiction rather than to allow the reader to arrive at conclusions.

Social and political concerns were better expressed in several works of nonfiction. As soon as he had finished *Les Faux-Monnayeurs*, Gide, accompanied by Marc Allégret, left for an extended trip through Africa. His *Voyage au Congo* (1927; translated as *Travels in the Congo*, 1929) and *Le Retour du Tchad: Carnets de route* (1928; translated as *Return from Lake Chad* in *Travels in the Congo*, 1929) are written in the usual Gidian diary style and reveal, as did *Les Nourritures terrestres*, his ever-present capacity for ecstasy and

wonderment before newly discovered natural environments and cultures. But the descriptions of a lush nature and the spontaneity and grace of the people are accompanied by comments revealing abject poverty and impossible working conditions. Gide is especially shocked by the atrocities committed by the concessionary companies. In addition to the travel descriptions themselves, several letters and reports sent to the French authorities by Gide succeeded in provoking a parliamentary debate and investigation. Gide's intervention had positive results, and the concessions were not renewed.

This growing social concern naturally led to what became Gide's most important preoccupation during the 1930s, his attraction to communism. His interest began to surface in pages from the *Journal* published in 1931 in the *NRF*. At this time, both the Soviet Union and the French Communist party were encouraging the cooperation of leftist intellectuals in the fight against fascism. Gide's original concept of Communist Russia was an ideal one. He hoped to find a society which allowed the individual all the freedom which capitalist conformity made impossible, a society rid of the constraints of family and religion. In 1936 he was invited to visit the U.S.S.R., where he gave the funeral oration for Maxime Gorki. But Gide's trip to Russia awakened him to the failings of Russian communism and especially to its contradictions with his own beliefs. Rather than the ideal individualistic society he had imagined, he found a regime which purged all those whose politics differed from official doctrine and branded homosexuals as counterrevolutionaries. Gide's objections were stated somewhat discreetly in his *Retour de l'U.R.S.S.* (1936; translated as *Return from the U.S.S.R.*, 1937) and more adamantly in *Retouches à mon Retour de l'U.R.S.S.* (1937; translated as *Afterthoughts: A Sequel to "Back from the U.S.S.R.,"* 1938). His connection with official communism was therefore short-lived.

Another genre Gide used in the 1930s was the drama. Early in his career, he had composed two very original and searching plays on themes similar to those of *L'Immoraliste*: *Le Roi Candaule* (King Candaules, 1901) and *Saül* (1903), which were produced, if somewhat tardily, by major figures in the theater, A. -F. Lugné-Poë and Jacques Copeau. Other works, such as *Philoctète* (1899) and *Le Retour de l'enfant prodigue*, can loosely be called closet drama, because of their dialogue form; these two were even performed. They attest to the importance of dialogue and other theatrical features in his composition. In 1931 he returned to drama with *Œdipe*, a rendering of the Oedipus legend that embodies his own particular humanism, incorporating strong individualistic features but also an element of social responsibility.

Another major event of this period was the sudden death of Gide's wife in 1938. His suffering was so great that he was even incapable of keeping up the *Journal* to which he was usually so faithful. Madeleine Gide died on 17 April and the first *Journal* entry after that is 21 August. Perhaps the best appraisal of the significance of this loss for Gide is that of La Petite Dame in the notebook entry dated April 19-June 10: "Il a perdu son contrepoids, la mesure fixe avec quoi il confrontait ses actes, sa vraie tendresse, sa plus grande fidélité; de son dialogue intérieur, l'autre voix s'est tue" (He has lost his counterweight, the fixed standard with which he confronted his acts, his real tenderness, his greatest loyalty; the other voice of his inner dialogue has been silenced).

Grief and remorse over Madeleine's death caused Gide to write and publish *Et nunc manet in te* (1947), a self-accusatory account of their relationship (including previously unpublished diary passages) in which, according to certain writers (lifelong friend Jean Schlumberger, for example, who attempted in *Madeleine et André Gide*, 1956, to attenuate the severity of Gide's mea culpa), Gide exaggerates Madeleine's suffering. As is the *Journal* kept from 1889 to 1949 and the memoirs (*Si le grain ne meurt* and *Ainsi soit-il ou les jeux sont faits*, 1952; translated as *So Be It; or, The Chips are Down*, 1959), *Et nunc manet in te* is but another Gidian attempt to "tell all" and thus reach a state of ultimate sincerity and moral *dépouillement* (stripping).

Perhaps the war had some role in shaking Gide out of his agony over his wife's death and causing him to resume action and participation in events. In 1941 he withdrew from the *NRF* in protest against its direction by collaborators such as Drieu La Rochelle. In 1942 he left for North Africa and for three years, until the war's end, lived in Tunis and Algiers. This was a time for reflection, reading, and following the events of the war. The impossibility of free thought and literary activity and the fear of having his manuscripts confiscated prevented Gide from returning to France. The period was, however, fruitful, for the *Journal* pages written from 1942 to 1945 represent an excellent chronicle of the North African campaign.

Gide's last major work and one which has been defined by many critics as representing the sum of his life experience is *Thésée* (1946). In *Thésée* Gide returns to the first-person autobiographical *récit*, supposedly narrated orally. Thésée tells his own story in three stages: his childhood (emphasizing both sensual awareness and the acceptance of discipline); his adventures in Crete (the need to confront monsters and deal with lovers); the founding of Athens (political awareness and responsibility). As he had done before in such works as *Le Prométhée mal enchaîné*, (1899), *Saül* (1903), and *Œdipe* (1931; translated in *Two Legends*, 1950), Gide reinterprets a legend according to his own preoccupations and evolving doctrines. Thésée's accomplished feats and his emancipation from tradition can be seen to correspond to obstacles overcome and "monsters" conquered during Gide's life.

In order to understand the implications of this work one needs to place it in a historical context and movement. Not only does Thésée's char-

Gide with his daughter Catherine in 1947 (courtesy of Catherine Gide)

acter symbolize the ideal culmination of the Gidian effort, but he also represents the type of hero being celebrated at the same time by existentialist writers such as Sartre and Anouilh. Sartre's *Les Mouches* (*The Flies*, 1943), also based on Greek legend, appeared in 1943, and Anouilh's *Antigone* (1942), whose Créon resembles Thésée, was written in 1944. With *Thésée* Gide shows his modernism, having evolved from the ideal artificiality of symbolism toward the statement of a pragmatic, active way of life.

Whereas in the play *Œdipe* Gide meant to criticize the mystification of blind faith, in *Thésée* he celebrates an attitude which finds the only value in acts themselves and rejects all transcendent principles as criteria for judgment. This difference is clearly expressed in the dialogue between Thésée and Œdipe which concludes the *récit*. Thésée engages in all the variety that experience offers him but is never held back, hindered, or mystified by any one adventure. He always remains in control of his destiny. He refuses, for example, to allow Ariane (Ariadne) to unwind the ball of yarn but holds on to it himself, thus choos-

ing his own limits. Dédale (Daedalus), the architect of the labyrinth, must have had Thésée in mind, for only those who maintain self-control are allowed to escape. This Gidian principle is often overlooked by readers taken up by the lyricism of such works as *Les Nourritures terrestres*, but one should be reminded of Ménalque refusing to drink and stating: "je tiens la sobriété pour une plus puissante ivresse; j'y garde ma lucidité" (I believe that sobriety is an even more powerful drunkenness since it allows me to keep my lucidity).

Thésée has learned the lesson which escapes heroes like Alissa and the pastor but finally enlightens Bernard in *Les Faux-Monnayeurs*. There are no absolute truths or principles according to which one can fashion one's life. Being is in becoming and one must "suivre sa pente pourvu que ce soit en montant" (follow one's inclination, provided it leads uphill). *Thésée* seems to offer a definition of the ideal existential man, the synthesis of a mentality which Gide and his positive characters strove to achieve.

Three important events occurred during the last years of Gide's life. In 1947 Oxford University granted him an honorary doctorate. During the same year he earned the Nobel Prize for literature and so finally achieved international acclaim. On 13 December 1950, two months before his death, he was able to attend with great joy the premier performance of his play *Les Caves du Vatican*, with a script taken from the novel and directed by Jean Meyer at the Comédie-Française.

André Gide died in Paris on 19 February 1951.

Letters:

André Gide, *Lettres* (Liège: A la Lampe d'Aladdin, 1930);

Correspondance Francis Jammes-André Gide 1893-1938, edited by Robert Mallet (Paris: Gallimard, 1948);

Marcel Proust, *Lettres à André Gide*, includes letters by Gide (Neuchâtel & Paris: Ides et Calendes, 1949);

Correspondance, 1899-1926, Paul Claudel-André Gide, edited by Mallet (Paris: Gallimard, 1949); translated by John Russell as *The Correspondence, 1899-1926, between Paul Claudel and André Gide* (New York: Pantheon, 1952);

Correspondance, 1909-1926, Rainer Maria Rilke-André Gide, edited by Renée Lang (Paris: Corrêa, 1952);

Correspondance Paul Valéry-André Gide 1890-1942, edited by Mallet (Paris: Gallimard, 1955); abridged and translated by June Guicharnaud as *Self-portraits: The Gide-Valéry Letters, 1890-1942* (Chicago: University of Chicago Press, 1966);

Correspondance André Gide-Charles Péguy 1905-1912, edited by Alfred Saffrey (Persan: Imprimerie de Persan-Beaumont, 1958);

The Correspondance of André Gide and Edmund Gosse, 1904-1928, edited by Linette F. Brugmans (New York: New York University Press, 1959; London: Owen, 1960);

Correspondance André Gide-Arnold Bennett 1911-1931: Vingt ans d'amitié littéraire, edited by Brugmans (Geneva & Paris: Droz & Minard, 1964);

Correspondance André Gide-Roger Martin du Gard 1913-1951, edited by Jean Delay, 2 volumes (Paris: Gallimard, 1968);

Jean Cocteau, *Lettres à André Gide*, edited by J.-J. Kihm, includes letters by Gide (Paris: Table Ronde, 1970);

Correspondance André Gide-François Mauriac, 1912-1950, edited by Jacqueline Morton (Paris: Gallimard, 1971);

Correspondance d'André Gide et Georges Simenon, edited by Francis Lacassin and Gilbert Sigaux (Paris: Plon, 1973);

Charles Brunard, *Correspondance avec André Gide et souvenirs* (Paris: La Pensée Universelle, 1974);

Gide and Albert Mockel, *Correspondance (1891-1938)*, edited by Gustave Vanwelkenhuyzen (Geneva: Droz, 1975);

Henri Ghéon and Gide, *Correspondance*, edited by Jean Tipi and Anne-Marie Moulènes, 2 volumes (Paris: Gallimard, 1976);

Correspondance André Gide-Jules Romains, edited by Claude Martin (Paris: Flammarion, 1976);

Gide and Jacques-Emile Blanche, *Correspondance: 1892-1939*, edited by Georges-Paul Collet (Paris: Gallimard, 1979);

André Gide-Justin O'Brien, Correspondance 1937-1951, edited by Morton (Lyons: Centre d'Etudes Gidiennes, 1979);

Correspondance André Gide-Dorothy Bussy, 1918-1951, edited by Jean Lambert, notes by Richard Tedeschi, 3 volumes (Paris: Gallimard, 1979, 1981, 1982); translated by Tedeschi as *Selected Letters of André Gide and Dorothy Bussy* (London: Oxford University Press, 1983);

Deutsch-französische Gespräche 1920-1950: La Correspondance de Ernst Robert Curtius avec André Gide, Charles Du Bos et Valery Larbaud, edited by Herbert and Jane M. Dieckmann (Frankfurt: Klostermann, 1980);

Gabrielle Vulliez, *La Tristesse d'un automne sans été: Correspondance de Gabrielle Vulliez avec André Gide et Paul Claudel (1923-1931)* (Bron: Centre d'Etudes Gidiennes, Université Lyon II, 1981);

Gide and François-Paul Alibert, *Correspondance: 1907-1950*, edited by Martin (Lyons: Presses Universitaires de Lyon, 1982);

André Gide-Jean Giono, Correspondance 1929-1940, edited by Roland Bourneuf and Jacques Cotnam (Lyons: Centre d'Etudes Gidiennes, 1984);

D'un monde à l'autre. La Correspondance André Gide-Harry Kessler (1903-1933), edited by Claude Foucart (Lyons: Centre d'Etudes Gidiennes, Université Lyon II, 1985);

Gide, *Correspondance avec Jef Last (1934-1950)*, edited by C. J. Greshoff (Lyons: Presses Universitaires de Lyon, 1985);

Anna de Noailles and Gide, *Correspondance (1902-1928)*, edited by Claude Mignot-Ogliastri (Lyons: Centre d'Etudes Gidiennes, Université Lyon II, 1986);

Gide and Thea Sternheim, *Correspondance (1927-1950)*, edited by Foucart (Lyons: Centre d'Etudes Gidiennes, Université Lyon II, 1986);

Gide, *Correspondance avec Francis Viélé-Griffin (1891-1931)*, edited by Henry de Paysac (Lyons: Presses Universitaires de Lyon, 1986);

Gide and Jacques Copeau, *Correspondance*, edited by Jean Claude, 2 volumes (Paris: Gallimard, 1987);

Gide, *Correspondance avec André Ruyters (1895-1950)*, edited by Martin and Victor Martin-Schmets (Lyons: Presses Universitaires de Lyon, 1987).

Interview:

Eric Marty, *André Gide, qui êtes-vous?* (Paris: La Manufacture, 1987).

Bibliographies:

Arnold Naville, *Bibliographie des écrits d'André Gide 1891-1952* (Paris: Guy le Prat, 1949);

Jacques Cotnam, *Bibliographie chronologique de l'œuvre d'André Gide 1889-1973* (Boston: G. K. Hall, 1974);

Cotnam, *Inventaire bibliographique et index analytique de la correspondance d'André Gide, publiée de 1897 à 1971* (Boston: G. K. Hall, 1975);

"Inventaire des traductions des œuvres d'André Gide," *Bulletin des Amis d'André Gide*, nos. 28, 29, 30, 31, 35, 42, 46, 58 (1975-1983);

Claude Martin and others, *La Correspondance générale d'André Gide*, fascs. 1-8, 1879-1951 (Lyons: Centre d'Etudes Gidiennes, Université Lyon II, 1985).

Biographies:

Jean Schlumberger, *Madeleine et André Gide* (Paris: Gallimard, 1956); translated by Richard H. Akeroyd as *Madeleine and André Gide* (Tuscaloosa, Ala.: Portals Press, 1980);

Jean Delay, *La Jeunesse d'André Gide*, 2 volumes (Paris: Gallimard, 1956-1957); abridged and translated by June Guicharnaud as *The Youth of André Gide* (Chicago: University of Chicago Press, 1963);

Claude Martin, *André Gide par lui-même* (Paris: Sevil, 1963);

George D. Painter, *André Gide, A Critical Biography* (New York: Atheneum, 1968);

Pierre de Boisdeffre, *Vie d'André Gide 1869-1951: Essai de biographie critique* (Paris: Hachette, 1970);

Maria van Rysselberghe, *Les Cahiers de la Petite Dame*, 4 volumes, Cahiers André Gide (Paris: Gallimard, 1973-1977);

Martin, *La Maturité d'André Gide: De "Paludes" à "l'Immoraliste" 1895-1902* (Paris: Klincksieck, 1977).

References:

André Gide, nos. 1-7, special issues of *Revue des Lettres Modernes* (1970-   );

Archives André Gide, nos. 1-5, Archives des Lettres Modernes (Paris: Minard, 1964-   );

Arthur E. Babcock, *Portraits of Artists. Reflexivity in Gidean Fiction 1902-1936* (Columbia, S.C.: French Literature Publications, 1982);

Christopher D. Bettinson, *Gide—Les Caves du Vatican* (London: Arnold, 1972);

Bettinson, *Gide: a Study* (Totowa, N.J.: Rowman & Littlefield, 1977);

Germaine Brée, *André Gide, l'insaisissable Protée* (Paris: Les Belles Lettres, 1953); revised and enlarged in English as *André Gide* (New Brunswick: Rutgers University Press, 1963); French version revised and enlarged (Paris: Les Belles Lettres, 1970);

Bulletin des Amis d'André Gide, 15 volumes to date (Lyons: Centre d'Etudes Gidiennes, Université de Lyon II, 1968-April 1985; Montpellier: Centre d'Etudes Littéraires du XXᵉ Siècle, Université de Montpellier III, July 1985-   );

Cahiers André Gide (Paris: Gallimard, 1969-   );

Elaine D. Cancalon, *Techniques et personnages dans les récits d'André Gide*, Archives André Gide, no. 2 (Paris: Lettres Modernes, 1970);

Karin Nordenhaug Ciholas, *Gide's Art of the Fugue: A Thematic Study of "Les Faux-Monnayeurs"* (Chapel Hill: University of North Carolina Press, 1974);

Thomas Cordle, *André Gide* (New York: Twayne, 1969);

Alain Goulet, *"Les Caves du Vatican": Etude méthodologique* (Paris: Larousse, 1972);

Goulet, *Fiction et vie sociale dans l'œuvre d'André Gide*, 2 volumes (Paris: Minard, 1984-1985);

W. Wolfgang Holdheim, *Theory and Practice of the Novel* (Geneva: Droz, 1968);

G. W. Ireland, *Gide, A Study of His Creative Writings* (London: Oxford University Press, 1970);

N. David Keypour, *Gide, écriture et réversibilité dans "Les Faux-Monnayeurs"* (Paris: Didier/Erudition/Montreal: Presses de l'Université de Montréal, 1980);

Philippe Lejeune, *Exercices d'ambiguïté. Lectures de "Si le grain ne meurt" d'André Gide* (Paris: Lettres Modernes, 1974);

David Littlejohn, ed., *Gide. A Collection of Critical Essays* (Englewood Cliffs, N.J.: Prentice-Hall, 1970);

Martine Maisani-Léonard, *Gide ou l'ironie de l'écriture* (Montreal: Presses de l'Université de Montréal, 1976);

Roger Martin du Gard, *Notes sur André Gide 1913-1951* (Paris: Gallimard, 1951); translated by John Russell as *Notes on André Gide* (London: Deutsch, 1953);

Eric Marty, *L'Ecriture du jour, Le "Journal" d'André Gide* (Paris: Seuil, 1985);

James H. McLaren, *The Theatre of André Gide: Evolution of a Moral Philosopher* (Baltimore: Johns Hopkins University Press, 1953);

Daniel Moutote, *Les Images végétales dans l'œuvre de Gide* (Paris: Presses Universitaires de France, 1970);

Moutote, *Index des idées, images et formules du "Journal" d'André Gide* (Lyons: Centre d'Etudes Gidiennes, 1985);

Moutote, *Le Journal d'André Gide et les problèmes du moi 1889-1925* (Paris: Presses Universitaires de France, 1968);

Maurice Nadeau and Philippe Clerc, *Album Gide* (Paris: Gallimard, 1985);

H. J. Nersoyan, *André Gide. The Theism of an Atheist* (Syracuse: Syracuse University Press, 1969);

Justin O'Brien, *Index détaillé des quinze volumes de l'Edition Gallimard des "Œuvres complètes" d'André Gide* (Asnières-sur-Seine: Prétexte, 1954);

Kevin O'Neill, *André Gide and the "Roman d'aventure"* (Sydney: Sydney University Press, 1969);

Catharine H. Savage, *André Gide: L'évolution de sa pensée religieuse* (Paris: Nizet, 1962);

Susan M. Stout, *Index de la Correspondance André Gide-Roger Martin du Gard* (Paris: Gallimard, 1971);

Wylie Sypher, "Gide's Cubist Novel," *Kenyon Review*, 11 (Spring 1949): 291-309;

Michael J. Tilby, *Gide, "Les Faux-Monnayeurs"* (London: Grant & Cutler, 1981);

C. D. E. Tolton, *Gide and the Art of Autobiography. A Study of "Si le grain ne meurt"* (Toronto: MacLean-Hunter Press, 1975);

Helen Watson-Williams, *André Gide and the Greek Myth: A Critical Study* (Oxford: Clarendon Press, 1967).

Papers:

Fifty of Gide's manuscripts and about 12,000 letters are deposited at the Bibliothèque Littéraire Jacques Doucet, Paris. These manuscripts are listed in the *Catalogue de Fonds Spéciaux de la Bibliothèque Littéraire Jacques Doucet* (Boston: G. K. Hall, 1972). The manuscripts of almost all of Gide's novels are in this collection with the exception of *Les Faux-Monnayeurs*, which is privately held.

Jean Giraudoux

(29 October 1882-31 January 1944)

Will L. McLendon
University of Houston

BOOKS: *Provinciales* (Paris: Grasset, 1909);
L'Ecole des indifférents (Paris: Grasset, 1911);
Retour d'Alsace (Paris: Emile-Paul, 1916);
Lectures pour une ombre (Paris: Emile-Paul, 1917); translated by Elizabeth S. Sargent as *Campaigns and Intervals* (Boston & New York: Houghton Mifflin, 1918);
Simon le pathétique (Paris: Grasset, 1918; revised, 1926);
Amica America (Paris: Emile-Paul, 1918);
Promenade avec Gabrielle (Paris: Gallimard, 1919);
Elpénor (Paris: Emile-Paul, 1919); translated by Richard Howard, with the assistance of Renaud Bruce (New York: Noonday Press, 1958);
Adorable Clio (Paris: Emile-Paul, 1920);
Suzanne et le Pacifique (Paris: Emile-Paul, 1921); translated by Ben Ray Redman as *Suzanne and the Pacific* (New York & London: Putnam's, 1923);
Siegfried et le Limousin (Paris: Grasset, 1922); translated by Louis Collier Willcox as *My Friend from Limousin* (New York & London: Harper, 1923);
La Prière sur la Tour Eiffel (Paris: Emile-Paul, 1923);
Juliette au pays des hommes (Paris: Emile-Paul, 1924);
Visite chez le prince (Paris: Emile-Paul, 1924);
Hélène et Touglas; ou, Les Joies de Paris (Paris: Sans Pareil, 1925);
Le Couvent de Bella (Paris: Grasset, 1925);
Premier Rêve signé (Le Dernier Rêve d'Edmond About) (Paris: Emile-Paul, 1925);
Bella (Paris: Grasset, 1926); translated by J. F. Scanlan (New York & London: Knopf, 1927);
Anne chez Simon (Paris: Emile-Paul, 1926);
Les Hommes tigres (Paris: Emile-Paul, 1926);
Le Cerf (Paris: Cité des Livres, 1926);
A la recherche de Bella (Liège: A la Lampe d'Aladin, 1926);
La Première Disparition de Jérôme Bardini (Paris: Editions du Sagittaire, 1926; translated as "The

Jean Giraudoux (photograph by D. R.; courtesy of Les Editions Bernard Grasset)

First Disappearance of Jérôme Bardini" in *The Best French Short Stories of 1925-1926*, edited by Richard Eaton (Boston: Small, Maynard, 1926);
Eglantine (Paris: Grasset, 1927);
Marche vers Clermont (Paris: Cahiers Libres, 1928);
Le Sport (Paris: Hachette, 1928);
Siegfried (Paris: Grasset, 1928); translated by Philip Carr (New York: L. MacVeagh, Dial Press/ Toronto: Longmans, Green, 1930);
La Grande Bourgeoise; ou, Toute Femme a la vocation (Paris: Editions Kra, 1928);

Amphitryon 38 (Paris: Grasset, 1929); translated in *Three Plays* (1964);

Le Signe (Paris: Emile-Paul, 1929);

Stéphy (Geneva: Kundig, 1929);

Aventures de Jérôme Bardini (Paris: Emile-Paul, 1930);

Rues et Visages de Berlin (Paris: Editions de la Roseraie, 1930);

Racine (Paris: Grasset, 1930); translated by P. Mansell Jones (Cambridge, U.K.: Fraser, 1938);

Fugues sur Siegfried (Paris: Lapina, 1930);

Judith; tragédie en trois actes (Paris: Emile-Paul, 1931);

Je présente Bellita (Paris: Grasset, 1931);

Mirage de Bessines (Paris: Emile-Paul, 1931);

La France sentimentale (Paris: Grasset, 1932);

Berlin (Paris: Emile-Paul, 1932);

Fontranges au Niagara (Paris: Cahiers Libres, 1932);

Intermezzo (Paris: Grasset, 1933); translated in *Plays* (1967);

Combat avec l'ange (Paris: Grasset, 1934);

Tessa, ou la nymphe au cœur fidèle, adapted from Margaret Kennedy and Basil Dean's play *The Constant Nymph* (Paris: Grasset, 1934);

Fin de Siegfried (Paris: Grasset, 1934);

La Guerre de Troie n'aura pas lieu (Paris: Grasset, 1935);

L'Impromptu de Paris (Paris: Grasset, 1937);

Electre (Paris: Grasset, 1937; translated by Winifred Smith as *Electra* in *From the Modern Repertoire*, second series, edited by Eric Bentley (Denver: University of Denver Press, 1952);

Supplément au voyage de Cook (Paris: Grasset, 1937);

Et moi aussi, j'ai été un petit Meaulnes (Paris: Emile-Paul, 1937);

Les Cinq Tentations de La Fontaine (Paris: Grasset, 1938);

Pour ce onze novembre (Paris: Grasset, 1938);

Cantique des cantiques (Paris: Grasset, 1938);

Alsace et Lorraine (Paris: Gallimard, 1939);

A propos de la rentrée des classes (Paris: François Bernouard, 1939);

Choix des élues (Paris: Grasset, 1939);

Ondine (Paris: Grasset, 1939); translated in *Plays* (1967);

Pleins Pouvoirs (Paris: Gallimard, 1939);

Le Futur Armistice (Paris: Grasset, 1940);

Réponse à ceux qui demandent pourquoi nous faisons la guerre et pourquoi nous ne la faisons pas (Paris: C.I.D., 1940);

Combat avec l'image (Paris: Emile-Paul, 1941);

Littérature (Paris: Grasset, 1941);

Le Film de la Duchesse de Langeais, d'après la nouvelle de H. de Balzac (Paris: Grasset, 1942);

L'Apollon de Marsac (Rio de Janeiro: Supplement to *Dom Casmurro*, no. 5, 10 July 1942);

Sodome et Gomorrhe (Paris: Grasset, 1943); translated by Herma Briffault as *Sodom and Gomorrah* in *Makers of the Modern Theater*, edited by Barry Ulanov (New York, Toronto & London: McGraw-Hill, 1961);

Le Film de Béthanie; texte de "Les Anges du péché" d'après le scénario de R.L. Bruckberger, Dominican, Robert Bresson, Jean Giraudoux (Paris: Gallimard, 1944);

Ecrit dans l'ombre (Monaco: Editions du Rocher, 1944);

Armistice à Bordeaux (Monaco: Editions du Rocher, 1945);

La Folle de Chaillot (Neuchâtel & Paris: Ides et Calendes, 1945);

Portrait de la Renaissance (Paris: Jacques Haumont, 1946);

Sans pouvoirs (Monaco: Editions du Rocher, 1946);

L'Apollon de Bellac (Neuchâtel & Paris: Ides et Calendes, 1946);

Visitations (Neuchâtel & Paris: Ides et Calendes, 1947);

Pour une politique urbaine (Paris: Editions Arts et Métiers Graphiques, 1947);

De Pleins Pouvoirs à Sans pouvoirs (Paris: Gallimard, 1950);

La Française et la France (Paris: Gallimard, 1951);

Les Contes d'un matin (Paris: Gallimard, 1952);

Pour Lucrèce (Paris: Grasset, 1953);

Oeuvre romanesque, 2 volumes (Paris: Grasset, 1955);

La Menteuse [fragment], *suivi de Les Gracques* (Paris: Grasset, 1958);

Portugal, suivi de Combat avec l'image (Paris: Grasset, 1958);

Oeuvres littéraires diverses (Paris: Grasset, 1958);

Théâtre, 4 volumes (Paris: Grasset, 1959);

Three Plays, translated by Phyllis La Farge with Peter H. Judd (New York: Hill & Wang, 1964)—comprises *Siegfried, Amphitryon 38,* and *Electre;*

Plays, translated by Roger Gellert (New York: Oxford University Press, 1967; London: Methuen, 1967)—comprises *Amphitryon 38, Intermezzo,* and *Ondine;*

Or dans la nuit: Chroniques et préfaces littéraires (1910-1943) (Paris: Grasset, 1969);

La Menteuse (Paris: Grasset, 1969); translated by Richard Howard as *Lying Woman* (New

York: Winter House, 1972; London: Gollancz, 1972);

Carnet des Dardanelles (Paris: Le Bélier, 1969);

Souvenir de deux existences (Paris: Grasset, 1975);

Théâtre complet, edited by Jacques Body (Paris: Gallimard, "Bibliothèque de la Pléiade," 1982).

PLAY PRODUCTIONS: *Siegfried*, Paris, Comédie des Champs-Elysées, 3 May 1928;

Amphitryon 38, Paris, Comédie des Champs-Elysées, 8 November 1929;

Judith, Paris, Théâtre Pigalle, 4 November 1931;

Intermezzo, Paris, Comédie des Champs-Elysées, 1 March 1933;

Tessa, Paris, Théâtre de l'Athénée, 14 November 1934;

La Guerre de Troie n'aura pas lieu, Paris, Théâtre de l'Athénée, 22 November 1935;

Supplément au voyage de Cook, Paris, Théâtre de l'Athénée, 22 November 1935;

Electre, Paris, Théâtre de l'Athénée, 13 May 1937;

L'Impromptu de Paris, Paris, Théâtre de l'Athénée, 4 December 1937;

Cantique des cantiques, Paris, Comédie-Française, 13 October 1938;

Ondine, Paris, Théâtre de l'Athénée, 4 May 1939;

L'Apollon de Marsac, Rio de Janeiro, Municipal Theatre, 16 June 1942; Paris, Théâtre de l'Athénée, 19 April 1947;

Sodome et Gomorrhe, Paris, Théâtre Hébertot, 11 October 1943;

La Folle de Chaillot, Paris, Théâtre de l'Athénée, 22 December 1945;

Pour Lucrèce, Paris, Théâtre Marigny, 6 November 1953.

MOTION PICTURES: *La Duchesse de Langeais*, screenplay by Giraudoux, 1942;

Béthanie, screenplay by Giraudoux and R. L. Bruckberger, 1943.

OTHER: "L'Orgueil," in *Les Sept Péchés capitaux*, edited by Jacques de Lacretelle (Paris: Editions Kra, 1927);

"Barbe," in *D'Ariadne à Zoé, Alphabet galant et sentimental* (Paris: Librairie de France, 1930);

Alfred de Musset, *Contes et nouvelles*, introduction by Giraudoux (Paris: Cité de Livres, 1931);

Adrienne Thomas, *Catherine Soldat*, preface by Giraudoux (Paris: Stock, 1933);

Annette Kolb, *Mozart*, preface by Giraudoux (Paris: A. Michel, 1938);

Evelyn Waugh, *Diableries*, preface by Giraudoux (Paris: Grasset, 1938);

"Discours liminaire," in *La Charte d'Athènes* (Paris: Plon, 1943);

Hommage à Marivaux, introduction by Giraudoux (Paris: Claude Sézille, 1944);

Théâtre complet de Marivaux, preface by Giraudoux (Paris: Editions Nationales, 1946).

PERIODICAL PUBLICATIONS: "Conversations canadiennes," *Idées Modernes*, 1 (February 1909): 323-331;

"L'Olympiade de 1924," *Revue Hebdomadaire*, 9 (1920): 330-333;

"Avant et après les jeux olympiques," *Annales Politiques et Littéraires* (18 November 1932): 442;

"Le Prix du football," *Annales Politiques et Littéraires* (16 December 1932): 550;

"Amateurs et professionnels," *Annales Politiques et Littéraires* (23 December 1932): 577; (30 December 1932): 605; (6 January 1933): 23;

"La Ligue des droits urbains," *Marianne* (19 April 1933);

"Pour un plus beau Paris (Faculté de Médecine)," *Marianne* (26 April; 3, 10, 17, 31 May; 14 June 1933);

"Les Responsables," *Marianne* (19 July; 6 September 1933);

"La Tragédie: Hier, aujourd'hui," *Conferencia*, 20 (1 October 1933): 385-398;

"Place Saint-Sulpice," *Marianne* (7 February 1934);

"Les Ecrivains, gardiens du domaine national," *Marianne* (16 May 1934);

"La Querelle de la Comédie," *Conferencia*, 24 (1 December 1934): 621-634;

"Les Travaux de France," series of five lectures, *Conferencia*, 8 (1 April 1939): 415-432; 9 (15 April 1939): 462-478; 10 (1 May 1939): 537-553; 11 (15 May 1939): 587-604; 12 (1 June 1939): 635-648;

"Une Dictature de l'urbanisme," *Comoedia* (19 February 1944);

"L'Aménagement de la France," *Echo des Etudiants* (31 March 1944).

Known primarily as one of the major French playwrights of the first half of the twentieth century, Jean Giraudoux scored his early literary successes with the novel, as evidenced by the fact that his *Siegfried et le Limousin* (1922; translated as *My Friend from Limousin*, 1923) was named co-winner of the Prix Balzac in 1922 (Emile Baumann's *Job le prédestiné* shared the honor). The previous year he had produced the fanciful novel *Suzanne et le Pacifique* (1921; translated as *Suzanne and the Pacific*, 1923) and well before that, in 1918, what amounts to his first true novel, *Simon le pathétique* (Simon the Sensitive). Other prose narratives of his formative years tend to defy standard classifications but can best be designated as short stories and travel notes all linked by a common thread of the author's experiences as a child in the French provinces.

Jean Giraudoux was born on 29 October 1882 in Bellac (Haute-Vienne) into a family of modest means. His father, Léger Giraudoux, was a minor official with the Department of Highways. With his parents, especially his mother, Anne Lacoste Giraudoux, and with his older brother, Alexandre, Giraudoux felt comfortable. He attended elementary school in Bellac and other provincial towns and studied at the lycée at Chateauroux for seven years, and then at the lycée Lakanal in Paris. To these surroundings and determinants were added strong doses of the military (World War I) and the diplomatic, since Giraudoux began his career in the French Foreign Service in 1910.

By 1928, when he produced his first work for the theater, *Siegfried* (an adaptation of his novel), Giraudoux was forty-six and had seven novels to his credit. While it is true that theatrical works became the major thrust of his literary efforts after *Siegfried* and *Amphitryon 38* (1929), it is significant that he returned intermittently to the novel as the more appropriate form for presenting dramas of contemporary men and women. Little critical attention has yet been paid to the dialectic so clearly indicated by the preponderance of ancient and classical themes and settings for his theater and of exclusively modern ones for his novels. There are a few exceptions, to be sure, notably in the theater with *Siegfried, Intermezzo* (1933), and *La Folle de Chaillot* (The Madwoman of Chaillot, 1945); but the novels are resolutely devoted to the contemporary scene. The intellectual and artistic disputation and discrimination involved here would seem to be ordered around Giraudoux's perception that the theater offered him richer opportunities than the novel for portraying universal aspects of the human plight in a way palatable to the public. The symbolic register to be exploited in the theater through the use of biblical characters and themes, Greek myth, and Roman history was a strong temptation for a novelist so attuned to the overtones of language as was Giraudoux, for one

who, in his earliest prose works, had frequently admitted to being seduced by the hidden significance of words and their near-magical qualities.

His two earliest books, *Provinciales* (1909) and *L'Ecole des indifférents* (School for Apathetics, 1911), are replete with indications of the power that words exercised over the young Giraudoux's mind: the former is a collection of vignettes of small-town life with touches reminiscent of an early Giraudoux literary idol, Jules Renard; the latter volume, striving for a more sophisticated tone, provides portraits of three young men, Jacques "the Selfish," Don Manuel "the Lazy," and Bernard "the Weak." Both books, particularly *L'Ecole des indifférents,* approach the style Giraudoux was soon to exploit in his novels, and the three young men strongly resemble the hero of the future novel *Simon le pathétique.* One suspects all these works of being strongly autobiographical, dealing as they do with the velleities of adolescents and young men seeking to reconcile artistic sensitivity and emotional and social equilibrium. Allusions to Giraudoux's experiences at the Ecole Normale Supérieure, where he completed his *licence ès lettres* in advanced German studies in 1904 and graduated at the top of his class in 1905, abound in these early books, as do references to his stay in Munich later in 1905. But it was his first trip to America as an exchange student at Harvard University for the 1906-1907 academic year that lent to young Giraudoux's manner and appearance a veneer of transatlantic sophistication that both surprised and intrigued such friends and future diplomatic colleagues as the urbane Paul Morand.

The "curious narcissism" that the critic Gonzague Truc noted early in Giraudoux's career is apparent on every hand in these first works—an observation confirmed by the author himself in a 1928 interview with A. de Luppé: "J'écris toujours à la première personne parce que je ne veux pas faire l'artifice de créer un autre personnage" (I always write in the first person because I do not wish to resort to the trick of creating another character). There is what one might describe as splitting of the personality, which begins in *Provinciales* and expands noticeably in *L'Ecole des indifférents* with Bernard "the Weak," who engages in dialogues with himself and indeed organizes his life in the Latin Quarter of Paris, where Giraudoux himself once occupied a flat, as though he had a roommate. He converses with his imaginary friend at the sidewalk cafés, comments on the pretty girls that pass

Giraudoux with Louis Jouvet, the actor and producer who strongly influenced Giraudoux's development as a playwright (courtesy of R. Laffont)

by, finds life generally wonderful, "mais il y était un peu seul" (but he was a bit lonely). This splitting of the self is often indicated through exploitation of a mirror technique in *Simon le pathétique.* The observant hero of this novel constantly notices one of his previous personalities, one of those little fellows dressed in black who looks very much like a brother, to paraphrase the poet Musset, but like a younger brother, since Simon is always a step ahead of him.

A kind of sentimental education, *Simon le pathétique* seems lacking in plot, like most of the subsequent novels. The persistently introspective nature of the narrative multiplies the faults of Simon's personality: Simon "the Anemic," Simon "the Tender," the "Wishy-Washy," "the Unstable," all vie for attention and are compared like so many Siamese twins. In the long run the splitting of the personality amounts to creation of scapegoats who relieve the hero of his flaws and their consequences, a major theme Giraudoux would develop fully in *Aventures de Jérôme Bardini* (1930). Jérôme feels that he has experienced many things by proxy as he looks at various old photographs of his former selves: the boy in first communion garb, the soldier who had carried the full backpack, and so forth.

As a sergeant in the 298th Infantry Regiment Giraudoux was wounded in the battle of the Marne in 1914 and later detached to special duty first in the Dardanelles, then in Portugal. Finally, in 1917 he was assigned by Philippe Berthelot, his mentor in the foreign service, to accompany a military-cultural mission that included the eminent philosopher Henri Bergson to the United States. Their destination was Cambridge, Massachusetts, and Harvard University, a homecoming after almost ten years for Giraudoux. At Harvard his roommate had been André Morize, who later made his career as a professor of French and founded, with Stephen Freeman, the French summer school at Vermont's Middlebury College. The ties were to endure, as evidenced by Giraudoux's visit to Middlebury in 1939, on the eve of the next war, just prior to his returning to France to assume his duties as propaganda minister. The second visit to New England in 1916-1917 together with his other wartime experiences furnished Giraudoux with the materials and inspiration for three books, *Lectures pour une ombre* (1917; translated as *Campaigns and Intervals,* 1918), the nostalgic and charming *Amica America* (1918), and *Adorable Clio* (1920). Though none of these can be called novels, their narrator-heroes are immediately recognizable as avatars of Jacques, Bernard, Don Manuel, and Simon.

Just as in his war diary *Lectures pour une ombre* almost all harsh detail is omitted in favor of poetic and fanciful descriptions, so in *Amica America* the accent is on the picturesque as perceived by a witty young French officer whose duties brought him into contact with rich, educated, often eccentric Americans. The serenity of the holiday episode entitled "Repos au lac Asquam" (Rest at Lake Asquam) is echoed over ten years later in the touching interlude between the couple Stéphy and Jérôme in *Aventures de Jérôme Bardini* at a comparable New England retreat. Taken all together these writings born of his wartime experiences constitute a maturing process and appear, on the surface, to be a nostalgic farewell to his childhood and youth. Giraudoux, however, would always yearn for the purity and innocence of those years and would people the novels and plays of his maturity with heroes—and particularly heroines—whose uppermost desire is for recapturing something of the paradise lost. To this end they learn that they must separate themselves from the horde, renounce bourgeois contentment and security, and, in short, pursue careers of evasion. Suzanne on her desert isle, in

Suzanne et le Pacifique; Jérôme Bardini, who abandons his family in France and pursues anonymity in the United States; Isabelle, heroine of the play *Intermezzo;* Edmée, in the 1939 novel *Choix des élues* (The Chosen Ones); and finally Nelly, in the posthumously published novel *La Menteuse* (1969; translated as *Lying Woman,* 1972), are prime examples of this enduring compulsion to achieve a higher felicity than secure, humdrum careers and existences can offer.

With tongue in cheek Giraudoux referred to his first published novel, *Simon le pathétique,* as a "mutilé" (a war casualty) when answering Jacques Doucet's request to acquire a manuscript draft of the book for his literary collection now in the Bibliothèque Sainte-Geneviève in Paris. Giraudoux claimed that as the German armies were approaching Paris in July 1914 two chapters had been hastily burned by an overwrought employee of the paper *Opinion* where the novel was appearing in serial form (July-August 1914) with the title *Simon.* The label "mutilé" is apt, but Giraudoux's suggestion that the war might have had a hand in the matter is mostly fanciful, the party responsible for the fragmentation and mutilation being more likely the undecided novelist himself. The crossword puzzle of chapters and sections, both those omitted from one version (1918) to the next (1926) or rebaptized or telescoped, is clear indication of Giraudoux's affinity with his doubting, hesitating hero. Simon is the prototype of the young man whose overly refined education keeps him from mixing freely with the crowd, however much he might wish to, who disdainfully distances himself, all the while poking fun at his own hesitancy and prudishness. Simon's girlfriend Anne wonders: "Derrière quel voile vivez-vous?. . . Il me semble parfois que rien ne vous atteint" (What kind of screen are you living behind?. . . I sometimes get the feeling that nothing can reach you). Like T. S. Eliot's character J. Alfred Prufrock, Simon seems to believe "There will be time, there will be time/To prepare a face to meet the faces that you meet . . ./ And indeed there will be time/To wonder, 'Do I dare?' and 'Do I dare?'/Time to turn back and descend the stair." Prufrock and Simon indeed have much in common, including the propensity for repetition. The raillery of a Jules Laforgue also comes to mind, for this young poet of the generation just preceding Giraudoux's and much admired by Eliot endured even less gracefully than Giraudoux or Eliot his sensitiveness and modesty. Ironic banter such as there is in *Simon le*

pathétique is, to be sure, a device for inflicting upon oneself a punishment that would be unendurable, coming from another person.

This young Simon, one discovers, has had precisely the same childhood and youth as Giraudoux, has pursued the same studies, taken the same trips, and affords a fuller picture than any of the characters from the earlier books. The first chapters, written before the outbreak of the war and entitled "L'Ecole du sublime" (School of the Sublime), reveal that Simon, always at the head of his class, has delayed choosing a profession as long as possible, "flown the coop," and traveled widely. Simon has been welcomed at every turn to rich and aristocratic circles and has returned to Paris where his friends and former classmates come to visit but leave him with nothing so much as the impression of his own superiority. Their accolades and praise for his accomplishments lead Simon to request his reader not to mistake him for a vain person when he admits: "Je n'étais pas tout à fait imparfait" (I wasn't entirely imperfect).

The body of the novel is a fragmented and rather unconvincing narrative of Simon's amorous dallyings. As John H. Reilly has pointed out in *Jean Giraudoux* (1979), Giraudoux had little interest in creating three-dimensional characters in *Simon le pathétique* or in pursuing psychological development. The confusion of traits and personalities among the three female protagonists, Gabrielle, Hélène, and Anne, testifies to the constant reshuffling of parts of the manuscript; and, as Reilly notes, Anne "may share some of the traits of Suzanne Boland, Giraudoux's future wife." They were married in 1918, had one son, Jean-Pierre, and were separated but not divorced at the time of Giraudoux's death in 1944. Comparing the published text of *Simon le pathétique* with a manuscript version, it is possible to theorize about this overlapping of the female roles and the personal reasons underlying certain of Giraudoux's omissions. The novel has been much criticized for its lack of solid, traditional construction, among other flaws, perhaps because some readers have failed to grasp the essential irony of the novel, that is, that Simon seems to wander blindly about in the world of his tastes and passions precisely because Giraudoux, at the time he wrote his first books, was trying rather desperately to find his own way and chose to heap genteel and somewhat subtle mockery on his own head. The wording of the title is significant: Giraudoux intends to show just how much a refined and overly sensitive young man bent on stylizing all his emotions is hoodwinked by his very qualities, just how *pathétique* he can be. He is like certain bees that construct unusually sculptured combs: "Mais aucun miel ne les baigne" (But no honey flows in them), as Giraudoux observes.

The appearance in 1919 of the lighthearted and witty *Elpénor,* a spoof of Homer's *Odyssey,* allowed Giraudoux fully to indulge his taste for the *boutade* (whimsical flash of wit) and the *canular* (farcical comment or prank), a part of his schoolboy and Ecole Normale heritage. If *Elpénor* is to be counted a novel, then it is the only one that prefigures the skillful use that Giraudoux would later make of classical themes and devices in his plays. Just as ten years later he was to take surprising liberties with the purported activities of Jupiter and Alcmena in *Amphitryon 38,* so Giraudoux here seizes on a minor reference in the adventures of Ulysses and his men to a sailor named Elpénor to spin a hilarious apocryphal tale that can best be appreciated by those who, like its author, have benefited or suffered from rigorous study of Greek and the classics.

Suzanne et le Pacifique marks a clear turning point in the novelist's development. Here for the first time he embarks on the creation of a fantasy world of attitudes that will in some measure compensate for life's disappointments and imperfections, which he was finding more and more intolerable as he advanced in his career and social contacts. The heroine, Suzanne, the embodiment of all that is bright and wholesome in provincial France, after a series of travels finds herself shipwrecked on a desert Pacific island and judges that she is destined "à jouer le rôle d'une Française seule dans une île" (to play the role of a Frenchwoman alone on an island). This is Giraudoux's way of stating that every creature, every action, situation, and object has been somehow foreordained and fits somewhere into the cosmic pattern. Suzanne, undismayed, soon makes her isolated domain the center of the universe, convincing herself that every event taking place in that vast human society from which she is now separated is occurring with her in view, for the eventual purpose of bringing her back home. And this is how she maintains contact with the universe more closely than if her island paradise were linked by radio with all the great capitals of the world. When she daydreams about France, for instance, she sees a pastureland in the Nivernais region dotted with sheep that will one day be loaded on a boat bound for her island. Or she thinks of Brittany, and Saint-Brieuc, where she sees a group of sailors gathered in some cabaret: the sailors who will be members of her rescue crew. But their boat cannot leave yet, because, as Suzanne's sixth sense informs her, the third ring of the starboard anchor is still waiting on a workman's bench at the Creusot foundry: "l'ouvrier avait la grippe, la pneumonie le menaçait" (the worker had the flu and was in danger of getting pneumonia). Or yet another reason: the ship must wait because the jar of pickles destined to sit on the captain's mess table is still at the bottling plant. All supposition is carefully excluded from this absolute world of the rigorous stylist that Giraudoux is becoming: it is not, for example, "l'ouvrier *devait* avoir la grippe" (the worker *probably* had the flu) but rather the affirmation "avait la grippe" (had the flu).

Sometimes, as she lies on the deserted beach, Suzanne gets the impression that the rescue boat is leaving, that somewhere a gigantic ship is being put to sea, since she feels the water suddenly rising to cover her heels. The possibilities of such mental games are obviously unlimited, and for Suzanne, as for Giraudoux, it is important to account for each object and each event, however small, just as the mathematician approaches absolute truth by adding still another factor to the equation in an infinite series. The universe is thus reduced by Giraudoux's x-ray view to a vast, logical, and perforce human schema, the exact opposite of the senseless and inhuman universe of certain of his well-known contemporaries. It is Giraudoux's special use of the enumeration technique that makes him not a forerunner of the "chosistes" (phenomenologists) but a true "ensemblier" (coordinator, decorative artist, one who "brings it all together"). Impressed as he was by the vacuity of the human lot, he attempts through enumeration to link humanity to the whole of creation. Through such methods the birch tree that will supply the pulp for the first newspaper that Suzanne will read after she is rescued becomes as irreplaceable in the structure of her universe as is the molecule of hydrogen to the glass of water. And it would doubtless be shown that all creation takes part in the arrival of Suzanne's rescue ship if only she—and Giraudoux—had eternity to enumerate. As scintillating, as witty as these games may be, the very magnitude of the vistas opened up in such stylistic fireworks overawes and discourages the reader. There is little or no basis for emotional involvement with such a protagonist as Suzanne.

Publisher's advertisement for the 1955 illustrated edition of Giraudoux's novels

Siegfried et le Limousin is atypical of the novelistic style Giraudoux had embarked upon with *Suzanne et le Pacifique* and was to exploit in most of his other novels. Along with *Aventures de Jérôme Bardini, Siegfried et le Limousin* is exceptional in that it has a traditional plot and allows the reader to follow a certain rectilinear and chronological unfolding of events. The meanderings and musings that are the stuff of most of the other novels are held to a minimum here. The fact that *Siegfried et le Limousin* deals with topics deriving from the recent world war, and in particular with Franco-German relations, doubtless accounts for its relative popularity at the time it was co-winner of the Prix Balzac in 1922. On the level of Giraudoux's personal life and career as a diplomat the novel is a landmark, treating as it does with great sensitivity the affinities and incompatibilities of the two temperaments, the two cultures that he knew best, the French and the German. Through his studies–Giraudoux prepared for but did not pass the *agrégation d'allemand* (highest university competitive examination in German for access to a university teaching career)–and through his travels and personal con-

tacts, Giraudoux had developed a keen insight into things German. It was this understanding and love of many aspects of Germany in addition to Giraudoux's rather sorry performance as commissioner of propaganda in 1939-1940 that led several of his compatriots seriously to misjudge his attitudes and motives during the Nazi Occupation. For example, Roger Allard, who spent many years on the literary staff of the *Nouvelle Revue Française,* remarked about 1950 that "l'esprit de Giraudoux n'est pas très français" (Giraudoux's way of thinking is not very French). Mutual understanding and appreciation, reconciliation where possible, these are the major themes of *Siegfried et le Limousin,* based on a case of amnesia in a French soldier who is left alive but without uniform or identification on the battlefield. Thus Jacques Forestier is discovered by the enemy, nursed back to health, reeducated, and, with the new identity of Siegfried von Kleist, soon after the war rises to an important position in German intellectual and political life, working tirelessly and instinctively toward a reconciliation of the two cultures. Much of what can appear optimistic and constructive in this novel should be read as an assessment by Giraudoux of the virtualities of human nature, for in the end–as is so often the case in Giraudoux's future works– the goals are not to be realized. Siegfried rediscovers his French identity and returns home. A generation later the "Trojan" war *will* take place, despite the ironic title of Giraudoux's best-known play, *La Guerre de Troie n'aura pas lieu* (1935; adapted by Christopher Fry for the English-speaking stage and published under the titles *Tiger at the Gates,* 1955, and *The Trojan War Will Not Take Place,* 1983).

The very serious question of practical compromise in facing life's problems forms the unlikely nucleus of *Juliette au pays des hommes* (Juliette in the Land of Men, 1924), a witty, airy, and seemingly superficial novel much in the spirit of *Suzanne et le Pacifique.* Juliette, a charming young provincial woman engaged to the handsome and wealthy young Gérard, finds that she must set her curiosity at rest before taking the marriage vows. She must explore all the facets of her inclinations and nature that might draw her to other men and see if she can gather them all up somehow and bestow them on Gérard. Giving herself one month to accomplish this feat, Juliette heads for Paris and experiences a series of encounters with men of many types: a botanist, an archaeologist, a writer, a mad Russian would-be lover—all of whom afford Giraudoux opportunities at satire of man's tendency toward overspecialization, onesidedness, and fragmentation of the larger self. What Juliette learns is to accept her own limitations as well as those of her fiancé, her province, in short, her little world. Being at one with these is far more important than pursuing some alluring but undefined or unrealizable goal. In this sense *Juliette au pays des hommes* represents Giraudoux's flirtation with that temptation all true artists must face: compromise, abandonment of the arduous path that leads to the ideal.

In this otherwise unremarkable novel Giraudoux has inserted what appears to be a gratuitous episode; the beginning of chapter six reads: "Juliette vint me voir aussi" (Juliette came to see me too). And soon afterward the author, alluding to his own works such as *Elpénor*, reads to Juliette some pages he has just written entitled "Prière sur la Tour Eiffel" (Prayer on the Eiffel Tower). They constitute what at that time amounted to Giraudoux's literary credo and had been published the previous year, 1923, in a limited deluxe edition. Their inclusion in the novel is not unwarranted, since the ideas contained in the "prayer" do fit into what Juliette is in the process of learning about self-limitation and compromise.

The "trilogy" of novels *Bella* (1926), *Eglantine* (1927), and *Aventures de Jérôme Bardini* (1930) was belatedly and only briefly designated by Giraudoux as "Histoire des Fontranges" (History of the Fontranges) on the title page of a deluxe edition of *Bella* published by Grasset in 1929. The 1926 first edition bears no such subtitle but does contain the notation that a sequel to be entitled "Bellita" was in preparation. This highly significant bit of information attests to the uncertainties of a writer who was struggling with contingencies far more basic than a proposed title; actually he was struggling with thematic materials that eluded him throughout the next novel—*Eglantine*, as it turned out—and doubtless created several of the frustrations that in turn generated *Aventures de Jérôme Bardini*, the first section of which had been published in a limited edition the same year as *Bella*.

It is well known that *Bella* was written in a spirit of loyalty to his friend and protector in government circles, Philippe Berthelot, whose ups-and-downs with Raymond Poincaré, a former president of France and later prime minister, furnished the materials of the novel. The work may have vindicated Berthelot in some minds of the charges of favoritism and intervention in a banking scandal; but *Bella* did its author little professional good. Already his colleagues in ministerial circles were finding that Giraudoux was a less than totally committed civil servant in his role as director of the Department of French Works Abroad, a bureaucratic ancestor of the present-day French Cultural Services. *Bella* gave many of them the distinct impression that Giraudoux had overstepped the bounds of propriety in seeking, through a novel, and therefore publicly, to clear his mentor Berthelot of charges brought by the Poincaré clan. The long-since-forgotten quarrel between these two politicians is transparently veiled in the struggles between the Rebendarts (Poincaré) and the Dubardeaus (Berthelot) in the novel. The angel of reconciliation in their midst is Bella, the attractive young widow of a Rebendart, and she is in love with Philippe Dubardeau, a son of the head of his clan, René Dubardeau. Just as in *Siegfried et le Limousin*, the grand scheme of reconciliation of the two feuding entities fails to bear fruit, thus further confirming Giraudoux's developing pessimism. But artistic problems as well grew out of *Bella*. The labor of composition of this novel gave birth to what might be called "off-shoot" chapters, by-products that Giraudoux usually marketed as limited edition deluxe booklets. The announced novel "Bellita" actually never appeared as such, but the brief *Je présente Bellita* (I Introduce Bellita) did make a limited-edition appearance in 1931.

It was the character of the Baron de Fontranges, Bella's genial father and representative of all that was reassuring in traditional France, who inspired Giraudoux to develop a trilogy. The baron occupies center stage along with the heroine and Moïse, a banker, in the sequel entitled *Eglantine* and also plays a major part in Jérôme Bardini's adventures. However, Giraudoux was never able fully to integrate his structural concepts while composing these novels, primarily because he could not resist the temptation to experiment in all directions, simultaneously, as it were, once he had found a sufficiently intriguing theme or set of characters. The novelist, unlike the playwright, did not have the benefit of a Louis Jouvet to offer him severe but constructive criticism. The resulting plethora of off-shoot chapters (some separately published, others included in *La France sentimentale*) bears clear testimony to this artistic dilemma: *Le Couvent de Bella* (Bella's Convent, 1925); *Hélène et*

Touglas; ou, Les Joies de Paris (Helen and Touglas; or, The Pleasures of Paris, 1925); *A la recherche de Bella* (Looking for Bella, 1926); *Je présente Bellita* (the final version of a text entitled "Gilbertain et le Pape" [Gilbertain and the Pope], 1931); *Attente devant le Palais Bourbon* (Waiting in Front of the Chamber of Deputies, 1932); *Français amoureux aux Jeux olympiques* (Frenchmen in Love at the Olympic Games, 1932); *Fontranges au Niagara* (Fontranges at Niagara Falls, 1932).

Giraudoux did envisage his prose works as a whole, as a sort of uninterrupted chronicle of present time. Precisely in 1932, when publication of the last of these off-shoots of *Bella* dealing with the Fontranges family was being completed, Giraudoux told Georges Charensol in an interview: "Un livre, une pièce ne se trouve nullement séparée de celle qui le précède, de celle qui le suit. Chaque œuvre en elle-même ne compte pas. Je n'ai pas la préoccupation du livre, mais de la série des livres" (A book or a play is in no wise separate from the one that precedes it or the one that follows it. Each work by itself doesn't count. I'm not concerned with one book, but with the series of books). To the reader of the trilogy the series is quite obvious, since Fontranges and Indiana, characters already introduced in *Bella* and *Eglantine*, reappear in *Aventures de Jérôme Bardini*.

Whereas the vacillations of Eglantine's affections between the aging Fontranges, representative of French traditionalism, and the equally mature Moïse, representative of Near Eastern exoticism, constitute one of the least rewarding of Giraudoux's novels, Jérôme Bardini's moral and artistic dilemmas command immediate attention and prove to be Giraudoux's best claim to having produced a readable and engaging novel, one that appears to be withstanding the test of time reasonably well. Instead of his usual charming if evanescent female protagonist, Giraudoux has chosen this time the mature but still vigorous Bardini to incarnate the moral dilemma which regularly left the author torn "between two truths or two lies," as the Ghost in his play *Intermezzo* puts it. Having achieved a near perfect score in all the standard categories of success—a beautiful and loving wife, a healthy male heir still in the cradle, considerable wealth, local respect and prestige—Jérôme Bardini feels so strong a call to explore the other possibilities in life that he decides to disappear, to abandon his family, even his country, and seek to create a new self in the New World. This is the challenge, movingly related in some of Giraudoux's finest prose, in the section entitled "La Première Disparition de Jérôme Bardini" (separately published in 1926). Part Two, "Stéphy" (published separately in 1929), relates the idyllic encounter with a young New York girl who is the epitome of purity and unassuming, even anonymous, devotion. But this charming love affair evoking many amusing aspects of life in Manhattan in the 1920s as observed by Giraudoux's prismatic vision can end only in a stalemate, since Jérôme is incapable of measuring up to Stéphy's performance in every category. Recognizing this fact in all modesty, Stéphy decides to make the break with their happiness and to "emigrate" from the "divine season" to the "human" one. Like her elder sisters Suzanne and Juliette, or like Edmée, yet-to-be heroine of *Choix des élues*, Stéphy feels that by walking out on Jérôme she has walked out of the terribly confining jail of ideal happiness.

The final section, entitled by Giraudoux "The Kid," relates Jérôme's involvement with a runaway boy whom he befriends and shelters in his hotel room in Niagara Falls. Jérôme's fascination with the simplicity and purity of childhood leads to his near worship of the Kid, whose portrait and actions are reminiscent of silent movies starring Jackie Coogan. But this infatuation and adoration must also come to an end, for society, in the person of the welfare worker, Mr. Deane, intervenes, having been alerted to the existence of this unlikely couple. Himself a former abandoned child, Mr. Deane is the voice of understanding and reason in his heart-to-heart talk with Jérôme: "Cher Monsieur . . . adorer l'enfance, c'est la pire hérésie. Songez ce à qui vous restera, dans quelques années, de votre divinité: un homme" (My dear sir . . . to adore childhood is the worst kind of heresy. Just think what will be left of your divinity in a few years: a man).

But while they have been talking, the sick child, alerted to danger, flees into the bleak winter night at Niagara Falls. Jérôme tracks the little fugitive through the snow in the direction of the falls and finds him half frozen hiding in a factory building. Their brief reconciliation scene is set amidst the *inhuman* surroundings of "discreet" factory machinery, where all is order, precision, and security from human intervention: "Tout semblait calculé, dans cette salle de mécanothérapie pour géants, de façon à couvrir pour le bien d'un enfant toutes les rumeurs mauvaises du monde" (Everything in that hall of mechanotherapy for giants seemed calculated so as to cover up the evil sounds of the world for the good of a child). In a final chapter, like a deus ex machina, old Fontranges, Jérôme's godfather, turns up in America and attempts to rescue Jérôme from himself, gently leading him back to the fold. On board the steamer returning to Europe they discuss Jérôme's disenchantment with the human state, his lack of belief in the values he once held dear. He admits having lost all trust in his colleagues, all faith in the notion of "great men" who might some day help humanity out of its impasse. Jérôme bitterly recalls how in his youth he had believed in genius: "Presque tout le temps que j'aurais pu, dans ma jeunesse, passer avec des femmes, je l'ai consacré aux hommes de génie. C'est avec eux que j'ai eu mes rendez-vous, mes déchirements" (During my youth nearly all the time that I could have spent with women I devoted to men of genius. It was with them that I had my affairs and my heartbreaks). But at the outset of these "liaisons" there had been a misunderstanding about the meaning of the word genius; no man, when you come down to it, has genius, Jérôme concludes.

Giraudoux's wrestlings with the dark angels of despair had begun in earnest and would continue unabated, particularly in such plays as *La Guerre de Troie n'aura pas lieu*, *Sodome et Gomorrhe* (1943), and the posthumously published *Pour Lucrèce* (1953; adapted by Fry as *Duel of Angels*, 1958). If many a page of these and other works appears to celebrate the human condition and mankind's efforts to strike an ideal balance between the animal and the vegetable kingdoms, as he likes to designate them, it should not be assumed that Giraudoux really believed in achievement of this ideal. In a spirit akin to that often echoed in Albert Camus's last writings, Giraudoux the ecologist, as well as the humanist and artist, affirms his determination to proclaim that life is beautiful and worth living, that human beings are kind and generous, knowing all the while that just the opposite is true. This is the ultimate message of *Pour Lucrèce*, whose victimized and dying heroine bitterly adds (in a manuscript variant) that she is expiring in such a negative faith "ne fût-ce que pour l'emporter sur vous" (if only to get back at you). Only in the effort, not in the achievement, is there any temporary salvation or semblance of victory.

This paradoxical stance is evident as well in Giraudoux's private and public efforts in the realm of urbanism. As an active member of the Urban League of Paris he crusaded throughout the 1930s and until his death early in 1944, dur-

ing the darkest moments of the Nazi Occupation, for the cause of saner urban policies. Despite his numerous articles about city planning, recreational facilities, architectural and other aesthetic concerns in journals and newspapers, Giraudoux had little cause to be encouraged by such successful lobbying efforts as those of the wine-and-spirits interests that preserved their extensive enclave of the Halle aux Vins (Wine Market) in the 5th *arrondissement,* a prime location then being promoted by Giraudoux and the Urban League for the projected new school of medicine of the University of Paris. The present quarters of this medical school, built soon after the war and sandwiched between ancient houses on the narrow rue des Saints-Pères, clearly demonstrate just how scandalously shortsighted and absurd the municipal authorities indeed were. Echoes of bitter setbacks such as this can be heard in *La Folle de Chaillot.*

The dichotomy of the inner self that began early in Giraudoux's career, the almost Rousseauesque coexistence of the optimist and the pessimist, amounts to artistic cyclothymia. With increasing insistence the outlooks of the optimists—Suzanne, Juliette, Eglantine, Isabelle (*Intermezzo*), Andromache (*La Guerre de Troie n'aura pas lieu*), Giraudoux the urbanist—are offset by the despairing and often fierce attitudes of the pessimists—Jérôme Bardini, Ulysses (*La Guerre de Troie*), Judith, Electra, even Ondine, and most particularly the heroines of the last two important dramas, Lia (*Sodome et Gomorrhe*) and Lucile (*Pour Lucrèce*). And it is through study of his writings on urbanism and social matters in conjunction with study of his novels and plays that one can best perceive the unity of design in Giraudoux's work. The directness of style in his articles on urbanism and the sociopolitical documents *Pleins Pouvoirs* (Full Powers, 1939), *Sans pouvoirs* (Powerless, 1946), and *La Française et la France* (The French Woman and France, 1951) should not lead one to conclude that they are totally detached from the more convoluted and sophisticated literary works. The preoccupations of the social man and the artist are the same. In an interview with André Lang in 1935 Giraudoux opined: "L'écrivain a, dans la société actuelle, un rôle immense à jouer. . . . La littérature est incorporée à la vie" (In today's society the writer has a tremendous role to play. . . . Literature is incorporated into life).

To preserve the childlike purity of humanity whenever possible, to restore it when it is lacking, this is the goal of the idealist Giraudoux who, in his "Prière sur la Tour Eiffel," likens himself to a wizard and a "little Messiah" for small things and animals. And although he speaks about this very personal and idealistic world of his in a fanciful and poetic fashion in *Suzanne et le Pacifique, Amphitryon 38*, and *Judith*, one would err in assuming that the same themes and attitudes cannot be expressed simply and straightforwardly in an article on sport, "Le Prix du football" (The Football Prize, 1932): "Pour rendre sensible cette entente de l'homme et des éléments, l'écrivain est, en somme, amené à recréer ce premier moment de joie sportive que fut celui de la création, à nous donner sa description de l'Eden" (In order to make this understanding between man and the elements felt the writer is led, in the long run, to re-create that first moment of athletic joy that was Creation, led to give us his own description of Eden). There can be little doubt that Giraudoux's love of a radiant and healthy human race as so often expressed in his propagandistic writings on sport, urbanism, and other social concerns is the same love that wells up in the heart of Judith's lover Holophernes, who considers himself to be "l'ami des jardins à parterre, des maisons bien tenues, de la vaisselle éclatante sur les nappes" (the friend of gardens bordered with flower beds, of well-kept houses, of dishes sparkling on the tablecloths). The same love also fills the heart of the god Jupiter (*Amphitryon 38*) who delights in contemplating "de grands et beaux corps sculptés à l'avant de l'humanité comme des proues" (great beautiful bodies sculptured at the forefront of humanity like prows).

Despite superficial divergencies there is in the basic plots of the novels and plays a startling homogeneity if one views them from the vantage point of the couple. They unwaveringly consist of man's efforts and woman's efforts to comprehend and adapt to the opposite sex. The promise of some measure of success is clearly offered in the works from *Simon le pathétique* through *Amphitryon 38*. After *Aventures de Jérôme Bardini*, however, the balance shifts and dramas of mutual incomprehension gain the upper hand. It can be assumed that this change reflects the increasing difficulties in the author's relationship with his wife. It has been observed by Paul Morand in his *Giraudoux: Souvenirs de notre jeunesse* (1948) that from the time that Giraudoux was appointed inspector general of French consular establishments throughout the world in the early 1930s

his private life began to resemble more and more that of the uprooted Bardini. In any case all the plays and novels produced after that time reflect an increasing skepticism in regard to the couple. The extraordinary inner vision of his heroes and heroines, even the early ones, presupposes by definition a disenchantment with reality, some malaise or fear that prompts them to retreat ever further into the safety zone which isolates them from the rank and file of humanity. The end point of such retreat is total solitude. Edmée, heroine of the last novel published during Giraudoux's lifetime, *Choix des élues* (1939), languishes in the idea of a world "où les rapports entre les êtres n'auraient jamais été que des flexions, des consentements, des transparences" (where relations between human beings would have been nothing more than flexions, assents, and transparencies). It has been asserted that disillusionments associated with the author's earliest years became the ingredients of obsessive scenes, one of which is the image in the mirror, central to *Simon le pathétique*. This narcissistic twist, the epitome of solitude, crops up with regularity; it is stunningly transmuted in the play *Judith* by the series of farewells the heroine bids to her former selves, as well as in *Pour Lucrèce* by Paola's revelation to Lucile that their "dialogue" is in truth a monologue.

Bardini's attempts at moving outward toward conjugal understanding prove to be but a "croisade sans croix vers l'inaccessible" (a crossless crusade toward the unattainable). Even the demure and tender Stéphy, who seems to be all sweetness and purity, is impregnated with that cruelty which characterized Giraudoux's future heroines: even while dreaming of her possible life with the mysterious Jérôme–the "Shadow," as she calls him–Stéphy is thinking ahead to her future life of "vengeance sur les hommes" (revenge against men) when, after the brief interlude with Jérôme, she will marry some anonymous and totally different male. The virgin Stéphy muses that whereas she feels ready to grant all the privileges and joys of love to the "Shadow," she will not do as much for the husband. Although she is an excellent cook her husband can simply eat canned foods, and furthermore she will make him open the cans himself! To forestall his trying to take her arm she will be careful to load it with packages, and if he insists on smoking, then she herself will stick the cigarette in his disgusting mouth. All these musings are far from being childish daydreams; they are the forerunners of the dis-

Portrait of Giraudoux by Vuillard (Rapho)

integration of all couples as announced by Lia's shrill retorts to her husband Jean in *Sodome et Gomorrhe,* now familiar reactions amplified to the point of horror.

As if to ward off some imminent catastrophe, Giraudoux for a while charges certain couples–Jérôme and Stéphy, Hector and Andromache (*La Guerre de Troie n'aura pas lieu*), Hans and Ondine–with offering up to the universe the symbol of a united pair of human beings. But they are all flawed in some respect, and one learns from one of the minor plays, *Supplément au voyage de Cook* (1937; adapted by Maurice Valency as *The Virtuous Island,* 1956), that it is not *a* couple but *the happy* couple alone that can forestall the universal catastrophe: "Ce n'est pas la question des couples qui compte, en ce bas monde, mais celle des couples heureux!" (It's not the matter of couples that counts in this old world but the matter of happy couples!). And only one couple apparently escapes the cruel destiny of Giraudoux's world; it can be cited here without upsetting the totally pessimistic pattern since it is a couple created by someone else, by Balzac, and only adopted and adapted by Giraudoux. In choosing to retell Balzac's story of Antoinette and Montriveau in his film *La Duchesse de Langeais* in 1942, scarcely two years before his death, Giraudoux doubtless was recreating a fantasy. The star of that wartime movie was the actress Edwige Feuillère, with whom he was emotionally involved, his marriage having long since disintegrated.

Another work that fits tightly into this pattern of despondency is the 1934 novel *Combat avec l'ange* (Struggle with the Angel), offering further study of the incompatibility of reality and the ideal, the impossibility of full and enduring understanding between the sexes. It is a strangely uneven and unduly complicated tale of the lovely South American woman, Maléna Paz, who, like Jérôme and Edmée, would appear to have every material, social, and intellectual reason to be happy in life, but whose private demon incites her to neurotic attempts to become acquainted with unhappiness. The intricacies of her unlikely story and its intertwining with the threads of a political and diplomatic plot reminiscent of *Bella*– and doubtless of the author's professional experiences–engender continuous struggles for the reader and make for dull reading. Here, as in the posthumously published *La Menteuse*, composed at about the same time, Giraudoux is far from achieving a successful transposition of his amorous and emotional problems to the artistic plane. Only in the theater with *Sodome et Gomorrhe* and *Pour Lucrèce* did he manage to sound the open diapason of despair and resentment over the human condition that is so unconvincingly suggested in *Combat avec l'ange*.

The reappearance of the characters Fontranges and Eglantine toward the end of *La Menteuse* clearly links this novel to the Bella-Bardini series of texts, whose composition is thus spread over the ten-year period 1926-1936. The heroine, Nelly, is but another unconvincing variant of Bella, Maléna, and Edmée; the urbane hero, Reginald, suggests the author's idealization of himself. Their love affair in Paris is carried on in an atmosphere evocative of Giraudoux's own milieu and so provides further evidence of the private motives that led him, according to his son Jean-Pierre in his postface to the 1969 edition of the novel, to forgo publication of the novel in his lifetime. Whatever claims may be made for *La Menteuse* as an example of Giraudoux's gift for writing a "psychological" novel, the fact remains that implicit in its tedious exploitation of tricky metaphor and various linguistic conceits is the notion that the heroine's psychological problems can be resolved through manipulation of language. Thus Giraudoux willy-nilly devalorizes suspense and disengages the reader from true involvement in his characters' concerns.

Indeed throughout his career Giraudoux the novelist was more often severely criticized than praised, although such critics as Robert Brasillach, Benjamin Crémieux, Edmond Jaloux, and René Lalou found much to admire in his concepts as well as his prose style. But, despite such brief and relative success as *Siegfried et le Limousin* may be said to have enjoyed, the novels as they appeared never attracted readers in numbers comparable to Giraudoux's theater public. When, in 1928, the play *Siegfried* was first performed even Giraudoux's staunchest admirers and friends found themselves more or less on the same side of the fence as his detractors. Almost universally they had assumed that the extravagant language of the novelist would be the playwright's nemesis. Few if any of them had foreseen the near miracle of reconciliation that would be wrought in Giraudoux's theater by the conjunction of symbolically rich subject matter (the ancient, the mythi-

cal, the universal) and the equally fertile linguistic register already perfected by Giraudoux in his novels. The rapid succession of brilliant theatrical successes—only *Judith* was not at first in this company—might easily have convinced their author that efforts at the novel were no longer worth his while. Yet Giraudoux persisted until the end of his life in writing novels all of whose subjects appear to be derived not from myth or history but from personal experience. Their settings often correspond to those of Giraudoux's travels: New York, Los Angeles, Canada, Latin America, Paris, while their subject matter corresponds to intimate, personal concerns. But the linguistic acuity and prowess so evident in the novels, being generally unsustained by correspondingly valid feats of structure and plot, almost inevitably yielded an artificiality dubbed "précieux." However much the reader's sensitivity might be tickled by the meandering of Suzanne's fancy as she muses on her Pacific island, however sophisticated Simon's amorous anguish or Nelly's amorous rationalizations, such niceties have not been deemed by the reading public to be the stuff of a good novel. Real-life modern men and women simply do not behave like the heroes or the heroines of Giraudoux's novels. In contrast, the characters in plays such as *La Guerre de Troie n'aura pas lieu*, *Intermezzo*, *Amphitryon 38*, and *L'Apollon de Bellac*, because they are lifted through their nonrealistic settings to a universal plane, have not only survived, they are also quite popular. But few readers of the novels can be found, if one judges by personal inquiry and the printers' statistics. Even advanced students of modern French literature find Giraudoux's novels tedious, often inaccessible in their allusions, and psychologically baffling.

Letters:

Lettres, edited by Jacques Body (Paris: Klincksieck, 1975);

"Correspondance entre Jean Giraudoux et Louis Jouvet," edited by Brett Dawson, *Cahiers Jean Giraudoux*, no. 9 (Paris: Grasset, 1980): 20-122.

Interviews:

Frédéric Lefèvre, "Jean Giraudoux," in his *Une heure avec . . .*, fourth series (Paris: Gallimard, 1924), pp. 141-151;

"De la façon de faire comprendre et goûter les auteurs modernes," *Cahiers de la République des*

Lettres, des Sciences et des Arts, 1 (15 April 1926): 70;

A. de Luppé, "Jean Giraudoux," *Le Correspondant,* 311 (25 May 1928): 509-523;

Georges Charensol, *Comment ils écrivent* (Paris: Montaigne, 1932), pp. 103-106;

André Lang, "L'Enchanteur Jean Giraudoux," in his *Tiers de siècle* (Paris: Plon, 1935), pp. 216-221.

Biographies:

Laurent LeSage, *Jean Giraudoux: His Life and Works* (University Park: Pennsylvania State University Press, 1959);

Georges Lemaître, *Giraudoux. The Writer and His Work* (New York: Ungar, 1972).

References:

René-Marill Albérès, *Esthétique et morale chez Jean Giraudoux* (Paris: Nizet, 1957);

Jacques Body, "A la lumière du manuscrit de *Souvenirs de deux existences* de Giraudoux," *Studi Francesi,* 20 (May-August 1976): 265-268;

Body, *Giraudoux et l'Allemagne* (Paris: Didier, 1975);

Body, "Nationalisme et cosmopolitanisme dans la pensée de Giraudoux," in *Actes du Congrès de l'Association Internationale de Littérature Comparée* (The Hague & Paris, 1966), pp. 534-540;

Cahiers de l'Association Internationale des Etudes Françaises, special issue on Giraudoux, 24 (May 1982);

Cahiers Jean Giraudoux (Paris: Grasset, 1973-   );

Morton M. Celler, *Giraudoux et la métaphore. Une Etude des images dans ses romans* (The Hague & Paris: Mouton, 1974);

Centenaire de Jean Giraudoux (1882-1944). La Jeunesse de Jean Giraudoux en Berry (Châteauroux: Association Amicale des Anciens Elèves du Lycée Jean Giraudoux, 1983);

Robert Cohen, *Giraudoux. Three Faces of Destiny* (Chicago: University of Chicago Press, 1968);

Aurel David, *Vie et mort de Jean Giraudoux* (Paris: Flammarion, 1967);

Brett Dawson, "De Harvard au Quai d'Orsay (avril 1908-juin 1910)," *Revue d'Histoire Littéraire de la France,* 83, nos. 5-6 (September-December 1983): 711-724;

Luc Decaunes, "En relisant *Bella,* ou Jean Giraudoux romancier," *Marginales,* 98 (November 1964): 1-10;

Esprit Créateur, issue on Giraudoux, 9, no. 2 (Summer 1969);

Jean-Pierre Giraudoux, *Le Fils* (Paris: Grasset, 1967);

"Giraudoux en son temps," proceedings of the colloquium held at the Collège de France, 11 December 1982, *Revue d'Histoire Littéraire de la France,* 83, nos. 5-6 (September-December 1983): 707-908;

Charles Krance, "Giraudoux's *Suzanne et le Pacifique.* Text, Topoi, and Community," *Australian Journal of French Studies,* 14 (May-August 1977): 164-173;

Laurent LeSage, *L'Œuvre de Jean Giraudoux, Essai de bibliographie chronologique, I* (Paris: Nizet, 1956);

LeSage, *L'Œuvre de Jean Giraudoux, II* (University Park: Pennsylvania State University Press, 1958);

Charles P. Marie, *Giraudoux aux sources du sens* (Besançon: Editions Austrasie, 1983);

Marie, *La Réalité humaine chez Giraudoux* (Paris: Pensée Universelle, 1975);

Chris Marker, *Giraudoux par lui-même* (Paris: Editions du Seuil, 1954);

Georges May, "Giraudoux et les Etats-Unis," *French Review,* 49 (May 1976): 1041-1054;

Will L. McLendon, "Les 'Antennes' des héros de Giraudoux," *Esprit Créateur,* 9 (Summer 1969): 118-127;

McLendon, "A Compositional Aspect of Giraudoux's Novels: The 'Offshoot' Chapter," *Orbis Litterarum,* 23, no. 3 (1968): 233-246;

McLendon, "Giraudoux and the Impossible Couple," *PMLA,* 82, no. 2 (May 1967): 197-205;

McLendon, "Giraudoux and the Split Personality," *PMLA,* 73, no. 5 (December 1958): 573-584;

McLendon, "Giraudoux, champion de l'urbanisme," *Le Bayou,* 58 (Summer 1954): 69-75;

McLendon, "Un Mutilé de Giraudoux: *Simon le pathétique,*" *French Review,* 31, no. 2 (December 1957): 99-108;

McLendon, "Sang de l'exégète," *French Review,* 32, no. 2 (December 1958): 178-179;

Paul Morand, *Giraudoux: Souvenirs de notre jeunesse* (Geneva: La Palatine, 1948);

Agnes Raymond, *Jean Giraudoux: The Theatre of Victory and Defeat* (Amherst: University of Massachusetts Press, 1966);

Raymond, "Première Ebauche d'un profil stylistique de Giraudoux," *Language and Style,* 6, no. 1 (Winter 1973): 39-47;

John H. Reilly, *Jean Giraudoux* (Boston: Twayne, 1979);

Gonzague Truc, "M. Jean Giraudoux et le modernisme littéraire," *Grande Revue,* 110 (1923): 547-561.

Papers:
Manuscripts and letters by Giraudoux are at the Bibliothèque Nationale, Fonds Giraudoux; the Bibliothèque de l'Arsenal, Fonds Louis Jouvet; the Bibliothèque Sainte-Geneviève, Fonds Jacques Doucet; the Pennsylvania State University Libraries; and the University of Texas (Austin), Harry Ransom Humanities Research Center.

Jacques de Lacretelle

(14 July 1888-2 January 1985)

Douglas W. Alden
University of Virginia

SELECTED BOOKS: *La Vie inquiète de Jean Hermelin* (Paris: Grasset, 1920);

Silbermann (Paris: Gallimard, 1922); translated by Brian Lunn (London: Benne, 1923; New York: Boni & Liveright, 1923);

La Bonifas (Paris: Gallimard, 1925); translated by Winifred Stephens Whale as *Marie Bonifas* (London & New York: Putnam's, 1927);

Lettres espagnoles (Paris: Emile Chamontin, 1926);

Quatre Etudes sur Gobineau (Liège: A la Lampe d'Aladin, 1926);

Aperçus (Paris: M. Lesage, 1927);

Aparté: Colère–Journal de Colère–Dix Jours à Ermenonville (Paris: Gallimard, 1927);

L'Ame cachée (Paris: Gallimard, 1928);

Etudes (Paris: Picart, 1928);

Histoire de Paola Ferrani (Paris: Flammarion, 1929);

Amour nuptial (Paris: Gallimard, 1929); translated by Edwin Granberry as *A Man's Life* (New York: Holt, 1931);

Le Retour de Silbermann (Paris: Editions du Capitole, 1929);

Le Demi-dieu; ou, Le Voyage en Grèce (Paris: A la Société d'Edition "Le Livre," 1930); republished as *Le Demi-dieu; ou, Le Voyage de Grèce* (Paris: Grasset, 1931); revised as *Le Voyage de Grèce* (Paris: Fayard, 1955);

Sabine, volume 1 of *Les Hauts Ponts* (Paris: Gallimard, 1932);

L'Enfance d'une courtisane (Paris: Editions de France, 1932);

Jacques de Lacretelle (courtesy of Mme Yolande de Lacretelle)

Les Fiançailles, volume 2 of *Les Hauts Ponts* (Paris: Gallimard, 1933);

Les Aveux étudiés (Paris: Gallimard, 1934);

Années d'espérance, volume 3 of *Les Hauts Ponts* (Paris: Gallimard, 1935);

La Monnaie de plomb, volume 4 of *Les Hauts Ponts* (Paris: Gallimard, 1935);

L'Ecrivain public (Paris: Gallimard, 1936);

Qui est La Rocque? (Paris: Flammarion, 1936);

Discours de réception de M. Jacques de Lacretelle à l'Académie Française et réponse de M. Abel Hermant (Paris: Gallimard, 1938);

Morceaux choisis (Paris: Gallimard, 1938);

Croisières en eaux troubles (Paris: Gallimard, 1939);

L'Heure qui change (Geneva: Milieu du Monde, 1941);

Libérations (New York: Brentano's, 1945);

Le Pour et le contre, 2 volumes (Geneva: Milieu du Monde, 1946);

Idées dans un chapeau (Monaco: Editions du Rocher, 1946);

Deux Cœurs simples (limited edition, Geneva: G. Cramer, 1947; trade edition, Paris: Gallimard, 1953);

Une Visite en été (Paris: Gallimard, 1953);

Le Tiroir secret (Paris: Wesmael-Charlier, 1959);

Les Maîtres et les amis: Etudes et souvenirs littéraires (Paris: Wesmael-Charlier, 1959);

La Galerie des amants (Paris: Perrin, 1963);

L'Amour sur la place (Paris: Perrin, 1964);

Talleyrand (Paris: Hachette, 1964);

Face à l'événement. "Le Figaro," 1826-1966 (Paris: Hachette, 1966);

Victor Hugo (Paris: Hachette, 1967);

Anthologie de lettres d'amour, 2 volumes (Paris: Perrin, 1968);

Introduction au théâtre de Racine (Paris: Perrin, 1970);

Portraits d'autrefois, figures d'aujourd'hui (Paris: Perrin, 1973);

Journal de bord (Paris: Grasset, 1974);

Les Vivants et leur ombre (Paris: Grasset, 1977);

Quand le destin nous mène (Paris: Grasset, 1981).

TRANSLATIONS: Mary Webb, *Sarn,* translated by Lacretelle and Madeleine T. Guéritte (Paris: Grasset, 1930);

Webb, *La Renarde,* translated by Lacretelle and Marie Canavaggia (Paris: Catalogne, 1933);

Emily Brontë, *Haute Plainte,* translated by Lacretelle and Yolande de Lacretelle (Paris: Gallimard, 1937);

Robert Goodyear, *Mrs. Loveday,* translated by Lacretelle and Yolande de Lacretelle (Paris: Robert Laffont, 1949).

When Jacques de Lacretelle died in 1985 at the age of ninety-six the daily *Figaro* called him the last French moralist. It would have been more correct to say that he was the last traditional novelist. Between the two world wars he was acclaimed as one of France's leading novelists and achieved membership in the venerable Académie Française at the early age of forty-eight. His traditionalism accounted for his initial successes in a period when French literature was still trying to return to its past, in spite of the dadaists and surrealists, but it inevitably doomed him to oblivion after World War II when the traditional values of French classicism succumbed first to existentialism and then to the New Novel.

A friend and admirer of Proust and Gide, Lacretelle took little more from them than the first-person narrative, hardly a new invention since it bore the hallmark of the eighteenth century. Whenever he tried to renew his writing, he returned to an archaic form, the omniscient author who knows all and explains all, the preferred technique of the nineteenth-century realists. Throughout his career he alternated these two forms with a surprising regularity.

Tall and handsome, even in his later years, he was a public figure only as an assiduous member of the Académie. Maladjusted as a child and as a young man, his literary success had given him a new confidence and his 1933 marriage a sense of serenity which compensated for a feeling of isolation due to the deafness which began in his early youth. Although a frequent lecturer, especially in foreign countries, he avoided the limelight and, in later years, was more interested in his country estates.

In spite of his *particule* (the *de* in his name), he had only married into the nobility, and, although he was at ease in this milieu, he was basically at variance with the usual aspirations of this social caste, for the Lacretelles had always been nineteenth-century liberals. The great-grandfather, Charles Lacretelle, was a bourgeois from Lorraine who came to Paris before the Revolution and who was famous for his liberal views. During the Empire he became a professor at the Sorbonne and a member of the Académie and, during the Restoration, was honored by a *particule,* which he never used. By marriage, his son Henri acquired the château of Cormatin and, assuming his *particule,* lived as a country gentleman; but he was also a friend and neighbor of the poet Alphonse de Lamartine who was soon to play a role in the revolution of 1848; it was, in fact, Henri de Lacretelle who headed the local revolution in Mâcon. Jacques de Lacretelle was born at Cormatin (Burgundy) in 1888, the son of

Amaury de Lacretelle and his wife, née Juliette Brouzet. He spent his childhood abroad since his father was a minor diplomat. Although he had a few childhood memories of Cormatin during vacations, all that was lost when Cormatin was sold in 1898 at the death of his father. At ten Jacques de Lacretelle went to Paris with his mother, who was related to one of the capital's most liberal clans clustered around Pauline Menard-Dorian, later to become a model for Proust's Madame Verdurin. Lacretelle grew up surrounded by Hugos, Daudets, Lockwoods, and Charcots. During the Dreyfus affair he knew all of the leading figures of the Dreyfus camp.

In such surroundings, Jacques de Lacretelle should have been a precocious child, but he was not. He was difficult and often rebellious. At the Lycée Janson-de-Sailly he was such a mediocre student that his mother withdrew him and, boarding him with a Protestant pastor whom he detested, put him in the Lycée of Versailles. She finally let him return to Janson, but he twice failed the baccalaureate examination and never took it again. It is ironic that this *cancre* was later to write the purest French prose and to be called upon to preface the French classics as though he were the arbiter of French classicism. Through family influence Lacretelle became a banker for eighteen months; after he was fired, he did nothing constructive but travel for the next few years. During the war he served for a brief time in the trenches, fell ill, and was discharged. But during the war he read Proust's *Du côté de chez Swann* (*Swann's Way*, 1913), went to visit this still unknown author, and, encouraged by Proust's friend Reynaldo Hahn, began to write.

His own adolescent revolt was the subject of his first novel, *La Vie inquiète de Jean Hermelin* (1920). Although there are Proustian overtones, the novel is traditional in form, being related from the omniscient point of view in the clearest prose. In themselves the events are not autobiographical, and one can only wonder whether the hero's thwarted sex life has any basis in reality. The novel was an immediate success because of the vogue for novels of adolescence, and Lacretelle was invited to enter the "holy of holies," the circle of the *Nouvelle Revue Française*.

Now the aesthetic pendulum was to swing the other way, for the next novel he wrote was to have a narrator as a participant. Lacretelle later referred to this unpublished manuscript as "Le Roman protestant." The narrator was to have been a Protestant, and his Protestant conscience

Lacretelle (seated, wearing bow tie) and others gathered around André Gide, Pontigny, 1923. Clockwise from left: Jean Schlumberger, Lytton Strachey, Mme Théo van Rysselberghe, Mme Mayrisch, Boris de Schloezer, Gide (holding book), André Maurois, Johan Tielrooy, Roger Martin du Gard, Jacques Heurgon, Funck-Brentano, Albert-Marie Schmidt, Pierre Viénot, Marc Schlumberger, Lacretelle, and Pierre Lancel.

was to have caused him to intervene in the lives of others. Lacretelle's mother was a Protestant from the Midi, but she never practiced any religion during her son's lifetime. Hence Lacretelle had largely to imagine his Protestant setting, though perhaps reading Gide helped him. Before he had gone far, Lacretelle interrupted his writing to compose a short story, "La Mort d'Hippolyte" (The Death of Hippolytus) (published in the *Revue Hebdomadaire* and later in his *L'Ame cachée* [The Hidden Soul, 1928]), a modern transposition of the Greek legend which every French child knew through Racine's *Phèdre*. This was a lesson in subtle logic and clarity. With this experience, Lacretelle returned to the first episode of his Protestant novel and expanded it into his masterpiece, the novel *Silbermann*, published in 1922, first in *La Nouvelle Revue Française* and then in book form.

Silbermann is the story of a precocious young Jew whom the Protestant narrator befriends and defends against persecution in the lycée, only to succumb to the persuasion of his less idealistic parents who believe that Silbermann is not a suitable companion for their son. Written in a chastened style and with a logic so subtle as to be unobtrusive, this novel is essentially cold because of the aesthetic principle which dominates. Silbermann is a tragic figure, but, as with so many Lacretelle characters, the tragedy is observed by someone on the outside, and it is the reader's responsibility to imagine the emotions. Short though it is and archaic in a sense, since it is in the lineage of the so-called psychological novel beginning with Madame de La Fayette's *La Princesse de Clèves* (1678), *Silbermann* is one of the great novels of the twentieth century.

Lacretelle abandoned "Le Roman protestant," although he was later to use another fragment of it in the short story "Le Christ aux bras étroits" (The Christ with the Upstretched Arms), published first in *La Revue de Paris* and then in *L'Ame cachée*. He now decided that he owed it to himself to become a great author in the true novelistic tradition of Balzac and Flaubert. The result was *La Bonifas* (1925; translated as *Marie Bonifas*, 1927), a long novel about a homely provincial child dominated by her father, ostracized by her fellow townsmen when she seems to be the lesbian which she is at heart, and finally transformed into a heroine when she organizes her town to resist the German occupation. Lacretelle always insisted that this was his best novel, perhaps because it conformed to his ultimate ideal of what a novel should be. For the modern reader its structure is too logical and its omniscience too artificial. Nevertheless Lacretelle was innovating in writing about a lesbian, although his novel is anything but clinical (the word *lesbian* is never mentioned).

Again the pendulum swings back as the narrator technique dominates in the next novel, *Le Retour de Silbermann* (The Return of Silbermann), published first in the weekly *Candide*. It is not the same novel that is known by this title today. In the first half the Protestant narrator has become a cynical debauchee who, in spite of occasional twinges of his Protestant conscience, causes his wife's death because of his indifference. This narrator is writing a novel entitled *Silbermann*. When he gives his manuscript to their nursemaid Hélène Mossé to read, the latter inexplicably disap-

pears. After his wife's death, the narrator rediscovers Hélène, who becomes his mistress, and through her he learns of the final defeat and death of Silbermann, for she had been Silbermann's mistress before becoming a nursemaid. When preparing to have his text published in book form, Lacretelle found Hélène Mossé to be too contrived; he therefore suppressed her and separated his text into two novels, *Amour nuptial* (Marital Love, 1929) and *Le Retour de Silbermann* (1929). *Amour nuptial*, often compared to Gide's *L'Immoraliste* (*The Immoralist*, 1902), was a success and won the novel prize of the Académie Française, whereas the simultaneous publication of *Le Retour de Silbermann* resulted in the eclipse of Lacretelle's second novel. It was republished later in a volume that also included *Silbermann*, which is unfortunate because the combined publication denigrates the hero of the original novel. Lacretelle said that he wanted to individualize Silbermann; he should have left him with his more heroic attributes.

In 1933 Lacretelle married Yolande de Naurois, a woman much younger than he, whom he had met not many years before when she was just eighteen. They had three children. The marriage introduced a considerable change into the life of a man who had been a bachelor for so long.

In his next novel, *Les Hauts Ponts* (1932-1935), he returned to the omniscient technique. In 1930 he had finished a translation of Mary Webb's *Precious Bane* and was eager to go back to the soil and, vicariously, to his birthplace, Cormatin. Instead of Burgundy, he chose the Vendée as his setting and spent some time in Fontenay-le-Comte before writing. This novel, originally planned for five "volumes" and ultimately reduced to four, appeared gradually over the next five years, first in periodicals and then in book form. His friend Roger Martin du Gard, author of the saga *Les Thibault* (1922-1940), had insisted that to achieve greatness, Lacretelle would also have to write a saga. Lacretelle's long novel is a nostalgic evocation of life in the nineteenth century and relates the fate of the château of Les Hauts Ponts, which is lost through the profligacy of its owner and then regained by his daughter Lise who seduces and blackmails her mother's former lover to get the necessary money, only to lose the castle again through the profligacy of her son. There are autobiographical elements, for Cormatin was once saved by a somewhat similar sacrifice of virtue. In discussing this novel before he wrote it, Lacretelle said that, this time, he was going to avoid the pitfall of concentrating on the analysis of one character, as he had done in *La Bonifas*. There are not only many characters and many subplots but the author makes a point of transferring the central intelligence from one character to another, so that they appear more human than Lacretelle's characters usually do. *Les Hauts Ponts* was Lacretelle's greatest effort and may well someday be considered his greatest novel. Although the first volume, *Sabine* (1932), received great acclaim, the others—*Les Fiançailles* (The Engagement, 1933), *Années d'espérance* (Years of Hope, 1935), and *La Monnaie de plomb* (The Lead Coin, 1935)—were less successful and *Les Hauts Ponts* seemed almost forgotten when the last volume appeared. Already literary tastes were changing radically, as Malraux and then Céline spread their violence through literature, as Gide made his trip to Moscow, and as World War II seemed to loom on the horizon.

From the beginning of his literary career, Lacretelle wrote short stories, travel books, and innumerable articles, mostly literary criticism which, for short periods, he contributed regularly to periodicals or newspapers. Few of these articles were political, but, as the next war approached, Lacretelle became increasingly critical of the Popular Front then governing France and expressed envy of what he perceived to be benevolent dictators (Mussolini and Salazar but never Hitler). He even supported the right-wing (and potential French dictator) Colonel François La Rocque but only after his organization had disbanded its storm troopers under government order. His pamphlet *Qui est La Rocque?* (1936) did little to improve his own stature after the war. During the war he lived on the Côte d'Azur and wrote regularly in the *Figaro* (which had taken refuge at Lyons), eventually joining its board of directors. After the Liberation, which he greeted in a series of enthusiastic articles, later collected under the title *Libérations* (1945) and published in New York, he felt himself to be the butt of attacks from some unknown quarter and ceased abruptly to write regularly for the *Figaro*, limiting himself to an occasional literary "chronique" on the front page.

Before the war he had begun to write a new novel, *Le Pour et le contre* (Pro and Con); he continued to write during the war and, in 1946, had it published in Geneva because of the promise of many more copies than Gallimard would or could provide because of the paper shortage.

The pendulum was still working but with a slight variation. Instead of using a narrator, the novelist creates a central character, Olivier Le Maistre, a writer whose career, both literary and personal, parallels very closely that of Jacques de Lacretelle. After living in his *garçonnière* as a handsome bachelor in the flamboyant 1920s, Le Maistre in his late forties suddenly marries a young woman scarcely out of her teens and has a happy marriage until he makes the mistake of revealing a former "mariage blanc" (unconsummated marriage), which shocks this conservative wife brought up in the Catholic tradition. His own infidelity and her attempted infidelity occur while they are in America at the outbreak of the war. Like Gide's Edouard in *Les Faux-Monnayeurs* (*The Counterfeiters*, 1926), Le Maistre is always writing and talking about his novel *Le Pour et le contre*, but he never writes it because his ship is torpedoed by the Germans on the way back to France. The trip to America at the outbreak of the war, the discrepancy in the ages of the spouses (Yolande de Naurois was twenty-one when she married Lacretelle), and many other details are manifestly autobiographical. Whether Le Maistre's unconventional life before his marriage is autobiographical may never be known, but there are suggestions that this part is authentic because, throughout Lacretelle's minor writings before his marriage, there parades a narrator usually named Damville, often considered an alter ego of Lacretelle, who is as cynical and disabused as Le Maistre himself during his bachelorhood.

Le Pour et le contre is an enormous novel, 664 pages long with 153 characters with names and 91 without names. Since the pendulum has now swung the other way, there is no omniscient analysis but no dominant narrator either; instead, for the first time in one of Lacretelle's novels, the characters talk. What they say or sometimes do reveals their natures, but mainly they just talk. This small talk, as well as the philosophical and literary talk, clearly results from Lacretelle's intention to modernize himself by imitating Aldous Huxley, whose title *Point Counter Point* (1928) makes Lacretelle's title seem like a poor translation. Although he does not mention Huxley in the novel, Lacretelle had reviewed the English author several years before. The main characters of *Le Pour et le contre* belong to the literary Bohemia of the 1920s, and the minor characters are all writers of the *NEJ* (Nouvelles Editions des Jeunes), an acronym which manifestly stands for the *NRF*. The entire *Nouvelle Revue Française* group and many other writers are present in disguise, from Rivière to Gallimard, from Martin du Gard to Cocteau and Radiguet. Did Lacretelle hope that his readers would be interested in identifying these characters as readers have been interested in identifying Proust's originals? At any rate this book aroused little interest, and, to this day, it is often overlooked.

In a scene reminiscent of the dinner of the Argonautes in *Les Faux-Monnayeurs* (but the basis of the scene was a real episode, a dinner in honor of the Belgian dramatist Fernand Crommelynck, said Lacretelle later), Olivier Le Maistre confronts the new generation and realizes that he is out of step. Lacretelle, too, seemed to have come to that realization. Though he never gave up his Trocadéro apartments (he occupied two of them with a garden overlooking the square) and never deserted the social and official life of Paris, morally he retreated first to his two country houses at Montfort-l'Amaury, then to his villa at Cabourg next to the Grand Hôtel immortalized by Proust in the Balbec episodes, and finally to his estates, the château de Brécy and the château d'O. Nothing important was to be written in the many years that he lived on, although his talent for writing never diminished. The pendulum, however, was still swinging. In 1946 type was set for the deluxe edition of a short novel entitled *Deux Cœurs simples,* but it did not appear until 1952 because Valentine Hugo did not finish the illustrations. Evidently Lacretelle was unconcerned about having this work appear in print. The novelette is so visibly inspired by Flaubert's *Un Cœur simple* (1877) that its plot need not be recounted. In its careful structure it is an artistic success, but its whimsicality is insufficient to move the reader. In 1953 Gallimard published the commercial edition of the novelette and also a play by Lacretelle, *Une Visite en été* (A Summer Visit). For years Lacretelle had been looking for a producer but with no success, for this well-constructed play is singularly undramatic, being based on a system of psychological analysis and on the eternal triangle of the old drawing-room comedy. Some polite attention was paid to *Deux Cœurs simples,* whereas the play went unnoticed.

Lacretelle never formally took leave of creative literature, and his personal correspondence reveals at least one more attempt to write a novel; but his heart was not in it. Being under no pressure to earn a living by his pen, he wrote mainly for his own pleasure the kind of rambling essay, erudite but with a personal touch, which he had always practiced even in his most productive years. Several volumes of essays, plus a brief autobiography, *Le Tiroir secret* (The Secret Drawer, 1959), appeared over the next thirty years. Rereading this production, one understands why *Le Figaro* (whose history he also wrote in *Face à l'événement* [Facing the Event, 1966]) called him the last French moralist. During these years he seemed to live primarily with the great French classics and with the great minds of France's past. He never lost the ability to write in that typical smooth-flowing classical French which had characterized his best work. In 1954 he created a furor in the Académie Française when, in his speech receiving the Duc de Lévis-Mirepoix, he roundly criticized the archroyalist Charles Maurras, whose place the duke was taking. The liberalism of his ancestors was cropping up in spite of the aristocratic veneer which he had acquired over the years. After that he never engaged in controversy, not even with the New Novelists or structuralists whom he simply chose to ignore.

Near the end of his life, however, when he was eighty-nine, he did speak out against the New Novelists in a very curious novel which seems to be a last will and testament, *Les Vivants et leur ombre* (The Living and their Shadow, 1977). It is a curious novel because it consists of four almost unrelated parts. The first section is a vivid evocation of the salon of Madame Menard-Dorian perceived through the eyes of a young narrator. How much of this is fiction and how much reality it is impossible to say, but fiction takes over in the next two parts as the narrator tells first the story of Léone and then of Haghers, both of whom were guests of Madame Menard-Dorian. Since the narrator is hardly present when he describes Léone's life through two unsuccessful marriages and a final affair, this part reads like a typical Lacretelle omniscient novel. In the next part, however, the narrator carries the burden of the action as he goes to Hong Kong and then to Macao in search of Haghers, who seems to be a combination of Gide's Ménalque from *L'Immoraliste* and Malraux's Grabot from *La Voie royale* (The Royal Way, 1930). Even the humanistic dialogue in which the narrator and Haghers engage sounds as if it might have been written by Malraux. In the final section Lacretelle seems to have discarded his narrator and to be speaking for himself as he visits the graves of the Menard-Dorians in Paris's Père La-

Lacretelle with his wife, the former Yolande de Naurois, in Alexandria, 1933 (courtesy of Mme Yolande de Lacretelle)

chaise cemetery and exorcizes his own demons, first of all Haghers and then the surrealists and the New Novelists. In his last line he defends his right to be free of all religions and to refuse the afterlife. Once again it is the nineteenth-century positivist who surfaces.

If *Les Vivants et leur ombre* was to have been a last will and testament, there was a final codicil, *Quand le destin nous mène* (When Fate Leads Us, 1981), published when Lacretelle was ninety-three. This small volume contains two *récits*, the first of which, entitled "Laurence," ranks with the polished work of *L'Ame cachée*. The narrator loves the mysterious and rebellious heroine who seems to be sensually attracted to him but falls in love with a gigolo and then commits suicide when the gigolo deserts her. The second *récit*, "Un Innocent," telling the story of an unhappy Jew at the time of the Popular Front of Léon Blum, seems to be the remnant of an earlier project for a novel. None of Lacretelle's final work relates to his personal life, and, in the end, he is once again the objective writer which he always aspired to be.

References:

Douglas W. Alden, *Jacques de Lacretelle: An Intellectual Itinerary* (New Brunswick: Rutgers University Press, 1958);

Alden, "Jacques de Lacretelle for and against Proust," *Romanic Review*, 41 (April 1950): 108-124;

André Beaunier, "Un Romancier: M. Jacques de Lacretelle," *Revue des Deux Mondes*, seventh series, 28 (1 August 1925): 698-709;

Benjamin Crémieux, "Amour nuptial; Le Retour de Silbermann," *Annales Politiques et Littéraires* (1 January 1930);

Abel Hermant, "La Vie inquiète de Jean Hermelin," *Le Gaulois*, 21 August 1920;

Edmond Jaloux, "La Bonifas," *Les Nouvelles Littéraires*, 25 July 1925;

Frédéric Lefèvre, "Une Heure avec Jacques de Lacretelle," in his *Une Heure avec...*, third series (Paris: Gallimard, 1925);

André Maurois, "Jacques de Lacretelle de l'Académie Française," *Les Nouvelles Littéraires* (14 November 1936);

Maurois, "Lacretelle," in his *Etudes Littéraires,* volume 2 (New York: Editions de la Maison Française, 1944);

Henri de Régnier, "*Sabine,*" *Le Figaro,* 11 April 1932;

André Rousseaux, "M. Jacques de Lacretelle, Grand Prix du Roman," *Candide* (26 June 1930).

Paul Léautaud
(18 January 1872-22 February 1956)

Raymond Mahieu
University of Antwerp

SELECTED BOOKS: *Le Petit Ami* (Paris: Mercure de France, 1903); translated in *The Child of Montmartre* (1959);

Henri de Régnier (Paris: E. Sansot, 1904);

Le Théâtre de Maurice Boissard, as Maurice Boissard, 2 volumes (Paris: Gallimard, 1926, 1943; revised, 1958);

Passe-Temps (Paris: Mercure de France, 1929);

Propos d'un jour (Paris: Mercure de France, 1947);

Journal littéraire, 19 volumes (Paris: Mercure de France, 1954-1966); translated and abridged by Geoffrey Sainsbury as *Journal of a Man of Letters, 1898-1907* (London: Chatto & Windus, 1960);

Journal particulier, 2 volumes (Monte Carlo: Editions du CAP, 1956);

Œuvres: Le Petit Ami précédé d'Essais et suivi d'In Memoriam et Amours (Paris: Mercure de France, 1956); *Le Petit Ami, In Memoriam,* and *Amours* translated in *The Child of Montmartre* (1959);

Bestiaire (Paris: Grasset, 1959);

The Child of Montmartre, translated by Humphrey Hare (London: Bodley Head, 1959; New York: Random House, 1959)—comprises *Le Petit Ami, In Memoriam,* and *Amours*;

Poésies (Paris: Le Bélier, 1963);

Passe-Temps II (Paris: Mercure de France, 1964);

Le Petit Ouvrage inachevé (Paris: Le Bélier, 1964);

Journal particulier. 1933, edited by Edith Silve (Paris: Mercure de France, 1986).

Paul Léautaud (photo Izis, courtesy of Raymond Mahieu)

OTHERS: *Poètes d'aujourd'hui. 1880-1900. Morceaux choisis,* edited by Léautaud and Adolphe van Bever (Paris: Mercure de France, 1900; revised and enlarged, 2 volumes, 1908; 3 volumes, 1929);

Stendhal: Les Plus Belles Pages, introduction and notes by Léautaud (Paris: Mercure de France, 1908);

Fagus, *Lettres à Paul Léautaud,* foreword and notes by Léautaud (Paris: La Connaissance, 1928);

Fernande Olivier, *Picasso et ses amis,* preface by Léautaud (Paris: Stock, 1933);

Ylla, *Chats,* preface by Léautaud (Paris: Editions O. E. T., 1935);

Catalogue de l'Exposition Paul Verlaine, preface by Léautaud (Paris: Université de Paris, Bibliothèque Littéraire Jacques Doucet, 1946);

Marie Dormoy, *Le Chat Miton,* preface by Léautaud (Paris: Editions Spirale, 1951).

The place occupied by Paul Léautaud in the history of the French novel is undoubtedly a marginal one; indeed, this writer's celebrity is mainly due to his work in genres other than the novel, namely dramatic criticism, memoirs, essays, and reflections, which appeared in periodicals and which were collected in various compilations of his work, and his imposing *Journal littéraire* (1954-1966; translated in part as *Journal of a Man of Letters,* 1960). Nevertheless, his venture into novel-writing was an important stage in the trajectory this student of the self followed in search of his own identity, and the texts that belong to this vein, although they are not numerous, show a quality which justifies the interest that has been given to them.

Paul Léautaud, who was born in Paris on 18 January 1872, was the illegitimate child of a precarious couple. He was abandoned a few days after his birth by his mother, Jeanne Forestier (an almost unknown actress), left to a wet nurse, and later educated by an old servant in the house of his father, Firmin Léautaud (an actor who became a prompter in the famous theater of the Comédie-Française); thus his childhood was lonely and melancholy. Secretly obsessed by the absence of the woman who had given birth to him, whom he did not see again, except now and then for a couple of hours, disturbed, and misunderstood by his father, with whom he had no affinity, he experienced powerfully his Oedipal situation, which curiously made him resemble the writer whom he later was to place above all others: Stendhal. His studies were modest; he attended only primary schools, first in Paris and later, from 1882 till 1886, in Courbevoie, a working-class suburb of Paris, to which his father had moved. Although he suffered in an environ-

ment he experienced as hostile, developing his tendency to retire within himself, he did make a friend who was to play a very important role in his literary début: Adolphe van Bever.

At fifteen Léautaud was forced to begin working. The small jobs he held for years without any enthusiasm contributed nothing to his integration into society; on the contrary, they led to an attitude of individualistic anarchism, which he was to keep for the rest of his life. Even when, from 1895 onward, he achieved a certain professional stability as a lawyer's clerk, it was clear that for him genuine life lay elsewhere. From 1889 on, literature furnished him with another life, the only one that would count for him henceforth. Influenced by his friend van Bever, he devoted himself to reading, associated with aspiring poets and artists, attended performances of the Théâtre de l'Œuvre (an avant-garde theater where works by Ibsen, Maeterlinck, and Jarry were performed), and became well acquainted with the staff of the *Mercure de France,* which gave him the opportunity to become a friend of the poet Paul Valéry.

He also started to write. His first productions were mainly lyrical poems, inspired (at least on the level of theme) by the breaking up with his first mistress, Jeanne Marié. From 1893 to 1895 the *Courrier Français,* an illustrated weekly, published twelve poems by Léautaud in which the influence of François Coppée and of Baudelaire is particularly recognizable. In 1895 and 1896 the *Mercure de France* accepted two pieces by Léautaud, the second of which showed the influence of Mallarmé. This influence, together with that of Maurice Barrès, is visible in his following, less lyrical works, which, according to the expression of the period, he called "proses": texts without any precise rules. The popularity of this generic experiment at the end of the century seems to be related to a crisis in the novel at the same time. From 1896 till 1900, Léautaud had five texts published in the *Mercure de France* in the following order: two "essais de sentimentalisme," one other "essai," a piece entitled "L'Ami d'Aimienne" (Aimienne's Friend), and one "essai de sentimentalisme." All are meditations written in an extremely mannered style, in which denial of the world and an egotism fed by memories are remarkable and in which the narcissistic purpose gradually acquires a dimension of critical judgment, irony, and dilettantism.

The first years of the twentieth century undoubtedly constitute the most intensive period of

Léautaud's life and career. On a personal level he passed through several crises which completed his break with the legacy of his childhood. In the field of literature, where he was achieving a certain status and notoriety, he gradually discovered, through an important and complex series of texts, what was to become his favorite working field.

But first he had to rid himself completely of the past. In 1901 Léautaud saw his mother for a few days at the bedside of a dying aunt, an encounter which crystalized all the needs and desires from the first days of his life. But the incestuous dream, built on frustration, which seemed to come to life in this encounter, failed. After a short period of intimacy between the two and an exchange of correspondence in which the loving tone quickly gave way to incomprehension, Jeanne Forestier—who had started a new life in Geneva, where she had married a physician—definitely ended their relationship in 1902. The following year it was Léautaud's father's turn to abandon him. The death of Firmin Léautaud meant for his son a certain reconciliation with the father image, but it also awakened an anxiety-ridden fascination with death, which never left him. To these crucial changes in his life he added another by bringing to a definitive end in 1903 his intermittent relationship with Georgette Crozier—the only woman he had truly loved. The almost domestic life he led from 1898 onward with Blanche Blanc (a liaison which was to last for seventeen years) was a dull reflection of the true partnership he had despaired of finding; such would be the case, to an even greater degree, in his later relationships. The last challenge he faced and last compromise was the working life. From 1902 till 1906 Léautaud worked for a judicial administrator and finally received some professional satisfaction; but his contempt for the world and, above all, his wish to give literature the first place in his life led to his resignation and to the decision to accept, early in 1908, a position as secretary for the *Mercure de France*—a modest job, but one that gave him the spare time in which to write.

One of his major literary pursuits during this period was criticism. His first publication was *Poètes d'aujourd'hui* (Poets of Today, 1900), in collaboration with Adolphe van Bever. This anthology, supplemented with notes and bibliographic information, was an important episode in literary history to the extent that it acquainted a whole generation with the poetry of their time. It also gave

Léautaud's mother Jeanne Forestier, who abandoned her son shortly after his birth in 1872 (courtesy of Raymond Mahieu). His obsession with her absence is reflected most clearly in the 1903 novel Le Petit Ami.

Léautaud the chance, through his often reserved commentaries, to indulge in some personal writing. He continued his commentaries a few years later in two short essays devoted to contemporary writers he knew well, *Henri de Régnier* (published separately in 1904) and "Marcel Schwob" (in the 15 March 1905 issue of the *Mercure de France*), in which the works under discussion are subordinate to the subjectivity of the critic. This is even truer for the considerable body of criticism he devoted to Stendhal, beginning shortly after the turn of the century, including the article which appeared in *L'Ermitage* in March 1905 ("Le Stendhal-Club"), some short scholarly pieces, and a collection of Stendhal's work, which appeared in 1908. This criticism devoted to the author he admired more than any other also gave Léautaud a chance to express himself and to reaffirm his own personality.

In the meantime the study of the self made a novelist of Léautaud—almost in spite of himself. An autobiographical project, conceived in 1901, led him to write three personal narratives—*Le*

Petit Ami, In Memoriam, and *Amours* (translated in a single volume as *The Child of Montmartre,* 1959)–the first of which at least is significant in the history of the novel. *Le Petit Ami* (published in the *Mercure de France* in 1902 and in book form the following year) does not have a plot, properly speaking; written in the first person, it is rather like a montage, strongly marked by reflexivity, in which memories of childhood and evocations of the present life of the narrator alternate. Two worlds are linked together here: on the one hand the world of a lonely child eager for tenderness, a world now gone but remembered with a great sense of accuracy and detail; on the other, a world both present and imaginary against which the writing takes place, the Paris of brilliant music halls in which the narrator is the "petit ami" of kind prostitutes. On the one hand, there is confrontation in the past with events and suffering; on the other, there is a surrender outside of time to an easy existence in which nothing is to be taken seriously. But the dreams and the actual experiences depend on each other: the reveries and the emotions of the "petit ami" are fed with images of childhood, and, inversely, childhood can be signified only by the mediation of the desire for irresponsibility, which the frame of remembering represents in the hallucinatory mode. This tension between the two parts, which creates the uniqueness of the work, is built around an absence, that of the mother. The incurable nostalgia underlying Léautaud's first writings (poems as well as "essais") reaches an extreme intensity in *Le Petit Ami*. Even the fact that Léautaud's final encounter with his mother took place while he was writing the book makes no difference: the account of this meeting finds a place in the text, but the temporary materialization of the phantom of the mother does not change the system of deficiency that determines the structure of the novel. Reexperienced in the act of writing, the unexpected episode does not prevent the book from remaining in the ambiguous balance between personal mythology and reality.

The success of *Le Petit Ami,* for which Léautaud always had a deep affection, made him aware of his position as a writer. His publisher believed so much in the value of the book that he proposed *Le Petit Ami* for the first Prix Goncourt in 1903, but the novel did not win. Although he was launched on his career, Léautaud did not immediately exploit the vein of his first success; only in 1905 did he write and have published (in

the *Mercure de France*) his second narrative, *In Memoriam*. His hesitation was based on critical reflection: in spite of the qualities he saw in his first novel, he was embarrassed by what for contemporary readers is its merit–its composite character in which imagination and memory are mixed. Thus, more and more concerned with the simple truth, the writer intended to tell what he had actually experienced himself in *In Memoriam*, which is devoted to the life and death of his father. The structure of the novella, in two parts, each with a very different rhythm, one about the past of his childhood and the other about the recent death of his father, establishes a dramatic contrast between the slowness and monotony of far-off days and the violent intensity of a death that is reported in detail. In addition, the constant irony of the text gives it a kind of indecisiveness, so that it simultaneously appears as a present revenge against his oppressive father of the past and as the confession, possible at last, of a love that had been censored. Structuring autobiographical data with means borrowed from the novel, *In Memoriam* reveals a moment of unique balance in the work of Léautaud.

This is not the case in the third narrative, *Amours,* published the following year, 1906, in the *Mercure de France*. As his career progressed, he turned increasingly away from the novel; *Amours* was to be exclusively autobiographical, devoted to his "histoires de femmes" or affairs with women. Written quickly, the work, which includes an account of the relationship between Léautaud and Jeanne Marié, shows a noticeable loss of density in comparison with his former narratives: the story is simply a linear one; the interaction between past and present is lost in a continual mockery which dissipates all ambivalence. In short, in the effort of wanting to rid his writing of the imaginative, he produced a work of remembrance which ends in an impasse in so far as it does not allow the self to recognize and reaffirm itself. In his pursuit of his own identity, Léautaud discovered with *Amours* that the road to systematical autobiography turned him away from his target; and after some last abortive attempts at autobiography, he gave up definitively.

What can be seen negatively as the forsaking of his autobiographical ambitions can also be seen positively, since it allowed him to define his future orientation. He renounced concessions to imagination and comprehensive projects and turned toward the form of the fragment, in which the writer asserts himself only by means of reference to what is external to him, defining his presence by either his adhesion or, especially, by his opposition to the world around him. This vein was explored by Léautaud in a series of short impressions and memoirs that parallel his longer writings. These appeared in reviews from 1904 to 1906 and were collected subsequently, some of them posthumously. His various texts of criticism belong to this phase of his writing, although in these he calls upon the writing of others in order to "write himself." There is another form of literature that satisfies the principles of egotism and to which he attaches more and more importance during this period, namely his diary.

Since 1893 Léautaud had been writing the work he was to continue throughout his life: his immense *Journal littéraire*. At the start he kept the journal only irregularly, and entries for the first years are rather thin. From 1903 onward, however, the diary is regular and extensive. The nature of its contents is revealing; after having indulged somewhat in introspection and having used its pages for commentary and as a reservoir of strictly literary texts, Léautaud modified it until it became essentially the chronicle of his own life and his world, one that follows the double principle he had chosen to follow: fragmentation (a diary by definition provides a broken discourse) and support of external facts (the extent of his specifically intimate observations continually declines). As early as 1907 he observed: "Au fond, je crois que tout mon plaisir d'écrire se bornerait très bien à ce 'journal,' en le faisant plus complet, avec plus de détails. Mes histoires personnelles, pour livres, j'y ai tant pensé, qu'elles ne m'intéressent plus assez à écrire" (I believe basically that all my pleasure of writing could be very well confined to this "journal" if I made it more complete, with more details. I have thought so much about my personal stories, that they no longer interest me enough to write them down).

In the following years the author's career developed in such a way that this supposition became a certainty. From 1908 to 1914 his life became more settled on both the literary and the private levels. On a personal level he found a source of income, modest but sufficient for his way of life, in his work for the *Mercure de France,* and he also found a place in an intellectual environment. He concluded that his life had acquired its definitive form and that he had little left to discover, in love, friendship, literature, or art. Léautaud began to turn increasingly inward in a feeling of failure. This state of mind was confirmed (and stressed) when he moved to a suburban house in Fontenay-aux-Roses (to the south of Paris) where he remained until his death; the author who had dreamed of a carefree and brilliant life in Paris found himself lost in the suburbs, obliged to travel a considerable distance every day. It must be noted that this change was the price he had to pay for a passion that had become increasingly important: his love for animals. In his house in Fontenay Léautaud took in wandering cats and dogs with an extraordinary solicitude which was no doubt easier for him to show to animals than people but which also confirmed him, as he saw the repeated scenes of pain and death, in his conviction that evil reigned universally.

In these conditions writing acquired for him inevitably a negative dimension. It was to be mainly writing *against something.* He found a starting point when he was offered the position of dramatic critic for the *Mercure de France* at the end of 1907. Under the pen name of Maurice Boissard he reported on theatrical productions in Paris, providing his readers with an idea of the performances and his judgment on them, and also using his columns as an excuse for a study of the self which assumed almost a dramatic form. Through the abundant reflections, confidences, and anecdotes of Maurice Boissard–presented to his readers as an old, rich patron of the arts, and an amateur writer–Léautaud provided an ongoing dramatization which was, like his other writings, an exercise in self-cultivation.

About half of the Boissard columns were written before 1914. The disguise they provided allowed Léautaud to elaborate and gradually enclose himself in another character. He had long dreamed of becoming a dandy; but not being able to realize this dream in a positive way for practical reasons, he took on the opposite character in which irony and aggressivity were combined with willful neglect of his appearance. For the rest of his life he displayed in literary circles the fully developed character of a cynical and ragged philosopher coming from an imaginary eighteenth century. This character was to play a determining role in his activity as a writer. If one considers the evolution of the *Journal littéraire* during this period, one can see that its pages, supposedly private, became more and more dependent on this disguise, which had become a second nature and which doubtless was a compensation for the masquerade he pursued in life. Léautaud

1954

Vendredi 10 Septembre — Le matin
lettre de Jean Denoël, de Juan les Pins,
m'informant qu'il vient de lire dans
le _Figaro_, que Rouveyre aurait été
renversé par une auto et transporté
à l'Hôtel Dieu, et me demandant si
je sais quelque chose, de le lui dire, et
si c'est grave.

Je lui ai répondu que je ne sais
absolument rien, qu'il écrive à la
concierge de Rouveyre, avec un timbre
pour sa réponse.

Singulier nature que j'ai. Cela me
laisse absolument froid.

La lettre de Denoël est datée d'hier
jeudi. L'accident est relaté dans le
Figaro du même jour. Il aurait donc
eu lieu la veille, mercredi

J'ai aussi écrit quelques mots à
Jean Marchand, (adressés chez Plon,
ignorant son adresse rue du Bac, lui
demandant ce qui s'est passé, qu'on l'ait
remplacé par Pierre Sipriot, que, moi,
ce qu'on m'en a dit. (François Sentein,
comme je l'ai noté), est tout à son avantage,
que je ne lui demande pas de me le dire,
si un peu délicat, qui en tout cas, pour
moi, je le regrette.

6 heures du soir — L'assemblage
des textes _Journal_ pour _La Table Ronde_
m'a donné un travail, depuis quatre ou
cinq jours, même pas encore terminé.
Si, pour certains passages, ce Pierre
Sipriot me demande des suppressions,
ce à quoi je m'attends un peu et auxquelles
je me refuserai, causant peut-être le renvoi
du manuscrit, j'aurai fait tout ce travail
pour rien.

Léautaud's entry for 10 September 1954 in the Journal littéraire *(Collection of Raymond Mahieu)* wrote to find himself, surely, but he also wrote at least as much to recognize himself in the form constructed in his writing. At the same time he wrote to make himself recognizable to future readers to whom his pages–a sort of archive of the self– were directed. Such a project, both limited and infinite, fit so well Léautaud's ambitions and narcissism alike that even before World War I it had become his principal activity.

Although in 1914 Léautaud still had more than forty years to live, from that period onward, for neither the biographer nor the critic do his life and literary production offer great interest. He remained with the *Mercure de France* until 1941, when he was dismissed because of a disagreement with the director. After that he devoted himself exclusively to his animals and his writing. His emotional life was confined to the mediocrity to which he had resigned himself. Among its salient episodes were the long and sordid relationship he had from 1914 till 1934 with a difficult woman named Anne Cayssac (he called her "le Fléau"–the Plague) and, from 1933 onward, his amorous relationship with Marie Dormoy, in whom he found a devoted friend until the end. His name and that of Maurice Boissard were often before the public since he continued his dramatic criticism till 1923 (in the *Mercure de France* till the autumn of 1921 and later on in the *Nouvelle Revue Française* and the *Nouvelles Littéraires*). A careful examination of his whole production reveals that it consists of a rather limited number of reminiscences, reflections and anecdotes, often coming from old sources, sometimes from his diary, and also of recastings of early texts, indefatigably reorganized and modified. (A number of incomplete reworkings of *Le Petit Ami* and of *In Memoriam* exist.) For example, Léautaud's volume published in 1929 under the title *Passe-Temps* is a compilation of texts that had already appeared two or three times in various publications. The only project that he really pursued and that was truly stimulating to him was the *Journal littéraire*, in which the description of the details of daily life and the gossip of literary life steadily acquired importance.

The sort of myth Léautaud formed around his person solidified in literary circles and received, toward the end of his life, wide publicity. In 1950 and 1951, thanks to a series of radio conversations with Robert Mallet (published in 1951), the eccentric and corrosive old man that he had become suddenly turned into a personality for millions of listeners. The result was that Léautaud acquired a much wider audience than before. This new status, and also the untiring efforts of Marie Dormoy, made possible the publication of the first two volumes of the *Journal littéraire* during his lifetime. When he died on 22 February 1956, the official recognition he received from the literary establishment was such that the survival of his works was assured, without their having to be rediscovered, although such a critical rediscovery would have been deserved.

Letters:
Lettres, 1902-1918 (Paris: Editions Mornay, 1929);
Lettres à ma mère (Paris: Mercure de France, 1956);
Lettres à Marie Dormoy (Paris: A. Michel, 1966);
Correspondance, 1912-1955, by Léautaud and André Billy (Paris: Le Bélier, 1968);
Correspondance générale de Paul Léautaud, edited by Marie Dormoy (Paris: Flammarion, 1972).

Interviews:
Entretiens avec Robert Mallet (Paris: Gallimard, 1951);
André Gillois, Interview with Léautaud, in his *Qui êtes-vous ?* (Paris: Gallimard, 1953).

Bibliography:
Albert Kies, "Les Livres de Paul Léautaud," *Revue des Amateurs* (October-November 1945).

Biographies:
Marie Dormoy, *Léautaud* (Paris: Gallimard, 1958);
Dormay, *La Vie secrète de Paul Léautaud* (Paris: Flammarion, 1971);
Raymond Mahieu, *Paul Léautaud. La Recherche de l'identité (1872-1914)* (Paris: Lettres Modernes / Minard, 1974).

References:
Etienne Buthaud, Index to Léautaud's *Journal littéraire,* in volume 19 of the *Journal* (Paris: Mercure de France, 1966);
Buthaud, "Paul Léautaud. Basoche et littérature," *Mercure de France,* 1143 (November 1958): 423-446;
Marie Dormoy, "Histoire du Journal," in volume 19 of Léautaud's *Journal littéraire* (Paris: Mercure de France, 1966);

Dormoy, "Paul Léautaud," in her *Souvenirs et portraits d'amis* (Paris: Mercure de France, 1963);

Dormoy, ed., *Paul Léautaud* (Paris: Mercure de France, 1969);

René-Louis Doyon, "Léautaud par ci, par là et ailleurs," *Livrets du Mandarin*, sixth series, 2 (Fall 1959): 1-24;

John A. Green, "Marcel Schwob and Paul Léautaud, 1903-1905," *Modern Language Quarterly*, 29 (December 1968): 415-422;

James Harding, *Lost Illusions. Paul Léautaud and His World* (Rutherford, N.J.: Fairleigh Dickinson University Press, 1974);

Hubert Juin, "Les Secrets de Paul Léautaud," *Magazine Littéraire*, 64 (May 1972): 55-59;

Raymond Mahieu, "Stendhal, tentation de Léautaud," *Stendhal Club*, 52 (15 July 1971): 309-323;

Robert Mallet, Lise Dubief, and Marie-Laure Prévost, *Paul Léautaud*, catalogue of the December 1972 exhibition (Paris: Bibliothèque Nationale, 1972);

Henri Martineau, "Paul Léautaud," *Divan*, 295 (July-September 1955): 165-178;

W. Somerset Maugham, "Three Journalists," in his *Points of View* (London, Melbourne & Toronto: Heinemann, 1958);

Mercure de France, special issue on Léautaud, 1125 (May 1957);

Maurice Nadeau, "Diogène en banlieue sud," in his *Littérature présente* (Paris: Corrêa, 1952);

Jean Penard, "Paul Léautaud et la Comédie humaine," *Critique*, no. 163 (December 1960): 1034-1049;

Gaëtan Picon, "Paul Léautaud et *Le Petit Ami*," in his *L'Usage de la lecture*, volume 2 (Paris: Mercure de France, 1961);

"Pour les quatre-vingts ans de Paul Léautaud," by Adrienne Monnier and others, special section of *Mercure de France*, 1062 (February 1952): 193-254;

Samuel de Sacy, "Léautaud implacable et singulier," *Actualité littéraire*, 66-67 (March-April 1960): 7-12;

Jean Selz, "Paul Léautaud ou le paradoxe de l'écrivain," *Lettres Nouvelles*, 37 (April 1956): 559-569;

Edith Silve, *Paul Léautaud et le Mercure de France. Chronique publique et privée, 1914-1941* (Paris: Mercure de France, 1985);

Marcel Thiébaut, "De Léautaud à Henry Bidou," in his *Entre les lignes* (Paris: Hachette, 1962);

Thiébaut, "Paul Léautaud," *Revue de Paris*, 66 (October 1959): 141-150;

Seymour S. Weiner, "Sincerity and Variants: Paul Léautaud's *Petit Ami*," *Symposium*, 14 (Fall 1960): 165-187.

Papers:

Léautaud's papers are in the Bibliothèque Littéraire Jacques Doucet in Paris.

Roger Martin du Gard

(23 March 1881-22 August 1958)

Grant E. Kaiser
Emory University

BOOKS: *L'Abbaye de Jumièges (Seine-Inférieure)* (Mondidier: Grau-Radenez, 1909);

Devenir! (Paris: Ollendorff, 1909);

L'Une de nous (Paris: Grasset, 1910);

Jean Barois (Paris: Nouvelle Revue Française, 1913); translated by Stuart Gilbert (New York: Viking, 1949; London: Bodley Head, 1950);

Le Testament du Père Leleu (Paris: Gallimard, 1920);

Temoignage: In memoriam (Paris: Imprimerie Grou-Radenez, 1921);

Le Cahier gris, part 1 of *Les Thibault* (Paris: Gallimard, 1922); translated as *The Gray Notebook* in *The Thibaults* (1926);

Le Pénitencier, part 2 of *Les Thibault* (Paris: Gallimard, 1922); translated as *The Penitentiary* in *The Thibaults* (1926); translated as *The Reformatory* (1933, 1934);

La Belle Saison, part 3 of *Les Thibault*, 2 volumes (Paris: Gallimard, 1923); translated as *The Springtime of Life* in *The Thibaults* (1926); translated as *High Summer* in *The Thibaults* (1933, 1934);

The Thibaults, 2 volumes, translated by Madeleine Boyd (New York: Boni & Liveright, 1926)—comprises *Le Cahier gris*, *Le Pénitencier*, and *La Belle Saison*;

Noizemont-les-Vièrges (Liège: A la Lampe d'Aladdin, 1928);

La Gonfle (Paris: Gallimard, 1928);

La Consultation, part 4 of *Les Thibault* (Paris: Gallimard, 1928); translated as *The Consulting Day* in *The Thibaults* (1933, 1934);

La Sorellina, part 5 of *Les Thibault* (Paris: Gallimard, 1928); translated in *The Thibaults* (1939);

La Mort du père, part 6 of *Les Thibault* (Paris: Gallimard, 1929); translated in *The Thibaults* (1939);

Dialogue (Paris: Claude Aveline, 1930);

Confidence africaine (Paris: Gallimard, 1931);

Un Taciturne (Paris: Gallimard, 1932; revised edition, Paris: Gallimard, 1948);

Roger Martin du Gard (photo Harlingue)

Vieille France (Paris: Gallimard, 1933); translated by John Russell as *The Postman* (London: Deutsch, 1954; New York: Viking, 1955);

The Thibaults, 2 volumes, volume 1 translated by Stephen Haden Guest, volume 2 translated by Stuart Gilbert (London: Lane, 1933, 1934)—comprises *Le Cahier gris*, *Le Pénitencier*, *La Belle Saison*, and *La Consultation*;

L'Eté 1914, part 7 of *Les Thibault*, 3 volumes (Paris: Gallimard, 1936); translated by Gilbert as *Summer 1914* (London: Lane, 1940);

The Thibaults, translated by Gilbert (London: Lane, 1939; New York: Viking, 1939)—comprises *Le Cahier gris*, *Le Pénitencier*, *La Belle Saison*, *La Consultation*, *La Sorellina*, and *La Mort du père*;

Epilogue, part 8 of *Les Thibault* (Paris: Gallimard, 1940); translated in *Summer 1914*, enlarged edition (1941);

Summer 1914, enlarged edition, translated by Gilbert (New York: Viking, 1941)—comprises *L'Eté 1914* and *Epilogue*;

Notes sur André Gide, 1913-1951 (Paris: Gallimard, 1951); translated by Russell as *Notes on André Gide* (London: Deutsch, 1953); Russell's translation also published as *Recollections of André Gide* (New York: Viking, 1953);

Le Lieutenant-Colonel de Maumort, edited by André Daspre (Paris: Gallimard, 1983).

Collection: *Œuvres complètes,* 2 volumes (Paris: Gallimard, 1955).

PLAY PRODUCTIONS: *Le Testament du Père Leleu,* Paris, Théâtre du Vieux-Colombier, 6 February 1914;

Un Taciturne, Paris, Comédie des Champs-Elysées, 28 October 1931.

OTHER: Olivia (Dorothy Bussy), *Olivia,* translated by Martin du Gard (Paris: Steele, 1949).

Many of the statements on Martin du Gard made by his friend André Gide lack the perception of distance. But Gide did make one statement which turned out to be true. He said that of all the contemporary non-precious writers in France, it was only Martin du Gard who counted. With the passing of time Jean Schlumberger, Jules Romains, Georges Duhamel are less and less read. Martin du Gard, however, bears reading and rereading. In part, his continued popularity is the result of his special gift for making his characters come alive. Each generation is able to appreciate them according to its own sensitivities. In his first works he had a tendency to try to oblige the reader to read with him a certain view of the world, but he learned that what was most important was a sense of living reality which opens the reader's perception of the world to new possibilities. Since the posthumous publication of *Le Lieutenant-Colonel de Maumort* in 1983, it seems clear that his claim to being read by posterity will rest on two works, or perhaps three: *Jean Barois* (1913; translated, 1949), *Les Thibault* (1922-1940; translated, 1926-1941), and possibly *Confidence africaine* (African Confession, 1931). His prose fiction is superior to his theater, perhaps because he came to consider drama an inferior genre, useful for him only when there was a gap in the urge to write novels.

Roger Martin du Gard was born on 23 March 1881 at his paternal grandparents' home,

69 boulevard Bineau, Neuilly-sur-Seine. His father, Paul Martin du Gard, was a lawyer; his mother, Madeleine Wimy Martin du Gard, was the daughter of a stockbroker. Martin du Gard's brother, and only sibling, Marcel, was born in December 1884.

While many of the details of his early youth are unknown, it has been ascertained that in October 1892 he became a part-time boarder at the Ecole Fénelon in the rue Général Foy in Paris. He took classes in the fifth, fourth, and third grades at the Lycée Condorcet. He was not a good student except in history and French composition. In January 1896 his father placed him in Passy as a boarding student with Louis Mellerio, who had studied at the Ecole Normale Supérieure. Here he discovered an artistic and intellectual milieu in which he was encouraged to join discussions and to read from Mellerio's extensive library. Mellerio taught him the importance of establishing a plan for everything he wrote, much as an architect might do. He completed his first baccalaureate in July 1897, and in October he became a student at the Lycée Janson-de-Sailly. After taking his second baccalaureate in July 1898, he entered the Sorbonne in November to prepare his *licence ès lettres.*

When he failed his examinations in July 1899, he took the qualifying examinations and was admitted to the Ecole des Chartes. The years 1900 to 1902 were spent at the Ecole but he failed the examinations for the second year and entered military service. In 1903 he returned to the Ecole, repeated his examinations, and was awarded a certificate as historiographer-paleographer in December 1905. His thesis, published in 1909, concerned the partially ruined Abbey of Jumièges in Normandy.

He claimed later that he entered the Ecole des Chartes without the knowledge of his parents and simply to pass the time until he could launch the career he hoped for: writing. But he never underestimated the influence the school had on him, by increasing his awareness of the past in its relation to the present and by inspiring in him a feeling of moral obligation to do rigorous research.

In February 1906 he married Hélène Foucault, the daughter of a Parisian lawyer, and in July 1907 their only child, Christiane, was born. In December 1929 she married Martin du Gard's best friend, Marcel de Coppet, a governor of the colonies.

The history of his novel-writing before *Jean Barois* contains more failures than successes. It is notable that Martin du Gard had a vision of quality for himself such that he did not publish his first novel-writing efforts. During his four-month honeymoon in North Africa, he began writing "Une Vie de saint" (The Life of a Saint) almost entirely in dialogue form, but he came to realize that this infinitely detailed story of a priest lacked the necessary vigor. He set it aside, a lesson learned from his masters at the Ecole des Chartes, and in 1908 took some courses in psychiatry from some of the best specialists of the day.

He realized that he would rediscover his equilibrium only when he returned to his literary writings. In the spring of 1908 he took his wife and child to Barbizon, in the forest at Fontainebleau, where in several weeks he wrote *Devenir!* (Becoming, 1909), a novel about a failed writer. The purpose was to exorcise his own fear of failure. In the novel the failed writer is doubled by another writer who has method, who works hard, and who suggests a future success.

Having *Devenir!* published by Ollendorff attested to Martin du Gard's talent for a writing career. This novel was undoubtedly the most unplanned, spontaneous novel he ever wrote, a work written in a free and easy, almost conversational style which resembles that of his letters.

The novel is divided into three sections: *Vouloir!* (Willing!), *Réaliser?* (Realizing?), and *Vivre.* (Living.). The punctuation marks used in the section titles, like that in the title of the book, help suggest a certain grandiloquence typical of youth. André Mazerelles, the writer as failure, is a full-blown case of *bovarysme*, full of desires, short on success. He convinces himself that he can write as well as the authors he reads and elaborate theories for a new novel that are on a level with theirs. All this takes place in the section headed significantly *Vouloir!* His moments of brilliance are always in the company of others, but he is incapable of the solitude considered necessary by Bernard Grosdidier, the potentially successful writer. André finally settles into the life of a rich country gentleman, but even in this role it is difficult to call him a success. His laziness encourages him to give up all pretensions. Finally his wife dies in childbirth (in scenes reminiscent of Gide's *L'Immoraliste*, 1902), and he consoles himself with the companionship of the maid. Bernard, at the end of the novel, has not yet succeeded in his writing enterprise, but all signs

suggest that with enough time he will have his novels published.

Evident in *Devenir!* is a pattern Martin du Gard will follow in each of his major novels, that of creating two principal characters, both of whom are, or become, writers of one sort or another. In *Devenir!* André's relationship to the world around him is indirect, filtered through literature, and therefore false. He has a "literary" manner for seeing painting, for listening to music, for dreaming of women; his own writing is merely derivative. He is a nonwriter. Bernard, in contrast, dislikes talking about literature and is capable of ripening his own tastes and capacities in solitude. He understands himself. He is a protowriter. If this first novel is flawed, it clearly shows Martin du Gard's capacities. The family background against which André fights provides a real conflict. The self-delusions of his personality are clearly delineated. Bernard's solidity remains unobtrusive, yet real. There is no sense here of the thesis novel.

Encouraged by the reaction of his friends to his first novel, he launched into another work, "Marise," the life of a woman, but decided after several months that he would destroy the manuscript, with the exception of one small episode, which was later published under the title *L'Une de nous* (One of Us, 1910). The publication of this brief volume was perhaps evidence of the fierce desire he felt to prove that he was capable of continuing to write. He later condemned the work as arising from an outmoded naturalism, and he was not wrong. *L'Une de nous* is the story of a congenitally weak man who is married to his cousin. When the husband seems to have gained strength, they have sexual relations, which causes him to have an incapacitating stroke. The wife, pregnant, sinks into a deep despair, fearful that her baby will inherit the husband's congenital weakness. The critics had nothing to say about the novella, and Martin du Gard had all remaining copies destroyed during World War I. He refused to allow the work to be included in his *Œuvres complètes* when they later appeared in a 1955 Gallimard Pléiade edition.

Martin du Gard's next novel, *Jean Barois*, was his first "serious" novel. It was the realization of his continuing ambition to write a novel composed entirely, or almost entirely, of dialogue. Even at this early stage in his career Martin du Gard had a clear idea that he had a gift for dialogue, which proved finally to be one of the strong points of his work. Later, when he returned to a more conventional form in *Les Thibault*, he confided to André Gide in a letter his feeling that he could not succeed unless he were writing scene or direct dialogue.

Jean Barois is the story of the life of its hero from his early youth until his death. The all-inclusive pattern reveals the influence on Martin du Gard of Tolstoy, George Eliot, Romain Rolland, and other novelists of sweeping frescoes. Another pattern, this one repeating that of *Devenir!*, is that the author follows the principal hero as he is on the rise, but when his life is in decline, Martin du Gard brings in a secondary hero as a replacement. The rise of this second and more successful hero offsets the failure of the principal hero.

In this case Jean Barois lives a life full of personal conflicts and also a life immersed in the crises of the time, especially the struggle between science and religion and the Dreyfus Affair. Progressively freeing himself from religious beliefs and family ties, Jean Barois affirms his individuality in terms of his philosophy, in his social life and in his political life. Old age, however, leads him to abandon his aggressively liberated stance and he returns to the comforts of religion. This return to the faith of his childhood is accompanied by the rise in the novel of his double, Marc-Elie Luce, who is both more convinced of his beliefs than was Jean Barois and less convincing as a character. Luce is perhaps the one character created by Martin du Gard who leaves an impression of being too stiff, too idealized, and too idealistic. Martin du Gard wrote, in a 1914 letter to Gide, that he wanted to make the lives of his characters so intense that the reader, facing them, would feel himself in the face of reality. He specifically speaks of Jean Barois in this context, hoping that his creation will be accepted as a prime evidence, but he does not mention Luce.

The difference between André Mazerelles of *Devenir!* and Jean Barois is that the latter has the power to write. He publishes voluminously and is editor of his own journal, *Le Semeur* (The Sower). His life and writings are governed by principles of order, coherence, unity, and affirmation. His writing becomes an instrument of knowledge and understanding. He is not a novelist, but an essayist. Luce likewise writes solidly historical, philosophical, and political pieces.

The difference between Jean Barois and Marc-Elie Luce is that Jean's active writing career begins with his liberation from religion and ends with his return to religion, while Luce, never reli-

gious, never ceases to write. Non-writing is a sign of disorder and failure, a fall from the grace of lucidity. Written history is textually identified with narrative discourse. In this novel Martin du Gard includes quotations which purport to be from the writings of his protagonists. In some cases these are borrowed from relevant writings of such historical figures as Bernard Lazare or from the stenographic court records (including footnotes) of Zola's trial in the Dreyfus case. In *Jean Barois* writing has become an act in what might be considered an early form of Sartre's *engagement*.

After the publication of *Jean Barois* in 1913, Martin du Gard and his wife began working with Jacques Copeau at the Théâtre du Vieux-Colombier. Then came World War I. Martin du Gard served as a sergeant in a transport division for the entire duration of the war. After his demobilization Martin du Gard rejoined Jacques Copeau's theater group, then left in 1920 in order to begin working on his magnum opus: *Les Thibault*. He first planned to use the grandiose title "Le Bien et le mal" (Good and Evil), which gives some idea of the themes and scope he had in mind. He had Gide's encouragement, and by May 1920 he had established a plan for this lengthy work. He moved to Clermont (Oise) where he worked in solitude all week, spending the weekends with his wife and daughter in Paris.

Discipline and hard work led to the publication in rapid succession of *Le Cahier gris* (*The Gray Notebook*) in April 1922, *Le Pénitencier* (*The Penitentiary* in May 1922, and the two volumes of *La Belle Saison* (*The Springtime of Life*) in October 1923. It was during the early 1920s that what had been a literary friendship with André Gide developed into a close personal friendship.

It was also during this period that Martin du Gard attended for the first time the Décades de Pontigny, sponsored by Paul Desjardins, to which the best literary minds of the time were invited. In 1924 Martin du Gard buried his father, who died of a stroke. In 1925 he purchased Le Tertre, a seventeenth-century castle at Bellême (Orne), in Normandy, where he continued to work on the following volumes of *Les Thibault*. Two additional volumes appeared in the spring of 1928: *La Consultation* (*The Consulting Day*) and *La Sorellina* (The Little Sister). *La Mort du Père* (Death of the Father), part six of *Les Thibault*, was published in March 1929. During the post-1925 period he spent considerable time restoring Le Tertre, even climbing the ladders with the work-

Martin du Gard and André Gide in 1922

men as he reconstructed his castle to his tastes.

During this same period he enjoyed a certain sense of fixity, of being settled in his life. He was following an already established plan for *Les Thibault* and settling into a comfortable existence on the scale of the upper bourgeoisie. He was later to say, in the midst of violent upheavals in his life: "I thought life was like that."

Then came a series of shocks. His daughter Christiane married his best friend, Marcel de Coppet. This event was profoundly disturbing to him, as his letters to Gide reveal. Barely a year later, he and his wife had an automobile accident after which he spent months in a cast at a Le Mans clinic. It was also during this period that he wrote *Confidence africaine*, the story of a "natural" incest. His months at the clinic left him much time to reappraise the progress he was making on *Les Thibault*. When he realized that he had a project far too ambitious to accomplish, he destroyed an almost completed volume, "L'Appareillage" (Getting Under Way), in order to organize a new plan for the rest of *Les Thibault*.

It was at Cassis in the south of France that he wrote much of the next published volume, *L'Eté 1914* (1936; translated as *Summer 1914,* 1940), which required extensive research concerning the coming of World War I. During the win-

ter of 1934 he moved to Nice, where he completed the three volumes of *L'Eté 1914,* and by November 1936 when they were published, he seems to have surmounted his crisis. After a lengthy visit to Rome, he returned to Le Tertre in the summer of 1937, where he wrote much of the final volume of *Les Thibault,* entitled *Epilogue* (1940; translated, 1941).

The 1930s brought him his moments of greatest glory. On 22 October 1937 he was awarded the Grand Prix Littéraire de la Ville de Paris for *L'Eté.* Then on 10 November he learned in Nice that he had been awarded the Nobel Prize for literature. Typically modest, Martin du Gard traveled to Sweden with his wife to receive the award, but he went to great lengths to avoid reporters and journalists. On his return trip he traveled through Germany.

On the eve of World War II Martin du Gard went with his wife for a stay in Martinique, where he finished *Epilogue,* returning to France with great difficulty, by way of the United States and Italy, after war was declared in September 1939. By December Martin du Gard was back in Nice. In January 1940 *Epilogue* was published, completing his vast eighteen-year enterprise.

Forced to flee from the advancing German troops, he left Le Tertre, which was used by the occupying German army, and by August 1940 he

Martin du Gard in 1922 (standing at right) with other key members of the group associated with the Nouvelle Revue Française: *André Gide (seated in front), Jean Schlumberger, and Jacques Rivière*

had again taken up residence in Nice where he stayed until the end of the war, except for a brief period before the Allied invasion of 1944. He was on a list of suspects and decided to move further inland to avoid being incarcerated. In 1949 Hélène, his wife, died.

A prostate operation in 1956 left him weakened, and during 1957, typically well organized, he put his papers in order, shipping to the Bibliothèque Nationale in Paris several trunks of materials, including a diary and letters not to be opened until thirty years after his death. He still had the strength to sign, along with André Malraux and François Mauriac, a protest against the seizure of Henri Alleg's book *La Question* and to ask for a cessation of torture in the Algerian war. Martin du Gard died on 22 August 1958 of a heart attack. He was buried in a cemetery at Cimiez (Nice), beside his wife, on a hill overlooking the sea.

The genesis and structure of *Les Thibault* warrant close examination. Martin du Gard's first inclination when he began to plan the work was to write another dialogue novel after the style of *Jean Barois*, knowing that one of his strong points in writing was the life he could instill into characters through conversations. However, when he took one scene and wrote it in two different styles, once as dialogue and once in a more conventional form, he discovered that the dialogue version was much longer and much more cumbersome than the more traditional one. It was too unmanageable for a long novel.

He therefore decided to compose what became *Les Thibault* as a traditional third-person narrative. It was not lacking in dialogue; in fact, much of the novel, indeed many of the best scenes, which are the main building-block of the work, are composed of dialogue, except that Martin du Gard gives his omniscient narrator the freedom to comment instead of adhering rigidly to the dramatic format.

These scenes, tableaux or moments of existence in the lives of the characters, may be brief or long, covering periods ranging from a day to several weeks, and there are long or short intervals of time that pass between the events of one novel and those of the next. For example, *Le Cahier gris* takes up five days, after which a year passes before the action of the second novel, *Le Pénitencier*, which narrates a series of events which lasts several weeks. Between the action of that book and the third in the series, *La Belle Saison*, five years have passed.

In some cases successive scenes actually double back upon each other, covering the identical time frame but with different characters involved. Several different perspectives are thus possible on a single event. This is true only of the volumes up to and including *La Mort du père*, since *L'Eté 1914* is organized according to the chronology of the forty-four days leading up to World War I, that is 28 June to 10 August 1914. The war years are passed over until several weeks before the armistice of 1918. Thus *Les Thibault* is not a war novel. *Epilogue,* the action of which takes place between 3 May and 18 November 1918, picks up Antoine's trace; the entire volume is in the form of his diary. He is portrayed as the doctor who cannot cure himself. As a medical officer, Antoine was on an inspection trip at the front line, checking to see that gas masks were being used by the men, when, he, without his own mask, was caught in a wave of gas, from which he ultimately dies. A fitting end to the novel, his diary allows him to speculate on the war, on humanity, on the Thibault family, and in an almost cosmic way, on the future of the human race.

Much has been said by critics about the close relationship between Antoine Thibault, the elder of the two brothers whose lives and experiences the work traces, and his creator, Martin du Gard. It is prudent, however, to bear in mind Martin du Gard's statement concerning the roles of Antoine and Jacques, the younger brother in *Les Thibault*: "Un tel sujet m'offrait l'occasion d'un fructueux dédoublement: j'y voyais la possibilité d'exprimer simultanément deux tendances contradictoires de ma nature" (Such a subject offered me the occasion for a fruitful duplication: I saw in it the chance to express simultaneously two contradictory tendencies of my nature). One is inclined to agree with André Malraux, who said that all of Martin du Gard's reason may have lined up on the side of Antoine, but all of his passion was with Jacques.

While Martin du Gard was besieged by young readers who felt their kinship with Jacques, the novelist thought it necessary to remind them that he shared Antoine's view that his brother, who is headstrong, rebellious, and of an artistic temperament, acted like an imbecile. But at another moment Martin du Gard stated that he was himself an "instinctive imbecile"; imbecile here would seem to indicate simply the opposite of rational. This was certainly one of the characteristics the creator shared with his character Jacques, for whatever efforts Martin du Gard may have made to subject his instinctive nature to his rationality, or even to the discipline he learned at the Ecole des Chartes, the best moments in his writing are indisputably those when his spontaneous self took the upper hand.

It was the rational control of Marc-Elie Luce of *Jean Barois* that gave to that character a somewhat idealized, somewhat stilted air, while in most sections of *Les Thibault*, both Jacques and Antoine move with the grace of a glider, their apparent spontaneity being the guarantee of their life.

"Tout ce que j'ai à dire passe automatiquement dans mes *Thibault*" (Everything I have to say passes automatically into my *Thibault*), Martin du Gard once said, and it is clearly important to discern how his statements passed into the novel. For instance, even if he expresses in the text opinions that are his own, they are normally offset by opposing arguments or characters. Such is the case, for example, in the debate between Antoine and the Abbé Vécard, who discuss religion after the death of Père Thibault. The debate is divided so evenly between the two characters that it is best summed up with the expression by which it ends: "Cloisons étanches" (watertight compartments). At other times Martin du Gard has the reader of *Les Thibault* see a given event through two different perspectives. Such is the case in the interview between Jacques and Professor Jalicourt at the moment Jacques is making important decisions about his future life. The professor's version of that visit is presented first, then later Antoine hears his brother's version, the two being quite dissimilar.

On a larger scale the same structural pattern of opposition and balance is evident in the novel as a whole. In contrast to the Roman Catholic family, the Thibaults, there is the Protestant family, the Fontanins. Both families have a role of considerable importance to play in the novel. Although it is clearly the Thibaults who occupy the center stage, the Fontanins act as a foil, allowing for perceptions into different social milieus of the day but not interfering with the central concentration on the triumvirate of Père Thibault and his two sons.

Although they both reside in the summer at Maisons-Laffitte, the two families have never had any contact before Jacques Thibault and Daniel de Fontanin meet. The father of the Protestant family is a philanderer who appeals to women on a basis of sentimentality and his good looks. He is more often absent than not. There is something rather common about this portrayal, although Martin du Gard is careful not to let his presentation of the personality fall to the level of melodrama. The Protestant family also gives the author the chance to amuse himself with the portrayal of the Christian Scientist pastor, whom he compares to a whirling dervish. Madame de Fontanin is the most likable member of the Fontanin family, perhaps because of her basic belief in the goodness of all people. Her instincts in that direction are carried to ridiculous extremes when it comes to her husband. The respect she shows for other people's ideas and feelings is a model of charity. Martin du Gard treats her with an amused respect. It is possible to perceive an unstated love between her and Antoine, even though they have only a few meetings. Among the Thibaults—the Catholic family—the father, Oscar, carries his religion almost to the point of fanaticism; he is stuffy and sanctimonious. (There is no mother—a parallel to the Fontanins' usually absent father.) In short, neither Roman Catholic nor Protestant belief is really treated with much indulgence by Martin du Gard. The children in both families seem to have abandoned their religious belief, or at least it has taken peripheral and sublimated forms in their lives. One can readily say that Jacques has a form of religiousness in him, but it has moved in the directions of social welfare, poetry, and myth. He has been called the last romantic hero, and romanticism, by its seeking of the grand and the grandiose and its admiration for the overpowering figure, contains elements of religion.

One of the interesting features of the Roman Catholic-Protestant relationship in the novel is what Jacques and Daniel make of their reading of Gide's *Les Nourritures terrestres* (1897; translated as *The Fruits of the Earth*, 1949). They both discover the book as adolescents. For Daniel it becomes an open doorway to an instinctual, easygoing, flaccid existence, a choice favored perhaps also by his mother with her indulgence and optimism. Jacques seems to understand better the dangers in such a book and he sees in it, paradoxically, a call to self-denial, to a more aggressive form of life, perhaps once more under the influence of his own family environment.

What joins the two families even more than the friendship of the two sons, for eventually that friendship breaks down, is the relationship between Jacques and Jenny de Fontanin, the daughter. There is a developing love affair in which Jacques feels himself torn in several different directions, one of which is toward Jenny. He does finally choose her as his mistress and they have a child born after Jacques's death. On the future of the child, Jean-Paul, Antoine will place his fears and hopes for the future of the human race. The relationship of the two lovers is a brief one, and—one is tempted to say—happily so. For both are in search of absolutes, and there is a strong sense that had they stayed together for a long period of time, their harmoniously tense and awkward relationship could never have withstood the pressures. As the story evolves, Jacques dies and Jenny pursues her life with their son in such a way that Jacques is idealized according to her own perceptions of him.

But that is after all one of the characteristics of myth: a general pattern is established which serves as a guide for living, yet an infinite variety of historical circumstances or of personal charac-teristics may contribute to the immediate perception of that general mold. That Martin du Gard was interested in myth may be seen by his story of the passenger waiting for the train that never comes, published in the 1958 homage issue of the *Nouvelle Revue Française*.

Of all of Martin du Gard's creations, Jacques is perhaps the most mythical, along with Rachel, one of Antoine's mistresses, and Père Thibault, whose mythical role is suggested by the fact that he is regularly referred to simply as "father." Jacques is absent at the beginning of the novel, which opens after he and Daniel have run away from school. He is the subject of a prolonged search. Mythical too is the strong sense he has of his own destiny throughout the novel. His youthful complaint: "Avoir des ailes, pour les briser, hélas, contre les barreaux d'une prison!" (Ah, to have wings, only to break them against the bars of a prison!), is finally prophetic when his plane crashes, resulting in a broken leg, as he drops pacifist tracts over the front lines in August 1914. His pseudonyms (J., Jacques le Fataliste, J. Mühlenberg, Jack Baulthy, Jean-Sébastien Eberle), the anonymity of the pacifist tract, and, finally, a board labeled FRAGIL (a makeshift splint attached to his leg), by which he is known just before being shot by a scared, retreating French soldier, all suggest a search for an identity or rather the individual forms which his universal identity adopts at given moments. Even his identification with a descent into the hell of an unspeakable life, followed by an idyllic stay in the mountains of Mühlenberg, Switzerland, suggests the archetypal nature of his experiences. To be identified with places suggests that one is dealing with a character who goes beyond the limits of personality. Yet he is finally neither Icarus nor Christ nor that other representation of Christ, the pelican, who feeds her young with her own blood, although all of these are called up by textual references. Neither is he the historical figure Lauro de Bosis, who distributed tracts from an airplane over Rome. He is a combination of all these, the ultimate rebel in search of himself.

Jacques is finally, in his own day, a development of issues raised by the earlier novel *Jean Barois*, for the same problems of the individual and his potential commitment to society are raised in *Les Thibault* in a different context. Even though many in the group of socialists in Switzerland, with whom Jacques affiliates himself, look up to him as a leader, he can never be deeply involved in the group. His nature is to remain al-

Gallimard promotional card with drawing by
Berthold Mahn

ways on the periphery.

Despite Martin du Gard's stated aim to give life to his characters and let his readers draw their own conclusions, when one has read the whole of *Les Thibault* or the whole of each of the novels that make it up, one becomes aware of a certain direction, of a certain authorial point of view. The primary mode for the directionality of the novels is their structure. The architectural whole is much more important than any given, particular argument. Martin du Gard commented, in a letter to Gide in 1927, on his work methods, comparing himself to a sculptor, eliminating the excess from the outside in, little by little. He prided himself on his reconstruction of his castle, Le Tertre, wrote a series of letters to his grandson that he called "Letters from the Architect," and, in composing his literary works, considered the architecture of his novels of prime importance.

With the exception of the spontaneous *Devenir!* he always began with quantities of cards in a file. He arranged the cards according to episodes, placed them in a time frame, and then started writing. He always claimed that he worked best from events that were in the past as opposed to current events. Using his card-file method, he recorded events that he could redis-

cover months hence and reconstruct in accord with a certain plan.

In her *Histoire du roman français depuis 1918* (1950) Claude-Edmonde Magny condemns the rupture at the middle of *Les Thibault*, after the death of the father, as an artistic lapse. Her criticism, infrequently countered, overlooks the fact that this break serves a structural and functional purpose. She is right to say that the tone, the mood of the story, changes. But she is wrong not to see that "rupture" is one of the markers of this novel. The novels form a sort of diptych in which the structures of the first half of the novel parallel the structures of the second half: the family structures of part one parallel the structures of the family of nations which are "ruptured" and disintegrate in the second half.

There is a deep irony in Martin du Gard's way of pursuing these structures. To take an example: while he was writing *L'Eté 1914* during the 1930s, it became painfully evident that the world was riding a dangerous path toward catastrophe. *L'Eté 1914* is filled with the hopes of the Socialists that they will be able to prevent the war, and in *Epilogue* Antoine speaks with intense hope of Woodrow Wilson and the League of Nations. Yet at the time of writing those passages, Martin du Gard knew that the next war was coming and that the League of Nations was a failure. He wrote to Gide in 1933 that there was a stunning analogy between 1933 and 1913-1914. The supreme irony is that war was declared in September 1939, while Martin du Gard was finishing *Epilogue*. He must have had some bitter thoughts as he wrote the final section of *Les Thibault*.

It would be quite unfair to say that the apparent rupture between the first and the second half of *Les Thibault* is complete. The diplomat Rumelles introduces the topic of politics into conversations at Antoine's medical office in *La Consultation*, well in advance of the war, and it is clear, as more than one critic has seen, that the death of Père Thibault is also the death of a certain moneyed bourgeoisie and a certain way of life. This is to say that there is in his death the echo of a social consciousness which extends far beyond the limits of one particular family.

Martin du Gard rooted his stories in history, yet he was never satisfied with a purely historical dimension. What he sought, as he explained to Gide, was to reach feelings buried deep in all people and waiting to be discovered. In this regard there is a profoundly Jungian side to Martin du Gard's writings: the search for the collective unconscious.

There is also a deeply existential side to his writings, especially *Les Thibault*, an aspect which was certainly one of the reasons that he had such a strong appeal for Albert Camus, who wrote the preface for the 1955 Pléiade edition of Martin du Gard's complete works. Among these existential directions is the belief that one really knows a man only after his death. The self-righteous, prudish, authoritarian Père Thibault leaves among his papers some indications that his life also had other more relaxed directions. Martin du Gard also anticipates the existential belief that a person defines himself more by his actions than by his words. Antoine is not a writer during most of the novel, and in fact he is a man of few words. Yet the author defines the detective turn of his mentality and of the novel from the very first pages. This desire for truth is a characteristic which also helps make of Antoine a good doctor, but at the end of his life, like André Mazerelles, Bernard Grosdidier, Jean Barois, Marc-Elie Luce, and Jacques Thibault, Antoine becomes a writer. But one must be careful to understand "writer" here not as one who plays with words but rather as one who performs an act. Writing is Antoine's contribution to medical science (as he observes the progress of his own illness) and also to the formation of the personality of Jean-Paul.

Likewise, the existential all-pervasiveness of death as the ultimate arbiter, as the final fact which governs human life, is everywhere in *Les Thibault*. All the major heroes face death, each in his own fashion: Père Thibault hypocritically and fearfully, Jacques Thibault heroically, and Antoine Thibault medically and stoically.

It is interesting to note that Antoine is one of the few doctors in literature who is actually observed practicing medicine. It is true that he specializes in problems of language (that is, how words can convey the experience of illness) and shows some tendencies toward psychiatry (the influence of Martin du Gard's having studied with some famous psychiatrists of his day), but this portrayal merely serves to highlight the human qualities, which are not smothered under the scientific surface which Antoine must acquire. It also makes of Antoine a person who attempts to think through his problems. For example, on the question of euthanasia, he refuses adamantly to consider mercy killing for the Héquet child, who is condemned in any case. This decision is based upon the doctor's respect for life. Yet he also rec-

ognizes that he had some kittens drowned that very morning, and when the time comes, he and Jacques together agree, without saying a word, that he will give the final injection to Père Thibault. "Au nom de quoi?" (In the name of what?) is one of the big questions of his life. One of the principles of his life, articulated in Martin du Gard's correspondence with Gide, is that one should not allow oneself to be blinded by the individual; that is, questions of the human race, of mankind in general, override questions of the individual personality.

The minor characters of the novel all have specific roles to play. Rachel, who becomes Antoine's mistress, is one of the influences that open Antoine up to new adventures in the world. Gise, who grows up in the Thibault family almost as a sister although she is not a blood relative, is a sexual temptation for both Jacques and Antoine. Monsieur Chasle, the private secretary of Père Thibault, provides comic relief. There is a whole world of other minor characters: Anne de Battaincourt, another of Antoine's mistresses, one who shows a seamy side of existence and provides Antoine with some moments of serious reflection; Lisbeth, who initiates Jacques to erotic pleasure; Rumelles, who gives a sort of official version of the political scene; Dédette, whose accident brings together Antoine and Rachel; and many, many more.

Mystery is an important element in *Les Thibault*. The novel opens with the givens of a detective story: a problem—missing children—and the attempt—Antoine's—to solve the problem rationally. It becomes clear that problem-solving is a characteristic of Antoine's mentality, and late in the novel Jacques refers to his brother as a detective. There is mystery in Jérôme de Fontanin's philandering, in Rachel's former existence, as well as in the existence she leads after leaving Antoine to return to Africa, in Jacques's maneuvers as he plays spy games before the outbreak of World War I, and in Antoine's attempts to locate his missing brother (both in *Le Cahier gris* and in *La Sorellina*, when Jacques has disappeared again). There is also an air of mystery when Jacques apparently sends flowers to Gise in England. Gise does not share her secret with the family, but she assumes, contrary to Père Thibault's belief, that Jacques is alive and that he loves her.

Incest as a theme appears in Jacques's story within the novel, "La Sorellina," in which a brother and sister have sexual relations, and in the story of Rachel's background. The best expression of this theme, however, is in Martin du Gard's novella entitled *Confidence africaine,* in which he wished to show how an incestuous relationship could come about and even be continued for four years, quite naturally. This is certainly one of Martin du Gard's best pieces of writing, a small masterpiece in which he handles a delicate subject with poise and equanimity. It also resulted in a long debate between himself, Gide, and their mutual friend Dorothy Bussy over the implications, artistic or other, of the child born of this incestuous relationship, who is sickly and finally dies.

Although the first of his plays, *Le Testament du Père Leleu* (Daddy Leleu's Will), was performed by Jacques Copeau's Théâtre du Vieux-Colombier in 1914 and published in 1920, then revived at the Comédie-Française in 1938, his drama never had the public acceptance of his novels, which always sold well for Gallimard. *Le Testament du Père Leleu* is a story of peasant greed and maliciousness in which the deceiver is deceived. His second play, *La Gonfle* (Dropsy), is a peasant farce written in the dialect of the Berry region. Published in 1928, it has never been produced. His third play, *Un Taciturne* (A Taciturn Man, published in 1932), is the story of a man who makes the discovery of his own homosexuality. It was produced by Louis Jouvet. He also wrote a book of rural sketches entitled *Vieille France* (1933; translated as *The Postman,* 1954), which is a biting and black satire of a small rural village.

Martin du Gard's hope at the end of his life was to complete the long book which he started after finishing *Les Thibault* and which finally appeared under the title *Le Lieutenant-Colonel de Maumort.* Martin du Gard referred to this book as his "posthumous" publication, and indeed it was posthumously published, twenty-five years after his death, in 1983. He changed the format several times, from letters, to diary, to novellas, during the eighteen years he worked on it. André Daspre did a magnificent job of sifting the papers and preparing the work for publication in a more or less readable form, providing 250 pages of notes to accompany the 1,059 pages of text in the Pléiade edition. (For this work Daspre received the Prix de l'Edition Critique for 1983.) Its final form is that of memoirs, written by a septuagenarian who wants to write the story of his happy life. One is reminded that Flaubert said that it is impossible to write about a happy life.

André Gide declared in 1948, after listening to a reading of some pages of *Le Lieutenant-Colonel de Maumort,* that they were among the best Martin du Gard had ever written. It does not seem likely that this judgment will be vindicated. There are some readers, it is true, who have praised the volume. However, the reader of *Le Lieutenant-Colonel de Maumort* feels himself buried under the weight of analytical memoirs. There is an excessiveness about this work which is not found in any of Martin du Gard's earlier works, even the long ones. Supposing, or knowing, that it would be a posthumously published work, he kept writing at it as if he did not want to construct an ending. But then, what can one criticize in an unfinished work? Who can say, had Martin du Gard lived twenty years more, what the final form of these memoirs might have been? In spite of some excellent pages, *Le Lieutenant-Colonel de Maumort* will never come close to replacing *Les Thibault,* or *Jean Barois,* or even *Confidence africaine* as Martin du Gard's best work. He was always at his best in that indeterminate area between the novel and the theater, where his characters are actively, even existentially, engaged in living out their lives, in animated contact with each other, generally expressing themselves in the author's well-crafted dialogue.

Letters:

Correspondance avec André Gide, 2 volumes (1913-1934 and 1935-1951) (Paris: Gallimard, 1968);

Correspondance avec Jacques Copeau, 2 volumes, edited by Claude Sicard (Paris: Gallimard, 1972);

Correspondance générale, 2 volumes, edited by Maurice Rieuneau, André Daspre, and Sicard (Paris: Gallimard, 1980).

References:

Denis Boak, *Roger Martin du Gard* (Oxford: Clarendon Press, 1963);

Jacques Brenner, *Martin du Gard* (Paris: Gallimard, 1961);

Catharine Savage Brosman, "André Gide and Roger Martin du Gard: For and Against Commitment," *Rice University Studies,* 59 (Summer 1973): 1-8;

Albert Camus, "Roger Martin du Gard," *Nouvelle Revue Française,* 34 (1955): 641-671;

Haakon Chevalier, "French Literature Before the Wars; Two Attitudes: 1914 and 1939," *French Review*, 16 (January 1943): 197-205;

André Daspre and Jochen Schlobach, eds., *Roger Martin du Gard. Etudes sur son œuvre.* (Paris: Klincksieck, 1984);

Trevor Field, "The Internal Chronology of *Jean Barois*," *Studi Francesi*, 50 (May-August 1973): 300-303;

Folio, special issue on Martin du Gard, no. 13 (October 1981);

René Garguilo, *La Genèse des "Thibault" de Roger Martin du Gard* (Paris: Klincksieck, 1974);

Robert Gibson, *Roger Martin du Gard* (London: Bowes & Bowes/New York: Hillary House, 1961);

John Gilbert, "Symbols of Continuity and the Unity of *Les Thibault*," in his *Image and Theme: Studies in Modern French Fiction* (Cambridge: Harvard University Press, 1969), pp. 124-148;

Irving Howe, "Martin du Gard: The Novelty of Goodness," in his *The Decline of the New* (New York: Harcourt, Brace & World, 1970), pp. 43-53;

Stuart H. Hughes, "Martin du Gard and the Unattainable Epic," in his *The Obstructed Path: French Social Thought in the Years of Desperation* (New York: Harper & Row, 1966), pp. 107-120;

Grant Kaiser, "Jacques Thibault: masque et mythe," in *Fiction, Form, Experience*, edited by Kaiser (Montreal: Editions France-Québec, 1976), pp. 114-127;

Kaiser, "Roger Martin du Gard devant la critique," *Studi francesi*, 59 (1976): 248-262;

Kaiser, "Roger Martin du Gard's *Jean Barois*: An Experiment in Novelistic Form," *Symposium*, 14 (Summer 1960): 135-141;

Claude-Edmonde Magny, *Histoire du roman français depuis 1918* (Paris: Editions du Seuil, 1950);

Nouvelle Revue Française, special issue on Martin du Gard, new series 12 (December 1958);

Martha O'Nan, "Form in the Novel: André Gide and Roger Martin du Gard," *Symposium*, 12 (Spring-Fall 1958): 81-93;

O'Nan, "Lettre autographe et bibliographie," *Folio*, 13 (1981): 70-76;

Réjean Robidoux, *Roger Martin du Gard et la Religion* (Paris: Aubier, 1964);

Leon Roudiez, "The Function of Irony in Roger Martin du Gard," *Romanic Review*, 48 (December 1957): 275-286;

Robert Roza, "Roger Martin du Gard: Master Builder of the Novel," *American Society Legion of Honor Magazine*, 38 (1967): 73-88;

Catharine Savage, *Roger Martin du Gard* (New York: Twayne, 1968);

David Schalk, *Roger Martin du Gard: The Novelist and History* (Ithaca, N.Y.: Cornell University Press, 1967);

Claude Sicard, *Roger Martin du Gard. Les Années d'apprentissage littéraire. (1881-1910)* (Lille: Atelier Reproduction de Thèses, Université Lille III, 1976);

Sonia Spurdle, "Tolstoy and Roger Martin du Gard's *Les Thibault*," *Comparative Literature*, 23 (Fall 1971): 325-345;

Susan M. Stout, *Index de la Correspondance André Gide-Roger Martin du Gard* (Paris: Gallimard, 1971);

Michael John Taylor, *Martin du Gard: Jean Barois* (London: Arnold, 1974);

Philip Thody, "The Politics of the Family Novel: Is Conservatism Inevitable?," *Mosaic*, 3 (Fall 1969): 87-101;

Eugen Weber, "The Secret World of *Jean Barois*," in *The Origins of Modern Consciousness*, edited by Ed Weiss (Detroit: Wayne State University Press, 1965), pp. 79-109;

Renée Fainas Wehrmann, *L'Art de Roger Martin du Gard* (Birmingham, Ala.: Summa, 1986);

W. D. Wilson, "Martin du Gard's *Epilogue*: A Problem of Closure," in *Perspectives on Language and Literature* (Mona, Jamaica: University of the West Indies, 1985), pp. 144-160;

Wilson, "The Theme of Abdication in the Novels of Roger Martin du Gard," *Neophilologus*, 59 (April 1975): 190-198;

John Wood, "Roger Martin du Gard," *French Studies*, 14 (April 1960): 129-140.

Papers:

Martin du Gard's papers are deposited at the Bibliothèque Nationale.

François Mauriac

(11 October 1885-1 September 1970)

Slava M. Kushnir
Queen's University

SELECTED BOOKS: *Les Mains jointes* (Paris: Falque, 1909);

L'Adieu à l'adolescence (Paris: Stock, 1911);

L'Enfant chargé de chaînes (Paris: Grasset, 1913); translated by Gerard Hopkins as *Young Man in Chains* (London: Eyre & Spottiswoode, 1961; New York: Farrar, Straus & Cudahy, 1961);

La Robe prétexte (Paris: Grasset, 1914); translated by Hopkins as *The Stuff of Youth* (London: Eyre & Spottiswoode, 1960);

La Chair et le sang (Paris: Emile-Paul, 1920); translated by Hopkins as *Flesh and Blood* (London: Eyre & Spottiswoode, 1954; New York: Farrar, Straus, 1955);

Petits Essais de psychologie religieuse (Paris: Société Littéraire de France, 1920);

Préséances (Paris: Emile-Paul, 1921); translated by Hopkins as *Questions of Precedence* (London: Eyre & Spottiswoode, 1958; New York: Farrar, Straus & Cudahy, 1959);

Le Baiser au lépreux (Paris: Grasset, 1922; New York: Macmillan, 1922); translated by James Whitall as *The Kiss to the Leper* (London: Heinemann, 1923); translated in *The Family* (1930);

Le Fleuve de feu (Paris: Grasset, 1923); translated by Hopkins as *The River of Fire* (London: Eyre & Spottiswoode, 1954);

Génitrix (Paris: Grasset, 1923); translated in *The Family* (1930);

La Vie et la mort d'un poète (Paris: Bloud & Gay, 1924);

Le Mal (Paris: Grasset, 1924); translated as *The Enemy* in *The Desert of Love and The Enemy* (1949);

Le Désert de l'amour (Paris: Grasset, 1925); translated by Samuel Putnam as *The Desert of Love* (New York: Covici, Friede, 1929); translated in *The Desert of Love and The Enemy* (1949);

Orages (Paris: Champion, 1925);

François Mauriac in the 1930s (courtesy of Claude Mauriac)

Bordeaux (Paris: Emile-Paul, 1926); republished in *Commencements d'une vie* (1932);

Coups de couteau (Paris: Trémois, 1926);

Le Jeune Homme (Paris: Hachette, 1926);

Proust (Paris: Lesage, 1926);

La Province (Paris: Hachette, 1926);

Un Homme de lettres (Paris: Lapina, 1926);

Thérèse Desqueyroux (Paris: Grasset, 1927); translated by Eric Sutton as *Thérèse* (London: Secker, 1928; New York: Boni & Liverwright, 1928);

Conscience, instinct divin (Paris: Emile-Paul, 1927);

Destins (Paris: Grasset, 1928); translated by Eric Sutton as *Destinies* (London: Secker, 1929; New York: Covici, Friede, 1929);

Le Démon de la connaissance (Paris: Trémois, 1928);

La Vie de Jean Racine (Paris: Plon, 1928);

Le Roman (Paris: L'Artisan du Livre, 1928);

Supplément au Traité de la concupiscence de Bossuet (Paris: Trianon, 1928);

Divagations sur Saint-Sulpice (Paris: Champion, 1928);

Dieu et Mammon (Paris: Capitole, 1929); translated by Bernard and Barbara Wall as *God and Mammon* (London: Sheed & Ward, 1936);

Mes plus lointains souvenirs (Paris: E. Hazan, 1929); republished in *Commencements d'une vie* (1932);

La Nuit du bourreau de soi-même (Paris: Flammarion, 1929);

Trois Récits (Paris: Grasset, 1929);

Ce qui était perdu (Paris: Grasset, 1930); translated as *That Which Was Lost* in *That Which Was Lost and The Dark Angels* (1951);

The Family, translated by Lewis Galantière (New York: Covici, Friede, 1930)—comprises *Le Baiser au lépreux* and *Génitrix*;

Paroles en Espagne (Paris: Hartmann, 1930);

Trois Grands Hommes devant Dieu (Paris: Capitole, 1930);

Blaise Pascal et sa sœur Jacqueline (Paris: Hachette, 1931);

Le Jeudi saint (Paris: Flammarion, 1931); translated by Marie-Louise Dufrenoy as *The Eucharist: The Mystery of Holy Thursday* (New York & Toronto: Longmans, Green, 1944);

Souffrances et bonheur du chrétien (Paris: Grasset, 1931); translated by Harold Evans as *Anguish and Joy of the Christian Life* (Wilkes-Barre, Pa.: Dimension, 1964);

Commencements d'une vie (Paris: Grasset, 1932)—comprises *Bordeaux* and *Mes plus lointains souvenirs*;

Le Nœud de vipères (Paris: Grasset, 1932; New York: Macmillan, 1932); translated by Warre B. Wells as *Vipers' Tangle* (London: Gollancz, 1933; New York: Sheed & Ward, 1933);

La Drôle (Paris: Hartmann, 1933);

Le Mystère Frontenac (Paris: Grasset, 1933); translated by Hopkins as *The Frontenac Mystery* (Lon-

don: Eyre & Spottiswoode, 1952); republished as *The Frontenacs* (New York: Farrar, Straus & Cudahy, 1961);

Le Romancier et ses personnages (Paris: Corrêa, 1933);

Discours de réception à l'Académie Française et réponse de M. André Chaumeix (Paris: Grasset, 1934);

Journal [I] (Paris: Grasset, 1934);

La Fin de la nuit (Paris: Grasset, 1935); translated as *The End of Night* in *Thérèse* (1947);

Les Anges noirs (Paris: Grasset, 1936); translated as *The Dark Angels* in *That Which Was Lost and The Dark Angels* (1951);

L'Education des filles (Paris: Corrêa, 1936);

Vie de Jésus (Paris: Flammarion, 1936); translated by Julie Kernan as *Life of Jesus* (London: Hodder & Stoughton, 1937; New York: Longmans, Green, 1937);

Journal [II] (Paris: Grasset, 1937);

Asmodée (Paris: Grasset, 1938); translated by Basil Bartlett as *Asmodée; or, the Intruder* (London: Secker & Warburg, 1939); translated by Beverly Thurman as *Asmodée* (New York: French, 1959);

Plongées (Paris: Grasset, 1938);

Les Chemins de la mer (Paris: Grasset, 1939); translated by Hopkins as *The Unknown Sea* (London: Eyre & Spottiswoode, 1948; New York: Holt, 1948);

Les Maisons fugitives (Paris: Grasset, 1939);

Journal [III] (Paris: Grasset, 1940);

Le Sang d'Atys (Paris: Grasset, 1940);

La Pharisienne (Paris: Grasset, 1941); translated by Hopkins as *Woman of the Pharisees* (London: Eyre & Spottiswoode, 1946; New York: Holt, 1946);

Le Cahier noir, as Forez (Paris: Editions de Minuit, 1943); bilingual edition (London: Burrup, Mathieson, 1944);

Le Bâillon dénoué, après quatre ans de silence (Paris: Grasset, 1945);

Les Mal-Aimés (Paris: Grasset, 1945);

La Rencontre avec Barrès (Paris: Table Ronde, 1945);

Sainte Marguerite de Cortone (Paris: Flammarion, 1945); translated by Bernard Frechtman as *Saint Margaret of Cortona* (New York: Philosophical Library, 1948);

Du côté de chez Proust (Paris: Table Ronde, 1947); translated by Elsie Pell as *Proust's Way* (New York: Philosophical Library, 1950);

Thérèse, translated by Hopkins (London: Eyre & Spottiswoode, 1947)—comprises *Thérèse Desqueyroux, Thérèse chez le docteur, Thérèse à l'hô tel,* and *La Fin de la nuit;* republished as *Thérèse: A Portrait in Four Parts* (New York: Holt, 1947);

Journal d'un homme de trente ans (Paris: Egloff, 1948);

Passage du malin (Paris: Table Ronde, 1948);

The Desert of Love and The Enemy, translated by Hopkins (London: Eyre & Spottiswoode, 1949; New York: Farrar, Straus & Cudahy, 1958)–comprises *Le Désert de l'amour* and *Le Mal;*

Mes Grands Hommes (Monaco: Editons du Rocher, 1949);

Journal [IV] (Paris: Flammarion, 1950);

La Pierre d'achoppement (Monaco: Editions du Rocher, 1951); translated by Pell as *The Stumbling Block* (New York: Philosophical Library, 1952); translated by Hopkins (London: Harvill, 1956);

Le Feu sur la terre; ou, Le Pays sans chemin (Paris: Grasset, 1951);

Le Sagouin (Paris: La Palatine, 1951); translated by Hopkins as *The Little Misery* (London: Eyre & Spottiswoode, 1952); Hopkins's translation republished as *The Weakling* in *The Weakling and The Enemy* (1952);

That Which Was Lost and The Dark Angels, translated by J. H. F. McEwen and by Hopkins (London: Eyre & Spottiswoode, 1951)–comprises *Ce qui était perdu* and *Les Anges noirs;*

Galigaï (Paris: Flammarion, 1952); translated by Hopkins as *The Loved and the Unloved* (New York: Pellegrini & Cudahy, 1952; London: Eyre & Spottiswoode, 1953);

Lettres ouvertes (Monaco: Editions du Rocher, 1952); translated by Mario A. Pei as *Letters on Art and Literature* (New York: Philosophical Library, 1953);

La Mort d'André Gide (Paris: Estienne, 1952);

The Weakling and The Enemy, translated by Hopkins (New York: Pelligrini & Cudahy, 1952)–comprises *Le Sagouin* and *Le Mal;*

Ecrits intimes (Geneva & Paris: La Palatine, 1953);

Journal [V] (Paris: Flammarion, 1953);

L'Agneau (Paris: Flammarion, 1954); translated by Hopkins as *The Lamb* (London: Eyre & Spottiswoode, 1955; New York: Farrar, Straus & Cudahy, 1955);

Paroles catholiques (Paris: Plon, 1954);

Bloc-notes, 1952-1957 (Paris: Flammarion, 1958);

Mémoires intérieurs (Paris: Flammarion, 1959); translated by Hopkins (London: Eyre & Spottiswoode, 1960; New York: Farrar, Straus & Cudahy, 1960);

Le Nouveau Bloc-notes, 1958-1960 (Paris: Flammarion, 1961);

Ce que je crois (Paris: Grasset, 1962); translated by Wallace Fowlie as *What I Believe* (New York: Farrar, Straus, 1963);

De Gaulle (Paris: Grasset, 1964); translated by Richard Howard (London: Bodley Head, 1966; Garden City: Doubleday, 1966);

Nouveaux Mémoires intérieurs (Paris: Flammarion, 1965);

D'autres et moi, edited by Keith Goesch (Paris: Grasset, 1966);

Mémoires politiques (Paris: Grasset, 1967);

Le Nouveau Bloc-notes, 1961-1964 (Paris: Flammarion, 1968);

Un Adolescent d'autrefois (Paris: Flammarion, 1969); translated by Jean Stewart as *Maltaverne* (London: Eyre & Spottiswoode, 1970; New York: Farrar, Straus & Giroux, 1970);

Le Nouveau Bloc-notes, 1965-1967 (Paris: Flammarion, 1970);

Le Dernier Bloc-notes, 1968-1970 (Paris: Flammarion, 1971);

Maltaverne (Paris: Flammarion, 1972).

Collections: *Œuvres complètes,* 12 volumes (Paris: Fayard, 1950-1956);

Œuvres romanesques et théâtrales complètes, 3 volumes, edited by Jacques Petit (Paris: Gallimard, 1978-1981).

PLAY PRODUCTIONS: *Asmodée,* Paris, Comédie-Française, 22 November 1937;

Les Mal-Aimés, Paris, Comédie-Française, 1 March 1945;

Passage du Malin, Paris, Théâtre de la Madeleine, 9 December 1947;

Le Feu sur la terre, Lyons, 12 October 1950; Paris, Théâtre Hébertot, 7 December 1950.

OTHER: Blaise Pascal, *Les Pages immortelles de Pascal,* edited by Mauriac (Paris: Corrêa, 1940; New York: Editions de la Maison Française, 1941); translated by Doris E. Troutman as *The Living Thoughts of Pascal* (New York: Longmans, Green, 1940; London: Cassell, 1941);

Alfred Dreyfus, *Cinq Années de ma vie, 1894-1899,* preface by Mauriac (Paris: Fasquelle, 1962);

Jean-René Huguenin, *Journal,* preface by Mauriac (Paris: Seuil, 1964);

Maurice Barrès, *L'Œuvre de Maurice Barrès,* 20 volumes, preface by Mauriac (Paris: Club de l'Honnête Homme, 1965-1968);

Michel Suffran, *Sur une génération perdue*, preface by Mauriac (Bordeaux: Samie, 1966);

Suffran, *Jean de la Ville de Mirmont*, preface by Mauriac (Paris: Seghers, 1968).

François Mauriac is without doubt one of the most important and prolific French authors of this century. His death on 1 September 1970 marked the close of a career unlikely to be paralleled in the literary history of France. A poet, he began his literary career with the publication in 1909 of a collection of poems, *Les Mains jointes* (Clasped Hands), reviewed with enthusiasm by the established writer Maurice Barrès, who predicted celebrity for the young author. To this Mauriac added in 1925 *Orages* (Storms), and in 1940 *Le Sang d'Atys* (The Blood of Atys), a long poem on which he worked intermittently for close to ten years. A literary critic, Mauriac meditated on the art of fiction in such works as *Le Roman* (The Novel, 1928) and *Le Romancier et ses personnages* (The Novelist and his Characters, 1933). A Christian moralist, author of numerous essays on Catholic thinkers and saints (Saint Margaret of Cortona, Pascal, Lacordaire) and of the poignant *Vie de Jésus* (1936; translated as *Life of Jesus*, 1937), author of autobiographical works, the most noted of which are *Commencements d'une vie* (Beginnings of a Life, 1932) and *Mémoires intérieurs* (Interior Memoirs, 1959), a playwright who wrote four plays—*Asmodée* (1937; translated as *Asmodée; or, the Intruder*, 1939), *Les Mal-Aimés* (The Ill-loved, 1945), *Passage du malin* (Passing of the Evil One, 1948), and *Le Feu sur la terre* (Fire on Earth, 1951), Mauriac is, however, above all a novelist.

One might say that for Mauriac the novel is the genre where the poet, the moralist, the critic, the autobiographer, and the dramatist meet. The poet is present in the novel, for Mauriac is a twentieth-century master of poetic prose; it is, in fact, in the novel that he attained his greatness as a poet. Mauriac's very approach to the novel was that of a poet, drawing fables from a limited field of experience protected against the outside world by the force of these fables' original impact upon the mind. Mauriac also brought to the novel a symbolist technique, reflecting the influence of Baudelaire and the symbolist movement in France. The human heart was for him a microcosm of the universe, which in turn was an objectification of the mind. This mutual interpenetration of cosmos and man is essentially poetic and deeply symbolist. What is more, the ex-

tent of this symbolist framework, in which the four elements play a most significant role, is the work of a highly original mind. For to create his strikingly tangible universe, Mauriac uses, within the general symbolism of fire, water, earth, and air, a great deal of sensory symbolism, above all, olfactory impressions, but also auditory, visual, and tactile images. The sense symbolism becomes most effective in synthetic combinations, where odors, sounds, sights, and touch fuse at the most dramatic movements of a novel.

The moralist and the critic are present in Mauriac's novels because the author does not hesitate to make digressions that reveal the moralist; he intervenes at certain moments and comments on the actions of his characters or even predicts their destiny. He is also able to suppress these interventions and to modify or develop his novelistic technique by incorporating into his novels the results of critical reflections or dialogues with other writers about the art of fiction. The case in point here is his polemic with Jean-Paul Sartre, who accused him of omniscience–of playing God with his characters–and the subsequent modifications that he brought to his novels as, for example, in *La Pharisienne* (1941; translated as *Woman of the Pharisees*, 1946).

The autobiographer is intimately present in the novel because Mauriac's novels are, at a very deep level, autobiographical, representing his own tendencies and potentialities, his own deep-rooted inner conflict developed and transformed by creative imagination. Mauriac himself claimed that his novels were an externalization of "my own debate, my own drama, my own destiny."

Finally most of Mauriac's novels, at least those written in the 1920s, present a highly dramatic structure. At a time when the modern novel tended toward sprawling prolixity, Mauriac, the author of *La Vie de Jean Racine* (Life of Racine, 1928), was not concerned with a detailed account spread over a period of years of the physical existence of his characters, but focused, like Racine, on the brief moments of the character's flowering. There are no moments of rest in his fiction, no intersecting of plots except in one or two later novels such as *La Pharisienne*. The novels are tightly constructed; the action, as in Racine, starts in medias res, at the height of characters' passions, when the crisis is near. The plot is always quick-paced, relentless in its movement. As the American critic of Mauriac, Michael Moloney, points out in *François Mauriac: A Critical Study* (1958): "Essentially the art of Mauriac is a 20th century adaptation of the art of Racine." Or one could say with Nelly Cormeau, author of *L'Art de François Mauriac* (1951), that the Mauriac novel is the form the contemporary tragedy has taken.

In dealing with Mauriac as a novelist, one must not forget the unity between the man and the novelist. Mauriac's first novel, *L'Enfant chargé de chaînes*, was published in 1913 (translated as *Young Man in Chains*, 1961), but as a boy of thirteen, he had written a charming novel of about thirty-five pages entitled "Va-t-en" (Go away), in which he already revealed his gift for social satire and his keen interest in very strong human passions. In 1969, at the age of eighty-four, one year before his death, Mauriac wrote his last novel, partly autobiographical, about an adolescent from the past, *Un Adolescent d'autrefois*, translated into English as *Maltaverne* (1970). At the end of his life Mauriac returned to fiction and to the topic of adolescence, the privileged age in his novels, as if to explicate, before dying, the deeper meaning implicit in all his previous novels. He planned a sequel to *Un Adolescent d'autrefois*, dictating, because of failing eyesight, to his wife, who typed all his manuscripts, contributed her comments, and thus participated to a certain extent in the poetic process. He fell into a coma while dictating and died a month later. Born a poet, Mauriac died a poet (the word "poetry" is used here not in a generic sense but in a sense approximating that of literary creation), considering always that his writing was the stuff of his life, that his work and his life were inseparable, or one, both part of the same vital process toward maturity, unification of self, and God.

In addition to poetry, essays, drama, and fiction, there is, however, another field in which Mauriac became prominent. In 1932, after emerging from a spiritual crisis in his life as well as from a serious illness—cancer of the vocal cords—Mauriac turned to political journalism. He remained in the political arena until his death in 1970, having contributed hundreds of articles to such newspapers and journals as *Echo de Paris*, *Sept*, *Temps Présent*, *Figaro*, *Figaro Littéraire*, *Table Ronde*, and *Express*. He brought to journalism on the one hand his inimitable style, a blend of lyricism and polemics, on the other hand his vibrant faith, his scrupulous Catholic conscience.

Mauriac strikes many readers as a profound but narrow writer, exploring a limited field of experience, rewriting the same novel. "Je fais toujours le même livre" (I continue to write the same book), he once said. Among French writers, he was the most French, supremely Gallic, even in his appearance, intensely devoted to his country, her problems, her culture, professing a distaste for travel and, although well informed about foreign literatures and cultures, he indeed had nothing cosmopolitan about him. He was also a son of Gascony, a *bordelais*, attached to his native region with the same poetic passion as to his childhood, celebrating this remote corner of France in every one of his novels. He was, finally, his whole life an outspoken Catholic, evolving within his Catholicism from a rigid, almost Jansenist position to a more tolerant Christian worldview but never once hesitating in his faith. Yet this writer, so *bordelais*, so French, so Catholic, attracted readers and admirers from outside France and outside the Church. His works have been translated into all major languages of the world. This truly universal appeal that his work had during his lifetime and continues to have today is undoubtedly the best indication of Mauriac's greatness.

Criticism of Mauriac's fiction has been hampered from the beginning by a confusion made by critics between Mauriac the artist and Mauriac the man, the public figure, who was a devout and militant Catholic. They assume that religion played a most important role in his fiction. Thus a Catholic critic, Henri Clouard, claimed in his 1962 history of French literature that "le problème du salut, le jet lumineux de la foi chrétienne et catholique traversant les confuses avidités de l'homme plongé dans l'immédiat: voilà le thème essentiel du roman mauriacien" (the problem of salvation, the luminous springing forth of Christian and Catholic faith traversing the confused desires of man plunged in the immediate: that is the essential theme of Mauriac's novels).

Mauriac himself contributed to the misunderstanding by making public statements about his fiction, in interviews or essays, that is, outside his fiction, or by intervening in a rather heavy-handed fashion at the end of the novel, as in *Le Désert de l'amour* (1925; translated as *The Desert of Love*, 1929), and telling the reader that only God could bring solace to his characters. Later he would restrict his comments to prefaces (*Thérèse Desqueyroux*, 1927; translated as *Thérèse*, 1928) or postfaces (*Galigaï*, 1952, translated as *The Loved and the Unloved*, 1952), both vehicles of ideology at odds with the implied meaning of the novel. This tendency to impose upon the reader a certain interpretation of his novels testifies to a conflict in Mauriac between the artist and the Catholic. The devout Catholic often felt ill at ease about his art, considering his poetry a channel for the indulgence of the senses and his portrayal of human passions a possible source of scandal to his Catholic readers. Artistic freedom appeared as moral laxity; however, moral integrity spelled the death of his art.

Thus the critics, considering Mauriac a Catholic novelist, disregarded the specific nature or tenor of his imaginative writing which is poetic and symbolic. They treated his novels as commodities, concerned only with their moral implications and their impact upon certain readers. Mauriac was finally forced to explain: "Je ne suis pas un romancier catholique; je suis un catholique qui écrit des romans" (I am not a Catholic novelist; I am a Catholic who writes novels). Indeed if many of Mauriac's novels could be loosely viewed as a portrayal of man's fallen nature, of man as a sinner in need of divine grace, this interpretation is too facile; it does not account for the richness, for the psychoanalytical complexity of Mauriac's characters, and, furthermore, it hardly applies to such important novels as *Génitrix* (1923; translated in *The Family*, 1930) or *Thérèse Desqueyroux*. In fact in Mauriac's novels the issue is not eternal salvation, but rather human happiness. Many of Mauriac's characters are totally pagan, such as Félicité and Fernand Cazenave in *Génitrix*. Thérèse Desqueyroux, the central character of Mauriac's fiction, is totally, unequivocally un-Christian in all her responses to life, a complete stranger to religion, despite the fact that Catholicism is practiced extensively in her class. God is absent from the preoccupations of Mauriac's characters and when he becomes a presence in their lives, as for Louis in *Le Nœud de vipères* (1932; translated as *Vipers' Tangle*, 1933), it is as a result of an altogether different activity, central to Mauriac's and to his heroes' concerns.

Despite the ideological and, therefore, censoring statements concerning his own fiction, Mauriac did offer, on several occasions, important information about his method of writing. Describing himself as an "instinctive writer," he claimed in an interview with Frédéric Lefèvre in 1924 that his writing was "entirely subconscious." In *Le Romancier et ses personnages* as well as in many other essays and interviews, he explained that he wrote the first draft of a novel very quickly, sometimes in three weeks, always in isolation from his family and from the external world. His writing

was compulsive: he was often surprised by the content of his novels and by the conduct of his characters, whom he could not control. Concentrating intensely upon a theme, he did not deliberately structure his novels: control in his fiction was basically organic. He claimed that he neither observed nor described, but rediscovered. He rediscovered through the medium of art his childhood and his adolescence, which were the true material of his books. Indeed Mauriac's novels, although written in Paris where he spent most of his life, are all set in the Bordeaux region, the context of his childhood, where the fundamental conflicts were laid down, the knot was tied, where, above all, he became aware of his poetic vocation. The physical distance Bordeaux-Paris parallels the temporal distance childhood-adult age. Art was an opening of the door shut behind him at the age of twenty. This pattern of departure from childhood and of return to it through creative memory is repeatedly represented in his novels.

Mauriac was born in Bordeaux, 11 October 1885, the fourth child of Jean-Paul and Claire Coiffard Mauriac. Jean-Paul Mauriac, a banker, died when his son François was not quite two, and the family moved in with Claire Mauriac's mother, who also lived in Bordeaux. In 1904 Mauriac completed his *baccalauréat*, and in 1906 he earned a *licence ès lettres*, writing a thesis entitled "Les Origines du franciscanisme en France" (The Origins of Franciscanism in France). In 1907 he went to Paris in order to prepare for entering the Ecole des Chartes. After failing on his first entrance examination he was accepted in November 1908. But six months later he resigned in order to devote himself entirely to literature. What decided him was an invitation by Charles-Francis Caillard, director of the *Revue du Temps Présent*, to collaborate as poetry editor and an offer to publish his first volume of verse for the sum of 500 francs. *Les Mains jointes* appeared in November 1909 and was highly praised by Barrès, who detected in it "the poetry of a child of a happy family," a "charming gift of spirituality" but with "a mad note of voluptuousness." This early recognition by a master was a turning point in Mauriac's career, bringing him to the attention of the critics, gaining for him friends such as Robert Vallery-Radot and the poet André Lafon, and opening several salons, among them that of Mme Alphonse Daudet, where he met Léon Daudet, Jean Cocteau, and Marcel Proust.

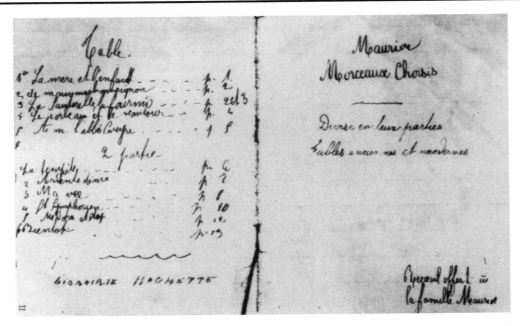

Table of contents and title page for a booklet of "fables" Mauriac wrote for his family when he was twelve
(courtesy of Claude Mauriac)

In 1911 Mauriac was already working on his first novel, *L'Enfant chargé de chaînes*, which appeared in 1913, shortly before his marriage to Jeanne Lafon on 3 June. In 1914, which witnessed the birth of Claude, the first of his four children, he produced his second novel, mellow and poetic, *La Robe prétexte* (translated as *The Stuff of Youth*, 1960). When World War I broke out, Mauriac was rejected by the army for physical disability, but joined the sanitary service. Sent to Salonika, he contracted a fever and had to be repatriated. On his recovery, he completed his third novel, *La Chair et le sang* (1920; translated as *Flesh and Blood*, 1954), begun in 1914. Mauriac's production of fiction in its beginnings coincides with marriage, fatherhood, and the experience of war.

At the heart of Mauriac's fiction there is an image of the reptile. It is mentioned in *Thérèse Desqueyroux*, the masterpiece of the 1920s, written in the middle of the moral crisis he was undergoing from 1926 to 1929, and associated with a "terrible power" in *Thérèse*, sometimes "destructive," a fatality which was already suggested by the chain image in the title of his first novel. The symbol of the reptile is used again in another great novel, written soon after the resolution of Mauriac's crisis, in 1932: *Le Nœud de vipères*. The reptilian symbol, therefore, refers to two major characters of Mauriac's fiction and is used at two critical moments in Mauriac's life and literary career.

The reptile is a version of the snake, the most earthly of animals, symbolizing a link between the vegetal and the animal kingdoms, the primal underlying unity of all life forms. A symbol of great complexity, the reptile first of all connotes an archaic, collective order. "The snake is also used as are other reptiles to refer to the primordial, the most primitive strata of life," according to Juan Eduardo Cirlot's dictionary of symbols. This primitive aspect of the symbol applies both to the biological and the psychic life of man. In neurology one speaks of the "reptilian brain," the most ancient part of the human brain comprising the hypothalamus and the archicortical parts, the seat of instincts and feelings, while the neocortex is the center of linguistic and intellectual functions. Thus from the very beginning there is inscribed in man a duality—a conflict between the instincts and the intellect. All Mauriac's heroes are born with a powerful sensuous nature. The titles—*Le Fleuve de feu* (1923; translated as *The River of Fire*, 1954), *La Chair et le sang*—refer to sensuality. Mauriac also said that emotion and feelings—the visceral—are the very root of his art, thus agreeing with the poet Paul Valéry that "l'esthétique c'est l'esthésique" (the aesthetic is the esthesic). In Freudian interpretation the reptile also refers to the most primitive and physical life of man, to the maternal and to sexuality. The relationship between the Mother and the Son is central to Mauriac's fiction. The Mother—

Mauriac during World War I (courtesy of Claude Mauriac)

charged with energy and becoming animated in certain circumstances. If Mauriac does not mention archetypes, he does accord great importance to heredity or "la race." Mauriac's characters inherit certain features of their personalities either from the father or the mother, and this is always clearly stipulated in every novel.

In Christian mythology the reptile is associated with the tree of life (the tree is a basic symbol in Mauriac's fiction) but also with death or evil (*Le Mal*–Evil, but translated as *The Enemy* [1949]–is the title of an early Mauriac novel published in 1924). There is, of course, a link between life or good and death or evil, for evil is part of life. Life is energy, good or creative, if properly channeled into the service of life, destructive or evil if blocked in its flow–if it becomes a knot, a tangle–leading to the division of the self and sometimes to crime. *Le Nœud de vipères* refers to such energy blocked by hate and vengeance. A block in energy leads either to a regressive state, a vegetative existence like that of Fernand Cazenave in *Génitrix,* or to a deviated course, an uncontrollable unleashing of energy or crime. Mauriac's heroes are often criminals. Louis seeks revenge, Thérèse poisons, Gradère (*Les Anges Noirs,* 1936; translated as The Dark Angels, 1951) kills, Costadot (*Les Chemins de la mer,* 1939; translated as *The Unknown Sea,* 1948) identifies with a murderer, Gajac (*Un Adolescent d'autrefois*) identifies with a rapist. Crime or destruction is the other side of creation. One must untangle the knot, let creative energy flow freely.

The reptile, therefore, suggests energy and duality, for energy implies both the opposition of poles and ultimately the unity of self. Mauriac, the disciple of Dostoyevski, stated that the novelist's function was to write about the complexity of man, about his illogical and multifaceted nature. Dualism is the chief feature of the Mauriac hero who is the *ange noir* (black angel)–the oxymoron implies a pair of opposites and their ultimate fusion in a new image–the *homo duplex*–to use the expression of Baudelaire, Mauriac's favorite poet. But Baudelaire's dual man, in whom the fundamental human duality between the senses and the intellect is experienced with a particular intensity, is precisely the artist or the poet.

The symbol of the reptile, the "nœud de vipères," in Mauriac's novels comes directly from the second stanza of "Bénédiction," the opening poem of Baudelaire's *Les Fleurs du mal* (*The Flowers of Evil*–an oxymoronic title). The poet–the knot of vipers–appears at the outset, a child in

Genetrix–is a powerful and omnipresent figure, refracted through a series of Phèdre-like characters and other surrogates determining the Son's future emotional and intellectual development. However, all Mauriac heroes are also gifted with a superior intelligence. The reptile in them is sensuality, but the reptile also is the duality of the sensuous and the intellectual inscribed in the human brain. Thérèse, who is referred to as an "ange de passions" (angel of passions), is also supremely intelligent, known for her critical inquisitive mind in the whole region. Louis in *Le Nœud de vipères* is a brilliant lawyer.

The primitive aspect of the reptile applies also to the psychic life of man. Reptile refers to the lowest stratum of the psyche, the seat of archetypes–innate structures, not Platonic but a result of ancestral experience. Akin to biological instincts, the archetypes are autonomous complexes chains, cursed by his mother. Mauriac's fiction is a subtle exploration of the origin of poetic vocation, of the Frontenac mystery, in the phrase that provides the title for the 1933 novel. This vocation is destiny: *L'Enfant chargé de chaînes, Destins* (1928; translated as *Destinies*, 1929)–the titles are significant. It is an innate drive, perhaps an archetype, often inherited from the father's side. "Si je suis né poète . . . ," says Mauriac's alter ego Yves Frontenac. The poet is gifted with a sensuous nature–*Le Fleuve de feu*–so powerful that all passion becomes frustration, *Le Désert de l'amour*. Mothering is crucial to the development of the senses as well to that of the intellect.

In Mauriac's fiction the widowed mother–a Jocasta figure–transfers her unsatisfied love to her son, the only one or the youngest. Through her sensuous attachment to the son (in *Le Mal* the mother is split into two contrasting figures: Thérèse Dézaymeries, Fabien's saintly mother, and Fanny, Thérèse's childhood friend, who becomes Fabien's mistress); Jocasta makes him a poet, but, a two-faced figure, a Janus, she can also kill the poet in him (*Génitrix*), stifle his development through her possessiveness. Reptile– heredity, sexuality–is at once evil and the tree of life, and ultimately wisdom. Mauriac's poets are obsessed by the problem of evil, operating through their art a descent into hell in order to face the Shadow or the evil in them, accept it, and transcend it. Thérèse's train journey is such an exploration of the darker side of her self. Louis, in *Le Nœud de vipères*, accomplishes the journey through writing.

The artist is the dual man, a black angel, a criminal, who through the mysterious power of self-expression can reach beyond the conflictual tendencies of his nature and attain creative order of the self. Art is this "terrible power," transmuting evil into wisdom and life. The artist channels the ambivalent primitive energy into art, untangles the "knot of vipers" so that the "mystery" does not become "ce qui était perdu"–"that which was lost," as the title of Mauriac's 1930 novel and its translation in 1951 would have it. Art is the way–"le chemin" (the title of the 1939 novel *Les Chemins de la mer*, literally means The Roads Which Lead to the Sea,–a notion not fully conveyed in the title of the English translation, *The Unknown Sea*)–of transmuting or structuring desire–*la Mère*–into its literary equivalent or metaphor–*la mer*. *La mère, la mer*–mother and sea– are homonyms in French and symbols of each other. The road that leads to the sea is the road that leads to Genetrix and to childhood, but also the road of return, of transformation of human desire into the permanence of art. Art resolves contradictions. In *La Vie de Jean Racine* Mauriac wrote: "Devenir un autre, rester le même, c'est une folie sans doute que de prétendre résoudre cette antinomie" (To become another, yet to remain the same, it is madness to wish to resolve this contradiction). However, in 1969, one year before Mauriac's death, the hero of *Un Adolescent d'autrefois*, Alain Gajac, stated this: "Je suis devenu un autre tout en demeurant le même" (I have become a different man while remaining the same).

In Mauriac's second novel, published in 1914, *La Robe prétexte* (a basic novel, since a part of it was written before *L'Enfant chargé de chaînes*), José Ximénès, the friend and guide of the hero-poet Jacques, points the way to self-realization and gives the key to the understanding of all Mauriac's fiction: "Le goût de la réussite je ne pense pas qu'il soutienne longtemps des âmes de notre qualité. Ce qui les pousse en avant, c'est cette force terrible qui entraînait ton père loin du berceau où tu étais un petit enfant–la vocation enfin!" (The taste for success, I do not think that it can long support minds of our quality. What pushes them onward is this terrible power which took your father away from you when you were a little child–the artistic vocation!).

Mauriac's novels can be divided into three categories corresponding to the three major stages both in his life and in the evolution of his heroes. His first four novels are apprentice works, largely autobiographical, introducing a particular type of hero–"le poète en herbe," or the budding poet. The second group comprises the masterpieces of the 1920s which made Mauriac famous. In these poignant, tragic narratives the central character is always a mutilated personality, a poet who fails to realize his vocation, succumbing to such obstacles as religion, society (both viewed as hostile to art), or sexuality (dissipation or passion for woman, which mobilizes all men's energy). In the end the hero dies psychologically or even physically. This period corresponds to Mauriac's own fear of his artistic nature, to the conflict in him between his art and his religious and moral conscience, culminating in the spiritual crisis of 1926-1929. The third group includes the novels of the 1930s, written during the decade of Mauriac's election to the presidency of the Societé des Gens de Lettres (1932) and to the

Page from the manuscript for Mauriac's 1923 novel Génitrix (Bibliothèque Municipale de Bordeaux, courtesy of Claude Mauriac)

Académie Française (1933). Less tragic in tone, more complex, written after resolution of the crisis, these manifest new confidence on the part of Mauriac in his capacity to reconcile the two "destinies" in his life: his poetic vocation, inherited from his father, and his Catholic faith, inculcated in him by his devout mother when he was a child. In most of these novels the hero is a poet who conquers the obstacles, writes, and thus arrives at the unity of self often symbolized by a turning of the whole of his being to God.

The first novels, somewhat awkward and groping in technique, contain the basic polarizations of Mauriac's artistic vision, providing basic patterns for what is to come. It is significant that religion occupies little space here, except in *L'Enfant chargé de chaînes,* in which the hero is temporarily attached to a social Catholic movement called "Amour et Foi"—Love and Faith—resembling Le Sillon, the Christian Democratic movement of Marc Sangnier. In these works religion is simply part of the young man's heritage, at best a source for him of aesthetic and sensuous enjoyment. The hero in each of these early apprentice novels is a budding poet. In *L'Enfant chargé de chaînes* the twenty-year-old Jean-Paul Johanet has his poems published in obscure journals. In *La Robe prétexte* Jacques is the narrator of the book one is reading, telling about his adolescence, about the formative years in which he became conscious of his vocation. A similar situation exists in *Préséances* (1921; translated as *Questions of Precedence,* 1958). In *La Chair et le sang* Claude is going through an apprenticeship in life which makes him a writer.

Mauriac's budding poet is systematically presented through the three activities which are essential to his life: dreaming, walking, and, above all, reading, which incorporates the first two (meditation on words while wandering from page to page). The wandering, even in a crowded street, is always a "multitude, solitude," as Baudelaire said, providing a release from social identity, an almost Dionysiac practice of one's subjectivity at a level where sensations, images, feelings are enjoyed without the control of the intellect. In *Un Adolescent d'autrefois* Alain Gajac will explain how in his Parisian wanderings he feels anonymous and liberated from all constraints: "A Bordeaux j'étais le fils Gajac qui avait peur des autres, mais à Paris je ne suis personne, aussi inconnu qu'un être humain peut l'être" (In Bordeaux I was the Gajac son who was afraid of others, but in Paris I am no one, as unknown as possible). Reading is an-

other modality of the subjective voyage, a true passion distinguishing the poet from his philistine society. "La lecture est . . . toute ma vie" (Reading is . . . the whole of my life), in the words of Alain Gajac. For Jean-Paul Johanet, of *L'Enfant chargé de chaînes,* reading is a narcissistic search for himself, but also a penetration of another's world, indeed, a "multitude, solitude."

The passion for reading is not simply a civilizing and liberating study of man, a means toward the spiritual tempering of the individual and a better world. Mauriac, author of *Mémoires intérieurs,* in which he explored his own sensitivity through the books he loved to read, knew well the role played by intertextuality in the making of a poet. He showed how books, expecially those read in childhood, influenced his way of thinking, seeing the world, and writing, how one writes a text in the context of others. Reading—reading for pleasure, for the sake of reading—exalts narcissism, nourishes a passion for words, gives examples of style and techniques. Without reading there is no writing: all Mauriac's fiction attests to this law. The passion for reading satisfies the sensuous and cognitive forces of one's being and is already a sign of election, a prelude to the work of art.

These first novels introduce another important Mauriac character: the friend of the poet, a doppelgänger figure, but also a guide who confirms the hero in his vocation. Vincent, in *L'Enfant chargé de chaînes,* who used to listen to Jean-Paul's poetry when they were in school; Edward, in *La Chair et le sang,* who introduced Claude to the more sophisticated world of poetry and music; José, the solitary stranger in *La Robe prétexte,* who instructed Jacques to follow in the footsteps of his father, a Gauguin-like character who abandoned his family and went to Tahiti in search of inspiration; Augustin, in *Préséances,* a Rimbaud-like figure, are all figures of the guide. They are based on Mauriac's own extremely positive experience of friendship. That is the way they appear in the autobiographical novels. But this character undergoes modifications in the novels of the 1920s in which the creative imagination overpowers the autobiographical element. In these works the friend is absent, physically or psychologically, from the hero's life and consequently the hero fails to become a poet.

At the same time the figure of the friend is born out of a deep longing for the father who died when the hero—like the author—was a child, who possessed literary tastes but did not develop them. Precisely the son will go further than the fa-

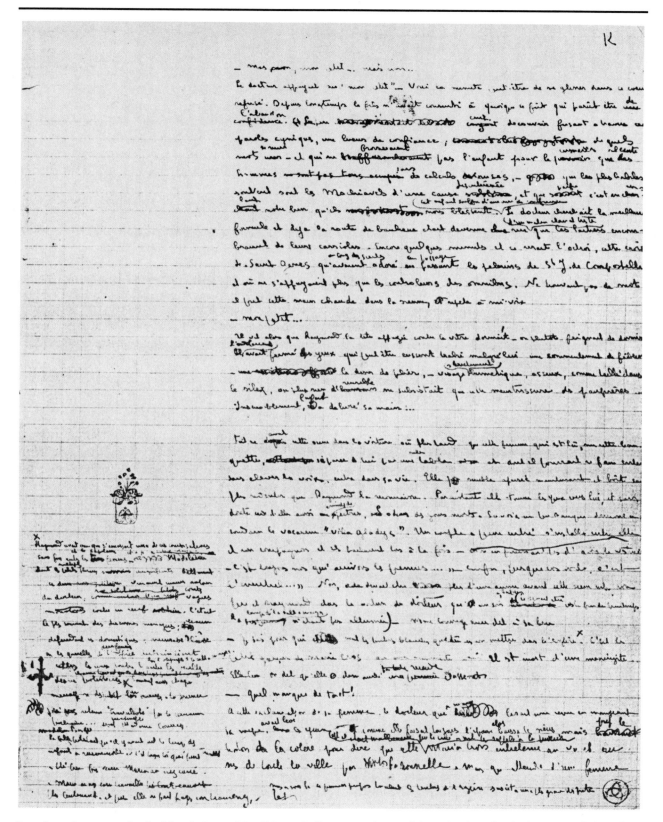

Page from the manuscript for Mauriac's novel Le Désert de l'amour, *winner of the 1925 Grand Prix du Roman de l'Académie Française (Bibliothèque Municipale de Bordeaux, courtesy of Claude Mauriac)*

ther. The friend, therefore, is a messenger from the father's world, the masculine counter pole to the mother's influence. Messenger of the father, he is the spirit leading the son on the road to self-identity or salvation, which in Mauriac's fiction is bound up with the practice of art.

Mauriac's first novels introduce all the important themes which are developed and orchestrated in the later novels, above all, the theme of the divorce between absolute values of childhood and adolescence–their purity and idealism–and the relativity of the external world. This theme is traditional in the novel, but Mauriac brings to the treatment of it his own lyrical tone. His mature novels show that only artistic creation, which permits the confrontation with the Shadow, can provide, through its synthetic or transformative power, a bridge between the overprotected childhood and the threatening adult world characterized above all by sexuality. In Mauriac's fictional universe creativity becomes the condition for the acceptance of or coming to terms with reality.

Le Baiser au lépreux (1922; translated as *The Kiss to the Leper*, 1923), a true masterpiece, Mauriac's first great success (his first book to exceed the sale of 3,000 copies and reach a broad public), free of the hesitancy and confusion of plot typical of first novels, marks the beginning of the second stage in Mauriac's fictional output, in which the central character is always a mutilated poet. On a superficial level, the novel is a story of the failure of a provincial, middle-class Christian marriage arranged for material and social reasons by the two families through the intervention of the parish priest. It is also a sexual drama, the failure of love and above all of sexual union, which is seen as degrading. But there is another level: the failure of the central character, Jean Péloueyre, to realize his poetic vocation and thus transcend his suffering in art. Michael Moloney called Péloueyre a "potential Keats" and correctly observed that "Mauriac dramatizes the poet in Jean."

Jean Péloueyre, with his sad, ugly face and morbid sensitivity, loves solitary walks through the fields and through poetry and philosophy. He is above all fascinated with Nietzsche's *Beyond Good and Evil*, a most significant title; he dreams of writing a vast work entitled "The Will to Power and Sanctity" in which he will reformulate the foundations of Christian morality. Jean Péloueyre dreams of a wider morality–a transformation of Christian ethics in the direction of a new tolerance, beyond the traditional good and

evil. A few years later another Mauriac character, Maryan of *Le Démon de la connaissance* (The Demon of Knowledge, 1928), will harbor the same ambition. But Péloueyre does not realize his dream. He becomes discouraged, wasting his passion on a woman, the beautiful Noémi, who, although desirous of love and fulfillment, is forced to marry him for his wealth and family prestige. He goes to Paris, the city of liberation, but is unable to free himself from the city of Bordeaux which he carries within him. He wastes his time, taking refuge in cafés and in churches (both seen as symbols of the womb), thinking of Noémi, rather than throw himself into the streets and crowds of Paris, or dream, read, and create. The narrator stipulates that not once does Péloueyre enter a library while in Paris. He returns to Bordeaux and in despair contrives to catch tuberculosis from a sick friend and die. In his agony he does not pray but recites Corneille.

Jean Péloueyre is killed by the alliance of three forces that are systematically presented in Mauriac's fiction as hostile to the poet, to the life of the mind and of literary creation: the family, microcosm of society, the Church, here represented by the parish priest who pushes Jean into a disastrous marriage, and woman, who represents nature and sexuality. There is no counter to this triple influence, no friend or guide, no masculine figure to help Péloueyre. His friend Daniel Trasis has neglected him; his father, a mediocre egocentric figure, is absorbed by his own narrow bourgeois interests and, after Jean's death, will force Noémi to give up all idea of remarriage. Mauriac said that Jean is an antidote to Nietzsche, the "exaltavit humilis" of the Magnificat. But this is Mauriac the Catholic making an ideological statement about his fiction from outside. The novel gives a totally different impression–that of a useless, absurd sacrifice of youth, love, and, above all, of poetic talent, to the forces of mediocrity, hate, and death represented by the family and the Church. Passion, a sign of quality in Mauriac's character, has not been channeled by Jean into a creative form; it has destroyed him. Stifled by his experience of Bordeaux, Jean is unable in Paris to reach beyond the contraries, to transform his passion into a spiritual equivalent, a new synthesis, new life.

In *Génitrix*, another masterpiece, possessing "something of the luminous simplicity of nightmare," according to the British critic Cecil Jenkins in *Mauriac* (1965), Fernand Cazenave is also a potential poet but mutilated by woman. Here the mystery of woman is illuminated by the fact that she is a possessive mother. Félicité–the name is ironic–is a caricature of all Mauriac mothers, a strong, authoritative, passionate woman, sexually unhappy, unfulfilled in her marriage. She transfers her unsatisfied love to her son Fernand, all the more so since she has lost one male child. The novel is a story of the various ways this Jocasta figure paralyzes her son's emotional development, making him weak, thoroughly dependent on her, emotionally impotent. Fernand dreams of self-expression. In fact, he has a habit of cutting out, from a book by Epictetus, various maxims, pasting and arranging them in a collage, thus hoping to obtain through this type of *bricolage*, this child's play, not only pleasure and liberation but also the meaning of life and death. The collage, accompanied by the libidinal relief and the higher purpose, expresses the artistic tendency in Fernand, made absurd by its immature, undeveloped aspect. It is, however, interesting to note that well before the modern critics Roland Barthes and Jacques Derrida, Mauriac called attention to the ludic and libidinal aspects of art.

Félicité Cazenave is not simply a grotesque embodiment of the bourgeois rage to own, as has been suggested by some superficial and reductive criticisms of Mauriac. *Génitrix* is a truly remarkable book in which the terrible possessive aspect of the Jocastian mother who kills her son emotionally and psychologically is expressed with unprecedented force. Fernand is unable to break away from his particular Jocasta; he behaves at the age of fifty like a child cut off from adult reality, completely alone in a matrocentric universe, hostile to intellect and to creativity, with no masculine figure to counterbalance the pull of the feminine. Fernand is stifled by his mother, who continues to have a hold on him, even after her death. At the end he is a living corpse, cared for by a servant, Marie Lados, a surrogate mother figure.

This book is outstanding for its cosmic symbolism. Passions are expressed in terms of climate and vice versa, but there is also often a contrast between the ugliness of the inhabitants and the beauty and grandeur of landscape–the *landes*–of the Bordeaux region. The novel is also outstanding for its nearly complete absence of any Christian element.

In 1928 Mauriac conceived another memorable character who reminds one of Fernand. Auguste Duprouy of "Le Rang" (Rank), a short story providing a scathing condemnation of the bourgeoisie of the Bordeaux region, is a man pos-

sessed with a poet's sensitivity and a brilliant mind. There are hints of greatness about him. But he is literally immolated by the female family–his mother and his two sisters who prevent him from pursuing his studies, from marrying, and from leaving Bordeaux. He dies of hunger while trying to pay for the funeral of his sister.

Le Désert de l'amour, winner of the 1925 Grand Prix du Roman de l'Académie Française, is another study of a mutilated personality, of a young man, potentially a poet, unable to come to terms with an Oedipal situation. There is no reference here to writing. But Raymond Courrèges has a passionate nature, a sign of election in Mauriac's fiction. Curiously he seems to share this vocation with Maria Cross, whom he loves and who is also gifted with a certain intellectuality and a taste for reading. As an intellectual woman, however, she is doomed in her bourgeois society, which permits women to be only wives, mothers, or mistresses.

Humiliated in his adolescence by Maria Cross, who is also loved by his father and is therefore a surrogate for the mother, Raymond spends all his passion venging himself on other women and leading a life of debauchery. At the end of the novel the narrator intervenes to tell the reader that only God could save Raymond. The opinion, expressed in a clumsy fashion and given completely outside the awareness of Raymond, who is a total stranger to religion, shocks the reader. It is as if Mauriac himself did not realize at that time the function of art and creativity and felt obliged to give a Catholic ending to his novel. The meaning implicit in the novel is different.

Raymond is another victim of the matrocentric universe. He has no one to confirm him in his uniqueness, to recognize the specific needs of his nature. His father, although a noted physician, is always absent, a weak, ineffectual figure. His friends are shallow, unable to introduce him to the higher things in life–to art and literature, which would enable him to synthesize the aspirations of his adolescence and the relativity of the adult world. Raymond does not read–a capital sin in Mauriac's novels–and, therefore, is unable to understand his own heart, to apply a more imaginative approach to his situation. He cannot come to terms with woman, he cannot transform the bad mother (frigid, part virgin, part prostitute) into the good mother, a source of inspiration.

Le Désert de l'amour has been analyzed with mastery by two critics: Cecil Jenkins in *Mauriac* and Conor Cruise O'Brien in *Maria Cross* (1954). They remind the reader that in Mauriac's Jansenist world sex is destiny, essential, yet morally and emotionally inaccessible. And the very image of this ambivalence is the stained Madonna, Maria Cross. *Maria* suggests sanctity, higher motherhood. *Cross* suggests that woman for the Mauriac hero always turns into a mother and that is the cross to which he is nailed. This dilemma is symbolically formalized in *Le Désert de l'amour*.

One should add, however, that if sex indeed is destiny in Mauriac's heroes, it is because the poetic vocation is also a destiny. It is for the poet, not for the other characters, that sex is inevitable, yet morally and emotionally inaccessible. The incestuous drive, the mistress-mother-saint syndrome, and inhibition are closely linked with the destiny of the poet.

Thérèse, the best known of all Mauriac fictional heroes, is the central character of this period of Mauriac's life, a key figure for the understanding of the rest. In the novel entitled *Thérèse Desqueyroux* she does not write but she dreams of writing: made a virtual prisoner by her husband in their home in Argelouse, ill, feverish, she imagines herself in Paris, a distinguished and admired novelist. What is more, in the first version of the novel published under the title *Conscience, instinct divin* (Consciousness, Divine Instinct, 1927), she actually does write, addressing a letter-confession to a priest and thus prefiguring another confession, that of Gabriel Gradère in *Les Anges noirs*. She also writes a short story entitled "Thérèse à l'hôtel," which, in fact, is cast in the form of Thérèse's diary. Finally it is interesting to observe that *Thérèse Desqueyroux* was written in 1927 at the height of Mauriac's spiritual crisis, at the same time as the essay *La Vie de Jean Racine* and the novel *Destins*. These three works form a trilogy in the exploration of the theme of human division. Thérèse is in a sense a doppelgänger of Racine and both are doubles of Mauriac himself. In *Destins* one has a further illustration of the cleavage within the artist's personality. Bob Lagave, the sensualist, representing the excesses of the flesh–and Pierre Gornac, the ascetic and intellectual, representing the excesses of the spirit–are the two opposite sides of the same personality and epitomize, as Mauriac claimed himself, the author's own profound contradiction. Both die, Bob physically, Pierre by burying himself in a monastery, because each represents a tendency in its extreme one-sidedness. Only an interaction, a living synthesis of contraries, can produce life.

If, in the later novel *La Fin de la nuit* (1935; translated as *The End of the Night,* 1947), Thérèse does not write, that is precisely the reason why she is dying. She has dissipated her heart (she dies of heart failure) and her life in impossible love affairs instead of channeling her energy into a more creative form. An avid reader in her youth of the popular books of Charles-Paul de Kock, of the essays of Sainte-Beuve, of Napoleonic history, she is now too weak to walk, dream, and read; she spends her time sitting in cafés, a sad, gaunt figure. Mauriac once said that he could not find a priest to convert Thérèse on her deathbed: that is because in his novels only writers find redemption. Mauriac seems also to be making a statement about the feminine condition. A woman gifted with an intellectual and especially artistic personality is not only viewed as a monster by the bourgeois society but she is a victim also of the fatality of sex. For she cannot possess that exalted relationship with the mother which is the determining factor in the artistic vocation. The absence of the mother in Thérèse's life may in fact reflect what is a law of nature in Mauriac's novels. Jocasta neglects her daughters, as suggested in *Les Chemins de la mer,* and transfers her love to the male child; Jocastian mothering by its very definition implies the mother and the child of the opposite sex. And even if there were an exalted and passionate relationship between the mother and the daughter, it would not be accompanied by the torment and the guilt which characterizes the love between Jocasta and the son.

Thérèse is the epitome of duality, the "reptile" in her. Resembling all the other Mauriac heroes, she represents the artist's lack of adaptation to the world yet also his deep attachment to it. Two women are at war in her: the "Thérèse landaise," conservative, conformist, proud to have married a Desqueyroux, passive yet passionate, sensually bound up with the sun-parched landscape of the Landes, with the scent of pine trees and the sound of cicada and the wounded birds; and the "other Thérèse," whose cold, critical, and aggressive intelligence is known in the whole region. Narcissistic, egocentric, exploring herself in the books she reads, she is also curious about others, and wishes to communicate and love. Her propensity for talking, arguing, confessing herself is a sign of a deep need for self-expression. But there is no one to listen to her. Her mother died when she was an infant; her father, a local politician, was never interested in her; her friend Anne and Thérèse's husband, Bernard, possess the provincial detestation of books and all things intellectual and do not understand her; her Aunt Clara, a surrogate mother figure, is completely deaf. Only Jean Azévédo, Anne's lover, confirms Thérèse as a unique individual who should break through the family wall. He represents the pole of Paris where Thérèse will arrive at the end, but he is not really a guide; he is too shallow and too one-sided and he does not point the way to creativity. He does, however, bring Thérèse self-awareness at a time when her individuality is submerged by pregnancy and motherhood, when she functions exclusively as the wife of Bernard and the receptacle of the future inheritor of the combined properties of the Larroques and the Desqueyroux. The irony is that the offspring is a girl, Marie.

Thérèse moves between these two extremes, these two opposite poles of her soul–Argelouse, "une extrémité de la terre," and Paris, the capital of the world, between the two men in her life representing the contrary forces of her psyche: Bernard Desqueyroux, heavy as the sound of his name, solid as rock and earth, a bourgeois rooted in the land and the peasant customs of his region, and Jean Azévédo, light and free as the vowels of his name suggest, an uprooted intellectual, a Jew, John–apostle of the new gospel of the realization of the self. Thérèse will abandon both in the end, for each represents not a synthesis of contraries, but the opposing tendency in its radical form.

At the height of her division bordering on schizophrenia, Thérèse resorts to crime. The crime is a radical expression of her neurosis. It is as if the repressed part of her–the free, intelligent, and independent woman–demands to be heard. If division led Mauriac to writing, to the expression of his contradiction, it leads Thérèse to crime. For crime is to a degree a substitute for novel-writing. "Un livre est un acte violent" (A book is a violent act), said Mauriac. The British critic Martin Turnell has suggested in *The Art of French Fiction* (1959) that Mauriac's novels are "symbolical Acts of Violence which give the illusion of escape from the trap." Thérèse's crime is akin to an artistic process: it appears sudden but is linked to neurosis, to a long frustration, as art is, but it lacks the concomitant discipline and the ultimate balance provided by art; it is progressive–

three times Thérèse poisons Bernard, increasing the doses, torturing him, never killing him; it is half-conscious, compulsive, mobilizing all Thérèse's energy; and it is in a sense intellectual, motivated by curiosity and desire to reach Bernard at a deeper level of his self; finally it leads to liberation. In a truly Nietzschean fashion Mauriac establishes a link between neurosis, crime, and creativity. Art is almost a sacerdotal activity, the Way of Grace, implying neurosis and crime, yet also, by unifying the disparate elements into a creative form, leading to salvation. This is why three characters occupy such an important place in Mauriac's fiction: the criminal, the priest, and the artist.

As a result of her descent into hell, symbolized by her train journey and her subsequent expiation in Argelouse, Thérèse arrives at the comprehension of the truth of her personality. One spring day in Paris–the season and the place of liberation in Mauriac's fiction–she will formulate this new knowledge into language: the contrary tendencies in her not only exist but are also indispensable to her survival–they cannot be sacrificed. A third term is needed, integrating the opposites–the call of Argelouse or tradition and the call of Paris or freedom, reaching beyond good and evil. This third term, in Thérèse's case, can only be literary creation.

"Sortir du monde . . . mais comment et où aller?" (Leave the world . . . but how and go where?), Thérèse once remarks, echoing almost word for word the questions of Maria Cross: "Où aller? . . . Où irait-elle?" (Go where? . . . Where would she go?). Thérèse goes further than her predecessors: she commits a crime, she operates a descent into hell and arrives at an understanding of the "evil" in her. It will be up to those who follow her–Mauriac's heroes of the 1930s–to complete the journey and transmute their suffering into a work of art. One leaves Thérèse, as if drunk with her new freedom and her discovery of herself, on the sidewalk of a Parisian street–a threshold to a new life–ready to throw herself into the crowd. The ending of the book is both promising and ominous–completely open.

In Mauriac's novels the poet is pitted against a certain social milieu–that of the provincial bourgeoisie of the Bordeaux region. There are glimpses of the Parisian bohemian circles, presented as shallow and impersonal, of degenerate aristocracy, of peasants of the Landes who, however, differ little from the bourgeois, being basically of the same stock, joined in the common

Mauriac and André Gide, Pontigny, 1929

worship of the land, differing only in wealth and social prestige. But it is essentially the bourgeoisie that Mauriac presents in his novels, painting a scathing portrait of his class. This class is conservative, acquisitive, materialistic, wary in the management of its wealth, fearful of risk and change. All progress is feared, unless it is commercial. It is a highly conformist and hypocritical society, for conformism breeds hypocrisy: appearance, name of family, social prestige are the only features which count. Through its routine, ordered existence this society wants to build a protective wall against anguish, disintegration, and death. This drive for solidity and permanence—for what Sartre called the being-in-itself—explains the bour-

geois suspicion of intellect and outside influence: intellectuals, artists, foreigners, above all Jews (Azévédo in *Thérèse Desqueyroux*) are perceived as agents of change and disorder.

Bourgeois society in Mauriac's fiction is in its final stage of disintegration, petrified, as if ready to crumble—a decaying family, a dying race. It is so enclosed in itself that its families favor inbreeding in order to prevent division of property. This is an incestuous society, a society of cousins whose consanguinity is a result of a defensive attitude to life. Decay is suggested by the theme of the end of the family, which reveals a presentiment of the end of one's class. This society of sons, who inherit the wealth and assure the continuity of the family name, is in fact dying, for the offspring is often a girl (Marie in *Thérèse Desqueyroux*), or the son dies (*Le Baiser au lépreux*) or enters a monastery (*Destins*) or there is no offspring (*Génitrix*). From the artistic point of view decay is suggested through imagery, through symbolic use of weather and the narrowing of space.

Mauriac, however, did not wish to destroy his class. In many of his essays he accorded considerable importance to the family–the microcosm of society, a traditional disciplinary force, and a model of social hierarchy. He claimed that the defects of the middle class were the defects of all social classes in an advanced state of development, and he considered them to be characteristic not of a class but of human nature. So if he used the Bordeaux middle class as a backcloth in his novels, it was not by choice but by fate: it was the class he knew best. Since his art thrives on reminiscence, he draws upon the experience of his childhood; he is dependent upon the bourgeoisie of southwestern France for the creation of atmosphere and place. One can say, therefore, that the bourgeoisie occupies an important place in Mauriac's fiction for artistic or aesthetic reasons.

First of all, the bourgeoisie is the antagonist of the poet, the obstacle which the poet will have to recognize and transcend. The contrast between the two is brought out precisely through the three activities indulged in by the poet but condemned as dangerous and unproductive by the middle class: walking, dreaming, and reading. In *Préséances* the narrator tells how, as an adolescent, he was obliged to hide his passion for reading from the sons of the great families of Bordeaux, who considered reading a "vice." Vice, for the bourgeois suspects that reading either breeds solitary enjoyment or leads to change– both considered dangerous to the middle-class ethic. But the poet is also, as Thérèse came to realize, part of the bourgeoisie. The indelible stamp of his social origin will remain. The function of society, in Mauriac's fiction, is to manifest the duality of the hero.

Secondly the evocation of the bourgeoisie gives unity to Mauriac's fiction. His portrayal of society is restricted to a certain geographical area and also isolated in time (the end of the nineteenth and the beginning of the twentieth centuries). In addition many of Mauriac's characters mentioned or appearing in one novel reappear in another, although not as systematically as in Balzac, thus providing a picture of a closely interre-

lated society and giving cohesion to Mauriac's fictional world.

The scathing portrait of the bourgeoisie is therefore a by-product of a more intimate, artistic vision, a result of memories and imagination, not of an ideological conviction. But this does not make the portrait less scathing or weaker. On the contrary, its involuntary aspect gives it greater force, because it comes not from a conscious intention but from depth of feeling experienced in youth, when the impact of the world upon a sensitive soul was particularly strong. Like Balzac who, although a royalist, showed that the society of the *ancien régime* was condemned, Mauriac in the 1920s circulated in the conservative orbit, yet his fiction suggests a vision of society and of its mechanisms that is at odds with bourgeois ideology.

Technically Mauriac's fiction, with its social content, appears traditional. It respects all the major novelistic conventions: a coherent plot, a realistic setting, a clear situation distinguishing between what is to be taken as actually happening and what is dreamed or remembered, characters who are real human types, never anonymous (anonymity being one of the chief features of the modernist novel). It is not parodic of former novels nor is it concerned with a purely semiotic basis of reality. It is teleological, exploring the hidden life at its source, aiming at the revelation of the mystery of life which thus constitutes its telos and determines everything which precedes it. It is, therefore, representative, pointing, as though through a windowpane, to the actual world and to actual historical events. Yet, despite its overall *vraisemblance*, or transparence, this fiction also draws attention to its own "literariness," a feature which is endemic to the New Novel in France.

Mauriac was always much preoccupied with style, revealing a very self-conscious attitude to language. He was close to the new novelists when he said that he was always rewriting the same book, when he experienced language as a system of signifiers in its materiality and sensuality, often reading parts of his novels aloud, seeing and hearing language, when he recognized in literature the importance of play and pleasure, that is, its ludic and erotic aspects.

Mauriac employed techniques which at the time were modern and which continued to be applied thirty years later in the new novel, but more radically and thoroughly. These included, above all, cinematic effects: close-ups (*Le Désert de l'amour*), flashbacks and traveling (*Thérèse Desqueyroux*), switching of point of view, thus imi-

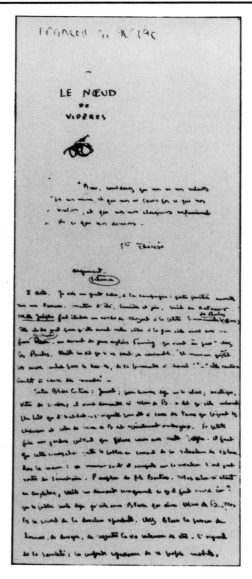

From the manuscript for Mauriac's 1932 novel, one of the first written after his spiritual crisis of 1926-1929 (courtesy of Claude Mauriac)

tating the displacement of the camera. *Destins* was technically inspired by the cinema. At the same time the abundant use of rhetorical devices and imagery such as metaphor, which undermines fiction by rejecting mimesis, superbly analyzed by Jean Touzot in his *La Planète Mauriac* (1985), contributed further to make these novels, despite their realistic or "transparent" aspect, consummate works of art and therefore artificial and opaque. The brevity and concentration of these novels also demanded high degrees of stylization or art. But it is especially through a certain narrative strategy called represented discourse or free indirect style, of which Mauriac is a master in

France, that his novels, above all *Thérèse Desqueyroux*, refer to themselves, pointing not to the world beyond them but to language which constitutes them, thus subverting representation.

In represented discourse the author places himself in the experiential field of the character, adopts his point of view but without withdrawing, as if assisting the character in the expression of his thoughts. The style, therefore, lends itself well to the exploration of the inner life of characters, for it abolishes authorial omniscience as well as the restrictions of the first-person narrative. In the depiction of mental states it permits rapidity, economy, flexibility and seems to foster narratorial realism. Furthermore it can draw the reader more intimately into the text, a process that is also the ambition of the new novelists. For if one cannot determine the origin of the discourse—whether it is the narrator or the character speaking—perhaps, as one critic has suggested, it is the reader who is speaking, identifying more easily with the ambiguous discourse. Mauriac's use of represented discourse is always lyrical, not ironical, as in Flaubert's works. However, represented discourse can have the opposite effect. Since this style implies a duality which is impossible in real life, it is in fact unreal, *invraisemblable*. It does not refer to an actual voice, but to an amalgam of two voices—the narrator's and the character's—which is its essence. The indetermination of the vocal origin of the discourse makes a vocal rendering of it impossible. The style, therefore, occurs chiefly in a "silent register," that of prose fiction; it is a literary, nonrepresentational style, making of Mauriac's fiction, which is primarily the writing of individual adventures in the world, a linguistic experience, an adventure in writing.

In 1929 Mauriac produced *Trois Récits* (Three Narratives)—short stories which had been separately published in 1926 and 1928, roughly at the same time as *Thérèse Desqueyroux*, *La Vie de Jean Racine*, and *Destins*, that is, in the middle of his spiritual crisis. They deal with the dual problem of art and the realization of human personality. *Coups de couteau* (Stabbings) is about an artist-painter who tortures his wife with a confession of his love for a younger woman, in whom in fact he worships his own youth. The story may be symbolic of any novelist's situation with regard to his family. *Un Homme de lettres* (A Man of Letters) is a story about a writer and his relationship with two women. In the most interesting of the three stories, *Le Démon de la connaissance*, a

Mauriac with Francis Jammes, Paris, 1937 (courtesy of Claude Mauriac)

young musician, who is an intellectual devoted to Nietzsche and wishing to become a writer, hears mysterious voices telling him to discover the "secret of his soul" and use both the good and the evil in him to realize the secret that is his personality. "Ecrire, écrire! Et que mes livres soient le commentaire de l'âme qu'à chaque instant je me crée" (To write and write. So that my books become a commentary on my soul that I create at every moment), says Maryan. The story resumes the old debate, inaugurated by *Le Baiser au lépreux,* about Nietzsche versus Christ, but now adds to it a truly Jungian dimension. Maryan wants a synthesis of pagan and Christian values as well as a conciliation of the diverse and contradictory tendencies of his own nature. His friend Lange, however, is afraid of such an ambition, considering it hostile to the humility preached by Christ.

Lange represents fidelity to tradition while Maryan wants a wider faith accommodating both tradition and modernism and which would not repress anything but rather integrate all the aspects of man in a harmonious whole. Lange and

Maryan embody Mauriac's own conflict, beginning in 1926, between the exigencies of his artistic nature and his Catholic conscience. Mauriac seems to be on the side of Lange, but the story anticipates his future development, marked by a deeply synthetic work, *Dieu et Mammon* (1929; translated as *God and Mammon,* 1936), and the wider Christianity at which he would arrive in the 1930s.

Mauriac's novels of the 1920s are informed by the painful conflict culminating in the moral crisis and the "conversion" of 1929. *Souffrances et bonheur du chrétien* (1931; translated as *Anguish and Joy of the Christian Life,* 1964) refers to this crisis and to this conversion and seems to give to the crisis a religious character. The conflict was exacerbated by an open letter, both eulogistic and taunting, written by André Gide to Mauriac and published in the *Nouvelle Revue Française* in 1928. Gide spoke of Mauriac's "compromise" which allowed him to love God without "losing sight of Mammon." The crisis was not really religious, for Mauriac never lost his faith. It was a complex experience, a mid-life crisis, partly a result of a conflict between the artist and the Catholic in Mauriac, between his emotional dilemmas and his rigid Catholicism. The artist rebelled against the strictures imposed upon his sensuality and his art by religion. The Catholic, afraid that his portrayal of human passions might bring scandal to his Catholic readers, was alarmed at that revolt. Art appeared as Mammon, the opposite of God. But in 1929 in *Dieu et Mammon*–the conjunction *et* is significant–Mauriac accepted his nature and his art as part of that nature, with all the risks that it entailed. He saw his novels as part of a natural process that could not be stopped, short of mutilating his own nature. The reading of Nietzsche had not been in vain. *Dieu et Mammon,* a retort to Gide, seemed to transcend the conflict between "good and evil," marking a new phase in the individuation process as well as a veritable assumption on Mauriac's part of his identity as a poet. By fully accepting his vocation or destiny, he transfigured it into freedom. He proclaimed himself a poet, exalting his vocation as his very life, a Calvary but also a road of salvation. Mauriac's conversion was in fact a conversion to literature.

The novels of the 1920s constituted a transcendent attempt at self-liberation through projection, a practice of self, revealing what was hidden or latent, producing a new tolerance, a new view of religion. Years later, in *Mémoires intérieurs*, Mauriac would express this new awareness in these terms: "La vie religieuse ne bride pas, elle satisfait au contraire l'exigence poétique, non comme un conte de fées qui serait vrai, mais comme une vision cohérente de l'être–tout en laissant assez d'incertitude, assez de mystère et d'ombre pour entretenir cette inquiétude sans laquelle l'art n'existerait pas si, comme je le crois, toute œuvre est une tentative de réponse au "que sommes nous? d'où venous-nous? où allons-nous?" (Religious life does not repress, on the contrary it satisfies poetic exigency, not as a fairy tale that would be true, but as a coherent vision of being. It leaves enough incertitude, mystery, shadow in order to nourish that anxiety without which art would not exist, if, as I believe, every artistic work is an attempt to reply to the question: What are we? Where are we going? From where do we come?). These final questions seem to echo the questions of Maria Cross, Raymond, and Thérèse. But this time Mauriac suggests an answer.

Mauriac emerged into the 1930s a new man, redoubling his activity, embarking on a truly new phase of creativity. His novels of the 1930s reflect this transformation. Almost all contain a conversion, as if he wanted to multiply his own experience by producing copies of it. This conversion, skillfully integrated into the fabric–structure and imagery–of the novel, is indeed an existential turning to God, but it occurs as a result of creative activity–reading and writing. The older critical view of Mauriac purging in the 1930s his work of "unhealthy" elements such as sensuality in order to flower into a great Catholic novelist has been completely abandoned. Sensuality actually flows with unprecedented power in *Le Nœud de vipères* and in *Les Chemins de la mer*. But this sensuality is no longer feared; it is confronted and integrated into a new synthesis which gives it meaning. The opposite view of Mauriac declining as a novelist in the 1930s is also outdated. For how can one compare *Génitrix*, for all its power and concentration, to the magnificent *Le Nœud de vipères* or *Le Chemins de la mer* or the technically complex *La Pharisienne*? The novels of the 1930s, vaster, more ambitious, synthetic, represent in Mauriac's career a definite achievement, one of lasting importance.

These novels of the 1930s were accompanied by a series of other activities of a highly synthetic nature. In 1932, Mauriac produced an autobiographical work: *Commencements d'une vie,* composed of seven chapters which were published in 1929 under the title *Mes plus lointains souvenirs* (My Earliest Memories), and four chapters published in 1926 under the title *Bordeaux.* What was dispersed–memoirs, impressions–was collected, unified, and viewed as forming the "beginnings of a life." Only a man confident of his identity, perceiving his life or a part of his life as a complete and unified whole, could write such an autobiographical work. His spiritual crisis resolved, Mauriac emerged into the 1930s a new man whose life had a meaning, a direction. In *Dieu et Mammon* and in the preface to *Trois Récits* he actually spoke of the joy of seeing in the middle of his life his personality finally emerge. This new conception of his self involved some fabrication and imagination; but the feeling of this identity was very strong. Mauriac had defined himself as a poet and he fixed this identity, of which he was sure, in an autobiographical form. For autobiography and the novel can be viewed as different modalities of the same effort to construct a self.

Mauriac's novels were a self-exploration, associated with struggle and suffering. Autobiography, on the contrary, is usually born out of conversion, out of a feeling of victory over disorder. It is a *bilan,* a summing-up, a diachronic grasp of self. And so *Commencements d'une vie* tells the genesis of Mauriac's personality grasped in its essence: the genesis of his poetic vocation. Mauriac writes of the epoch privileged by all autobiographies because, as the child is father to the man, the seed of everything is in childhood. *Commencements d'une vie* is not a collection of scattered impressions but a rational selection of those memories which are coherent, which confirm what the author now knows: he is a poet. "Si j'avais su, alors, regarder en moi, j'eusse pu déchiffrer mon destin futur avec plus de sûreté que dans les plis de mes mains" (If I had been able then to look into myself I could have deciphered my future destiny with more certainty than in the folds of my palm). Thus, for example, Mauriac speaks now of his "unhappy" childhood. Yet this is contradicted by other descriptions of this period of his life that attest to the contrary—the fact that his childhood was extremely happy, protected, traversed by moments of mysterious ecstatic joy. The problem lay elsewhere. The alternation of extreme feelings—of joy and suffering—was a sign of the child's propensity for intense emotional states, especially suffering. The unhappiness resulted in fact from the child's inability to relate his exalted happiness to the external world. What is more, the child dramatized his feelings, played at being solitary and ignored, as if he knew by instinct that this play was an exercise to become a man of letters. He is a poet, said Mauriac, who enjoys watching himself suffer and who needs to suffer.

Commencements d'une vie is a seminal text, radiating intertextuality into the novels which precede it and those which follow it, a prism of Mauriac's themes. It ends on a meditation of destiny now recognized and therefore possessed.

> Chaque destinée humaine comporte une révélation où comme dans la Révélation chrétienne, les prophéties ne prennent de sens que lorsque les événements les ont éclairées. Bordeaux te rappelle cette saison de ta vie où tu étais entouré de signes que tu ne sus pas interpréter. Alors, la ville maternelle touchait doucement toutes les plaies douloureuses de ton coeur et de ta chair pour que tu fusses averti et que tu te prémunisses contre le destin: elle t'a exercé à la solitude, à la prière, à plusieurs sortes de renoncements. En prévision des jours futurs, elle t'emplissait de visages grotesques ou charmants, de paysages, d'impressions, d'émotions, enfin de tout ce qu'il faut pour *écrire.*

> (Each human destiny implies a revelation where, as in Christian Revelation, the prophecies become meaningful only when events have illuminated them. Bordeaux reminds you of the season of your life when you were surrounded by signs which you did not know how to interpret. The Maternal city then would softly touch all the painful wounds of your heart and your flesh so that you would be warned and that you would fortify yourself against destiny: it trained you to bear solitude, to pray, to renounce certain pleasures. In prevision of future days, it filled you with grotesque or charming faces, with landscapes, with impressions, emotions, in fact, with everything that one needs *to write.*)

The very year Mauriac produced his autobiographical work he turned to journalism and was to remain in the political arena until the end of his life. The interest in the self and the past coincides with an opening to the collective and to the future of society. This coincidence is significant. One must remember that Saint Augustine was at once the author of *Confessions* and of *The City of God,* that if Rousseau wrote *Confessions,* he also wrote *Le Contrat social.* There seems to be a link between autobiography (self-conception) and utopia (vision of the desired society), between the myth of the individual and the social myth. At the heart of autobiography is a paradox: the unique individual discovers himself also a man, linked to a group, not just an *I* but a *we.*

In his first postconversion novel, *Le Nœud de vipères,* old Louis (his surname is never given), a brilliant lawyer now retired, begins to write, at the age of sixty-eight, what is part diary and part memoir. Louis is pushed into writing by an extreme situation: years of solitude and frustration in his marriage, illness (heart disease), and the proximity of death. He begins his narrative on Holy Thursday, which is also his birthday. At the end of his narrative, which is a descent into hell to confront before death his childhood, the mother, his love/hate relationship with his wife Isa and his children, he arrives, after years of hate and revenge, at understanding and forgiveness—at resurrection. The process of writing untangles the knot of contrary tendencies, releasing the flow of creative energy. The story is in fact about a writer, possessing the features of all Mauriac's poets—intense narcissism and desire to communicate, high intelligence, a complex, sensitive nature yet capable of coldness and cruelty–but prevented from pursuing a literary career by his mother, who pushed him into law and into amassing a fortune. By writing Louis expresses his nature and thus understands it better. He goes further than Thérèse: he becomes a writer and he will be saved. Writing appears as a way of salvation, the road leading to faith and God–God perceptible to the heart, not to the mind, in Pascal's words. Before dying, Louis is indeed touched by grace but this grace–this change of heart–is brought about by the practice of writing.

Le Mystère Frontenac of 1933 has been hailed as a hymn to the family. Mauriac seems to be making amends for his severe indictment of the family in *Le Nœud de vipères*. In fact, this novel is quite explicitly a story of a poet, Yves Frontenac, a tender and optimistic story because it is more directly autobiographical because Yves Frontenac, the alter ego of Mauriac, succeeds, as the author did, in realizing his vocation. The whole family here participates in the poet's vocation while the poet appears as a transcendent sum total of all the ancestral traits. For Yves inherits his talent from his father; he is raised by a Jocastian mother, authoritarian, possessive yet intelligent and tender, who grants her youngest son the freedom to go to Paris in order to launch his literary career; his older brother Jean-Louis serves as the friend and guide of the poet. The poetic vocation is exalted, compared to a holy, priestly vocation, a road of self-sacrifice ultimately leading to self-realization.

Les Anges noirs is another novel about a poet, Gabriel Gradère (Gabriel: a Black Angel, an oxymoron; Gradère: the surname connotes progress or scaling). An orphan, like all other Mauriac poets, excessively sensitive and sensuous yet also brilliant, Gradère was corrupted already in his childhood by his cruel father and by women who were attracted to him: Aline, the prostitute, who took care of him in his youth when he was poor and ill, Adila, eight years older, who became his wife; both are surrogates of the mother, the two faces of Jocasta–Aline the bad mother, Adila the good mother.

The novel is in its first part a letter written by Gradère to a priest, Alain Forcas, whom Gradère calls his double. The second part is told in the third person. But it is clear that the written confession to the priest, which is a descent into hell, a rediscovery of childhood and youth through the medium of writing, has an influence on the events in the second part of the book. But given the complex, half-conscious nature of some of these events, the third person, more discreet, indirect, oblique, is a more suitable method of relating them. The descent into hell liberates pent-up energies and Gradère will confront the anima–the mystery of woman, always a mother, the feminine which is also a mirror of his soul. He will kill Aline (Adila is already dead, killed by Gradère's cruelty), and thus liberate himself from woman. The brutal killing of Aline, which shocks many readers, is in fact a symbolic killing of the negative aspects of woman-mother. That is why it brings liberation and a turning to God.

It is noteworthy that in 1936, the year Mauriac created Gradère, his greatest sinner-criminal, he also produced his *Vie de Jésus*. Jesus, significantly, is no longer seen as simply the crucified one, but rather as "une nourriture pour le corps autant que pour l'esprit" (a nourishment for the body as well as for the soul), a fusion of contraries, a symbol of wholeness or the self.

The beautiful novel *Les Chemins de la mer*, written at the height of Mauriac's maturity and published in 1939 (translated as *The Unknown Sea*, 1948), deals explicitly with a poet, Pierre Costadot (*le costaud* [the sturdy one?]–the surname suggests strength, as does the Christian name Pierre), author of a long poem entitled "Cybèle," which, like the poem *Le Sang d'Atys*, which Mauriac was completing at the time for publication in 1940, presents itself as a synthesis of pagan and Christian values. The preceding novels seem to have liberated the poet in Mauriac's fiction. Mauriac now directly explores the poet's specific nature, above all his sensuality, which flows freely in this novel in its various forms: the sensuality contained in the relationship between Jocasta and the son; that of the poet in love with a young woman–a sublimated mother figure; a young girl's sexual awakening and her love for her fiancé; homosexuality, represented by Landin. The relationship with the possessive, castrating mother has been sublimated or transmuted into Costadot's platonic love for a young girl–the sister of the friend–Rose Revolou. Rose is a substitute for the young mother, the *soror* of the alchemists, a symbol of wisdom. She is the final metamorphosis of the woman-mother in Mauriac's fiction. The poetic vocation is clearly viewed here as the primary source of self-definition, of psychic integration and fulfillment. It is stated, albeit in a somewhat cursory manner, that Pierre Costadot arrives at happiness.

Among the later novels such as *La Pharisienne* (1941; translated as *Woman of the Pharisees*, 1946), *Le Sagouin* (1951; translated as *The Little Misery*, 1952), *Galigaï* (1952; translated as *The Loved and the Unloved*, 1952), *L'Agneau* (1954; translated as *The Lamb*, 1955), the first two deserve mention. *La Pharisienne*, an ambitious novel technically, with many secondary characters and subplots, is another portrait of the poetic personality drawn against the backdrop of the Bordeaux middle class. It is about Louis Pian, the narrator of the story, his sister Michèle, who replaces to a certain extent his deceased mother, and his friend and later brother-in-law Jean de Mirbel, son of the noted novelist the Countess de Mirbel. Mauriac again explores the Oedipal complications in the life of a poet through the triangular relationship of the poet-sister-friend. This is also a story of conversion: Brigitte Pian converts from a rigid, almost Jansenist Catholicism to a more tolerant worldview, a more permissive and forgiving Christianity and, above all, to literature, art, and love.

Le Sagouin is a short but poignant novel about a mutilated child-poet. Mauriac returned to the formula of the 1920s for this work, as if to show his readers that he was still capable of producing a powerfully concentrated and tragic narrative. Little Guillou, an ugly duckling, is a genius, gifted with a poetic temperament: he is brilliant, an avid reader, also a dreamer, full of active imagination. But he is all alone in the female family, hated by his mother, Paule, a woman of the middle class who despises in him the living image of her sick, degenerate, aristocratic husband, Baron Galéas de Cernès. One day Guillou meets Robert Bordas, an intellectual, a militant leftist, a teacher. His life is transfigured; his imagination and sensitivity are intensified by the hope of being tutored by Bordas and of meeting his son Jean-Pierre, a boy of Guillou's age who undoubtedly could become a friend and a guide. But Bordas has only scorn for aristocracy and will not agree to seeing Guillou on a regular basis. When he hears one day of the death—by drowning—of both Guillou and his father he refuses ever to forgive himself for his indifference. The novel is a poignant exploration of the psyche of a child-poet sacrificed by the combined forces of family and society, the latter represented by two social classes: degenerate aristocracy and republican bourgeoisie.

In 1969 Mauriac produced his last complete novel, *Un Adolescent d'autrefois* (translated as *Maltaverne*, 1970). It is as if with this novel written at the end of his career he wanted to explicate the implicit meaning of all his earlier novels. Alain Gajac, the hero-narrator of the novel, is the final metamorphosis of the Mauriac poet. An accomplished writer, since it is his narrative that one reads, he resembles all the other Mauriac poets. He is an orphan, raised by a widowed mother to whom he is much attached, a mother as strong a personality as Félicité Cazenave, yet tender as Blanche Frontenac. She belongs to the group of the positive Jocastian mothers in Mauriac's fiction. She does not care for her son's intellectuality and literary tastes, but she does realize that he is a "chosen one" and permits him freedom to pursue his literary vocation. Although a believer, Alain is critical of the narrow Catholicism of his class. He holds in execration bourgeois materialism, egoism, and conformism, yet he is very much part of this milieu, the very type, as he admits, of the "fils Gajac." He goes through an emotional and sexual apprenticeship with his young mistress Marie, to some extent a surrogate mother, as the name indicates, and his intellectual and literary ambitions are supported by two friends—figures of the guide—André Donzac and Prudent Duberc. It is Donzac who serves as narratee, the one to whom the narrator is telling his story, one who apparently comments on the text and gives advice, although this action is not represented in the novel.

In Gajac Mauriac for the last time epitomizes the conflict between Bordeaux, the maternal city, representing nature, traditional values, what is given, and Paris, the opposite pole, symbolizing more masculine values associated with the father and the life of the mind and freedom. Gajac is the first Mauriac hero who will clearly formulate the truth of the Mauriac conflict: that between Bordeaux and Paris one cannot choose, for to choose would be tantamount to a mutilation of the self. Yet not to choose could kill. In fact, the conflict must be lived and transcended. Only a third term, a vaster whole fusing the two calls of body and of spirit, can solve the dilemma. Gajac will leave Bordeaux, Jocasta, and her kingdom, for Paris, the city of liberation, where he will transform the capital amassed in childhood and adolescence into a work of art, that third term providing the resolution of the clash of polarities. In Paris he will distance himself from Bordeaux, only to realize it, to understand and transform it, to return to it through the medium of art.

Bordeaux is the real subject of all his works, Mauriac once said. Gajac, the last hero of Mauriac, finally provides an answer to the question posed by the first hero, Jean-Paul Johanet of *L'Enfant chargé de chaînes:* "Mon Dieu, pourquoi suis-je enfant chargé de chaînes?" (My God, why am I a child burdened by fetters?): precisely in order to bear them, to suffer, to nourish the poetic vocation. Gajac comes to know that writing is for him the only way, the way of suffering but also the way of truth and eternity. "Ecrire pour que rien ne se perde" (To write so that nothing is lost). Writing unifies what is multiple and dispersed. On the eve of his departure for Paris, he feels as if he were leaving for another world where he will be reborn. He understands that "un livre broché à trois francs sera l'aboutissement de toute cette souffrance. Le nouvel homme en moi manifestera sa force et son courage en osant utiliser pour son avancement le destin qui sera devenu la matière d'un livre broché à trois francs" (the outcome of all this agony will be a three-franc paperback. The new man born within me must show his strength and courage by daring to exploit for his own advancement the destiny which will have become the substance of a three-franc paperback).

All the key words of Mauriac's fiction are here: *souffrance, livre, nouvel homme, force, destin.* Writing or the exercise of poetic vocation will bring a creative order of the self, beyond the contraries of good and evil. It appears as a quasi-Kierkegaardian fusion of the aesthetic, the ethical, and the religious dimensions of life, the Way of Balance and of Self.

As a political commentator, Mauriac left a permanent mark on French journalism. He brought to journalism both style–his superb artistry, skillfulness in polemics–and substance–forty years of meditation on political and social events. His newspaper articles are at once a record of an individual response to everyday social and political reality and a diary of the French nation. Above all, Mauriac was the creator of a new type of journalistic article particularly suited to his temperament: the *bloc-notes.* This loose genre, a *fourre-tout* or holdall, permitted him to use a multiplicity of styles and techniques–dialogue, narrative, personal meditation, portrait, satire–and treat a variety of subjects. Political comments are interspersed with memories, religious meditations, reflections on literature. The *bloc-notes* thus becomes a fusion of two registers: the lyric and the polemic, a synthesis of the two meanings of

Cover for Mauriac's collection of newspaper articles written from 1952 to 1957 (courtesy of Claude Mauriac)

the French word *journal:* the newspaper, a public account of events in the world, and the diary, an account of an intimate individual experience. The ephemeral political event somehow acquires quality or eternity through the resonance it elicits in the psyche of the poet-journalist. The *bloc-notes,* by integrating the public and the private, the social and the psychological domains of personality, aims in its own way at that union of opposites for which Mauriac seemed to search all his life.

Mauriac had been interested in political and social questions since his youth. His political ideas underwent development through the years, but their roots were in the encounters of his childhood and adolescence spent in a wealthy bourgeois Catholic family, a traditionalist family, but one in which political issues were freely debated. Mauriac's political awareness was intensified by a family conflict which in turn seemed to exteriorize his own political division. On the one hand there were the Coiffards, his mother's family, staunchly conservative, practicing a rigid, almost

Jansenist brand of Catholicism. On the other hand, there were the Mauriacs, republican (at a time when republican was an antonym of both Catholic and conservative), anticlerical, free-thinking. Mauriac was deeply devoted to his strong-willed Catholic mother, who raised him in a conservative atmosphere. Every day he read the *Action Française* of Charles Maurras, from whom he contracted a lofty idea of France and of her destiny, a suspicion of parliamentary democracy and a taste for law, order, and authority. But he also had a deep longing for his absent father, from whom he felt he had inherited his literary vocation as well as his critical mind and his anticlericalism.

One should add that Mauriac's artistic nature, sensitive and emotional, reacted keenly to the severe Catholicism which was imposed upon him. This Catholic education intensified his scrupulous nature, made him prone to feel guilt at being rich while others suffered, incited him to ask questions and reject the moral comfort so characteristic of his class. It made him receptive to Marc Sangnier's movement Le Sillon. If Sangnier's intellectual confusion and working-class style repulsed the bourgeois and the aesthete in Mauriac, Sangnier nevertheless deeply influenced his political outlook. From Sangnier he learned that patriotism must not be placed above Christian duty and social justice, that politics and Christian principles must not be viewed as incompatible or independent of each other. This conflict in Mauriac's early life between conservatism and liberalism was echoed by another family contrast: his oldest brother Pierre, the future dean of the right-wing faculty of Bordeaux (a stronghold of the Action Française movement between the two wars), was a staunch Maurrassian, while his brother Jean, a priest, was an ardent *Sillonniste*, responsible for introducing Mauriac to Sangnier.

Thus Maurras and Sangnier, whose doctrines had a lasting effect on Mauriac's political conduct, both attracted and repulsed him. Maurras made him a nationalist; Sangnier gave him social conscience. Mauriac never failed to present his private political history in a dialectical light, dramatizing, with a true artist's urge, the two opposite strands of his life, considering his bourgeois upbringing and his admiration for Maurras on the one hand, his affective Catholicism and the lesson of Le Sillon on the other to be the basic ingredients of his political creed. His subsequent responses to political events present a pattern of regular, almost too perfectly balanced fluctuations between conservative and leftist positions. If one strand surfaces above the other in a given historical period, if Mauriac leans, for example, toward the Left, then the opposite tendency toward the Right somehow manifests itself in the following period, as if by compensation, thus revealing a deep need for the conciliation of conflicting tendencies.

Mauriac contributed lectures and articles with some political content early in his career, for example, to the *Revue Montalembert* shortly after his arrival in Paris. In 1914 he contributed, under the pseudonym of François Sturel, twelve political articles to the Parisian *Journal de Clichy*, directed by Daniel Fontaine, who in fact deserves credit for pushing Mauriac into journalism. In 1919 some of his journalism appeared in a more important conservative newspaper, the *Gaulois*. Mauriac reveals himself in these early articles to be a skilled polemicist, a Christian social conservative defending Catholic values against corrupt and radical France. Yet these articles reveal a conflict between his bourgeois upbringing tinged with *barrésisme* (cult of one's individuality) and his sympathy for social Catholicism and announce his future liberalism and pragmatism. For example, Mauriac is rather prudent in his denunciation of bolshevism, recommending flexibility and dialogue. This journalistic activity, however, was abandoned for poetry, essays, fiction.

It was only in 1932 as a result of his moral crisis and his "conversion" that he turned again to journalism. At this point in his career there is in his work a complex interaction of moral, literary, and social factors. The "new man" emerging into the 1930s, more confident both in his faith and in his artistic powers, and with the events of the 1930s pressing themselves upon his consciousness, was embarking on a new stage of life, renewing himself and his art in relation to the wider world, attempting to examine this world more closely. But there may have been another reason for returning to journalism. His crisis was in part a conflict between his moral and social conscience on the one hand and his literary art on the other. Mauriac no longer considered literary freedom to be moral laxity. But he still wanted to go on writing with a conscious Catholic outlook. This could not be done in the novel, a genre in which the uniqueness of the individual network of desires, feelings, impulses prevails, independent of the author's conscious intentions. Journalism, however, appeared able to accommodate moral exigencies with aesthetics, a direct defense of Christian values without the sacrifice of art.

Mauriac began by contributing in 1932 to the conservative newspaper the *Echo de Paris,* a paper reflecting his own leaning at the time toward the side of law and order. But he did not take long to adopt an independent course with regard to the events of the 1930s. It was the Spanish Civil War which became the turning point in the evolution of his political ideas. It kept him in the political arena, permitting the journalist to supersede the novelist, and it pushed him away from the Right.

After some hesitation at the beginning of the war when Franco appeared to most Catholics as a crusader against Communist barbarism, Mauriac joined a small circle of liberal Catholics grouped around such leftist and Christian Democratic papers as *Sept* and *Temps Présent.* He had no illusions about the Republican side, feeling that Spain was being exploited by foreign powers, but he was particularly offended by Franco's effort to bind his own cause, the cause of the Right, with that of the Church. Mauriac's denunciation of Franco was unequivocal and courageous since he risked alienation from his family, his friends, his class.

The second event which helped push Mauriac even further to the left and hastened the maturation of his political observations was the Second World War. Again Mauriac initially welcomed the party of law and order—that of Marshal Henri Philippe Pétain. But he quickly switched allegiance to General Charles de Gaulle and his resistance movement. During the Nazi occupation of France, he was part of the intellectual resistance, denouncing Nazi ideology in the poignant pseudonymously published *Le Cahier noir* (Black Notebook, 1943; translated, 1944). The liberation of Paris, 25 August 1944, revealed a writer transformed: given the proportion of his writing devoted to the political scene and the confidence with which he expressed his opinions, it was clear that Mauriac had embarked on a second career, that of a political commentator in sympathy with the Christian Democrats who soon, in 1946, took power in France. At first he even played the part of a professional newspaperman, attending press conferences and debates in the Assembly, but later commenting on the issues from an independent personal perspective.

The great theme of his writings in this immediate postwar period was the need for the reconciliation of enemies, for burying the ideological differences in the common cause—that of rebuilding a strong France. The working classes' role—and that meant the Communists' role—in the Resistance was such as to demand recognition. Christians and Communists could cooperate. Mauriac sought to establish a dialogue with the French Communists, whom he deemed necessary to establish a unified Left in France. This interlude was probably also inspired by his distrust and envy of American prestige and power. Mauriac never said a single word about millions suffering in Soviet concentration camps. But he did condemn the policies of Andrei Zhdanov and commented in numerous articles on the famous trials that took place in the Soviet satellite countries from 1947 to 1951. His effort toward a *rapprochement* with the Communists ended in a fiasco. With the intensification of the Cold War, he found himself drawn again into the more politically conservative and pro-American camp.

But Mauriac pleaded for national unity in another way. He manifested courage in condemning the excesses of the purge of political collaborators which took place from 1944 to 1949. He considered Christian charity and the more practical issue of national reconciliation to be more important than strict justice. He did not dare defend Maurras, whom he considered responsible for collaboration, nor Pétain, for whom, however, some years later he had kind words. But he pleaded for mercy for his fellow writers such as Henri Béraud and especially Robert Brasillach, the novelist, critic, and editor-in-chief of the collaborationist paper *Je Suis Partout,* executed on de Gaulle's order in 1945.

In 1945 Mauriac was named Grand Officier de la Légion d'Honneur. In 1947 he received an honorary degree from Oxford. In 1952 he was awarded the Nobel Prize for literature. This coincided with the outbreak of violence in the French protectorate of Morocco. Mauriac claimed that the honor he received made him more aware of his social and political responsibility as a writer and as an intellectual. He embraced with enthusiasm the cause of the Moroccan and Tunisian struggle for independence, becoming president of the association France-Maghreb, attacking on the back page of the *Express* the leaders—usually Christian Democrats—of the Fourth Republic for their ineffectiveness and their shortsightedness, moving again into the orbit of the Left. He gave his full support to only one leader of the fourth Republic: the Radical Pierre Mendès-France, who terminated the Indochina war in 1954. This aroused fury in the militant Catholic milieus, for Mendès-France was a notorious adversary of government subsidies to the so-called *écoles libres*–the Catholic schools in France. In 1956, despite his pronounced anticolonialism, Mauriac failed to comprehend the nature of events in Algeria.

In 1958 Mauriac welcomed the return to power of General de Gaulle, the "premier des nôtres," as he called him in a well-known article written in 1944. In his view de Gaulle was the only man capable of resolving the Algerian problem. During the Fifth Republic, Mauriac gave ardent support to de Gaulle's handling of the Algerian war which ended in Algeria's independence in 1962, as well as to de Gaulle's subsequent political and social policies, becoming thus almost an unofficial "historiographe du roi." He remained an ardent Gaullist to the end of his life. His Gaullism was in a sense responsible for his death. On 27 April 1969, the day de Gaulle lost his referendum and fell politically, Mauriac, as if by intuition of the disaster, also took a fall, a physical one, sustaining a broken shoulder. He died the next year on 1 September 1970.

Mauriac's Gaullism has been viewed as a return to the models of his youth–the nationalists Maurras and Barrès–that is, to an elitist reactionary position. It has been also described as romantic, a fascination with a great leader of his age, a solitary, misunderstood man standing above all battles. However, Mauriac disagreed with this view, claiming that his Gaullism was basically pragmatic: there was no one better equipped to govern France. Furthermore Mauriac saw in de Gaulle a living synthesis of the Right and the Left–of a bourgeois nourished in his youth by the lofty philosophy of Maurras, a patriot, yet a practicing Christian, possessing respect for all individuals and pursuing social policies in accordance with the ethics of the Christian Left. Thus de Gaulle reflected for Mauriac his own search for a conciliation of the two contrary strands in his political outlook.

Mauriac's Gaullism was at best a temporary synthesis, for the conflict between opposite political tendencies was never resolved. Perhaps one could say that for this poet and political observer, for this intensely private man and celebrated public figure, for this patriot and admirer of Maurras and this social Catholic and adversary of Maurras, for this anti-Fascist who fought and wept for Brasillach, for this anticolonialist who remained silent when Algeria took up arms, the real, the definitive synthesis could come only in

eternity or in Christ, in whom alone he had a continuing, childlike, total trust.

Mauriac's achievement as a writer is often of very great quality. A few of his novels reel toward melodrama, but in a writer of his prolific output this is not surprising. Mauriac is, first of all, a consummate artist, bringing to literature his distinctive tone, a symbolist style, new techniques. He is a great Catholic essayist who maintained his faith in its public application against all opposition and who produced writings which, as Cecil Jenkins put it, "through the reality of their tensions bear witness to the continuance of the Christian sense of life as an element in the culture of his time." His fiction can be viewed as one of the most complete attacks mounted on the middle class in this century. He is a complex psychologist, defining his novelistic enterprise in Freudian terms, providing insight into human sexuality. However, his fiction can also be read in a Jungian light, as giving form to the darkest part of man while at the same time constituting a search for wholeness of self. Above all Mauriac is the explorer in the modern novel of the poet's psyche and his predicament in the world. He belongs to a group of major representative writers of this century–Marcel Proust, Thomas Mann, Georges Bernanos, André Malraux–whose literary work postulates a value: this value is neither religion nor intellectuality, neither tradition nor revolution, but human creativity. Art for them is a "duty," a "mission"–the very words used in *Le Mystère Frontenac*–a quasi-sacerdotal activity able to bring a new creative order of the self, give meaning and justification to life.

In 1959 in his *Mémoires intérieurs,* the old Mauriac meditated on the child he was at the age of seven and the mysterious joy he experienced at many moments of his childhood. He hoped that death would bring about the revelation of the "source"–of the mystery behind the joy. This search for the source–the source of the poetic vocation–is precisely the chief concern of Mauriac's fiction. Mauriac has not solved the mystery. As an American Freudian critic, Matthew Besdine, put it: "The mystery of creativity is still a mystery." However, Mauriac went further perhaps than any other writer in his attempt to elucidate the mystery. By meditating on the nature of artistic vocation, on its genetic origins, on the conditioning factors–both affective and intellectual–which determine the flowering of genius, by suggesting that talent is both innate and a result of education and environment, a destiny, yet re-

Mauriac in 1970, the year of his death (courtesy of Claude Mauriac)

quiring freedom, industry, and discipline, by analyzing the conditions of being an artist and by linking art with the modern concept of the self, Mauriac has shed new light on the mystery and thus has made a substantial contribution to human knowledge.

Letters:

Jean Labbé, "Choix de lettres de Francis Jammes à François Mauriac," *Table Ronde* (February 1956): 86-108;

Corespondance André Gide–François Mauriac, 1912-1950, edited by Jacqueline Morton (Paris: Gallimard, 1971);

Correspondance entre François Mauriac et Jacques-Emile Blanche (1916-1942), edited by Georges-Paul Collet (Paris: Grasset, 1976);

Lettres d'une vie (1904-1969), edited by Caroline Mauriac (Paris: Grasset, 1981);

Lettres de François Mauriac à Robert Vallery-Radot, 1909-1931, Cahiers François Mauriac, no. 12 (Paris: Grasset, 1985).

Interviews:

Frédéric Lefèvre, "François Mauriac," in his *Une Heure avec . . . ,* first series (Paris: Gallimard, 1924);

Jean Marchand, "François Mauriac," *Paris Review,* 1 (Summer 1953): 33-39;

Maxwell A. Smith, "My Interview with Mauriac," *American Society Legion of Honor Magazine* (Winter 1963);

Fernand Séguin rencontre François Mauriac (Montreal: Editions de L'Homme, 1969; Ottawa: Editions Ici Radio-Canada, 1969);

François Mauriac. Souvenirs retrouvés: Entretiens avec Jean Amrouche, edited by Béatrice Avakian (Paris: Fayard/Institut National de l'Audiovisuel, 1981);

Les Paroles restent, edited by Keith Goesch (Paris: Grasset, 1985).

Bibliography:

Keith Goesch, *François Mauriac: Essai de bibliographie chronologique, 1908-1960* (Paris: Nizet, 1965).

References:

Marc Alyn, *François Mauriac* (Paris: Seghers, 1960);

Ernst Bendz, *François Mauriac: Ebauche d'une figure* (Paris: Messageries du Livre, 1946);

John T. Booker, "Mauriac's *Nœud de vipères:* Time and Writing," *Symposium,* 35 (Summer 1981): 102-115;

Catharine Savage Brosman, "Point of View and Christian Viewpoint in Thérèse Desqueyroux," *Essays in French Literature,* no. 11 (November 1974), 69-73;

Cahiers François Mauriac (Paris: Grasset, 1974-);

Centre Catholique des Intellectuels Français, *Le Chrétien Mauriac* (Paris: Desclée de Brouwer, 1971);

Bernard Chocon, *François Mauriac ou la passion de la terre* (Paris: Lettres Modernes, 1972);

Henri Clouard, *Histoire de la littérature française: Du symbolisme à nos jours* (Paris: Albin Michel, 1962);

Connaissance des Hommes, special issue on Mauriac, 46 (Autumn 1972);

Nelly Cormeau, *L'Art de François Mauriac* (Paris: Grasset, 1951);

Ramon Fernandez, *Préface à "Dieu et Mammon"* (Paris: Le Capitole, 1929);

Figaro Littéraire, special issues on Mauriac (15 November 1952; 7 September 1970);

Amélie Fillion, *François Mauriac* (Paris: Edgar Malfére, 1956);

Alexander Fischler, "Thematic Keys in François Mauriac's *Thérèse Desqueyroux* and *Le Nœud de vipères,*" *Modern Language Quarterly,* 40 (December 1979): 376-389;

John E. Flower, *A Critical Commentary on Mauriac's "Le Nœud de vipères"* (London: Macmillan, 1969);

Flower, "Form and Unity in Mauriac's *The Black Angels,*" *Renascence,* 19 (Winter 1967): 79-87;

Flower, *Intention and Achievement, An Essay on the Novels of François Mauriac* (Oxford: Clarendon Press, 1969);

Flower, "The Role of the Natural World in the Novels of François Mauriac," *Modern Languages,* 49 (June 1968): 55-61;

Flower, "Towards a Psychobiographical Study of Mauriac—the case of *Génitrix,*" in *Literature and Society: Studies in Nineteenth and Twentieth Century French Literature,* edited by C. A. Burns (Birmingham: Birmingham University Press, 1980), pp. 166-177;

François Mauriac. (Paris: Lettres Modernes/ Minard, 1975-);

Emile Glenisson, *L'Amour dans les romans de François Mauriac, essai de critique psychanalytique* (Paris: Editions Universitaires, 1970);

Keith Goesch, *François Mauriac* (Paris: Editions de l'Herne, 1985);

Graham Greene, "François Mauriac," in his *The Lost Childhood and Other Essays* (London: Eyre & Spottiswoode, 1951), pp. 69-73;

M. Grover, "The Inheritors of Maurice Barrès," *Modern Language Review,* 64 (July 1969): 529-545;

William Holdheim, "Mauriac and Sartre's Mauriac Criticism," *Symposium,* XVI, no. 4 (Winter 1962): 245-258;

Tony Hunt, "Fatality and the Novel: Tristan, Manon Lescaut and Thérèse Desqueyroux," *Durham University Journal,* 48 (June 1976): 183-195;

Martin Jarett-Kerr, *François Mauriac* (Cambridge: Bowes & Bowes, 1954; New Haven: Yale University Press, 1954);

Cecil Jenkins, *Mauriac* (Edinburgh & London: Oliver & Boyd, 1965; New York: Barnes & Noble, 1965);

Eva Kushner, *François Mauriac* (Paris: Desclée de Brouwer, 1972);

Slava M. Kushnir, *Mauriac journaliste* (Paris: Lettres Modernes, 1979);

Jean Lacouture, *François Mauriac* (Paris: Seuil, 1980);

Anne Gertrude Landry, *Represented Discourse in the Novels of François Mauriac* (Washington, D.C.: Catholic University of America Press, 1953);

Margaret Mein, "François Mauriac and Jansenism," *Modern Language Review,* 58 (October 1963): 516-523;

Elinor S. Miller, "The Sacraments in the Novels of François Mauriac," *Renascence,* 31 (Spring 1979): 168-176;

Michael Moloney, *François Mauriac: A Critical Study* (Denver: Swallow, 1958);

Robert North, *Le Catholicisme dans l'œuvre de François Mauriac* (Paris: Conquistador, 1950);

Kathleen O'Flaherty, "François Mauriac, 1885-1970: An Effort of Assessment," *Studies,* 60 (Spring 1971): 33-42;

Ruth Benson Paine, *Thematic Analysis of François Mauriac's "Génitrix," "Le Désert de l'amour" and "Le Nœud de vipères"* (University, Miss.: Romance Monographs, 1976);

Parisienne, special issue on Mauriac, 4 (May 1959);

Rima Drell Reck, "François Mauriac, the Novelist and the Moral Landscape," in her *Literature and Responsibility: The French Novelist in the Twentieth Century* (Baton Rouge: Louisiana State University Press, 1969), pp. 162-189;

T. Reed, "The Presentation of Direct Speech in *Thérèse Desqueyroux,*" in *Literature and Society: Studies in Nineteenth and Twentieth Century French Literature,* edited by C. A. Burns (Birmingham, U.K.: Printed by John Goodman for the University of Birmingham, 1980);

Revue du Siècle, special issue on Mauriac (July-August 1933);

Bernard Roussel, *Mauriac, le péché et la grâce* (Paris: Editions du Centurion, 1964);

Jean-Paul Sartre, "François Mauriac et la liberté," in *Situations I* (Paris: Gallimard, 1947), pp. 36-57;

Malcolm Scott, *Mauriac: the Politics of a Novelist* (Edinburgh: Scottish Academic Press, 1980);

Helena Shillony, *Le Roman contradictoire: une lecture du "Nœud de vipères" de Mauriac* (Paris: Lettres Modernes, 1978);

Pierre-Henri Simon, *Mauriac par lui-même* (Paris: Seuil, 1953);

Maxwell A. Smith, *François Mauriac* (New York: Twayne, 1970);

Smith, "Mauriac and the Theatre," *American Society Legion of Honor Magazine,* 37 (Spring 1966): 101-110;

Albert Sonnenfeld, "The Catholic Novelist and the Supernatural," *French Studies,* 22 (October 1968): 307-339;

Robert Speaight, *François Mauriac, A Study of the Writer and the Man* (London: Chatto & Windus, 1976);

Philip Stratford, *Faith and Fiction, Creative Process in Greene and Mauriac* (Notre Dame, Ind.: University of Notre Dame Press, 1963);

Michel Suffran, *François Mauriac* (Paris: Seghers, 1973);

Table Ronde, special issue on Mauriac (January 1953);

C. B. Thornton-Smith, "Sincerity and Self-Justification: The Repudiated Preface of *La Fin de la nuit,*" *Australian Journal of French Studies,* 5 (May-August 1968): 222-232;

C. D. E. Tolton, "The Revirement: A Structural Key to the Novels of François Mauriac," *Australian Journal of French Studies,* 12 (January-April 1975): 105-113;

Jean Touzot, *Mauriac avant Mauriac 1913-1922* (Paris: Flammarion, 1977);

Touzot, *La Planète Mauriac* (Paris: Klincksieck, 1985);

Touzot, ed., *François Mauriac* (Paris: Editions de l'Herne, 1985);

Philip Toynbee, "Literature and Life, 5: Mauriac: Impossible to Keep Silent!," *Observer,* 27 October 1957, p. 14;

Travaux du Centre d'Etudes et de Recherches sur Mauriac (Bordeaux: Université de Bordeau III, 1977-);

Martin Turnell, *The Art of French Fiction: Prévost, Stendhal, Zola, Maupassant, Gide, Mauriac, Proust* (London: Hamilton, 1959; New York: New Directions, 1959);

Fernand Vial, "François Mauriac Criticism: a Bibliographical Study," *Thought,* 27 (Summer 1952): 235-260;

Kathryn E. Wildgen, "Dieu et Mammon: Women in the Novels of François Mauriac," *Renascence,* 27 (Autumn 1974): 15-22.

Papers:

The majority of Mauriac's manuscripts can be found at the Bibliothèque Jacques Doucet in Paris; some have been deposited at the Bibliothèque Municipale of Bordeaux, while the manuscript of *Thérèse Desqueyroux* is at the Harry Ransom Humanities Research Center, University of Texas at Austin.

André Maurois
(Emile Salomon Wilhelm Herzog)
(26 July 1885-8 October 1967)

Lionel Dubois
De Paul University

BOOKS: *Les Silences du Colonel Bramble* (Paris: Grasset, 1918; Cambridge: Cambridge University Press, 1920); translated by Thurfrida Wake and Wilfrid Jackson as *The Silence of Colonel Bramble* (London & New York: Lane, 1919); revised edition of original French version (New York: Brentano's, 1943);

Ni ange, ni bête (Paris: Grasset, 1919; London & New York: Century, 1932);

Le Général Bramble (Paris: Grasset, 1920); translated by Jules Castier and Roland Boswell (London & New York: Lane, 1921; New York: Dodd, Mead, 1922);

Les Discours du Docteur O'Grady (Paris: Grasset, 1922); edited by E. G. LeGrand (Cambridge: Cambridge University Press, 1926); translated by Gerard Hopkins as *The Return of Doctor O'Grady* (London: Bodley Head, 1951);

Ariel; ou, La Vie de Shelley (Paris: Grasset, 1923); translated by Ella D'Arcy as *Ariel: A Shelley Romance* (London: Lane, 1924); D'Arcy's translation also published as *Ariel: The Life of Shelley* (New York: Appleton, 1924);

Dialogues sur le commandement (Paris: Grasset, 1924); translated by J. Lewis May as *Captains and Kings* (London: Lane, 1925; New York: Appleton, 1925);

Bernard Quesnay (Paris: Gallimard, 1926); translated by Brian W. Downs (London: Cape, 1927; New York: Appleton, 1927); revised and enlarged edition of original French version (Paris: Gallimard, 1928);

Meïpe; ou, La Délivrance (Paris: Grasset, 1926); translated by Eric Sutton as *Mape: The World of Illusion* (London: Lane, 1926; New York: Appleton, 1926); revised as *Les Mondes imaginaires* (Paris: Grasset, 1929);

Le Chapitre suivant (Paris: Editions Sagittaire, 1927); translated as *The Next Chapter; The War Against the Moon* (London: Kegan Paul, Trench, Trubner, 1927; New York: Dutton, 1928);

Conseils à un jeune Français partant pour l'Angleterre (Paris: Champion, 1927); translated in *A Private Universe* (1932);

Un Essai sur Dickens (Paris: Grasset, 1927); translated by Hamish Miles as *Dickens* (London: Lane, 1934; New York: Harper, 1935);

Quatre Etudes anglaises (Paris: Cahiers de la Quinzaine, 1927); revised as *Etudes anglaises* (Paris: Grasset, 1927);

Rouen (Paris: Emile-Paul, 1927);

La Conversation (Paris: Hachette, 1927); translated by Yvonne Dufour as *Conversation* (New York: Dutton, 1930);

La Vie de Disraëli (Paris: Gallimard, 1927); translated by Miles as *Disraeli: A Picture of the Victorian Age* (London: Lane, 1927; New York: Appleton, 1928);

Voyage au pays des Articoles (Paris: Schiffrin, 1927); translated by David Garnett as *A Voyage to the Island of the Articoles* (London: Cape, 1928; New York: Appleton, 1928);

Aspects de la biographie (Paris: Sans Pareil, 1928); translated by Sydney Castle Roberts as *Aspects of Biography* (Cambridge: Cambridge University Press, 1929; New York: Appleton, 1929);

Climats (Paris: Grasset, 1928); translated by Joseph Collins as *Whatever Gods May Be* (London: Cassell, 1929); Collins's translation also published as *Atmosphere of Love* (New York: Appleton, 1929);

Le Pays des trente-six mille volontés (Paris: Editions des Portiques, 1928); translated by Katharine I. Monro as *The Country of Thirty-six Thousand Wishes* (London: Heinemann, 1930); translated by Pauline Fairbanks (New York: Appleton, 1930);

Fragments d'un journal de vacances: Un Chapitre de ma vie (Paris: Hazan, 1929);

André Maurois (photograph by Gerald Maurois)

Supplément à Mélanges et pastiches de Marcel Proust [Le Côté de Chelsea] (Paris: Editions du Trianon, 1929); revised as *Le Côté de Chelsea* (Paris: Gallimard, 1932); translated by George D. Painter as *The Chelsea Way; or, Marcel in England* (London: Weidenfeld & Nicolson, 1966; New York: J. H. Heinemann, 1967);

Don Juan; ou, La Vie de Byron, 2 volumes (Paris: Grasset, 1930); translated by Miles as *Byron* (London: Cape, 1930; New York: Appleton, 1930);

Patapoufs & filifers (Paris: Hartmann, 1930); translated by Rosemary Benét as *Fatapoufs & Thinifers* (New York: Holt, 1940); translated by Norman Duncan as *Fattypuffs & Thinifers* (London: Lane, 1941);

L'Amérique inattendue (Paris: Editions Mornay, 1931); translated in part in *A Private Universe* (1932); republished in part in *En Amérique* (1933);

Lyautey (Paris: Plon, 1931); translated by Miles (London: Lane, 1931: New York: Appleton, 1931);

Le Peseur d'âmes (Paris: Gallimard, 1931); translated by Miles as *The Weigher of Souls* (London: Cassell, 1931; New York: Appleton, 1931);

Tourguéniev (Paris Grasset, 1931);

L'Anglaise et d'autres femmes (Paris: Nouvelle Société d'Edition, 1932); translated by Miles as *Ricochets: Miniature Tales of Human Lives* (London: Cassell, 1934; New York & London: Harper, 1935);

Le Cercle de famille (Paris: Grasset, 1932); translated by Miles as *The Family Circle* (London: Cassell, 1932; New York: Appleton, 1932);

Voltaire, translated by Miles (London: Davies, 1932; New York: Appleton, 1932); original French version (Paris: Gallimard, 1935);

A Private Universe, translated by Miles (London: Cassell, 1932; New York: Appleton, 1932)— comprises *Conseils à un jeune Français partant pour l'Angleterre, Mes Songes que voici*, and parts of *L'Amérique inattendue* and *Chantiers américains;*

En Amérique (Paris: Flammarion, 1933);

Chantiers américains (Paris: Gallimard, 1933); translated in part in *A Private Universe* (1932);

Edouard VII et son temps (Paris: Editions de France, 1933); translated by Miles as *King Edward and His Times* (London: Cassell, 1933); Miles's translation also published as *The Edwardian Era* (New York: Appleton-Century, 1933);

Introduction à la méthode de Paul Valéry (Paris: Editions des Cahiers Libres, 1933);

Mes songes que voici (Paris: Grasset, 1933); translated in *A Private Universe* (1932);

Byron et les femmes (Paris: Flammarion, 1934);

L'Instinct du bonheur (Paris: Grasset, 1934); translated by Edith Johannsen as *A Time for Silence* (New York & London: Appleton-Century, 1942);

Sentiments & coutumes (Paris: Grasset, 1934);

Magiciens et logiciens (Paris : Grasset, 1935); translated by Miles as *Prophets and Poets* (New York & London: Harper, 1935); Miles's translation also published as *Poets and Prophets* (London: Cassell, 1936); enlarged as *Points of View: From Kipling to Graham Greene* (New York: Ungar, 1968; London: Muller, 1969);

Malte (Paris: Editions Alpina, 1935);

Premiers Contes (Rouen: Defontaine, 1935);

Histoire d'Angleterre (Paris: Fayard, 1937); translated by Miles as *A History of England* (London: Cape, 1937); Miles's translation also published as *The Miracle of England* (New York & London: Harper, 1937);

La Machine à lire les pensées (Paris: Gallimard, 1937); translated by James Whitall as *The Thought-reading Machine* (New York & London: Harper, 1938),

Chateaubriand (Paris: Grasset, 1938); translated by Vera Fraser (London: Cape, 1938); Fraser's translation also published as *Chateaubriand: Poet, Statesman, Lover* (New York & London: Harper, 1938);

Un Art de vivre (Paris: Plon, 1939); translated by Whitall as *The Art of Living* (London: Hodder & Stoughton, 1940; New York & London: Harper, 1940);

Discours de réception à l'Académie française et réponse de M. André Chevrillon (Paris: Grasset, 1939);

Etats-Unis 39: Journal d'un voyage en Amérique (Paris: Editions de France, 1939);

Les Origines de la guerre de 1939 (Paris: Gallimard, 1939);

Tragédie en France (New York: Editions de la Maison Française, 1940); translated by Denver Lindley as *Tragedy in France* (New York & London: Harper, 1940);

Etudes littéraires, 2 volumes (New York: Editions de la Maison Française, 1941, 1944; Paris: SFELT, 1947);

Mémoires, 2 volumes (New York: Editions de la Maison Française, 1942); translated by Denver and Jane Lindley as *I Remember, I Remember* (New York & London: Harper, 1942); Lindley translation also published as *Call No Man Happy* (London: Cape, 1943); revised and enlarged as *Mémoires* (Paris: Flammarion, 1970); translated by Denver Lindley as *Memoirs, 1885-1967* (New York & London: Harper, 1970; London: Bodley Head, 1970);

Cinq Visages de l'amour (New York: Editions Didier, 1942); revised and enlarged edition translated by Haakon M. Chevalier as *Seven Faces of Love* (New York: Didier, 1944); revised and enlarged French edition published as *Sept visages de l'amour* (Paris: Jeune Parque, 1946);

Espoirs et souvenirs (New York: Editions de la Maison Française, 1943);

Toujours l'inattendu arrive (New York: Editions de la Maison Française, 1943);

Histoire des Etats-Unis, 2 volumes (New York: Editions de la Maison Française, 1943, 1944); translated by Denver and Jane Lindley as *The Miracle of America* (New York & London: Harper, 1944); original French version republished (Paris: Albin Michel, 1947); Lindley translation republished as *A New History of the United States* (London: Lane, 1948); original French version republished as *Histoire du peuple américain* (Paris: Editions Littéraires de France, 1955, 1956);

Eisenhower (New York: Didier, 1945); translated by Eileen Lane Kinney as *Eisenhower the Liberator* (New York: Didier, 1945);

Etudes américaines (New York: Editions de la Maison Française, 1945);

Franklin: La vie d'un optimiste (New York: Didier, 1945); translated by Howard Simon as *Franklin: The Life of an Optimist* (New York: Didier, 1945);

Terre promise (Paris: Flammarion, 1945; New York: Editions de la Maison Française, 1945); translated by Joan Charles as *Woman Without Love* (New York & London: Harper, 1945; London: Lane, 1948);

Journal (Etats-Unis 1946) (Paris: Editions du Bateau Ivre, 1946); translated in *From My Journal* (1948);

Conseils à un jeune Français partant pour les Etats-Unis (Paris: Jeune Parque, 1947);

Histoire de la France (Paris: Wapler, 1947); 2 volumes (New York: Editions de la Maison Française, 1947-1948); translated by Henry L. Binsse as *The Miracle of France* (New York: Harper, 1948); Binsse's translation republished as *A History of France* (London: Cape, 1949); revised and enlarged edition translated by Binsse and Hopkins (London: Cape, 1956; New York: Farrar, Straus & Cudahy, 1957); revised and enlarged edition of original French version (Paris: Albin Michel, 1958);

Les Mondes impossibles (Paris: Gallimard, 1947);

Retour en France (New York: Editions de la Maison Française, 1947); translated in part in *From My Journal* (1948);

Rouen dévasté (Rouen: Societé Normande des Amis du Livre, 1947);

From My Journal, translated by Charles (New York: Harper, 1948); republished as *My American Journal* (London: Falcon Press, 1950) —comprises *Journal (Etats-Unis 1946)* and parts of *Retour en France;*

Journal d'un tour en Amérique latine (Paris: Editions du Bateau Ivre, 1948); translated by Frank Jackson as *My Latin-American Diary* (London: Falcon Press, 1953);

Journal d'un tour en Suisse (Paris: Aux Portes de France, 1948);

A la recherche de Marcel Proust (Paris: Hachette, 1949); translated by Hopkins as *The Quest for Proust* (London: Cape, 1950); Hopkins's translation also published as *Proust: Portrait of a Genius* (New York: Harper, 1950);

Alain (Paris: Domat, 1950);

Nouveaux Discours du Docteur O'Grady (Paris: Grasset, 1950);

Le Dîner sous les marronniers (Paris: Deux Rives, 1951);

Cours de bonheur conjugal (Paris: Hachette, 1951); translated by Crystal Herbert as *The Art of Being Happily Married* (London: Bodley Head, 1953; New York: Harper, 1953);

Ce que je crois (Paris: Grasset, 1951; enlarged, 1952);

Destins exemplaires (Paris: Plon, 1952); translated by Helen Temple Patterson as *Profiles of Great Men* (Ipswich, U.K.: Tower Bridge, 1954);

Lélia; ou La Vie de George Sand (Paris: Hachette, 1952); translated by Hopkins as *Lelia: The Life of George Sand* (London: Cape, 1953; New York: Harper: 1953);

Lettres à l'Inconnue (Paris: La Jeune Parque, 1953); translated by John Buchanan-Brown as *To the Fair Unknown* (London: Bodley Head, 1957); Buchanan-Brown's translation also published as *To an Unknown Lady* (New York: Dutton, 1957);

La Vie de Cecil Rhodes, Œuvres Libres, new series 312, no. 86 (1953); translated by Rohan Wadham as *Cecil Rhodes* (London: Collins, 1953; New York: Macmillan, 1953);

Olympio; ou, La Vie de Victor Hugo (Paris: Hachette, 1954); translated by Hopkins as *The Life of Victor Hugo* (London: Cape, 1950); Hopkins's translation also published as *Olympio: The Life of Victor Hugo* (New York: Harper, 1956);

Portrait de la France et des Français (Paris: Hachette, 1955);

Aux innocents les mains pleines (Paris: La Table Ronde, 1955);

Robert et Elizabeth Browning. Portraits suivis de quelques autres (Paris: Grasset, 1955);

Périgord (Paris: Hachette, 1955);

Discours de réception de M. Jean Cocteau à l'Académie Française et réponse de M. André Maurois (Paris: Gallimard, 1955);

Louis XIV à Versailles (Paris: Hachette, 1955);

Les Roses de septembre (Paris: Flammarion, 1956); translated by Hopkins as *September Roses* (London: Bodley Head, 1958; New York: Harper, 1958);

La France change de visage (Paris: Gallimard, 1956);

Les Trois Dumas (Paris: Hachette, 1957); translated by Hopkins as *Three Musketeers: A Study of the Dumas Family* (London: Cape, 1957); Hopkins's translation also published as *The Titans: A Three-generation Biography of the Dumas* (New York: Harper, 1957);

Lecture, mon doux plaisir (Paris: Fayard, 1957); translated in part in *The Art of Writing* (1960);

Portrait d'un ami qui s'appelait moi (Paris: Wesmael-Charlier, 1959);

La Vie de Sir Alexander Fleming (Paris: Hachette, 1959); translated by Hopkins as *The Life of Sir Alexander Fleming, Discoverer of Penicillin* (London: Cape, 1959; New York: Dutton, 1959);

Dialogues des vivants (Paris: Fayard, 1959);

The Art of Writing, translated by Hopkins (London: Bodley Head, 1960; New York: Dutton, 1960)—comprises essays from *Lecture, mon doux plaisir* and other sources;

Le Monde de Marcel Proust (Paris: Hachette, 1960); translated by Moura Budberg, with the assistance of Barbara Creed, as *The World of Marcel Proust* (London: Angus & Robertson, 1974; New York: Harper & Row, 1974);

Pour piano seul: Toutes les nouvelles de André Maurois (Paris: Flammarion, 1960); translated by Adrienne Foulke as *The Collected Stories of André Maurois* (New York: Washington Square Press, 1967);

Paris (Paris: F. Nathan, 1961);

Adrienne; ou, La Vie de Madame de La Fayette (Paris: Hachette, 1961); translated by Hopkins as *Adrienne: The Life of the Marquise de La Fayette* (London: Cape, 1961; New York: McGraw-Hill, 1961);

Histoire parallèle des Etats-Unis et de l'U.R.S.S., 4 volumes by Maurois and Louis Aragon, (Paris: Presses de la Cité, 1962); volume 3 translated by Patrick O'Brien as *From the New Freedom to the New Frontier: A History of the United States from 1912 to the Present* (New York: McKay, 1963; London: Weidenfeld & Nicolson, 1963);

De Proust à Camus (Paris: Perrin, 1963); translated by Carl Morse and Renaud Bruce as *From Proust to Camus: Profiles of Modern French Writers* (Garden City: Doubleday, 1966; London: Weidenfeld & Nicolson, 1967);

Choses nues (Paris: Gallimard, 1963);

Napoléon (Paris: Hachette, 1964); translated by D. J. S. Thomson (London: Thames & Hudson, 1964; New York: Viking, 1964);

De Gide à Sartre (Paris: Perrin, 1965);

Histoire de l'Allemagne (Paris: Hachette, 1965); translated by Stephen Hardman as *An Illustrated History of Germany* (London: Bodley Head, 1966; New York: Viking, 1966);

Prométhée; ou, La Vie de Balzac (Paris: Hachette, 1965); translated by Norman Denny as *Prometheus: The Life of Balzac* (London: Bodley Head, 1965; New York: Harper & Row, 1966);

Au commencement était l'action (Paris: Plon, 1966);

Soixante ans de ma vie littéraire, suivi de Le Rôle de l'écrivain dans le monde d'aujourd'hui (Périgueux: Fanlac, 1966);

Lettre ouverte à un jeune homme sur la conduite de la vie (Paris: A. Michel, 1966); translated by Frances Frenaye as *Open Letter to a Young Man* (New York: J. H. Heinemann, 1968);

D'Aragon à Montherlant (Paris: Perrin, 1967);

Trois Portraits de femmes: La Duchesse de Devonshire, La Comtesse d'Albany, Henriette-Marie de France (Paris: Hachette, 1967);

Nouvelles Directions de la littérature française (Oxford: Clarendon Press, 1967);

La Conquête de l'Angleterre par les Normands (Paris: Albin Michel, 1968);

Les Illusions (Paris: Hachette, 1968); translated as *Illusions* (New York: Columbia University Press, 1968);

Le Chapitre suivant: 1927, 1967, 2007 (Paris: Nouvelle Librairie, 1979).

Collection: *Œuvres complètes*, 16 volumes (Paris: Grasset, 1950-1956).

PLAY PRODUCTION: *Aux innocents les mains pleines*, Paris, Comédie-Française, 2 March 1955.

André Maurois was born Emile Salomon Wilhelm Herzog in Elbeuf, France, in 1885. His family, manufacturers originating from German-occupied Alsace, had taken refuge in the Seine Maritime area following the 1871 defeat of France in the Franco-Prussian War. The author of *Bernard Quesnay* often mentioned his father, Ernest Herzog, a very simple and rigorous man. About his mother, Alice Lévy-Rueff Herzog, it is known only that she had studied the classics in Paris and that she had initiated her son to poetry and the classics. This attentive mother personally managed the education of her son and two daughters and taught them reading and writing.

André Maurois's school was a simple private school. His teachers included, as professor of piano, the father of the musician Marcel Dupré and, as professor of German, Fraulein Bussmann, aunt of the future German chancellor Heinrich Brüning. After this beginning, the young Maurois entered the petit lycée d'Elbeuf where he studied Latin, French, and mathematics. He was at the head of his class. In 1897 he continued his studies at the Lycée Corneille in Rouen, where Flaubert had been a student. It was the time of the Dreyfus affair, and for a young Jew, the school atmosphere was not always pleasant. As an adolescent, Maurois suffered from poor health and had to wear a back brace because of spinal curvature. He was an excellent student, first in his class, and won many prizes, making some of his fellow students envious. Although he had to endure their malevolence for a while, with his simple, unassuming nature he soon gained their respect. Within two years his

Maurois working in the family factory at Elbeuf, 1925 (courtesy of the estate of André Maurois)

health improved and, leaving his brace, he began physical training, at which he excelled.

The year 1901 was an important year for him. That year he started studying philosophy with Emile-Auguste Chartier, who later took the pseudonym of Alain. This fascinating master organized his course as a Socratic dialogue, a form which Maurois found exciting. More spiritualist than materialist, Chartier praised the classical traditions but appreciated the effects of such authors as Saint-Simon who ignored the stylistic standards of some of his seventeenth-century contemporaries yet created a striking and enduring style of his own. In 1901 Chartier had not had work published yet, but he was an exceptional professor: a free-minded, sincere, and persuasive man. Maurois was permanently impressed by his ideas and shaped his own concepts and beliefs in accordance. At the same time, Chartier noticed the spirit of his student. In a 1902 letter addressed to his best friend, Elie Halévy, Chartier described Maurois as "definitely *First class*, unreservedly."

At the end of the school year Maurois won the first prize in philosophy at the Concours Général, a prestigious national competition among the best students of France. He then had a long conversation with his mentor, who advised him to pursue his dream of becoming a writer: "follow the examples of Balzac or Stendhal. First, observe men at work: enter your father's factory and stay there for some years."

The young Maurois did not follow this advice immediately. At eighteen years of age, in 1903, he graduated with a *licence ès lettres* from the University of Caen. With his studies ended, he became a soldier. He was appreciated by his superiors and finished his one year of military service as a sergeant. Then he recalled Chartier's words and entered the family wool mill. At first he was bored, but eventually he acquired a liking for the mill and became a leader who succeeded in seeing the business through a financially difficult period. At night he read Montaigne, Chateaubriand, Hugo, and Balzac. During this time, he maintained close contact with Chartier, who was then teaching in Paris. In 1912 the young provincial industrialist married a young Polish woman, Janine de Szymkiewicz. This marriage with a Catholic foreigner surprised his parents, but Maurois managed to overcome their objections.

In August 1914 when World War I began, Maurois was mobilized in the French army as an interpreter because of his fluency in the English language. He became a liaison officer assigned to the British army and saw destruction and death daily in the trenches. In these terrible conditions he wrote a book concerning his companions' stoicism, dignity, and impassiveness in facing danger. The French staff, in fear of the British officers' reaction, ordered him to use a pseudonym, and the book was published in 1918 under the name, then unknown, of André Maurois. André was the first name of a cousin killed by the enemy; Maurois was the name of a little village near Cambrai where he was stationed. This first book, *Les Silences du Colonel Bramble* (translated as *The Silence of Colonel Bramble*, 1919) was an immediate success. Its sequel was *Les Discours du Docteur O'Grady* (1922; translated as *The Return of Doctor O'Grady*, 1951). In these two books Maurois portrays himself as Aurelle, an interpreter who depicts with classical refinement and reserve facets of the British character: courage, cold humor, and phlegm.

After the success of *Les Silences du Colonel Bramble*, Maurois tried to produce a historical fiction, *Ni ange, ni bête* (Neither Angel nor Beast), in 1919, about the engineer Philippe Viniès's adventures in love and politics during the 1848 French revolution. Clustered around this character are the historical figures of Alphonsede Lamartine and Louis-Marc Caussidière. Viniès, who takes part in the revolt, is deprived of his appointment as a state engineer and is forced to go in exile. The novel ends at this point, with an allusion to the rise of the Second Empire on the final page. Having saved society and reassured the landowners, the new government celebrates. This book, which was conceived during the war, has many elements of a good novel but the main character is not strong.

Chartier was right: it is only by direct observation of men that a writer can be a creator. After the war, Maurois returned to the factory to resume his former life. In 1918 his wife had suffered a nervous breakdown. In 1924 she fell ill with septicemia and died at age thiry-one, leaving three children. Maurois's fifth book, *Ariel*, a fictionalized biography about Shelley's life, full of irony and bitterness, had just been published in

1923. In 1925 his father died. The writer-businessman became distraught. At the age of forty Maurois gave up the family business. In 1926 he came out of his depression when he married Simone de Caillavet. Coming from a family devoted to letters, enthusiastic about poetry, she encouraged her husband's vocation. Henceforth, the life of Maurois became indistinguishable from his work.

Maurois's next novels are much more cohesive. They constitute a unit, comparable to the *Comédie humaine* (*The Human Comedy*) of Balzac, since the same characters and locations reappear. There are six works belonging to the same cycle: *Bernard Quesnay* (1926; translated, 1927), *Climats* (1928; translated as *Whatever Gods May Be*, 1929), *Le Cercle de famille* (1932; translated as *The Family Circle*, 1932); *L'Instinct du bonheur* (1934; translated as *A Time for Silence*, 1942), *Terre promise* (1945; translated as *Woman Without Love*, 1945), and *Les Roses de septembre* (1956; translated as *September Roses*, 1958). All these novels deal with the problems of marriage, especially the problem of mutual understanding, and in each the same sentimental disappointments can be found.

In *Bernard Quesnay* the factory at Pont-de-l'Eure, modeled on the Herzog factory, is the dominant controlling force, and its shadow strongly influences the characters of the story. Maurois here frees himself from the tortures that obsessed him in his youth at the factory: the rivalries, the daily worries, the competition and the price struggles, the problems of the workers' psychology and class conflict. In this oppressive atmosphere, Bernard Quesnay steals some moments away from the factory to see his mistress, Simone Beix. He would like to marry her, to take her with him to Pont-de-l'Eure, but she considers the factory as a rival. She wants to possess completely her lover's heart and attentions. The marriage will never take place. Bernard will grow older alone while working every day in the factory, his only family. In contrast, his brother Antoine, a dreamer, leaves the factory to secure his private happiness.

Climats, the second novel in the cycle, is generally considered Maurois's masterpiece for its memorable characters, its subtle psychology, and its interesting bi-partite structure, which affords two opposing points of view. It was a best-seller in France and also sold widely in Spanish, Russian, and other languages. The atmosphere and theme recall those of the previous novel. The action takes place in Gandumas, in the Limousin re-

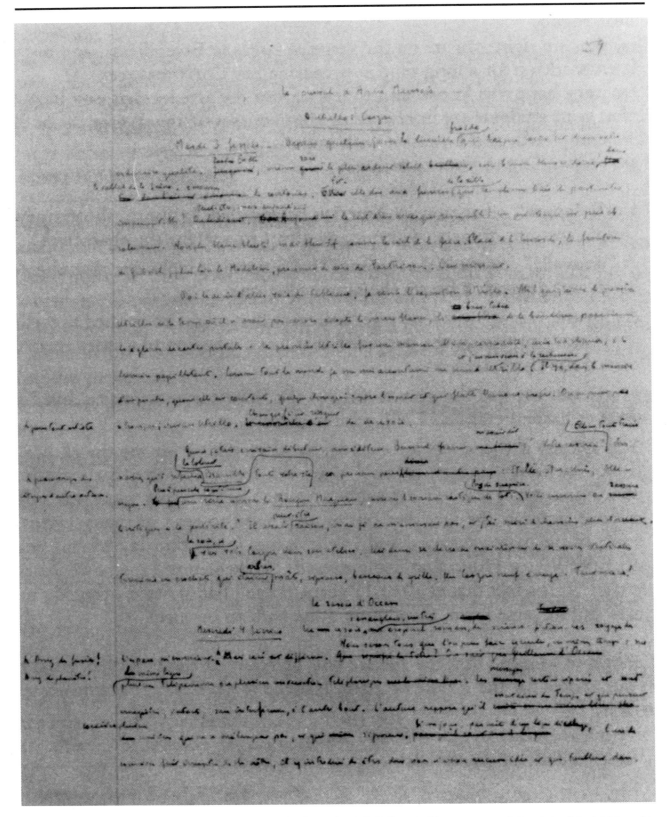

Pages from Maurois's journal (Jack Kolbert Archives, courtesy of the estate of André Maurois)

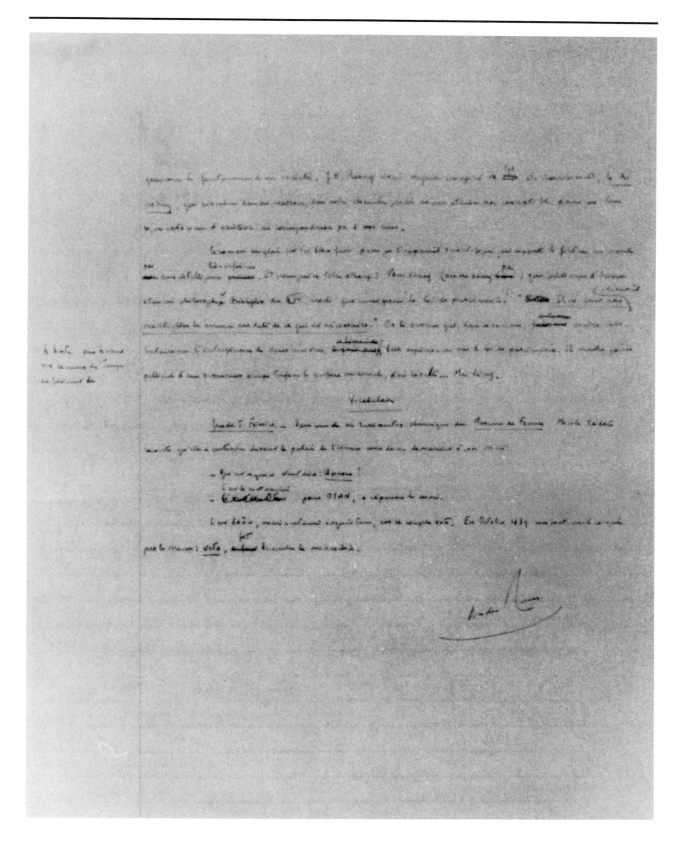

gion. Philippe Marcenat, like Bernard Quesnay, works hard in his factory. But being passionate, tender, generous, he finds someone to love, the blonde Odile Malet, the girl of his dreams. She allows herself to be conquered but soon gets bored with her busy husband. Finally, they are divorced. Then the dark-haired Isabelle de Cheverny enters his life, but reality cannot erase the image of the ideal woman that obsesses Philippe's mind. Although Philippe and Isabelle marry, he is unfaithful to her, ever seeking the sentimental climate that will provide him happiness. Will he ever find it with the patient Isabelle? The last pages allow one to think so briefly, but the premature death of Philippe leaves the question unanswered.

The remaining four novels in the cycle recast and expand themes set forth in the first two. In *Le Cercle de famille*–considered by some Maurois's most biting work because of its bitter criticism of an adulterous woman and her complacent husband–a central conflict is that between mother and daughter; in *L'Instinct de bonheur,* a couple must come to terms with the wife's former love affair and the child born of this relationship; *Terre promise* chronicles a woman's disappointing and ultimately unsuccessful search for physical, emotional, and intellectual fulfillment; and *Les Roses de septembre* deals with the complications and infidelities that threaten the marriage of a celebrated novelist, Guillaume Fontane. Fontane, like most of Maurois's heroes, will not transform his life. He is too wise to sacrifice his partner for an occasional passion, and in the end understands the strength of his union with his wife. He finally realizes that what he appreciates most is his domestic harmony. And the lesson of this novel is that it is useless, in full maturity, to seek happiness in adventures reserved for young men.

Rather than creating new fictional worlds, these works consist primarily of socially conservative observations of the French people and their morality. Therefore, it is not surprising that Maurois's role as a novelist was soon overshadowed by his later nonfiction works–essays, biographies and, most important, historical writings. A sampling of titles attests to the diversity of his interests: *Dialogues sur le commandement* (1924; translated as *Captains and Kings,* 1925), *Quatre Etudes anglaises* (Four English Studies, 1927) and its revision, *Etudes anglaises* (1927), *Aspects de la biographie* (1928; translated as *Aspects of Biography,* 1929), *Mes songes que voici* (Here Are My Dreams, 1933;

translated 1932), *Cinq Visages de l'amour* (1942; revised and enlarged edition translated as *Seven Faces of Love,* 1944), and *Alain* (1950).

According to Maurois, the biographer who studies his hero from documents must make a being made of flesh arise from heaps of papers. If not, he is lost. The search for the truth needs serious documentation, just as the depiction of personality is a matter of art. For Maurois the choice of the subject is important: "Some lives are as naturally beautiful as spontaneous works of art." After setting down the rules of the genre in *Aspects de la biographie,* Maurois composed some of the best biographies in French literature. His skills as historian and psychologist are obvious in these substantial volumes. Most of his subjects are writers, English or French, several of whom were also statesmen: Shelley, Byron, Chateaubriand, Hugo, George Sand, the Dumas family, Dickens, Turgenev, the Brownings, Disraeli. There are also contemporary figures–Proust, Edward VII of England, Marshal Lyautey of France, Sir Alexander Fleming, the discoverer of penicillin, and the American general Dwight D. Eisenhower–and the interesting biography of the little-known Adrienne de La Fayette, wife of the Marquis de La Fayette.

Among all these biographies, his *Vie de Disraëli* (1927; translated, 1927) is considered one of his best efforts. But in all of them the intuitive sharpness of Maurois's analyses and the formal subtleties of his narration are evident. The earlier biographies borrow from the techniques of fiction to such a degree that they sometimes read like novels: *Ariel; ou, La Vie de Shelley* (1923; translated as *Ariel: A Shelley Romance,* 1924); *Don Juan; ou, La Vie de Byron* (published and translated in 1930). In later works his style progressed toward sobriety, without losing its power of suggestion (*Chateaubriand* [published and translated in 1938]; *A la recherche de Marcel Proust* [1949; translated as *The Quest for Proust,* 1950], *Prométhée; ou, La Vie de Balzac* [1965; translated the same year as *Prometheus: the Life of Balzac*]).

Maurois may tell the amorous adventures of Chateaubriand, or those of Byron, Hugo, or George Sand: it is the same irony that shows up at every moment. But irony does not exclude sympathy. Maurois seems to have appreciated the weaknesses and worries of mankind as well as its heroism and glory. Another aspect of his style consists in the pleasant contrast of words and the flexibility of sentences which produce Maurois's characteristic musicality and harmony. The style

Maurois, his second wife, Simone de Caillavet Maurois, and three of their children (courtesy of the estate of André Maurois)

of André Maurois is characterized, above all, by sobriety and clarity. He is never effusive; as he once remarked, he has "contained rather than pushed" his style. Maurois's most characteristic sentence is short and simple, and he is fond of the humorous image. He also elaborates images over a long, developed sentence, a process which recalls the technique of Proust. The same image also sometimes reappears in subsequent passages, like a recurrent theme song. In Maurois's well-known pastiche of Proust, *Le Côté de Chelsea* (1929; translated as *The Chelsea Way*, 1966), the illusion is perfect.

During his lifetime Maurois was honored with many awards. He received honorary doctorates from Princeton, Oxford, Edinburgh, and Heidelberg and was given the Grande Croix de la Légion d'Honneur, the highest decoration in France. He was elected to the Académie Française in 1938. Widely known and appreciated, he was notably popular in Great Britain and in the United States, where he spent several years teaching at Princeton during World War II.

In the fall of 1967 Maurois was hospitalized with an acute abdominal condition. He died on 8 October and was honored four days later with a state funeral held in the courtyard of the Académie Française. Until the very last, in spite of terrible suffering, he never lost his cordiality, which has become legendary.

A novelist, essayist, biographer, lecturer, and writer of popular magazine articles, André Maurois was always faithful to the rationalism of his master, Alain (Chartier). He resisted modernism, from the philosophy of Bergson to psychoanalysis and existentialism. He refused to follow slavishly both old and new literary fashions. His thinking and his art are characterized by clarity, balance, and beauty, avoiding the ambiguity which has seduced so many modern novelists and biographers.

References:

Michel Droit, *André Maurois* (Paris: Editions Universitaires, 1953);

Amélie Fillon, *André Maurois romancier* (Paris: Société Française d'Editions Littéraires et Techniques, 1937);

L. Clark Keating, *André Maurois* (New York: Twayne, 1969);

Jack Kolbert, *The Worlds of André Maurois* (Selinsgrove, Pa.: Susquehanna University Press/

London & Toronto: Associated University Presses, 1985);

Maurice Roya, *André Maurois* (Paris: Editions de la Caravelle, 1934);

Jacques Suffel, *André Maurois* (Paris: Flammarion, 1963).

Paul Morand
(13 March 1888-23 July 1976)

Bruno Thibault
University of Delaware

SELECTED BOOKS: *Lampes à arc* (Paris: Sans Pareil, 1920);

Feuilles de température (Paris: Sans Pareil, 1920);

Tendres Stocks (Paris: Gallimard, 1921); translated by H. I. Woolf as *Green Shoots* (London: Chapman & Dodd, 1923);

Ouvert la nuit (Paris: Gallimard, 1922); translated by Vyvyan B. Holland as *Open All Night* (London: Chapman & Dodd, 1923; New York: T. Seltzer, 1923);

Fermé la nuit (Paris: Gallimard, 1923); translated by G. P. C., C. B. P., and H. M. as *Closed All Night* (London: Chapman, 1924; New York: T. Seltzer, 1925);

Poèmes (1914-1924) (Paris: Sans Pareil, 1924);

Lewis et Irène (Paris: Grasset, 1924); translated by Holland as *Lewis and Irene* (London: Chatto & Windus, 1925; New York: Boni & Liveright, 1925);

L'Europe galante, volume 1 of *La Chronique du XXe siècle* (Paris: Grasset, 1925); translated by Guy Chapman as *Europe at Love* (London: Knopf, 1926; New York: Boni & Liveright, 1927);

Rien que la terre (Paris: Grasset, 1926); translated by Charles-Emile Roche as *Earth Girdled* (London: Knopf, 1926); translated by Lewis Galantière as *Nothing but the Earth* (New York: McBride, 1927);

Rain, Steam and Speed—Pluie, vapeur et vitesse—(after Turner) (Paris: Champion, 1926);

Le Voyage (Paris: Hachette, 1927); translated by Erich Posselt and Sinclair Dombrow (New York: Heron Press, 1930);

Paul Morand

Bouddha vivant, volume 2 of *La Chronique du XXe siècle* (Paris: Grasset, 1927); translated by Eric Sutton as *The Living Buddha* (London: Knopf, 1927); translated by Madeleine

Boyd (New York: Holt, 1928);

East India and Company (New York: Boni, 1927);

Magie noire, volume 3 of *La Chronique du XX* *siècle* (Paris: Grasset, 1928); translated by Hamish Miles as *Black Magic* (London: Heinemann, 1929; New York: Viking, 1929);

U.S.A. 1927 (Paris: Sans Pareil, 1928);

Paris-Tombouctou (Paris: Flammarion, 1928); republished as *A. O. F. de Paris à Tombouctou* (Paris: Flammarion, 1932);

Hiver caraïbe (Paris: Flammarion, 1929);

Champions du monde, volume 4 of *La Chronique du XX* *siècle* (Paris: Grasset, 1930); translated by Miles as *World Champions* (London: Heinemann, 1931; New York: Harcourt, Brace, 1931);

New-York (Paris: Flammarion, 1930); translated by Miles (New York: Holt, 1930; London: Heinemann, 1931);

Route de Paris à la Méditerranée (Paris: Firmin-Didot, 1931);

Papiers d'identité (Paris: Grasset, 1931);

1900 (Paris: Editions de France, 1931); translated by Mrs. Romilly Fedden as *1900 A.D.* (New York: Payson, 1931); original French version revised (Paris: Flammarion, 1942);

Air indien (Paris: Grasset, 1932); translated by Desmond Flower as *Indian Air* (London: Cassell, 1933); Flower's translation republished as *Indian Air: Impressions of Travel in South America* (Boston & New York: Houghton Mifflin, 1933);

Flèche d'Orient (Paris: Gallimard, 1932); translated by Flower as *Orient Air Express* (London, Toronto & New York: Cassell, 1932);

Rococo (Paris: Grasset, 1933);

Londres (Paris: Plon, 1933); translated by Flower as *A Frenchman's London* (London: Cassell, 1934); original French version revised in *Le Nouveau Londres . . .* (1962);

Paris to the Life: A Sketch-Book, by Morand and Doris Spiegel, translated by Gerard Hopkins (London & New York: Oxford University Press, 1933);

France-la-doulce (Paris: Gallimard, 1934); translated by Stuart Gilbert as *The Epic-Makers* (London: Dickson, 1935);

Bucarest (Paris: Plon, 1935);

Rond-point des Champs-Elysées (Paris: Grasset, 1935);

La Route des Indes (Paris: Plon, 1935); translated as *The Road to India* (London: Hodder & Stoughton, 1937);

Les Extravagants (Paris: Gallimard, 1936);

Le Réveille-matin (Paris: Grasset, 1937);

L'Heure qu'il est (Paris: Grasset, 1938);

Méditerranée, mer des surprises (Tours: Mame, 1938);

Réflexes et réflexions (Paris: Grasset, 1939);

Chroniques de l'homme maigre, suivi de Propos d'hier (Paris: Grasset, 1941);

L'Homme pressé (Paris: Gallimard, 1941);

Feu M. le duc (Geneva: Milieu du Monde, 1942);

Petit Théâtre (Paris: Grasset, 1942);

Vie de Guy de Maupassant (Paris: Flammarion, 1942);

Propos des 52 semaines (Geneva: Milieu du Monde, 1942);

Excursions immobiles (Paris: Flammarion, 1944);

A la fleur d'oranger; Le Locataire; Le Bazar de la charité (Vevey: Clefs d'Or, 1946);

Le Dernier Jour de l'inquisition, suivi de Parfaite de Saligny (Paris: Table Ronde, 1947);

Montociel, rajah aux Grandes Indes (Geneva: Editions du Cheval Ailé, 1947); translated by Tony White as *Montociel, Rajah of Greater India* (London: Chapman & Hall, 1962);

Journal d'un attaché d'ambassade, 1916-1917 (Paris: Table Ronde, 1948);

L'Europe russe annoncée par Dostoïevsky (Paris: Pressédition, 1948);

Giraudoux, souvenirs de notre jeunesse (Geneva: Palatine, 1948);

Le Visiteur du soir: suivi de quarante-cinq lettres inédites de Marcel Proust (Geneva: Palatine, 1949);

Le Flagellant de Séville (Paris: Fayard, 1951); translated by Nora Wydenbruck as *The Flagellant of Seville* (London: Lehmann, 1953);

Hécate et ses chiens (Paris: Flammarion, 1954);

L'Eau sous les ponts (Paris: Grasset, 1954);

La Folle amoureuse (Paris: Stock, Delamain & Boutelleau, 1956);

Fin de siècle (Paris: Librairie Stock, 1957);

Le Prisonnier de Cintra (Paris: Fayard, 1958);

Le Lion écarlate, précédé de La Fin de Byzance et d'Isabeau de Bavière (Paris: Gallimard, 1959);

Bains de mer, bains de rêve (Lausanne: Guilde du Livre, 1960);

Fouquet ou, Le Soleil offusqué (Paris: Gallimard, 1961);

Le Nouveau Londres, suivi de Londres, 1933 (Paris: Plon, 1962);

La Dame blanche des Habsbourg (Paris: Laffont, 1963);

Tais-toi (Paris: Gallimard, 1965);

Nouvelles d'une vie, 2 volumes (Paris: Gallimard, 1965);

Monplaisir . . . en littérature (Paris: Gallimard, 1967);

Ci-gît Sophie-Dorothée de Celle (Paris: Flammarion, 1968); translated by Anne-Marie Geoghegan as *The Captive Princess: Sophia Dorothea of Celle* (New York: American Heritage Press, 1972);

Monplaisir . . . en histoire (Paris: Gallimard, 1969);

Discours de réception de Paul Morand à l'Académie Française et réponse de Jacques Chastenet (Paris: Gallimard, 1969);

Venises (Paris: Gallimard, 1971);

Poèmes (réunis) (Paris: Gallimard, 1973);

Les Ecarts amoureux (Paris: Gallimard, 1974);

L'Allure de Chanel (Paris: Hermann, 1976);

Monsieur Dumoulin à l'Isle de la Grenade (Paudex: Editions de la Fontainemore, 1976);

Les Extravagants: Scènes de la vie de bohème cosmopolite (Paris: Gallimard, 1986).

Collection: *Œuvres* (Paris: Flammarion, 1981).

Paul Morand is a writer who is today considered of the second rank. His literary activity spanned about sixty years; he wrote over sixty volumes. He remains best known for his early writings, in particular the short stories published in the 1920s. At the time when he began to write, Morand was greeted as a modernist par excellence. He introduced a new tone in French literature, a new style which represented a complete rupture with the polished works of the previous generation, as well as a refreshing and direct vision—brutal at times—of the modern world. Morand, however, was not a writer of ideas nor a theoretician of the novel. He was a witness: for him it was the eye that counted most. In *Papiers d'identité* (Identification Papers, 1931), he goes as far as to say, "Je me défends d'avoir des théories: les théoriciens n'en vivent pas et les créateurs risquent d'en mourir" (I refuse to have theories: theoreticians don't live by them, and artists risk death because of them).

Morand was born in Paris, on the rue Marbeuf, the only son of Marie-Louise (née Charrier) and Eugène Morand, a painter and playwright. His father was the curator of an annex of the Louvre museum and then became the director of the important Ecole des Arts Décoratifs. Thus the young Morand found himself in contact with the literary, theatrical, and artistic milieu of Paris: he met Marcel Schwob, Auguste Rodin, Sarah Bernhardt, Stéphane Mallarmé, and, through them, Oscar Wilde and Frank Harris.

In 1905 his failure to earn a baccalaureate degree made it necessary for him to take lessons from a young professor who was to become his friend for life: Jean Giraudoux. The following year he registered at the Ecoles des Sciences Politiques to prepare for a career in foreign affairs. From 1909 to 1912 he made several vacation trips to Italy, Spain, and Holland, and studied for an entire year in England. These travels—and especially his sojourns in London—had a tremendous influence on the formation of his personality: Morand learned to consider Europe as a whole and to identify the various national features and traditions he felt were on the verge of disappearing. In 1913 Morand passed brilliantly the entrance examination for the Ministère des Affaires Etrangères. At the outbreak of the war, the young attaché was sent to London for two years; he then moved to Paris (1916-1917), to Rome (1917), and to Madrid (1918). During his brief stays in Paris, Morand frequented the high-society salons and the circles of avant-garde reviews; he made lasting friendships with Jean Cocteau and Marcel Proust.

His first works appeared soon after the war ended. In 1920 he produced *Lampes à arc* (Arc-Lamps) and *Feuilles de température* (Temperature Records). These are short prose poems, intentionally prosaic, which describe the impact of the war on the four corners of Europe. These texts were equally influenced by Walt Whitman's lyricism and by Italian futurism: they celebrate "modern life"—the reign of speed, machines, statistics, and electricity. Morand is especially adroit in describing new and unusual settings of modern big cities—train stations, suburbs, factories, stadiums, docks, hotels, and nightclubs—and in making them poetic.

Tendres Stocks (1921; translated as *Green Shoots*, 1923) is a collection of three short stories about three young women, Clarissa, Aurora, and Delphine, drifting in wartime London. Through these characters Morand presents a keen observation of the evolution of morality and of the relationship between the sexes. Praised by André Breton, the book was immediately translated by Ezra Pound for the London firm Chapman and Dodd, but his translation was rejected and remained unpublished until 1984, when it was released by New Directions under the title *Fancy Goods*. The main characteristics of Morand's particular style are already present: eccentric characters, fast-paced narration, disorderly descriptions, unexpected and humorous imagery. "Le seul

Morand in the 1920s with fellow members of the jury for the Prix du Nouveau Monde. Left to right: Jean Giraudoux, Jean Cocteau, Jacques de Lacretelle, Morand, Bernard Fay, and Valery Larbaud.

reproche que je serais tenté de faire à Morand," declared Marcel Proust in his long and warm preface for the book, "c'est qu'il a quelquefois des images autres que des images inévitables" (The only fault I might be tempted to find with Morand is that he sometimes employs imagery which is not inevitable).

Ouvert la nuit (1922; translated as *Open All Night*, 1923), Morand's second story collection, enjoyed tremendous success. In less than two years after its publication, one hundred printings appeared, and the book has been regularly republished ever since. With *Ouvert la nuit*, the legend of a dandy and cosmopolitan Paul Morand, cynical seducer and fan of sports and speed, was born. *Ouvert la nuit*, like *Tendres Stocks*, narrates episodes in the lives of several women, victims of the moral and material disintegration of Europe. The themes of these stories are exoticism and eroticism, as the titles show: "La Nuit hongroise" (The Hungarian Night), "La Nuit turque" (The Turkish Night), "La Nuit catalane" (The Catalonian Night), "La Nuit romaine" (The Roman Night), and "La Nuit nordique" (The Nordic Night). In 1923 Morand provided a sequel to

Ouvert la nuit with *Fermé la nuit* (translated as *Closed All Night*, 1924), which portrays in a similar manner the lives of four colorful men: a German, an Irishman, a Frenchman, and an Oriental refugee in London.

These books clearly demonstrate that Morand was not interested in abstract types of humanity but that he researched the types of his time: revolutionary agitators, decayed aristocrats, professional sportsmen, successful businesswomen, political exiles, drug addicts, and so on. By the same token, the psychology of these characters is not traditional either. "On me reproche souvent de m'en tenir à l'exceptionnel, de ne pas chercher, en écrivant, l'humain et le permanent. . . . Aujourd'hui où toute une psychologie nouvelle nous apprend à voir que nos plus profonds abîmes ne sont jamais révélés en surface que par des actes en apparence manqués, étranges, illogiques, inexplicables,—est-il possible de faire grief aux jeunes écrivains de commencer par là? Pour moi, l'exceptionnel est une manière d'atteindre le permanent" (I am often accused of keeping to the exceptional and not seeking in my writings to establish the human and permanent el-

Publisher's notice for the third book in Morand's series La Chronique du XXe siècle

ements. . . . Today, when a whole new psychology teaches us that the deepest abysses of our moral life are never revealed on the surface, but are revealed by actions that are seemingly unintentional, weird, illogical, unexplainable–is it possible to take young writers to task for commencing on the same lines? For me, the study of the exceptional is a way of reaching the permanent).

The modernism of Morand is evident not only in his themes, settings, psychology, and characters but also in the narrative techniques he uses. These short stories are not so much stories as fragmentary and problematic portraits. Morand employs varying points of view and perspectives: he represents a city, a nation, or a char-

acter through opinions, descriptions, and minds that are contrasted and sometimes incompatible. He mixes documents with his narrations. In "La Nuit de Babylone" he uses stream of consciousness.

Starting in 1925, Morand's literary goals became more precise: he sought to "outdate" exoticism, that is, to replace the romantic exotic style with a new, more contemporary travel writing. That year, assigned to the French legation in Bangkok, Morand took a trip around the globe, visiting New York, Vancouver, Yokohama, Shanghai, Borneo, Ceylon, Aden, Djibouti, and Suez. *Rien que la terre* (1926; translated as *Earth Girdled*, 1926) is the account of this experience: an express voyage around the world, during which the traveler realizes that the earth is astonishingly small and that nothing can satisfy his appetite for exoticism any longer. "Nous allons vers le tour du monde à quatre-vingts francs. Tout ce qu'on a dit de la misère de l'homme n'apparaîtra vraiment que le jour où ce tarif sera atteint" (We are headed toward the tour of the world on eighty francs. All that we hear about man's misery will not really come to pass until this tariff is fixed). The originality of this travel diary stems from the fact that the author does not describe a specific country (although he devotes several pages to Siam, where he stayed for several weeks), but presents a portrayal of the whole earth as if seen at once, simultaneously.

In 1927 Morand asked for a leave of absence from the Ministère des Affaires Etrangères and was placed on the unattached list. He married the Romanian princess, Hélène Soutzo, whom he had known since 1916. With his wife he undertook a long series of travels outside of Europe: in 1927 he visited the United States once again; in 1928, French West Africa; in 1930, the West Indies; in 1931, South America; in 1935, the Middle East. These and earlier travels furnished the material for numerous travel diaries of uneven quality, and for several short stories and novels published under the collective title *La Chronique du XXe siècle* (The Chronicle of the Twentieth Century). The *Chronique* continues the enterprise of *Ouvert la nuit* and *Fermé la nuit*—to portray the crisis of the postwar period—but extends the framework to Asia in *Bouddha vivant* (1927; translated as *The Living Buddha,* 1927); to Africa in *Magie noire* (1928; translated as *Black Magic,* 1929); and to North America in *Champions du monde* (1930; translated as *World Champions,* 1931). In these books, Morand attempts to demonstrate that there is a struggle among the races just as there is a struggle among the classes. *Bouddha vivant,* through the fatal friendship of two young men, Renaud, the pragmatic Frenchman, and Jali, the Buddhist Siamese, shows how the civilizations of the East and the West fail to understand each other and are destined to destroy each other. *Magie noire* portrays the Negro race—in a somewhat caricatural manner—facing the present stage of world evolution and unable to cope with the standards of the whites.

In *Champions du monde,* as well as in *U.S.A. 1927* (1928) and *New-York* (1930; translated, 1930), Morand popularizes the modernist image of the United States: skyscrapers, financial em-

pires, booming technology, jazz, and racial intermingling. Morand sees "une Amérique optimiste, approvisionnée comme notre Europe à ses plus belles heures, bien au large sur son territoire, pleine d'égoïsme sur les bords et de générosité à l'intérieur, ... un pays que j'admire pour son estomac d'autruche, absorbant tout, ne restituant rien, une Amérique ne créant pas encore, fabriquant, mais du moins parfaitement heureuse" (an optimistic America, stocked as was our Europe in its best days, sailing easily over its territory, full of selfishness outside and of generosity inside, ... a land that I admire for its ostrichlike stomach that absorbs everything and restores nothing, an America still uncreative, fabricating but at least perfectly happy).

In 1930, however, the life and the work of Paul Morand began to take a new turn. The worldwide economic depression, the subsequent tense international atmosphere, and the difficulties encountered by France forced Morand to limit his travels. He settled in Paris and began a period of feverish activity. In 1932 he asked to be placed on active service and became the head of the tourist bureau in France. He also directed a series of short-story volumes, *La Renaissance de la nouvelle,* for the publishing house of Gallimard. In 1933 he joined the editorial board of the daily newspaper, *Figaro,* for which he wrote numerous articles later collected in several volumes: *Rond-point des Champs-Elysées* (Champs-Elysées Circle, 1935), *Le Réveille-matin* (The Alarm Clock, 1937), *L'Heure qu'il est* (The Time It Is, 1938), and *Réflexes et réflexions* (Reflexes and Reflections, 1939). These chronicles show Morand's involvement with politics, his growing concern about the social unrest in France, and his sympathy for the right wing. During this period, he associated with movie stars and producers, wrote several screenplays, and completed *France-la-doulce* (1934; translated as *The Epic-Makers,* 1935), a virulent satire which contributed, at least in part, to his reputation as an anti-Semite.

The most important publication of this transitional period is, however, *1900* (1931; translated that year as *1900 A.D.*), a work of history and memoirs of the Belle Epoque. In this book Morand recalls the old order and stability of the prewar period, its Victorian morals and traditions, as well as its carefree spirit and lightheartedness. There is a sense of nostalgia, but also of impatience, for Morand sees a parallel between 1900 and 1930. As he explained in the preface to a later edition: "En 1930 nous vivions alors une

André Maurois, Paul Valéry, and Paul Morand at the Château de Montmirail (Marne), July 1930
(courtesy of the estate of André Maurois)

dernière décade heureuse; notre déclin avait des tiédeurs de duvet et un capiteux parfum. Nous descendions vers 1939 comme 1900 descendait vers 1914, glissant dans l'abîme comme dans un plaisir" (In 1930 we were living one last happy decade; our decline had the tepidness of down and a heady perfume. We were descending toward 1939 as 1900 descended toward 1914, sliding into the abyss as into pleasure).

This nostalgia for the old order and the theme of modern decadence are found in his short stories of that period, for instance in "Milady," rightly considered one of Morand's masterpieces. Colonel Gardefort, a retired officer from Saumur, embodies all the traditional virtues of old France. A first-class horseman, he forms a passionate attachment to his mare, Milady, whom he trains to perfection. He is soon forced to sell her in order to provide for his material needs, but cannot adjust to life without the animal. On the property of the new owner, the Belgian banker Grumbach, Gardefort throws himself off a cliff with Milady, after having executed spectacular feats of horsemanship. This story, collected in *Les Extravagants* (The Eccentrics, 1936), clearly demonstrates that the ancient values of self-control, mastery, honor, sportsmanship, and independence can no longer survive in the modern world. Stylistically, the narration is striking because of its concise and traditional—almost

Balzacian—line, totally stripped of modernist imagery.

In 1938 Morand represented France at the Danube Talks. From 1939 to 1940 he directed the French Mission on Economic War in London. In July 1940, after the defeat of the French army, he returned to France, without orders, to offer his services to the provisional government in Vichy. The next year two works by Morand were published. *L'Homme pressé* (The Man in a Hurry, 1941) is a satire of his early modernist style, and a criticism of speed and haste. Pierre Niox spoils everything around him—love, friendship, fatherhood, career—because of his restless need to experience things quickly and to be always on the move. Morand explains: "On a souvent dit que j'étais un adorateur de la vitesse. Je l'ai en effet beaucoup aimée. Ensuite, moins. En cherchant à la mieux comprendre, je me suis aperçu qu'elle est loin d'être toujours un stimulant; elle est aussi un déprimant, un acide corrosif, un explosif dangereux à manier . . . " (It has often been said that I was a worshiper of speed. Indeed I loved it greatly once, but later on not so much. In trying to understand it better, I realized that it is far from acting always as a stimulant; it also has the effect of a depressant, a corrosive acid, an explosive dangerous to manipulate . . .). *L'Homme pressé* met with a mediocre reception because of the untimeliness of its theme.

Morand and his wife, Hélène Soutzo Morand, whom he married in 1927 (Atelier René-Jacques)

Chroniques de l'homme maigre (Chronicles of the Thin Man, 1941), a collection of previously published articles, was more in tune with the times. Here Morand advocates the pro-German "national revolution" organized by the Vichy regime.

In 1942 Morand became the director of movie censorship. At this time he opened a high-society salon, where various persons associated with the German collaboration and certain German intellectuals, such as Ernst Jünger, were received. In 1943 he was sent as ambassador to Bucharest and, in 1944, to Bern. At the Liberation his political functions with the Vichy government caused him to be banished from France. He began a life of exile and moral and material difficulty. From 1945 to 1950 Morand lived in Vevey, Switzerland, taking only short trips to Spain and Tangiers. He fell into semi-inactivity, writing very little, except for two books of memoirs on Giraudoux and on Proust and a study of Dostoyevski. In 1951, however, Morand produced an important novel, *Le Flagellant de Séville* (translated as *The Flagellant of Seville*, 1953), in which he chronicles the invasion of Spain by the armies of Napoleon, the fall of the Bourbons, the

reign of Joseph Bonaparte, and the restoration of 1813. This historical framework allowed Morand to describe the horrors of war, the defeat and the occupation, the dishonor and the exile he had recently experienced. Through the central character, Don Luis, a Castilian aristocrat accused of betraying his country and of collaborating with the enemy, Morand attempts to exculpate himself. The plot of this long novel, although conventional, is lively, and the characters are truly convincing. With *Le Flagellant de Séville,* Morand began to reach a new public, and a group of young writers, the "Hussars," led by Roger Nimier, rallied in his favor. In July 1953 the decree of revocation was annulled, and Morand returned to Paris.

His sojourn in Tangiers inspired Morand to write a short novel, *Hécate et ses chiens* (Hecate and her Dogs, 1954), in which his early themes, eroticism and exoticism, resurface. The action takes place in the 1920s. Clothilde is a woman who, like Hecate, the goddess of the moon, presents two faces: one pure and luminous, the other dark and wanton. She entangles her young lover, the narrator, in a cruel and masochistic relationship and finally pushes him to despair. Clothilde-Hecate also embodies the double face of modern Europe–prey, according to Morand, to all vices and excesses. *"Hécate et ses chiens* est un livre qui a inventé sa forme,"* wrote Roger Nimier in a prefatory note. "L'avantage des phrases sèches et des ellipses de Paul Morand, c'est de laisser au mystère la` place qu'il doit avoir: avec le mystère l'émotion est là, et la peur" (*Hécate et ses chiens* is a book which has invented its own form. The advantage of Paul Morand's dry sentences and ellipses is that they leave plenty of room for mystery: with mystery, emotion is present, and so is fear). Other works of similar style and themes, such as *La Folle amoureuse* (The Amorous Madwoman, 1956) and *Les Ecarts amoureux* (Amorous Follies, 1974), followed, but without the same success.

In 1968, at the age of eighty, Morand was elected to the Académie Française. (His first attempt to gain admittance in 1958 had failed because of the veto of General Charles de Gaulle, then president of the Republic.) The last years of Morand's life were dedicated to preparing various collections of his works, and to writing his autobiography, *Venises* (Venices, 1971). In this book he recounts his life through successive portraits of the city of Venice (hence the plural form of the title). He then presents himself as the witness of a forgotten era, and proclaims, "Je suis veuf de l'Europe" (I am Europe's widower). *Venises* received immediate general acclaim and struck the public by its unusual fragmentary form and despairing tone.

Letters:

Lettres à des amis et à quelques autres, edited by Ginette Guitard-Auviste (Paris: Table Ronde, 1978).

Bibliography:

Georges G. Place, *Paul Morand* (Paris: Editions de la Chronique des Lettres Françaises, 1975).

Biographies:

Jean-François Fogel, *Morand-Express* (Paris: Grasset, 1980);

Ginette Guitard-Auviste, *Paul Morand, légende et vérités* (Paris: Hachette, 1981);

Manuel Burrus, *Paul Morand, voyageur du vingtième siècle* (Paris: Séguier, 1986).

References:

Bernard Delvaille, *Paul Morand* (Paris: Seghers, 1966);

Ginette Guitard-Auviste, *Paul Morand* (Paris: Editions Universitaires, 1956);

Georges Lemaître, *Four French Novelists: André Gide, Marcel Proust, Jean Giraudoux, Paul Morand* (London & New York: Oxford University Press, 1938);

Stéphane Sarkany, *Paul Morand et le cosmopolitisme littéraire* (Paris: Klincksieck, 1968);

Marcel Schneider, *Morand* (Paris: Gallimard, 1971).

Papers:

Morand's papers are at the library of Vevey, Switzerland, and at the Institut de France (Académie Française) in Paris.

Charles-Louis Philippe

(4 August 1874-21 December 1909)

J. E. Flower
University of Exeter

BOOKS: *Quatre Histoires de pauvre amour* (Paris: Editions de l'Enclos, 1897);

La Bonne Madeleine et La Pauvre Marie (Paris: Bibliothèque Artistique et Littéraire, 1898);

La Mère et l'enfant (Paris: La Plume, 1900; revised edition, Paris: Gallimard, 1923);

Bubu de Montparnasse (Paris: Editions de la Revue Blanche, 1901); translated by Laurence Vail as *Bubu of Montparnasse* (Paris: Crosby Continental Editions, 1932; New York: Avalon, 1945);

Le Père Perdrix (Paris: Fasquelle, 1903); translated by Agnes Kendrick Gray as *A Simple Story* (New York: Knopf, 1924);

Marie Donadieu (Paris: Fasquelle, 1904); translated by Violet Hudson (London: Grey Walls Press, 1949);

Croquignole (Paris: Fasquelle, 1906);

Dans la petite ville (Paris: Fasquelle, 1911);

Faits divers (Nevers: Cahiers du Centre, 1911);

Charles Blanchard (Paris: Nouvelle Revue Française, 1913);

Les Contes du matin (Paris: Nouvelle Revue Française, 1916);

Chroniques du canard sauvage (Paris: Gallimard, 1923).

Charles-Louis Philippe

Although Charles-Louis Philippe liked to claim that his work was fundamentally apolitical and asocial, it does constitute an important link in the tradition of writing which takes working-class people and their environment for its principal subject. His treatment may lack the bite and satirical edge of Octave Mirabeau's writing; it may have none of Emile Zola's massive vision of a class-ridden society or of Jules Vallès's indignation at injustices and inequalities; nor does it have the political dimension that becomes increasingly characteristic of Henri Barbusse's work or, later, of Paul Nizan's. But Philippe does continue a tradition that was already apparent in the works of authors such as Hugo, Sand, Lamartine, and many minor writers in the early part of the nineteenth century who chose to romanticize, dig-

nify, and even idealize the peasant or workers. He also anticipates various aspects of nonmilitant proletarian and populist writing as it developed in the 1920s. The works of Henry Poulaille and Eugène Dabit, as well as the early writings of Louis Guilloux, all bear traces of similarity with his novels.

Louis Philippe and his twin sister, Louise, were born in Cérilly in the Bourbonnais. (He was "rebaptized" Charles-Louis by René Ghil in 1894.) His father was a cobbler who eventually made enough money to enjoy the last years of his life in some comfort. He served as the model for the title character of Philippe's posthumously published novel *Charles Blanchard* (1913). Despite

213

his humble background and some poor health, Philippe made his mark at the local school and subsequently at the lycées of Montluçon and Moulins, where he seemed destined for higher academic success. Any ambitions he may have had came to an end in 1894, however, when he failed the competitive examination for entry to the Ecole Polytechnique. A popular story claims that he was too inhibited by his small size to present himself for the examination, but in reality his interest in literature was already pulling him in another, conflicting direction. He sent some early poems to Mallarmé and René Ghil and had his first verse published in the Belgian review *Stella*. In 1895 he moved to Paris, where he worked for the health service and where, through Ghil, he became friendly with Louis Lumet and the group of artists and writers associated with the mildly socialist review *L'Enclos*. After a short spell back in Cérilly, during which he was declared unfit for military service because of necrosis of the jaw, he returned to Paris in 1896. He spent a brief period again with the health service before succeeding in an open competition for a post with the municipality. Here, with occasional promotions, he remained for the rest of his life.

With a secure, if modest, living assured, Philippe devoted as much time as possible to literature. In 1897 his first stories, *Quatre Histoires de pauvre amour* (Four Stories of Poor Love), were published at his own expense by Lumet's group. In these Philippe sympathizes with the lot of several representatives of the working class (tramps and a prostitute, for example) and suggests that their plight and indeed their crimes are the result of social pressures. This hint of social concern is paralleled by a clear sexual obsession which appears in later work and which admirers and critics have generally chosen to ignore. A year later two more stories, *La Bonne Madeleine et La Pauvre Marie* (Good Madeleine and Poor Marie), appeared, published again at Philippe's expense. These are stories of two village girls, both of whom eventually die because of lack of love. Their suffering, however, is sublimated, and the stories are heavy with religious sentimentality and a frequently inflated style. The two girls are clearly intended to be martyrs of their situation, but Philippe's choice of register, his authorial interventions, and his recourse to pastoral and religious imagery dilute any real social impact the stories may have had. This is not suffering such as it is experienced by Catherine Maheu in Zola's

Germinal (1885) or by the title character in the Goncourt brothers' novel *Germinie Lacerteux* (1864). Instead it is muted, and, as much of Philippe's subsequent work shows, it is to be accepted as part of the natural state of the working class.

In July 1898 Philippe met Maria Tixier, a flowermaker turned prostitute. From a letter (8 September 1898) to his Belgian friend Henri Vandeputte (the correspondence was published in 1911 as *Lettres de jeunesse à Henri Vandeputte*) Philippe's attitude toward her appears to smack of condescension: "Je m'intéresse à sa souffrance, j'aurais du plaisir à la former, comme j'ai du plaisir à former des petits enfants" (Her suffering interests me; I would like to train her in the way I have liked training small children). His influence and attempts to remonstrate with her seem to have had little effect. The book which would develop from this relationship, *Bubu de Montparnasse* (1901; translated as *Bubu of Montparnasse*, 1932), was not only based on first-hand knowledge but motivated by anger as well. It is the most overtly committed of all his novels and arguably the best as Philippe once again blames society and the economic currents at work within it for forcing young girls like Marie into vice. In its presentation and treatment of the theme of prostitution *Bubu de Montparnasse* should be compared with Zola's *Nana* (1880).

Before its appearance in 1901, however, Philippe had written, and again published at his own expense, *La Mère et l'enfant*. (The complete text would not appear until 1923.) Set, like its predecessors, in a world of poverty and suffering, this first-person narrative is addressed to the mother and describes the coming of age of Pierre Hardy (in large part a self-portrait) who reappears in *Bubu de Montparnasse*. Whether it is the comfort of home life that is described or the pain experienced in breaking away from the mother figure, the narrator seizes every opportunity for sentimental self-indulgence. Alterations in the novel's manuscript suggest that Philippe was aware of the need to trim some of his excesses, and to a degree the style in the 1923 version is more spare and popular in register than in the earlier one. Fundamentally, however, *La Mère et l'enfant* bears Philippe's hallmark, and only in *Bubu de Montparnasse* did he begin to write at length with more, though not total, sustained purposiveness and control.

According to his letters to Vandeputte, *Bubu de Montparnasse* was written with vigor and enthusiasm during the first six months of 1900.

Through his association with Maria–Berthe in the novel–Philippe amassed considerable documentation on the world of pimps and prostitutes. The novel traces Berthe's fortunes at the hands of a timid, sentimental but caring lover (Hardy) who tries to rescue her from her plight and her life in the control of her pimp Bubu. The latter ultimately wins her back, and Hardy is left to bemoan his lot and pass sententious comments on a society in which prostitutes have no choice: "Les filles publiques sont marquées dès l'origine comme des bêtes passives que l'on mène au pré communal" (prostitutes are marked from the beginning like cattle that allow themselves to be led without protest to the communal meadow).

This closing image is important. It underlines Philippe's passive acceptance of a society in which the rich and strong will always win: "Nous vivons dans un monde où les pauvres doivent souffrir" (We live in a world where the poor have to suffer). Indeed throughout the novel animal imagery is used to describe the passivity not only of prostitutes but also of the poor and weak in general. Many are fed to the all-consuming machine that is Paris, which crushes them unthinkingly in its jaws. Only the likes of Babu and his criminal (burglar and murderer) friend Jules seem to escape. But this view of a society divided between possessors and possessed goes beyond mere observation. Philippe clearly admires those who succeed–by whatever means–and this attitude removes some of the edge from his intended indignation. Although there is not the emphasis on the workings of an anonymous destructive force of the kind found in one of Zola's novels or in Barbusse's portrayal of war in *Le Feu: Journal d'une escouade* (1916; translated as *Under Fire: The Story of a Squad*, 1917), the acceptance of prostitution as economically unavoidable is clear.

Philippe claimed that about the time he was writing *Bubu de Montparnasse* he discovered the work of Nietzsche: "un remède à mes maux, un grand cordial qui me fait très fort" (a cure for my pains, a splendid tonic which does me a great deal of good). Some critics consider that in his admiration for the German philosopher is to be found the source of his approval of a character like Bubu. It seems more likely, however, that this element in his work has much deeper roots in an inferiority complex stemming from his small stature and lack of material and sexual success in life. It would also be rewarding to explore this theme in his work in the light of his relationship with his mother and his twin sister. In *Bubu*

de Montparnasse, as in most of his novels, there is a curious masochistic streak which goes beyond mere resignation. It is a mixture of indignation at the plight of those born to poverty, enjoyment of the suffering which necessarily follows from it, and, at the same time, repressed desire to be in a position of power himself. Ten years after he had written *Bubu de Montparnasse,* in a letter to André Ruyters, Philippe, reflecting on the novel, made an interesting and revealing remark: "Tu m'as vu à Paris, dans des temps où j'étais malheureux et affaibli. Mais vous ignorez tous et Van de Putte [*sic*] l'ignore aussi que je suis un homme très fort. On le sait maintenant autour de moi" (You saw me in Paris at a time when I was miserable and weak. But like everybody including Van de Putte you don't know how strong I am. People around me realize that now).

Whatever the psychological and personal inspiration for it, *Bubu de Montparnasse* is, of all Philippe's novels, the one which makes a social point most strongly. It was well received and secured his reputation as an important, if still somewhat marginal, writer, who would subsequently unsuccessfully compete for the Prix Goncourt in 1904 and 1906 with his novels *Marie Donadieu* and *Croquignole*. During the period 1901-1903 he wrote regular articles for *Le Revue Blanche* and *Le Canard Sauvage*. In 1903 his novel *Le Père Perdrix* (translated as *A Simple Story,* 1924) was published, by which time he had also received promotion in the Paris council partly because of the influence of the writer Maurice Barrès to whom Philippe gave a cat called Bubu. In *Le Père Perdrix,* based partly on Philippe's father's life, he once again deals with the contrast between the lives of the poor and those of the middle classes, though the latter are not simplistically presented as being purely exploitative. The novel also explores the theme of revolt through the refusal by Jean to conform to the dictates either of his bosses or his family. The author's admiration for someone strong enough to resist both pressures to conform and the conditioning forces of his upbringing is again clear, though at the end of the novel resignation prevails.

In his sixth novel, *Marie Donadieu* (1904; translated into English, 1949), Philippe returns to the theme of the disputed woman in a plot that recalls the Berthe-Hardy-Bubu triangle. The story was derived from an affair he had had with the mistress of a friend in 1901. In 1906 Philippe's last completed novel, *Croquignole,* was published. Again the contrast between the rich and the poor, the strong and the weak, is explored. The former is epitomized by Croquignole, who inherits money and abandons his dull office job to enjoy two years of carefree existence; the latter by Claude Buy (another alter ego of Philippe) and his colleagues. There is, however, an important difference between this and Philippe's previous novels. Both Croquignole and Angèle, the poor (but pure) seamstress he seduces–and whom Claude loves–commit suicide. For Croquignole freedom, once tasted, allows no return; for Angèle betrayal of her class is unforgivable. Rather than the celebration of freedom which some critics consider it, *Croquignole* is ultimately pessimistic. For the majority, Philippe suggests, there can be no alternative to resignation and acceptance of one's lot.

After *Croquignole* Philippe began *Charles Blanchard* (1913), a novel based on the life of his father, who had died in 1907. It would not be finished. From September 1908 to September 1909 he produced a weekly story for *Le Matin*. These were eventually collected and published in two volumes: *Dans la petite ville* (In the Small Town, 1911) and *Les Contes du matin* (Morning Stories, 1916). He became loosely attached as well to the group around André Gide and Jean Schlumberger who founded *La Nouvelle Revue Française*. Toward the end of 1909 Philippe developed typhoid and meningitis. He died on 21 December.

In September 1960 the review *Europe* published a short memorial tribute to Philippe including a bibliography and three homage articles, which quoted statements made earlier by Jean Giraudoux (who had spent some of his childhood in Cérilly) and Valery Larbaud. Almost without exception the contributors refer to his having been "of the people," a true recorder of the lives and emotions of his own class. Elsewhere Ray referred to him as a natural socialist: "Il était socialiste comme les nègres sont crépus: le socialisme était pour lui le sentiment d'une différence" (He was a socialist in the way that Negros have crinkly hair: for him socialism was being aware of a difference). But he was not a man of action, however much he may have aspired to be one. In an interview in 1905 he claimed that his real contribution was to write about the working class with which he was totally at one, a theme repeated throughout his correspondence with Vandeputte. Yet there is no doubt that such ambitions led both to sentimental-

ity ("I am most happy when I am sad") and to a straining for literary effect.

His descriptions and his use of simile and metaphor (attributed by some contemporaries to the influence of the symbolists) can be excessive and inappropriate. Jules and Bubu, discussing syphilis and observing passersby from a café terrace, are likened to Adam naming God's creatures on the day of creation. In *Croquignole* a description of Angèle clearly resembles a popular one of the Virgin Mary: "Parfois elle posait ses deux mains l'une sur l'autre, en croix, à la hauteur de ses seins, s'inclinait un peu vers la droite et battait des paupières en silence" (Sometimes she would cross her hands over her breast and quietly lean slightly to the right, her eyelids fluttering). In *Le Père Perdrix* brandy is described as "un ange aux ailes étendues" (an angel with outstretched wings). The mother's thoughts in *La Mère et l'enfant* are likened to a line of old shady lime trees. Muted, pastel shades are much in evidence, and some of the pastoral scenes in his work recall those of the poet Francis Jammes, whose writing Philippe much admired. Philippe also intrudes into his text a great deal to moralize or to address his characters and reader, but there are times when his perceptions are accurate and recorded in a precise, understated way.

In 1905 Léon Bloy, who had objected to the overtly political dimensions of the writings of Zola and Vallès, remarked about Philippe in an interview: "Cet écrivain n'a pas de talent, il a presque du génie. Du génie dans l'expression. C'est un homme tout à fait remarquable" (This writer doesn't have talent, he almost has genius, especially in his expression. He is quite remarkable). In later years Philippe was equally admired by Dabit and Poulaille for his authentic and sensitive picture of the poor, but he was scorned by Nizan and other left-wing militants whose conceptions of writing in the early 1930s could not accommodate such an irresolute view of the class struggle. Had he lived longer it seems unlikely that Philippe's preoccupations and style would have changed substantially, though it is impossible to estimate what impact World War I would have had. He and his work remain relatively neglected, but there is no doubting his place in a broadly defined tradition of left-wing writing during the last century. He also has an important place among writers of impressionistic, often self-indulgent, novels around the turn of the century. And there can be no doubt either that an analysis of the psychological inspiration of his entire œuvre would be extremely rewarding.

Letters:

Lettres de jeunesse à Henri Vandeputte (Paris: Nouvelle Revue Française, 1911).

References:

Gene J. Barbaret, "André Gide and Charles-Louis Philippe," *French Review,* 28 (May 1955): 477-484;

Europe, memorial tribute to Philippe, no. 377 (September 1960);

J. E. Flower, "Sentimentality and Resignation: Charles-Louis Philippe," in his *Literature and the Left in France* (London: Macmillan, 1983), pp. 50-64;

F. W. J. Hemmings, "The Russian Novel and the Disintegration of Naturalism. Charles-Louis Philippe," in his *The Russian Novel in France* (London: Oxford University Press, 1950), pp. 147-176;

Nouvelle Revue Française, special issue on Philippe, 3 (15 February 1910);

H. Poulaille, "Charles-Louis Philippe, le populisme et la littérature prolétarienne," *Cahiers Bleus,* no. 55 (March 1930);

Leo Spitzer, *Linguistics and Literary History* (Princeton: Princeton University Press, 1948);

Bruno Vercier, Introduction to Philippe's *Bubu de Montparnasse* (Paris: Garnier/Flammarion, 1978).

Marcel Proust
(10 July 1871-18 November 1922)

Douglas W. Alden
University of Virginia

BOOKS: *Les Plaisirs et les jours* (Paris: Calmann-Lévy, 1896); translated by Louise Varese as *Pleasures and Regrets* (New York: Crown, 1948; London: Dobson, 1950); translated by Varese, Gerard Hopkins, and Barbara Dupee as *Pleasures and Days, and Other Writings* (Garden City: Doubleday, 1957);

Du côté de chez Swann (Paris: Grasset, 1913); translated by C. K. Scott Moncrieff as *Swann's Way*, 2 volumes (London: Chatto & Windus, 1922; New York: Holt, 1922);

Pastiches et mélanges (Paris: Gallimard, 1919);

A l'ombre des jeunes filles en fleurs (Paris: Gallimard, 1919); translated by Scott Moncrieff as *Within a Budding Grove* (London: Chatto & Windus, 1924; New York: T. Seltzer, 1924);

Le Côté de Guermantes I (Paris: Gallimard, 1920); translated in *The Guermantes Way* (1925);

Le Côté de Guermantes II–Sodome et Gomorrhe I (Paris: Gallimard, 1921); *Le Côté de Guermantes II* translated in *The Guermantes Way* (1925); *Sodome et Gomorrhe I* translated in *Cities of the Plain* (1927);

Sodome et Gomorrhe II, 3 volumes (Paris: Gallimard, 1922); translated in *Cities of the Plain* (1927);

Sodome et Gomorrhe III: La Prisonnière, 2 volumes (Paris: Gallimard, 1923); translated by Scott Moncrieff as *The Captive* (London: Knopf, 1929; New York: A. & C. Boni, 1929);

Albertine disparue, 2 volumes (Paris: Gallimard, 1925); translated by Scott Moncrieff as *The Sweet Cheat Gone* (London: Knopf, 1930; New York: A. & C. Boni, 1930);

The Guermantes Way, 2 volumes, translated by Scott Moncrieff (London: Chatto & Windus, 1925; New York: T. Seltzer, 1925)—comprises *Le Côté de Guermantes I* and *Le Côté de Guermantes II*;

Le Temps retrouvé, 2 volumes (Paris: Gallimard, 1927); translated by Frederick A. Blossom as *The Past Recaptured* (New York: A. & C. Boni, 1932);

Chroniques (Paris: Gallimard, 1927);

Marcel Proust (photograph by H. Martinie)

Cities of the Plain, 2 volumes, translated by Scott Moncrieff (New York: A. & C. Boni, 1927)—comprises *Sodome et Gomorrhe I* and *Sodome et Gomorrhe II*;

Le Balzac de Monsieur de Guermantes (Neuchâtel: Ides et Calendes, 1950);

Jean Santeuil, 3 volumes (Paris: Gallimard, 1952); translated by Gerard Hopkins (London: Weidenfeld & Nicolson, 1955; New York: Simon & Schuster, 1956);

A la recherche du temps perdu, 3 volumes, edited by Pierre Clarac and André Ferré (Paris: Gallimard, Bibliothèque de la Pléiade, 1954);

Contre Sainte-Beuve, suivi de Nouveaux Mélanges, edited by Bernard de Fallois (Paris: Gallimard, 1954); translated by Sylvia Townsend

Warner as *On Art and Literature, 1896-1919* (New York: Meridian Books, 1958); Warner's translation of *Contre Sainte-Beuve* republished as *By Way of Sainte-Beuve* (London: Chatto & Windus, 1958);

Textes retrouvés, edited by Phillip Kolb and Larkin B. Price (Urbana: University of Illinois Press, 1968); revised and enlarged edition, Cahiers Marcel Proust, new series 3 (Paris: Gallimard, 1971);

Les Pastiches de Proust, edited by Jean Milly (Paris: Armand Colin, 1970);

Jean Santeuil; précédé de Les Plaisirs et les jours, edited by Clarac and Yves Sandre (Paris: Gallimard, Bibliothèque de la Pléiade, 1971);

Contre Sainte-Beuve: précédé de Pastiches et mélanges et suivi de Essais et articles, edited by Clarac and Sandre (Paris: Gallimard, Bibliothèque de la Pléiade, 1971);

Le Carnet de 1908, edited by Kolb, Cahiers Marcel Proust, new series 8 (Paris: Gallimard, 1976);

L'Indifférent (Paris: Gallimard, 1978);

Remembrance of Things Past, 3 volumes, translated by Scott Moncrieff and Terence Kilmartin (London: Chatto & Windus, 1981);

Matinée chez la princesse de Guermantes, edited by Henri Bonnet and Bernard Brun (Paris: Gallimard, 1982);

Poèmes, edited by Claude Francis and Fernande Gontier, Cahiers Marcel Proust, new series 10 (Paris: Gallimard, 1982);

La Prisonnière, edited by Milly (Paris: Flammarion, 1984);

La Fugitive (Albertine disparue), edited by Milly (Paris: Flammarion, 1986);

Le Temps retrouvé, edited by Brun (Paris: Flammarion, 1986).

Collection: *Œuvres complètes de Marcel Proust,* 10 volumes (Paris: Gallimard, 1929-1936).

OTHER: Jacques-Emile Blanche, *Propos de peintre: De David à Degas,* first series, preface by Proust (Paris: Emile-Paul, 1919).

TRANSLATIONS: John Ruskin, *La Bible d'Amiens* (Paris: Mercure de France, 1904);

Ruskin, *Sésame et les lys: Des trésors des rois* (Paris: Mercure de France, 1906).

In 1936 Léon Pierre-Quint claimed that the vogue for *A la recherche du temps perdu (Remembrance of Things Past)* was ended and that Marcel Proust was destined henceforth to interest only thesis writers at the Sorbonne. He was still the authority on Proust, having published the first biography in 1925, but he could not have been more mistaken, for Proust today is almost universally revered as the greatest French author of the twentieth century. His masterpiece comes closer than that of any other French writer of this century to being a summa, a literary monument. It continues the traditions both of the great seventeenth-century classical writers such as Madame de La Fayette, the Duc de Saint-Simon, and La Rochefoucauld, and of the nineteenth-century realists–Stendhal, Balzac, and Flaubert. Yet it is also highly innovative in technique and content. By his style alone Proust stands among the masters. His great work reveals the mind of a *moraliste* or commentator on mores, a great social novelist, a master psychologist, a comic writer, a highly original aesthetician, and a poet. Its characters range from members of the highest aristocracy through the leisured bourgeoisie and the professional class, to modest artists, bluestockings, and courtesans, and finally to servants from the peasant class. Themes as varied as music, visual arts, medicine, travel, nature, and diplomacy run through the text along with the most fundamental themes of the self, childhood and adolescence, love and sexuality, society, and artistic creation. It is a major fictional document on its time as well as a very intimate work. Its form can be called organic, since, like a tree, its structure combines logic and coherence with the capacity to expand greatly. Proust himself compared it to a cathedral, whose vast overall pattern is not visible until it is complete and which incorporates many smaller structures and countless decorative features.

Criticism from the 1970s and 1980s, in addition to a wealth of biographical and critical material from previous decades, attests to the multiple approaches one can take to Proust's work. While textual scholarship is still being pursued, the most recent critical examinations have tended to emphasize either narrative technique or psychological content. Proust is seen as a great narrative innovator; his manipulations of narrative time and voice, for example, are an early instance of techniques later used by certain New Novelists, as Gérard Genette showed in *Figures III* (1972; partially translated as *Narrative Discourse: An Essay on Method,* 1980), and Proustian technique contributed to creating a new conception of story line, plot, and narrator. Other critics view Proust as one of the most creative psychologists of the self;

Serge Doubrovsky, in *La Place de la Madeleine* (1974; translated as *Writing and Fantasy in Proust*, 1986), has shown how Proust used language and metaphor to conceal and reveal at once the most intimate obsessions of his psyche. As novel writing has become more complex with the advent of the so-called New Novelists, Proust's masterpiece has seemed to become increasingly simple, although the term simplicity hardly characterizes his long novel (it has 3,116 pages in the Pléiade edition of 1954, which is soon to be superseded by the publication of yet another revised text). Composed from approximately 1908 (if one does not include its early avatars, of which some traces persist in the finished work) until the last days of the author's life in 1922, published between 1913 and 1927 (the posthumous volumes thanks to the diligence of Proust's brother Robert and several editors), and originally issued in sixteen separate volumes, *A la recherche du temps perdu* consists of seven named parts, some of which are themselves divided into sections with titles.

When the first part of this vast work appeared in 1913 under the title *Du côté de chez Swann* (translated as *Swann's Way*, 1922), it was greeted with hostility because of the complexity of Proust's style. Alfred Humblot, who worked for the publisher Ollendorff and was one of the editors who had rejected Proust's manuscript somewhat earlier, wrote to Proust's friend Louis de Robert: "Cher ami, je suis peut-être bouché à l'émeri, mais je ne puis comprendre qu'un monsieur puisse employer trente pages à décrire comment il se tourne et se retourne dans son lit avant de trouver le sommeil" (Dear friend, I am perhaps a blockhead, but I cannot understand how a gentleman can use thirty pages to describe how he turns over in bed before getting to sleep). The passage to which Humblot alludes, which occurs at the very outset of the novel as the middle-aged narrator is remembering some of his past nocturnal experiences, is one of the most melodious in the French language and one of the most profound in suggesting the operations of the unconscious mind. When Proust had time to write with care, as he did throughout the composition of *Du côté de chez Swann*, he was one of the greatest masters of French style. Later, in his feverish haste to finish his novel before death overtook him (and it did overtake him before he could make the final touches on the last volumes), he was more attentive to what he had to say than to how he said it.

In the posthumously published fragments of the essay now entitled *Contre Sainte-Beuve* (1954; translated as *By Way of Sainte-Beuve*, 1958), Proust notes: "un livre est le produit d'un autre moi que celui que nous manifestons dans nos habitudes, dans la société, dans nos vices. Ce moi-là, si nous voulons essayer de le comprendre, c'est au fond de nous-même, en essayant de le recréer en nous, que nous pouvons y parvenir" (a book is the product of another personality than the one that we express in our habits, in society, in our vices. If we want to try to understand that personality we can succeed only by trying to recreate it deep inside us). Although the fragments of his essay on Sainte-Beuve antedate the writing of his great novel, Proust's rejection of the biographical method is a warning against using that method to interpret his work. Yet the very nature of his novel seems to impose a biographical method since it purports to be the life story of a man who, toward the end of the novel, suddenly calls himself Marcel. It is true that manuscript evidence shows that, while Proust used this name for his main character, or narrator, in some drafts of the novel, he later eliminated it in almost all passages, and, presumably, would have deleted it entirely, had he lived long enough to oversee himself the publication of his final volumes. Thus his last intention was to avoid establishing identity between himself and his narrator; and recent critics have taken care to avoid such an assimilation. It remains true that the work had its basis in autobiography and the reality Proust observed around him, and that many identifications can be made between his characters and their models. Unfortunately, so much research has been spent on relating Proust's novel to real events and persons that one essential fact has been obscured: whatever its undeniable connections with reality, *A la recherche du temps perdu* is a true novel since it is a work of the imagination in which the main events never really happened and the main characters in their final form never really existed. Nevertheless, it is useful for the literary biographer to draw on Proust's writings to form a picture of the man—on his correspondence, of course, but also his fictional masterpiece and the unfinished novel that preceded it, *Jean Santeuil* (published posthumously in 1952 and translated in 1955), in which there is less artistic transposition and arrangement of the facts of Proust's life through the 1890s than in the later work.

Marcel Proust was born in Paris on 10 July 1871. He was one of two sons of an eminent medical doctor, Adrien Proust, a professor at the Faculty of Medicine of the University of Paris, the author of several medical books, and a specialist in public hygiene who invented the "cordon sanitaire," or international quarantine, designed to prevent the spread of plague. He was a self-made man who came from relatively humble provincial origins described in detail by André Maurois in his *A la recherche de Marcel Proust* (1949). Adrien Proust's father was a shopkeeper in the small town of Illiers southwest of Chartres; his plans were that his son would enter the priesthood, but the young man made his way to Paris and a medical career instead. In religion Adrien Proust was a conformist, at least outwardly, but it is easier to imagine him as a typical nineteenth-century positivist, more interested in scientific discovery than in the afterworld. The narrator of *A la recherche du temps perdu* inherits this attitude toward science and religion. Like Proust, who, in real life, wrote newspaper articles in defense of the churches which were being desecrated at the time of the separation of church and state, the narrator is keenly interested in Gothic architecture and enjoys the "aubépines" (hawthorn) on the church altar at Combray but rejects belief in the afterlife. The narrator has a father but he has little to say about him. Even his profession is unknown, although he seems to have some connection with the Ministry of Foreign Affairs. The only time that the reader really senses his austere presence is in an episode to be treated below, when he tells the narrator's mother to sleep in her son's room to help him overcome his nervousness.

As for the fictional mother, it is difficult to characterize her too, except to say that she has all of the reflexes of a good bourgeoise, despises sham in others, disapproves of her son's cohabitation with his mistress in the family apartment, and wishes that her son would be more self-controlled and productive. For the son, she is always a haven of goodness and purity. Although she does not appear in the final pages of the novel, there is no reference to her death. It is as though Marcel Proust, the author, wished her to live on in his novel for eternity. Nevertheless the narrator, several times in the novel and particularly at the end when he is mentally reviewing the events of his life, blames her for his lack of willpower which began when she abdicated her responsibilities the night that he was so nervous as

a small boy. Thus blame is assessed in the novel, but there is no real resentment expressed.

The real-life situation is far more complex. The 1953 publication by Philip Kolb of *Marcel Proust: Correspondance avec sa mère* (translated as *Marcel Proust: Letters to His Mother*, 1956) shed a strange light on the relation between Proust and his mother, revealing a petulant Proust who, in his late twenties, should have been but was not behaving as a grown-up, a Proust incapable of coping with reality and continually pursued by his hovering mother. These letters, fragments of which had already been quoted by Maurois in his biography of Proust, seemed to confirm the conjectures made the year before when Bernard de Fallois pieced together for publication the fragments of a very different and much earlier version of *A la recherche du temps perdu*, the novel alluded to above and known as *Jean Santeuil*. Jean Santeuil loves his parents but, when they thwart him, he falls into violent rages. Most biographers assume that these rages are autobiographical. None has survived in *A la recherche du temps perdu*.

When Dr. Adrien Proust married Jeanne Weil on 3 September 1870, he married well, for his much younger and beautiful wife brought him a dowry of 200,000 francs and an enviable social position, since she belonged to a distinguished family. The fact that his father-in-law was a rich stockbroker was less important than the fact that his wife's uncle was a well-known statesman, minister of justice in 1848 and destined to become minister of justice again under the Third Republic. Finally elected senator for life, he was honored with "funérailles nationales" at his death in 1880. This great-uncle's wife had received many important people of the day, including Alphonse de Lamartine, Victor Hugo, George Sand, and Baron de Rothschild. The statesman bore the name Adolphe Crémieux which sounds French but, as most Frenchmen know, is Jewish. More obviously Jewish was the name of the doctor's new wife, Jeanne Weil. In 1870 Adrien Proust was probably not the least concerned that his wife was Jewish. Unlike many Jews who converted to Catholicism at the turn of the century, Mme. Proust remained faithful to her Jewish traditions, although she never imposed them on her sons. Thanks to the Weil fortune, which he inherited both from his mother and from her brother, Marcel Proust was always financially independent even though he often

photograph by Pierre Petit

Proust's parents, Dr. Adrien Proust and Madame Jeanne Weil Proust

claimed in his correspondence that he was on the verge of bankruptcy.

In *A la recherche du temps perdu,* neither parent is Jewish and thus the narrator is not either. Nevertheless, reading between the lines of the novel, Jean Recanati, in his *Profils juifs de Marcel Proust* (Marcel Proust's Jewish Profiles, 1979), discerns cases in which the narrator seems to react or is treated as though he were a Jew, a pariah in French society. For example, there is a scene in which the narrator is about to dine in a restaurant with his noble friend Saint-Loup. Momentarily separated from his friend, who is giving instructions to his coachman, the narrator is directed by the proprietor away from the section reserved for the aristocracy, into a room clearly intended for Jews (the main door leading into it is identified by the narrator as the door reserved for Hebrews); only when Saint-Loup enters and exclaims at seeing him there is he allowed to join the nobles at their table. This scene has its equivalent in the earlier *Jean Santeuil* when Jean, snubbed and insulted by Madame Marmet, an anti-

pathetic minor character, receives, at the same theater party, cordial treatment from the King of Portugal, who invites him for a private conversation. If one separates well-known facts from Recanati's conjectures, it is clear that there is no real evidence to suggest that Proust suffered from being half Jewish.

In 1896 he wrote to the minor poet Comte Robert de Montesquiou-Fezensac to explain his recent silence when Montesquiou started to discuss Jews (the conversation might have been apropos of Alfred Dreyfus, who had been sent to Devil's Island the year before). Proust's explanation: "C'est pour cette raison très simple: si je suis catholique comme mon père et mon frère, par contre, ma mère est juive" (It is for this very simple reason: if I am Catholic like my father and brother, in contrast, my mother is Jewish). From this statement one could conclude that Proust's half-Jewish background was not common knowledge. If he seems to have been reticent to discuss such matters at that time, two years later he was in the thick of things, seeking signatures for a pro-Dreyfus petition which appeared in *L'Aurore* the day after Emile Zola's *J'accuse* (I Accuse) was published there. During the various trials which ensued, young Proust was a passionate observer in the audience and recorded his experiences immediately in *Jean Santeuil*. These courtroom scenes were never transferred to *A la recherche du temps perdu*, in which the Dreyfus affair is simply part of the historical background. Whereas some characters, such as the Prince and Princesse de Guermantes, are, unlike most members of their class, strongly pro-Dreyfus (although on this matter they hide their feelings from each other), the narrator and even the Jew Charles Swann seem indifferent to the controversy. When Swann discusses with the narrator what the prince has just revealed to him, the reader gets the impression that the narrator is pro-Dreyfus, although he never says so. Although there is nothing Jewish about the narrator, not even his sympathies, the problem of Jewishness is present in the novel. Proust put the Jewish side of his heredity into two characters, Swann and Bloch. Swann, the assimilated red-haired Jew, is everything which, in his adolescence and youth, the narrator (and one could add, without hesitation, Marcel Proust) aspired to be: the elegant man-about-town who is received as an equal by the nobility. Bloch, in contrast, is the Jewish scapegoat whose *gaffes* at the reception of Madame de Villeparisis are comical but also moving because they reveal an inner struggle. Bloch's affected speech, in which he imitates the neoclassical style of the poet Leconte de Lisle, appears—much to the surprise of readers—in the early correspondence of Proust. He has caricatured himself in Bloch. He even appears anti-Semitic in his portrayal of Bloch's relatives.

Proust's younger brother, Robert, mentioned in the 1896 letter to Montesquiou, appears in a text entitled "Robert et le chevreau" (Robert and the Kid), which contains elements that Proust used elsewhere and which later became a key episode in "Combray" (the first section of the novel), in which the boy narrator bids adieu to the hawthorn bushes of which he is very fond. There is no brother in the final version of *A la recherche du temps perdu*. His absence has sometimes been construed as rejection by the author. From a psychoanalytic standpoint some have argued for sibling rivalry as the cause of Proust's neuroses and, by extension, of the neuroses of the narrator. Nevertheless, there seems to have been no overt rivalry. Proust's earliest correspondence reveals a real concern for his younger

brother, and friends speak of an enduring affection which united the two brothers. Robert Proust conformed to the bourgeois ideals of the Proust family, for he became a surgeon and as prestigious in the medical world as his father had been.

Other members of the Proust family are represented in the text, such as the maternal grandfather and an uncle who appear momentarily. Like the characters called a great aunt and the narrator's grandmother's sisters, whose models, if they existed, have never been identified, they are fleeting images rather than distinct characters. In contrast, the maternal grandmother is one of the most vivid characters in *A la recherche du temps perdu*. Biographers usually claim that Bathilde, who rushes about in the rain-soaked garden at Combray and tries to prevent her sisters from giving cognac to her husband, is closely modeled on the real Madame Nathé Weil. All that is known about Proust's grandmother is that she was well-educated and admired the seventeenth-century epistolary writer Madame de Sévigné. In the novel Bathilde has the same admiration, as does her daughter after her mother's death. One may also conjecture that Madame Weil had a hard time putting up with her husband, who must have been irascible and domineering. An early letter of Proust to his mother supports this view, as does the portrayal of the grandfather in *Jean Santeuil*. The reader of *A la recherche du temps perdu* is constantly impressed by the degree to which the narrator's affection for his grandmother seems to supplant his affection for his mother. In *Les Femmes chez Proust* (1971) Jeanine Huas maintains that this transference is a kind of revenge (belated, since Madame Proust was already dead when her son began writing his novel in earnest) because Proust's real mother had become indifferent in her later years. In any event there is incontrovertible evidence that Proust transferred two important events in his life from the real mother to the fictional grandmother. In a well-known episode in *Le Côté de Guermantes* (1920, 1921; translated in *The Guermantes Way*, 1925), the narrator, who is visiting his friend Robert de Saint-Loup in the imaginary town of Doncières, telephones his grandmother, whereas in *Jean Santeuil* it is the mother to whom the hero speaks by phone. The later version of this event is a masterpiece of subtlety, humor, and pathos. Although such a call would seem routine today, the narrator stresses that telephones were still unusual at that time; he has never before heard his grandmother's voice except in her presence. The difference is tremendous; all the tenderness of her love comes through strikingly when the operators, whom Proust calls Danaids of the Invisible, finally make the connection. (Like other episodes, involving automobiles and airplanes, the telephone exchange is a case where Proust re-creates for his readers the charm and wonder of modern inventions, then in their infancy.) Similarly, the episodes in which the narrator's grandmother becomes ill and dies are really based on the death of Proust's *mother*. He even incorporates into the text some of the quotations from Madame de Sévigné and other classical authors which, biographical evidence shows, Madame Proust pronounced during her last illness; however, the Molièresque doctors were a later embellishment, entirely invented. In the final volume of *A la recherche du temps perdu*, reviewing his life, the narrator again expresses his guilt at causing his grandmother's death because of his lack of will power. According to Huas, Madame Proust accepted and abetted his lack of will power to keep him unto herself. Be that as it may, if Proust still felt guilt in his later years, it was for another reason.

There is no doubt that Proust's real guilt feeling was for being a homosexual. Huas expresses the generally accepted view that his mother was a frigid woman uninformed about sex, indifferent to it and her husband's occasional infidelities. A different opinion is that expressed by Henri Bonnet in his *Les Amours et la sexualité de Marcel Proust* (1985). Bonnet places great credence in Maurice Duplay's statement, in his *Mon Ami Marcel Proust* (1972), that "Madame Proust connaissait les moeurs de son fils" (Madame Proust knew about her son's mores). In Proust's correspondence there are letters, written clandestinely during classroom recitations, which reveal that he was making discreet homosexual advances to his fellow *lycéens* but was being repulsed. The result was the ostracism and bullying described, but without explanation, in *Jean Santeuil*. There is also extensive correspondence with Reynaldo Hahn, the model for Henri de Réveillon in *Jean Santeuil*, giving evidence of a deep affection if nothing more. Later, as the correspondence reveals, Proust transferred his affection to Prince Antoine Bibesco and then to a dashing young noble and diplomat, Bertrand de Fénelon, whom he met in 1901. Particularly during a trip to Holland in 1902 he suffered intensely because of his inability to communicate with Fénelon on an emotional level, little suspecting that the latter was "bimetallic," to use their

Proust circa 1885 (photograph by Nadar)

term, that is to say, bisexual. When Proust learned later about Fénelon, he transformed his fictional counterpart, Robert de Saint-Loup, into a homosexual at the end of *A la recherche du temps perdu*. Fénelon, unintentionally, taught Proust all that he needed to know about unrequited love and jealousy. During these years when several friendships between him and other young men were established and then dissolved, Proust sought to hide his conduct from public view. In 1897 the journalist Jean Lorrain, himself a notorious homosexual, reviewed Proust's first published book and insinuated that Anatole France had prefaced the book through favoritism, and went on to suggest that his next volume would be prefaced by Alphonse Daudet, thanks to the influence of his son Lucien Daudet. To the readers of *Le Journal*, where Lorrain's review appeared, this was patently a reference to a homosexual relationship between Proust and his friend, the effeminate Lucien. Proust felt obliged to defend his honor and fought an inconclusive duel with Lorrain.

In his biography of Proust Maurois revealed for the first time the extent of Proust's homosexuality and insisted that Proust's claim to have loved young women from time to time, particularly Jeanne Pouquet when she was the fiancée of his friend Gaston de Caillavet, was a smokescreen. Maurois seems to have been a reliable source because he was married to the Caillavets' daughter Simone (who is the model for the daughter of Gilberte de Saint-Loup at the end of Proust's novel). In his monumental two-volume biography, *Marcel Proust* (1959, 1965), George D. Painter presents a "bimetallic" Proust, who, around the turn of the century, might have had heterosexual affairs with Laure Hayman and Louisa de Mornand, one a courtesan, the other an actress. When, as an invalid spending most of his time in bed during the second decade of the century, Proust was writing the second part of his masterpiece, *A l'ombre des jeunes filles en fleurs* (1919; translated as *Within a Budding Grove*, 1924), his sexual and emotional life reached a low ebb. Before the First World War he did get emotionally involved with a man named Alfred Agostinelli, who was killed in an airplane crash in 1914. After this relationship Proust patronized the homosexual brothel of Albert Le Cuziat (who in some respects is reflected in the fictional character Jupien), to which he gave some of the family furniture. In her *Monsieur Proust* (1973), Céleste Albaret, Proust's "gouvernante" (governess or housekeeper), maintained that Proust went to the brothel only for documentation of the final scene of the degradation of the fictional Baron de Charlus. But Bonnet has convincingly proved that Albaret was wrong by quoting from the unpublished notebooks of Marcel Jouhandeau. Jouhandeau's reports confirm those of Maurice Sachs in *Le Sabbat* (The Sabbath, 1946) concerning Proust's homosexual and sadistic activities in male brothels.

In *A la recherche du temps perdu* the narrator gradually discovers homosexuality in others and, like Swann with Odette, suffers from the belief that his mistress is a lesbian, but he is never in any way implicated himself. In fact, to the extent that the author's point of view, as distinct from that of the narrator, is present in the novel, one can say that, in spite of the eloquent plea for homosexuality in the opening pages of *Sodome et Gomorrhe*, one of the sections of *A la recherche du temps perdu* (published in 1921 and 1922), homosexuality is not presented in a favorable light. The homosexual Baron de Charlus is a kind of

modern Lear who, once the arbiter of the high society which the narrator hopes to penetrate, becomes in the end a social outcast and a complete degenerate.

One experience which the narrator has in common with Proust is that of his illness. Proust was born in his great-uncle's house at 96 rue de Lafontaine in the Auteuil section of Paris. His mother had been sent there by Dr. Proust, who had narrowly escaped death from a stray bullet during the Commune (the popular uprising during the siege of Paris by the Prussians) and who thought that bucolic Auteuil was safer than the center of the city. Proust was not a healthy child, perhaps because of his mother's anxiety. The narrator of Proust's novel falls ill at the age of fifteen and cannot make a projected trip to Venice and Florence. When, a little later, he is unable to go to the Champs-Elysées to meet Gilberte Swann, the girl with whom he falls in love as an adolescent (and who is the daughter of Charles Swann and Odette, his sometime mistress, later wife), he describes the symptoms in detail and explains that he has had asthma for some time. His illness stays with him throughout the novel, and he is frequently the object of solicitude and special care on the part of Saint-Loup. In *La Prisonnière* (1923; translated as *The Captive*, 1929), during his cohabitation with Albertine, the young woman he has brought to his house, illness often prevents him from going places with her. Near the end of the novel, during a great blank in the narrative, he spends "beaucoup d'années" in a sanatorium before making a final appearance at an afternoon reception of the Princesse de Guermantes.

Proust was even more prone to illness than his narrator. His first asthma attack occurred when he was nine, and his attendance at school was intermittent, especially in his early years. The only period of his life when he was relatively healthy was during his military service, which he began at the age of eighteen, but even then his commanding officer asked him to get a room in town because his asthma kept other soldiers awake. Gradually his daily schedule became so maladjusted that he slept most of the day and got up only at night. In 1905, after his mother's death, he read what the psychiatrists had to say about asthma and, following what he was sure were her wishes for his welfare, put himself in Dr. Sollier's sanatorium at Boulogne-sur-Seine from which he emerged after a few weeks, not cured but convinced that there was no cure.

Proust during his military service at Orléans, 1889-1890

Although there were afterwards to be many occasions on which Proust went to parties and dinners, even the theater, and also took short vacation trips, for the remainder of his life he was essentially a sick man. There were periods in which he reentered society, notably in 1917 and on isolated occasions when he emerged to observe reality or visit Le Cuziat's establishment, but for most of his last twelve or fifteen years he lived as an invalid. The ill health caused by asthma was compounded by his use of pharmaceutical products and by an undeniable psychosomatic element. In 1910 he decided that his bedroom in the apartment of Boulevard Haussmann to which he had moved late in 1906 should be insulated against sound, to which his

nerves had always been especially susceptible; thus came into being his famous cork-lined room, in which he lived until 1919 when the building was sold and he was obliged to move. Ultimately the neglect of his body, undernourishment, and large doses of coffee to keep himself awake were to kill him while Dr. Robert Proust looked on helplessly.

In retrospect at least the happy periods of Proust's life were limited to childhood. That is why in his novel he was so anxious to re-create the enchanted world of Combray. His few earliest readers immediately savored this enchantment when they read *Du côté de chez Swann*. Painter goes into elaborate detail to explain how this fictional town resembles the Illiers of Marcel Proust even though Proust has altered the geography and drawn on several churches to compose the one in Combray because the original was uninteresting.

The narrator's family circle, which Proust portrays at Combray, is, moreover, not a portrait of those relatives who really lived there, but rather a composite of family members and acquaintances from Paris. For instance, his maternal grandmother Weil did not visit Illiers, so that placing the narrator's maternal grandmother in the garden there is taking liberty with fact; similarly, Charles Haas, the elegant Paris clubman whom Proust took as the chief model for his character Charles Swann—although his acquaintance with him was very limited, if indeed it existed at all—had no relations in Illiers, although his fictional counterpart visits the narrator's family there. It was important, in fact, for Proust to establish connections at Combray between the narrator's family and Swann. For, since the latter serves as a forerunner of the narrator, a favorable model in some ways (he is an aesthete and a man of great taste) and an initiator, whose experiences with women, especially Odette de Crécy, heroine of the section of *Du côté de chez Swann* which is called "Un Amour de Swann" ("Swann in Love"), foreshadow those of the narrator later, he needs to be visible during the narrator's formative years. He is even connected to one of the two most crucial experiences of the narrator recounted in "Combray," the episode called the "drame du coucher" (good-night drama). In this episode Swann's presence at a family dinner is the obstacle that prevents the narrator, then a child, from receiving the customary good-night kiss from his mother. The anxiety he feels at being deprived of this "viatique" (viaticum), as he calls it, is such that he resolves to stay up and greet his mother when the guest departs. (The garden by which Swann arrives and departs is modeled not on that of the Illiers house but on Proust's great-uncle's house at Auteuil.) Swann is thus associated with anxiety and with the subsequent awful drama when the boy accosts his mother, who tries to scold him, but is prevented by the father, who suggests that, counter to her program of discipline for the boy, she go spend the night with the child. This episode is the source of the remorse that runs throughout the novel, as a psychological motivation and a theme.

The enchantment of childhood lingers on in the final segment of *Du côté de chez Swann*, "Noms de pays: le nom" (Place Names: the Name), when the adolescent narrator falls in love with Gilberte Swann and then gradually discovers that the love is only in his mind and is not reciprocated. Of the model for Gilberte, Proust once said to Céleste Albaret: "J'étais fou d'elle" (I was crazy about her). Marie de Bénardaky was dark-haired, not red-headed like Gilberte, and was the daughter of a wealthy Polish nobleman whose wife, according to Albaret, "avait la réputation d'aimer trop les aventures au champagne" (had the reputation of liking too well adventures flavored with champagne), which identifies her with Odette de Crécy, the mother of Gilberte Swann. It is not known what really happened between Proust and Marie de Bénardaky, and one may assume that the sexual episode in the bushes recounted in the novel was invented. It is unlikely that the Prousts approved of this playmate, but there is no indication that they were stern with their son, as were the parents of Jean Santeuil when they prevented him from seeing Marie Kossichef.

If the narrator's childhood and youth are composed of fragments of Proust's own experience, there is one enormous lacuna, the narrator's education. He alludes to attending *collège* or secondary school, but gives no details. Such details abound in *Jean Santeuil*, with Monsieur Beulier standing in for Proust's philosophy professor Alphonse Darlu. It is therefore difficult to understand why the narrator of *A la recherche du temps perdu* appears to be so uneducated (in truth, like Proust in real life, he dazzles his interlocutors with his knowledge and insights). Proust's education began at the age of nine in the Cours Pape-Carpentier, and two years later he entered the Lycée Fontanes (which soon changed its name to Lycée Condorcet). In the be-

ginning Proust's academic record was dismal because of his frequent absences but, when he was in "rhétorique"–the last two years of the lycée–it improved significantly under the influence of Darlu. In 1889 he received his bachelor's diploma and began his military service at Orléans. At this time normal military service was supposed to last five years, although it seldom did, so that it was advantageous, if one belonged to the right social class, to enroll in an officer-training program lasting only one year. Because those programs were about to be abolished, Proust enlisted in haste; when his time was up he would willingly have stayed on except that the officers were tired of this unmilitary creature at the bottom of his class. Although the narrator of *A la recherche du temps perdu* never serves in the army, it is obvious that his military experience enables the author to write the chapter on Doncières when the narrator visits Saint-Loup, who seems to be in an officer-training program, although a more advanced one than that in which Proust had been engaged. Back in Paris, which he had hardly left because he returned there every weekend to lead his social life, Proust was confronted with paternal pressure to plan a career. He enrolled simultaneously in the Faculty of Law of the University of Paris and in the independent Ecole Libre des Sciences Politiques. After two years, in 1892 he was doing well at "Sciences Po" but was failing in law. The next year, however, he obtained a *licence en droit*. A year later he received a *licence ès lettres* at the Sorbonne, his parents having sanctioned literary and philosophical studies at last. In September of the same year he wrote to his father that he was willing to prepare for the "concours des affaires étrangères ou celui de l'Ecole des Chartes" (competition for foreign service or the one for the School of Manuscript Research). He never prepared for either but, in 1895, entered the *concours* for an unpaid librarianship and, having succeeded, was appointed to the Bibliothèque Mazarine, the library of the Institut de France. He seldom performed his duties, annually asked for leave on the pretext of bad health, and was finally dismissed in 1900.

Proust's real interest during all of this time was society. It began when, at the age of seventeen, he invited his lycée friend Jacques Bizet and Bizet's mother, Madame Emile Straus, to share his box at the Odéon theater. Madame Straus was Jewish, although her first husband, the composer Jacques Bizet, was not. After his death she had married one of the wealthiest men in Paris.

She was beautiful and witty (her wit is reflected in the character of the Duchesse de Guermantes). It has often been said that Proust entered Jewish society before penetrating the nobility. Did not many of his friends bear Jewish names such as Robert Dreyfus, Reynaldo Hahn, Daniel Halévy, Léon Brunschvicg? In truth, there was no such thing as Jewish society. Madame Straus kept one of the leading salons of Paris, receiving important figures from all quarters, including writers, artists, and the nobility. In 1892 Proust met the Napoleonic Princesse Mathilde, whom he later depicted under her real name in his novel, but he was not yet frequenting the legitimate nobility of the so-called Faubourg Saint-Germain. (The distinction between the two nobilities is the subject of a long discussion in *A la recherche du temps perdu* when the narrator meets at Doncières the Prince de Borodino, an invented character modeled on a descendant of Napoleon whom Proust met during his military service in 1889.)

In 1889 Proust had met Madame Albert Arman de Caillavet, who was not noble in spite of the form of her name, her husband having misappropriated the de Caillavet from his country estate; she had been born Léontine Lippmann. The centerpiece of her salon was her lover, none other than Anatole France, who in Proust's novel is portrayed in part as the writer Bergotte and in part as the diplomat Norpois. Madame Arman's salon was so exclusive that Robert de Montesquiou had great difficulty getting invited. The latter was of particular interest to Proust because he knew all of the leading poets from Mallarmé on down but more especially because he was related to most of the great noble families of France. Proust's long correspondence with Montesquiou records a campaign of flattery, followed by misunderstandings and reconciliations because of the count's overbearing pride and tendency to be easily offended. Proust immortalized him by making him the Baron de Charlus.

Just as the narrator wanted Charlus to introduce him to the Duchesse de Guermantes or to her sister-in-law, the Princesse de Guermantes, Proust hoped that Montesquiou would get him an entrée into the exclusive milieu of the Comtesse Greffulhe or the Comtesse de Chevigné, reputed to be the most beautiful and elegant ladies of Paris. Since Montesquiou did not cooperate, Proust tried it on his own, for these ladies could be seen in the salons which he frequented, and, with Madame Chevigné, he even went through the hat-doffing procedure on the

Avenue de Marigny in which he has his narrator engage. Unlike the narrator who becomes a favorite of the Duchesse de Guermantes, Proust was never really intimate with these ladies and was annoyed much later when Madame de Chevigné was not flattered to have been portrayed in his novel. Members of the nobility have written articles to prove that Proust did not really know their social class. The truth is that Proust invented his Faubourg Saint-Germain, which never existed in the glorified and exclusive form in which he represents it. This is part of Proust's romanticism. However, he did become intimate with a group of young nobles in the last period of his social life. In 1901 he met Comte Gabriel de la Rochefoucauld and gradually added to his list of acquaintances Salignac-Fénelon, Duc Armand de Guise, Prince Léon Radziwill, Marquis Louis d'Albuféra, and other aristocrats.

In *Le Côté de Guermantes*, the narrator, then a young man, finds among his papers a childhood essay on the steeples of Martinville, which in "Combray" he had quoted in full. He decides to send it, revised, to the *Figaro*. Some 1,300 pages later, in the sixth part of the novel, the narrator opens his paper and finds it published, finally. Except for this one publication, the narrator does not seem to be an active writer, although at one point he does say that he made a mistake by imitating Bergotte and, when he is in Venice, he alludes to his translation of Ruskin (a task Proust took on shortly before Ruskin's death in 1900). By contrast, Proust's career as a writer began very early. Being a student in so intellectual a lycée as Condorcet produced immediate results in the form of writings for ephemeral literary periodicals, in this case, the *Revue Verte*, founded by Daniel Halévy and Jacques Bizet, and, on its demise, the *Revue Lilas*. There has been speculation that the narrator's childhood essay in "Combray," mentioned above, on "Les Clochers de Martinville" (The Steeples of Martinville) was based on a contribution by Proust to the *Revue Lilas*, but it seems more likely to have had its origin in Proust's description of the steeples of Caen, written in October 1907 and published the following month in the *Figaro*. (Some fragments of Proust's earliest publications have survived and have been republished in the 1971 Pléiade edition devoted mainly to *Contre Sainte-Beuve*.)

After leaving the lycée, from March 1892 to March 1893, while the magazine lasted, Proust was a contributor to *Le Banquet*, founded by the

Proust at twenty-one

same group of would-be authors. By this time Proust was composing book reviews and other texts of various lengths, not only for *Le Banquet* but also for other periodicals and even for the newspaper *Le Gaulois*. With the disappearance of their periodical, the *Banquet* group began to have material published in *La Revue Blanche*, a higher class avant-garde publication having works by Gide, Barrès, Verlaine, Mallarmé, and Heredia in its table of contents. Proust was for a time secretary of the Académie Canaque (the Cannibal Academy), a mock French Academy, established by the three daughters of Heredia to parody their father's attempts to be elected to the Académie Française. Proust's best known contribution to *La Revue Blanche* was an article "Contre l'obscurité" (Against Obscurity), a criticism of the reigning symbolist school and, by implication, of Mallarmé, for whom he later showed more respect in *A la recherche du temps perdu*. To *Le Banquet*, *La Revue Blanche*, and finally to *La Revue Hebdomadaire*, which even paid its authors, Proust contributed sketches and short stories, collected in 1896 in a deluxe volume entitled *Les Plaisirs et les jours* (translated as *Pleasures and Regrets*, 1948). Adorned by pictures of flowers by Madame

Madeleine Lemaire, who, combined with Madame Arman de Caillavet, was the model for the unforgettable Madame Verdurin in *A la recherche du temps perdu,* this volume became in 1897 the butt of sarcasm from two of Proust's literary associates, Robert Dreyfus and Jacques Bizet, in a dramatic skit, "Les Lauriers sont coupés" (The Laurel Trees Have Been Cut); in this amateur production at Bizet's house, they poked fun at the exorbitant price of the volume and at its snobbism.

From the apparently reluctant Anatole France, Madame Arman had managed to get a preface. France called Proust "notre jeune ami," a depraved Bernardin de Saint-Pierre and an ingenuous Petronius—in other words, a decadent. Proust would not have objected to the label, for he once applied it to himself in early correspondence. This term immediately calls to mind Joris Karl Huysmans's *A Rebours* (*Against the Grain,* 1884), in which the noble Des Esseintes, ever in search of the rare and perverse sensory experience, lives with a turtle encrusted with gems, and for long years closes himself off from the world in his eccentric abode. It was notorious that the original for Des Esseintes was Proust's friend Montesquiou. Although *Les Plaisirs et les jours* is not the epitome of decadence that Huysmans's book is, epithets such as "depraved" and "ingenuous" do apply. Proust's characters dwell usually in "Illyria," although occasionally they return to Parisian society, and they bear names like Baldassare or Cydalise. Although sometimes affected, the style is pure Francian, that is to say, simple sentences occasionally distinguished by rare words or images, the antithesis of Proust's mature style, which is syntactically complicated with far-reaching metaphors. Unread in its day, Proust's first book is very meaningful today in the light of *A la recherche du temps perdu*.

Biographers discover in "Cires perdues" (Lost Waxes) a description of Madame de Chevigné, whose birdlike appearance resembles that of the Duchesse de Guermantes; in "Sonate clair de lune" (Moonlight Sonata), a tribute to Proust's flirtation with (some say love for) Marie Finaly when he was a visitor at Les Frémonts, the Norman estate of Madame Laure Baignères on the Channel coast; and in "Critique de l'espérance à la lumière de l'amour" (Criticism of Hope in the Light of Love) the echoes of a disagreement with Reynaldo Hahn. Many sketches are prose poems on nature; others are character portraits in the manner of the seventeenth-century moralist La Bruyère. Technically the best

Proust with his mother, Jeanne Weil Proust, and his brother, Robert, circa 1896

short story, but the least important for future reference, is "La Mort de Baldassare Silvande, vicomte de Sylvanie" (The Death of Baldassare Silvande, Viscount of Sylvania), with which the volume opens. Seen first through the eyes of his small nephew, who fears to talk to his uncle known to be dying of something incurable, Baldassare goes on living an egocentric life with occasional love affairs and then seems to will his own death.

Much more important for the future are the numerous fictions in which Proust insists that love is subjective. Various characters, such as the Vicomtesse de Styrie in "Violante et la mondanité" (Violante and Mundanity), are tempted by unattractive individuals whose inferiority they immediately recognize and then live out their lives regretting that they did not succumb. In "Rêve" (Dream) a narrator finds Dorothy B. to be "sans charme et sans esprit" (without charm or intelligence) but his imagination goes to work in a kind of dream and for a short time he loves her. Caught up in the laws of habit,

a frequent theme in these sketches, love is not durable. In "Source des larmes qui sont dans les amours passées" (Source of Tears Which Are in Past Loves), Proust writes: "Nous savons qu'un jour celle de la pensée de qui nous vivons nous sera aussi indifférente que nous le sont maintenant toutes les autres qu'elle" (We know that someday she, on the thought of whom we live, will be as indifferent for us as are now all the others but her). More durable than love is jealously, as in "La Fin de la jalousie" (The End of Jealousy), the last piece in the volume. Honoré's unreasonable jealousy of Françoise survives his love for her and ends only with his death. One story, "La Confession d'une jeune fille" (A Girl's Confession), has fascinated biographers because it seems to be a blatant case of transposition of the sexes (as is "Critique de l'espérance à la lumière de l'amour") and an admission of Proust's guilt vis-à-vis his mother. Dying of a self-inflicted bullet wound, the young girl confesses to an interlocutor that she caused her mother's death when her mother accidentally spied on her while she was having intercourse with a former seducer who had reappeared on the eve of the girl's marriage. Proust omitted from *Les Plaisirs et les jours* another previously published story, "Avant la nuit" (Before Night), which is a preview of the major plot of *A la recherche du temps perdu*. In this story the heroine, also dying of a self-inflicted bullet wound, confesses to her masculine lover that she has killed herself from remorse at being a lesbian. The reason for the omission is obvious: apart from any moral considerations, two self-inflicted bullets were too much in one short volume.

No sooner was *Les Plaisirs et les jours* in press than Proust started to write another work, as letters to his mother and Reynaldo Hahn prove. Proust scholars originally did not attach any importance to what are vague allusions in the correspondence, and therefore the literary world was startled when, in 1952, Gallimard published the three-volume novel by Marcel Proust entitled *Jean Santeuil*. Despite its length (715 pages in the current Pléiade edition), Proust never finished the novel; nor did he intend to have it published in the form in which it appeared. It is composed of innumerable manuscript fragments pieced together by Bernard de Fallois, who first tried unsuccessfully to discover their inner coherence and then imposed his own order. Absorbed by his social life and beset by illness after he finished *Les Plaisirs et les jours*, Proust lacked the will power to create. Lacking even more was an understanding of what he was attempting to do. In 1899, discouraged by the very size of his incoherent manuscript, he abandoned his novel. In 1902 he added three more scenes to his novel, this time changing the name of one of his main characters from Henri de Réveillon to Bertrand de Réveillon in honor of Bertrand de Fénelon. Then he put his manuscript aside and used only memory to recall what he later wished to include in *A la recherche du temps perdu*.

The reader of *A la recherche du temps perdu*, when he goes back to *Jean Santeuil*, has continually a sensation of déjà vu. Illiers, appearing usually under its real name but occasionally called Eteuilles, is obviously an earlier version of Combray. Rejecting totally the earlier Fallois version, the editors of the Pléiade edition have redeciphered the fragments and rearranged them according to the apparent chronological age of the hero. The early episodes include scenes such as the mother's abdication (a foreshadowing of the *drame du coucher*), games with Marie Kossichef in the Champs-Elysées, and then life at Illiers, where the character who appears most frequently is a paternal uncle, vanished from *A la recherche du temps perdu*. Then Jean becomes friends with his lycée comrade, Henri de Réveillon, whom biographers identify with Reynaldo Hahn primarily because Proust and Hahn were guests at the eighteenth-century château of Réveillon belonging to Madame Madeleine Lemaire, the illustrator of *Les Plaisirs et les jours*. For psychoanalytic critics Henri de Réveillon is the brother figure, like Saint-Loup in the later novel. Henri is antithetical, stupid as a student but dazzling as a young man, a musician like Hahn (who was already a fine composer) but a candidate for the Ecole Polytechnique. When Henri takes his friend home to the family castle, where "Saint Louis avant de quitter Paris avait dit adieu à Geffroy II duc d'Aquitaine et de Réveillon" (Saint Louis before leaving Paris had taken leave of Geoffrey II, Duke of Aquitania and Réveillon), the duke and duchess immediately recognize the otherwise undemonstrated genius of Jean Santeuil and become his surrogate parents. By them Jean is twice saved, once (as noted) in the King of Portugal episode and once when the duke himself serves as Jean's second in a duel resulting from a false accusation of cheating at cards. Such episodes are extremely naive and even more naive is the portrait of the nobility, for it is hard for any reader of *A la recherche du temps perdu* to imagine the same

woman who served as the model for Madame Verdurin transformed into a duchess. Perhaps this bourgeois-like homelife of the Réveillons is a more accurate picture of the nobility in 1900, but it does not correspond to one's idea of that class after one has read the later novel.

Naive also is Proust's approach to the problem of the novel at this time. To give some initial form to his novel he employs the timeworn device of the "bouteille à la mer"–the bottle cast into the sea. In the preface a narrator and his friend at Beg Meil in Britanny meet a writer, "C.," who later dies and leaves them a manuscript, which is the novel that follows. Beg Meil is where Proust and Hahn, on vacation, introduced themselves to the American painter Thomas Alexander Harrison. This meeting with Harrison is the model for the meeting with the writer C. in *Jean Santeuil*, although C. himself is modeled chiefly on Maupassant, whom Proust knew in literary salons, in the late 1880s. Later, Harrison appears in *A la recherche du temps perdu* as the painter Elstir, whom the narrator and Saint-Loup meet under the same circumstances. In the course of describing the character and habits of C., the narrator defines the writer's aesthetic principles. C. is struggling with the problem of realism and has decided to write "des histoires rigoureusement vraies" (stories rigorously true). Not only must the minor characters be taken from reality but the principal character, according to C., must also be autobiographical. *Jean Santeuil*, however, ignores one essential ingredient of the traditional realistic novel: plot. Proust himself described the novel thus: "Ce livre n'a jamais été fait, il a été récolté" (This book was never made: it was harvested). When, from 1908 onwards, Proust wrote and organized the material that became *A la recherche du temps perdu*, he initially had similar difficulties with plot and structure.

As for the other ingredient of the realistic novel, character analysis, Proust knows the principles but usually follows Maupassant rather than Flaubert. His minor characters are usually presented in vignettes of linear development, their life stories being related as one unit somewhat in the manner of a Maupassant short story. In the case of Jean Santeuil and his parents, Proust seems to think that he has constructed characters since repeated apostrophes call upon the gentle reader to observe the technical progress that he has made but, as characters, the Santeuils, as well as the Réveillons, are miserable failures. Two di-

Proust at Evian, 1905 (Hôtel Splendide)

gressive forces are at work in Proust's prose to disrupt whatever inclination he has to write in the linear manner of the realists. The first is a desire to be lyrical, as is manifest in the descriptions of Illiers, where hawthorns and a camellia are more important than characters, or in the descriptions of the storm at Beg Meil. The second is a predilection for philosophical generalizations. The narrator says of C. in the preface: "Souvent son récit était interrompu par quelques réflexions où l'auteur exprime son opinion sur certaines choses, à la manière de certains romanciers anglais qu'il avait autrefois aimés. Ces réflexions, souvent très ennuyeuses pour le lecteur pour qui elles coupent l'intérêt et ôtent l'illusion de la vie, étaient ce que nous écoutions avec le plus grand plaisir . . . " (Often his account was interrupted by some reflections in which the author expresses his opinion concerning certain things, in the manner of certain English novelists that he had once

loved. These reflections, often very boring for the reader who loses interest and for whom the illusion of life is destroyed, were what we listened to with the greatest pleasure . . .). Scarcely, in *Jean Santeuil*, has Proust begun what promises to be a linear narrative than he digresses in a long generalization in which an editorial *nous* implicates the reader. His extremely long paragraphs already have the density of his mature style. The various stages of the extant manuscripts of *A la recherche du temps perdu* show that this complexity was often increased by further insertions, but the spontaneously written and seldom-corrected manuscript of *Jean Santeuil* shows that such complexity was natural in his thought processes.

Jean Santeuil does show development—progress in Proust's wisdom, in his style, and in his character presentation as he describes historical characters such as General Raoul-François de Boisdeffre and Colonel Georges Picquart (to whom, incidentally, when the colonel was a prisoner at Mont Valérien, Proust sent a copy of *Les Plaisirs et les jours*) during the Dreyfus trials. Similarly, when he recounts the affair of the Gisors sugar factories–a scandal based on the Panama scandal (which arose in the mid-1880s from a plan to build a canal, and in which Ferdinand Marie de Lesseps was convicted of fraud in 1893)– Proust reveals his ability to create character; the same is true for scenes in which Jean and Henri mingle with military officers at Provins (scenes that prefigure similar ones in the imaginary town of Doncières in *A la recherche du temps perdu*).

The penultimate section of the novel, entitled by the editors "De l'amour" (Concerning Love), assembles many unrelated texts recounting mainly Jean's love affairs after he has grown up. Back in the days of Réveillon, he had had a mysterious sexual encounter with a young lady who slipped into his bed. Now he has many encounters, usually with a woman named Françoise, but it is never quite clear whether that name always designates the same person. "De l'amour" begins with a discussion of Stendhal's essay by the same title but omits his theory of crystallization. The latter, which Proust knew well and which seems to have influenced his own theory of love, was an attempt by Stendhal to explain the psychological process of falling in love, in which he identified several stages. The most important of these is when, on a small kernel or crystal of inclination or predisposition that already exists, other feelings "crystallize," creating a complex of favorable feelings, that act like a magnet and to which each subsequent experience with the loved one adds additional force. The presence of an obstacle between oneself and the object is often a crucial factor. It is a process of self-persuasion, based on a small fact such as the color of a woman's eyes, or a phrase she said, but it ultimately has far more mental reality than reality in fact, and thus is impervious to exterior influences, until one begins to "decrystallize" or fall out of love.

This clearly supports Proust's views on the subjectivity of love, which, before illustrating masterfully in *A la recherche du temps perdu*, he demonstrates in an episode in *Jean Santeuil* where Jean is in love with Madame S. In a fit of jealousy Jean tries to surprise his mistress at home one night but taps on the wrong window; trying again in the daytime, he suspects that she is receiving another lover at that very hour. She later explains by letter why she did not open the door

for him. All these details are found in crucial episodes of "Un Amour de Swann," where Odette betrays Swann with his rival Forcheville and then explains that it was her "uncle."

In another episode readers of *A la recherche du temps perdu* will be surprised to discover a scene between Jean and Françoise which presages the one between Swann and Odette and later a similar one between the narrator and Albertine when he tries to get her to confess that she is a lesbian. When Jean is finally forgetting his unhappy love, it revives under the stimulus of a sonata of Camille Saint-Saëns, a fact which supports the view–disputed in the early days of Proust criticism–that the chief model for the sonata by Vinteuil–an invented character in *A la recherche du temps perdu*, whose music is often discussed and described and plays a role in the love affair of Charles Swann and Odette–is indeed music by Saint-Saëns. Jean's love revives one final time in a dream. These episodes and features show that Proust was, when he composed *Jean Santeuil*, already in possession of most of the plot elements for *A la recherche du temps perdu*, from the "bille d'agate" (agate marble), once belonging to Marie Kossichef, which Jean gives to his mistress, to the game of "furet" (ferret, or catch the ring on the string), which the narrator of the later work plays with Albertine. Monsieur de Lamperolles is the forerunner of Proust's later creation Charlus. Buried in these fragments are episodes of involuntary memory. Without knowing it, Proust already had the solution to his aesthetic problem: how to construct a novel.

In 1899 (the year that Dreyfus received a presidential pardon) Proust became even more enthusiastic about his discovery, made earlier in the decade through translated excerpts, of a kindred soul, the British aesthetician John Ruskin, who seemed to write in the same complicated sentences as Proust tried to use in capturing the impressions and experiences furnished by art and nature. By December 1899 he was engaged in translating some of *La Bible d'Amiens*. In 1900, when Ruskin died, Proust published an obituary article on him, followed by a longer piece that appeared in the *Figaro*, and later by a two-part essay "John Ruskin" in the *Gazette des Beaux-Arts*. He made several journeys to places such as Rouen and Venice, in order to see firsthand what his English predecessor had written about, and continued working on his translations with the help of his mother, who knew English much better than he did, at least at the outset, and of

Proust in Venice, where he worked on his translation of John Ruskin's The Bible of Amiens *published in 1904*

Reynaldo Hahn's British cousin, Marie Nordlinger. It matters little that one of the earliest scholarly articles on Proust two decades later pointed out minor flaws in his translation of *La Bible d'Amiens*, published in 1904 by Mercure de France: Proust's rendering was considered an outstanding literary achievement. In spite of his admiration for Ruskin, Proust, in articles and in his preface to *La Bible d'Amiens*, objected to the British writer's idolatry of works of art and to his moralizing.

Proust continued to translate Ruskin, turning to *Sesame and Lilies*, of which he translated the first part, "Of Kings' Treasuries" (an essay on reading), and then the second, "Of Queens' Gardens," but never the third.

Proust had not yet finished *Sésame et les lys* when the most dramatic event in his life occurred. On 26 September 1905, his mother died. The death of his father two years earlier had not produced the same shock. Despite his depression he was able to continue producing articles, of particular note one on Ruskin's subject of reading. "Sur la lecture" (On Reading), published first in *La Renaissance Latine* and then as the preface to *Sésame et les lys*, is a remarkable example of Proustian style. In unbroken paragraphs that go on for several pages and in melodious language that permits the uninterrupted flow of ideas and images, Proust evokes his own childhood memories. At one point in the history of Proust criticism, scholars regarded this essay as the turning point in his aesthetic development, and they attributed this new departure to the influence of Ruskin. Of course, the publication of *Jean Santeuil* proves that they were wrong; much of his aesthetic had already crystallized. After publication in periodicals, *Sésame et les lys* appeared in volume form in June 1906.

One of the debts which Proust felt he owed his mother was to write a great work of literature. In 1908 he started all over again. As Philip Kolb, editor of the *Correspondance de Marcel Proust* (1970-), pointed out in a 1958 article in the *Mercure de France,* Maurois was wrong in his conjectures that Proust started writing *A la recherche du temps perdu* three years earlier. The proof of the correct date is in a letter written "slightly before January 8, 1908," in which Proust is seeking information to compose "Robert et le chevreau," the first episode on Proust's agenda of "feuilles écrites" (pages written), quoted by Bernard de Fallois in his edition of *Contre Sainte-Beuve* and republished in Kolb's edition of *Le Carnet de 1908* (1976).

Momentarily Proust's energies were channeled in another direction. He began to have published in the *Figaro* a series of successful pastiches with, as his subject, the "affaire Lemoine," a celebrated hoax, just then coming to a conclusion, in which Henry Lemoine deceived even the international De Beer company into believing that he could make diamonds. Each pastiche was written in the style of a well-known author: Balzac, Flaubert, Sainte-Beuve, and others. As well as amusing sophisticated readers, this exercise increased Proust's own perception of stylistic problems. Some critics of Proust have said that the pastiches were the real new departure, that imitating the style of others gave Proust the desire to develop his own style.

Proust was still hesitating, however. His correspondence over this period reveals that he was planning an essay on Sainte-Beuve which he apparently never finished or at least never had published. Although his novel and his essay were scarcely started, the correspondence of the period records his attempts to find a publisher for both and eventually Proust refers to the "roman de Sainte-Beuve" (the Sainte-Beuve novel) as though essay and novel were one and the same. In 1954 Bernard de Fallois discovered and edited for publication *Contre Sainte-Beuve, suivi de Nouveaux Mélanges.* This volume included some preliminary sketches for the essay on Sainte-Beuve as well as a number of "avant-textes" (pre-texts) of *A la recherche du temps perdu* which he claimed were part of the essay but which were really manufactured by him from the notebooks for the novel. On this misleading evidence Proust critics constructed elaborate theories of how Proust's masterpiece grew out of *Contre Sainte-Beuve.*

When *Contre Sainte-Beuve* was republished in Pierre Clarac and Yves Sandre's 1971 Pléiade edition (that also included *Pastiches et mélanges* and *Essais et articles*), the editors reduced the essay from 152 to 101 pages. It includes a formal discourse attacking Sainte-Beuve's biographical method, an attempt to approach the subject informally in an account of a conversation between Proust and his mother, and sections on Nerval, Baudelaire, and Balzac, all of whom were maligned by Sainte-Beuve. Nerval and Baudelaire fare well in this defense, but Proust expresses extreme displeasure with Balzac's style while recognizing his genius. One other segment which the editors have retained is that which Fallois originally had separately published in 1950 as *Le Balzac de Monsieur de Guermantes,* in which the familiar name seems to be a convincing argument for the function of the text as a transition to *A la recherche du temps perdu.* An even more convincing argument is the piece which appears at the beginning of the Pléiade edition and which starts: "Chaque jour j'attache moins de prix à l'intelligence" (Each day I value intelligence less). Proust calls on writers to create a new literature of impressions, by which to convey something of themselves—the true subject of a writer. These impressions are to be based on involuntary memory, for which he gives three examples from his own experience: the cup of tea and toast (later the toast was ennobled as a *madeleine,* a kind of cake), the uneven paving stone, and the clink of a spoon on a dish (which now come at the end of *A la recherche du temps perdu*). The correct explanation for the relationship between the Sainte-Beuve and other critical sections and Proust's masterwork appears to be that *A la recherche du temps perdu* was not an outgrowth of the essay but that Proust was struggling with the idea of absorbing all of his aesthetic theories into one great work which would register his privileged moments and be a commentary on them. Was this to be a philosophical study or fiction? Proust was not quite sure and years later he was still wondering whether he should call his work a novel.

Proust thus started writing what was to become his masterpiece in the same manner that he had started *Jean Santeuil:* he composed fragments, not knowing how he would put them together. Some of these fragments attempt to record those privileged moments when he actually seemed to be in touch with his unconscious. At others he gave considerable prominence to dreams. When the unconscious was not function-

Marie de Bénardaky, the model for Gilberte Swann in Proust's A la recherche du temps perdu

ing, he put the highest premium on momentary inspiration which sometimes produced the rudiments of a character he would later develop but more often resulted in a lyrical sequence which he moved freely about in his novel or even fragmented (as he did with the magnificent sequence on the cries of the street vendors in Paris).

Since Proust was still composing and constructing his book at the time of his death, he kept most of his scribbles with the result that the record of the genesis and elaboration of *A la recherche du temps perdu* is almost complete. Seldom satisfied with a first draft, he rewrote his texts many times in his notebooks before he knew where he was going to put them. He often wrote upside down or in the margins and went back to use a blank page, so that the relationship and the chronology of these texts are intricate problems. For decades this mass of material was largely in the possession of Proust's niece, Madame Suzy Mante-Proust (her mother, Madame Robert Proust, had sold some of it which only recently has become available to scholars), who finally let Maurois and Fallois consult it, with imperfect results. In the early 1960s the Bibliothèque Nationale purchased the Mante-Proust collection, but systematic work did not begin until the inauguration of the *Bulletin d'Informations Proustiennes* in 1975. There has been only one attempt to understand the totality of Proust's manuscripts, Maurice Bardèche's brilliant two-volume synthesis *Marcel Proust, romancier* (Marcel Proust, Novelist), published in 1971.

In 1909 Proust read to his friend Georges de Lauris a manuscript two hundred pages long which is presumed to have included all of "Combray," the first section of *Du côté de chez Swann*. Next he wrote, according to Bardèche, the section on Balbec, which would later become part of *A l'ombre des jeunes filles en fleurs* and then inserted "Un Amour de Swann" and "Noms de pays" between the two other parts. In 1912 he thought he had a manuscript ready for publication and began to look in earnest for a publisher. In succession Fasquelle, Ollendorff, and the Nouvelle Revue Française rejected his work before a new and inexperienced publisher, Bernard Grasset, agreed to publish it at the author's expense. Grasset made no attempt to edit the text but passed it on to his printers, who printed all the typographical errors in the manuscript and added more of their own, especially when they had trouble reading some of the handwritten additions. The text of these proofs was published in Douglas Alden's 1978 book *Marcel Proust's Grasset Proofs: Commentary and Variants.* When Proust read his work in print for the first time, he was so displeased that he rewrote and rearranged his material at the proof stage; the result was *Du côté de chez Swann* (1913), which, although filled with typographical errors in its published form, was nevertheless the masterpiece as readers know it today. The leading critic of the day, Paul Souday of *Le Temps,* was unable to see beyond the typographical errors and upbraided Proust for not knowing the rules of French syntax, especially as regards the imperfect subjunctive. To be sure of at least some favorable publicity, Proust managed to place review articles written by his friends, the poet Jean Cocteau and Jacques-Emile Blanche, the painter who, years before, had done the well-known portrait of young Proust as a dandy. Originally he had planned for two volumes divided into "Le Temps perdu" (Time Lost) and *Le Temps retrouvé* (translated as *The Past Recaptured*) with the common title of "Les Intermittences du cœur" (Intermittencies of the Heart). At this point Proust's work was extended by another volume, *Le Côté de Guermantes,* to be added in the middle, and the general title was changed to *A la recherche du temps perdu.*

Du côté de chez Swann opens with a lyrical section called the "overture" in the English translation. Someone, not yet identified as the hero, is turning over in a semiawake state and recalling other bedchambers which are related to still others that appear in parts of the novel not yet written in 1913. There follows the scene of the mother's goodnight kiss, which the hysterical child always insists on having in spite of the guests, including Monsieur Swann, who are down below in the garden. Next comes another isolated scene, that of the magic lantern, which gives a more poetic projection to the story as it presents the villain Golo and the legendary ancestors of the Guermantes and introduces the theme of optical illusions, which calls into question the very existence of reality. Finally there comes the real introduction: the famous scene involving the cup of tea and the *madeleine*. The sensory experience of the tea and cake releases the flood of memories pent up in the narrator's unconscious mind, and the result is supposed to be the rest of *A la recherche du temps perdu*. On the surface this is as preposterous a beginning as the "bouteille à la mer" of *Jean Santeuil* but it is so poetic that this event, essentially outside the chronology of the novel in a kind of timeless vacuum (although it precedes the revelations of *Le Temps retrouvé*), assumes immediately its full meaning as a declaration of aesthetic principle. Even when the narrative voice says that he ceased to feel "médiocre, contingent, mortel," he does not yield to a mystical state. This is a psychological experiment which he must pursue to the end, concentrating all his powers on the analytical process.

In the course of organizing the publicity campaign for *Du côté de chez Swann*, Proust managed to get an interview with Elie-J. Bois of *Le Temps*. It is now generally believed that Proust wrote the interview himself. His first concern was to define his originality as a novelist and to signify his break with the tradition of "une action brève avec peu de personnages" (a brief plot with few characters). In his system of "psychologie dans le temps" (psychology in time), his characters are gradually revealed with all of their changes and contradictions as perceived not by an omniscient author but through the eyes of other characters. He goes on to say that his work is "une suite de 'Romans de l'inconscient'" (a series of novels of the unconscious) in which his originality is the distinction between voluntary and involuntary memory. In no sense, he continues, is he attempting to exploit a relationship with the reigning philosophy of Henri Bergson, since this distinction is not to be found in Bergson's work.

Whether or not Proust is a Bergsonian has been debated since the beginnings of Proust scholarship. In her succinct and objective study, *Bergson et Proust*, published in 1976, Joyce N. Megay

records seventy-one books and forty-four articles which attempt to settle this question. Although Proust was in 1892 an usher at the marriage of his cousin, Louise Neuberger, to Henri Bergson; although, the same year, he invited Bergson to dinner with Fernand Gregh; and although, in 1902, Bergson read to the Académie des Sciences Morales a report on Proust's translation of *La Bible d'Amiens*, Proust was never in close contact with Bergson and never had him as a professor at the Sorbonne (as Painter claims) for the simple reason that Bergson never taught at the Sorbonne. Furthermore, Proust's *cahiers* consulted by Megay prove that Proust read only one chapter of *Matière et mémoire* (*Matter and Memory*, 1896) in 1909, precisely to be sure that Bergson did not make the distinction between the two types of memory. He never read more of Bergson until, as he was reaching the end of *A la recherche du temps perdu*, he introduced a Norwegian philosopher who discusses Bergson and Boutroux.

It is surprising that, given his philosophical interests and knowledge, Proust was so uninformed about Bergson, the most influential philosopher of his day. Proust, however, had a different frame of mind and, as Henri Bonnet explains in *Alphonse Darlu, le maître de philosophie de Marcel Proust* (1961), was taught to admire Kant and to espouse a kind of "idealistic" realism ("idealism" being the nineteenth-century reply to some of the excesses of positivism). If Proust occasionally used such terms as *temps* and *durée* (time and duration), he never gave them a Bergsonian meaning. More recently, in her *Marcel Proust: Théories pour une esthétique* (1981), Anne Henry has argued convincingly that the strongest philosophical influences on Proust were Schopenhauer, Schelling, and particularly Tarde, a totally forgotten philosopher today. In reality, although a direct connection has never been established, Proust was more closely allied with the psychologists and psychiatrists of his time and undoubtedly knew his father's colleague, Dr. Jean Charcot, the director of the Salpêtrière Hospital and the mentor of Freud (with whom Proust had no dealings, however). Among the psychological philosophers of the time was Théodule Ribot who wrote about involuntary memory for several years in philosophical journals and whose ideas eventually reached laymen's periodicals. Proust always insisted that he arrived at his ideas independently but there seems to be some professional rivalry in his remark, in a letter to Walter Berry in 1919, that Ribot was a "philosophe de 25ᵉ

Proust (standing, third from left) at a picnic in the country. Proust's father, Dr. Adrien Proust, is seated at the right.

ordre." If Proust's ideas were his own, they nevertheless belonged to the intellectual climate of his times.

"Combray"—that is, the narrative—which is purportedly evoked by the cup of tea ("tilleul," linden tea, says Proust at the end of the *Madeleine* passage), is an outstanding literary creation. The narrative benefits from the profound observations of a mature narrator and from the spontaneous perceptions of a youthful narrator, that is, the figure who also says "I" but is from the past and who lives again in the mind of the older person. Both narrators speak and record but if they

explain, it is only in generalizations applicable to all humanity. Proust is no longer trying to build a character, because he is that character, whom he has merely to put down on paper as the character relives his life. In one sense, he is a prism through which reality is observed and sometimes distorted. In order to suggest the thought processes of the reminiscing older narrator, there is little chronology in "Combray," and the reader is often unsure of the age of the younger narrator, particularly when he encounters the insufferable Bloch who speaks in a jargon reminiscent of Leconte de Lisle. As Gérard Genette points out in his *Figures III*, Proust seldom relates one single event but rather presents several similar events overlaid, so that the predominant tense is the imperfect rather than the preterite, the normal tense in French narrative. Following thoughts as they develop is so characteristic of Proust's natural style of writing that jumping at random from one reminiscence to another seems quite natural too. "Combray" is a literary tour de force which appears chaotic but is carefully orchestrated. These reminiscences are lined up along a pattern of *déplacement,* that is to say, going from one place to another, such as going to Mass and coming back, or escaping what he calls the mediocre incidents of his personal life by "une vie d'aventures" (a life of adventures), that is, by reading. In spite of the intervening digressions, the reader is constantly reminded where the young narrator is and what he is doing.

Proust, it is clear, was by this point becoming a novelist in spite of himself. From the cup of tea emerges a very real Balzacian world, with its church tower in the distance and with its inhabitants peering out of their windows like the characters of the *Comédie humaine.* When the narrator's *tante* Léonie is described as though by an omniscient author and when her conversation is recorded with stenographic precision, the reader legitimately wonders how the young narrator can have remembered all of this and, indeed, whether he was even present to hear it. The same problem of plausibility occurs in the garden scene preceding the goodnight kiss. Proust was never to shed completely the trappings of the traditional realistic novelist despite his contention that everything is perceived through the prism of the narrator.

Confronting the proofs Grasset had prepared for *Du côté de chez Swann,* Proust approached the problem of revision in the same spirit. He had to make what he was writing more interesting. He polished up the banal conversation in the garden to make it more amusing, that is to say, more in the realistic tradition. He changed the locations of the subplot involving Legrandin which, although unfolding gradually, has many of the characteristics of a Maupassant short story, including a surprise ending in which it is discovered that Legrandin is a snob. In fact, was it not in the realistic tradition to place clues here and there to prepare what was coming? In the Bois interview Proust indicated clearly that this method of preparation was part of his system. At the last minute, as indicated by handwrit-

Charles Haas, the model for Swann in A la recherche du temps perdu

ten additions to the typescript, Proust decided to add a subplot concerning a scientist named Vington whose daughter, observed by the peeping-tom narrator, would engage in a lesbian scene. Like the Duchesse de Guermantes, whom the young narrator glimpsed in the Combray church, like Gilberte who made an obscene gesture that is commented on a few thousand pages later, like Madame de Saint-Loup, whose future presence at Combray was evoked in the beginning in order for the author to return to her at the end of *A la recherche du temps perdu* (in the Grasset proofs, before the change, Madame de Villeparisis had this function), Mademoiselle Vington was a preparatory figure: she led to Albertine, that is, was an early sketch of a lesbian and thus foreshadowed the much more important heroine Proust would create later. Rereading his text, Proust discovered that he had placed an omniscient biography of Vington beside the already existing omniscient biography of Swann in the garden scene. Hence he rewrote the Vington sequence completely, changed its locations in the text, and transformed the scientist into the composer Vinteuil, since he had decided that he needed a composer for future reference.

After "Combray" in *Du côté de chez Swann* comes "Un Amour de Swann." Rereading his manuscript at some early stage when it contained only the sections on Combray and Balbec, Proust must have decided that he would have to provide an antidote to the lengthy account of his childhood and adolescence which ran the danger of becoming boring. Since he also intended to have his narrator fall in love eventually, he thought that it would underline the seriousness of his work if he could give a graphic illustration of his theory of love at an earlier point in his narrative. Because there are brief passages in the notebooks which present a character Swann attracted to a series of young girls at Querqueville (the original name for Balbec), Maurois contended that "Un Amour de Swann" was a kind of crypt beneath the entire novel; in other words, that it was written first. That seems most unlikely. Proust was giving himself a lesson in the art of the novel before going on. Although he learned much from this experience he never again found it necessary to practice the art in this traditional form of which "Un Amour de Swann" is a masterly illustration.

Perhaps the most symmetrical novel in the French language, going in a perfect curve from indifference to love to indifference, "Un Amour de Swann" is the product of one continuous inspiration, already so near perfection that the proof version required little change before the final touches. The elegant aesthete Swann, received as an equal by the Guermantes, is indifferent to the beautiful courtesan Odette de Crécy, until his imagination goes to work when he sees in her a resemblance to Zephora in a painting by Botticelli. If a romantic were writing this story, it would be quite different: Swann's imagination would create an unreal Odette and this would lead to some unreal dénouement. For Proust, Odette remains real but that does not prevent the psychological machine within Swann from going into action. Love is, Proust insists, a subjective experience. Gradually Swann accepts her invitations, for she is interested in him and is momentarily free in a professional sense. He even goes with her to the receptions of the Verdurins, whom he finds charming although, if he had been in his right mind, that is, not inclined toward love, he would have seen them as bourgeois intellectual snobs. This is an illustration of one element in the crystallization process, as analyzed by Stendhal and illustrated by Proust. The predisposition to love has fixed itself on one object; henceforth, everything associated with that object acquires attractiveness. Swann truly believes he likes the Verdurins, because Odette likes them, and does his best to excuse to himself their vulgarisms and pretentiousness, not even realizing that he is lying to himself.

One night he arrives late at the Verdurins' and misses her. Again the psychological machine takes over, and he pursues her frantically throughout Paris but in vain until he encounters her quite late. This is the crux of the crystallization process. Swann has encountered an obstacle and has fallen in love. Adjusting the catleya orchid in her corsage while they ride in a carriage, he goes through all of the gentlemanly procedures of a seduction, which amazes Odette, who is not accustomed to being treated with such respect. After a brief period of happiness, Swann is suddenly expelled from the Verdurin clan because he has not been sufficiently subservient. The presence of a potential rival, the Comte de Forcheville, whom the Verdurins favor, plunges Swann into the next phase of the love process: jealousy. Odette is still his mistress, although they never live under the same roof, and Swann's increasing jealousy creates problems between them. One day Swann goes back into Faubourg Saint-Germain society, from which Odette is quite naturally excluded, and, at a reception of the Marquise de Saint-Euverte, hears a sonata (by Bertet in the proof version but by Vinteuil in the final text) which had once been the "hymne national" of their love and which now, by a process of involuntary memory, causes his old love to revive. By contrast Swann realizes that all he has left is jealousy. Yet jealousy is an illness over which he has no control. As his jealousy increases, he becomes tyrannical. Scrutinizing her language like a psychiatrist, he traps Odette into admitting something that he had never suspected, that she was out with Forcheville the night that he could not find her. Then he accuses her of being a lesbian, and she admits it but then retracts her statement with the remark that she made the admission only to stop him from tormenting her. Their relations never reach a dramatic climax. Swann's jealousy withers away when Odette goes off on a long journey with the Verdurins and one day Swann wakes up to the realization that he has loved "une femme qui ne me plaisait pas, qui n'était pas mon genre" (a woman who did not please me, who was not my kind).

Nevertheless the reader already knows that Swann ultimately marries Odette since the narrator has already told him so at the beginning of "Combray." Proust made several efforts in the Grasset proofs to explain away this inconsistency and then, in the final text, left only the explanation that Swann married Odette because otherwise she would not let him see their daughter, Gilberte, whose birth takes place during a gap in the narrative. Odette, of course, wanted marriage more than anything else. It was to be the beginning of her social ascension.

Critics of Proust, influenced also by the story of Albertine later on, have rejected his contention that his theory of love had universal application on the grounds that, in real life, Proust never knew reciprocated love except with his mother and grandmother. It should be noted that, on rare occasions, abandoning the convention that Swann is a central intelligence isolated from all other characters, the quasi-omniscient narrator provides a glimpse of what Odette is thinking and feeling. She does love Swann in her own way but finds it harder to take him as he grows more jealous.

Although there is never a digression in the narrative, "Un Amour de Swann" contains more than the love story of Odette and Swann. In his portrayal of the "petit clan" of the Verdurins, from Doctor Cottard to Professor Brichot, Proust has created, with all of the humor of the realists, some memorable characters. Likewise, when Swann attends the reception of Marquise de Saint-Euverte, Proust introduces the Duchesse de Guermantes, who bears at that moment her earlier title of Princesse des Laumes, and for the first time in his novel describes the inanities of a social gathering with the skill which he had been perfecting over the years by his occasional newspaper articles (a short piece of this kind is collected in *Les Plaisirs et les jours*).

The experience of writing "Un Amour de Swann" had taught Proust a lesson: that he could not create a long prose work of imagination without some attention to plot. According to evidence found by Bardèche in the notebooks, Proust next wrote "Noms de pays" but placed it before the section on Balbec, the part previously written. When Grasset told him that he already had too much type for one marketable volume, Proust cut "Noms de pays" in half and used the first half to complete *Du côté de chez Swann* because he felt that he needed to return to his main subject, the life of his narrator. In order to end with an artis-

tic flourish, he very arbitrarily excised the final paragraphs of "Noms de pays" and moved them also forward to the end of *Du côté de chez Swann*. In this passage, walking in the Bois de Boulogne like the courtesan Léonie Clomesnil in Proust's adolescence, Odette is evoked one last time (the aging narrator is supposed to have returned to the Bois), but this text is inappropriate at this point because Odette, as Madame Swann, has scarcely been mentioned yet, whereas she will be the main subject of the second part of "Noms de pays." No further changes were necessary in this first half of "Noms de pays," for Proust had already written a perfect text. It recasts the old story of Marie de Bénardaky in the Champs-Elysées, adding many more adventures coupled with the ups-and-downs of the narrator's emotions until he finally concludes: "Dans mon amitié avec Gilberte, c'est moi seul qui aimais" (In my friendship with Gilberte, I was the only one who was in love). This portion of the narrative is related in a uniform pattern in which action scenes in the Champs-Elysées alternate with scenes of brooding introspection at home.

In early 1914 Proust finished more manuscript and sent it to Grasset who had it set in type under the title *Le Côté de Guermantes*. Then, although it would have seemed unnecessary, he had Grasset reset what was left of the 1913 proofs (the overflow from the actual published volume) in which he had made almost no corrections except to expand the scene in which the narrator and Saint-Loup meet the painter Elstir for the first time. In 1934 Albert Feuillerat of Yale discovered a set of these 1914 proofs, described them in his *Comment Marcel Proust a composé son roman* but did not reproduce them so that they remained a kind of legend in Proust criticism. Feuillerat tried to deduce Proust's original text on the basis of two levels, an earlier lyrical and a later analytical Proust. This was ingenious work, but there was one basic fallacy: Proust had not yet written a continuous text going beyond the 1914 Grasset proofs. The 1914 proofs can be read in Alden's 1978 book. When Grasset was mobilized in World War I, publication ceased. With various doctor's certificates, Proust managed to escape mobilization although he was officially in the reserve. If he could not have his work published, at least he had time to polish his manuscripts and to write more.

Meanwhile an unusual event had taken place, which was destined to alter the rest of *A la recherche du temps perdu* significantly. In 1907

Proust had been at Cabourg and there had engaged the services of a professional chauffeur named Alfred Agostinelli (the model for the nameless chauffeur who drives the narrator and Albertine during their second sojourn in Balbec). In 1913 Agostinelli turned up on Proust's doorstep with Anna, whom he passed off as his wife, and obtained employment as Proust's secretary. Proust later wrote to Reynaldo Hahn: "J'aimais vraiment Alfred. Ce n'est pas assez de dire que je l'aimais, je l'adorais" (I was truly in love with Alfred. It is not enough to say that I loved him, I adored him). One day Agostinelli "escaped," or at least left Proust's employ, to learn to pilot an airplane on the Côte d'Azur. Proust had just written his only extant letter to Agostinelli, in which he notes that Agostinelli had been willing to help in returning the airplane that Proust had bought for him and that now he had refused, all of which suggests similar "Proustian" negotiations of the narrator with Albertine concerning a yacht and a Rolls Royce after she flees. On the very day Proust wrote the letter, he received from Anna a telegram saying that Agostinelli's plane had fallen into the Mediterranean and that he had drowned. A similar telegram announces Albertine's death from falling off a horse. These facts give substance to the belief that the model for Albertine is really Agostinelli.

It is commonly said that, but for Agostinelli, Albertine would never have existed because she was not in the proofs of 1914. That is not quite true, for researchers continue to turn up evidence that Proust always intended to confer a mistress on his narrator. In *Le Carnet de 1908* (1976) a sentence describes a mistress whom the narrator will keep "sans chercher à la posséder" (without seeking to have intercourse), a remark to be added to the debate about what happens between the narrator and Albertine. In the Grasset proofs, in the midst of the episode of the goodnight kiss, the text digresses to include an episode in which the narrator, years later, suffers the same anguish when he lingers outside "quelque bal, redoute ou première" (some ball, gala evening, or first night) trying to communicate with his estranged mistress. In the revised text this anxiety is attributed to Swann, doubtless as a preparation for the novelette to come. It is a curious fact that, when putting "Un Amour de Swann" into final form, Proust expanded the lesbian references with so many details that this seems to be a preview of the Albertine plot. In his preface to the 1984 Flammarion edition of *La

Prisonnière*, which is the fifth of the seven main parts (still another revision of Proust's text not to be confused with the revision promised by Gallimard's Pléiade editions), Jean Milly describes a passage in Proust's 1913 notebooks which outlines the Albertine plot up to the point at which she dances with Andrée. Thus it is quite clear that Proust's last-minute addition to the Grasset proofs, the Mademoiselle Vington (Vinteuil) episode, had a definite destination from the very beginning. The mistress of 1913 was originally named Maria but at some point her name was crossed out and replaced by "Albertine." Whether this change occurred before or after Agostinelli's fugue matters little, for he had nothing to do with that part of the Albertine plot. His contribution to that plot is evident in much later events, when Albertine escapes, dies, and lives on in the emotions of the narrator. According to Bardèche (but this is not confirmed by Milly), after Agostinelli's death Proust immediately wrote a very moving "pretext" which was the genesis of the 1925 volume of *A la recherche du temps perdu, Albertine disparue* (translated as *The Sweet Cheat Gone*, 1930).

During the war Proust requested and obtained release from his contract with Grasset and emigrated to the Nouvelle Revue Française and their publishing house Gallimard. Jacques Rivière, the director of their monthly periodical, had persuaded Gide and others that they had been wrong in rejecting Proust's manuscript several years before. In 1919 Gallimard published Proust's new volume, *A l'ombre des jeunes filles en fleurs,* which won the Prix Goncourt and brought him worldwide fame. (This honor was to be followed shortly by another: in 1920 he was made a *chevalier* in the Légion d'Honneur.) What was originally to be the text of this new volume was contained in the unused portions of the Grasset proofs of 1913. *A l'ombre des jeunes filles en fleurs* begins thus with the second half of "Noms de pays." The narrator unexpectedly receives from Gilberte an invitation to a "goûter" (children's afternoon snack) and this inaugurates a long symbiosis with Madame Swann during which the narrator gradually loses his love for Gilberte when she begins to avoid him. Rereading his text, however, Proust decided that this part needed a new plot, and he carefully designed one in which the narrator wills himself to forget Gilberte and finally succeeds. Probably undetected by the reader, there are now two time frames running parallel: one is the original

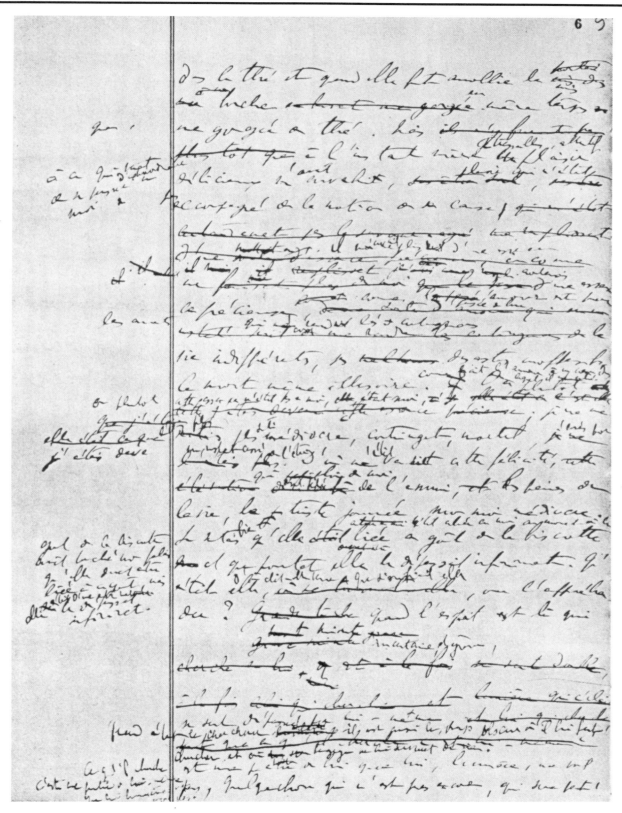

Page from the manuscript for Du côté de chez Swann, *the first book of* A la recherche du temps perdu
(Bibliothèque Nationale)

frame of a single tea party which Madame Swann is giving and the other is the long period of time during which the romantic narrator is killing off his love.

The second section of *A l'ombre des jeunes filles en fleurs* covers the narrator's first trip to Balbec with his grandmother. The structure of the original text in the 1913 proofs was essentially the same as in "Combray," a *déplacement* in the form of arrival and then finally departure from Querqueville (Balbec), punctuated with smaller *déplacements* such as the trip of the narrator and Saint-Loup to Rivebelle. Essentially without plot, the text already contained memorable scenes such as the narrator and his grandmother being snubbed by the personnel and guests of the Grand Hôtel until the Marquise de Villeparisis recognizes the grandmother as a childhood friend; such as the much anticipated arrival of the marquise's nephew, Saint-Loup, the perfect friend because he is a noble; and such as the equivocal encounter with the Baron de Charlus, who alternately insults and cajoles the amazed young narrator. In due course the narrator learns that all three of his new acquaintances are members of the Guermantes clan. Proust did not have to reread this original version to realize that it was far from perfect. He resolved to improve it by introducing immediately the new character of Albertine. By isolating the additions one perceives that this new plot develops with the logic and precision of a true novel. First the lecherous young narrator is attracted to a group of young girls, until he finally becomes aware that one of them must be the Albertine whom Gilberte once mentioned (an addition, of course, to the second half of "Noms de pays"). Finally he persuades his new friend Elstir to introduce him to Albertine in an amusing episode. Assimilated at last into the group of girls and young men, he annoys Albertine because of his stupidity while playing *furet*. At the very end of the Balbec sojourn, Albertine spends the night in the hotel and invites the narrator to her room, but she rings the servant's bell when he tries to kiss her. With Albertine gone, the narrator seems to forget her and to return to the state of loving the collectivity of young girls, an artistic conclusion to a carefully contrived plot. In making his additions, Proust was unconcerned about the original structure of his text and thus one finds the comical elevator boy announcing that the hotel is about to close for the season long before the Albertine

plot really develops. Obviously time is elastic for Proust.

In 1920 Gallimard published the next installment of Proust's novel as *Le Côté de Guermantes I* (translated in *The Guermantes Way*, 1925), the basic text of which was still part of the 1914 Grasset proofs. This part had already been so carefully composed that the only significant changes in the later elaboration were made in the Doncières episode, which was already symmetrically divided into morning events, afternoon events, and evening events. Compared to later sections of *A la recherche du temps perdu, Le Côté de Guermantes I* is well ordered and is sustained by one essential subject, the aristocracy, as illustrated by the Guermantes, a theme going back to the earliest stages of Proust's notebooks and thence to his childhood readings of Augustin Thierry, the author of histories of the Norman conquest of England and the Merovingian period, in which the foundations of the French nobility were laid. The essential plot of *Le Côté de Guermantes I* and *Le Côté de Guermantes II* (1921; translated in *The Guermantes Way*, 1925) is that of the narrator falling in love (these are his words although the reader will entertain doubts) with the duchess and then falling out of love when he discovers how unintelligent and affected she really is. As this section begins, the narrator's family have become tenants in the Hôtel de Guermantes in Paris and the Guermantes have become ordinary people, with the duke shaving contemptuously in front of the window and the duchess mistreating her servants (according to Françoise, the family servant, who has been in the novel since "Combray"). Then the narrator learns that the duchess has the most exclusive salon in Paris, and his imagination goes to work. Doffing his hat, he pursues her daily in the street because she waved to him at the theater; then he sees her, but does not talk to her, at the Villeparisis reception; and finally, in one of those unexpected events which punctuate *A la recherche du temps perdu*, she invites him to dinner because she has come to perceive him as a young genius. Even the episode of the narrator's visit to Doncières, where Saint-Loup is assigned as an officer to the military garrison, fits perfectly into the basic plot although it is a digression, since the narrator goes there in the vain hope that Saint-Loup will give him an introduction to his aunt, the duchess. For Proust the real subject is society. The Villeparisis reception occupies ninety-five pages and is chaotic because it is designed to reproduce the very chaos of such gatherings. The reception of the Duchesse de Guermantes in *Le Côté de Guermantes II* covers even more pages.

After publication of *A l'ombre des jeunes filles en fleurs*, it was relatively simple for Proust to prepare *Le Côté de Guermantes I* because he had the Grasset proofs. He decided to end the volume with an autonomous episode, the death of the grandmother, which could be placed anywhere in the narrative and which, conveniently, was already in print since it had appeared in the monthly *Nouvelle Revue Française*. This text became a bridge between the first and second Guermantes volumes: Proust split it in two, as if to say: "Continued in the next number," a procedure which he adopted to end each subsequent volume of *A la recherche du temps perdu*. When Proust sat down to write *Le Côté de Guermantes II*, except for the second half of his *NRF* text he had nothing but a blank notebook and, of course, reams of other unassimilated material in his other notebooks. The typescripts and proofs produced after the Grasset proofs had been exhausted are the subject of Alison Winton's *Proust's Additions: The Making of "A la recherche du temps perdu"* (1977). Working vertically in her concern to describe the evolution of individual parts, Winton delineates in the 1954 Pléiade edition certain texts older than the documents she was studying but does not provide commentary. Douglas Alden has contributed to the *Cahiers Marcel Proust* an essay on this earliest manuscript, the one which Proust started when he ran out of Grasset proofs.

This manuscript is contained in little notebooks of *papier écolier* very similar to the bluebooks used in American universities but without a cover. From 1914 or 1915 on (whenever he started) Proust divided his time between finishing the manuscripts needed for immediate publication and forging ahead in his basic manuscript. Céleste Albaret writes that she thinks it was in the spring of 1922 that Proust announced to her: "Cette nuit, j'ai mis le mot *fin*" (Last night I wrote the word *end*). And he added: "Maintenant je peux mourir" (Now I can die). He did die, of pneumonia, on 18 November 1922. He had not only managed to publish *Le Côté de Guermantes II* with its brief appendage, *Sodome et Gomorrhe I*, but had proofread *Sodome et Gomorrhe II* (1922; translated in *Cities of the Plain*, 1927), which stretched over three volumes when published the next year, had finished revising the manuscript of *La Prisonnière* (which he first called "Sodome

et Gomorrhe III"), and was working on revisions for what he wanted to call *La Fugitive* and what the Gallimard editors chose to call *Albertine disparue*, because a book by Rabindranath Tagore called *La Fugitive* had appeared in 1922. (The title has since been restored and has been used most recently in the 1986 Pléiade edition.) In his manuscripts also was the far from finished *Le Temps retrouvé* (1927; translated as *The Past Recaptured*, 1932).

When Proust looked down at his blank booklet, he was concerned about one problem: what to do with Albertine, who had not appeared in *Le Côté de Guermantes I*. He fumbled with different versions, crossed them out, and then left this surprising explanation: "Albertine, cette fois, rentrait à Paris plus tôt que de coutume. D'ordinaire elle n'y arrivait qu'au printemps" (Albertine, this time, was back in Paris sooner than customary. Ordinarily she arrived there only in the spring). Was this written before or after the revisions of *Le Côté de Guermantes I* ? At any rate, there it stands in the final text today as though Proust, in an antinovelistic spirit, disdained the ordinary logic of novels. Next Proust proceeded directly to the seduction of Albertine, conducted on a willing victim by an indifferent lecher. These and subsequent intimate scenes involving Albertine, which lack physical details (except for one scene in *La Prisonnière* in which she is lying asleep naked), have already inspired voluminous commentaries by Proust critics.

When Proust rewrote his text in further typescripts and on proofs, he had little time for structure but nevertheless became more of a novelist than ever because of the need to create plots which had little relation to his own biography. For example, the continuous text concerning Albertine in the basic manuscript is fragmented immediately, even as he proceeds, by two more interweaving plots. A letter from Saint-Loup tells the narrator how to go about seducing Madame de Stermaria (a character who appeared briefly in *A l'ombre des jeunes filles en fleurs* but who, as eliminated sections of the Grasset proofs indicate, was intended to be the love interest of the narrator at Balbec). With Albertine seduced, the narrator now humiliates her by having her help in arranging dinner for Stermaria in the Bois de Boulogne. Anticipation is always more than the narrator can stand, so it is a great shock to him when Stermaria sends last-minute regrets. Interrupting these two plots is a long digression on Saint-Loup's affair with Rachel, related from the

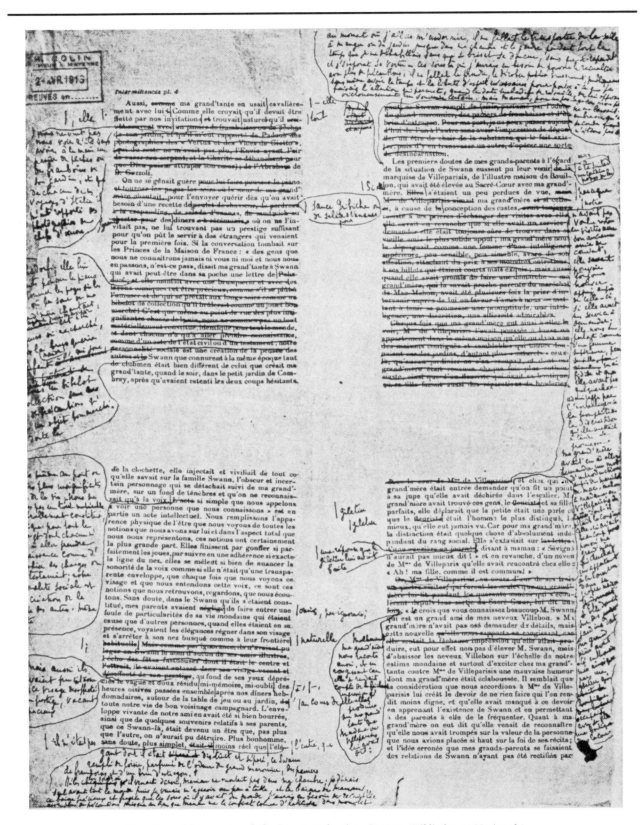

Proust's revisions on proofs for Du côté de chez Swann *(Bibliothèque Nationale)*

omniscient point of view and apparently intended as a retake of "Un Amour de Swann" in another key. Proust was well aware how readily readers can get lost in plots and digressions, so he formed the habit of reminding the reader whenever he gets back to the main subject.

Before he returned to the Albertine plot in earnest, Proust turned to the supply of other plots, events, lyrical passages, and wisdom in his notebooks. These were used to make up part of the substance of *Le Côté de Guermantes II, Sodome et Gomorrhe I* and *III,* and *La Fugitive* (1986). Swann reappears now and then and is shown dying of a chronic illness when his friend, the duchess, indifferently tries to go to the ball in her symbolic red shoes. Offstage, Odette marries Forcheville, and then Gilberte, after being momentarily pursued in the street by the lecherous narrator, who does not recognize her, penetrates Faubourg society under the name of Mademoiselle de Forcheville and marries Saint-Loup. In his notebooks Proust had the elements of another major plot which he never developed. It concerned the Baronne de Putbus's maid, whom the narrator was supposed to pursue and finally overtake at Padua, the city to which the early references to Giotto led in *Du côté de chez Swann.* In the final text the narrator goes to Balbec in pursuit of the maid but does not find her because the baroness has canceled the trip. He misses her again in Venice because he suddenly decides to run for the train to rejoin his mother.

The narrator's arrival at Balbec will provide the opportunity to use still another important text from the notebooks, the section entitled "Les Intermittences du cœur" (once Proust's title for the entire novel) in which, under the stimulus of tying his shoe, the narrator has a powerful involuntary memory in which the grandmother lives again. For Proust, the most important unfinished plot, except for that of Albertine, concerns Charlus who has reappeared frequently, looking more sinister each time. In *Le Côté de Guermantes II* the narrator goes to the rendezvous to which Charlus has summoned him, after having proposed, in the previous volume, to make him his protégé, as Vautrin does with Rastignac in Balzac's *Le Père Goriot.* However, the reception Charlus gives him is very cool, in contrast to his earlier offers of protection. The coolness is explained partly by the narrator's having told someone that he and Charlus were friends—an insult to the latter's immense pride, which can allow for only condescending relationships. Psychologically

speaking, it also reveals doubtless his paranoia—associated with his deviant behavior—and his fear that people will suppose the narrator to be his lover. When Charlus goes into a rage, the narrator, in exasperation, stamps on Charlus's tall hat just as Proust once trod on Fénelon's headgear.

Three times, when bringing Charlus into the narrative of his basic manuscript, Proust pasted in long passages from a dog-eared earlier manuscript. The first time was in connection with the conjunction of Charlus and Jupien, which the narrator, ever a peeping-tom, sees partially and then overhears—the same episode accompanied by Proust's commentary on homosexuality. In the basic manuscript this event takes place while the narrator waits for the duchess to return so that she can authenticate the invitation of the Princesse de Guermantes, which the narrator fears might be a hoax. While the narrator is waiting, he observes a flower waiting for fertilization by an insect; the conjunction between it and the bumble bee that arrives is compared to the curious pairing off of Charlus and Jupien. Proust attached so much importance to this homosexual episode that he finally isolated it as *Sodome et Gomorrhe I* at the end of *Le Côté de Guermantes II.* The second time that Proust used old text was in connection with the meeting of Charlus and the musician Morel on the station platform at Doncières, where the narrator and Albertine were in the situation of voyeurs. The third time was in the episode in which the Queen of Naples, like the Duchesse de Réveillon in a similar scene in *Jean Santeuil,* gives her arm to the staggering Charlus, who has just been cast out by the Verdurins and isolated from Morel, just as they once had cast out Swann and isolated him from Odette. In telling the story of Charlus in terms of traditional love patterns, even to the extent of insisting that the patterns of homosexual and heterosexual love were the same, Proust did not succeed in writing an artistic retake of "Un Amour de Swann." He added at random many other episodes: Morel persecuting a coachman, Morel in a brothel observed by Charlus, Charlus pretending to have a duel so as to excite Morel's sympathy, and Morel planning to seduce Jupien's daughter. One Charlus episode, which was in the basic manuscript, was omitted from the original edition of *Sodome et Gomorrhe II* and relegated to the notes section of the 1954 Pléiade edition, although Proust had clearly indicated in a note that he intended to use it elsewhere. It tells how the royal-born Princesse de Guermantes falls in love with

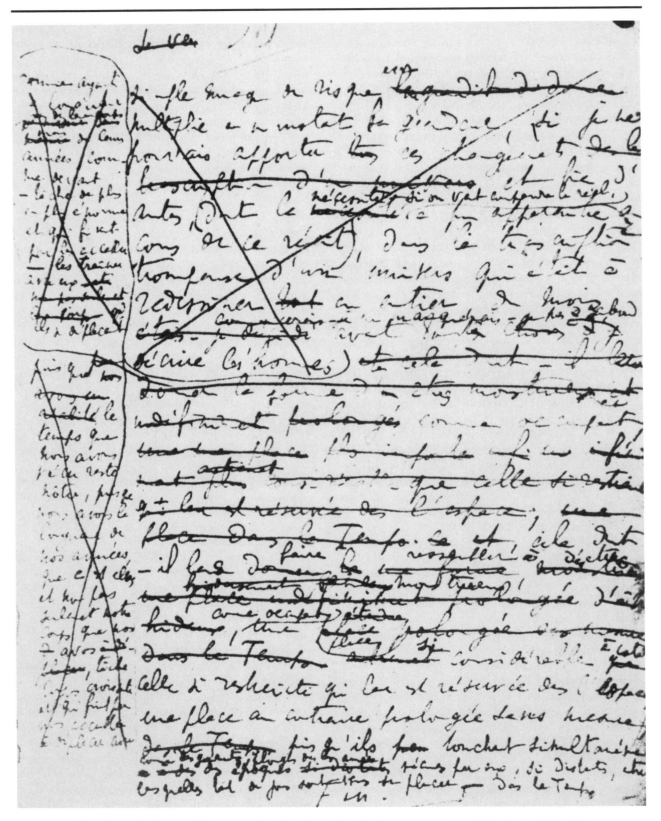

One of the final pages of the manuscript for A la recherche du temps perdu *(Bibliothèque Nationale)*

Charlus but loses out to a revolting "contrôleur d'omnibus" (omnibus conductor) (there is an allusion to this missing episode in *Le Temps retrouvé*).

During the composition of all of *Sodome et Gomorrhe II*, Albertine was still something of a problem for the author. Momentarily she had also been an emotional problem for the narrator in *Le Côté de Guermantes II* when she was late for her midnight rendezvous. Now, because the Baronne de Putbus was supposed to be one of their guests, the narrator gets himself invited to the summer estate of the Verdurins and thus the "petit clan," joined by Charlus pursuing Morel, comes back on stage, traveling to and fro on the train while the names of the stations reverberate in the background with poetic frequency. Albertine, posing as the narrator's cousin, gets involved in all this, but the long-anticipated Albertine plot does not come. This reminds the narrator of the scene near Combray he had witnessed, in a voyeuristic manner, as a boy, in which Mademoiselle Vinteuil and her woman friend had insulted sadistically the memory of the deceased composer Vinteuil, her father, and then had closed the shutters before engaging in what he supposed obscurely were acts of sexual perversion. (This episode in "Combray" had scandalized the poet Francis Jammes, although he was one of the narrator's earliest admirers).

The narrator whisks Albertine off to Paris to live in his family's apartment during his mother's prolonged absence. He never seems really to have loved her but now he is completely dominated by jealousy of her because of the lesbian connections she has had, and, he supposes, still has.

Except for some long digressions concerning Charlus, *La Prisonnière* has a unity which the immediately preceding volumes lacked, for the story of Albertine's sequestration unfolds with logic and precision. The narrator is happiest with Albertine when she is asleep or when she replaces his mother in conferring the goodnight kiss. At other times he does not trust her, engages (with utter stupidity) her friend Andrée to spy on her, sends Françoise to bring her back from a theater at the Trocadéro when he notices in the newspaper that a friend of Mademoiselle Vinteuil is in the play, and, finally, prevents her from attending the reception of the Verdurins where Morel is supposed to play a newly discovered work of the late Vinteuil with Mademoiselle Vinteuil as the honored guest. Finally he psychoanalyzes her language and so torments her with his interrogations that Swann's tormenting of

Proust in May 1921

Odette seems mild in comparison. Yet jealousy is replaced by indifference, and the narrator is on the verge of sending her away when she slams down a window in irritation and, a day or so later, leaves while the narrator sleeps.

La Fugitive is the story of jealousy surviving the death of the loved one and then eventually fading away because no emotion is permanent. First, with ambiguous messages because he has always been unduly subtle in dealing with people (like Proust, as the correspondence proves), the narrator tries to persuade Albertine to return, and then comes the fatal telegram announcing her death. Now the narrator experiences a suffering which he has never known before. In his memory he relives his life with Albertine and, in so doing, recalls many remarks which he had not particularly noticed at the time. Now is jealousy reborn and he sends Aimé, the maître d'hôtel from Balbec who has appeared in the narrative many times, to investigate Albertine's past in Touraine (and also in Nice, for there is a confusion in the text which Proust did not have time to remove). Facts do not help since facts belong to the outside world and, in the inner world, are often subject to doubt. Then the narrator brings in Andrée who, to make herself interesting, tells him anything he wants to know. Love and jealousy fade away as the narrator returns to an episodic normal existence and as he finally makes the trip to Venice with his mother, an expedition anticipated by the narrator even before Balbec and planned by Proust long before he invented Albertine. A telegram which he thinks comes from Albertine leaves him completely indifferent. Actually, as the reader learns later, the telegram is from Gilberte and *La Fugitive* ends with a visit to Gilberte who, now Madame de Saint-Loup, is having marital difficulties and is living in Swann's château de Tansonville in the environs of Combray.

The episode of the *septuor* of Vinteuil played by Morel at the Verdurin reception is the culmination of a long thematic development or succession of plots that involve, successively, three individuals: Bergotte, Elstir, and Vinteuil. Bergotte, as already noted, was present in the Grasset proofs and was the writer who so fired the youthful imagination of the narrator that, in accord with the Proustian principle that anticipation is always greater than realization, the narrator was disappointed when he met the great man at Madame Swann's while he was still on friendly terms with Gilberte.

For each of these three artists, Proust described one or more works of art which he invented but sometimes with certain models in mind. In Bergotte's case, the description is not extensive, although in "Combray" several pages are devoted to an account of the impressions his style leaves on the narrator, and elsewhere the narrator quotes a few phrases or terms Bergotte is said to have used. Perhaps Proust put little of Bergotte's "works" into his text because, although there are many models for him, the chief one is Anatole France, and France represented a kind of writing which the mature Proust had surpassed. Elstir (who was named Bergotte in an earlier fragment in *Jean Santeuil*) was likewise in the

1914 Grasset proofs and so was his painting of the imaginary port of Carquethuit, which Proust described in detail, inspired (as Juliette Monnin-Hornung has shown in her 1951 book *Proust et la peinture*) by the impressionists but especially by Turner's seascapes. Vinteuil was something of an afterthought, at least in the beginning. In "Combray" he was originally the scientist Vington, as has been noted. However, when Proust wrote "Un Amour de Swann," although he called him Berget, his role was fully defined. He was not only the musician whose sonata set the mnemonic processes of Swann in motion, he was also the creator of a fully described piece of music which scholars early identified as imitating Saint-Saëns, a piece of music which the dilettante Swann never understood. When, in the evolution of the text, the narrator understands that aesthetic message is not certain, it is evident that his understanding unfolds simultaneously with the Albertine plot. Almost without explanation (it was possibly the example of Swann whose story the narrator always seemed to know) one finds the narrator admiring Vinteuil's sonata, and Albertine often plays it for him, although the ambiguous text designates the instrument sometimes as a pianola and sometimes as a piano. The *septuor*, played by Morel at the Verdurins', reminds the narrator of past happiness with Albertine, but the experience is much deeper than that with Swann since it seems to tell him that art is greater than life. That is the ultimate message of *Le Temps retrouvé,* but art, in this final discussion, is not music: rather, it is literature.

Apparently it was the Gallimard copyreaders who decided where *Le Temps retrouvé* should start since the basic manuscript indicated no break. Their decision was to split the narrator's sojourn at Tansonville into two parts, as Proust was wont to do when beginning a new section of *A la recherche du temps perdu*. At Tansonville the narrator discovers that Swann's way and the Guermantes's way, which once seemed to be at opposite ends of the earth, are so close that they almost join. In a different form the same episode was intended for the Grasset proofs, but Proust crossed it out before sending his typescript to the printer. Of course, this is an allegorical way of representing the fusion of the bourgeoisie and the nobility by the marriage of Gilberte Swann and Robert de Saint-Loup. Already disappointed by his inability to recapture the past by visiting Combray, the narrator reads what purports to be an unpublished part of the Goncourt brothers' journal (a pastiche which mentions the Verdurins) and concludes that, since he cannot register reality directly like the Goncourts, he does not have the makings of a writer. The next episode shows the narrator on leave from his sanatorium and returning to wartime Paris, obviously an event which Proust could not have foreseen when he started *A la recherche du temps perdu*. The narrator now gives his impressions of civilian life at the time with the focus on the Verdurins, spies on Charlus in Jupien's brothel, and learns of the death of Saint-Loup at the front (but only after his *croix de guerre* is found near Jupien's brothel). On a second return from the sanatorium, presumably after the war though this is not entirely clear, he goes to the reception of the Princesse de Guermantes and, at this point, the reader returns to one of Proust's oldest texts, the one which he wrote as his conclusion at the same time that he wrote the opening pages of *A la recherche du temps perdu*. Pasted-in pieces of very old paper on the manuscript prove that some segments come from a text written many years before. A brief addition informs us that the original Princesse de Guermantes is now dead and that the prince has married the widowed Madame Verdurin, information that is of no consequence for the reception. Other additions create complications which Proust did not have time to eliminate: Cottard and Bergotte are both alive and dead; La Berma is dead and then lives again in an extraneous episode in which her rival, Rachel, causes her death; Morel wins a decoration and is also a deserter; the narrator meets Gilberte twice at the reception. As the narrator, momentarily in episodes from the old text, goes to the reception, he has three sensations of involuntary memory (two of which were once in *Contre Sainte-Beuve*). Then, in new text, while waiting in the prince's library because a concert is in progress, he has time to meditate for fifty-one pages on literary creation. In another sequence from old text, he joins the guests at last and finds that "chacun semblait s'être 'fait une tête' " (each one seemed to have put on a disguise). The quid pro quos which result are amusing and the changes point out to the astonished narrator that time has passed. Only Odette de Forcheville seems to have survived this aging process, though she wears the clothes of another era. Charlus is absent because, in the street, the narrator has just encountered him in a state of utter senility. After two more episodes of involuntary memory the narrator is finally convinced of his literary mission and the novel ends on the word

temps, for Proust once thought that time and the changes it produces in people were his main subject.

The romantic nostalgia for past time that characterizes the episode of the reception given by the Princesse de Guermantes was to close the novel and to give it its final tone. However, this episode, for all its interest, is less important than the fifty-one pages of discussion of involuntary memory, which Proust inserted. The narrator's three experiences of involuntary memory in this section lead him to a rediscovery of the past and also to the recognition that the exquisite pleasure granted by such an experience is akin to the aesthetic pleasure he had received from music, art, and literature. This awakens his latent, unfulfilled vocation as a literary artist. Through the narrator's voice, Proust presents his theory of art as an expression of truth, including one's own personal truth as evidenced by subjective experiences, including memory. He explores the role of impressions, of dreams, language, and especially metaphor, in literary creation.

While explicitly rejecting what he calls realism—that is, just the appearance of things, as presented by a "cinematographic parade"—he allows for and even insists upon the role of the intelligence in identifying and recreating the truths given by memory and impressions, that is, in literary creation. The narrator finally returns to the message which he has been holding back since the opening pages of the novel, namely that involuntary memory is useless until its workings have been analyzed by intellectual research and recorded on paper. In the Grasset proofs dealing with Combray and Balbec, he had long ago charted an itinerary leading to this conclusion. First, inspired to create, the youthful narrator can do no more than cry: "Zut!" When the moving steeples of Martinville, re-creating the illusions of the magic lantern, give him a new inspiration, he writes his essay but it is a failure because he has not yet learned that impressions, to be valid for literature, must be sifted through the memory or, better still, through the unconscious. In the Grasset proofs there was originally another fully developed example of involuntary memory set in motion by the odor of the worm-eaten "châlet de nécessité" (public toilet) in which the grandmother has a stroke (fragments of this text remain on page 241 of the Pléiade edition). Near Balbec the trees along the road to Rivebelle beckon to the narrator, but he does not heed them. In *Le Temps retrouvé* the narrator recalls

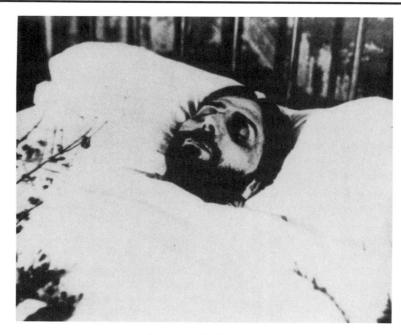

Proust on his deathbed

this itinerary but involuntary memory now has less importance. What really counts is the metaphor establishing unexpected relationships and providing the only effective means of communication between the artist and the other monads of this world. Thus one sees that Proust's art is essentially lyrical in spite of the reiterated desire to discover basic "laws." The narrator goes on to reject realism as practiced by members of that school or any literature, such as populism, which has a price tag–that is, a label–visibly displayed. Then he acknowledges his literary ancestors: Chateaubriand, Nerval, Baudelaire. Surprisingly, he does not mention his principles of character presentation but does insist on the subjectivity of love. He thanks Albertine (Albertine who did not love him, he now says) for all of the pain that his love for her caused him, for without that experience he would have been unable to express his emotions with such depth.

In the dedication to his late friend Willie Heath which begins *Les Plaisirs et les jours,* Proust wrote prophetically: "Quand j'étais tout enfant, le sort d'aucun personnage de l'histoire sainte ne me semblait aussi misérable que celui de Noé, à cause du déluge qui le tint enfermé dans l'"arche pendant quarante jours. Plus tard, je fus souvent malade, et pendant de longs jours je dus rester aussi dans l'arche.' Je compris alors que jamais Noé ne put si bien voir le monde que de l' 'arche, malgré qu'elle fût close et qu'il fît nuit sur la terre" (When I was a very small child, the fate of no character in the Bible seemed to me as miserable as that of Noah because of the flood which kept him shut up in the ark for forty days. Later I was often sick and for long days I had to remain also in the 'ark.' I understood then that never could Noah see the world better than from the ark, although it was closed up and although it was night on earth). When he wrote *A la recherche du temps perdu* Proust was truly in the ark. If he had not been there, he could never have penetrated so deeply into his own universe, both psychological and social. His vision of society was limited to the idle rich and to their servants. His psychological penetration was restricted by his own physical make-up. But no writer has penetrated such a universe more deeply or with greater emotion.

Letters:

Correspondance générale de Marcel Proust, 6 volumes, volumes 1-5 edited by Robert Proust and Paul Brach, volume 6 edited by Brach and Suzy Proust-Mante (Paris: Plon, 1930-1936);

Letters of Marcel Proust, translated and edited by Mina Curtiss (New York: Random House, 1949);

Marcel Proust: Correspondance avec sa mère, edited by Philip Kolb (Paris: Plon, 1953); translated and edited by George D. Painter as *Mar-*

cel Proust: Letters to His Mother (London: Rider, 1956; New York: Citadel Press, 1958);

Lettres à Reynaldo Hahn (Paris: Gallimard, 1956);

Choix de lettres, edited by Kolb (Paris: Plon, 1965);

Correspondance de Marcel Proust, 15 volumes to date, edited by Kolb (Paris: Plon, 1970-);

Correspondance Proust-Copeau, edited by Michael Raimond (Ottawa: Editions de l'Université d'Ottawa, 1976);

Marcel Proust and Jacques Rivière, *Correspondance (1914-1922),* edited by Kolb (Paris: Gallimard, 1976);

Selected Letters, 1880-1903, edited by Kolb, translated by Ralph Mannheim (Garden City, N.Y.: Doubleday, 1983; London: Collins, 1983).

Bibliographies:

Douglas W. Alden, "Bibliography," in his *Marcel Proust and His French Critics* (Los Angeles: Lymanhouse, 1940), pp. 171-259;

Philip Kolb, "Les Publications de Marcel Proust," in *Marcel Proust: Textes retrouvés,* edited by Kolb (Paris: Gallimard, 1971), pp. 263-290;

Larkin B. Price, *A Check List of the Proust Holdings at the University of Illinois Library at Urbana-Champaign* (Urbana: University of Illinois Library, 1975);

Victor E. Graham, *Bibliographie des études sur Marcel Proust et son œuvre* (Geneva: Droz, 1976);

Elizabeth Russell Taylor, *Marcel Proust and His Contexts: A Bibliography of English-Language Scholarship* (New York & London: Garland, 1981).

Biographies:

Léon Pierre-Quint, *Marcel Proust, sa vie, son œuvre* (Paris: Editions Kra, 1925); translated by Hamish and Sheila Miles as *Marcel Proust, His Life and Work* (New York: Knopf, 1927);

André Maurois, *A la recherche de Marcel Proust* (Paris: Hachette, 1949); translated by Gerard Hopkins as *The Quest for Proust* (London: Cape, 1950); Hopkins's translation also published as *Proust, Portrait of a Genius* (New York: Harper, 1950);

André Ferré, *Les Années de collège de Marcel Proust* (Paris: Gallimard, 1959);

George D. Painter, *Marcel Proust: A Biography,* 2 volumes (London: Chatto & Windus, 1959, 1965); also published as *Proust: The Early Years* and *Proust: The Later Years* (Boston: Little, Brown, 1959, 1965);

Marcel Plantevignes, *Avec Marcel Proust; Causeries souvenirs sur Cabourg et le boulevard Haussmann* (Paris: Nizet, 1966);

Maurice Duplay, *Mon Ami Marcel Proust; Souvenirs intimes,* Cahiers Marcel Proust, no. 5 (Paris: Gallimard, 1972);

Céleste Albaret, *Monsieur Proust,* as told to Georges Belmont (Paris: Laffont, 1973); translated by Barbara Bray (London: Collins, Harvill Press, 1976);

Henri Bonnet, *Les Amours et la sexualité de Marcel Proust* (Paris: Nizet, 1985).

References:

Douglas Alden, *Marcel Proust's Grasset Proofs: Commentary and Variants* (Chapel Hill: North Carolina Studies in the Romance Languages, 1978);

Jean Autret, *L'Influence de Ruskin sur la vie, les idées et l'œuvre de Marcel Proust* (Geneva: Droz, 1955);

Maurice Bardèche, *Marcel Proust, romancier* (Paris: Les Sept Couleurs, 1971);

Serge Béhar, *L'Univers médical de Proust, Cahiers Marcel Proust,* no. 1 (Paris: Gallimard, 1970);

William Stewart Bell, *Proust's Nocturnal Muse* (New York: Columbia University Press, 1962);

Leo Bersani, *Marcel Proust; The Fictions of Life and of Art* (New York: Oxford University Press, 1965);

Henri Bonnet, *Alphonse Darlu, le maître de philosophie de Marcel Proust, suivi d'une étude critique du "Contre Sainte-Beuve"* (Paris: Nizet, 1961);

Jacques Borel, *Proust et Balzac* (Paris: José Corti, 1975);

Germaine Brée, *Du temps perdu au temps retrouvé* (Paris: Belles Lettres, 1950); translated by C. J. Richards and A. D. Truitt as *Marcel Proust and Deliverance from Time* (New Brunswick: Rutgers University Press, 1955);

Brée, *The World of Marcel Proust* (Boston: Houghton Mifflin, 1966);

Bulletin de la Société des Amis de Marcel Proust et des Amis de Combray (Illiers-Combray, 1950-);

Bulletin d'Informations Proustiennes (Paris: Presses de l'Ecole Normale Supérieure, 1975-);

Cahiers Marcel Proust (Paris: Gallimard, 1927-1935; new series, 1970-);

Pierre Clarac and André Ferré, *Album Proust* (Paris: Gallimard, 1965);

Georges Daniel, *Temps et signification dans "A la recherche du temps perdu"* (Paris: Nizet, 1963);

Gilles Deleuze, *Marcel Proust et les signes* (Paris: Presses Universitaires de France, 1964); translated by Richard Howard as *Proust and Signs* (New York: Braziller, 1972);

Serge Doubrovsky, *La Place de la madeleine* (Paris: Mercure de France, 1974); translated by Carol Mastrangelo Bové and Paul Bové as *Writing and Fantasy in Proust* (Lincoln & London: University of Nebraska Press, 1986);

Albert Feuillerat, *Comment Marcel Proust a composé son roman* (New Haven: Yale University Press, 1934);

Wallace Fowlie, *A Reading of Proust* (Garden City, N.Y.: Doubleday, 1964);

Gérard Genette, *Figures III* (Paris: Seuil, 1972); translated in part by Jane E. Lewin as *Narrative Discourse: An Essay on Method* (Ithaca, N.Y.: Cornell University Press, 1980);

René Girard, ed., *Proust: A Collection of Critical Essays* (Englewood Cliffs: Prentice-Hall, 1962);

Victor E. Graham, *The Imagery of Proust* (Oxford: Blackwell, 1966);

Anne Henry, *Marcel Proust: Théories pour une esthétique* (Paris: Klincksieck, 1981);

Jeanine Huas, *Les Femmes chez Proust* (Paris: Hachette, 1971);

Pascal Alain Ifri, *Proust et son narrataire dans "A la recherche du temps perdu"* (Geneva: Droz, 1983);

Elizabeth R. Jackson, *L'Evolution de la mémoire involontaire dans l'œuvre de Marcel Proust* (Paris: Nizet, 1966);

Claude-Henry Joubert, *Le Fil d'or: Etude sur la musique dans "A la recherche du temps perdu"* (Paris: José Corti, 1984);

Murielle Marc-Lipiansky, *La Naissance du monde proustien dans "Jean Santeuil"* (Paris: Nizet, 1974);

Joyce N. Megay, *Bergson et Proust; Essai de mise au point de la question de l'influence de Bergson sur Proust* (Paris: J. Vrin, 1976);

Marie Miguet-Ollagnier, *La Mythologie de Marcel Proust* (Paris: Belles Lettres, 1982);

Jean Milly, *Proust et le style* (Paris: Minard, 1978);

Juliette Monnin-Hornung, *Proust et la peinture* (Geneva: Droz, 1951);

Allan H. Pasco, *The Color Keys of "A la recherche du temps perdu"* (Geneva: Droz, 1976);

Georges Poulet, *L'Espace proustien* (Paris: Gallimard, 1963); translated by Elliott Coleman as *Proustian Space* (Baltimore: Johns Hopkins University Press, 1977);

Jean Recanati, *Profils juifs de Marcel Proust* (Paris: Editions Buchet / Chastel, 1979);

Jean-Pierre Richard, *Proust et le monde sensible* (Paris: Seuil, 1974);

J[ulius] E[dwin] Rivers, *Proust and the Art of Love: The Aesthetics of Sexuality and the Life, Times & Art of Marcel Proust* (New York: Columbia University Press, 1980);

Brian G. Rogers, *Proust's Narrative Techniques* (Geneva: Droz, 1965);

Roger Shattuck, *Marcel Proust* (New York: Viking Press, 1974);

Shattuck, *Proust's Binoculars: A Study of Memory, Time and Recognition in "A la recherche du temps perdu"* (New York: Random House, 1963);

Robert Soupault, *Marcel Proust du côté de la médecine* (Paris: Plon, 1967);

Randolph Splitter, *Proust's "Recherche": A Psychoanalytic Interpretation* (Boston, London & Henley: Routledge & Kegan Paul, 1981);

Gareth Steel, *Chronology and Time in "A la recherche du temps perdu"* (Geneva: Droz, 1979);

Bernard Straus, *Maladies of Marcel Proust* (New York: Holmes & Meier, 1980);

Walter A. Strauss, *Proust and Literature: The Novelist as Critic* (Cambridge: Harvard University Press, 1957);

Jean-Yves Tadié, *Proust et le roman* (Paris: Gallimard, 1971);

Allison Winton, *Proust's Additions: The Making of "A la recherche du temps perdu"* (Cambridge: Cambridge University Press, 1977);

Jacques Zéphir, *La Personnalité humaine dans l'œuvre de Marcel Proust: Essai de psychologie littéraire* (Paris: Minard, 1959).

Papers:
Most of Proust's manuscripts are at the Bibliothèque Nationale, Paris. The University of Illinois library and the Harry Ransom Humanities Research Center at the University of Texas, Austin, have some manuscripts and numerous letters.

Raymond Radiguet

(18 June 1903-12 December 1923)

James P. Mc Nab
Guilford College

SELECTED BOOKS: *Les Joues en feu* (Paris: François Bernouard, 1920);

Devoirs de vacances (Paris: Sirène, 1921);

Les Pélican (Paris: Editions de la Galerie Simon,
1921); translated by Michael Benedikt and
George Wellworth as *The Pelicans* in *Modern
French Theater* (New York: Dutton, 1964 [pp.
117-129]; London: Faber & Faber, 1965);

Le Diable au corps (Paris: Grasset, 1923); translat-
ed by Kay Boyle as *The Devil in the Flesh*
(Paris: Crosby Continental Editions / New
York: H. Smith, 1932; London: Grey Walls
Press, 1949);

Le Bal du comte d'Orgel (Paris: Grasset, 1924); translated by Malcolm Cowley as *The Count's Ball*
(New York: Norton, 1929); translated by Violet Schiff as *Count d'Orgel Opens the Ball* (London: Harville, 1952; New York: Grove,
1953);

*Les Joues en feu: Poèmes anciens et poèmes inédits,
1917-1921* (Paris: Grasset, 1925); translated
by Alan Stone as *Cheeks on Fire: Collected
Poems* (London: Calder, 1976; New York: Riv-
errun, 1980);

Règle du jeu (Monaco: Editions du Rocher, 1957);

Gli Inediti, bilingual French-Italian edition of
works by Radiguet and others, edited by Li-
liana Garuti delli Ponti (Parma: Guanda,
1967).

Collections: *Œuvres complètes* (Paris: Grasset,
1952);

Œuvres complètes, 2 volumes, edited by Simone
Lamblin (Paris: Club des Libraires de
France, 1959).

PLAY PRODUCTION: *Les Pélican,* Paris, Théâtre
Michel, 24 May 1921.

Although Raymond Radiguet wrote many
poems and critical articles, it is as the author of
the two novels, *Le Diable au corps* (1923; translated as *The Devil in the Flesh,* 1932) and *Le Bal du
comte d'Orgel* (1924; translated as *The Count's Ball,*
1929), that he is best known. He is one of the lead-

*Raymond Radiguet (courtesy of Les Editions
Bernard Grasset)*

ers of that return to tradition loosely called "classicism." By a curious irony Radiguet's novels seem
detached from their period or even their century, whereas his brief life—and death—reflect visibly and even dramatically the turbulent period
after World War I when he came to maturity.

As the oldest of seven children whose father, Jules-Maurice Radiguet, eked out a meager
living as a cartoonist, Radiguet made an early decision to leave school and try to sell first his drawings, then his short writings. His mother,
Jeanne-Louise-Marie Tournier, was so busy with

her other children that she could spare little time for him. He was fifteen when, in 1918, he placed some drawings with the writer and editor André Salmon, a friend of his father. Like every other person who came in contact with Radiguet, Salmon was impressed by the maturity and intelligence of the short youth in hand-me-down clothes. He was reluctant to encourage Radiguet, fearing for him the moral dangers so prevalent in Paris in that turbulent time. But, having weighed these dangers against the limitations of Saint-Maur-des-Fossés, Radiguet's hometown on the eastern edge of the capital, he decided to help the boy. Salmon considered Radiguet's home circumstances to be "hideous"–"l'affreux Parc-Saint-Maur"–"une bastille bourgeoise" (a middle-class Bastille).

Before long, with the help first of Salmon, then of others, Radiguet was regularly contributing poems and critical pieces to newspapers and journals. The talents with which he came in contact were diverse and extraordinary, at a quite brilliant moment in the artistic history of the capital. Salmon introduced him to Max Jacob, a Breton Jewish poet who had converted to Christianity in 1909. Although Jacob and Radiguet did not remain in close contact for very long, Jacob's influence on the younger man remained strong. The artists with whom Radiguet became acquainted immediately recognized his prodigious talents, and, at a time of intense rivalries, vied for his attention.

The pace of Radiguet's life quickened. Indeed, for five years, he was caught up in a welter of activities, periods of intense creative activity but also, increasingly, a frenetic round that came to include heavy use of alcohol and drugs. For better and for worse, the preponderant influence in his life came to be Jean Cocteau. André Breton, the future leader of surrealism, tried to enlist Radiguet in the ranks of Dada and the avant-garde. After some hesitation, Radiguet accepted instead the advances–the word is entirely appropriate–of Cocteau. In so doing, he antagonized Breton and his group, who hated Cocteau, and gradually abandoned artistic experimentation. He became almost as much of a guide to Cocteau as the other was to him, steering him back toward traditional literary genres and models, such as the short psychological novel, verse in rhyme and strict meter, and especially a classical style: concise, probing, and characterized by litotes. They chose as their symbol the rose, dear to the sixteenth-century poet Ronsard. In truth, in

spite of his youth, Radiguet was better versed in the classics of French literature than was Cocteau.

World War I had swept aside social and sexual barriers, conventions, and distinctions, and its termination unleashed a frenzied energy that could be channeled constructively or be terribly destructive. Radiguet was drawn into this vortex. Thanks to Cocteau, he discovered Parisian high life, counting among his friends and acquaintances Erik Satie and the group of composers who were influenced by him known as "The Six"; Picasso; Gabrielle "Coco" Chanel; Proust; Juan Gris; Misia Sert; Jean and Valentine Hugo (Jean was the great-grandson of Victor Hugo); and many others. While Radiguet valued the friendship of Cocteau, in part out of real affection, in part out of opportunism, Cocteau's constant presence irritated the younger man. Once, for example, after an evening at the famous bar "Le Bœuf sur le toit" (The Ox on the Roof), in the company of Cocteau and his group, "The Mutual Admiration Society," Radiguet disappeared with his friend Constantin Brancusi, the sculptor. Cocteau was frantic with anxiety and jealousy. The two friends had gone, in dinner jackets, from Le Bœuf to the train station. In a gesture of defiance or independence, Radiguet took a train to Marseilles, then a boat to Corsica.

By 1923 Radiguet's achievements were real and recognized. From 1918 to 1921 he had written many poems. These included early, experimental pieces that appeared in journals and in a couple of collections, *Les Joues en feu* (Cheeks on Fire, 1920) and *Devoirs de vacances* (Summer Assignments, 1921). Some fourteen of the early poems, along with twenty others, rhymed and octosyllabic, would be published posthumously in a 1925 collection also entitled *Les Joues en feu* (translated as *Cheeks on Fire*, 1976). As a critic also, Radiguet was very visible, commenting upon the current literary scene, praising Cocteau, taking up a position against Dada. He had written a brilliant play, *Les Pélican* (1921), that bears comparison with Ionesco's better works. He had been involved in several playful but significant collaborative ventures with Cocteau, including the broadsheet "Le Coq" (The Rooster). Above all, he had written *Le Diable au corps*, a novel that was published in March 1923, and most of *Le Bal du comte d'Orgel*, which would not come out until 1924.

On the surface, or viewed from a distance, Radiguet seemed poised for a brilliant, productive future. In later years, Cocteau insisted upon the order, harmony, or preordained divine plan that governed Radiguet's life and death. In fact, it is an appalling lack of order, the sense of a life spinning out of control, of energy degenerating into entropy, that mark the final months. In the summer of 1923 Radiguet kept up his heavy drinking instead of switching to the milk and water that Cocteau claimed was his more customary summer regimen. At their beach retreat in Le Piquey, on the Bay of Biscayne, Radiguet was able to find alcohol, in spite of the best efforts of Cocteau and his friends to conceal it from him. By early September both Radiguet and Valentine Hugo, who had spent time with the group at the beach, complained of stomach pains. But whereas she was properly treated, his illness was misdiagnosed by Cocteau's personal physician. Both had in fact contracted typhoid from eating contaminated oysters. Radiguet lived on until December, in conditions of extraordinary disorder, at the Hotel Foyot, opposite the Luxembourg Gardens. In the last of a number of heterosexual affairs, to establish some distance between himself and Cocteau, he was living with a young woman called Bronya Perlmutter. Unwilling, in his words, to become a forty-year-old man called "Mme Jean Cocteau," he even entertained some thought of marriage. Instead, weakened by the abuses of those few fast years in Paris, he was taken to a clinic and died, alone and in agony, early in the morning of 12 December 1923. Cocteau was heartbroken and could not find the courage to attend the funeral. Grief and guilt over this death, and to a lesser extent over others, would attend Cocteau throughout much of his career.

Le Diable au corps reflects the best and not the worst of times that the two friends spent together. Radiguet wrote most of it in the summer of 1921 in Le Piquey. Its publisher, Bernard Grasset, was on the lookout for new, young authors, and in *Le Diable au corps* he recognized a work of genius. He was eager to sell as many copies as possible and orchestrated an unprecedented publicity campaign. Radiguet's photograph was prominently displayed in bookstore windows everywhere, and there was even movie newsreel coverage of Grasset grandly signing a check for 100,000 francs in payment to his young author.

While the publicity campaign that accompanied the publication of *Le Diable au corps* was considered vulgar and unseemly by many critics, it

did stimulate interest in the work and its author. Within a month of the novel's appearance, there were more than thirty reviews, most positive. An initial printing of six thousand copies was sold out immediately and other printings followed rapidly. Within one month, forty-one thousand copies had to be printed. To this day sales continue to be lively.

The story told in *Le Diable au corps* is a simple and traditional one. The first-person narrator, a mere youth, conducts a love affair with a young woman called Marthe, who is some three years older than he. Marthe has recently married, and her husband Jacques has gone off to fight against the Germans in World War I. Most of the action takes place in the Marne region, just east of Paris, the home of Marthe and of the narrator and, of course, of Radiguet himself. The narrative opens in March 1914, when the narrator is twelve. The war effects a suspension of normal order, rules, and constraints and allows the love affair to develop. But, with predictable inevitability, the armistice restores order. Jacques returns. Marthe dies in childbirth, and her husband assumes that the newborn son, fathered by the narrator, is his own. The narrator claims to detect in this outcome a pattern, the reestablishment of a proper order.

Le Diable au corps is largely autobiographical. Radiguet did indeed, at the age of fifteen, have an affair with a local married woman. When this fact came out, it added to the controversy that already surrounded his novel. What is most interesting about *Le Diable au corps,* however, is neither the circumstances of its appearance nor its autobiographical features, but a mastery of form that is extraordinary. At a time when the novel as a genre had fallen into some disrepute, Radiguet showed that it was an appropriate vehicle for the presentation of complexities of character and conduct.

For the first year or two of his career, Radiguet's writing was very much in the experimental mode that was flourishing in the immediate postwar period. But it did not take him long to elect as his own center or focus a respect for tradition. In simplified terms he veered from the left wing of letters to the right. *Le Diable au corps,* rejecting not just the avant-garde but also nineteenth-century realism and naturalism, links up with an old tradition in French literature.

Whereas Malraux, Sartre, and other writers of Radiguet's generation presented the reach of history, often in the form of catastrophe, as ineluctable, *Le Diable au corps* presents war not as the ines-

Radiguet in 1922, as sketched by Jacques-Emile Blanche (courtesy of René Radiguet)

capable intrusion of harsh reality, but rather as the temporary dismissal of reality. For the unnamed narrator war is not the accentuation of the normal suffering and death that attend life. Instead it is an opportunity, a liberation. He is able to enjoy a level of freedom and a range of experience that would otherwise have been inconceivable. War is a catalyst and a backdrop, not itself the center of interest.

In *Le Diable au corps* interest is centered upon the course of love and a young man's sentimental education. Critics might complain—as Roland Dorgelès and others did—that Radiguet shows no respect for France's fighting men. There is substance to this criticism. Jacques, the soldier—the only soldier presented in any detail in the book—is a hapless, uncomprehending cuckold. But *Le Diable au corps* is not a war novel as

such, meriting comparison with Dorgelès's own harrowing war story, *Les Croix de bois* (Wooden Crosses, 1919). It is more like works that antedate Radiguet's own century and the nineteenth and in fact go all the way back to the Middle Ages.

Radiguet's rejection of realism is consistent throughout *Le Diable au corps*. There is, for example, almost no physical description of the characters, while the settings, small towns on or near the Marne River, are barely identified—by a name, a brief notation, or just an initial. Real-life considerations relating to income, dress, eating habits, and all of those vital signs that crowd a novel by Balzac are noticeably absent from *Le Diable au corps*. From his critical writings it is clear that Radiguet intensely disliked the preponderant role given to ambition and material considerations in the novels of Balzac and Stendhal: "Les héros de Stendhal, de Balzac veulent arriver. Leur amour gêne leur arrivisme et vice-versa" (The heroes of Stendhal and Balzac wish to "make it." Their love gets in the way of their "making it" and vice versa). He deplored the emphasis placed upon money in the realist novel and considered this emphasis, paradoxically, an impoverishment. For his part, he did not hesitate: love is all in *Le Diable au corps*.

In effect, as the love grows between Marthe and the narrator they come to inhabit a world that is qualitatively different from that of those around them. The two live in a separate space and time, not within society, but against it, in contradiction of its values. Theirs is a world of the inside, of secrecy and intimacy, often a nocturnal world. The archetype or ideal model which, wittingly or unwittingly, appears to have inspired Radiguet is medieval courtly love. The conflict of values and perceptions that separates lovers and others, the primacy of the rituals of love over more manly virtues, as well as the emphasis upon the mysterious, cavelike attributes of Marthe's chamber are all reminiscent of *Tristan et Iseult* and other medieval romances. More specifically, the certainty that the lovers will be separated by the armistice, that final restoration of the order of day and society over night and love, is a clear echo of the medieval *alba* (aubade), the erotic poem of dawn, in which two lovers, joined inside the lady's chamber, are interrupted by the morning call of the world of the adults, imperious duty, the imperatives of authority.

There is an undeniable lack of suspense in *Le Diable au corps*. The reader knows in advance the likely time frame: events will probably—and do—come to an end in 1918. It is clear also that the outcome cannot be happy. On the other hand, the novelist achieves an astonishing "fit" between a believable story of the twentieth century and an enduring archetype. And, if Marthe is undeveloped as a character, since she exists only for and through her love, the same is not true of the narrator. He is far from simple. His perverseness surfaces on many occasions and is accurately suggested by the title of the work. Although Radiguet categorically denied that there is anxiety—angst—in this novel, at a time when anxiety was very much in vogue, there is, in the make-up of the narrator, a complexity and maladjustment rather characteristic of the early 1920s.

The summer of 1922 saw another period of prodigious creative effort on the part of both Radiguet and Cocteau. Cocteau worked on two novels, *Le Grand Ecart* and *Thomas l'imposteur*, a play, *Antigone*, and a long poem, *Plain-Chant*, in regular verse, celebrating his love for Radiguet, though not explicitly homosexual. Radiguet revised *Le Diable au corps*—Bernard Grasset had insisted on revisions to make it as nearly perfect as possible—and wrote much of his second and last novel, *Le Bal du comte d'Orgel*. It would not be published until July 1924, some seven months after his death. As he watched *Le Bal du comte d'Orgel* grow and take shape, Cocteau reacted with a show of astonishment and admiration, claiming in letters to his mother that it put to shame both Stendhal and Balzac. The comparison is hardly appropriate, given Radiguet's dislike of both, and the actual inspiration for the work is *La Princesse de Clèves*, Mme de La Fayette's seventeenth-century aristocratic masterpiece.

It is now clear that Cocteau did much more than congratulate his protégé. He helped shorten the work considerably, cleaned up grammar and spelling, made revisions, and provided a conclusion. For some fifty years Cocteau's efforts to conceal his own contribution to the final form of *Le Bal du comte d'Orgel*, as well as those of Bernard Grasset and Joseph Kessel, a reader for Grasset, went undetected. Cocteau emphatically denied that *Le Bal du comte d'Orgel* was anything but the work of Radiguet, working alone. Cocteau's motives cannot be attacked: he wished to secure for his friend a kind of consecration, comparable to that of another child prodigy, Rimbaud. And he continued his efforts when the book was published, contriving to obtain the best reviews possible. Cocteau's performance was an astonishing effort to reshape a whole life—that of Radiguet—to give to it an appearance of predetermined perfection and completeness, a mission accomplished.

Le Bal du comte d'Orgel was hailed as a landmark in the development of the psychological novel and continues to enjoy wide popular success. Critics as diverse as André Gide, Jacques Rivière, and Albert Thibaudet praised the work's maturity, the author's sureness of touch. The reader does have the impression of a work of considerable maturity, of an aesthetic vision that is distinguished by coherence and consistency. Although *Le Bal du comte d'Orgel* has been widely praised, there has, however, been relatively little attempt to understand just what Radiguet's contribution to the novel as a genre is. This contribution is real and significant and perhaps surprising.

The very first line of the novel is unusually adroit in evoking the principal themes that it will treat: the workings of the human heart, noble birth, and the survival of the past into the present. *Le Bal du comte d'Orgel* begins with a question: "Les mouvements d'un cœur comme celui de la comtesse d'Orgel sont-ils surannés?" (Are the stirrings of a heart like that of the Countess d'Orgel out of date?). The answer, which the novel will provide, is no. The unswerving virtue of the countess is as fascinating as the deviousness of vice.

The action of *Le Bal du comte d'Orgel* is minimal and brief. The story takes place from February 1920 to October of the same year. The narrative point of view is third-person omniscient. François de Séryeuse, a highly respected youth of twenty, goes to the Medrano Circus with his ambitious friend Paul Robin. There the two friends meet Anne and Mahaut, count and countess d'Orgel. For the duration of the novel François's fate will be linked to that of this attractive couple. In the ensuing months, François and Mahaut fall in love, though they scarcely admit this to themselves, let alone to one another. The activities that they share are slight: François occasionally has lunch with the couple, while his mother, who is a widow of thirty-seven, invites them to lunch in her home in Champigny, on the Marne, near Paris. With the coming of summer, many of the friends of Anne and Mahaut leave Paris, and François sees still more of the couple. It becomes clear to François and to Mahaut, separately, that they share tastes—for gardens and nature, for example—that are foreign to the husband. A crisis is reached in the fall. Mahaut, conscious of her love and troubled by it, pours out her feelings in a long letter of confession to François's mother. The mother complicates matters by assuring Mahaut that she is loved by François and by showing Mahaut's letter to her son. The conclusion provides no resolution. After a dinner at the Orgels' attended by François and a number of their friends, Mahaut opens her heart to her husband, confessing her love for François. But his resolute frivolity blinds him to her suffering. He merely advises his wife that they should carry on as though nothing had happened and that she should sleep.

The sources for *Le Bal du comte d'Orgel* are obvious. In the first place, Radiguet's initiation into Parisian high society brought him into contact with the count and countess de Beaumont, who held a lavish fancy dress ball each year. They had many traits in common with Anne and Mahaut, for whom they clearly served as models. It is not difficult to find a real-life counterpart for most of the characters of the novel, with François as an idealized representation of Radiguet himself. The other principal source, freely admitted by Radiguet, is *La Princesse de Clèves*. The theme of chaste love, evolving in a tightly knit aristocratic society, with a confession scene and a ball as important motifs, repeats important features of *La Princesse de Clèves*.

Le Bal du comte d'Orgel is an extraordinary accomplishment. The subject appears slight and the action almost nonexistent. No material necessity intrudes upon the lives that are presented. The reduction of material considerations in *Le Diable au corps* to the barest minimum is even more radical here. While the interiors that are mentioned are presumably elegant, they are not described. The many meals around which the friends gather are no doubt enticing, but no details or descriptions are given. The pattern that runs all through *Le Bal du comte d'Orgel* is a withholding of material information. This is reminiscent of French classical theater's dependence upon litotes, and at the same time, by suppressing material information in order better to focus on love, mood, and moral dilemma, Radiguet anticipates Nathalie Sarraute's *Tropismes* (1939).

It is clear from Radiguet's fragmentary writings about the novel that he was quite lucid in his conception of the genre: "Dans le roman d'amour tout doit être subordonné à l'amour–pas de soucis matériels. Le genre le plus profondément, gravement frivole" (In the novel about love, everything must be subordinated to love–no material cares. The most profoundly, gravely frivolous genre). He is successful in attaining this objective.

The image of the ball is a particularly effective, concentrated metonymy for the lives led by the characters in *Le Bal du comte d'Orgel*. The title is apt. Before Radiguet, many novelists, including Mme de La Fayette, Flaubert, and Proust, had also featured a ball as a narrative event of central importance. For these writers as for Radiguet, the ball entails grace and elegance, set patterns and conventions, and sexual attraction. But Radiguet rings a major change in his use of the ball. The ball of the title—a fancy dress ball organized by the count—does not take place in the novel. Much of the action involves the major characters in preparations for it. But, in something of an anticlimax, the novel stops before the much awaited event takes place. Nonetheless, the lives of the count and his entourage, elegant, repetitive, bound by convention, and rather gratuitous, readily call to mind the image of a ball. The fact that the ball of the title does not take place before the conclusion of the novel reinforces a sense that these lives, however elegant and graceful, ultimately lack fulfillment or consummation.

The principal characters of the novel are aristocratic anachronisms, cut off from vulgar reality, given over to propriety, elegance, protocol, and ritual. They are tightly bound first by etiquette, then by lineage. They are at the farthest remove from self-creating, self-projecting existentialist characters such as those of Sartre. The very time which they inhabit is a kind of double bind. They live in the present, very conscious of inescapable protocol. But more important, even when they are quite unaware of this, their character and conduct are shaped and determined by the heavy weight of the past: not just their own, but a historical, ancestral one. Mahaut, for example, is of ancient, feudal lineage. Her husband Anne, on the other hand, is of more recent court nobility. At every level it is this ancestral past and the differences it implies that separate the two. It explains her gravity and his levity, her love of nature and his love of artifice.

François and his mother are unaware of their own aristocratic background. Nonetheless, François is recognized as an equal in noble circles, and Mme de Séryeuse behaves like a noblewoman in spite of herself. Eventually, François and Mahaut come to realize that he is indeed aristocratic and a distant cousin of Mahaut.

Those characters whose past is not ancient, who are in effect free to evolve in the present, are not portrayed sympathetically, as having any depth. Paul Robin is a social climber, very much a product of the nineteenth century. And an American woman, Hester Wayne, about whose childhood, parentage, or ancestry the reader learns nothing, is presented in caricatural terms: she is a shrill, unrefined seductress, the antithesis of the purity of Mahaut.

The ideology that underlies *Le Bal du comte d'Orgel* is deeply reactionary and quite pessimistic. Characters are either heirs, carrying a heavy ancestral freight, or superficial. Freedom of action is largely an illusion; current actions are often merely the latest cycle in a pattern of repeti-

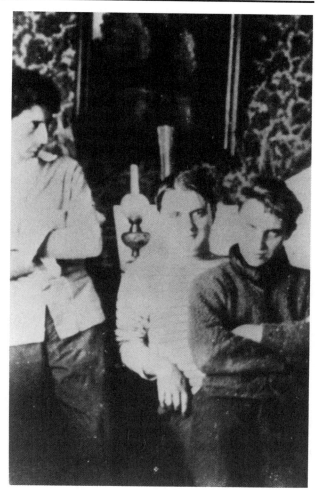

*Jean Cocteau, Georges Auric, and Raymond Radiguet, 1923
(Bibliothèque Littéraire Jacques Doucet)*

tion and recurrence. Moreover, the differences that separate individual from individual run deep, having been inherited from the past. All through *Le Bal du comte d'Orgel*, there is a consistent and complete pattern of difficulty of communication, and no example of an enduring, loving marital relationship. Moreover, at the edge of the aristocratic little world, outside forces threaten to overpower it. The Bolshevik Revolution lurks in the background as a threat of events to come; one of its victims is a friend of the Orgels. The undifferentiated mass of the people occasionally encroaches upon the world in miniature of the count and his friends, suggesting that a future leveling of society will take place.

Radiguet's description of the novel of love as "profondément, gravement frivole" is more than a mere *boutade*. In frivolity untrammeled by day-to-day cares, material concerns, or existential projects, Radiguet sets out to reveal the workings of an essential core of being, laying it bare especially in the crisis of love. What he shows is far from reassuring. He chronicles a world of grace and elegance, but one that is disappearing, trapped by its past and doomed to extinction.

Those who knew Radiguet have described an inscrutable, extremely lucid, and rather cold figure, always looking on with some skepticism, revealing little of himself, sparing of word and gesture. This economy, these powers of observation and analysis, are very much in evidence in both *Le Diable au corps* and *Le Bal du comte d'Orgel*. They recall some of France's great classical moralists, including La Rochefoucauld and La Bruyère.

In his life and death, Radiguet was very much a part—in fact an appropriate symbol—of his times. But his significance as a writer derives from his ability to stand back from his times and not remain embroiled in them. His novels reflect his ability to eliminate all the accretions from realism, and all the confusion of his own turbulent period, in order to focus upon what he considered essential and of lasting significance: the attempt to understand the human heart.

Biographies:

Keith Goesch, *Raymond Radiguet, étude biographique* (Paris & Geneva: La Palatine, 1955);

Margaret Crosland, *Raymond Radiguet: A Biographical Study with Selections from His Work* (London: Owen, 1976).

References:

Gabriel Boillat, *Un Maître de 17 ans, Raymond Radiguet* (Neuchâtel: La Baconnière, 1973);

Clément Borgal, *Radiguet* (Paris: Editions Universitaires, 1969);

H. A. Bouraoui, "Radiguet's *Le Diable au corps:* Beneath the Glass Cage of Form," *Modern Language Quarterly*, 34 (March 1973): 64-77;

Pierre Chanel, ed., "Raymond Radiguet, Jean Cocteau," *Cahiers Jean Cocteau*, 4 (1973);

Serge Dieudonné, "Cocteau entre soi-même et Radiguet," *Cahiers Jean Cocteau*, 8 (1979): 193-206;

Jean-Jacques Kihm and Elizabeth Sprigge, *Jean Cocteau: The Man and the Mirror* (New York: Coward-McCann, 1968);

James P. Mc Nab, *Raymond Radiguet* (Boston: G. K. Hall, 1984);

David Noakes, *Raymond Radiguet* (Paris: Seghers, 1952);

Nadia Odouard, *Les Années folles de Raymond Radiguet* (Paris: Seghers, 1974);

Andrew Oliver, "*Le Bal du comte d'Orgel*, structure, mythe, signification," *Revue des Langues Modernes*, 81, fasc. 1 (1975): 109-120; 82, fasc. 1 (1977): 161-184;

Philippe R. Pérébinossoff, "Amusement and Control: The Theatricals of Raymond Radiguet's *Count d'Orgel*," *Romance Notes*, 17 (Fall 1976): 131-136;

Claude-Marie Senninger-Book, "*Le Bal du comte d'Orgel*, une *Princesse de Clèves* du vingtième siècle," *Symposium*, 17 (Summer 1963): 130-143;

Francis Steegmuller, *Cocteau: A Biography* (Boston: Little, Brown, 1970).

Romain Rolland
(29 January 1866-30 December 1944)

Megan Conway
Tulane University

SELECTED BOOKS: *Les Origines du théâtre lyrique moderne. Histoire de l'opéra en Europe avant Lully et Scarlatti* (Paris: A. Fontemoing, 1894);

Aërt (Paris: Cahiers de la Quinzaine, 1898);

Les Loups, as Saint-Just (Paris: Georges Bellais, 1898); translated by Barrett H. Clark as *The Wolves* (New York: Random House, 1937); translated by John Holmstrom as *The Hungry Wolves* (London & Glasgow: Blackie, 1966);

Le Triomphe de la raison (Paris: Revue d'Art Dramatique, 1899);

Danton (Paris: Revue d'Art Dramatique, 1900); translated in *The Fourteenth of July and Danton* (1918);

Millet, translated by Clementia Black (London: Duckworth/New York: Dutton, 1902);

Le Quatorze Juillet (Paris: Editions des Cahiers, 1902); translated in *The Fourteenth of July and Danton* (1918);

Le Temps viendra (Paris: Ollendorff, 1903);

Le Théâtre du peuple: Essai d'esthétique d'un théâtre nouveau (Paris: Suresnes, 1903); translated by Clark as *The People's Theater* (New York: Holt, 1918; London: Allen & Unwin, 1919);

La Montespan (Paris: Editions de la Revue d'Art Dramatique, 1904); translated by Helena Van Brugh De Kay as *The Montespan* (New York: Heubsch, 1923; London: Jarrolds, 1927);

Jean-Christophe, part 1, 4 volumes (Paris: Ollendorff, 1905-1906)—comprises *L'Aube, Le Matin, L'Adolescent,* and *La Révolte*; translated by Gilbert Cannan as *Jean-Christophe: Dawn, Morning, Youth, Revolt* (New York: Holt, 1910); Cannan's translation also published in 2 volumes as *John Christopher: Dawn and Morning* (London: Heinemann, 1910) and *John Christopher: Storm and Stress* (London: Heinemann, 1911);

Michel-Ange (Paris: Librairie de l'Art Ancien et Moderne, 1905); translated by Frederick Street as *Michelangelo* (New York: Duffield, 1915);

photograph by Almassy

La Vie de Michel-Ange (Paris: Hachette, 1907); translated by Frederic Lees as *The Life of Michael Angelo* (New York: Dutton, 1912; London: Heinemann, 1912);

Vie de Beethoven (Paris: Hachette, 1907); translated by B. Constance Hull as *Beethoven* (London: Drane, 1907; New York: Holt, 1917);

Musiciens d'aujourd'hui (Paris: Hachette, 1908); translated by Mary Blaiklock as *Musicians of To-day* (New York: Holt, 1914; London: Kegan Paul, 1915):

Musiciens d'autrefois (Paris: Hachette, 1908; revised, 1908); translated by Blaiklock as *Some Musicians of Former Days* (New York: Holt, 1915; London: Kegan Paul, Trench, Trübner, 1915);

Jean-Christophe à Paris, part 2 of *Jean-Christophe*, 3 volumes (Paris: Ollendorff, 1908)—comprises *La Foire sur la place, Antoinette,* and *Dans la maison;* translated by Cannan as *Jean-Christophe in Paris: The Marketplace, Antoinette, The House* (New York: Holt, 1911); Cannan's translation also published as *John Christopher in Paris* (London: Heinemann, 1911);

Théâtre de la Révolution (Paris: Hachette, 1909)—comprises *Danton, Le Quatorze Juillet,* and *Les Loups;*

Jean-Christophe. La Fin du voyage, part 3 of *Jean-Christophe,* 3 volumes (Paris: Ollendorff, 1910-1912)—comprises *Les Amies, Le Buisson ardent,* and *La Nouvelle Journée;* translated by Cannan as *Jean-Christophe. Journey's End: Love and Friendship, The Burning Bush, The New Dawn* (New York: Holt, 1913); Cannan's translation also published as *John Christopher. Journey's End* (London: Heinemann, 1913);

Haendel (Paris: Alcan, 1910); translated by A. Edgefield Hull as *Handel* (London: Paul, Trench, Trübner, 1916; New York: Holt, 1916);

Vie de Tolstoï (Paris: Hachette, 1911); translated by Bernard Miall as *Tolstoy* (London: Unwin, 1911; New York: Dutton, 1911);

L'Humble vie héroïque: Pensées choisies (Paris: E. Sansot, 1912);

Les Tragédies de la foi (Paris: Hachette, 1913)—comprises *Saint-Louis, Aërt,* and *Le Triomphe de la raison;*

Au-dessus de la mêlée (Paris: A l'Emancipatrice, 1915); translated by C. K. Ogden as *Above the Battle* (Chicago: Open Court, 1916; London: Allen & Unwin, 1916);

Aux peuples assassinés (La Chaux-de Fonds: Edition des Jeunesses Socialistes Romandes, 1916);

Salut à la Révolution russe, by Rolland, P.-J. Jouve, H. Guilbeaux, and F. Masereel (Geneva: Editions de la Revue Demain, 1917);

The Fourteenth of July and Danton: Two Plays of the French Revolution, translated by Clark (New York: Holt, 1918); *The Fourteenth of July* republished separately (London: Allen & Unwin, 1919);

Pierre et Luce (Paris: Ollendorff, 1918); translated by Charles de Kay as *Pierre and Luce* (New York: Holt, 1922);

Empédocle d'Agrigente et l'âge de la haine (Paris: La Maison Française, 1918); revised in *Empédocle, suivi de L'Eclair de Spinoza* (Paris: Du Sablier, 1931);

Colas Breugnon (Paris: Albin Michel, 1919); translated by Katherine Miller (New York: Holt, 1919); enlarged edition of original French version (Geneva: Edito-Service, 1971);

Liluli (Paris: Editions du Sablier, 1919); translated (New York: Boni & Liveright, 1920);

Les Précurseurs (Paris: Editions de l'Humanité, 1919); translated by Eden and Cedar Paul as *The Forerunners* (London: Allen & Unwin, 1920; New York: Brace & Howe, 1920);

Voyage musical aux pays du passé (Paris: Hachette, 1920); translated by Miall as *A Musical Tour through the Land of the Past* (New York: Holt, 1922);

Clerambault: Histoire d'une conscience libre pendant la guerre (Paris: Albin Michel, 1920); translated by Miller as *Clerambault: The Story of an Independent Spirit during the War* (New York: Holt, 1921); Miller's translation republished as *Clerambault, or One Against All* (London: Jackson, Wylie, 1933);

La Révolte des machines; ou, La Pensée déchaînée (Paris: Editions du Sablier, 1921); translated by William A. Drake as *The Revolt of the Machines; or, Invention Run Wild: A Motion Picture Scenario* (Ithaca, N.Y.: Dragon Press, 1932);

Les Vaincus (Antwerp: Editions Lumière, 1922);

L'Ame enchantée, part 1, *Annette et Sylvie* (Paris: Ollendorff, 1922); translated by Ben Ray Redman as *Annette and Sylvie* (New York: Holt, 1925; London: Butterworth, 1927);

L'Ame enchantée, part 2, *L'Eté* (Paris: Ollendorff, 1923); translated by Eleanor Stimson and Van Wyck Brooks as *Summer* (New York: Holt, 1925; London: Butterworth, 1927);

Mahatma Gandhi (Paris: Stock, 1924); revised and enlarged (Paris: Delamain, Boutelleau, 1924); translated by Catherine D. Groth as *Mahatma Gandhi, The Man who Became One with the Universal Being* (New York & London: Century, 1924; London: Swathmore, 1924);

Le Jeu de l'amour et de la mort (Paris: Editions du Sablier, 1925); translated by Eleanor Stimson Brooks as *The Game of Love and Death* (New York: Holt, 1926);

Pâques fleuries (Paris: Editions du Sablier, 1926); translated by Eugene Löhrke as *Palm Sunday* (New York: Holt, 1928);

L'Ame enchantée, part 3, *Mère et fils*, 2 volumes (Paris: Albin Michel, 1927); translated by Van Wyck Brooks as *Mother and Son* (New York: Holt, 1927; London: Butterworth, 1927);

Les Léonides (Paris: Editions du Sablier, 1928); translated by Löhrke (New York: Holt, 1929);

Souvenirs d'enfance (La Charité-sur-Loire: Delayance, 1928);

Beethoven. Les Grandes Epoques créatrices, 7 volumes (Paris: Editions du Sablier, 1928-1945); volume 1 translated by Ernest Newman as *Beethoven the Creator* (London: Gollancz, 1929; New York: Harper, 1929);

Essai sur la mystique et l'action de l'Inde vivante, 2 volumes (Paris: Stock, Delamain & Boutelleau, 1929-1930); volume 1 translated by E. F. Malcolm-Smith as *The Life of Ramakrishna* (Mayavati, Almora, Himalayas: Advaita Ashram, 1929); Malcolm-Smith's translation republished as *Prophets of the New India* (New York: Boni, 1930; London: Cassell, 1930); volume 2 republished as *The Life of Vivekananda and the Universal Gospel* (Mayavati, Almora, Himalayas: Advaita Ashram, 1931);

Paroles de Renan à un adolescent (Paris: Editions de la Belle Page, 1930);

Goethe et Beethoven (Paris: Editions du Sablier, 1930); translated by G. A. Pfister and E. S. Kemp (New York & London: Harper, 1931);

Jean-Christophe, definitive edition, 5 volumes (Paris: Albin Michel, 1931-1934);

A Declaration by Romain Rolland, address to the World Congress against War, Amsterdam 1932 (New York: American Committee for Struggle Against War, 1932);

L'Ame enchantée, part 4, *L'Annonciatrice*, published as *La Mort d'un monde* (Paris: Albin Michel, 1933) and *L'Enfantement*, 2 volumes (Paris: Albin Michel, 1933); translated by Amalia De Alberti as *The Death of a World* (New York: Holt, 1933; London: Butterworth, 1933); and *A World in Birth* (New York: Holt, 1934);

L'Ame enchantée, definitive edition, 4 volumes (Paris: Albin Michel, 1934);

Quinze Ans de combat, 1919-1934 (Paris: Rieder, 1935); translated by K. S. Shelvanker as *I Will Not Rest* (London: Selwyn & Blount, 1935; New York: Liveright, 1937);

Par la révolution, la paix (Paris: Editions Sociales Internationales, 1935);

Compagnons de route, essais littéraires (Paris: Editions du Sablier, 1936);

Valmy (Paris: Editions Sociales Internationales, 1938);

Robespierre (Paris: Albin Michel, 1939);

Le Voyage intérieur (Paris: Albin Michel, 1942); translated by Elsie Pell as *Journey Within* (New York: Philosophical Library, 1947); revised and enlarged edition of original French version (Paris: Albin Michel, 1959);

Péguy, 2 volumes (Paris: Albin Michel, 1945);

Le Seuil, précédé du Royaume du T (Geneva: Editions du Mont-Blanc, 1946);

Le Périple (Paris: Emile-Paul, 1946);

De "Jean-Christophe" à "Colas Breugnon"; Pages de journal (Paris: Editions du Salon Carré, 1946);

Souvenirs de jeunesse (1866-1900); Pages choisies (Lausanne: Guilde du Livre, 1947);

Essays on Music, edited by David Ewen (New York: Allen, Towne & Heath, 1948);

Les Aimées de Beethoven (Paris: Editions du Sablier, 1949);

Inde: Journal 1915-1943; Tagore, Gandhi, Nehru et les problèmes indiens (Paris: Editions Vineta, 1951; enlarged, Paris: Albin Michel, 1960);

Journal des années de guerre 1914-1919 (Paris: Albin Michel, 1952);

Mémoires et fragments de Journal (Paris: Albin Michel, 1956);

Beethoven, les grandes époques créatrices, definitive edition (Paris: Albin Michel, 1966).

PLAY PRODUCTIONS: *Aërt*, Paris, Théâtre de l'Œuvre, 3 May 1898;

Morituri, Paris, Théâtre de l'Œuvre, 18 May 1898;

Le Triomphe de la raison, Paris, Théâtre de l'Œuvre, 21 June 1899;

Danton, Paris, Théâtre Civique, 30 December 1900;

Le Quatorze Juillet, Paris, Théâtre de la Renaissance-Gémier, 21 March 1902;

Le Jeu de l'amour et de la mort, Paris, Théâtre de l'Odéon, 29 January 1928.

OTHER: *Encyclopédie de la musique et dictionnaire du conservatoire*, 11 volumes, volumes 2 and 3 include contributions by Rolland (Paris: Delagrave, 1913-1931);

Stendhal, *Vies de Haydn, de Mozart, et de Métatase*, preface by Rolland (Paris: Champion, 1914);

Marcelle Capy, *Une Voix de femme dans la mêlée*, preface by Rolland (Paris: Ollendorff, 1916);

Ananda Coomaraswamy, *La Danse de Çiva: Quatorze essais sur l'Inde*, translated from the English by Madeleine Rolland, preface by Rolland (Paris: Reider, 1922);

La Jeune Inde, recueil d'articles de Mahatma Gandhi, 1919-1922, translated by Hélène Hart, introduction by Rolland (Paris: Stock, 1924);

Vie de M.-K. Gandhi, écrite par lui-même, preface by Rolland, *Europe*, 25 (January-April 1931): 465-490;

Maksim Gorky, *Eux et nous*, preface by Rolland (Paris: Editions Sociales Internationales, 1931);

"Un Message de Romain Rolland . . . : Faisons face à l'ennemi," address to the Brussels Peace Conference, *L'Humanité* (6 and 11 September 1936);

Nicolas Ostrovski, *Et l'acier fut trempé*, translated from the Russian by V. Feldman, preface by Rolland (Paris: Editions Sociales Internationales, 1936);

Les Pages immortelles de Rousseau, choisies et expliquées par Romain Rolland (Paris: Corrêa/New York: Longmans, Green, 1938); translated by Julie Kernan as *The Living Thoughts of Rousseau presented by Romain Rolland* (New York & Toronto: Longmans, Green, 1939);

"A Rilke. Souvenir de son voisin," in *Rilke et la France*, essays and memoirs by Edmond Jaloux and others (Paris: Plon, 1942);

Alexeï Remizov, *La Maison Bourkov*, translated from the Russian by Robert and Zénitta Vivier, preface by Rolland (Paris: Editions de Pavois, 1946).

PERIODICAL PUBLICATIONS: *Saint Louis, Revue de Paris* (1 March 1897): 87-137; (15 March): 358-395; (15 April 1897): 571-593;

"La Musique en Allemagne au dix-huitième siècle," *La Revue de Paris* (15 February 1906): 852-882;

Les Trois Amoureuses, Revue d'Art Dramatique et Musical, 21 (1906): 169-191, 249-275, 333-348;

"Shakespeare. Pour le tricentenaire de la mort du poète," *Journal de Genève* (17 April 1916);

"Déclaration de l'Indépendance de l'Esprit," *Humanité* (26 June 1919);

"Du rôle de l'écrivain dans la société d'aujourd'hui," *Commune*, 2 (May 1935): 929-935;

"Retour de Moscou," *Commune*, 3 (October 1935): 129-133;

"Nécessité de la révolution," *Europe*, 50 (15 July 1939): 289-302;

"Message to the International Music Congress, 1939, New York," *Musical Quarterly*, 25 (October 1939): 510-512;

"Mon Séjour chez Gorki," *Lettres Françaises* (9 March 1960).

Romain Rolland's tremendous output of plays, novels, music criticism, biographies, polemics, and correspondence has secured for him a place in European letters and thought. Well known and widely read in his day, he was the apostle of an idealism which holds less appeal for modern audiences. Much of his writing seems dated. Readers are no longer shocked by illegitimacy, pacifism, or communism, and enough time has passed since the world wars that the sense of immediacy needed to appreciate much of Rolland's work has vanished. Yet perhaps it is because of these very reasons that Rolland will be remembered, for his work stands as a reflection of the complex and conflicting issues of the world in which he lived.

During his lifetime and for several years after his death, Rolland commanded a tremendous popular and intellectual following. In 1926 a special issue of the journal *Europe* was devoted to the writer in honor of his sixtieth birthday. Ten years later the newspapers were full of details about a special celebration–"Hommage de la France à Romain Rolland"–in honor of his seventieth birthday. *L'Humanité* reported that thousands were turned away owing to the overwhelming turnout. André Gide presided over the event, which included speeches and coordinated meetings of various clubs also honoring Rolland. A year after his death a book of collected essays, tributes, and poems was published under the fitting title of *Hommages à Romain Rolland*. Eulogistic articles appeared in several journals, and, in 1955 and again in 1965, *Europe* dedicated a special issue to Rolland. The 1965 issue included the schedule for a week of radio programming devoted to Rolland's life and works.

Although Rolland's popularity has waned significantly in the West, he remains highly regarded in the Soviet Union. A huge celebration was held in Moscow in 1966 honoring the one-hundredth anniversary of the writer's birth. A book written in collaboration by two of Russia's foremost Rolland scholars was published especially to commemorate the event. Included in the volume was a list of all the publications on Rolland scheduled to appear in 1966 for the jubilee. In the USSR alone there were 159 entries covering Rolland's musical works, his political writings, and his novels. By 1969 over three million copies of Rolland's works had appeared in Russian. To the present day Rolland remains popular as the subject of Soviet critical inquiry and the bulk of contemporary work on the author comes from Russia and the Soviet block countries.

Romain Edmé Paul Emile Rolland was born on 29 January 1866 in Clamecy in the department of Nièvre. His father, Emile Rolland, a native of one of the small neighboring towns, carried on the family tradition and was a highly esteemed, fourth-generation notary. His mother, Antoinette-Marie Courot Rolland, was the daughter of a local family of farmers and notaries who had lived in the area for several generations. Of highly disparate natures, the separate influences of Rolland's parents are quite evident in Rolland's life and works. His father belonged to the old French bourgeoisie that was intensely republican; his ancestors had been ardent revolutionaries. Emile Rolland was well known around town and enjoyed his position, a strikingly different attitude from that of his wife. She was of a retiring nature and preferred devotion and religious piety to worldly distractions. The tendency toward religious introspection she bequeathed to her son along with a great love of music had a lasting influence on Rolland's intellectual formation.

Rolland had two sisters. Both were named Madeleine and both of them played significant roles in his life. The first Madeleine was two years younger than her brother. In June of 1871, when she was three, the family went to vacation at the beach at Arcachon. The little girl had not been well, but, as it seemed to be nothing serious, the family was not overly concerned. Thus it was a great shock to her five-year-old brother when she died overnight after suffering six hours of agony, caused presumably by diphtheria. The specter of death haunted young Rolland, strengthened by the fact of his own delicate

health and a weakness of the lungs inherited from his mother's side of the family. He never outgrew his physical infirmities: illness plagued him throughout his life.

If Madeleine's death was a shock to Rolland, it was a crushing blow to Madame Rolland, who brooded for years over the loss of her child. Despite the well-meaning efforts of her neighbors, the young mother clung tenaciously to her grief. When a second daughter was born to her the next year, she named the baby Madeleine, for the first Madeleine had appeared to her in a vision shortly before the birth. This new daughter does not seem to have lessened the mother's grief. She did, however, offer companionship to Rolland, whom she helped considerably in later life because of her English scholarship.

His childhood years at Clamecy were important. From Rolland's own testimony, the most distinguishing feature of the very old town was its tranquility. The surrounding countryside of gently rolling green, the ancient houses, and the old church of St. Martin all radiated peace and calm. In this peaceful environment Rolland as a sickly child built up a comfortable dream world. If at times the world around him seemed to hold him like a prison, freedom was found in books, in music, and in the promise of the canal that flowed next to the house where he lived. When the barges passed by, Rolland could imagine himself on them, escaping to discover the rest of the world. Music was perhaps the best freedom. The works of Beethoven and of Mozart helped him transcend the parameters of his own existence and gave him a taste of the sublime. Even the homey music of the bells of St. Martin was a cause for joy and a symbol of liberty. In the library sheltered in an unused wing of the house, Rolland built a fortress of dreams; in a ring of chairs which he arranged in a magic circle he made the acquaintance of Shakespeare and other authors.

Schooling at Clamecy, however, fell short of what Madame Rolland desired for her son. Her plan to send him to school in Paris did not include the delicate Romain facing the capital alone, so she engineered the relocation of the entire family. If this seems surprisingly ambitious for the still-brooding mother, Rolland later explained that she no longer felt comfortable in Clamecy. In any event, the move must have taken a great amount of determination. Emile Rolland had to sell his respected private practice and accept a subordinate position in a Paris

Rolland and his sister Madeleine, circa 1880 (courtesy of R. Laffont)

bank. Even Madame Rolland's father joined in the move, which took place in October 1880.

The world of Paris presented a rude awakening for the sheltered boy from the Nivernais. The city seemed to him full of corruption and decay, underscored no doubt by his continuing preoccupation with death. He endured two desperately unhappy academic years at the Lycée Saint-Louis where he passed two *baccalauréat* examinations. In the fall of 1882 Rolland entered the Lycée Louis-le-Grand. There he spent the next four years preparing for the Ecole Normale Supérieure. His classmates at Louis-le-Grand included Paul Claudel and André Suarès, with whom he attended concerts. During this time, however, he developed no close friendships nor was he inspired by any of his professors. His love of music became a passion that lifted him periodically out of his unhappiness. He heartily defended Wagner, reveled anew in Beethoven, and was enraptured by the force of a full symphony orchestra. He also discovered Spinoza, renewed his acquaintance with Shakespeare, and, much to his

mother's anguish, renounced his faith. Academically, however, he was only a moderately successful student. Twice he failed the entrance examinations before he was admitted to the Ecole Normale in November of 1886.

Although Rolland had begun his studies in philosophy, he chose history and geography as the subjects for his second year, thinking that they would offer him a greater scope than the set philosophy and literature courses. Perceiving definite patterns in history, he arrived at a belief he repeatedly held and abandoned during his life that time is nonlinear; past, present, and future exist concurrently. During this period he also developed his ideas on heroism and decided to contact those whom he considered to be living heroes. Among these were Renan, Edmond de Goncourt, Ibsen, and Tolstoy. While his results were somewhat less than satisfactory, he eventually received a long letter from Tolstoy, later published by Charles Péguy in his *Cahiers de la Quinzaine*. Rolland conceived a lasting admiration for Tolstoy, whose works affected him greatly.

Rolland circa 1886 (photograph by Piron)

Most of his third year at the Ecole Normale was spent working diligently to prepare for the history *agrégation*, which he passed, placing eighth, in August 1889. Despite all his efforts to that end, Rolland hated the prospect of teaching. Fate intervened and an appointment opened up at the Ecole Française d'Archéologie de Rome. Unwillingly, for the prospect of so much action was not at all to the liking of one who by his own admission preferred a dreamy torpor, he decided to accept the post. The two years he spent in Rome proved to be the happiest, and some of the healthiest, of his life.

His research took up only a measure of his time and he profited from his freedom to learn about Rome and himself. His quite considerable pianistic talent was discovered and he was soon a desired guest at many official and private dinners. In January 1890 he met Malwida von Maysenbug who, despite the forty-eight-year difference in their ages, became his great friend, confidante, and mentor. She was an idealist who believed in such causes as the emancipation of

women and she numbered among her close friends many great men, including Wagner and Nietzsche. She and Rolland carried on a voluminous correspondence until her death in 1903. At von Maysenbug's apartment he also made the acquaintance of two sisters, Antonietta and Sofia Guerrieri-Gonzaga. Seeing the elder girl yawn during one of their conversations, Rolland turned his attention to the younger Sofia. Only sixteen at the time and rather shy, she provided Rolland with material for his dream world and inspired many of his later creations.

During these two years in Rome he decided to write plays. His first, "Empédocle," was never finished. "Orsino," completed but never published, inspired by the character in *Twelfth Night*, is notable for the idea expressed in the last line, where the hero dies shouting "Death does not exist!" Rolland began a third play, "Les Baglioni," but before it was finished, he left Italy in July 1891 in the company of Malwida von Maysenbug.

Back in Paris, Rolland once again faced the prospect of teaching, this time postponed by a year's leave of absence on the grounds of poor health. He finished "Les Baglioni" in October. In January and February he wrote a play in verse, "Niobé," then started on a fifth drama, "Caligula." These plays were not written for his amusement only. The dreamer took his wares to most of the theaters in Paris only to meet refusals and rejection everywhere. His failures were not only literary. He also applied for posts at the Bibliothèque Nationale, the Luxembourg Museum, and the Louvre and was turned down in every case. His emotional life was more successful. On 11 April 1892, he dined at the home of a professor of classical philology at the Collège de France. There he met the professor's daughter, Clotilde Bréal. They had a deep love of music in common and her playing of Wagner commanded Rolland's respect. Perhaps part of Clotilde's attraction was the fact that she was Jewish and Rolland had become passionately aware of the persecution of the Jews during his stay in Rome. Although he had developed a close friendship with André Suarès, also Jewish, during their years at the Ecole Normale, Rolland later admitted that at the time of meeting Clotilde he knew very little about Judaism. Experiencing a desire to make reparations for society's anti-Semitic attitudes, Rolland offered his hand and his heart and the two became engaged that summer. They were married without a religious ceremony on 31 October

1892. The next month they left Paris for Rome, where Rolland was on a brief official mission for the Ecole des Beaux Arts, thanks to the intervention of Clothilde's father.

During the six months that the couple remained in Rome, Rolland carried on research for the doctoral thesis that his father-in-law had made a condition of the marriage. When the couple returned to Paris, Rolland taught a course in art history first at the Lycée Henri IV, then in 1894-1895 at Louis-le-Grand. Meanwhile he was working on his dissertation, *Les Origines du théâtre lyrique moderne. Histoire de l'opéra en Europe avant Lully et Scarlatti* (The Origins of Modern Lyric Theater. History of European Opera before Lully and Scarlatti), published in 1894. In 1895 he received the degree of *docteur ès lettres*. In 1894-1895 he also taught a course on morals at the Ecole Jean-Baptiste Say. While reviewing the traditional views of ethical behavior, he began to codify his own ideas about social responsibility that would play such a great part in his life and writings. In November of 1895, he began teaching art history at the Ecole Normale, where he stayed until he was transferred to the Sorbonne in 1903. Never having desired to be a professor, he found that his professional duties did not bring him a great deal of satisfaction nor did they provide financial independence. Rolland complained unhappily in a letter written in 1896 to his friend Suarès of having to live off his wife's dowry.

Teaching and work on his dissertation did not keep him from doing what to him was truly important—writing plays. In July of 1893 he finished "Caligula." The first six months of 1894 he spent working on its twin, "Le Siège de Mantoue" (The Siege of Mantua). He continued his struggle to get his work published or produced. The Comédie-Française turned down "Niobé," the *Revue de Paris* rejected "Les Baglioni," the *Mercure de France* refused "Le Siège de Mantoue," and a letter from Rolland to Sarah Bernhardt was ignored. Undismayed he turned his hopes to the provinces and to Germany but his luck did not improve. Not one of his five earliest plays was ever produced or published. Early in 1896 Clotilde Rolland intervened and sent *Saint-Louis*, a tragedy written between September 1894 and August 1895, to Jules Lemaître, who, with difficulty, had it accepted by the *Revue de Paris*. It took a year before the play appeared and, when it did, critical reception was less than favorable. Nevertheless Rolland was pleased. At last he had had something published, a step in the right direction.

A two-month visit to Germany in the summer of 1896 was the catalyst for two projects that had long been in the planning stage. That fall he began writing *Aërt*, another play, and *Jean-Christophe*, a long, multi-volume novel which he correctly foresaw would take him years to finish. Both portray the struggle of a hero against the world. The play, as well as two others Rolland undertook shortly afterward, *Le Triomphe de la raison* (The Triumph of Reason, 1899) and *Les Vaincus* (The Vanquished; published in unfinished form in 1922), ends in the suicide of the protagonist. *Aërt* was accepted by the Théâtre de l'Œuvre in June 1897 and performed one night only on 3 May 1898 to a moderately receptive audience. His next play, staged as *Morituri* but known by its published title, *Les Loups* (1898), was produced at the same theater only fifteen days later and elicited a considerably different reaction.

Les Loups (translated as *The Wolves*, 1937), published under the pseudonym Saint-Just, a Revolutionary figure much admired by Rolland, is set in Mainz in 1793 and portrays the conflict between justice and the good of the state. The principal characters include Quesnel, a commissioner of the Convention, and three officers in the Republican army—an academician, a former butcher, and an ex-aristocrat. A spy is caught and he accuses the former nobleman, d'Oyron, of treason. By the close of the play, the other three characters know the charge is false but d'Oyron is executed nevertheless—in the best interests of the country.

Rolland expected to provoke his audience with this deliberate echo of the Dreyfus affair, which had caused a great amount of social and political furor. Dreyfus, a captain in the French army, was accused of divulging military secrets to the Germans. In December of 1894 Dreyfus, a Jew, was convicted in a secret court-martial and sentenced to life imprisonment on Devil's Island. Many prominent people, including Zola, believed that a great injustice had been committed and they led a protest that finally ended in 1906 when a later trial vindicated the captain. In the meanwhile, France was torn between those who supported the army, those who fought against the persecution of the Jews, and others who believed that justice had been ignored. Rolland himself had not always been in full support of the captain. In November 1897 Rolland had written to Malwida von Maysenbug that, although his wife and her father believed completely in the innocence of Dreyfus, he could not share their conviction. His lack of sympathy was a result, no doubt, of the fact that his marriage with Clotilde was on shaky ground. He later changed sides, although, other than writing *Les Loups*, he never took an active part in the controversy surrounding the affair.

Reactions to the play were not what Rolland had expected. By his own admission, he intended the play to be a glorification of France, great no matter what the circumstances, not a show of support for Dreyfus. In fact, the play angered the military, thrilled liberals and socialists, and left the Jews unsatisfied. But, at last, his work attracted some attention.

Rolland himself seems to have found inspiration in the work. During the summer following the production of the play, he conceived the idea for a whole cycle of plays about the French Revolution, of which *Les Loups* and a play written earlier, *Le Triomphe de la raison*, would be a part. Full of enthusiasm, Rolland set to work on a new piece, *Danton*, of which he finished the first version in November 1898. He read the play to his wife and her father, who were in no way encouraging. His father-in-law, a practical man, criticized Rolland's passion for writing plays in general and professed a concern over Rolland's obsession with the Revolution, which he considered to have a disturbing influence.

The breach in ideas was a serious one. By the summer of 1900, Rolland and his wife were spending long periods of time apart. In February 1901 Rolland officially separated from Clotilde and moved in temporarily with his parents. Their divorce became final in May of the same year.

The difficulties in his emotional life did not dampen his enthusiasm for the Revolutionary plays. Rolland revised *Danton* (1900) and wrote yet another play, *Le Quatorze Juillet* (1902; translated as *The Fourteenth of July*, 1918). From 1898 to 1902 all four of the Revolutionary plays were produced and requests for translations reached Rolland from Italy, Russia, and Germany. The Revolution, however, was not Rolland's only preoccupation. He suffered severe health problems during this period, including tuberculosis and heart trouble. Surprisingly he was still incredibly busy. He wrote articles of musical criticism for several journals, principally the *Revue de Paris*. From 1901 to 1903 he taught courses in music history at two successive girls' schools in addition to the

Rolland at the time he was writing his biography of Beethoven, the first of three books in his series "Vie des hommes illustres"

course he was still teaching at the Ecole Normale. Despite all his efforts, he was still terribly poor. He lived the solitary life of a hermit in the tiny apartment where he read, studied, played the piano, and began to write something other than plays. He began in earnest a biography of Beethoven and his long-contemplated novel, *Jean-Christophe*.

Vie de Beethoven (1907; translated, 1907), the first of three books Rolland designated his "Vies des hommes illustres" (Lives of Illustrious Men), was first published in *Cahiers de la Quinzaine* (January and September 1903) under the auspices of Charles Péguy, as had been the case for three of the Revolutionary plays. The biography was rather short, concentrating on Beethoven as a man and on his life rather than on Beethoven as a composer. Beethoven was one of Rolland's personal heroes and his life demonstrated how a great man could control sorrow, specifically sorrow associated with physical suffering. Written for a popular audience, the work was well received.

In February 1904 the first part of Rolland's best-known work, *Jean-Christophe*, was published in *Cahiers de la Quinzaine*. The novel occupied much of the next nine years of the author's life. Before publication in ten volumes by the Parisian firm Ollendorff (1905-1912), it appeared in ten volumes with seventeen installments in the *Cahiers*: *L'Aube* (Dawn) and *Le Matin* (Morning), February 1904; *L'Adolescent* (The Adolescent), January 1905; *La Révolte* (Revolt), November 1906-January 1907; *La Foire sur la place* (The Fair in the Square), March 1908; *Antoinette*, March 1908; *Dans la maison* (In the House), February 1909; *Les Amies* (The Friends), January-February 1910; *Le Buisson ardent* (The Burning Bush), October-November 1911; *La Nouvelle Journée* (The New Day), October 1912. From 1910 to 1913 Gilbert Cannan's three-volume English translation of the entire saga appeared under the titles *Jean-Christophe: Dawn, Morning, Youth, Revolt* (1910), *Jean-Christophe in Paris: The Marketplace, Antoinette, The House* (1911), and *Jean-Christophe. Journey's End: Love and Friendship, The Burning Bush, The New Dawn* (1913).

Jean-Christophe is the life story of a German musician, Jean-Christophe Kraft. *L'Aube* begins with the infancy of the title character, and his parents and surroundings are shown through the perceptions of a baby. The next three volumes follow Christophe through his childhood and formative years to the threshold of manhood. His musical genius is apparent early and he is eager to get out into the world but his widowed mother begs him to stay with her. His energies are devoted to composing and he begins to chafe against the restrictive, conventional ideas of music. Because of an altercation with some German soldiers, Christophe is forced to flee his native land and go to Paris to make his fortune as a musician, composer, and pianist.

Volumes five, six, seven, and part of eight are all set in Paris. Rolland makes use of his German hero's visit to France to criticize many aspects of German and French society. *La Foire sur la place* is a bitter critique of the literary and artistic circles of Paris. In this volume Christophe comes face-to-face with the cultural world of Paris and is disgusted by the corruption he finds there. Overwhelmed he is unaware of the chaste love he has inspired in one of his music students, a young Italian girl, Grazia, based on Sofia Guerrieri-Gonzaga. Neither he nor his music finds acceptance in the world of fashionable music, so he withdraws and concentrates on composition. He nearly starves to death. Then he meets Olivier Jeannin, a sensitive, refined, finely built intellectual, the French counterpart to the best of German enthusiasm that Christophe represents. Volume six, *Antoinette*, tells the story of the early lives of Olivier and his sister Antoinette, whom Christophe had met once in Germany. In *Dans la maison*, volume seven, the two young men, now best friends, have moved in together, and from Olivier Christophe learns to appreciate the good side of French culture. Olivier also teaches his friend to understand and feel affection for the common people. Later, in volume eight, Olivier's marriage and Christophe's success cause the two to drift apart. Christophe discovers that his mysterious benefactor is none other than Grazia, now the wife of an Austrian ambassador. It is now Christophe's turn to fall in love, but she feels only friendship for him and leaves with her husband for America. In volume nine, *Le Buisson ardent*, after the failure of Olivier's marriage, Olivier and Christophe are together again and become involved in political unrest. During a May Day riot, Olivier is seriously wounded, and Christophe kills a policeman and is forced to flee. Friends spirit him out of the country to Switzerland, where he receives word that Olivier has died. Grief robs him of his creative genius until another crisis reawakens his creativity. In the last volume, *La Nouvelle Journée*, an aged Christophe has returned to Paris and there he finds success, friendship, and affection. New sorrows assail the old composer but he can face these now because of his previous experiences.

Jean-Christophe is a story of heroes and a story of moral responsibilities. Like the "illustrious men" about whom Rolland was writing at the same time, Christophe and Olivier are models to be followed. Rolland meant for their attitudes and their ways of learning and dealing with problems to be examples for his readers. The two main characters are both biographical and autobiographical. Rolland called Christophe his "shadow"; Olivier—with the intentional echo of Roland and Olivier from *La Chanson de Roland*—was his double. Closely modeled upon Rolland's greatest personal hero, Christophe resembles Beethoven, particularly in the first three volumes of *Jean-Christophe*, in which details are borrowed directly from Beethoven's early life. Christophe is a musical genius and, as such, he represents the musician that Rolland wished to have been, the novelist's fantasized self. Olivier is closer to Rolland's real self, but both figures put their beliefs into action, something that Rolland advocated unceasingly although he never quite managed to do so himself. He was always too busy writing.

From the time the first volumes were published, *Jean-Christophe* attracted both public and critical attention. Critics admired the musical arrangement of the book; the story line was popular among more general readers. Because of its biting criticism, *La Foire sur la place* was less well received, as were some of the later volumes, but critical opinion was generally very favorable up to the beginning of World War I. Then the tide was swayed by a change in public opinion which, with the advent of the war, turned more patriotic and nationalistic, and the German Jean-Christophe was no longer acceptable as a hero or as a critic of French society. After the war the series regained its admirers and it remains Rolland's most popular work.

While writing *Jean-Christophe*, Rolland kept up his habit of working on several projects simultaneously. He continued writing articles on musicology and in 1908 produced two books on musicians: *Musiciens d'aujourd'hui* and *Musiciens d'autrefois* (translated as *Musicians of To-day*, 1914, and *Some Musicians of Former Days*, 1915). He became interested in Michelangelo and wrote two books on the famous artist. *Michel-Ange*, published in 1905 and translated in 1915, was an analysis of the Italian's works. *La Vie de Michel-Ange*, the second of the "Vies des hommes illustres," appeared the next year in *Cahiers de la Quinzaine*, was published by Hachette in 1907, and translated as *The Life of Michel Angelo* in 1912. This biography shows how the great artist deals with a type of sorrow much different from that of Beethoven. Michelangelo's tragedy was that he was born with the spirit of discontent against which he had to struggle constantly. Since the struggle was not successful, Michelangelo's life had no consolation, although it showed great heroism.

In Rolland's own life there had been some consolation. In 1905 he received the Vie Heureuse prize, and in 1909 he was named to the Légion d'Honneur. His writing was finally earning recognition. Unfortunately his physical health suffered a severe blow. On 28 October 1910 Rolland was run over by an automobile. He spent the next three months in bed and convalesced slowly in Italy and then in France. With the intention of writing an article, he spent some of his time rereading Tolstoy, who had died in De-

cember of 1910. The article developed into a book, and the third biography of the "Vies des hommes illustres," *Vie de Tolstoï*, was published both in Paris and in English translation in New York during 1911. Tolstoy's form of heroic suffering differs yet again, for this hero has chosen his lot for himself. The biography won the approval of Tolstoy's family for its sympathetic portrayal of the Russian writer who had so inspired Rolland in his youth.

Owing primarily to the accident, Rolland had been on leave from the Sorbonne for two years when he submitted his resignation in July 1912 in order to devote himself more fully to his literary efforts. The completion of *Jean-Christophe* was liberating—"En me séparant de Christophe je n'éprouve . . . qu'un sentiment de délivrance" (Separating myself from Christophe, I experience only a feeling of deliverance). Rolland went back to Switzerland in April of the following year. He stayed there for six months and relaxed by writing *Colas Breugnon* (published and translated into English in 1919). This novel, whose title character might have been one of Rolland's own forebears, portrays the bon-vivant attitudes of the paternal side of his family. During his stay in Switzerland, the Académie Française awarded Rolland the Grand Prix de Littérature. He was not particularly enthusiastic at winning the prize. His mind was becoming increasingly preoccupied with philosophical and social concerns.

The beginning of 1914 marked a change in Rolland's literary output. For the next four years he put aside most of his creative writing and concentrated on spreading his ideas of internationalism. After a few months in Paris, he had returned to Switzerland and was there when war broke out. Exempt from military service by reasons of age and ill health, he decided to stay in Switzerland. Though at first he joined in the general exultation at the declaration of war, he began to decry the destruction that it entailed. He clung to the illusion of the possibility of an honorable war with the opponents Germany and France able to respect each other despite differences of opinion. He believed that a spirit of internationalism, a united brotherhood of citizens of every country, was more important than nationalist distinctions and to further this doctrine, he wrote the most famous of his wartime articles, "Au-dessus de la mêlée" ("Above the Battle"). The title was the cause of much misinterpretation by those who saw in it Rolland vaunting his own superiority or underscoring the aloofness of his life in Switzerland. The main point of the article was that young men were dying in vain and that it was up to the European elite to rise above the call of nationalism and build a City whose consciousness would be free from the injustice and chauvinism of individual nations, a refuge for liberated souls of all nations. Rolland appealed to fellow intellectuals to demonstrate for peace instead of making war and thus became a figurehead of pacifism for the next several years.

"Au-dessus de la mêlée" and many of his other numerous wartime articles were first published in the *Journal de Genève* but in November 1915 they were collected in a book, bearing the title of the best known, published in Paris. The book raised a storm of protest in France. It was officially denounced, its author ostracized, and, for a while, the circulation of the essays was prohibited. Rolland was undaunted. Sales of the book went to benefit the Agence Internationale des Prisonniers de Guerre, in whose behalf Rolland's energies were engaged from October 1914 to July 1915. Organized under the auspices of the International Red Cross, the agency was located in Geneva. Rolland was deeply devoted to the purposes of the International Red Cross and when, in 1916, he was awarded the Nobel Prize for 1915 for literature, he divided the prize money between the Red Cross and several French charities. *Au-dessus de la mêlée* was published in English translation in 1916.

After giving up his work with the Agence Internationale, Rolland left Geneva for several other Swiss residences and returned once more to creative writing. In 1916 he conceived and began a novel about a new type of hero not cast in the traditional heroic mold. Clerambault is a quiet little man whose struggle takes place in the realm of thought rather than in the world like that of Jean-Christophe. Rolland's intention was to call the book a "roman-méditation," a combination novel and meditation, with the title "L'Un contre tous" (One against All). However, after his experience with "Au-dessus de la mêlée," he was afraid this title might also be misunderstood. When the novel was completed and published in 1920, it bore the title *Clerambault: Histoire d'une conscience libre pendant la guerre*. In this work, translated as *Clerambault: The Story of an Independent Spirit during the War* (1921), Rolland advocates the necessity of individual thought as a check on the masses. The outlook for humanity is gloomy and pessimistic. Even more cynical is the author's allegorical drama, *Liluli*, published the previous year

and translated in 1920. The subject is war and the one character left unscathed by the battle is buried in an avalanche. The heavens are empty; God is ineffective. Not surprisingly, critics saw the play as Rolland's abandonment of faith.

Rolland's next work after *Clerambault*, the short novel *Pierre et Luce*, conceived and written in 1918, translated into English in 1922, was also inspired by the war. The plot is derived from the tragic bombing by the Germans of a Parisian church. A shell caused the roof to collapse, killing several people and wounding many others. The title characters, two innocent lovers, are killed in a similar tragedy but not before Rolland has expounded on his ideas of the concurrence of past, present, and future.

The year 1919 marked Rolland's return to Paris instigated by the news of his mother's stroke. He arrived 4 May; she died fifteen days later. Rolland remained in Paris for the next two years. In April of 1921 he left for Switzerland. The following April he rented the Villa Olga in Villeneuve on Lake Geneva and moved there with his sister Madeleine and their father. Rolland leased the villa for the next sixteen years and there he did most of the work on his next major creative undertaking.

The plan for another serial novel had been conceived as early as 1912 but Rolland had put it aside first to work on *Colas Breugnon* and then again when the war intervened. This cycle would have a female protagonist—the counterpart of Jean-Christophe. He called it *L'Ame enchantée* (The Soul Enchanted). Begun in 1921, it appeared in four parts with seven volumes between 1922 and 1933. The first two parts, *Annette et Sylvie* and *L'Eté* (Summer), were written in quick succession and each published the year after its completion, in 1922 and 1923 respectively; English translations of both appeared in 1925. These volumes are the best known and most critically appreciated of the series. Two years passed taken up with other projects before Rolland began the third part, *Mère et fils* (Mother and Son), which appeared in French and in English translation in 1927. Rolland put off the last part, *L'Annonciatrice* (literally, The Female Messenger), for over three years and when he finally started working on the manuscript in October 1929, he was repeatedly sidetracked by other projects and interests.

Simply put, the complex novel is the story of Annette Rivière's enchantment and disenchantment with the world of materialism. Rolland him-

From the manuscript for Rolland's "Déclaration de l'Indépendance de l'Esprit," a manifesto calling for a universal brotherhood of the Mind, published in L'Humanité, *26 June 1919 (Stefan Zwieg,* Romain Rolland: The Man and His Work, *1921)* self considered it "le drame silencieux de la famille moderne" (the silent drama of the modern family). *Annette et Sylvie* opens in 1900, when Annette, long motherless, loses her father and discovers that she has an illegitimate half sister, Sylvie. Annette seeks her out and the two become close friends despite the disparity of their upbringing. Because of their independent natures, the two eventually drift apart but stay in touch. Annette becomes affianced to Roger Brissot but, unfortunately, he wants a traditional marriage based on the inequality of the sexes and Annette cannot accept his point of view. She breaks off the engagement and discovers that she is pregnant. *L'Eté* opens after the birth of her son, Marc. Ignoring public opinion, Annette is quite happy with her unwed motherhood but soon she faces the painful loss of her fortune and must teach for a living. Still hoping to find love, she meets an old school chum, Julien Davy. She dreams of marriage but because of Julien's timid spirit of conformity, plans fall through. Later, Annette becomes the mistress of a surgeon. This relationship is no more successful than the others and Annette breaks it off, not wishing to be a slave to passion. Meanwhile Marc grows away from his mother. Annette can do nothing to reach him and this failure plus that of her love affairs are trials to her development that she must overcome in order to be free to start a new life. The book closes as Annette nears her fortieth birthday and war is declared.

The focus of the novel shifts in the next part. Experiences from Rolland's own life and statements of his ideas abound in *Mère et fils*. Here Annette takes a job teaching in a provincial boys' school where, like Rolland at the Lycée Saint-Louis, she is confronted with the corruption and mediocrity of the students. More and more alienated from his mother, Marc attends a Parisian boarding school and begins to mix with a crowd of anarchists. Annette forms an attachment to a wounded soldier who wants nothing so much as to see his dearest friend, an Austrian who is now a prisoner of war. Deeply touched by this friendship that surmounts nationalism (the unmistakable voice of Rolland), Annette helps the Austrian escape so that he can see his dying friend. She returns to Paris where she finds that her son has learned to appreciate her. Marc discovers the identity of his father, now politically prominent, and seeks him out only to be disgusted by his pompous views. The young man is about to be

drafted and is making plans to run away when the armistice is declared.

The last volume, *L'Annonciatrice*, written so much later than the rest, is the most politically aware and the least interesting to modern readers, although it was favorably received by certain critics at the time. When it opens Annette is leaving Paris as the governess of a Rumanian family. She does not occupy the post long, for Annette flees, fearing for her life, in order to escape the advances of her employer. Back in Paris she develops a stormy relationship with a newspaper publisher named Timon whom she eventually converts to the Soviet cause. Marc, revolted by capitalism, scarcely works. Terribly poor, he refuses the help of Sylvie, now rich, and falls desperately ill. He is nursed back to health by Assia, a Russian immigrant, who wins him to communism. They marry and have a son, Vania, a true child of the communist world, who scorns the bourgeois values of his grandmother. Marc leaves Assia to fight fascism and is killed by the Black Shirts in Italy. Sylvie dies and Assia leaves Annette to go to the United States to remarry and, no doubt, further the cause of communism. A new world is being born.

For Rolland's contemporary readers, the novel's sense of immediacy was inescapable. The action ends in 1933, the same year the last volume was published. As a whole the work attracted much attention. Critics saw it as another step in Rolland's fight for freedom and compared it to *Jean-Christophe*. Because of the novel's quantity of philosophical commentaries, Rolland was variously seen as a prophet and social critic. Reactions, especially to the last volume, depended greatly on the political leanings of the critic. Rolland's advocacy of socialism and communism gained for him both acclaim and violent dislike. More recently Annette's fierce spirit of independence and the intimate view of her loves and psyche have earned Rolland some recognition as an early advocate of women's rights.

In order to understand fully the forces at work in *L'Ame enchantée*, it is helpful to consider Rolland's other interests during the novel's preparation. Over the years he was becoming more and more involved with the pacifist and communist movements, and his increasing commitment to those ideas can be seen in the successive volumes of *L'Ame enchantée*. Additionally several critics have noted traces of mysticism in the novel directly related to Rolland's growing preoccupation with the philosophies of the East.

Rolland and Gandhi, 1931

While Rolland had been attracted to Indian religions as early as 1898, his interest was sparked in 1914 by an article written by Ananda Coomarswamy advocating a world policy for India. The article bore a dedication to Rolland and the two men began a correspondence that lasted several years. In 1916 another Indian, Rabindranath Tagore, spoke out in favor of Rolland. They began to correspond and met for the first time in April 1921.

Rolland continued his Eastern studies and wrote a biography of Mahatma Gandhi that was initially published in the first volume of *Europe*, a journal founded by Rolland in 1923 in collaboration with several other writers; it appeared in book form in 1924 and in English translation under the title *Mahatma Gandhi, The Man who Became One with the Universal Being.* Gandhi was another of Rolland's heroes, a leader to be admired for his wisdom and his great, active courage. The book was an enthusiastic portrait of the Indian; it was widely read and sold well.

Rolland's correspondence soon expanded to include Gandhi and Jawaharlal Nehru as well as several other Indians. In 1926 he entertained first Nehru, then Tagore at Villa Olga at Villeneuve. Madeleine Rolland, who for the past several years had translated various essays and articles for her brother, now proved an invaluable asset as an interpreter. These meetings provided the inspiration for the last volume of *L'Ame*

enchantée and for another long work, *Essai sur la mystique et l'action de l'Inde vivante* (Essay on the Mystique and Action of Living India). The first volume of the work was published in 1929 and bore the title *La Vie de Ramakrishna* (translated as *The Life of Ramakrishna*, 1929). The second, *La Vie de Vivekananda et l'Evangile universel*, appeared the next year (and in English translation as *The Life of Vivekananda and the Universal Gospel* in 1931). In these books Rolland is trying to show that there is a "universal gospel" that presupposes an essential accord between Hinduism and Christianity. He proceeds to defend Eastern doctrine to the West and vice versa. His efforts were crowned by another visit from Tagore in August 1930 and one by Gandhi, who arrived for a short stay the following month.

Between the writing of *Mahatma Gandhi* and the visits of Tagore and Nehru in 1926, Rolland took time away from his Indian studies and the writing of *L'Ame enchantée* to pursue his interest in the French Revolution. It was time to complete the project for the cycle of revolutionary plays abandoned at the turn of the century. In 1924 he wrote *Le Jeu de l'amour et de la mort* (published in 1925; translated as *The Game of Love and Death* in 1926; produced in 1928), set in March of 1794. The title of his next play, *Pâques fleuries* (1926), translated as *Palm Sunday* (1928), hints that the seeds of revolution are already planted and waiting to blossom forth. This play is the pro-

Rolland and Maksim Gorky in Moscow, 1935

logue of the whole cycle and the action occurs in 1774. Much of the tension of the play results from the fact that, unlike the audience, the characters are ignorant of the Terror that is to come. The story of *Les Léonides* (1928; translated, 1929) takes place twenty-three years after that of *Pâques fleuries*. The characters are the same or the descendants of the characters of the earlier play but now the moving force on the horizon is Bonaparte. The play ends on an optimistic note—class barriers formerly so rigid have now dissolved. The drama that completed the eight-play series was not written until 1938. *Robespierre*, Rolland's last play, published in 1939, was an effort to justify the actions of the figure whom Rolland considered the greatest man of the Revolution. Fate, inexorable fate, dictated the revolutionary hero's actions. The play is the glorification of revolution, which, by now, Rolland had come to believe was often necessary in order to establish peace and the ideal republic.

Despite Rolland's devotion to political and social idealism, he never lost his passion for music. His work on Beethoven had only begun with the early biography. In 1928 he produced the first

part of a monumental project on his favorite composer, *Beethoven. Les Grandes Epoques créatrices* (1928-1945). The first volume was subtitled *De l'Héroïque à l'Appassionata* (From the Eroica to the Appassionata) and was translated under the title *Beethoven the Creator* (1929). The work begins with Beethoven in his thirtieth year, for it is not so much a biography as a study of Beethoven's creativity and production. Critics reviewed the volumes favorably but generally agreed that a prior technical knowledge of musical composition and of Beethoven's sonatas was helpful to the reader.

Work on the larger project was deferred for several years but in the meanwhile, Rolland produced *Goethe et Beethoven* (1930; translated, 1931). This piece is a study of the German poet intended to remind the public that he was the "greatest poet of modern Europe" and it was only right that he should have met the greatest of musicians. Meant for a wider audience than *Les Grandes Epoques créatrices*, *Goethe et Beethoven* is much less technical than the earlier work.

The next volumes of *Les Grandes Epoques créatrices* appeared much later. The two volumes of *Le Chant de la Résurrection* (The Song of the Resurrection, 1937) concentrate on the years of the composer's life between 1816 and 1823. Rolland analyzes the technical aspects of Beethoven's last sonatas and the Mass in D. The last part of the study, *La Cathédrale interrompue* (literally, The Interrupted Cathedral), equally technical, was published in three volumes. *La Neuvième Symphonie* (The Ninth Symphony) and *Les Derniers Quatuors* (The Last Quartets) appeared in 1943. *Finita Comoedia* appeared in 1945, after Rolland's death.

In 1923 a young Russian widow had written to Rolland about her impressions of *Jean-Christophe*. This was the beginning of a correspondence that led to a meeting in August 1929. Both parties appear to have been pleased with the encounter and the next year Rolland asked Marie Kodachova to come to live with him in Switzerland. In 1931 she came to Villeneuve to be his companion, secretary, and nurse.

Rolland's health was very poor and in August of 1932, he was too ill to assume in person the chairmanship of the World Congress Against War. Instead he sent a statement, published in pamphlet form in 1932, to be read on his behalf. Perhaps it is just as well that Rolland was unable to go for, under the influence of current political affairs, his Russian companion and his own Revolutionary plays, Rolland's ideas of pacifism were undergoing a radical change. He no longer believed that social change could be effected by nonviolence. While he deplored the idea of a capitalistic war, war to establish the "Revolution"– the new order–was often a regrettable necessity. More and more, it seemed to Rolland that Russian communism represented the hoped-for new order. He spoke up often in support of the USSR and in praise of Lenin, a position which no doubt was partially responsible for his election to the Academy of Science of Leningrad in 1932. Because of his beliefs Rolland refused the Goethe medal that the German government under Chancellor Hitler awarded him in April 1933. He wrote and published several articles condemning the German government. These, as well as the rest of his postwar polemics that had appeared in the Communist newspaper *Humanité*, were later collected into two books: *Quinze Ans de combat, 1919-1934* (translated as *I Will Not Rest*, 1935) and *Par la révolution, la paix* (By Revolution, Peace), both published in Paris in 1935.

Rolland's enthusiasm for Russia led to a trip to the Soviet Union during the summer of 1935, accompanied by Marie Kodachova, whom he had married the year before. He went to see Maksim Gorky, with whom he stayed, but wherever Rolland stopped he was met with a warm welcome. Upon his return from Russia, he highly praised Stalin and the vitality of the Soviet people under the direction of the Communist party. In Rolland's opinion the political developments in the USSR represented the hope of civilization and he pledged his continuing efforts to defend her against all detractors. He was particularly impressed with the Soviet youth and wrote laudatory articles that were published both in Europe and in Russia.

Later the same summer Rolland took another trip, this time to visit the region of his birth, the Nivernais. He began to think about returning to France and in September of 1937, he bought a house in Vézelay, a small town not far from Clamecy. The next May, after sixteen years, he gave up the lease on the Villa Olga and moved the household to Vézelay. Rolland had several projects waiting to be finished: his play, *Robespierre*, the last of his works on Beethoven, his personal memoirs, and *Le Voyage intérieur* (1942; translated as *Journey Within*, 1947), a collection of thoughts and introspective studies written primarily from 1924 to 1926. He launched into these endeavors and a literary study of his friend Péguy with his customary verve but neither they nor his continuing battle with tuberculosis could keep Rolland from raising his voice against the worsening political situation in Europe. He protested against the violation of human rights and scathingly condemned Hitler's Germany. When war was declared in September 1939, he wrote declaring himself unreservedly on the side of "the democracies and of France," who were in such terrible danger from Germany. Nevertheless he still believed in his ideal of internationalism–the German people themselves were not the enemy; they had been led astray by a despot who needed to be destroyed. With the approaching end of the war came a new belief in the destiny of France. Rolland had witnessed enough acts of heroism and sacrifice to assure him that the mission of an eternal France was to defend the cause of liberty. Caught up in this enthusiasm, Rolland finally succumbed to tuberculosis and died at Vézelay on 30 December 1944 at the age of seventy-eight.

At the end of his life Rolland seems to have experienced a renewal of religious feeling. This was definitely not a reconversion to Catholicism as Claudel tried to interpret it, but a belief in some unseen, divine power. In light of the mysticism inherited from his mother that threads its way in and out of Rolland's literary texts, such a religious reawakening is not surprising. In fact, in Rolland's work taken as a whole, vacillation and contradiction seem to be the rule rather than the exception. His opinion about the Dreyfus case is one example of many that show a turnabout in point of view and a distinct reluctance to take a stand. Similarly he alternately accepted and rejected pacifism, then communism. Revolution was first denounced but later seen as a necessary means to an end. In *Jean-Christophe* Rolland promotes individualism and the importance of individual action. Collective and social action compete with individualism but finally dominate *L'Ame enchantée*. He believed that he was devoted to action but the testimony of his life shows that, in reality, he practiced detachment over participation. In many ways he was guilty of the attitude he so hotly protested when critics accused him of being superior and withdrawn in his "Au-dessus de la mêlée." Although ostensibly fighting for a better Europe and a better world, his plea was addressed to the European elite, not the common man, and the City of God would be newly created, not formed from an existing community. In his efforts to remain above the battle, distant from the passions and emotions that clouded the war years, Rolland often came across not as a prophet or watchdog, but simply as a man unable to take a firm stand. Consequently during World War I the French considered him pro-German while the Germans thought of him as a Francophile. Although critics of this period found fault with his changeability, it is perhaps this characteristic that will guarantee his place in literary history.

Two factors, however, remain stable throughout his works and his life—his enduring love of music and his belief in heroes. Music was a passion that filled his life. It was a source of beauty and truth, of enjoyment and inspiration that never faltered. And Beethoven, as "the greatest of all composers," was Rolland's greatest hero. There were many other heroes as well—the other "illustrious men," Michelangelo and Tolstoy; Tagore and Gandhi; Robespierre and Saint-Just; Goethe; Gorky. Although Rolland found some of these heroes less than perfect, his belief in heroism remained unshaken. He created new heroes including Orsino, the prince Aërt, Christophe and Olivier. If his heroes are splendid examples of the triumph and strength of the individual,

they are no less a testimony to Rolland's belief in the spirit of internationalism, for they transcend the constraints of nationalism. German, Italian, Indian, Russian as well as French, Rolland's heroes represent his belief in the essential brotherhood of man and the possibility of world peace.

Letters:

Rolland and Tagore, edited by Alex Aronson and Krishna Kripalani (Calcutta: Visva-Bharati, 1945);

Lettres de Romain Rolland à un combattant de la Résistance (Paris: Rodstein, 1949);

Cahiers Romain Rolland (Paris: Albin Michel, 1948-)—volumes 1-3, 5-8, 10-26 include letters by Rolland;

Europe, special issue on Rolland, 109-110 (January-February 1955)—includes letters by Rolland;

Romain Rolland, Lugné-Poë: Correspondance, 1894-1901, edited by Jacques Robichez (Paris: L'Arche, 1957);

Europe, special issue on Rolland, 439-440 (November-December 1965)—includes letters by Rolland;

Lettres de Romain Rolland à Marianne Czeke dans la Bibliothèque de l'Académie des Sciences de Hongrie, edited by Györgyi Safran (Budapest: Publications Bibliothecae Academiae Scientiarum Hungaricae, 1966);

Etudes de Lettres, special issue on Rolland, second series 9, edited by E. Buenzod and G. Guissan (Lausanne: Faculté des Lettres, 1966)—includes letters by Rolland;

Bon Voisinage. Edmond Privat et Romain Rolland. Lettres et documents, Cahiers Suisses Romain Rolland (Neuchâtel: La Baconnièrel/Paris: Albin Michel, 1977).

Interviews:

"Romain Rolland, Before War Began, Prophesied German Revolution," *New York Times*, 4 November 1917, VII: 8;

Lucien Price, "Romain Rolland et Villa Olga," *Yale Review*, new series 20 (December 1930): 273-292; republished in Price's *We Northmen* (Boston: Little, Brown, 1936);

Price, "Romain Rolland Converses," *Atlantic Monthly*, 156 (December 1935): 718-726; republished in Price's *We Northmen* (Boston: Little, Brown, 1936);

Louis Aragon, Interview with Rolland, *Cahiers du Bolchévisme* (15 March 1936);

Dilip Kumar Roy, Interview with Rolland, in his *Among the Great* (Bombay: N. M. Tripathi, 1945), pp. 5-63.

Bibliographies:

William Thomas Starr, *A Critical Bibliography of the Published Writings of Romain Rolland* (Evanston: Northwestern University Press, 1950);

N. A. Vaksmakher, A. V. Païeskavya, and E. L. Galperina, *Romain Rolland: Index bio-bibliographique* (Moscow: Editions du Livre de l'Union Soviétique, 1959).

Biographies:

Marcel Doisy, *Romain Rolland* (Brussels: Editions La Boétie, 1945);

René Arcos, *Romain Rolland* (Paris: Mercure de France, 1950);

Jean-Bertrand Barrère, *Romain Rolland par lui-même* (Paris: Seuil, 1955);

Barrère, *Romain Rolland, l'âme et l'art* (Paris: Albin Michel, 1966).

References:

Dushan Bresky, *Cathedral or Symphony: Essays on Jean-Christophe* (Bern: Lang, 1973);

René Cheval, *Romain Rolland, l'Allemagne et la guerre* (Paris: Presses Universitaires de France, 1963);

Maurice Descotes, *Romain Rolland* (Paris: Editions du Temps Présent, 1948);

Bernard Duchatelet, *La Genèse de "Jean-Christophe" de Romain Rolland* (Paris: Lettres Modernes/Minard, 1978);

Frederick John Harris, *André Gide and Romain Rolland: Two Men Divided* (New Brunswick: Rutgers University Press, 1973);

Hommages à Romain Rolland (Geneva: Editions du Mont-Blanc, 1945);

Marcelle Kempf, *Romain Rolland et l'Allemagne* (Paris: Nouvelles Editions Debresse, 1962);

Arthur Levy, *L'Idéalisme de Romain Rolland* (Paris: Nizet, 1946);

Harold March, *Romain Rolland* (New York: Twayne, 1971);

Dragoljub-Dragan Nedeljkovia, *Romain Rolland et Stefan Zweig* (Paris: Klincksieck, 1970);

Jacques Robichez, *Romain Rolland* (Paris: Hatier, 1961);

David Sices, *Music and the Musician in "Jean-Christophe": The Harmony of Contrasts* (New Haven & London: Yale University Press, 1969);

William Thomas Starr, *Romain Rolland and a World at War* (Evanston: Northwestern University Press, 1956);

Ronald A. Wilson, *The Pre-War Biographies of Romain Rolland and Their Place in his Work and the Period* (London: Oxford University Press, 1939);

Stefan Zweig, *Romain Rolland: The Man and His Work*, translated by Eden and Cedar Paul (New York: T. Seltzer, 1921).

Jules Romains
(Louis Farigoule)

(26 August 1885-14 August 1972)

William T. Starr
Northwestern University

SELECTED BOOKS: *Le Bourg régénéré, petite légende* (Paris: L. Vanier, 1906);

La Vie unanime (Paris: L'Abbaye, 1908);

Un Etre en marche (Paris: Mercure de France, 1910);

Manuel de déification (Paris: E. Sansot, 1910);

L'Armée dans la ville (Paris: Mercure de France, 1911);

Mort de quelqu'un (Paris: E. Figuière, 1911); translated by Desmond MacCarthy and Sydney Waterlow as *The Death of a Nobody* (London: Latimer, 1914; New York: Huebsch, 1914);

Puissances de Paris (Paris: E. Figuière, 1911);

Les Copains (Paris: E. Figuière, 1913); translated by Jacques Le Clerq as *The Boys in the Back Room* (New York: McBride, 1937);

Odes et prières (Paris: Mercure de France, 1913);

Sur les quais de la Villette (Paris: E. Figuière, 1914); republished as *Le Vin blanc de la Villette* (Paris: Gallimard, 1923);

Europe (Paris: Gallimard, 1916);

Cromedeyre-le-Vieil (Paris: Gallimard, 1920);

Donogoo-Tonka, ou Les Miracles de la science (Paris: Gallimard, 1920); translated and adapted by Gilbert Seldes as *Donogoo* (New York: Federal Theatre Project, 1937);

La Vision extra-rétinienne et le sens paroptique, as Louis Farigoule (Paris: Gallimard, 1920; enlarged, 1921); translated by C. K. Ogden as *Eyeless Sight: A Study of Extra-retinal Vision and the Paroptic Sense* (London & New York: Putnam's, 1924);

Le Voyage des amants (Paris: Gallimard, 1920);

Amour couleur de Paris (Paris: Gallimard, 1921);

Monsieur Le Trouhadec saisi par la débauche (Paris: Gallimard, 1921);

Psyché, 3 volumes: *Lucienne, Le Dieu des corps, Quand le navire . . .* (Paris: Gallimard, 1922-1929); *Lucienne* translated by Waldo Frank (New York: Boni & Liveright, 1924); all three volumes translated by John Rodker

Jules Romains in 1948 (photograph by Roger Viollet)

as *The Body's Rapture* (Oxford: Boriswood, 1933; New York: Liveright, 1933);

Petit Traité de versification, by Romains and G. Chennevière (Paris: Gallimard, 1923);

Knock, ou Le Triomphe de la médecine. Monsieur Le Trouhadec saisi par la débauche (Paris: Gallimard, 1924); translated by Hanley Granville-Barker as *Doctor Knock* (London: Benn, 1925; New York: French, 1925); translated by James B. Gidney as *Knock* (Woodbury, N.Y.: Barron's, 1962);

Le Mariage de Le Trouhadec; La Scintillante (Paris: Gallimard, 1925); *La Scintillante* translated by F. Vernon as *The Peach*, in *Modern One-act Plays from the French* (New York: Holt, 1933);

Le Dictateur (Paris: Gallimard, 1925);

Chants des dix années (Paris: Gallimard, 1928);

Volpone, adapted from Ben Jonson's play by Romains and Stefan Zweig (Paris: Gallimard, 1929);

Le Déjeuner marocain (Paris: Gallimard, 1929);

Jean le Maufranc (Paris: Gallimard, 1929); revised and republished in *Musse; précédé de la première version, Jean le Maufranc* (Paris: Gallimard, 1929);

Pièces en un acte: La Scintillante; Amédée et les messieurs en rang; Démétrios; Le Déjeuner marocain (Paris: Gallimard, 1930);

Problèmes d'aujourd'hui (Paris: Editions KRA, 1931); revised as *Problèmes europeéns* (Paris: Flammarion, 1933);

Les Hommes de bonne volonté, 27 volumes: *Le 6 octobre, Crime de Quinette, Les Amours enfantines, Eros de Paris, Les Superbes, Les Humbles, Recherche d'une église, Province, Montée des périls, Les Pouvoirs, Recours à l'abîme, Les Créateurs, Mission à Rome, Le Drapeau noir, Prélude à Verdun, Verdun, Vorge contre Quinette, La Douceur de la vie, Cette Grande Lueur à l'est, Le Monde est ton aventure, Journée dans la montagne, Les Travaux et les joies, Naissance de la bande, Comparutions, Le Tapis magique, Françoise, Le 7 octobre* (Paris: Flammarion, 1932-1946); translated by W. B. Wells and Gerard Hopkins as *Men of Good Will*, 14 volumes (New York: Knopf, 1933-1946; London & Toronto: Dickson, 1933-1946);

Le Couple France-Allemagne (Paris: Flammarion, 1934);

Boën, ou La Possession des biens (Paris: Gallimard, 1935);

Visite aux Américains (Paris: Flammarion, 1936);

L'Homme blanc (Paris: Flammarion, 1937);

Cela dépend de vous (Paris: Flammarion, 1939);

Sept Mystères de destin de l'Europe (New York: Editions de la Maison Française, 1940); translated by Germaine Brée as *Seven Mysteries of Europe* (New York: Knopf, 1940; London & Melbourne: Hutchinson, 1941);

Salsette découvre l'Amérique (New York: Editions de la Maison Française, 1940); translated by Lewis Galantière as *Salsette Discovers America* (New York: Knopf, 1942; London: Hutchinson, 1942);

Grâce encore pour la terre! (New York: Editions de la Maison Française, 1941);

Nomentanus le réfugié (New York: Editions de la Maison Française, 1943; Paris: Table Ronde, 1945);

Bertrand de Ganges (New York: Editions de la Maison Française, 1944); republished in *Bertrand de Ganges, Suivi de Nomentanus le réfugié* (Paris: Flammarion, 1947);

Retrouver la foi (New York: Editions de la Maison Française, 1944; Paris: Flammarion, 1945);

Le Colloque de novembre. Discours de réception de Jules Romains à l'Académie Française et réponse de Georges Duhamel de l'Académie Française (Paris: Flammarion, 1946);

Le Problème numéro un (Paris: Plon, 1947);

Pierres levées (Paris: Flammarion, 1948);

Le Moulin et l'hospice (Paris: Flammarion, 1949);

Salsette découvre l'Amérique, suivi de Lettres de Salsette (Paris: Flammarion, 1950);

Violation de frontières (Paris: Flammarion, 1951); translated by Hopkins as *Tussles with Time* (London: Sidgwick & Jackson, 1952);

Interviews avec Dieu, as John W. Hicks (Paris: Flammarion, 1952);

Saints de notre calendrier: Goethe, Balzac, Hugo, Baudelaire, Gobineau, Zola, Strindberg, France, Zweig, Gide, Chennevière, Fargue (Paris: Flammarion, 1952);

Maisons (Paris: Seghers, 1953);

Examen de conscience des français (Paris: Flammarion, 1954); translated by Cornelia Schaeffer as *A Frenchman Examines His Conscience* (London: Deutsch, 1955);

Situation de la terre (Paris: Flammarion, 1954); translated by Richard Howard as *As It Is on Earth* (New York: Macmillan, 1962);

Passagers de cette planète, où allons nous? (Paris: Grasset, 1955);

Le Fils de Jerphanion (Paris: Flammarion, 1956);

Le Roman des douze, by Romains and others (Paris: R. Julliard, 1957);

Une Femme singulière (Paris: Flammarion, 1957); translated by A. Pomerans as *The Adventuress* (London: Muller, 1958);

Souvenirs et confidences d'un écrivain (Paris: Fayard, 1958);

Le Besoin de voir clair: Deuxième rapport Antonelli (Paris: Flammarion, 1958);

Hommes, médecins, machines (Paris: Flammarion, 1959);

Mémoires de Madame Chauverel, 2 volumes (Paris: Flammarion, 1959, 1960);

Les Hauts et la bas de la liberté (Paris: Flammarion, 1960);

Pour raison garder (Paris: Flammarion, 1960);

Un Grand Honnête Homme (Paris: Flammarion, 1961);

Portraits d'inconnus (Paris: Flammarion, 1962);

Ai-je fait ce que j'ai voulu? (Paris: Wesmaël-Charlier, 1964);

Lettres à un ami, 2 volumes (Paris: Flammarion, 1964, 1965);

Lettre ouverte contre une vaste conspiration (Paris: A. Michel, 1966); translated by Harold J. Salemson as *Open Letter Against a Vast Conspiracy* (New York: J. H. Heinemann, 1968);

Marc-Aurèle, ou L'Empereur de bonne volonté (Paris: Flammarion, 1968);

Amitiés et rencontres (Paris: Flammarion, 1970).

PLAY PRODUCTIONS: *L'Armée dans la ville,* Paris, Théâtre de l'Odéon, 4 March 1911;

Cromedeyre-le-Vieil, Paris, Théâtre du Vieux-Colombier, 26 May 1920;

M. Le Trouhadec saisi par la débauche, Paris, Comédie des Champs-Elysées, 14 March 1923;

Amédee et les messieurs en rang, Paris, Comédie des Champs-Elysées, 15 December 1923;

Knock, ou Le Triomphe de la médecine, Paris, Comédie des Champs-Elysées, 15 December 1923;

La Scintillante, Paris, Comédie des Champs-Elysées, 7 October 1924;

Le Mariage de Le Trouhadec, Paris, Comédie des Champs-Elysées, 31 January 1925;

Le Dictateur, Paris, Comédie des Champs-Elysées, 5 October 1926;

Démétrios, Paris, Comédie des Champs-Elysées, 9 October 1926;

Jean le Maufranc, Paris, Théâtre des Arts, 1 December 1926; revised as *Musse, ou l'école de l'hypocrisie,* Paris, Théâtre de l'Atelier, 21 November 1930;

Volpone, adapted from Ben Jonson's play by Romains and Stefan Zweig, Paris, Théâtre de l'Atelier, 23 November 1928;

Le Déjeuner marocain, Paris, Théâtre Saint-Georges, 9 February 1929;

Boën, ou La Possession des biens, Paris, Théâtre de l'Odéon, 4 December 1930;

Donogoo, ou Les Miracles de la science, Paris, Théâtre Pigalle, 25 October 1930;

Le Roi masqué, Paris, Théâtre Pigalle, 19 December 1931;

L'An mil, Paris, Théâtre Sarah-Bernhardt, 5 March 1947.

PERIODICAL PUBLICATIONS: "Ode génoise," *Nouvelle Revue Française,* 22 (1 May 1924): 517-537;

L'An mil, Revue de Paris, 54 (May 1947): 3-20; (June 1947): 29-50; (July 1947): 18-50;

"Ce Siècle avait dix ans: Une jeunesse littéraire," *Conférencia,* 38 (15 December 1949): 483-498.

Jules Romains's principal fictional works appeared on the French literary scene shortly after the major works of Marcel Proust; some of the important works of Roger Martin du Gard, author of *Les Thibault* (1922-1940), preceded Romains's works, and the novels of Georges Duhamel were appearing at about the same time as those of Romains. In spite of the stature of the first two and keen competition from the third, Romains's novels found an important place on the literary scene in France. Animated by a new broad conception of society, although perhaps not as penetrating in this respect as the nineteenth-century novels of Honoré de Balzac, and infused with an optimism as great as the pessimism of Emile Zola and the naturalist school, the novels made their way very quickly among a broad reading public. They represent a continuation of the older humanistic tradition, but infused with a new vision of society, a society torn loose from many of its traditional values by the catastrophe of World War I. To many, Romains's novels seemed to offer a significant and penetrating picture and analysis of the society of the times. The considerations on war, the depiction of it and analysis of its causes, lent an importance to these works that few others of the time possessed.

Jules Romains, dramatist, poet, essayist, and novelist, was born Louis-Henry-Jean-Farigoule on 26 August 1885 in Saint-Julien-Chapteuil. He received all of his education in Paris, where his father, Henri Farigoule, was a teacher. Romains completed his studies at the Lycée Condorcet, where he was awarded the diplomas in letters and in sciences in July 1901. In July 1904 he received a scholarship which permitted him to study for a diploma in belles lettres at the Sorbonne. The next year he passed the competitive examination for enrollment in the Ecole Normale Supérieure and earned a *licence ès lettres.* Before he could enroll, he had to spend a year of obligatory military service, so that it was not until October 1906 that he actually entered the celebrated Ecole Normale, situated in rue d'Ulm in

Paris. In July 1907 he was awarded diplomas in physiology and botany; in July 1908 he earned a diploma in histology. The combination of these two diplomas entitled him to a *licence ès sciences*. At the termination of his three years of study at the Ecole Normale, he was awarded in 1909 the title of *agrégé* in philosophy, which authorized him to teach in any of the state secondary schools or in the schools of law, pharmacy, or medicine.

Religion played an important role in his evolution. As a child he showed a sincere and profound piety during his catechism lessons and at his first communion in the church of Notre-Dame-de-Clignancourt in Paris. As he grew older doubts began to torment him and, after long and painful debates within himself, he abandoned the faith of his childhood. He found help and comfort in his reading of Lucretius's *De rerum natura* (On the Nature of Things) and many years later confessed that one of the sources of his poetic inspiration was this crisis of religious conscience.

As a youngster Romains had listened attentively to his father who read to the assembled family Zola's *La Débâcle* (1892), a novel of the Franco-Prussian War of 1870-1871, which ended in the defeat of France. A few years later Romains saw Zola himself in Paris, where the novelist was giving public readings. Along with Balzac, Zola was later an important influence on Romains as a novelist. Among his favorite authors, Anatole France occupied an important place; in 1923 Anatole France asked the younger writer to repeat his experiments with extraretinal vision, eyeless sight ("vision extra-rétinienne") for him in the former's apartment in Saint-Cloud. The experiment had been published in 1920 as *La Vision extra-rétinienne et le sens paroptique* (translated as *Eyeless Sight: A Study of Extra-retinal Vision and the Paroptic Sense*, 1924).

Romains's education included not only the French classics of the seventeenth and eighteenth centuries, but also nineteenth-century poets, such as Victor Hugo, a major influence, and Charles Baudelaire, whom Romains was exposed to outside the classroom. His studies of German also brought him into contact with German authors, especially of Schiller, whose works seem to have served as models for some of Romains's later works; his admiration for *Don Carlos* (1787) was enduring. Henri Bergson with his philosophy of intuition, the *élan vital*, and the *élan initial* and the theories of the sociologist Emile Durkheim concerning the psychology of social groups had an important influence on his thinking and writing.

In October 1903, as Romains and his friend Georges Chennevière were walking in the rue d'Amsterdam in Paris, the former had a sudden vision of the unity of the city and all its components, with a collective consciousness. They proceeded to call their intuition of collective wholes *Unanimisme,* and to take it as a point of departure for literary works.

Romains met the poet and future novelist Georges Duhamel in 1907, at the home of the young writer René Arcos, and he soon became one of Duhamel's closest friends. His later excursions into what he called unanimism grew in part out of his early feelings of group dynamics in Paris and out of his association, in 1906, with the Groupe de l'Abbaye, an experiment in communal living organized in part by Duhamel. Duhamel later wrote about the experiences of this group (which included Arcos, Charles Vildrac, Georges Périn, Georges Chennevière and Luc Durtain) in one of the volumes of his *Chronique des Pasquier* (1933-1944; translated as *The Pasquier Chronicles,* 1937-1946). The Abbey was located near Créteil, within easy commuting distance of Paris. Unlike the core members of the group, Romains did not reside there but visited frequently. The experiment played a crucial role in Romains's formulation of unanimism, a theory holding that the psychology of the group–social, political, or intellectual–is of primary importance in the motivation and orientation of the individual. The individual, and particularly the poet, Romains held, can be powerful only when he merges with a larger, and more important, collective whole. Although unanimism grew in part out of the work of Durkheim, Romains was one of the first to enlarge the scope of this new sociology by making it the basis of his writings. In Romains's first formulations unanimism was a benevolent force, but the destruction and carnage of World War I caused him to reflect on the dangers of group dynamism.

Some of Romains's first poems were first published in the periodical *La Phalange,* directed by Jean Royère, a young poet himself who encouraged other young poets. Viélé-Griffin, the older symbolist poet, was the journal's protector, and Albert Thibaudet, poet and critic, was one of the contributors; others were René Ghil, Luc Durtain, Georges Chennevière, and Guillaume Apollinaire. Through these young writers Romains met such painters and critics as Max Jacob, André Salmon, Pablo Picasso, and Marie Laurencin. In 1908, his long poem *La Vie unanime* (The

Unanimist Life) was published. In it he emphasized the collective consciousness of the group—household, neighborhood, city, province, nation, or nations. His other volumes of poetry published before World War I were: *Un Etre en marche* (Someone Walking, 1910), and *Odes et prières* (Odes and Prayers, 1913).

In the fall of 1909 Romains began to teach at the lycée in Brest, where he remained for one year. In 1910 he became closely associated with the well-known theatrical producer and director André Antoine. At the same time he was writing a play, *L'Armée dans la ville* (The Army in the City, 1911). The subject was a war between two great modern nations and the occupation of the one country by the victorious army of the other. According to Romains, when he was at work on this play he was deeply involved in developing the idea of unanimism, and he attached great importance to the theatrical expression of his philosophy. When he discussed the work with Antoine, he was told to bring the completed text, and it would be read—and produced, if suitable. *L'Armée dans la ville* was presented at Paris's Odéon theater, 4 March 1911.

In October 1911 Romains was appointed to the faculty of the lycée at Laon, near Paris, where he established residence. In 1911 and 1912 he seems to have taught at the Ecole Polytechnique and Saint-Cyr (a military academy). His first wife, Gabrielle Gaffé (known as G. G.), was the daughter of a colleague of Romains's father. G. G. had married a draftsman of the French national railway system in 1906 and was divorced in 1911. Romains celebrated his marriage to her during Easter vacation, 1912. After their marriage Romains and G. G. went to Italy and to the Côte d'Azur where Romains later bought a small dwelling in Hyères. In 1913 he traveled in Switzerland, Holland, and Belgium.

As a poet Romains had definite ideas concerning the essence of poetry and the role of the poet. Like Victor Hugo, he believed in the poet as a seer. Poetry, he wrote, does not live "on the moon." It has its roots in a particular time, in the humanity of a particular epoch. Truly creative poetry must transform, by means of its own light, the world it faces and the objects it evokes, no matter how trivial and contemporary. Poetry and literature in general are privileged instruments for the conquest of the universe by the soul and the psyche of man. Their function, almost mystic, is to constitute the farthest point of the conscious awareness of reality. For Romains, as for other

Romains at the time of his association with producer-director André Antoine. In 1911 Antoine staged Romains's first play, L'Armée dans la ville, *in Paris at the Théâtre de l'Odéon (photograph by Marlingue).*

poets of his generation, Rimbaud was a true precursor: he taught through his example a prophetic consciousness of the world as it lies before the living soul and he continued in the tradition of Charles Baudelaire, for whom poetry was the autonomous exploration of the universe by the human soul.

In poetry Romains found a particularly apt medium to express his conception of unanimist life. In his 1958 memoirs *Souvenirs et confidences d'un écrivain* (A Writer's Memories and Confidences), he wrote that he had always more liking for what joins men rather than for what divides them. He affirmed his belief that there is virtue in union, that unity seems to engender forces inherent in itself, especially when the creation of an epoch—whether social or intellectual—is at hand.

At the outbreak of World War I, as a member of the auxiliary army, Romains was charged with the administration of the Service des Allocations, or dependents' allotments service in an office in Paris. Here he remained for two years. In 1916 he was appointed temporary instructor in the Collège Rollin, and his volume of poems, *Europe,* appeared. In October 1917 he was named professor of philosophy at the University of Nice, where he stayed until after the war.

In *Europe* Romains expresses his horror of what seemed to him a European civil war. The continent, rather than the nation, becomes the unanimist group, which, unfortunately, seems bent on its own destruction. With his belief in unanimism and in the power of the poet, Romains campaigned against war more vigorously than perhaps any other French poet of the time. He compared the outbreak of conflict to the relapse of a rehabilitated drug addict: the war of 1914-1918 interrupted a process of social rehabilitation in which war was being eliminated from the human psyche and opened the way for more of the same barbarous attitudes and actions. Romains's campaign against war is one of several important themes in various volumes of his major work, the novelistic series *Les Hommes de bonne volonté* (1932-1946; translated as *Men of Good Will,* 1933-1946).

Like *Les Hommes de bonne volonté,* Romains's early novels deal with crowd psychology and unanimistic philosophy. His first novel, *Mort de quelqu'un* (1911, translated as *The Death of a Nobody,* 1914) has as its subject the death of a solitary apartment-dweller completely unknown to his neighbors—a death which gives the other tenants a new sense of unanimity and solidarity before this phenomenon common to all mankind. By his use of simultaneous actions and his eschewing of a hero, or dominant character, Romains made *Mort de quelqu'un* interesting in technique as well as content. It was followed by the humorous novel *Les Copains* (1913; translated as *The Boys in the Back Room,* 1937), partially set in the provincial town of Ambert which Romains had visited on a tour along the Loire undertaken during his days as a student at the Ecole Normale Supérieure.

The theme of this novel is a humanism—the sort in which the humanist finally succumbs to a paralyzing complacency of which he himself is aware, and which, he realizes, will negate his plans conceived in a moment of rapt vision. The novel narrates in a series of comic episodes the plot to regenerate a unanimist consciousness in the quiet provincial towns of Ambert and Issoire. It presents a group of practical jokers, reminis-

cent of those Romains knew in his student days, who descend on the two small towns, shaking the one out of its torpor and causing the inhabitants of the other to flee in terror. The youths claim to have restored the "pure act," anticipating perhaps the notion of the "acte gratuit" (gratuitous act), developed by André Gide in *Les Caves du Vatican* (1914; translated as *The Vatican Swindle,* 1925) after he had first introduced it in *Le Prométhée mal enchaîné* (1899; translated as *Prometheus Illbound,* 1919). *Les Copains* was dear to the author, who wrote in *Souvenirs et confidences d'un écrivain* that the characters were true comrades and that when he felt depressed he often thought of them. In contrast to this novel, *Psyché,* (1922-1929) in three volumes, *Lucienne, Le Dieu des corps,* and *Quand le navire . . .* (all translated in 1933 as *The Body's Rapture*), is almost a psychological novel, treating the topic of ideal love, on both the intellectual and the physical plane, through the couple Lucienne and Pierre Febvre. The first volume, which tells of their meeting and the formation of their powerful attachment, narrowly missed winning the Prix Goncourt for 1922.

Romains's long series of novels, *Les Hommes de bonne volonté,* is one of the most imposing extended works of fiction written in France since Balzac and Zola. The enterprise is vaster than that of Zola, who limited himself to re-creating the life of one family (a large family, to be sure) during the Second Empire. Moreover, Romains differs from Balzac and Zola by having each volume of his series (except for the last two) depend on preceding ones. His works lack, however, the breadth and intensity of the earlier novelists; neither the characters nor the ambience in which they move seems as sharply and penetratingly evoked. Nevertheless, *Les Hommes de bonne volonté* remains an important modern novel, although few of the twenty-seven volumes are still widely read.

The series was planned as a panorama of French society from 1908 to 1933. The story line begins in Paris, 6 October 1908, and moves to the French provinces, to various foreign countries, then back to the provinces, and finally to Paris, where it ends, on 7 October 1933. The first four volumes are a kind of introduction. The first novel in the series, *Le 6 octobre* (*The Sixth of October*), covers one day in 1908 when news of the crisis in the Balkans, which eventually brought about World War I, appears in the Parisian newspapers while the people of Paris, unaware of the significance of these events, go

Romains with T. S. Eliot in London, 1949

about their daily affairs as usual. The two most important characters of the series as a whole, Jean Jerphanion and Pierre Jallez, appear first in volumes two and three, *Crime de Quinette* (*Quinette's Crime*, based in part on the Landru case, a French version of the case of Jack the Ripper) and *Les Amours enfantines* (*Childhood's Loves*). The two men probably represent two sides of Romains's own character, the practical and the sensitive. Romains's use of these two permits the discussion of a wide variety of contemporary topics and the introduction of a large amount of autobiographical material. The next several volumes of *Les Hommes de bonne volonté* introduce the themes of sentimentality and sexuality as well as new groups of characters, some of which are in sharp contrast to one another and which, brought together by the author, are to form a complete picture of society.

Jean Jerphanion and Pierre Jallez, whom the reader first meets in the Ecole Normale Supérieure, where they are "internes" (students who live in and study there), stand out as the most memorable of the characters. They take long and frequent walks throughout Paris through which the author brings the city in all its varied character before the reader and discusses all sorts of social, philosophical, and even psychological questions. Volumes fifteen and sixteen,

Prélude à Verdun (*Verdun. The Prelude*) and *Verdun*, were written in the late 1930s, under the threat of a second impending war, and reflect a weakening of the optimism which is expressed in the general title of the series. In these two volumes Romains typifies the selfishness and self-sacrifice, the horrors and bravery displayed in one important World War I battle and thus of war itself. The battle is seen through the eyes of few characters, but the novelist maintains his unanimist perspective of whole armies functioning as a unit. Romains's unanimism, however, is in these later works a force that negates the individual rather than promoting his value. *Prélude à Verdun* and *Verdun* are among the best novels in the series. The last volumes of *Les Hommes de bonne volonté* deal with the disillusion of post-World War I France, the utopian vision in Russia, the negative menace of another collective movement, Fascism, and the beginnings of Nazism in Germany.

Romains's dramas are among his best and most enduring works. The violence that can be the result of group hysteria is the dominant theme of the verse drama *Cromedeyre-le-Vieil* (1920), concerning an isolated mountain village, where the men far outnumber the women and raid a neighboring village to even the balance. In another text written during the same period, as a film scenario for a project of the poet Blaise

Cendrars, which never materialized, *Donogoo-Tonka, ou Les Miracles de la science* (1920; translated as *Donogoo*, 1937) violence is replaced by relatively innocuous fraud.

The plot involves the geographer Le Trouhadec, title character of two later comedies, *Monsieur Le Trouhadec saisi par la débauche* (Monsieur Le Trouhadec Seized by Debauchery, 1921), and *Le Mariage de Le Trouhadec* (Trouhadec's Marriage, 1925). He is a professor of geography at the Collège de France and a candidate for election to the prestigious Institut de France. But he has discovered that a South American town, Donogoo-Tonka, which he described years before, does not exist, and he fears being unmasked as a fraud. Lamendin, who earlier appeared in *Les Copains*, proposes to assist him by creating the town. This is done by means of an enormous publicity campaign that appeals to greed: the lure of gold draws numerous pioneers, who ironically really do find mineral wealth and whose mining camp becomes a prosperous city, of which Lamendin then seizes dictatorial control. The play satirizes modern advertising, the public response to it, academic pedantry, and pseudo-science. It also contains unanimist elements, the new city being a unit. However, the city's creator and leader is not truly one with it, as would be the case ideally according to unanimism; he is instead a trickster and an exploiter.

In 1930 Romains turned the scenario into a play called *Donogoo*. In the author's eyes it was an important play because of its unanimistic themes: the action of an idea on the masses, the propagation of this idea through and by the masses independent of its true value, the fabrication of a myth and a mystique, the aptitude of men to endow with real existence those ideas in which they believe with sufficient conviction, the fecundity of myth which can produce both good and evil, and the role of a leader whether he be a puppet or a true leader of men.

Romains's best play is *Knock, ou, Le Triomphe de la médecine* (1924; translated as *Doctor Knock*, 1925). The well-known actor and producer Louis Jouvet triumphed as the title character and hero. *Knock, ou, Le Triomphe de la médecine* is a lighthearted comedy concerning a charlatan who convinces the members of an entire town that they are sick and need his services and his medicines. A similar dramatic success, starring Jouvet again, was his play *Le Dictateur* (1925).

Romains was extremely conscious of national and international movements and events, and was politically active. Even before the Congrès de Tours (1922), the meeting in Tours at which the socialist party divided into two groups, the SFIO (Section Française de l'Internationale Ouvrière, or French Section of the Socialist Party) on the one hand, and the Parti Communiste Français on the other, he had begun to collaborate on the newspaper that was later to become the official organ of the French Communist Party, *L'Humanité*. At the request of Jean Jaurès, the socialist leader, he was responsible for the newspaper's poetry section.

Since his days as a student at the Ecole Normale, Romains had been a frequent and enthusiastic traveler. His first postwar trip was in 1921, when he went on a cruise which included North Africa, Barcelona, Spain, and the island of Sardinia. In 1924 he made his first trip to the United States to attend the P.E.N. Congress, the first of many such meetings in which he participated. The following year he went to Berlin, where he spoke at the Berlin City Hall on the subject of Franco-German relations, asserting: "Nous jurons qu'il n'y aura plus jamais entre nous le front des armées" (We swear that henceforth there will never be front lines of armies between us).

In 1926 he attended the meetings of the P.E.N. Congress in Berlin, where he again spoke of Franco-German relations and met Albert Einstein. In 1933 he attended the meetings of the same club, of which he would be elected president in 1936, at Dubrovnik, where his authority made itself felt as he brought about the exclusion of the German delegation composed of Nazis. In 1927 he went to Vienna to the centenary celebration of Beethoven's death, where he represented *L'Illustration*, a fashionable illustrated magazine of current events. There he met and conversed with Sigmund Freud. Among his acquaintances of this time he counted the Italian writer Luigi Pirandello; the two of them dined together and discussed plans (which never materialized) to collaborate in the writing of a play with a Mediterranean theme.

During the year 1934 he attended a congress in Rome and then went to Venice, where he was invited to a state banquet. Toward the end of that year, he went to visit the prominent politician Pierre Laval, to whom he carried a message from Goebbels in Hitler's name. His association with these members of the Nazi party was unfortunate but was typical of his varied and sometimes contradictory associates and ideas. In 1935, in London, he dined with Stefan Zweig, the Austrian writer of Jewish descent with whom he had collaborated in the late 1920s on an adaptation of Ben Jonson's play *Volpone*. Romains had been one of the defenders of Maurice Maeterlinck whose symbolist play *Pelléas et Mélisande* (1892) had aroused sharp controversy because of its defense of adultery and its unconventional technique, and Maeterlinck invited him to his home, Les Abeilles. In 1935 Romains, Maeterlinck, Duhamel, and other representatives of France were guests of honor of the Portuguese government. Romains spent the winter and spring of 1936 in Nice, where he held the chair of philosophy at the University of Nice and continued his association with Zweig. Early in the same year he made the acquaintance of the novelist Roger Martin du Gard, whom he met almost daily.

In December 1938 Hendrik de Man called on him in the name of the King of Belgium to head a mission of a very difficult and delicate nature to Edouard Daladier's government in France. The kings of Sweden, Norway, Denmark, and Belgium and the Queen of Holland, in a conference at Oslo, had conceived the project of an official conference for peace in which the "Big Four" (England, Germany, Italy, and France) were to take part. Romains was designated to sound out secretly Prime Minister Daladier.

After his 1936 divorce from G. G., following a two-year separation, Romains celebrated his second marriage, on 18 December 1936, to Lisa Dreyfus, daughter of a wealthy businessman, and the couple took up residence in an apartment in the Faubourg Saint-Honoré in Paris. The poet Paul Valéry was a witness to the ceremony. On 31 October 1938 Romains met the French president Vincent Auriol at a banquet for the Anciens Combattants de la Haute Garonne (Veterans from the Haute Garonne). Some time before the outbreak of World War II, he had been invited to teach at Mills College in California; after visiting Spain and Portugal, he and his wife arrived in New York on 15 July 1940.

After some two years in the United States he took up residence in Mexico City, where he became one of the directors of the Institut Français au Mexique. In 1945 he was again in the United States; in New York his public lectures under the auspices of the Alliance Française were well attended by audiences who were especially enthusiastic following the liberation of France from Nazi occupation the previous summer and fall.

After his return from exile in the United States and Mexico, and throughout his last decades, Romains remained very active and productive, remarkably so for a man no longer in his middle years. Romains was elected to the Académie Française in 1946. He was later designated to represent that body at the funeral of French statesman Edouard Herriot. In 1950 Romains served as president of the Fêtes de Paris commission, preparing for the bimillenary celebration of the founding of the city of Paris. His books in all genres reveal an author greatly concerned with social and moral questions, and often despairing of the quality of life in postwar Europe and even the possibility that mankind would survive to the next century. In that way, he was as *engagé*, or committed, as the writers who were the darlings of postwar France, and he had, through his radio broadcasts, done as much as many of them to contribute to the Allied victory; but his tone was that of a wise elder rather than a contemporary, and he did not have the wide appeal of Sartre and others. Many of his later works are, moreover, distinctly inferior to earlier ones; other reveal that he did not have the acute political, social, and philosophical insights to which he often laid claim. Among his postwar creative works, *L'An mil* (The Year One Thousand, 1947), his last play to be staged, contrasts fear, manipulation, and greed with philosophical serenity and the ability to enjoy life. Another play, "Barbazouk" (1963), never performed in France, treats the theme of power in an Oriental setting and with a plot involving a king and a commoner who switch roles.

In the novel *Le Moulin et l'hospice* (The Mill and the Hospice, 1949), set in the sixteenth century, Romains deals with the topic of intolerance during the religious wars and the efforts of reasonable and enlightened people to preserve their lives and culture in the face of fanaticism. Another fictional work, *Le Fils de Jerphanion* (Jerphanion's Son, 1956), while not a part of *Les Hommes de bonne volonté*, can be seen as a sequel, but the son of the title turns out to be morally inferior to the heroes of the earlier books, a fact that reflects the author's pessimism and disappointment with the generation that came to adulthood after World War II. Romains also produced another series of novels, consisting of *Une Femme singulière* (The Adventuress, 1957), *Le Besoin de voir clair* (The Need to See Clearly, 1958), and

Romains conferring on André Maurois the distinction of Grand Officier de la Légion d'Honneur, 1954
(photograph by Gérald Maurois)

two volumes of *Mémoires de Madame Chauverel* (1959, 1960), purportedly the memoirs of the heroine. These works are, unfortunately, inferior to the best of his earlier fiction and of less intrinsic interest to many readers, since the author eschews the attempt to portray a large segment of society and deal with the most pressing problems of Europe in this century, and instead creates an implausible plot based on political and sexual intrigue.

Romains also published a number of lengthy essays and historical volumes, on topics such as the atomic bomb and war, which he qualified as *Le Problème numéro un* (Problem Number 1, 1947), literary figures, whom he called *Saints de notre calendrier* (Saints of Our Calendar, 1952), and the Fourth Republic. Under the name John W. Hicks he published *Interviews avec Dieu* (1952), in which a journalist ostensibly interviews God—a Deity far removed from the Biblical portrait, who is silent on many central theological questions. Romains also published *Maisons* (Houses, 1953), a volume of poetry, and essays on Alexander the Great, Napoleon, Galileo, and Marcus Aurelius; the latter he called, as the title puts it, *Marc-Aurèle, ou L'Empereur de bonne volonté* (1968), a reminder of the "men of good will" of his long novel series. In *Ai-je fait ce que j'ai voulu?* (Did I Do What I Wanted?, 1964) and *Amitiés et rencontres* (Friendships and Meetings, 1970), Romains looked back over his own career and reminisced about literary figures he had known; his judg-

ments on Charles Péguy and André Gide are harsh, whereas his portrait of his friend Chennevière is generous and tender. *Amitiés et rencontres* was Romains's last book. He died in Paris on 14 August 1972, twelve days before his eighty-seventh birthday.

Romains's works, especially his fiction and his best plays, certainly deserve a permanent place in twentieth century French literature. Despite his poetic writings and certain idealistic elements in his thought, he can be seen as having created one of the monuments of modern realism. *Knock* remains a favorite of readers and theater goers, *Mort de quelqu'un* is not only an excellent example of a unanimist vision but also anticipates to some degree later developments in fiction that feature the collectivity, and the books dealing with Verdun, as well as other volumes in *Les Hommes de bonne volonté*, can be considered important and revealing works concerning the war and society in France in the first third of this century. As a poet, his reputation has suffered considerable eclipse, perhaps because, despite his innovative unanimist vision, he insisted on retaining rhyme and other features of classical prosody, and, while accepting departures such as the fourteen-syllable line, argued that versification should become more complex than before, a position that goes against the trends of the century. Some of what he thought to be his most important accomplishments, including his work on extra-retinal vision and the philosophic and psychological grounding of unanimism, has never been appreciated by the public as he wished, and in his latter years he acquired a jaundiced view of the critics and scholars, along with a sense of disappointment inspired by the indifference of the reading public to many of his works, a disappointment which was not entirely offset by his election to the Academy and his prosperity. In some ways he produced too much, of uneven quality, and his frequent prolixity has not found favor with those who prefer a chiseled style and understatement and suggestion. Nor has the *roman-fleuve* or series novel been highly regarded as a genre since the advent of the New Novelists. Yet his powerful, often moving depictions of people and society, informed by a vision that sees them as a whole, and his incisive character portraits have many admirers, and, along with imposing fictional series by such novelists as Proust, Martin du Gard, and Duhamel, *Les Hommes de bonne volonté* remains a major work of social realism in France.

Letters:

Correspondance Jacques Copeau-Jules Romains, Cahiers Jules Romains, 2 (Paris: Flammarion, 1978);

Correspondance André Gide-Jules Romains, edited by Claude Martin (Lyon: Publications du Centre d'Etudes Gidiennes, 1979).

References:

Actes du colloque Jules Romains. Paris. Bibliothèque nationale, 17-18 février 1978 (Paris: Flammarion, 1979);

Douglas W. Alden, "The News on October 6," *Romance Notes,* 12 (Spring 1971): 235-243;

Alden, "Quinette, Landru, and Raskolnikoff," *French Review,* 43 (December 1969): 215-226;

Harry Bergholz, "Jules Romains and his 'Men of Good Will,'" *Modern Language Journal,* 35 (April 1951): 303-309;

Madeleine Berry, *Jules Romains, sa vie, son œuvre* (Paris: Editions du Conquistador, 1953);

Berry, "L'Œuvre poétique et romanesque de Jules Romains," *Cahiers de la Compagnie Madeleine Renaud-Jean-Louis Barrault,* 3, no. 9 (1955): 27-34;

Denis Boak, *Jules Romains* (New York: Twayne, 1974);

Germaine Brée and Margaret Guiton, "Georges Duhamel and Jules Romains: Men of Good Will," in their *An Age of Fiction* (New Brunswick: Rutgers University Press, 1957);

Cahiers Jules Romains (Paris: Flammarion, 1976-1982);

John Cocking, "Jules Romains and Unanimism." *World Review,* new series, 27 (May 1951): 33-37;

Etiemble, "Déchéance de Jules Romains ou le danger de la déification," *Temps Modernes,* 2 (July 1947): 154-162;

Wallace Fowlie, "The Novel of Jules Romains," *Southern Review,* 7 (Spring 1942): 880-892;

Philippe Jolivet, "Le Comique dans le théâtre de Jules Romains," *Orbis Litterarum,* 11 (1956): 229-236;

Jolivet, "*Les Hommes de bonne volonté* de Jules Romains, technique et style," *Nottingham French Studies,* 1 (May 1962): 39-49;

Jolivet, "Le Théâtre poétique de Jules Romains." *Orbis Litterarum,* 9 (1954): 120-128;

A. E. A. Naughton, "Jules Romains Pasticheur," *Modern Language Review,* 56 (January 1961): 24-27;

P. J. Norrish, *The Drama of The Group* (Cambridge: Cambridge University Press, 1958);

Norrish, "Romains and 'L'Abbaye,'" *Modern Language Review,* 52 (October 1957): 518-525;

Aaron Schaffer, "Jules Romains Despairs of Men of Good Will," *American Scholar,* 17 (Spring 1948): 191-200;

Ben Stoltzfus, "Unanimism Revisited," *Modern Language Quarterly,* 21 (September 1960): 239-245;

Leland Thielemann, "The Problem of Unity and Individualism in Romains' Social Philosophy," *Modern Language Quarterly,* 2 (1941): 249-262;

Harold H. Watts, "Jules Romains: The Quinette Beneath the Skin," *Rocky Mountain Review,* 10 (Spring 1946): 125-135;

Clotilde Wilson, "Sartre's Graveyard of Chimeras: *La Nausée* and *Mort de quelqu'un,*" *French Review,* 38 (1965): 744-753.

Jean Schlumberger

(26 May 1877-25 October 1968)

Jean-Pierre Cap
Lafayette College

SELECTED BOOKS: *Poèmes des temples et des tombeaux* (Paris: Mercure de France, 1903);
Le Mur de verre (Paris: Ollendorff, 1904);
Heureux qui comme Ulysse . . . (Paris: Cahiers de la Quinzaine, 1906);
Epigrammes romaines (Paris: Bibliothèque de l'Occident, 1910);
L'Inquiète Paternité (Paris: Nouvelle Revue Française, 1911);
Les Fils Louverné (Paris: Nouvelle Revue Française, 1914);
Un Homme heureux (Paris: Gallimard, 1920);
La Mort de Sparte (Paris: Gallimard, 1921);
Le Camarade infidèle (Paris: Gallimard, 1922);
Le Lion devenu vieux (Paris: Gallimard, 1924);
Dialogues avec le corps endormi (limited edition, Paris: Champion, 1925; trade edition, Paris: Gallimard, 1927);
L'Amour, le prince et la vérité (Paris: Sans Pareil, 1927);
Césaire, ou La Puissance de l'esprit (Paris: Gallimard, 1927);
L'Enfant qui s'accuse (Paris: Gallimard, 1927);
Les Yeux de dix-huit ans (Paris: Gallimard, 1928);
Saint-Saturnin (Paris: Gallimard, 1931); translated by Dorothy Bussy as *The Seventh Age* (New York: Dodd, Mead, 1932); Bussy's translation republished as *The Seventh Age; or, Saint Saturnin* (London: Gollancz, 1933);
Sur les frontières religieuses (Paris: Gallimard, 1934);
Histoire de quatre potiers (Paris: Gallimard, 1935);
Plaisir à Corneille (Paris: Gallimard, 1936);
Essais et dialogues (Paris: Gallimard, 1937);
Stéphane le Glorieux (Paris: Gallimard, 1940); translated by W. G. Corp as *Stefan the Proud* (London: Seagull Press, 1946);
Jalons (Marseilles: Sagittaire, 1941; New York: Brentano's, 1941; London: Penguin, 1945);
Nouveaux Jalons (Marseilles: Sagittaire, 1943);
Le Procès Pétain. Avant-propos et notes d'audience. Blessures et séquelles de la guerre (Paris: Gallimard, 1949);
Théâtre (Paris: Gallimard, 1949);

Jean Schlumberger (photograph by Laure Albin-Guillot)

Eveils (Paris: Gallimard, 1950);
Madeleine et André Gide (Paris: Gallimard, 1956);
Passion (Paris: Gallimard, 1956);
Rencontres. Feuilles d'agenda. Pierres de Rome (Paris: Gallimard, 1968).
Collection: *Œuvres*, 7 volumes (Paris: Gallimard, 1958-1961).

PLAY PRODUCTIONS: *On naît esclave,* by Schlumberger and Tristan Bernard, Paris, Théâtre du Vaudeville, 4 April 1912;
Les Fils Louverné, Paris, Théâtre du Vieux-Colombier, 1913;
La Mort de Sparte, Paris, Théâtre du Vieux-Colombier, 1921;
Césaire, ou La Puissance de l'esprit, Paris, Théâtre de la Chimère, 1922.

OTHER: Roger Martin du Gard, *Les Thibault*, preface by Schlumberger (Monte Carlo: Seuret, 1960-1961).

PERIODICAL PUBLICATIONS: "Enquête sur les sentiments: L'Instinct paternel," *Bulletin de l'Union pour la Vérité* (May 1909); "Le Visiteur de minuit; un acte de Jean Schlumberger," *L'Avant-Scene*, no. 66 (1958): 44-50.

Jean Schlumberger regarded himself primarily as a novelist and, indeed, both his experimental and traditional fiction constitute significant contributions to the genre. He is, however, perhaps best known today for his role as critic and administrator for the influential *Nouvelle Revue Française*, his participation in the founding of the Théâtre du Vieux-Colombier, and his lifelong friendship with André Gide.

Born into a wealthy Protestant family in Guebwiller, Alsace, on 26 May 1877, the son of Paul and Marguerite deWitt Schlumberger, Schlumberger was the great-grandson of the historian François Guizot on his mother's side. At fifteen Schlumberger left his native province, then a part of Imperial Germany, in order not to incur military service obligation in Germany. In Paris he studied the humanities at the Lycée Condorcet and later the history of religion at the Sorbonne. Before turning to literature, Schlumberger envisaged entering the ministry and traveled to Palestine. Also, he participated in the "Universités Populaires" movement, which in France was even less successful than it was in England. In 1899 he married Suzanne Weyher, a painter. They settled in Paris in a fifth-floor apartment near the Luxembourg Gardens which Jean Schlumberger occupied until his death. They had a son and two daughters. During the early years of their married life, they made two extended trips to Florence and Rome which were sources of inspiration for her painting and his poetry. Later, in addition to frequent stays at Braffy near the Val Richer, François Guizot's former estate in Normandy, and on the French Riviera, Schlumberger traveled in England, Germany, Switzerland, and, each year during the 1930s, to Morocco for a visit with his daughter, Monique, who had settled in that country.

Schlumberger began his literary career as a poet with *Poèmes des temples et des tombeaux* (Poems of Temples and Tombs, 1903), Goethean in inspiration and Parnassian in form, as are his *Epi-grammes romaines* (Roman Epigrams, 1910), and simultaneously as a novelist with *Le Mur de verre* (The Glass Wall, 1904). This first novel, with its symbolistic ambience, followed contemporary literary trends more closely than his poetry did. Its theme is the impossibility of complete or true communication between a couple in love. The plot explores the tragic dissolution of a marriage as the young bride is consumed by a languor caused at least in part by her disappointment with this grave imperfection of love. Although the book was well received, soon Schlumberger disavowed it as he began his friendship with Gide, who, like him, had Norman ties. From this time onward he was influenced by Gide and became preoccupied by the desire to innovate. *Heureux qui comme Ulysse . . .* (Happy He Who like Ulysse . . . , 1906), titled after a quotation from a sonnet by Du Bellay, marks his true beginning as a fiction writer. This work, later expanded into the triptych *L'Inquiète Paternité* (Restless Paternity, 1911), was much admired by Gide and his friends for its concise style. It consists of three dialogues presenting the points of view of a husband returning after a long absence, his wife who in his absence had a son by her husband's friend, and the bewildered child. The central theme of this curious work is the possibility that "elective paternity" may be preferable to natural paternity.

In addition to helping establish the *Nouvelle Revue Française*, in which he played a key role, writing its declaration of principles, "Considérations," and administering it from 1909 to 1911, Schlumberger participated in the founding of the Théâtre du Vieux-Colombier, the most important experimental theater in France on the eve of World War I. Although he dedicated considerable energy to writing for the theater, most of his plays had only what the French call a "succès d'estime": *Les Fils Louverné* (The Louverné Sons, produced in 1913), *La Mort de Sparte* (The Death of Sparta, 1921), and *Césaire, ou La Puissance de l'esprit* (1922). While Schlumberger attached greatest importance to *La Mort de Sparte*, his *Césaire* is deeper and much more innovative. It presents a purely psychological confrontation between a strong personality and a weak one, which is crushed.

Although to the end of his life he remained a great admirer of the theater and especially of that of Paul Claudel, after World War I Schlumberger wrote more fiction than plays. In 1920 he composed *Un Homme heureux* (A Happy Man), the story of a happily married and successful man, who leaves his comfortable bourgeois environment, completely severing all ties in order to work and live as a lumberjack in Oregon. His only apparent motive is his dread of the anesthetic effects of comfort and happiness on his sense and spirit. Thus, the adventure resides in the psychological and spiritual experiment undertaken by the principal character. Generally, this novel was misunderstood, and some critics have remarked that it deserved much greater success.

In *Le Camarade infidèle* (The Unfaithful Comrade, 1922), Schlumberger ridicules and demystifies a typical patriotic lie: the legendary halo, completely fake in this case, surrounding the memory of a soldier killed in the war. For humanitarian and patriotic reasons, the widow has been led to believe by authorities and her husband's comrades that the dead man had been an exemplary soldier who had died heroically. A comrade goes as far as to console the widow in person, with the farcical result that he falls in love with her. Schlumberger was neither antipatriotic nor cynical; he merely wanted to show how truth also can be a casualty of war.

Ostensibly, *Le Lion devenu vieux* (The Lion Grown Old, 1924) is the story of the last month in the life of Cardinal de Retz (1613-1679). In fact, the seventeenth-century French churchman, whose personal life had been quite controversial to many because of his numerous amorous affairs with women, was conscious of his role as a historical figure. At the end of his life he tried to preserve the truth about himself, recorded in his memoirs, which were published in 1717. He feared they might be mutilated by well- or ill-intentioned censors (as indeed they were). Schlumberger tells his story dramatically in the first person in the form of a detailed confidential report by the cardinal's aide. Coincidentally, at the time he was writing this novel, Schlumberger was trying to persuade Gide not to publish certain parts of his diary for fear that these might jeopardize his stature as a writer, and indeed some of Retz's more resounding statements in defense of truth could have been uttered by Gide. In spite of its stylistic quality, thematic depth, and interest, *Le Lion devenu vieux* met with the total indifference of the public.

Schlumberger's 1928 work, *Les Yeux de dix-huit ans* (Eighteen-Year-Old Eyes), is a collection of five Browning-like interior monologues. "Au bivouac" is the dressing-down by an officer of a young conscript accused of cowardice. More generally, it deals with the relationships between

men in war. "Les Yeux de dix-huit ans" relates a quasi-hallucination which a mature man confides to a young man who reminds him very much of himself at eighteen. "Testament" is the spiritual drama of a dying man who in his quest for God has renounced a normal life only to find despair. "L'Enseveli" records the thoughts of a man who is buried alive yet facing death bravely, without any religious faith. Finally, "Heia Mater . . . " reflects the oriental belief that the dead continue to exist among the living to the extent that the survivors preserve in their lives a place for the dead, a notion which deeply influenced Schlumberger after the death of his wife in 1924.

Saint-Saturnin (1931; translated as *The Seventh Age,* 1932) is Schlumberger's longest, most complex and ambitious novel. Like Gide in *Les Faux-Monnayeurs* (*The Counterfeiters,* 1926), in *Saint-Saturnin* Schlumberger opted for a freer fictional structure in which the voices of a number of characters belonging to different generations and conditions express diverse points of view. This polyphony is heard against the background of a nature which, knowing only the changes of seasons, discreetly teaches the protagonists about the cycle of life and the precariousness of human dignity, which is based on sanity. The subject itself, aging and its consequences for the individual and his family, had rarely been treated when Schlumberger wrote *Saint-Saturnin.* Numerous other themes important to Schlumberger are woven into the fabric of the novel. The relationship between spouses, conflicts between parents and children, and solitude are all treated in the context of an upper-middle-class French family of the 1920s. He focuses on the way in which the entire family faces the tragedy of senility as it afflicts one of its most beloved and most respected members. *Saint-Saturnin* was well received both in France and abroad and remains Schlumberger's major literary achievement, earning for him an honorable place among French novelists of the first half of the twentieth century.

Histoire de quatre potiers (The Story of Four Potters, 1935) is about four men who in the midst of the Depression decide to form a small company. Schlumberger had great faith in private enterprise, especially when it involved a group of friends. His optimism also led him to believe that a few individuals could change the course of events, albeit on a small scale. Set in Normandy and against the broader background of the world Depression, this polyphonic novel, a psychological study of a group of men living and

Pierre Viénot, André Gide, Roger Martin du Gard, and Jean Schlumberger at one of "Les Décades de Pontigny," the yearly gatherings of intellectuals instituted by Paul Desjardins

working together in a situation with moments of tension and anguish as well as humor, can be interpreted as an attempt by four individuals to react collectively against very difficult economic conditions. One can also read this story as an allegory of the founding of the *Nouvelle Revue Française* and the first heroic years of the review's existence. If all the characters in the novel do not correspond exactly to the principal figures of the review, it is perhaps because Schlumberger intended to tease some of his friends. For example, the oldest member of the small community is considerably older than his partners and older than Gide. Also, he has a burlesque affair with the maid-cook who is even older than he. In *Histoire de quatre potiers* a certain superficiality arises from the abstract presentation of physical work and, as in all of Schlumberger's novels, there is a lack of interest in the working class. This, however, is a shortcoming common to many prominent French writers in the twentieth century.

In *Stéphane le Glorieux* (1940; translated as *Stefan the Proud*, 1946), his last novel, Schlumberger chose again the first-person narration, a structure which Gide had long preferred because of the credibility it inspires in the reader. Again, as in *Le Camarade infidèle*, the subject is the effect of war. He found the theme of his story almost twenty years earlier in the Japanese No *Atsumori*. Partly because of the exotic origin of his inspiration, Schlumberger chose to place the action of his story in an unspecified country of the Balkans toward the end of the nineteenth century. The narrator is a medical doctor who has observed the effects of the psychological wound mysteriously inflicted on the brave soldier Stéphane Saleck. After returning from a war in which he had been a hero, Stéphane's behavior has become increasingly strange. Finally, he leaves his wife and son to live in seclusion. His conduct inspires a variety of interpretations, and in his dying moments Stéphane entrusts the mystery of his life to the doctor. In a brilliant commando action Stéphane had killed somewhat treacherously a young soldier who bore great physical resemblance to his own son but who was spiritually much superior. Although praised for his bravery, Stéphane is destroyed by growing remorse. Throughout the story are the intertwined themes of paternal love–Stéphane's love for his own disappointing son–and remorse for killing a superior young man such as he would have wished his son to be. The glorious wartime deed ironically causes him to lose all happiness and even the will to live. Together with Schlumberger's short work "Au bivouac," *Stéphane le Glorieux* is among the most profound statements on war in French literature in the last half-century.

Beginning in the 1930s, Schlumberger turned increasingly to genres other than fiction. In 1934 he composed *Sur les frontières religieuses* (On the Frontiers of Religious Thought), a series of essays which express the highly personal thoughts of a humanist who has long since ceased to hold any religious belief. In 1936 the tercentenary of Corneille's tragedy *Le Cid*, *Plaisir à Corneille* (Corneille with Pleasure), a much-acclaimed study on the seventeenth-century French dramatist, was published. The intent of this chronological study of Corneille's plays was to defend the great playwright against his detractors and, above all, to expose the beauty of his poetry and ideals to the admiration of those who did not know him. Interestingly, Schlumberger's position was in opposition to that of Gide, who was an unconditional admirer of Racine. Together with Robert Brasillach, Schlumberger contributed to the revival Corneille has enjoyed since the 1930s.

At the outbreak of World War II, he felt the urgency to write for the general public. In a series of short essays, published in the *Figaro,* he reflected on the French people, their culture, the selfishness of the bourgeoisie, certain negative aspects of French life, always attempting to explain the disaster of 1940 and show how France might survive as a great nation. These essays and a few earlier ones on ethical and aesthetic themes were included in *Jalons* (Landmarks, 1941) and *Nouveaux Jalons* (New Landmarks, 1943). Although without documentary importance, Schlumberger's essay on the trial of Marshal Philippe Pétain, head of Vichy France (*Le Procès Pétain,* 1949), is an exemplary attempt at an impartial examination of France's wartime leader in a historical perspective.

Schlumberger's last major works are of greater significance to literary historians than to critics. *Eveils* (Beginnings, 1950) is an engaging autobiography in which Schlumberger recounts the major events of his life to 1914, including the beginnings of his friendship with Gide as well as the founding of the *Nouvelle Revue Française* and of the Théâtre du Vieux-Colombier. In the numerous accounts of these major events which he wrote subsequently, he did not significantly add to the version found in *Eveils*. As a friend of Gide and his wife for some forty years, Schlumberger was convinced that Gide had left in his writing a portrait of his wife Madeleine that was neither accurate nor fair. In his *Madeleine et André Gide* (1956), using all existing documents to which, as his friend's executor, he had access, he scrupulously attempted to paint a truthful portrait of Madeleine and to describe the couple's life together with fairness. His testimony remains both valuable and admirable.

Schlumberger's last significant work, *Passion* (1956), is a volume of short stories in epistolary form on the theme of blind love. However, the last story, "Noces d'argent" (Silver Wedding), presents the alternative of a wise marital love based on trust and understanding rather than passion. After 1956 he published very little else.

Extremely modest, Schlumberger never attracted the attention of a large public. However, the "happy few" who have read his works admire them and hold him in great esteem. His fiction represents some of the best of twentieth-century classicism, in which a searching but disciplined style is joined to psychological analysis, character portrayal, and moral considerations. The substantial body of literary criticism he produced is similarly illustrative of the aesthetic principles that were at the heart of the *Nouvelle Revue Française* in its early decades: essentially the criteria of intelligence and artistic quality, whatever the particular topic or style of the work.

Letters:

Jacques Rivière-Jean Schlumberger. Correspondance 1909-1925, preface by Jean-Pierre Cap (Lyons: Centre d'Etudes Gidiennes, Université Lyon II, 1980).

References:

Auguste Anglès, *André Gide et le premier groupe de la "Nouvelle Revue Française." La Formation du groupe et les années d'apprentissage 1890-1910* (Paris: Gallimard, 1978);

Anglès, "Jean Schlumberger ou le mur de verre," *Nouvelle Revue Française* (November 1963): 824-842;

Marcel Arland, "Jean Schlumberger," in his *Essais et nouveaux essais critiques* (Paris: Gallimard, 1952), pp. 195-198;

Jacques Brenner, "Notes pour un portrait," *Nouvelle Revue Française* (March 1969): 379-383;

Pierre Brisson, *Vingt Ans du "Figaro," 1938-1958* (Paris: Gallimard, 1959), pp. 172-175;

Jean-Pierre Cap, "Jean Schlumberger et la *Nouvelle Revue Française* 1909-1914," *Esprit Créateur,* 14 (Summer 1974): 99-109;

Cap, *Techniques et thèmes dans l'œuvre romanesque de Jean Schlumberger* (Geneva: Peret-Gentil, 1971);

Cap, "Une Amitié littéraire: Jacques Rivière–Jean Schlumberger," *Présence Francophone,* 5 (Autumn 1972): 107-112;

Marie Delcourt, *Jean Schlumberger, essai critique* (Paris: Gallimard, 1945);

André Gide, *Préfaces* (Neuchâtel & Paris: Ides et Calendes, 1948), pp. 143-148;

Hélène Harvitt, "Jean Schlumberger: Grand Prix National des Lettres 1955," *American Society Legion of Honor Magazine,* 27 (Spring 1956): 9-23.

Papers:
Most of Jean Schlumberger's papers are at the Fonds Doucet, Bibliothèque Sainte-Geneviève, and at the Bibliothèque Nationale, both in Paris.

Appendix: Nobel Laureates

The first Nobel Prize for Literature was awarded in 1901 to the French poet Sully Prudhomme. Since that time eleven French writers have won the prize—more than from any other country. Of the eight French novelists who received the prize, four made their reputations during the period 1900-1930 covered by this volume. In recognition of this unusual concentration of Nobel laureates in a single literary period, the following appendix comprises the citations, presentations, and acceptance remarks of the four prize-winners: Romain Rolland, Roger Martin du Gard, André Gide, and François Mauriac.

ROMAIN ROLLAND
1915

"as a tribute to the lofty idealism of his literary production and to the sympathy and love of truth with which he has described different types of human beings"

[In the spring of 1915 news reached Rolland that he was under consideration for the Nobel Prize. Because of World War I, no winner was announced until November of the following year, when Rolland was honored with the award for 1915. He gave no acceptance speech.]

ROGER MARTIN DU GARD
1937

"for the artistic vigour and truthfulness with which he has pic-
tured human contrasts as well as some fundamental aspects of
contemporary life in the series of novels entitled
Les Thibault"

photo Harlingue

Presentation

by

Per Hallström
Permanent Secretary of the Swedish Academy

The recipient of the Nobel Prize in Literature for 1937, Roger Martin du Gard, has dedicated most of his activity to a single work, a long series of novels with the collective title, *Les Thibault* (1922-40). It is a vast work both in the number of its volumes and in its scope. It represents modern French life by means of a whole gallery of characters and an analysis of the intellectual currents and the problems that occupied France during the ten years preceding the First World War, a gallery as full and an analysis as complete as the subject of the novel permitted. The work has therefore taken a form especially characteristic of our era, called the "roman fleuve" in the country of its origin.

The term designates a narrative method that is relatively little concerned with composition and advances like a river across vast countries, reflecting everything that is found on its way. The essence of such a novel, in large as well as small matters, consists in the exactitude of this reflection rather than in the harmonious balance of its parts; it has no shape. The river lingers at will and only rarely does the undercurrent disturb the smooth flow of its surface.

Our age can hardly be called calm; on the contrary, the speed of the machines accelerates the rhythm of life to the point of agitation. It is strange, therefore, that in such an age the most popular literary form, the novel, should have developed in a totally opposite direction, and by so doing have become only the more popular. Still, if the novel offered us the satisfying world of fantasy, one could explain this phenomenon in psychological terms as a sort of poetic compensation for the frustrations of daily life. But it is precisely the heart-rending anguish of reality that the novel takes such time to sound and to emphasize.

Nevertheless, the novel is there, with its boundless substance, and the reader finds a certain solace in the heightened awareness which he acquires from the inevitable element of tragedy inherent in all life. With a kind of heroism, it swallows reality in large draughts and encourages us to bear even great sufferings with joy. The reader's aesthetic demands will be satisfied in isolated sections of the work which are more condensed and therefore better suited to call forth his feelings. *Les Thibault* does not lack such sections.

The essential characters of the novel are three members of the same family: the father and two sons. The father remains in the background; his passive role, one of weight and massiveness, is presented by a special technique. The two sons and the countless secondary characters of the work are presented in a dramatic manner. Unprepared by anything in the story, we see them before us, acting and speaking in the present; and we are given a detailed and complete description of the setting. The reader must be quick to grasp what he sees and hears, for the capricious and irregular rhythm of life beats everywhere. He is helped in his task by the writer's most perfected tool: the analysis of his heroes' thoughts, expressed beyond words, an insight into the darkness which engenders conscious actions. Martin du Gard goes even further; he shows how thoughts, feeling, and the will can be transformed before becoming words and acts. Sometimes exterior considerations–habit, vanity, or even a simple gaucherie–alter expressions and personality. This examination, at once subtle and bold, of the dynamic processes of the soul obviously constitutes Martin du Gard's most original and most remarkable contribution to the art of characterizing human beings. From the aesthetic point of view, this is not always an advantage, for the analysis may appear cumbersome when its results do not seem necessary to the story.

This introspective method is used even for the father's character, but it is less complicated in his case. His personality is already clear-cut and complete at the beginning of the novel, for he belongs to the past. Events of the present no longer affect him.

He is a member of the upper middle class, conscious of his status and his duties, a faithful servant of the Church and a generous benefactor of society, full of prudent advice. He really belongs to a generation before his own, to the France of the July Monarchy; that is why he is to come into more than one conflict with the next generation, in particular with his sons. But this conflict rarely reaches the verbal level, for the old man is too convinced of his proper worth to engage in discussions. Hence the perennial theme of the opposition of youth to age is not specially treated here.

The representative of age appears above all in an attitude of introspection and immutability; he relies heavily and complacently on all that he thinks wise and just. No word can influence him. In the isolation of his life, one might see the whole tragedy of age if he were not himself so completely unaware of the possibility of such a tragedy.

He is characterized rather by comic traits; profounder sentiments are expressed only at the time of his death, in the face of his human destiny. This expression is not direct but results from a strictly objective, concrete description of the long martyrdom of his agony. It is a moving description despite its minute detail. Up to now he had been considered only from without, with the exception of some rare instances when he had revealed what, even in him, was hidden behind the façade he presented to the world.

The difference between him and his oldest son receives little emphasis. Antoine Thibault is a doctor. Entirely absorbed by his profession, his father's moral and ethical points of view are entirely alien to him. Morality is replaced in him by an intense and conscientious devotion to research and to the exercise of his profession. Master of himself, prudent, tactful, he has not the least desire for opposition; he has not even time to think of it. He is a man ambitious for the future. At first he is occasionally a little fatuous, but he soon commands respect by his work.

Antoine becomes a sympathetic representative of the intellectuals of his day, full of ideas, without prejudices in his conceptions, but as a determinist convinced of the inability of the individual to change whatever the general course of events may be. He is not a revolutionary.

Quite different is his brother Jacques, who is several years younger. The latter is too close to the writer's heart to suffer any criticism. He is the hero of the work, and the exterior world is examined and judged according to his ideals. His father's responsibility for his evolution is considerable, but actually Jacques, by his whole nature, is destined to be a revolutionary. When the story begins, he is a schoolboy of fourteen in a college run by priests. Although he dislikes and neglects his studies, he commands respect by his intelligence. The catastrophe occurs when he discovers a friend among his schoolmates, and their affection, at this dangerous period of adolescence, takes an exalted and seemingly erotic form. Their feelings are betrayed by their letters, misinterpreted (as, indeed, they are bound to be) by the priests who intervene with disciplinary measures. The strict surveillance and the very intrusion into his emotional private life are an unbearable offense to Jacques. Futhermore, he has to await his father's rage, stirred up by this scandal. His revolt is expressed in action. He carries along his friend in his escape far from all yokes, those he endured and those he feared in a hostile and harsh world. He feels that his whole being, in the grip of romantic poetry and of more dangerous tendencies, is irreconcilable with the real world. Seeking happiness and freedom, the two boys leave for Africa, but their visionary project is destroyed in Marseilles by the efforts of the police who had been alerted.

On his return, his father, in an excess of pedagogic zeal, makes a psychological mistake; he condemns his son to solitary confinement in a reformatory founded by himself. The oppression of this confinement causes Jacques' indomitable personality to emerge even stronger and fiercer. The account of this development is the most moving episode in the work.

After he has been released owing to his brother's influence, Jacques is permitted to pursue his studies, his only consolation. He does brilliantly and is easily accepted by the Ecole Normale, the supreme goal of all ambitious and talented students and the open door to all top literary or scientific careers. But Jacques cannot be attracted by an official career that for him is only a void and an illusion; he soon sets out for adventure and reality. Once more the boy escapes to Africa, but this time he succeeds and he remains absent from the narrative for a long time.

He is seen again when Antoine discovers his residence—in Switzerland among the revolutionaries—and brings him back to their father's deathbed. He arrives too late for a reconciliation, even if one considered a reconciliation between these two diametrically opposed concepts of life possible. The old man does not recognize him, but Jacques feels a deep sorrow, for he is not one of those people who, obsessed with mankind's future happiness, begin by stifling every trace of humanity in themselves.

Such is the outline of Jacques' inner life as far as it is known. For the rest he remains rather elusive, as before, but we notice the author's great appreciation of his faculties and of his character.

We get to know him fully when the novel approaches its conclusion and at the same time its height of epic grandeur—in the summer of 1914 just before the world catastrophe. Jacques is in Geneva, having left Paris soon after his father's death in order to escape the necessity of inheriting a fortune in a society which he scorns. He belongs to a group of socialist and communist reformers whose immediate mission is to halt the threat of war by the revolt of the masses. The description of these agitators is one of the least successful passages in the book; the overall impression, whether intended or not, is that these men are not worthy of their mission.

But Jacques' stature increases in everyone's eyes when he leaves Geneva and returns to Paris to accomplish his mission. His development is moral rather than intellectual; his actions have no great results, but he saves his soul. The description of the last days of July in Paris, with Jacques wavering between hope and despair in this surcharged atmosphere, is a veritable *tour de force* in Martin du Gard's novelistic achievement. The history of this period revives, reawakens, as far as the masses' role is concerned. But, as almost always, the role is not decisive. The masses are impotent, blind, and in this case even less familiar than usual with the game of politics that causes such tragedies. The author himself seems not to be particularly initiated, but he is tolerant and human, and his description, as far as it goes, is truthful.

Against the background of this bewildering anxiety there occurs a brief but highly illuminating episode of a completely different character. Jacques meets again a young girl with whom he had almost fallen in love several years before, but from whom he had run away as he had run away from everything else. This time the true spark is kindled between them. This fatal love story is one of the most significant episodes in the novel; it is profoundly felt and rendered in all its pure beauty precisely because it is restricted to the dimensions that the breathless

flight of days imposes on the story. It lasts only a short time, but that is enough to give it a tragic and simple beauty.

When all the political illusions vanish for Jacques at the declaration of war, he recreates for himself a new illusion, born of his despair and of his will to sacrifice. Right at the front lines he tries to ward off the catastrophe by appealing from an airplane to the two opposing armies, seeking to inspire in them a common revolt and a desire to overthrow the powers which hold them captive. Without hesitating he leaves Paris and the woman he loves.

The adventure is stamped with the same schoolboy romanticism and lack of reality as was his first flight out of the world, but Jacques nonetheless carries out his plan with his customary energy. His call for revolution is printed in Switzerland, the airplane and pilot are ready, the expedition begins. It will not last long, for he has hardly flown over the battlefield when the plane crashes and catches fire with its whole load, men and bundles of paper. Jacques himself falls, a heap of bruised and burned flesh, among the retreating French troops. All his perception is restricted to a vague sensation of the bitterness of defeat and to unbearable and infinite physical torments, which are finally relieved by the bullet of a compatriot tired of dragging along this ill-fated person whom he holds to be a spy anyhow.

It is difficult to imagine a bitterer dénouement to a tragedy or a crueller irony in a defeat. But Martin du Gard did not direct his irony toward his hero. Perhaps he wanted to show the brutality and the cruelty of world events as opposed to idealistic tendencies. His bitterness is certainly justified here, but the long detailed description of the whole episode becomes almost intolerable in its scrupulous exactitude.

Jacques Thibault, as we finally get to know him, lives in our memory as a heroic figure. Without the least grandiloquent attitude or word, this upright, silent, and reserved man receives at last the seal of grandeur: grandeur of will and courage. Whenever the novel centres on him, the writer's untiring work achieves persuasive eloquence. After his pointed and sceptical analysis of the human soul, which almost consumes its object with its often extreme exactness in detail, through the most minute realism possible, Martin du Gard finally pays homage to the idealism of the human spirit.

Acceptance

The presence of so many illustrious persons assembled under the patronage of His Highness, the Crown Prince, heightens the emotions that I feel at finding myself here and hearing the words of praise that have just been addressed to me. I feel rather like an owl, suddenly roused from its nest and exposed to the daylight, whose eyes, used to the dark, are blinded by dazzling brightness.

I am proud of the exceptional mark of esteem the Swedish Academy has bestowed on me, but I cannot conceal my surprise from you. Ever since I felt your favour lie upon and almost overwhelm me, I have asked myself how to interpret it.

My first thought was of my country. I am happy that in making a *French* author its choice for this year, the distinguished Swedish Academy has thought fit to glorify our French literature in particular. On the other hand, I know some great poets among my compatriots, noble and powerful minds, whom your votes might have chosen with much better reason. Why then am I today in this place of honour?

The demon of vanity, never completely silenced, at first whispered to me some flattering presumptions. I even went so far as to ask myself whether by granting this distinction to the "man without dogma" that I profess to be, the Academy did not wish to emphasize that in this century, when everyone "believes" and "asserts", it is perhaps useful that there should be some who "hesitate," "put in doubt," and "question"—independent minds that escape the fascination of partisan ideologies and whose constant care is to develop their individual consciences in order to maintain a spirit of "inquiry" as objective, liberal, and fair-minded as is humanly possible.

I should also like to think that this sudden honour acknowledges certain principles dear to me. "Principles" is a big word to be used by a man who says that he is always ready to revise his opinions. I must, however, admit that in the practice of my art I have imposed upon myself certain guidelines to which I have tried to be faithful.

I was still very young when I encountered, in a novel by the English writer Thomas Hardy, this reflection on one of his characters: "The true value of life seemed to him to be not so much its beauty, as its tragic quality." It spoke to an intuition deep within me, closely allied to my literary vocation. Ever since that time I have thought that the prime purpose of the novel is to give voice to the tragic element in life. Today I would add: the tragic element in the life of an individual, the tragedy of a "destiny in the course of being fulfilled."

At this point I cannot refrain from referring to the immortal example of Tolstoy, whose books have had a determining influence on my development. The born novelist recognizes himself by his passion to penetrate ever more deeply into the knowledge of man and to lay bare in each of his characters that individual element of his life which makes each being unique. It seems to me that any chance of survival which a novelist's work may have rests solely on the quantity and the quality of the individual lives that he has been able to create in his books. But that is not all. The novelist must also have a sense of life in general; his work must reveal a personal vision of the universe. Here again Tolstoy is the great master. Each of his creatures is more or less secretly haunted by a metaphysical obsession, and each of the human experiences that he has recorded implies, beyond an inquiry into man, an anxious question about the meaning of life. I admit that I take pleasure in the thought that, in crowning my work as a novelist, the members of the Swedish Academy wished to pay indirect homage to my devotion to that unapproachable model and to my efforts to profit from the instruction of his genius.

I should like to conclude with a more sombre hypothesis, although I am embarrassed to disturb this festive mood by arousing those painful thoughts that haunt all of us. However, perhaps the Swedish Academy did not hesitate to express a special purpose by drawing the attention of the intellectual world to the author of *L'Eté 1914 [Summer 1914]*.

That is the title of my last book. It is not for me to judge its value. But at least I know what I set out to do: in the course of these three volumes I tried to revivify the anguished atmosphere of Europe on the eve of the mobilizations of 1914. I tried to show the weakness of the governments of that day, their hesitations, indiscretions, and unavowed desires; I tried above all to give an impression of the stupefaction of the peaceful masses before the approach of that cataclysm whose victims they were going to be, that cataclysm which was to leave nine million men dead and ten million men crippled.

When I see that one of the highest literary juries in the world supports these books with the prestige of its incontestable authority, I ask myself whether the reason may not be that these books through their wide circulation have appeared to defend certain values that are again being threatened and to fight against the evil contagion of the forces of war.

For I am a son of the West, where the noise of arms does not let our minds rest. Since we have come together today on the tenth of December, the anniversary of the death of Alfred Nobel (that man of action, "no mere shadow," who in the last years of his life seems indeed to have put his supreme hope in the brotherhood of nations), permit me to confess how good it would be to think that my work—the work that has just been honoured in his name—might serve not only the cause of letters, but even the cause of peace. In these months of anxiety in which we are living, when blood is already being shed in two extreme parts of the globe, when practically everywhere in an atmosphere polluted by misery and fanaticism passions are seething around pointed guns, when too many signs are again heralding the return of that languid defeatism, that general consent which alone makes wars possible: at this exceptionally grave moment through which humanity is passing, I wish, without vanity, but with a gnawing disquietude in my heart, that my books about "Summer 1914" may be read and discussed, and that they may remind all—the old who have forgotten as well as the young who either do not know or do not care—of the sad lesson of the past.

ANDRÉ GIDE
1947

"for his comprehensive and artistically significant writings, in which human problems and conditions have been presented with a fearless love of truth and keen psychological insight"

Presentation

by

Anders Österling
Permanent Secretary of the Swedish Academy

On the first page of the remarkable journal kept by André Gide for half a century, the author, then twenty years old, finds himself on the sixth floor of a building in the Latin Quarter, looking for a meeting place for "The Symbolists," the group of youths to which he belonged. From the window he looked at the Seine and Notre Dame during the sunset of an autumn day and felt like the hero of a Balzac novel, a Rastignac ready to conquer the city lying at his feet: "And now, we two!" However, Gide's ambition was to find long and twisting paths ahead; nor was it to be contented with easy victories.

The seventy-eight-year-old writer who this day is being honoured with the award of the Nobel Prize has always been a controversial figure. From the beginning of his career he put himself in the first rank of the sowers of spiritual anxiety, but this does not keep him today from being counted almost everywhere among the first literary names of France, or from enjoying an influence that has persisted unabatedly through several generations. His first works appeared in the 1890's; his last one dates from the spring of 1947. A very important period in the spiritual history of Europe is outlined in his work, constituting a kind of dramatic foundation to his long life. One may ask why the importance of this work has only so recently been appreciated at its true value: the reason is that André Gide belongs unquestionably to that class of writers whose real evaluation requires a long perspective and a space adequate for the three stages of the dialectic process. More than any of his contemporaries, Gide has been a man of contrasts, a veritable Proteus of perpetually changing attitudes, working tirelessly at opposite poles in order to strike flashing sparks. This is why his work gives the appearance of an uninterrupted dialogue in which faith constantly struggles against doubt, asceticism against the love of life, discipline against the need for freedom. Even his external life has been mobile and changing, and his famous voyages to the Congo in 1927 and to Soviet Russia in 1935—to cite only those—are proof enough that he did not want to be ranked among the peaceful stay-at-homes of literature.

Gide comes from a Protestant family whose social position permitted him to follow his vocation freely and to devote greater attention than most others can afford to the cultivation of his personality and to his inner development. He described this family milieu in his famous autobiography whose title *Si le grain ne meurt . . .* (1924) [*If It Die . . .*] is taken from St. John's words about the grain of wheat that must die before its fruition. Although he has strongly reacted against his Puritan education, he has nonetheless all his life dwelled on the fundamental problems of morality and religion, and at times he has defined with rare purity the message of Christian love, particularly in his short novel, *La Porte étroite* (1909) [*Strait Is the Gate*], which deserves to be compared with the tragedies of Racine.

On the other hand, one finds in André Gide still stronger manifestations of that famous "immoralism"—a conception which his adversaries have often misinterpreted. In reality it designates the free act, the "gratuitous" act, the liberation from all repressions of conscience, something analagous to what the American recluse Thoreau expressed, "The worst thing is being the slave dealer of one's soul." One should always keep in mind that Gide found some difficulty in presenting as virtue that which is composed of the absence of generally recognized virtues. *Les Nourritures terrestres* (1897) [*Fruits of the Earth*] was a youthful attempt from which he later turned away, and the diverse delights he enthusiastically sings of evoke for us those beautiful fruits of southern lands which do not bear keeping. The exhortation which he addresses to his disciple and reader, "And now, throw away my book. Leave me!," has been followed first of all by himself in his later works. But what leaves the strongest im-

309

pression, in *Nourritures* as elsewhere, is the intense poetry of separation, of return, captured by him in so masterly a fashion in the flute-song of his prose. One rediscovers it often, for example in this brief journal entry, written later, near a mosque at Brusa on one May morning: "Ah! begin anew and on again afresh! Feel with rapture this exquisite tenderness of the cells in which emotion filters like milk . . . Bush of the dense gardens, rose of purity, indolent rose in the shade of plane trees, can it be that thou hast not known my youth? Before? Is it a memory I dwell in? Is it indeed I who am seated in this little corner of the mosque, I who breathe and I who love thee? or do I only dream of loving thee? . . . If I were indeed real, would this swallow have stolen so close to me?"

Behind the strange and incessant shift in perspective that Gide's work offers to us, in the novels as well as in the essays, in the travel diaries, or in the analyses of contemporary events, we always find the same supple intelligence, the same incorruptible psychology, expressed in a language which, by the most sober means, attains a wholly classic limpidity and the most delicate variety. Without going into the details of the work, let us mention in this connection the celebrated *Les Faux Monnayeurs* (1926) [*The Counterfeiters*], with its bold and penetrating analysis of a group of young French people. Through the novelty of its technique, this novel has inspired a whole new orientation in the contemporary art of the narrative. Next to it, put the volume of memoirs already mentioned, in which the author intended to recount his life truthfully without adding anything that could be to his advantage or hiding what would be unpleasant. Rousseau had had the same intention, with this difference, that Rousseau exhibits his faults in the conviction that all men being as evil as he, none will dare to judge or condemn him. Gide, however, quite simply refuses to admit to his fellows the right to pass any judgment on him; he calls on a higher tribunal, a vaster perspective, in which he will present himself before the sovereign eye of God. The significance of these memoirs thus is indicated in the mysterious Biblical quotation of the "grain of wheat" which here represents the personality: as long as the latter is sentient, deliberate, and egocentric, it dwells alone and without germinating power; it is only at the price of its death and its transmutation that it will acquire life and be able to bear fruit. "I do not think," Gide writes, "that

there is a way of looking at the moral and religious question or of acting in the face of it that I have not known and made my own at some moment in my life. In truth, I have wished to reconcile them all, the most diverse points of view, by excluding nothing and by being ready to entrust to Christ the solution of the contest between Dionysus and Apollo."

Such a statement throws light on the intellectual versatility for which Gide is often blamed and misunderstood, but which has never led him to betray himself. His philosophy has a tendency toward regeneration at any price and does not fail to evoke the miraculous phoenix which out of its nest of flames hurls itself to a new flight.

In circumstances like those of today, in which, filled with admiring gratitude, we linger before the rich motifs and the essential themes of this work, it is natural that we pass over the critical reservations which the author himself seems to enjoy provoking. For even in his ripe age, Gide has never argued in favor of a full and complete acceptance of his experiences and his conclusions. What he wishes above all is to stir up and present the problems. Even in the future, his influence will doubtless be noted less in a total acceptance than in a lively controversy about his work. And in this lies the foundation of his true greatness.

His work contains pages which provoke like a defiance through the almost unequalled audacity of the confession. He wishes to combat the Pharisees, but it is difficult, in the struggle, to avoid shocking certain rather delicate norms of human character. One must always remember that this manner of acting is a form of the impassioned love of truth which, since Montaigne and Rousseau, has been an axiom of French literature. Through all the phases of his evolution, Gide has appeared as a true defender of literary integrity, founded on the personality's right and duty to present all its problems resolutely and honestly. From this point of view, his long and varied activity, stimulated in so many ways, unquestionably represents an idealistic value.

Since Mr. André Gide, who has declared with great gratitude his acceptance of the distinction offered him, has unfortunately been prevented from coming here by reasons of health, his Prize will now be handed to His Excellency the French Ambassador.

Acceptance

read by

Gabriel Puaux
French Ambassador

It would no doubt be of little purpose to dwell on my regrets at not being able to be present on this solemn occasion nor to have my own voice bear witness to my gratitude, compelled as I am to forgo a trip that promised to be both pleasant and instructive.

I have, as you know, always declined honours, at least those which as a Frenchman I could expect from France. I confess, gentlemen, that it is with a sense of giddiness that I suddenly receive from you the highest honour to which a writer can aspire. For many years I thought that I was crying in the wilderness, later that I was speaking only to a very small number, but you have proved to me today that I was right to believe in the virtue of the small number and that sooner or later it would prevail.

It seems to me, gentlemen, that your votes were cast not so much for my work as for the independent spirit that animates it, that spirit which in our time faces attacks from all possible quarters. That you have recognized it in me, that you have felt the need to approve and support it, fills me with confidence and an intimate satisfaction. I cannot help thinking, however, that only recently another man in France represented this spirit even better than I do. I am thinking of Paul Valéry, for whom my admiration has steadily grown during a friendship of half a century and whose death alone prevents you from electing him in my place. I have often said with what friendly deference I have constantly and without weakness bowed to his genius, before which I have always felt "human, only too human." May his memory be present at this ceremony, which in my eyes takes on all the more brilliance as the darkness deepens. You invite the free spirit to triumph and through this signal award, given without regard for frontiers or the momentary dissensions of factions, you offer to this spirit the unexpected chance of extraordinary radiance.

Prior to the acceptance, Arne Tiselius, Deputy Chairman of the Nobel Foundation, made the following comment: "Unfortunately, Mr. André Gide, due to ill health, has had to give up his original intention to attend the ceremonies. We regret this, indeed, and would like to extend our reverence and our sympathy to the venerable master of French literature whose genius has so profoundly influenced our time."

FRANÇOIS MAURIAC
1952

"for the deep spiritual insight and the artistic intensity with which he has in his novels penetrated the drama of human life"

Presentation

by

Anders Österling
Permanent Secretary of the Swedish Academy

The student of François Mauriac's works will be struck from the very first by the insistence with which Mauriac devotes himself to describing a precise milieu, a corner of land one can point to on a map of France. The action of his novels nearly always unfolds in the Gironde, the Bordeaux region, that old vine-growing country where chateaux and small farms have taken possession of the earth, or in the Landes, the country of pine trees and sheep pastures where the song of the cicadas vibrates in the lonely spaces and where the Atlantic sounds its far-off thunder. This is Mauriac's native country. He considers it his calling to describe this singular region and its people, especially those who own the land; and it can be said that his personal style partakes of the restrained energy which twists the branches of the grape vines and of the pitiless clarity of the light which falls from a torrid sky. In that sense, this writer, who is read the world over, is undeniably and markedly a man of the province, but his provincialism does not exclude the great human problems of universal scope. If one wants to dig deep one must first and always have a ground to thrust one's pick into.

Mauriac had a more than usually restricted childhood; he grew up in the shelter of a milieu in which the maternal influence made itself strongly felt, an influence which did not cease to act on his adolescent sensitivity. There is reason to believe that he had painful surprises later when he made contact with the outside world. Guided until then by pious advice, he had not suspected that evil dominated reality to such an extent as it appears in all the monotony and indifference of everyday life. Catholic by birth, brought up in a Catholic atmosphere which became his spiritual country, he has, in short, never had to decide for or against the Church. But he has on several occasions re-examined and publicly specified his Christian position, above all in order to question whether the demands a realist's position made on the writer could be reconciled with the commandments and prohibitions of the Church. Apart from these inevitable and insoluble antinomies, Mauriac, as a writer, uses the novel to expound a particular aspect of human life in which Catholic thought and sensitivity are at the same time background and keystone. Hence, his non-Catholic readers may to a certain extent feel that they are looking at a world foreign to them; but to understand Mauriac, one must remember the one fact without which no account of him can be complete: he does not belong to the group of writers who are converts. He himself is conscious of the force that gives him those roots which permit him to cite a great and stern tradition when he probes souls overwhelmed by the weight of their faults and scrutinizes their secret intentions.

Mauriac has been assured a central position in modern literature for so long and so unquestionably that the denominational barriers have almost lost all importance. Whereas many writers of his generation who had a fleeting glory are almost forgotten today, his profile stands out more and more distinctly with the years. In his case it is not a question of fame achieved at the price of compromise, for his sombre and austere vision of the world is scarcely made to please his contemporaries. He has always aimed high. With all the power and all the consistency of which he is capable, he has tried to continue in his realistic novels the tradition of such great French moralists as Pascal, La Bruyère, and Bossuet. To this let us add that he represents a tendency toward religious inspiration which, particularly in France, has always been an extremely important element of spiritual formation. If I may in this context say a few words about Mauriac as a distinguished journalist, we must not forget, in the interest of European thought, his work in that field, his commentaries on daily events, the entire side of his literary activity which deserves public esteem.

But if he is today the laureate of the Nobel Prize in Literature, it is obviously above all because of his admirable novels. Suffice it to name a few a masterpieces such as *Le Désert de l'amour*

(1925) [*The Desert of Love*], *Thérèse Desqueyroux* (1927) [*Thérèse*], and its sequel *La Fin de la nuit* (1935) [*The End of the Night*], *La Pharisienne* (1941) [*Woman of the Pharisees*], and *Le Nœud de vipères* (1932) [*The Knot of Vipers*], without intending to say how far the artistic qualities of these works place them in a class apart; for everywhere, in the whole series of Mauriac's novels, are found unforgettable scenes, dialogues, and situations, so mysteriously and so cruelly revealing. The repetition of the same themes could create a certain monotony, but his acute analyses and sure touch awaken the same admiration with each new encounter. Mauriac remains unequalled in conciseness and expressive force of language; his prose can in a few suggestive lines shed light on the most complex and difficult things. His most remarkable works are characterized by a purity of logic and classic economy of expression that recall the tragedies of Racine.

The voiceless anxiety of youth, the abysses of evil and the perpetual menace of their presence, the deceitful temptations of the flesh, the ascendancy of avarice in the life of material goods, the havoc of self-satisfaction and pharisaism—these are the motifs that constantly reappear under Mauriac's pen. Small wonder that in his wielding of such a palette, he has been accused of blackening his subjects without cause, of writing as a misanthrope. But the response he gives is that, on the contrary, a writer who bases his whole concept of the world on grace and sees man's supreme recourse in God's love has the feeling of working in a spirit of hope and confidence. We have no right to doubt the sincerity of this declaration, but it is evident that in practice sin attracts him more than innocence. He detests what is edifying, and while he never grows tired of portraying the soul that persists in evil and is on its way to damnation, he generally prefers to bring down the curtain at the moment when the consciousness of its misery is about to push the soul toward repentance and salvation. This writer limits himself to the role of witness to the negative phase of this evolution, leaving all the positive side to the priest, who does not have to write a novel.

Mauriac himself once said that everyone is free to seek satisfaction in a literature that beautifies life and permits us to escape from reality, but the predilection which most people have for this kind of literature should not make us unjust toward the writers whose vocation is to know man. It is not we who hate life. Those alone hate life who, not being able to bear the sight of it, falsify it. The true lovers of life love it as it is. They have stripped it of its masks, one by one, and have given their hearts to this monster at last laid bare. In one of his controversies with André Gide, he returned to the cardinal point of this thought in affirming that the most complete sincerity is the form of honour which is linked to the writer's craft. Most often Tartuffe is made to appear under the ecclesiastical costume, but Mauriac assures us that this personage is found much more frequently in the midst of those supporting the theory of materialistic progress. It is easy to deride the principles of morality, but Mauriac objects to such derision; as he has stated quite simply, "Each of us knows he could become less evil than he is."

This simple phrase is perhaps the key that opens the secret of good in the chapters of Mauriac's work, the secret of their sombre ardour and their subtle disharmony. His plunges into the midst of man's weaknesses and vices are more than the effect of a mania pushed to virtuosity. Even when he analyzes reality without pity, Mauriac preserves a last certainty, that there is a charity which passes understanding. He does not lay claim to the absolute; he knows that it does not exist with virtue in the pure state, and he views without indulgence those who call themselves pious. Faithful to the truth which he has made his, he strives to describe his characters in such a way that, seeing themselves as they are, they would be stricken with repentance and the desire to become if not better, at least a little less evil. His novels can be compared to narrow but deep wells at the bottom of which a mysterious water is seen glistening in the darkness.

Dear Sir and colleague—In the few moments at my disposal I could speak about your work only in a sketchy manner. I known how much it deserves admiration; I also know how difficult it is to do it justice, to make general statements without ignoring the specific characteristics of your work. The Swedish Academy has awarded you this year's Novel Prize in Literature "for the deep spiritual insight and the artistic intensity with which you have in your novels penetrated the drama of human life."

There remains for me to extend to you the most heartfelt congratulations of the Swedish Academy, this younger sister of your venerable Académie Française, and to ask you to receive the Prize from the hands of His Majesty the King.

Acceptance

The last subject to be touched by the man of letters whom you are honouring, I think, is himself and his work. But how could I turn my thoughts away from that work and that man, from those poor stories and that simple French writer, who by the grace of the Swedish Academy finds himself all of a sudden burdened and almost overwhelmed by such an excess of honour? No, I do not think that it is vanity which makes me review the long road that has led me from an obscure childhood to the place I occupy tonight in your midst.

When I began to describe it, I never imagined that this little world of the past which survives in my books, this corner of provincial France hardly known by the French themselves where I spent my school holidays, could capture the interest of foreign readers. We always believe in our uniqueness; we forget that the books which enchanted us, the novels of George Eliot or Dickens, of Tolstoy or Dostoevsky, or of Selma Lagerlöf, described countries very different from ours, human beings of another race and another religion. But nonetheless we loved them only because we recognized ourselves in them. The whole of mankind is revealed in the peasant of our birthplace, every countryside of the world in the horizon seen through the eyes of our childhood. The novelist's gift consists precisely in his ability to reveal the universality of this narrow world into which we are born, where we have learned to love and to suffer. To many of my readers in France and abroad my world has appeared sombre. Shall I say that this has always surprised me? Mortals, because they are mortal, fear the very name of death; and those who have never loved or been loved, or have been abandoned and betrayed or have vainly pursued a being inaccessible to them without as much as a look for the creature that pursued them and which they did not love—all these are astonished and scandalized when a work of fiction describes the loneliness in the very heart of love. "Tell us pleasant things," said the Jews to the prophet Isaiah. "Deceive us by agreeable falsehoods."

Yes, the reader demands that we deceive him by agreeable falsehoods. Nonetheless, those works that have survived in the memory of mankind are those that have embraced the human drama in its entirety and have not shied away from the evidence of the incurable solitude in which each of us must face his destiny until death, that final solitude, because finally we must die alone.

This is the world of a novelist without hope. This is the world into which we are led by your great Strindberg. This is would have been my world were it not for that immense hope by which I have been possessed practically since I awoke to conscious life. It pierces with a ray of light the darkness that I have described. My colour is black and I am judged by that black rather than by the light that penetrates and secretly burns there. Whenever a woman in France tries to poison her husband or strangle her lover, people tell me: "Here is a subject for you." They think that I keep some sort of museum of horrors, that I specialize in monsters. And yet, my characters differ in an essential point from almost any others that live in the novels of our time: they feel that they have a soul. In this post-Nietzschean Europe where the echo of Zarathustra's cry "God is dead" is still heard and has not yet exhausted its terrifying consequences, my characters do not perhaps all believe that God is alive, but all of them have a conscience which knows that a part of their being recognizes evil and could not commit it. They know evil. They all feel dimly that they are the creatures of their deeds and have echoes in other destinies.

For my heroes, wretched as they may be, life is the experience of infinite motion, of an indefinite transcendence of themselves. A humanity which does not doubt that life has a direction and a goal cannot be a humanity in despair. The despair of modern man is born out of the absurdity of the world; his despair as well as his submission to surrogate myths: the absurd delivers man to the inhuman. When Nietzsche announced the death of God, he also announced the times we have lived through and those we shall still have to live through, in which man, emptied of his soul and hence deprived of a personal destiny, becomes a beast of burden more maltreated than a mere animal by the Nazis and by all those who today use Nazi methods. A horse, a mule, a cow has a market value but from the human animal, procured without cost thanks to well-organized and systematic purge, one gains nothing but profit until it perishes. No writer who keeps in the centre of his work the human creature made in the image of the Father, redeemed by the Son, and illuminated by the Spirit, can in my opinion be considered a master of despair, be his picture ever so sombre.

For his picture does remain sombre, since for him the nature of man is wounded, if not corrupted. It goes without saying that human history as told by Christian novelist cannot be based on the idyll because he must not shy away from the mystery of evil.

But to be obsessed by evil is also to be obsessed by purity and childhood. It makes me sad that the too hasty critics and readers have not realized the place which the child occupies in my stories. A child dreams at the heart of all my books; they contain the loves of children, first kisses and first solitude, all the things that I have cherished in the music of Mozart. The serpents in my books have been noticed, but not the doves that have made their nests in more than one chapter; for in my books childhood is the lost paradise, and it introduces the mystery of evil.

The mystery of evil—there are no two ways of approaching it. We must either deny evil or we must accept it as it appears both within ourselves and without—in our individual lives, that of our passions, as well as in the history written with the blood of men by power-hungry empires. I have always believed that there is a close correspondence between individual and collective crimes, and journalist that I am, I do nothing but decipher from day to day in the horror of political history the visible consequences of that invisible history which takes place in the obscurity of the heart. We pay dearly for the evidence that evil is evil, we who live under a sky where the smoke of crematories is still drifting. We have seen them devour under our own eyes millions of innocents, even children. And history continues in the same manner. The system of concentration camps has struck deep roots in old countries where Christ has been loved, adored, and served for centuries. We are watching with horror how that part of the world in which man is still enjoying his human rights, where the human mind remains free, is shrinking under our eyes like the "peau de chargin" of Balzac's novel.

Do not for a moment imagine that as a believer I pretend not to see the objections raised to belief by the presence of evil on earth. For a Christian, evil remains the most anguishing of mysteries. The man who amidst the crimes of history perseveres in his faith will stumble over the permanent scandal: the apparent uselessness of the Redemption. The well-reasoned explanations of the theologians regarding the presence of evil have never convinced me, reasonable as they may be, and precisely because they are reasonable. The answer that eludes us presupposes an order not of reason but of charity. It is an answer that is fully found in the affirmation of St. John: God is Love. Nothing is impossible to the living love, not even drawing everything to itself; and that, too, is written.

Forgive me for raising a problem that for generations has caused many commentaries, disputes, heresies, persecutions, and martyrdoms. But it is after all a novelist who is talking to you, and one whom you have preferred to all others; thus you must attach some value to what has been his inspiration. He bears witness that what he has written about in the light of his faith and hope has not contradicted the experience of those of his readers who share neither his hope nor his faith. To take another example, we see that the agnostic admirers of Graham Greene are not put off by his Christian vision. Chesterton has said that whenever something extraordinary happens in Christianity ultimately something extraordinary corresponds to it in reality. If we ponder this thought, we shall perhaps discover the reason for the mysterious accord between works of Catholic inspiration, like those of my friend Graham Greene, and the vast dechristianized public that devours his books and loves his films.

Yes, a vast dechristianized public! According to André Malraux, "the revolution today plays the role that belonged formerly to the eternal life." But what if the myth were, precisely, the revolution? And if the eternal life were the only reality?

Whatever the answer, we shall agree on one point: that dechristianized humanity remains a crucified humanity. What worldly power will ever destroy the correlation of the cross with human suffering? Even your Strindberg, who descended into the extreme depths of the abyss from which the psalmist uttered his cry, even Strindberg himself wished that a single word be engraved upon his tomb, the word that by itself would suffice to shake and force the gates of eternity: "crux ave spes unica." After so much suffering even he is resting in the protection of that hope, in the shadow of that love. And it is in his name that your laureate asks you to forgive these all too personal words which perhaps have struck too grave a note. But could he do better, in exchange for the honours with which you have overwhelmed him, than to open to you not only his heart, but his soul? And because he has told you through his characters the secret of his torment, he should also introduce you tonight to the secret of his peace.

Books for Further Reading

The following list includes a number of histories of French literature that deal with the period 1900-1930 and other volumes bearing on the literary trends of the early decades of the century in France or concentrating on more than one author treated in this volume. This list is necessarily very restrictive. Additional sources, both general and specific, are listed in the major bibliographies of criticism on modern French literature. Among them, in addition to the annual *MLA International Bibliography*, are a work indispensable for scholars, Douglas W. Alden and Richard A. Brooks, *A Critical Bibliography of French Literature*, volume 6: *The Twentieth Century*, 3 parts (Syracuse: Syracuse University Press, 1979); Douglas W. Alden, et al., eds., *French XX Bibliography: Critical and Biographical Reference for the Study of French Literature Since 1885* (New York: French Institute-Alliance Française, 1949-1985; Selinsgrove, Pa.: Susquehanna University Press, 1986-   ), which is not annotated but lists primary works and book reviews as well as critical works; Otto Klapp, *Bibliographie der französischen Literaturwissenschaft* (Frankfurt: Klosterman, 1960-   ), not annotated, but very thorough and particularly good for European criticism; and the bibliography in *Revue d'Histoire Littéraire de la France*, edited by René Rancœur (formerly a quarterly or annual section of the journal, now printed as issue number 3 of each volume). Major collections of manuscripts from modern French writers are at the Bibliothèque Nationale in Paris, the Bibliothèque Littéraire Jacques Doucet in Paris, and the University of Texas at Austin.

Albérès, René Marill. *L'Aventure intellectuelle du XXe siècle, 1900-1950*. Paris: Nouvelle Edition, 1950. Revised and enlarged as *L'Aventure intellectuelle du XXe siècle: Panorama des littératures européennes 1900-1963*. Paris: Albin Michel, 1959.

Albérès. *Bilan littéraire du XXe siècle*. Paris: Aubier, 1956. Revised edition, 1962. Later revised edition, Paris: Nizet, 1971.

Albérès. *Histoire du roman moderne*. Paris: Albin Michel, 1962. Revised editions, 1967-1971.

Bersani, Leo. *Balzac to Beckett: Center and Circumference in French Fiction*. New York: Oxford University Press, 1970.

Boisdeffre, Pierre de, ed. *Dictionnaire de littérature contemporaine 1900-1962*. Paris: Editions Universitaires, 1962. Revised edition, Paris: Editions Universitaires, 1963.

Brée, Germaine, and Margaret Guiton. *An Age of Fiction: The French Novel from Gide to Camus*. New Brunswick, N.J.: Rutgers University Press, 1957. Revised as *The French Novel from Gide to Camus*. New York: Harcourt, Brace & World, 1962.

Brée and Pierre-Olivier Walzer. *Littérature française: Le XXe Siècle*, 2 volumes. Paris: Arthaud, 1975.

Brombert, Victor. *The Intellectual Hero: Studies in the French Novel, 1880-1955*. Philadelphia & New York: Lippincott, 1961.

Clouard, Henri. *Histoire de la littérature française, du symbolisme à nos jours*, 2 volumes. Paris: Albin Michel, 1947-1949. Revised editions, 1960, 1962.

Cocking, J. M., Enid Starkie, and Martin Jarrett-Kerr. *Three Studies in Modern French Literature*. New Haven: Yale University Press, 1960.

Cruickshank, John, ed. *French Literature and Its Background*, volume 6: *The Twentieth Century*. New York & London: Oxford University Press, 1970.

Faÿ, Bernard. *Panorama de la littérature contemporaine.* Paris: Editions du Sagittaire, 1925. Revised edition, 1929.

Fowlie, Wallace. *Climate of Violence: The French Literary Tradition from Baudelaire to the Present.* New York: Macmillan, 1967.

Fowlie. *A Guide to Contemporary French Literature: From Valéry to Sartre.* New York: Meridian, 1957.

Hatzfeld, Helmut. *Trends and Styles in Twentieth Century French Literature.* Washington, D.C.: Catholic University of America Press, 1957.

Magny, Claude-Edmonde. *Histoire du roman français depuis 1918.* Paris: Editions du Seuil, 1950.

Moore, Harry T. *Twentieth Century French Literature to World War II.* Carbondale: Southern Illinois University Press, 1966.

Nathan, Jacques. *Histoire de la littérature contemporaine.* Paris: Nathan, 1954. Revised edition, 1960.

Peyre, Henri. *The Contemporary French Novel.* New York: Oxford University Press, 1955. Revised as *French Novelists of Today.* New York: Oxford University Press, 1967.

Raimond, Michel. *La Crise du roman, des lendemains du naturalisme aux années vingt.* Paris: Corti, 1966.

Rieuneau, Maurice. *Guerre et révolution dans le roman français de 1919 à 1939.* Paris: Klincksieck, 1974.

Saurat, Denis. *Modern French Literature 1870-1940.* London: Dent, 1946; New York: Putnam's, 1947.

Stambolian, George, ed. *Twentieth Century French Fiction: Essays for Germaine Brée.* New Brunswick, N.J.: Rutgers University Press, 1975.

Tison-Braun, Micheline. *La Crise de l'humanisme: Le Conflit de l'individu et de la société dans la littérature française moderne,* 2 volumes. Paris: Nizet, 1958, 1967.

Tison-Braun. *L'Introuvable Origine: Le Problème de la personnalité au seuil du XXᵉ siècle.* Geneva: Droz, 1981.

Contributors

Douglas W. Alden...*University of Virginia*
Anna Balakian..*New York University*
Elaine D. Cancalon...*Florida State University*
Jean-Pierre Cap ....*Lafayette College*
Megan Conway ....*Tulane University*
Margaret Davies...*University of Reading*
Lionel Dubois...*De Paul University*
J. E. Flower ....*University of Exeter*
Grant E. Kaiser..*Emory University*
Slava M. Kushnir...*Queen's University*
Raymond Mahieu ....*University of Antwerp*
Will L. McLendon..*University of Houston*
James P. Mc Nab ....*Guilford College*
Helen T. Naughton ....*College of Notre Dame*
David O'Connell...*University of Illinois at Chicago*
Alain D. Ranwez...*Metropolitan State College*
William T. Starr ....*Northwestern University*
Bruno Thibault..*University of Delaware*
Elizabeth Richardson Viti...*Gettysburg College*

Cumulative Index

Dictionary of Literary Biography, Volumes 1-67
Dictionary of Literary Biography Yearbook, 1980-1986
Dictionary of Literary Biography Documentary Series, Volumes 1-4

Cumulative Index

DLB before number: *Dictionary of Literary Biography*, Volumes 1-67
Y before number: *Dictionary of Literary Biography Yearbook*, 1980-1986
DS before number: *Dictionary of Literary Biography Documentary Series*, Volumes 1-4

A

B

Cumulative Index

D

F

H

I

J

L

N

O

P

Q

R

S

U

V

W

Cumulative Index

7168

LIBRARY
ST. MICHAEL'S PREP SCHOOL
1042 STAR RT. - ORANGE, CA. 92667

7168